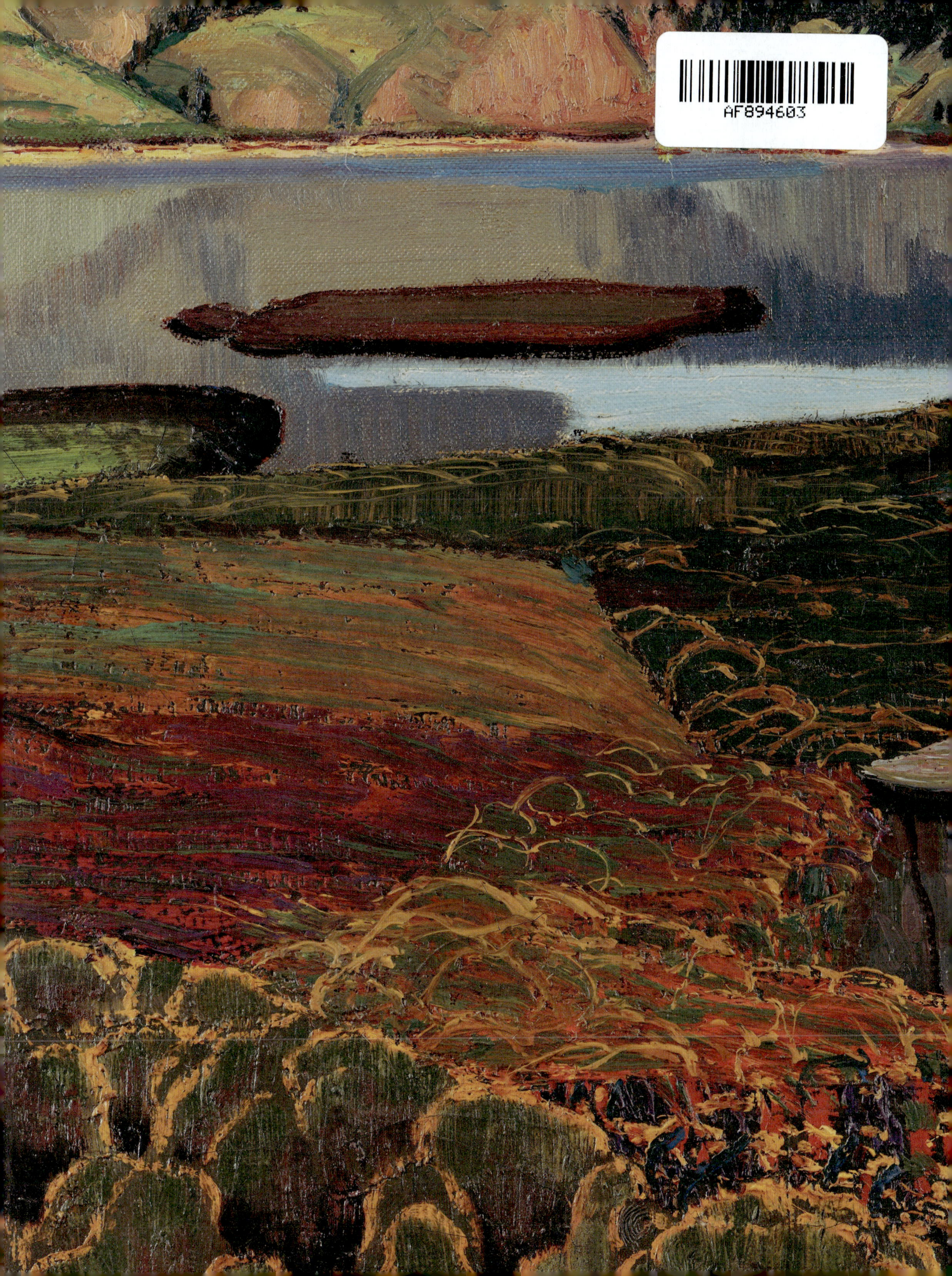

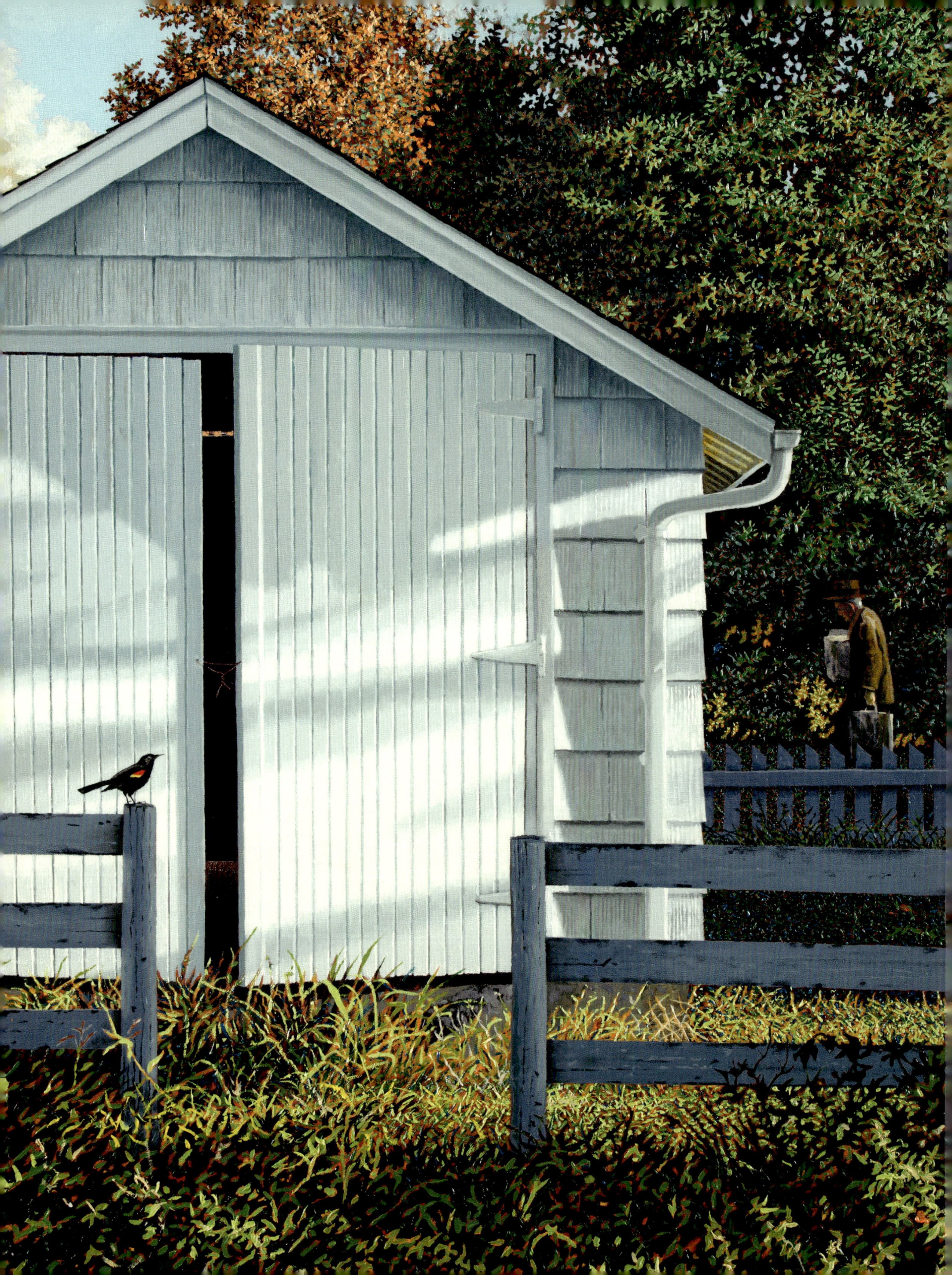

Edited by Jeremiah William McCarthy and Diana Thompson

FOR AMERICA

Paintings from the National Academy of Design

American Federation of Arts, New York
National Academy of Design, New York

Distributed by Yale University Press, New Haven and London

CONTENTS

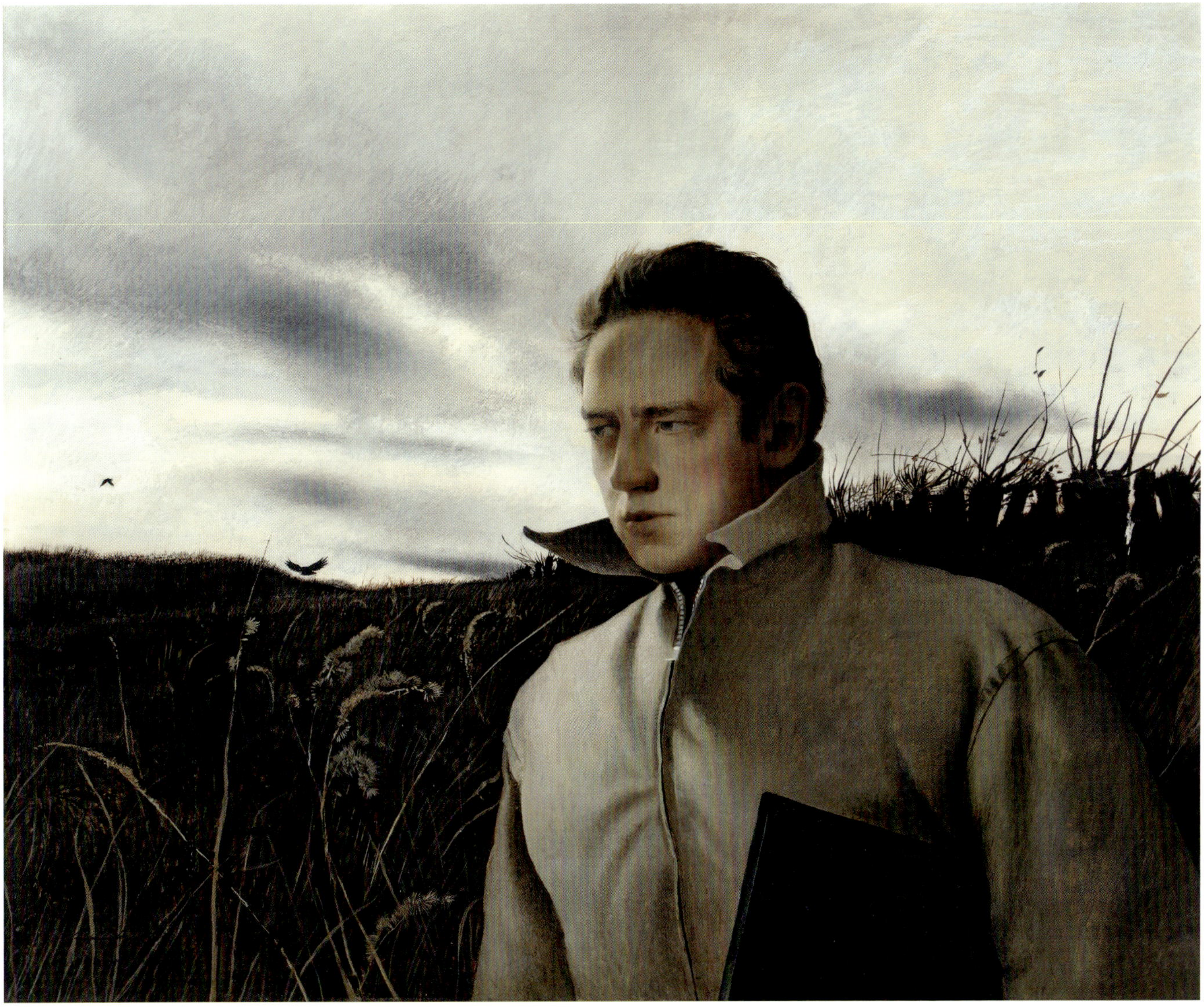

Andrew Wyeth, *Self-Portrait*, 1945. Egg tempera on gessoed panel, 25 × 30 in. (63.5 × 76.2 cm)

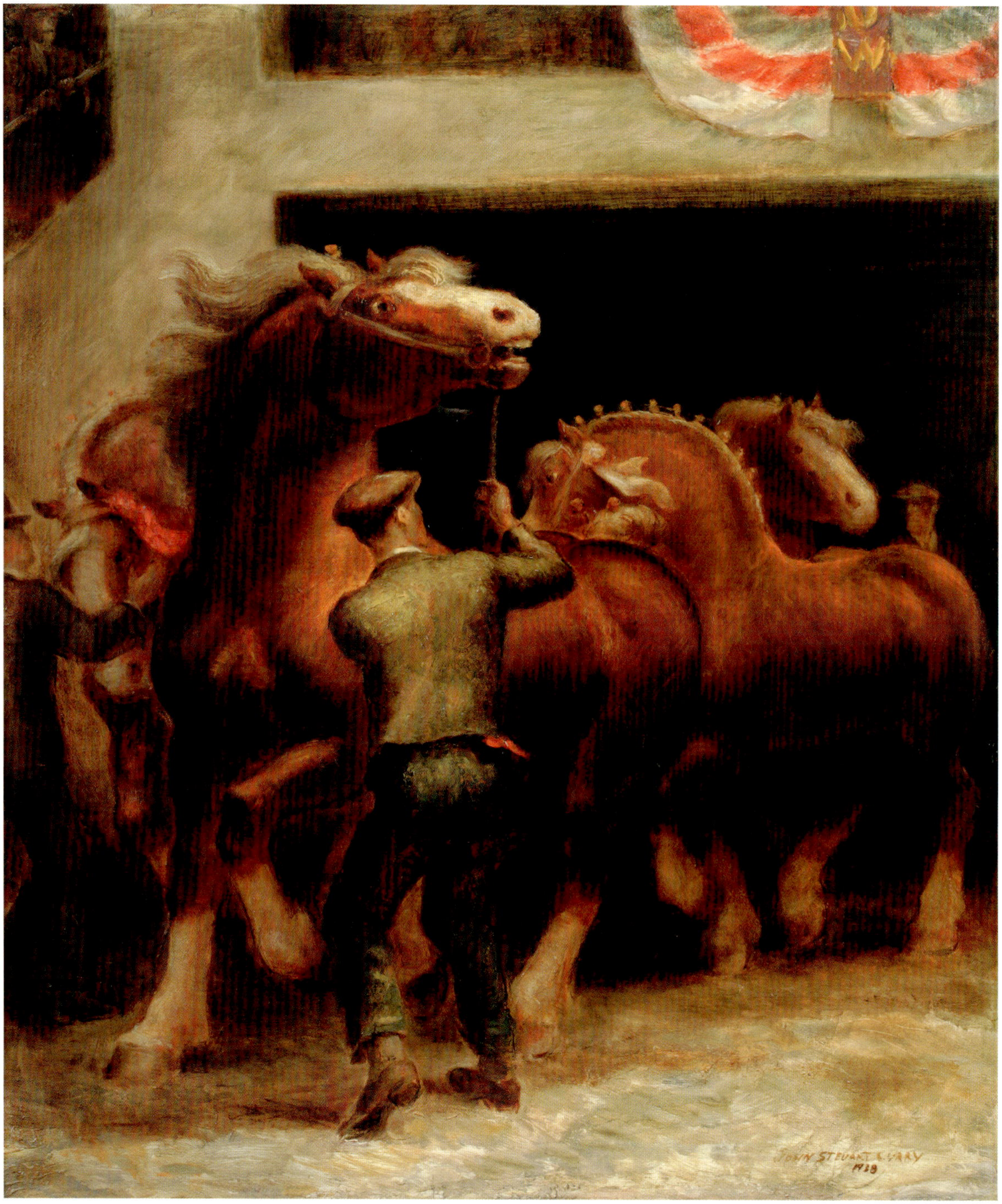

John Steuart Curry, *Belgian Stallions*, 1938. Oil on wood panel, 30 × 25 ½ in. (76.2 × 64.8 cm)

With over twenty-five exhibitions in our collaborative history, *For America: Paintings from the National Academy of Design* offers the opportunity to reflect on our institutions and the critical roles they have played in the development of American art. Conceived in 1825 by Samuel F. B. Morse and a group of forward-thinking individuals, the National Academy of Design (NAD) is the nation's oldest artist and architect honorary society. The American Federation of Arts (AFA)—born from a 1909 convocation of US government officials, including President William H. Taft; artists; and representatives of more than eighty institutions, including delegates from the NAD—is the leader in initiating traveling exhibitions that advance knowledge and appreciation of visual art in this country. Two legacies of action, then: the first establishing that artists know best the means for their own improvement, the second demonstrating that art is for all and should be brought to those who want and need it.

In these pages, we find examples of art's ability to make connections across differences of background, age, and belief. It is there in Cecilia Beaux's determined gaze, in the dynamism of John Steuart Curry's stallions, in the steady hands of Benny Andrews. The idea that art and artists are the lifeblood of a free society has been regularly challenged, but our two institutions have provided—indeed, will continue to provide—stalwart protection and advocacy for both.

That museums from the East to the West Coasts have joined this national tour is a testament to this mission. We offer our appreciation to strong partners at the Dayton Art Institute, New Britain Museum of American Art, The Society of the Four Arts, Dixon Gallery and Gardens, New Mexico Museum of Art, Figge Art Museum, and Crocker Art Museum. *For America* is a true collaboration between our institutions.

This remarkable publication is the work of the team at Matsumoto Incorporated, as well as our partners at Lucia | Marquand and Yale University Press. On behalf of our institution, we recognize the professionalism and dedication of our colleagues, including Elizabeth Abbarno, Shawna Gallancy, Frances Wu Giarratano, Brian Keliher, Julija Lazutkaite, Audrey Walen, and Shelley Wilson, of the AFA, and, at the NAD, Auzelle Epeneter and Mary Fisher. Most of all, we thank Jeremiah William McCarthy and Diana Thompson for their curatorial acumen and expertise.

A special debt of gratitude is owed to those who believed in the value of this project and made it possible through their financial support. They include AFA Chairman Emerita Jan Mayer and the JFM Foundation, Monique Schoen Warshaw, and Steph and Jody La Nasa.

Finally, to National Academicians everywhere, we are forever thankful for your vision.

Pauline Willis, Director and CEO, American Federation of Arts

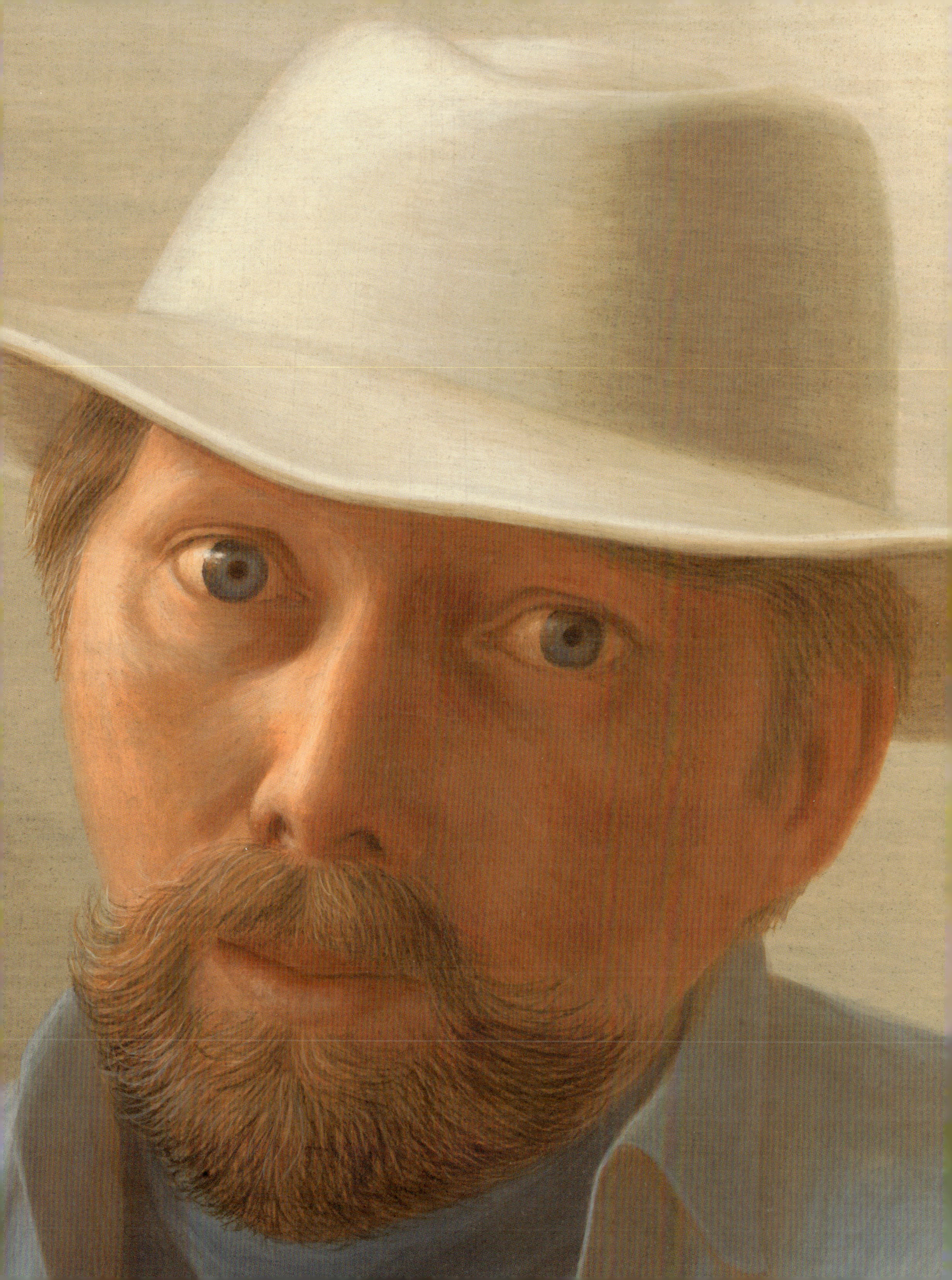

FOR AMERICA: AN INTRODUCTION

JEREMIAH WILLIAM MCCARTHY AND DIANA THOMPSON

Since its founding nearly two hundred years ago, the National Academy of Design has upheld a rule instituted in its first constitution and bylaws on December 16, 1826: any elected National Academician (NA) must offer a "specimen of his own production in the Arts of Design, to be preserved in the Gallery of the Academy."[1] In 1839, the constitution was amended with a proviso that individuals nominated to the rank of Associate National Academician (ANA), which almost always preceded the NA class of membership, must present a portrait of themselves to the Academy, whether painted by their own hand or that of a fellow artist.[2] Although this additional obligation was eliminated in 1994, when the associate level of membership was abolished, such gifts—of the latter, known as "diploma portraits," or the former, known as "diploma works"—are the defining feature of the Academy's collection and the conceptual spine of *For America: Paintings from the National Academy of Design*.[3] By reproducing artists' portraits in tandem with representative works from their oeuvre, this publication, and the exhibition that accompanies it, offer an unprecedented glimpse into the ways a group of American artists have viewed themselves and their painted worlds over the past two centuries.

Myriad approaches have been taken to the Academy's diploma requirements. In some cases, the artists whose gazes meet our own can be easily integrated into the terrains conjured by their work, and to revealing ends. When viewed in isolation, for example, the protagonists of George Tooker's intimate and haunting *Voice II* (or are they, rather, twins, each seeking its double across the presence of distance?) belong fully to the world of paint (p. 18). And in the artist's *Self-Portrait*, Tooker greets his viewer with a reticent stare and an enigmatic smile—just another character alongside his imaginary subjects (p. 19). Yet, when the two works are viewed together, and when we notice Tooker's hand resting on the ledge as if about to cross the threshold of his portrait into our own flesh-and-blood world, it becomes clear that both works toy with the border between image and reality, thus suggesting the permeability and interdependence of those two realms.

Although the Academy's 1839 constitution, as well as the subsequent revisions, stipulated a time limit of one year after election for diploma portraits, this regulation was rarely, if ever, enforced by the governing council.[4] Thus, a lengthy gap between an Academician's diploma portrait and diploma work could provide the opportunity to demonstrate growth, or to smuggle into the collection an alternative approach to the initial submission. Felicie Waldo Howell Mixter's *Self-Portrait* and *City Waterfront*—painted at least twelve years apart—document not only changes in her painterly technique but also her ever-evolving ideas concerning representation (pp. 138–39). In the searching self-portrait, painted when she was just twenty-five years old, there is none of the hard-edged, analytical certainty that governs the artist's later landscape and similar series in that vein, such as those she devoted to the streets and the façades of New England.

When painters are asked to turn their gaze on their peers, interpersonal relationships can be reflected in portraiture. Robert Frederick Blum and William Merritt Chase were intimate friends: the two traveled throughout Europe together in the first half of the 1880s, frequently depicted one another, and were elected ANAs in the same year. While some of Chase's critics perceived an aloofness in his figures, the artist's emotionally stirring portrait of Blum forges a deeper connection between the artists' well-known paintings *The Young Orphan* and *Two Idlers* (pp. 92–93), framing each in a new light.[5] In some cases, artists have submitted portraits for both of their diploma presentations, documenting peer networks or circles of influence. John Singer Sargent offered a profile of his friend Claude Monet as his diploma work to stand alongside his own likeness (pp. 96–97), signifying their bond and the older artist's decisive influence on the younger's development and production.

While we should not assume that all Academicians intended their two diploma submissions to be viewed in tandem—surely, some presented what was ready at hand and met the criteria, or offered the Academy a work they deemed less salable on the open market—many duos suggest otherwise. On April 5, 1926, for instance, Ernest L. Ipsen substituted a formal portrait of NAD president Edwin Howland Blashfield (p. 24), then in his final month of office, for the depiction of the noted explorer Robert Bartlett that had served as Ipsen's original diploma presentation. The artist's image of Blashfield consciously channeled both the dignity and the restraint of Blashfield's own diploma work, *Saint Michael* (p. 25), with which Ipsen was familiar from its exhibition at the Academy.

The Academy's collection is also populated with pairs that defy explanation. Consider Abbott H. Thayer, whose diploma portrait (p. 114) was long thought to be an autograph likeness until the discovery of a cache of letters at the Academy revealed the work to be from the hand of the artist's frequent travel companion George Of.[6] Of executed the portrait just in time to meet the one-year submission deadline strongly suggested by the Academy's council, likely with the understanding that at some point it would be finished by Thayer himself. Left today in its unfinished state, the work vibrates with uncanny intensity when viewed alongside Thayer's diploma work, *Winter Landscape* (p. 115), echoing the eccentric Academician's sketchy, formally innovative style.

In an effort to demonstrate artists' dialogues across time, and taking our cue from the Academy's collecting principles, we have combined on the basis of visual tropes or painterly concerns works that would otherwise be relegated to different movements or epochs. A comparison of the portraits of Eliza Greatorex and Will Barnet (pp. 20–21), each artist's stylus and sketchbook ready at hand, reveals timeless truisms: painting is a mode of inhabiting the world, mark making a way of recording all that and more. Other duos broach differing approaches to similar subject matter. Aaron Shikler's 1959 portrait of the writer and translator Claire Nicolas White, depicted within an ambiguous space and free of any symbolic context, channels the growing unease of the decade's end—and certainly none of the assurance and aspiration that mark John White Alexander's *Mrs. Thomas Hastings*, reproduced opposite it (pp. 22–23).[7] These juxtapositions allow a reader to trace, for the first time, the continuities and ruptures of painterly traditions as they unfolded over two centuries within the Academy.

One of the most vital legacies in American art, long championed by the nation's artists, has been an undaunted commitment to realism and painterly representation, especially the figurative tradition, and the Academy's collection evinces the institution's deep-rooted support for this sensibility. It includes numerous—in some cases, competing—interpretations of traditional studio genres, such as the still life, the nude, and the portrait. Remember, too, that although this painterly mode is enjoying a contemporary resurgence, as recent Academicians such as Kerry James Marshall, David Salle, and Dana Schutz reinvigorate its central questions, it has not yet been fully historicized, and our selection of work from the twentieth century aims to shine light on the accomplishments of artists whose work was too often overlooked in the waxing of postwar American abstraction and the ascendance of its formidable advocates and the institutions that bolstered it.[8]

The paintings reproduced in this volume not only present a visual document of the Academy's membership over the decades but also tell a story of American art from the 1800s to the present day. The earliest works outline the origins of the Academy and the concomitant rise of the Hudson River School and American genre painting. In the second half of the nineteenth century, scores of painters returned stateside after studying in the art centers of Düsseldorf, London, and Paris, shifting the emphases and transforming the pedagogy of the Academy and its associated school of fine arts. Then, as European avant-garde movements flourished in the early twentieth century, the Academy became a bastion for artists upholding a representational aesthetic; to strengthen its national profile during this period, the governing council expanded membership beyond the vicinity of New York City to important satellites such as Old Lyme, Connecticut (p. 102) and Taos, New Mexico (pp. 142–43).

The texts that follow touch upon such historical moments yet, en masse, expand this familiar assessment of the Academy and its members.[9] Synchronic essays devoted to single works, artistic pairings, or movements—for example, Susan Rather's careful reading of Samuel F. B. Morse's self-portrait miniature, revealing the identity of the "self-taught" artist's first teacher, and Elizabeth A. Spear's nuanced discussion of Hudson River School painting via the material conditions of the works' display—are balanced with diachronic essays that expound broader themes, such as the development of the figurative tradition or the appeal of Monhegan Island to artists over half a century. These two ways of viewing, which the art historian Erwin Panofsky termed "microscopic" and "telescopic"—the one close up, the other from far away—parallel the physical processes of making and looking at paintings.[10] The book and exhibition take as axiomatic that these approaches are simply attempts to activate works of art in novel and unexpected ways, and they are not intended to provide a comprehensive history of American painting. Finally, we have invited current National Academicians to write about individual works in the collection in single-page reflections, and their responses, recorded alongside the paintings that inspired them, constitute another pairing of sorts.

Some concluding notes on criteria are in order. Our decision to focus exclusively on painting stems from the early concerns of the Academy's founders: sixteen self-declared painters, one sculptor, two architects, and five engravers.[11] Although the Academy was largely resistant to modernism and its divergent threads as they unfurled throughout the twentieth century, such tendencies are not absent from the collection; still, early in the conversations that shaped this book and exhibition, we decided that the lesser known, and often critically overlooked, story of figuration and of artists working in a representational mode in the wake of abstraction and modernism would be a thoroughgoing thread. Additionally, although the Academy's collection includes still lifes from artists as stylistically diverse as John La Farge and William Bailey, we decided that that thematic and historical trajectory would be better explored in a separate exhibition.

Moreover, an academy, by its nature, is an exclusionary organization, and throughout its history, on occasion, the Academy has been resistant to change in one form or another. Until 1869, the membership body was drawn exclusively from the New York City area, and until the turn of the century, ANAs and NAs were culled from the previous year's annual exhibition. In 1967, Hughie Lee-Smith became only the second African American National Academician; exactly forty years earlier, Henry Ossawa Tanner had broken that barrier to become the first. And in 1992, the Academy nominated and elected its first female president, the painter Jane Wilson, who held the position for two years. That said, as this is a collection built by artists and not by acquisition committees or museum officials—an artists' art history, so to speak—there are remarkable portents within the Academy's holdings, years ahead of their time, which we have highlighted whenever possible. For example, rather than a likeness of himself, Charles White submitted *Matriarch* (p. 27)—a portrayal of his great-aunt Hasty Baines, born into slavery in 1857 on the Yellowley plantation in Ridgeland, Mississippi—as his diploma portrait.[12] Painted 110 years after her birth, in the thick of a decade rife with political and social unrest, the deeply personal work stood for White as a symbol of wisdom and courage—universal themes also explored in his mature work *Mother Courage II* (p. 26)—and today, as ever, the colloquy between the two works is edifying.

As the Academy is a living institution that counts 460 of today's leading artists and architects as members, selecting recent work for inclusion was a difficult undertaking.[13] We defined our task as follows: to end with paintings by current members whose work addresses contemporary concerns while harking back to the storied history of both this institution and this nation. Although the portrait requirement for Academicians was eliminated over two decades ago, many have continued to pay homage to it. Thus, Peter Saul's diploma work, a self-portrait (p. 277)—the only one the artist has made up to this point—is a fitting work to end the volume. It is our belief that such paintings can provide mirrors for the present, ways of imagining and grappling with the past, and, finally, dreams for a possible future.

1. The immediate precursor to the NAD, the New-York Drawing Association, came into being on November 8, 1825, when a group of thirty men—professional artists, amateurs, and students—led by Samuel F. B. Morse convened to discuss the formation of a union for the advancement of their profession; they resolved to meet three times each week for evening drawing sessions. At that time, the American Academy of the Fine Arts (founded December 3, 1802, and originally known as the New-York Academy of the Fine Arts) provided inconsistent access to and, on occasion, barred artists from the only collection of antique casts in New York City. As the burgeoning association became a threat to the academy's status, a half-hearted reconciliation was attempted, but it failed, and on January 14, 1826, the former officially broke with the latter and renamed itself the National Academy of the Arts of Design. The founders, following the conventions of the time, defined the four "arts of design" as painting, sculpture, architecture, and engraving, as against the broader moniker of "fine arts," which included poetry, music, landscaping, drama, and so on. On January 15, 1826, the group unanimously elected the first class of professional artists to the Academy's governing body, eight of whom went on to ensure the success of the fledgling organization: founding president Samuel F. B. Morse, founding vice president Henry Inman, Frederick S. Agate, Thomas Cole, Thomas Seir Cummings, William Dunlap, Asher B. Durand, and Charles C. Ingham. On May 6, 1829, the current name, National Academy of Design, was adopted. In 2012, to better reflect contemporary art practices, the four membership categories were reduced to two: the visual arts and architecture. Further details on the NAD's formation and development are available in two histories written by Academicians: Thomas Seir Cummings, *Historic Annals of the National Academy of Design, New York Drawing Association, Etc., with Occasional Dottings by the Way-side, from 1825 to the Present Time* (Philadelphia: George W. Childs, 1865), and Eliot Clark, *History of the National Academy of Design, 1825–1953* (New York: Columbia University Press, 1954). Also relevant are Samuel Isham, *The History of American Painting* (New York: Macmillan, 1944; first published 1905), 182–201; William Dunlap, *A History of the Rise and Progress of the Arts of Design in the United States*, 3 vols. (Boston: C. E. Goodspeed, 1918; first published 1834), 3:119–34; and Lois Marie Fink and Joshua C. Taylor, *Academy: The Academic Tradition in American Art; An Exhibition Organized on the Occasion of the*

One Hundred and Fiftieth Anniversary of the National Academy of Design, 1825–1975, exh. cat. (Washington, DC: Smithsonian Institution Press, 1975).

2. No regulation stated that such portraits needed to be painted by another Academician, and the collection includes many portraits by non-Academicians, such as Luigi Lucioni's diploma portrait (p. 162), painted by Leonebel Jacobs, a noted portraitist in her time. Until 1898, regulations limited the size of such works to 21 by 17 inches; thereafter, 30 by 25 inches was the maximum.
3. The moment of election to the Academy has always been considered separate from an Academician's diploma presentation(s). Today, members are elected through a confidential process in which each NA is eligible to nominate for membership up to three candidates—any living visual artist or architect who has made a significant impact on American culture. The nominating NA submits a letter of recommendation and letters of support from two fellow Academicians as well as a dossier on the nominee. Each year, the full membership body meets to present and discuss nominees, and afterward, a vote is cast. The entire process, from the call for nominations to the final vote, takes approximately seven months.
4. The one-year rule for submissions only applied to ANAs from 1839 through 1843; beginning with the constitution of 1844, the one-year rule for submissions applied to both ANAs and NAs.
5. Wendell Stanton Howard's assessment that Chase "never sounded those notes that come from the depth of the human heart" is symptomatic of that approach to his work; see "A Portrait by W. M. Chase," *Harper's Monthly Magazine* 113 (June 1906): 698. On Chase's superficiality, see "Mr. Chase's Pictures," *Chicago Daily Tribune*, September 15, 1889; "The Fine Arts: The Wm. M. Chase Exhibition," *Critic*, n.s., 7, no. 166 (March 5, 1887): 115; and H. Monroe, "Paintings in Chicago," *Art Amateur* 21, no. 5 (October 1889): 91.
6. See David B. Dearinger, ed., *Paintings and Sculpture in the Collection of the National Academy of Design, 1826–1925* (New York: Hudson Hills Press, 2004), 427.
7. Claire Nicolas White was married to a grandson of the architect Stanford White; Helen Hastings was the wife of the architect and Academician Thomas Hastings (ANA 1906; NA 1909).
8. For extended discussion, see Marshall N. Price, "Abstraction at the National Academy," in Price, ed., *The Abstract Impulse: Fifty Years of Abstraction at the National Academy, 1956–2006* (New York: National Academy Museum and School of Fine Arts; Hudson Hills Press, 2007), 15–20.
9. For an example of this treatment, see the ten chronological, thematic essays presented in *Artists by Themselves: Artists' Portraits from the National Academy of Design* (New York: National Academy of Design, 1983), 49–137.
10. See Erwin Panofsky, *Early Netherlandish Painting*, 2 vols. (Cambridge, MA: Harvard University Press, 1953), 1:182.
11. The painters were Frederick S. Agate, Thomas Cole, James Coyle, Thomas Seir Cummings, William Dunlap, John Evers, Charles C. Ingham, Henry Inman, Samuel F. B. Morse, John W. Paradise, J. Parisen, Rembrandt Peale, Edward C. Potter, Hugh Reinagle, Nathaniel Rogers, and D. W. Wilson; the sculptor, John Frazee; the architects, Martin E. Thompson and Ithiel Town; and the engravers, Asher B. Durand, Mosley J. Danforth, William Main, Peter Maverick, and Charles C. Wright.
12. This information is taken from a handwritten letter, penned by the artist's wife, Frances White, to Academy staff, dated a few months before Charles White's passing. Frances White's reference to a "Yellowby" plantation in Ridgeland, Mississippi, is likely a mistake of Yellowley plantation, owned by James Brownlow Yellowley from 1853 to 1896.
13. The Academy's collection includes more than 2,200 paintings, nearly half of them portraits.

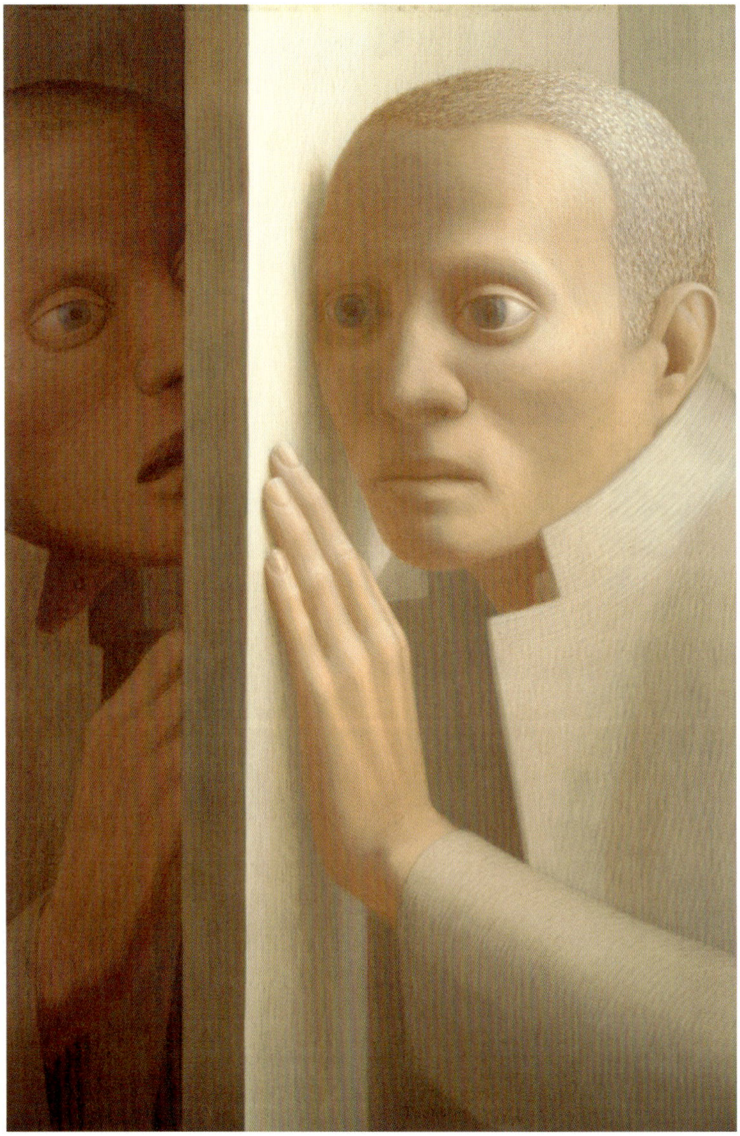

George Tooker, *Voice II*, 1972. Egg tempera on gessoed panel, 17 ½ × 11 ½ in. (44.5 × 29.2 cm)

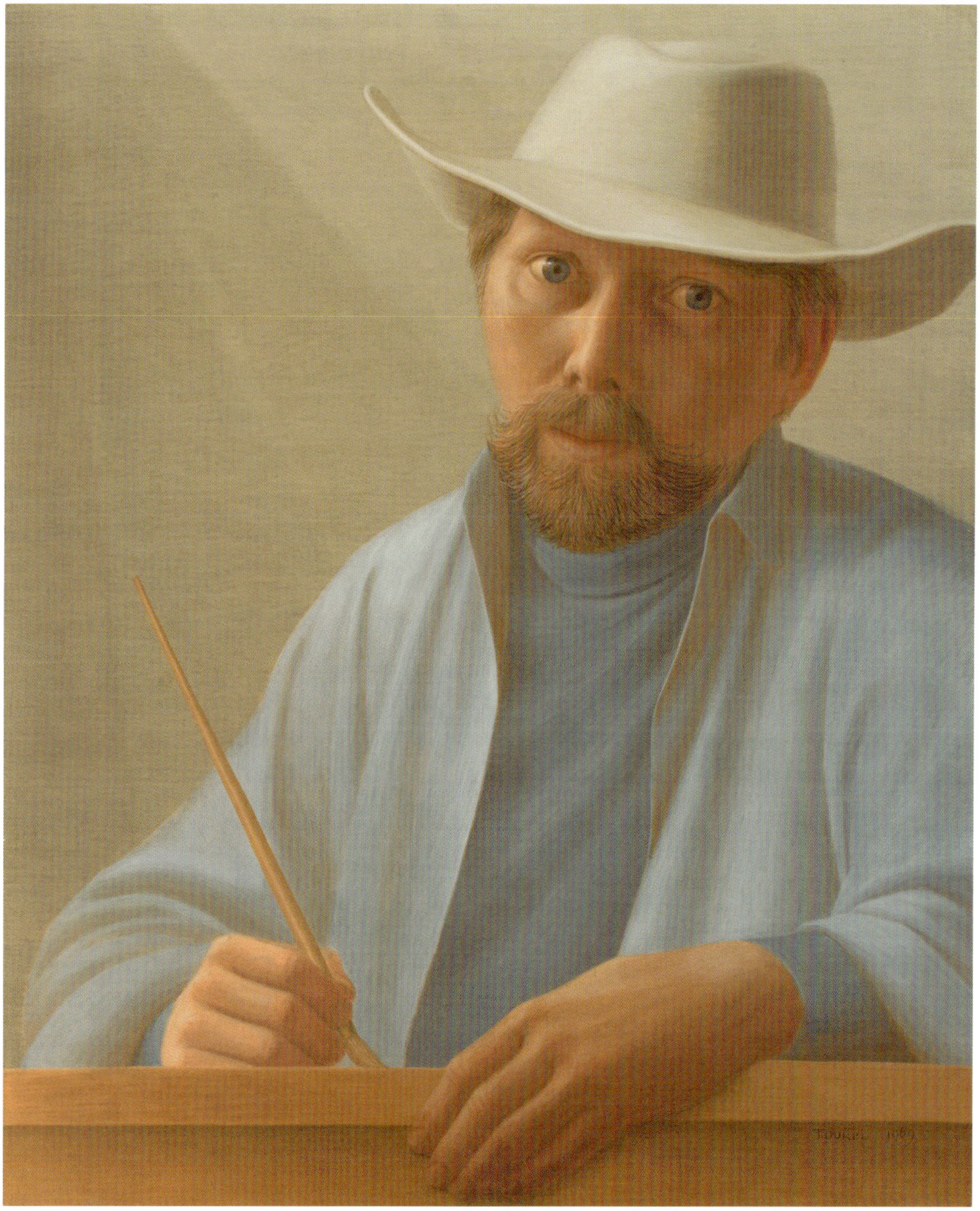

George Tooker, *Self-Portrait*, 1969. Egg tempera on gessoed panel, 24 × 19½ in. (61 × 49.5 cm)

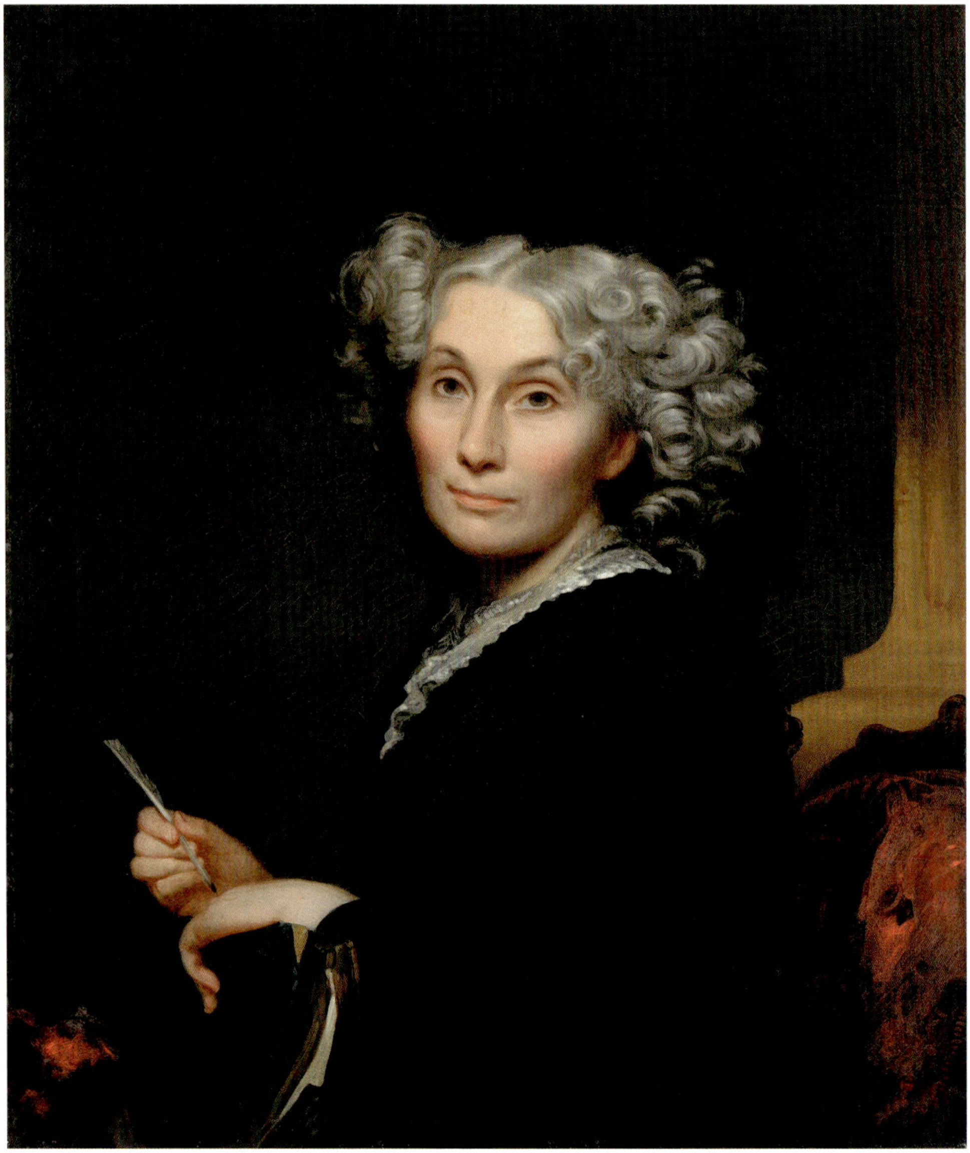

Ferdinand Thomas Lee Boyle, *Eliza Greatorex*, 1869. Oil on canvas, 30 × 25¼ in. (76.2 × 64.1 cm)

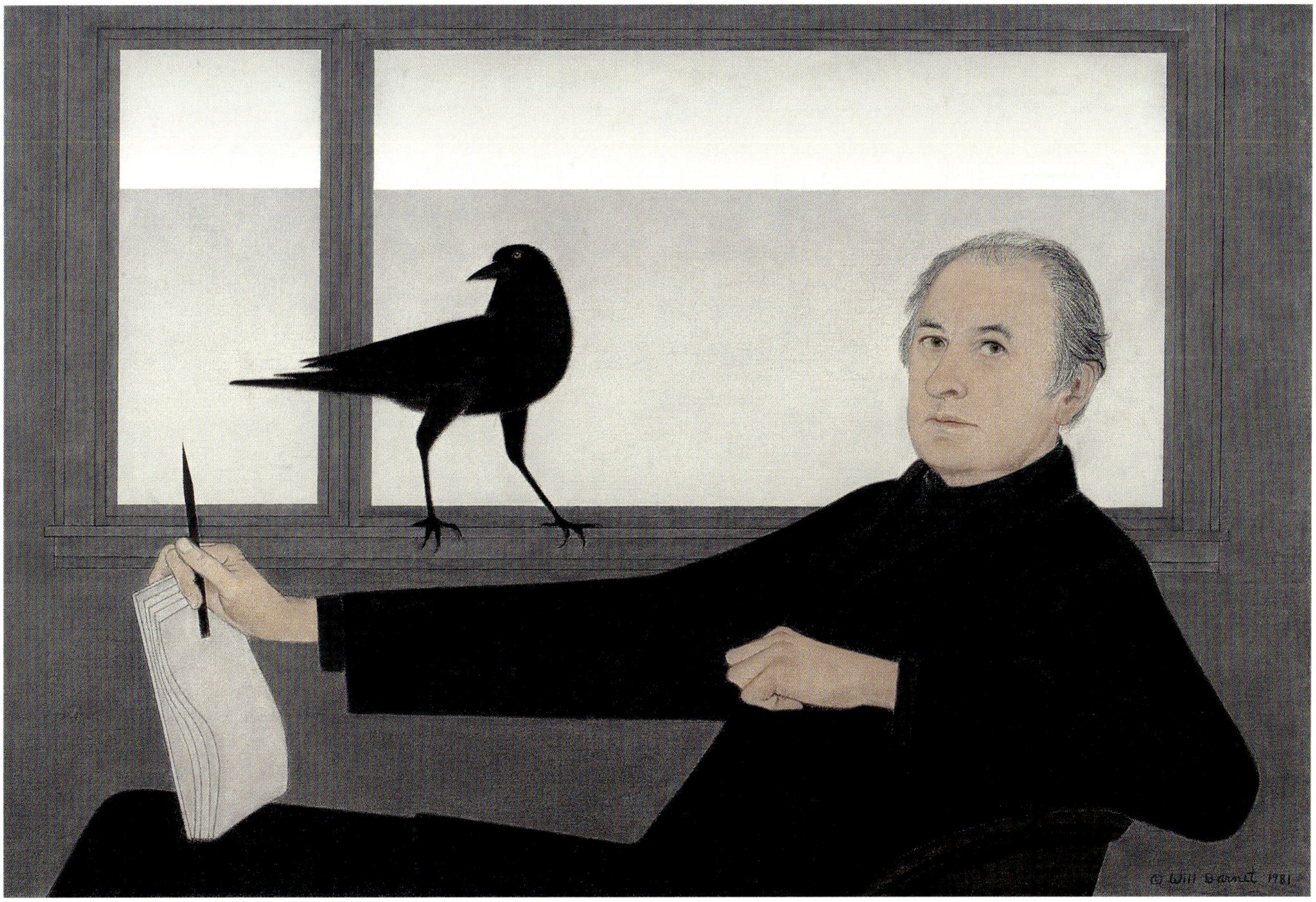

Will Barnet, *Self-Portrait*, 1981. Oil on canvas, 31 ⅛ × 45 ½ in. (79.1 × 115.6 cm)

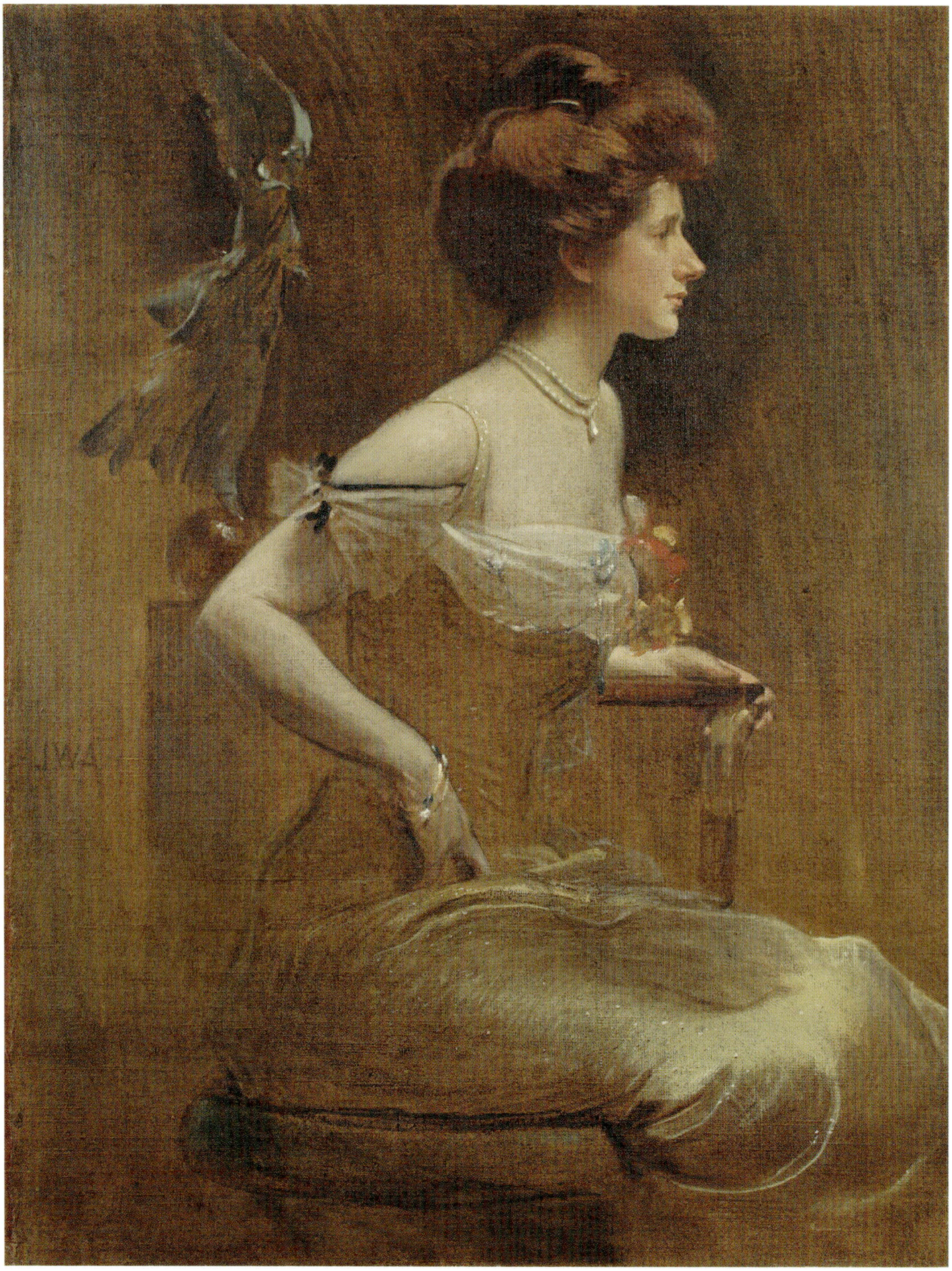

John White Alexander, *Mrs. Thomas Hastings*, 1901. Oil on canvas, 47 ½ × 35 ½ in. (120.7 × 90.2 cm)

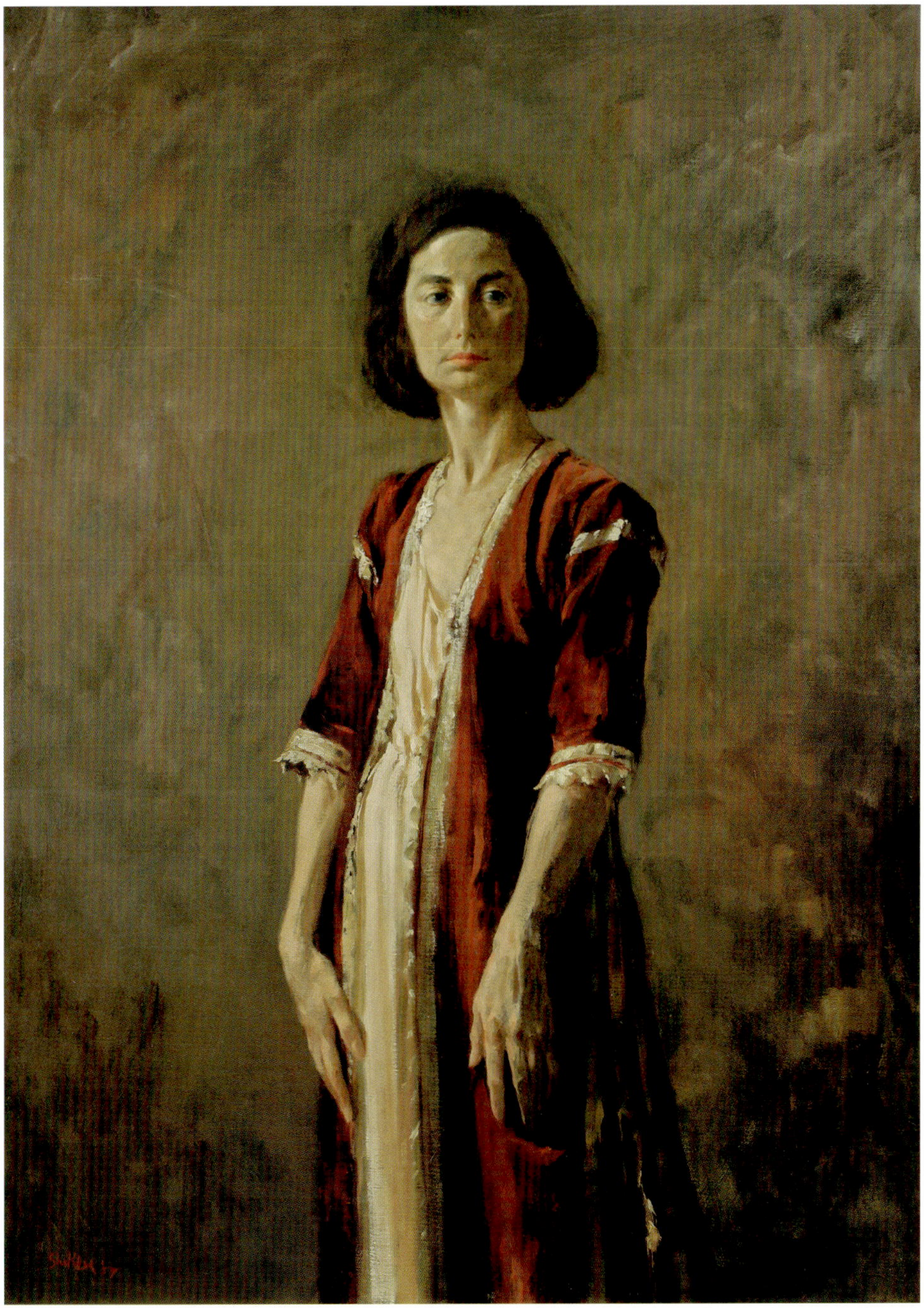

Aaron Shikler, *The Empire Coat*, 1959. Oil on canvas, 35 × 25 in. (88.9 × 63.5 cm)

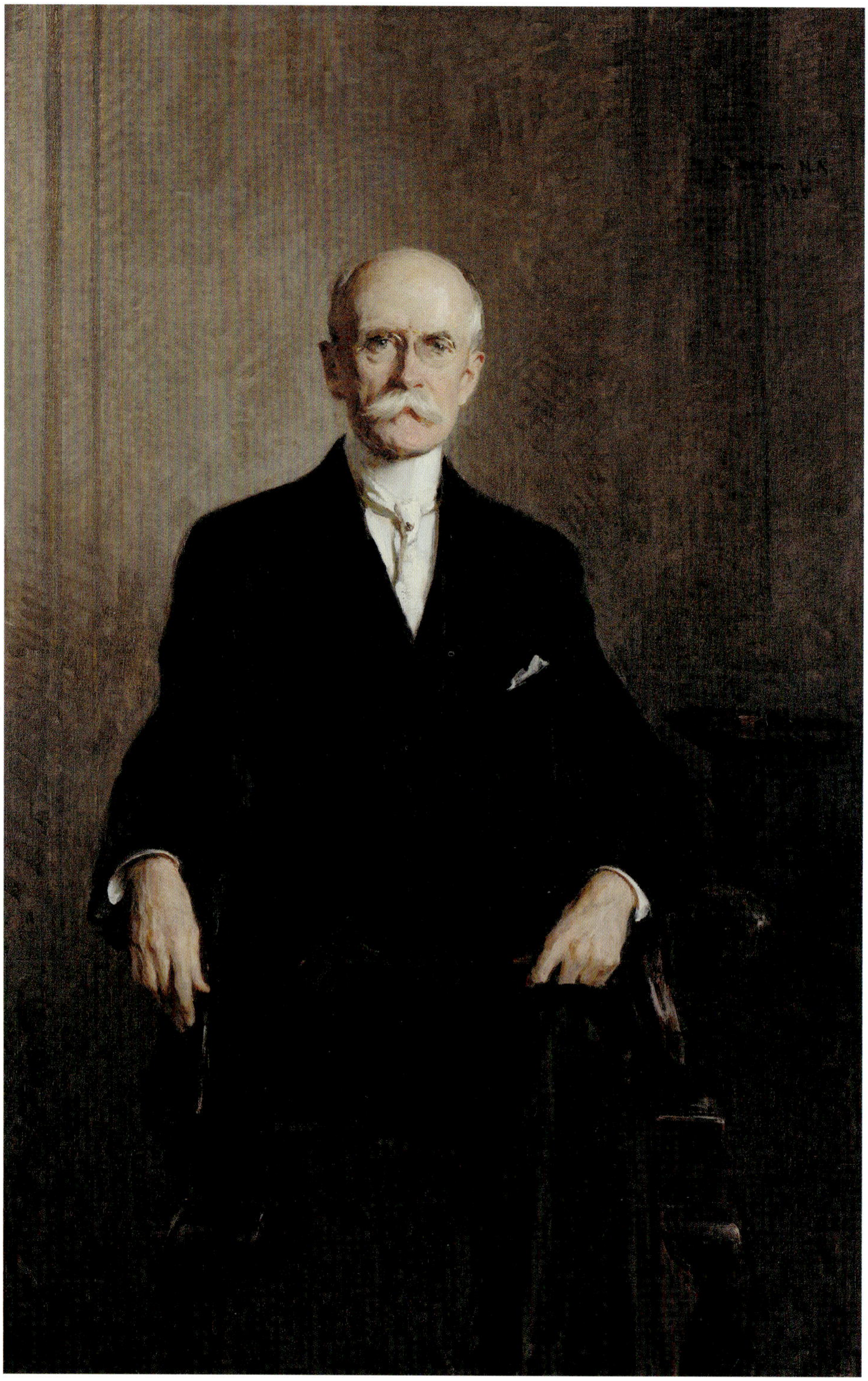

Ernest L. Ipsen, *Edwin H. Blashfield*, 1925. Oil on canvas, 60¼ × 38 in. (153 × 96.5 cm)

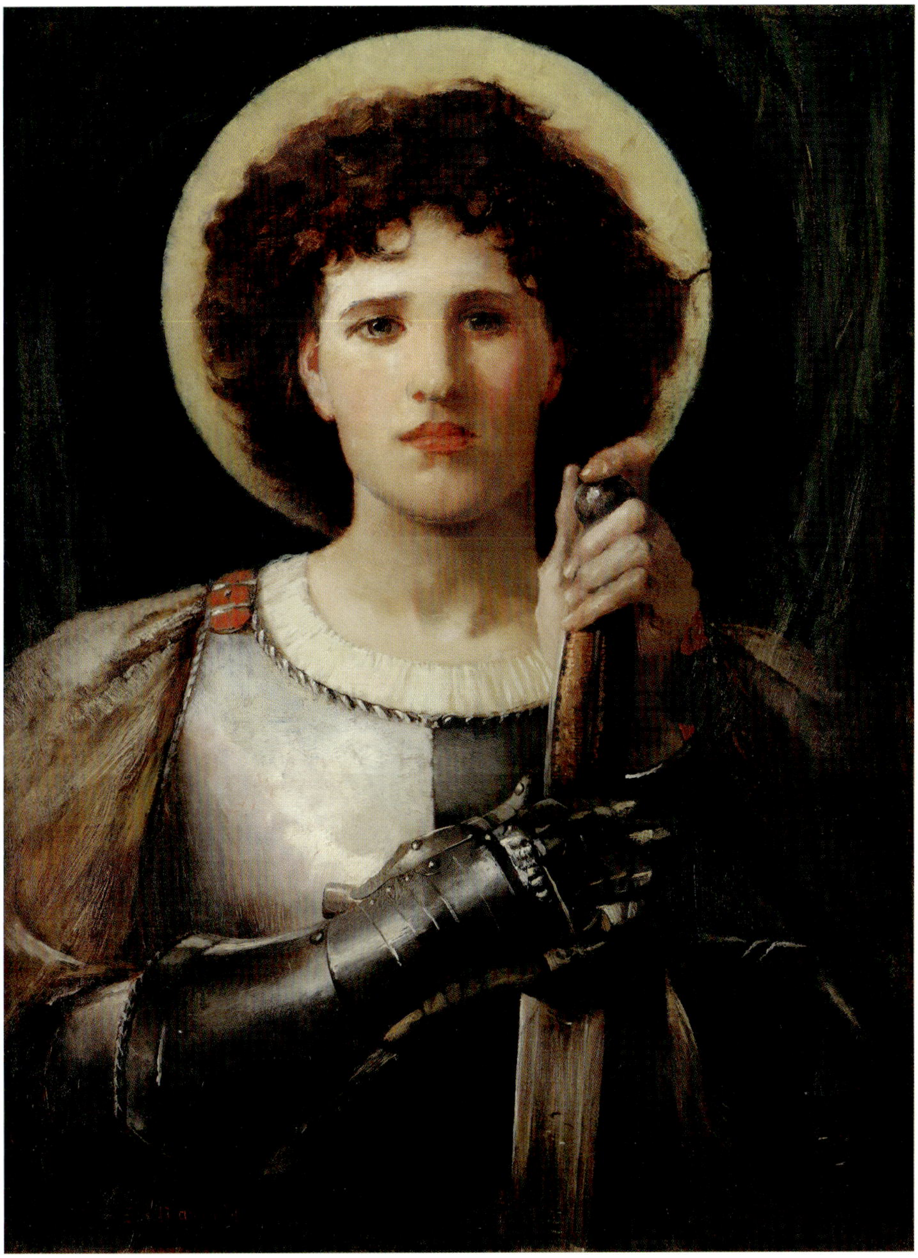

Edwin Howland Blashfield, *Saint Michael*, n.d. Oil on canvas, 30 ⅛ × 22 in. (76.5 × 55.9 cm)

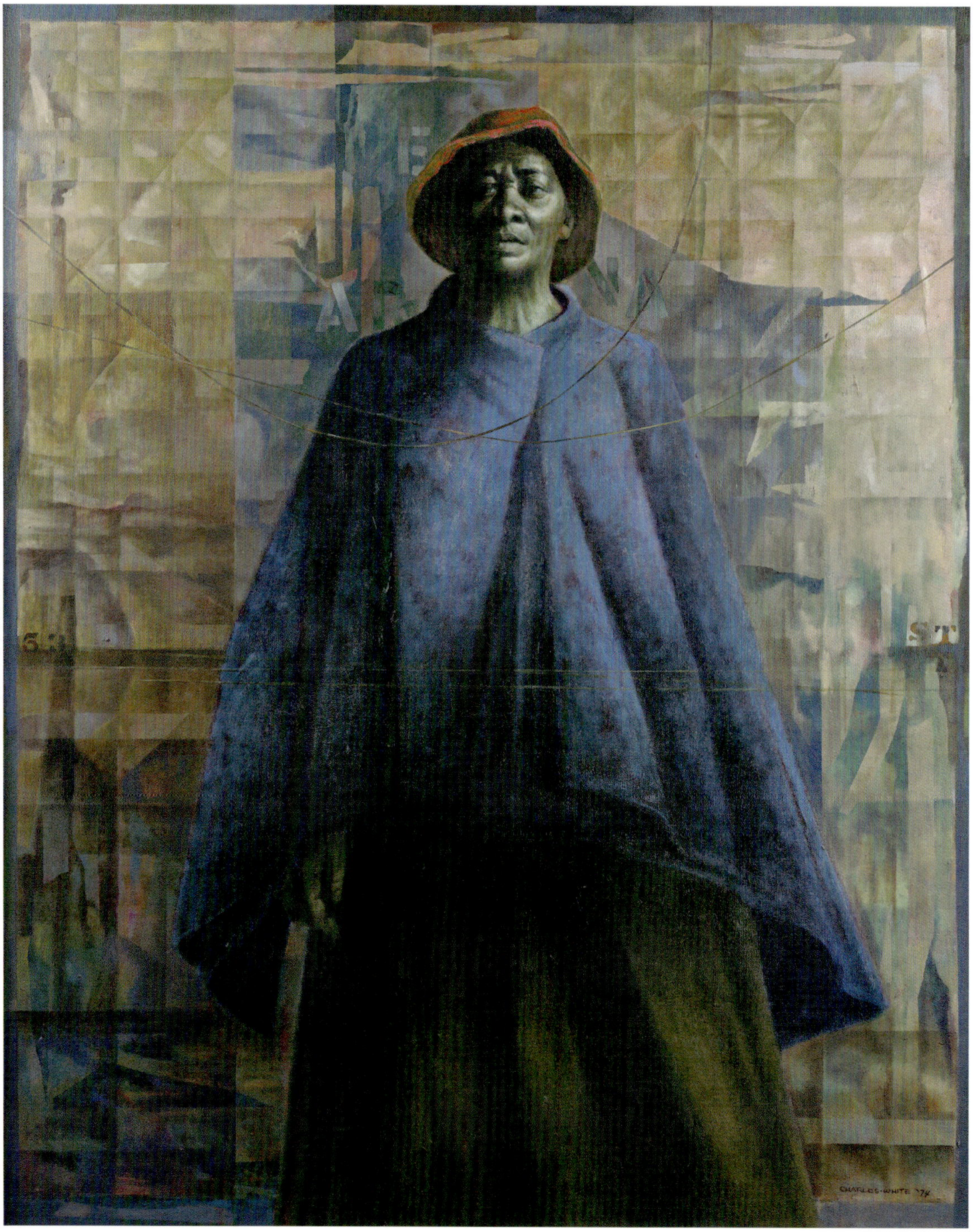

Charles White, *Mother Courage II*, 1974. Oil on canvas, 49 ¾ × 39 ⅞ in. (126.4 × 101.3 cm)

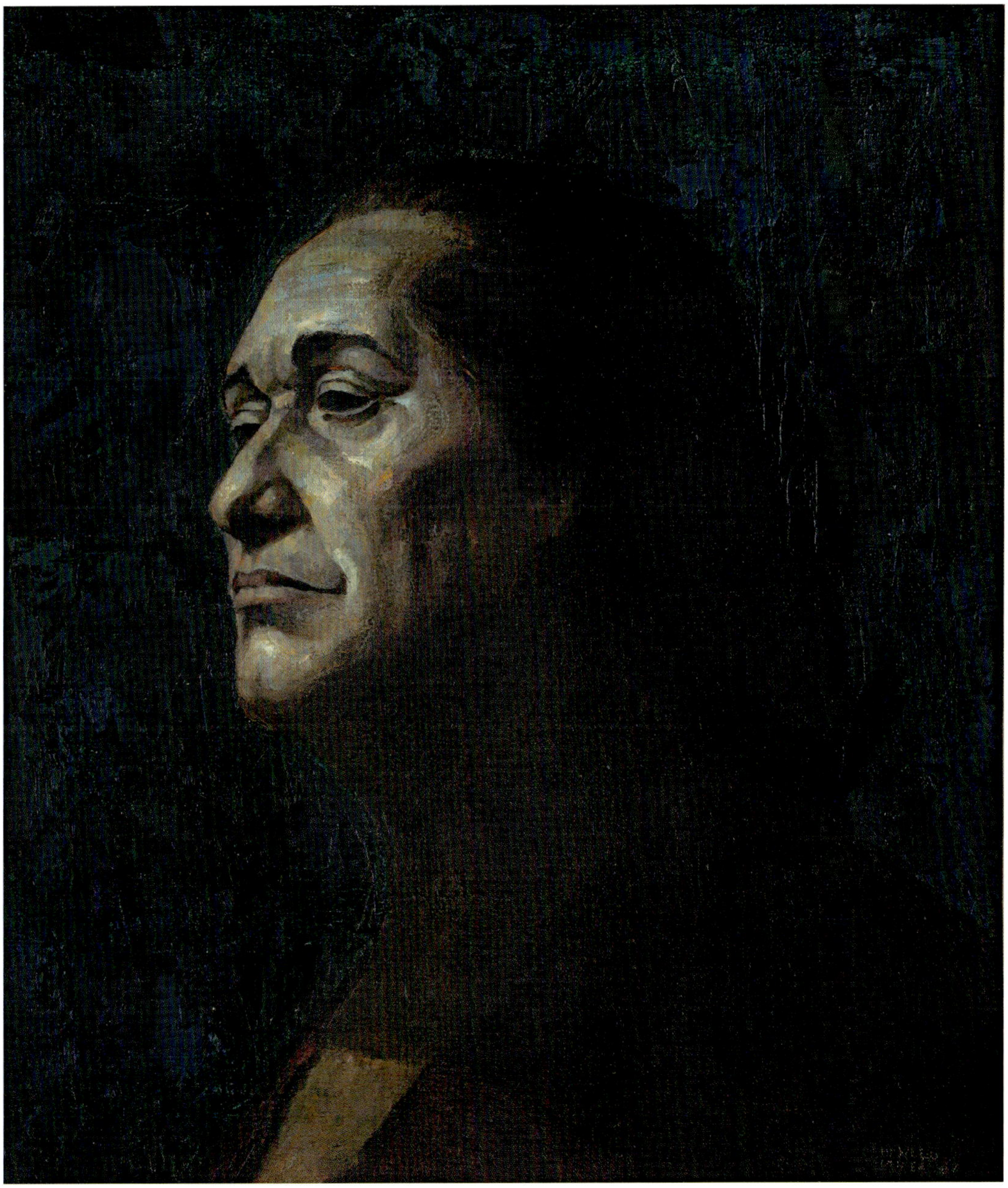

Charles White, *Matriarch*, 1967. Oil on canvas, 20 × 17 in. (50.8 × 43.2 cm)

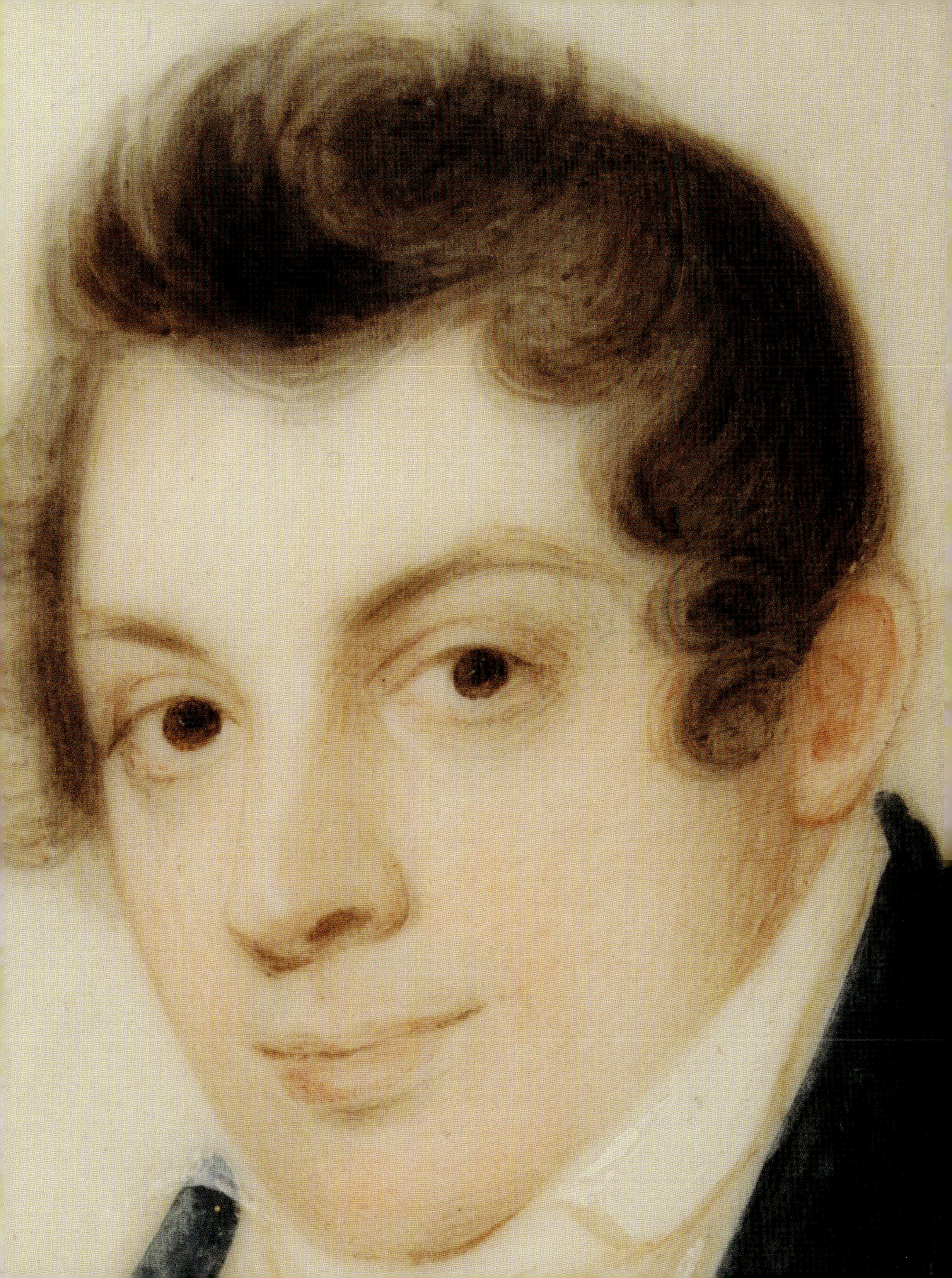

A FIRST TEACHER AND THE RESONANCE OF MINIATURE PAINTING: SAMUEL F. B. MORSE

SUSAN RATHER

Samuel F. B. Morse's modest public emergence as a painter—his earliest surviving works, in watercolor, include profile portraits on paper and a self-portrait miniature on ivory (p. 40)—can be dated to about 1809, when he was studying at Yale College and not yet twenty years old. Young people of Morse's social background often engaged in artistic pastimes, as he had done by 1802, but his resumption of those pursuits, in the face of uneven academic performance, was not auspicious for a son of the prominent New England minister and geographer Jedidiah Morse.[1] In the Anglophone world, a premodern view of painters as tradesmen or artisans had lingered through the eighteenth century, along with a perception of portraits, the only type of picture in demand, as useful but not especially imaginative.[2] Still, after graduating from Yale in 1810, Morse committed openly to art, embarking on a period of study in Boston with the noted and continentally trained painter Washington Allston. Allston's socially privileged origins, Harvard education, and demonstrated commitment to history painting—the most intellectual and inventive genre from an academic perspective—modeled a respectable future for the young Morse.

How Morse learned to paint before that time has not been investigated; most consider him self-taught. Amateurs, whether they took lessons or not, favored watercolor because it was less complicated, messy, and space-consuming than the old master medium of oil on canvas and therefore suitable for domestic (or dormitory) production. Morse evidently found encouragement from Yale students, professors, and community members. "My price is 5 dolls. for a miniature on ivory," he noted, "and I have engaged 3 or 4 at that price. My price for profiles is 1 doll. and every body is willing to engage me at that price."[3] Naked references to money do nothing to dispel the impression of a tradesman-like start in painting, at odds with the public-minded discourses of history painting. That academic language would become second nature to Morse after he arrived in London in 1811 and ran headlong into a corresponding antipathy for miniatures. Sir Martin Archer Shee, a future president of the Royal Academy of Arts, publicly scoffed that, owing to "the prompt means of subsistence which miniature-painting affords to every manufacturer of a face, [miniature painting] will always be the refuge of imbecility: a receptacle for the poor and disappointed in art."[4] In that context, Morse might well have been embarrassed by his modest artistic beginnings.

In the miniature self-portrait made while still at Yale, Morse appears relaxed and confident as he gazes out directly at the viewer (although in the process of making, the artist's eye met his own mirrored reflection). Smooth skin, wide-open eyes, arched brows, and upwardly curved lips convey friendly inquisitiveness. These facial features, framed by curls of hair, constitute a study in counterbalancing arcs, revealing that Morse was practiced in his art beyond mere description. Further, the artist's light touch of watercolor brush to ivory, when painting his face, yielded a material transparency that seems to project qualities of the subject himself. In contrast to the luminous face and bright white shirt, with its fashionably bowed cravat, Morse rendered the high-collared blue coat more densely, anchoring the composition. Unusually for a miniature, he included his hands, a critical feature because they hold tools that identify Morse as an artist: a palette, secured by the left thumb and fingers, and a brush, poised in the somewhat boneless hand of the strongly foreshortened right arm. Like most self-portraitists, Morse corrected the mirror's reversal, so the painting hand appears true.

Interestingly, Morse chose not to represent himself as making the work we see, an arguably more direct reminder than the left-right correction that pictures are not mirrors. His tools are the giveaway: an evidently wood-grained palette dotted with discrete spots of color, indicating pigments mixed with oil, which have enough substance to adhere where the artist placed them. Miniaturists, by contrast, typically used tiny ivory or porcelain palettes, powdered pigments (or cakes), water, and gum for the binding of colors and glazing. All might have been contained within a miniaturist's tidy toolbox (fig. 1), such as the one Charles Willson Peale included in a well-known portrait showing his brother, James, painting an oval miniature (ca. 1795; Mead Art Museum, Amherst, MA). Ovals still dominated at the time Morse fashioned his own likeness, their smooth contours conducive to being worn on the body, as was the custom for intimate portraits often bestowed as gifts. A rectangular format better suited Morse's purpose; very likely, the Yale self-portrait served at once to display his skills to prospective patrons for miniatures and to represent his aspiration (if not perhaps his immediate capacity) to paint in oils on canvas.[5]

A self-taught artist can learn by visual example, which the Morse family home certainly offered. By the 1790s, the same could be said for many households with children who did not become artists.

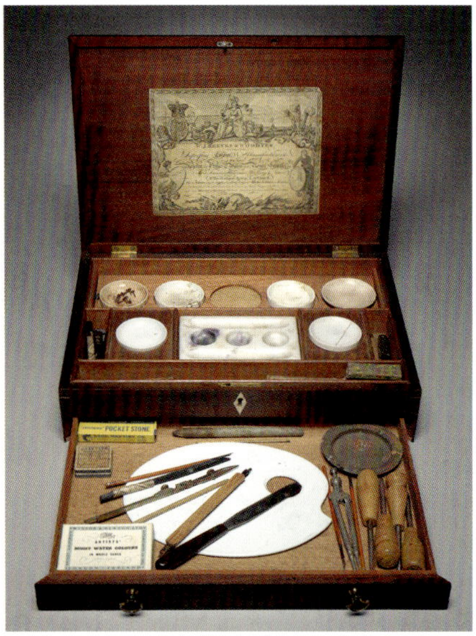

Fig. 1. Watercolor paint box, descended in the family of Rosina Cox Boardman, 1799–1816. Yale University Art Gallery, New Haven

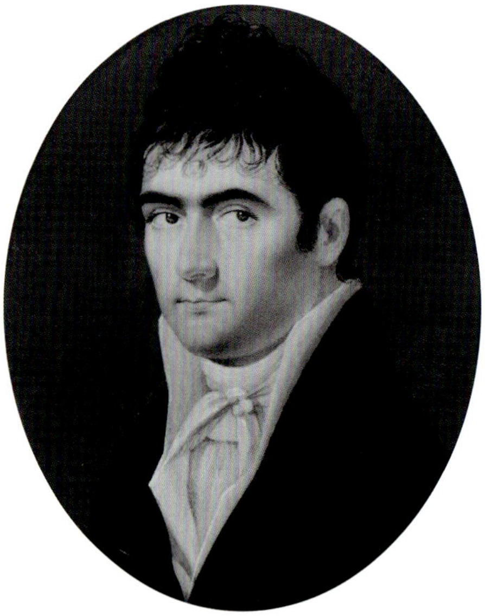

Fig. 2. Thomas Gimbrede, *Self-Portrait*, ca. 1805. Watercolor on ivory. Metropolitan Museum of Art, New York

Still, it is easy to imagine a child's fascination in seeing his three-year-old self gazing directly back from a canvas, as Morse could do with Edward Savage's double portrait of Samuel and his more remote father (ca. 1794; private collection).[6] And even now, the miniature portrait of Jedidiah by the little-known Nathaniel Hancock (ca. 1794; Yale University Art Gallery, New Haven) astonishes for its verso depiction, no greater in size than a large thumbprint, showing the geographer instructing a group of young women.[7] The wide popularity of miniatures leaves little doubt that Morse had the opportunity to see examples, but whether they alone could have coaxed from him the skill evident in his small self-portrait remains open to question.

Many artists in eighteenth- and early nineteenth-century America benefited from technical manuals, although Morse's access to such texts has not been established. Copies of Robert Dossie's multiply reissued *The Handmaid to the Arts* have been identified in the possession of forty-six American booksellers, repositories, and individuals; yet that text included a mere five pages on watercolor pigments and their preparation. A would-be miniaturist seeking more comprehensive guidance could do no better than *The Art of Painting in Miniature: Teaching the Speedy and Perfect Acquisition of that art without a master; By Rules so easy, and in a Method so natural as to render this charming Accomplishment universally attainable*. That book (identified in only five locations) includes sections on the difference between miniatures and other kinds of pictures; on the preparation, management, and uses of specific colors; on drawing, with particular attention to faces; and on the usefulness of prints. Consistent with the original 1676 French publication date, however, the author addressed painting on paper or vellum, not ivory, which had become the dominant support by 1752, when the book was last issued in English.[8]

Newspaper advertisements have proved a goldmine for understanding the arts in early America, and simply tapping that source pays quick dividends in regard to Morse. On May 14, 1807, the *Connecticut Journal* of New Haven ran the following notice:

> Dancing, Drawing, etc. Mr. Thos. Gimbrede, has the honour to Inform the Ladies and Gentlemen of this City, that he intends to spend the summer in New-Haven, and to teach the following branches of polite education, viz—DRAWING, DANCING, and FENCING, and the taking of MINIATURE LIKENESSES, or Profiles. Specimens of his Painting may be seen at the Book-Store of Beers & Howe. . . . N.B. He will give private lessons in any of the above branches.

A week later, Gimbrede publicized a partnership with "Mons. Value," in whose "room" the lessons would occur. Value, as his own advertisements in a different local newspaper attest, had been in New Haven since late 1806 teaching French, dancing, drawing, and music, for which he cited endorsements from Rev. Dr. Timothy Dwight, president of Yale College, and Benjamin Silliman, a professor of science.[9]

Morse was right there. On June 7, 1807, he informed his parents that he had thrown himself into French, detailing a twenty-four-hour cycle of study punctuated by recitation "to Monsieur Value." Within three months, the teacher had promised, the young man would be able to read any French book. Morse optimistically purchased examples at Beers and Howe, the booksellers Jedidiah Morse had charged with supplying Samuel's needs.[10]

Within a single month, then, Morse had several paths to an encounter with Gimbrede. He may have noticed the advertisement, probably encountered the miniaturist's work in the bookstore, and must have seen examples and learned about Gimbrede while attending his French lessons. Gimbrede was also French and a relatively recent émigré, affording Morse further opportunity to practice a language he was so intent on acquiring.

Gimbrede's commitment to teaching in those years (by the 1810s, he worked primarily as an engraver) may help to explain his tiny surviving oeuvre. A striking miniature of a wall-eyed gentleman bears the artist's signature along the obverse rim, while the protective case of another held a backing card, used to secure the ivory, marked "Presented / by the / Junior Class Y.C. / [illegible] / Aetat 25 / Gimbrede Pinxt." (fig. 2).[11] Although the latter work is catalogued as a self-portrait of about 1805, the basis for doing so is unclear. Surely the Yale junior class would not, as a collective entity, have presented Gimbrede with an example of his own painting, much less a self-portrait. (If so, the miniature would have to date to 1807, the only year in which Gimbrede, born in 1781, could

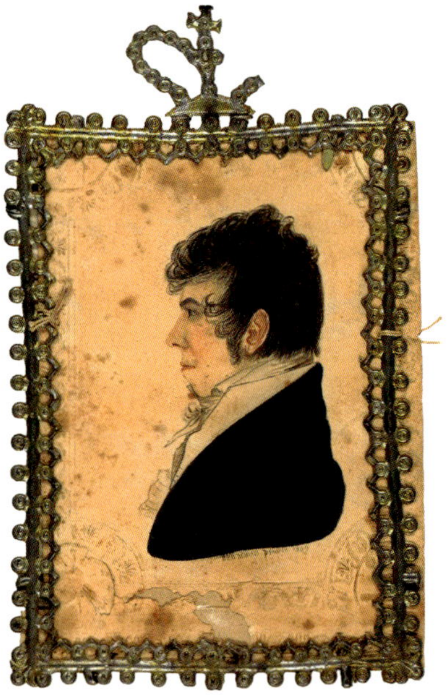

Fig. 3. Samuel F. B. Morse, *John Bartlett*, 1809. Watercolor on wove paper, with embossed design. Yale University Art Gallery, New Haven

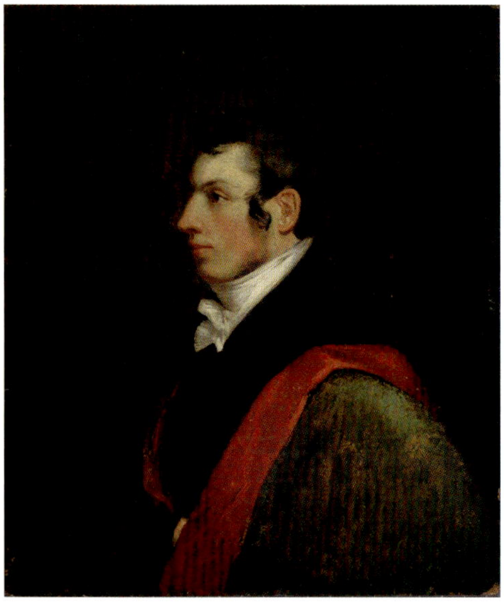

Fig. 4. Samuel F. B. Morse, *Self-Portrait*, 1812. Oil on millboard. National Portrait Gallery, Smithsonian Institution, Washington, DC

have been twenty-five years old and present in New Haven.) It makes more sense as a portrait by Gimbrede of someone else, possibly the recipient of the gift. Or perhaps the inscription has nothing to do with this miniature but was a practice text that became a bit of studio detritus, reused to secure in its frame a likeness that may or may not be a self-portrait.[12]

Strikingly, Gimbrede executed the miniature in grisaille, echoing the popularity of late eighteenth-century French drawings *à la manière noire*, in imitation of English mezzotints. Gimbrede knew such works firsthand, having trained in Paris with the miniaturist Jean-Baptiste Jacques Augustin, a savvy, technically innovative, and self-proclaimed (though not actual) autodidact. Miniatures enjoyed immense popularity in France, as elsewhere, and were generously represented in the annual Salon exhibitions, constituting 25 percent of portraits (themselves roughly 40 percent of all paintings) on display in 1801.[13] The need to compete with portraits in oil prompted French miniaturists to adopt more opaque backgrounds, as is evident in Gimbrede's signed miniature. American painters later favored darker grounds as well, but during the years around 1800, neither monochromy nor density of paint surface held any appeal relative to the English approach—used by Morse for his own self-portrait—which used the warm ivory to compositional advantage.

In addition to lessons in miniature painting, Gimbrede offered New Haven residents instruction in profile making. In his case, the practice needs to be disentangled from the proliferation of machine-made silhouettes that required only "three minutes sitting," as touted by an advertiser whose notice shared a column with Gimbrede's of May 1807.[14] Instead, judging from Morse's signed portraits of Gideon Tomlinson (ca. 1809; Yale University Art Gallery) and John Bartlett (fig. 3), Gimbrede taught students to make hand-drawn, watercolor-accentuated profiles on paper. Popular in England, France, and the United States, such portraits represented a step up from the cheap and ubiquitous cut profiles and yet were larger, quicker to produce, and less costly than miniatures on ivory. Tellingly, Morse signed his examples with the term "pinxit."

Gimbrede departed New Haven in late 1807, six months after first advertising there but long enough to provide Morse—assiduous in practicing what he loved—with sufficient skill to attract customers for portraits.[15] By August 1809, Morse reported happily, "I employ all my leisure time in painting. I have a great no. of persons engaged already to be drawn on ivory, no less than 7." Beyond the Yale students and faculty who dominate the known roster, Morse portrayed at least one female contemporary, "Miss [Caroline] Leffingwell," a granddaughter of the bookseller Isaac Beers. Morse and his sitters, the artist claimed, were all pleased with their likenesses, whether on ivory or paper.[16]

Morse had left such work behind and committed fully to oil painting by 1811, when he arrived in London for four years of study and mentoring from the American-born Benjamin West, second president of the Royal Academy. During that time, Morse made a copy in oils of West's head (p. 41) after an 1810 portrait by Sir Thomas Lawrence (Yale Center for British Art, New Haven), then in the subject's studio; the junior artist retained this token of West throughout his life.[17] Oil was the privileged medium at the academy's annual exhibitions at Somerset House, where the display of miniatures (so common at the Paris Salon) had long been contested. Small ivories, which appear clustered around a fireplace in a well-known engraving of the upstairs Great Room in 1787, were relegated in most years to poorly lit ground-floor space, along with watercolors on paper and sculptures. As watercolor surged in popularity in Britain after 1800, new organizations sprang up. Yet the Society of Painters in Water Colours (founded in 1804) barred from membership all miniaturists and other portrait makers, who, in turn, launched a more inclusive but short-lived society in 1807. In 1811, the leading miniaturists resumed showing at the Royal Academy (to which none, however, had been elected since 1791) after being granted a gallery next to the Great Room, only to find themselves again displaced to the lower rooms in 1812.[18]

It is easy to imagine that Morse adopted the superior attitude of the academic oil painter. He could not have declared himself an artist of large-scale historical subjects, like his acknowledged teachers Allston and West, more conspicuously than with *The Dying Hercules*, which won critical accolades at the Royal Academy's spring 1813 exhibition. In a contemporaneous second self-portrait, this time in oils (fig. 4), Morse appears poised—perhaps inadvertently—between the present and the recent past. The relatively small profile format (the work is roughly 11 by 9 inches) recalls his earlier practice, while his academic robes distinguish him as a man of real education, which few artists had; a Yale degree was significantly beyond the level of learning thought necessary for a history painter.

Sir Joshua Reynolds, the academy's first president and himself primarily a portraitist, proudly figured in various self-portraits his distinction as the recipient, in 1773, of an honorary doctorate of laws from Cambridge. The imposing version of 1780 (Royal Academy of Arts, London) cannot have failed to impress Morse when it was included in a comprehensive exhibition of Reynolds's work held in 1813 at the British Institution for Promoting the Fine Arts in the United Kingdom.[19] That event solidified Reynolds's posthumous reputation as founder of the British School and compounded British "sneers," which Morse found shocking, at the famously uneducated West.[20] West would soon recast his lot with his native country, relating, in John Galt's fabled biography of 1816, the previously unknown story of his colonial Pennsylvania youth and naming William Williams as the first teacher no one knew him to have had.[21]

Within the next decade, Morse started to build his own artistic legacy (unaware that his greatest impact would lie in the scientific pursuits that had intrigued him at Yale, to which he returned during the 1840s). At the age of just thirty-five, in 1826, he became the first president of the National Academy of Design, and in 1831, he began *Gallery of the Louvre*, setting out an ambitious program for the future of American art. The enormous, six-by-nine foot painting (fig. 5), begun in Paris, is studded with miniature (and stunningly anamorphic) versions of European masterworks, purposefully chosen and imaginatively reassembled in the majestic Salon Carré of the French national gallery, where the annual Salon exhibitions of contemporary painting took place. Back in New York by late 1832, Morse spent six months finishing the complex composition, populating the space with associates and friends.[22]

At the center, the artist himself appears in profile, guiding a young woman in her drawing. Behind them, occupying the brightest spot on the floor, a miniaturist (not firmly identified) sits absorbed at her compact easel, modeling that more accessible branch of painting. Just beyond her, conspicuously white in the intensely colored environment, the Louvre's famous Greco-Roman statue *Diana the Huntress* strides across her plinth. Morse had an abiding interest in sculpture, shared with his close friend the American sculptor Horatio Greenough, to whom the inclusion of *Diana* may refer.[23] An expanse of glowing red in a gold frame further sets the statue off—or does she call attention to it? A closer look reveals a neat arrangement of miniatures in their own tiny frames (fig. 6). Yet something seems odd: they hang too high to be inspected by a gallery visitor, for whom even basic proximity is denied by the statue and its plinth. Morse paid no heed to naturalism when he included the miniatures; their presence is purely symbolic.

Miniatures connect people in intimate ways. When Morse, probably around 1820, reencountered a Yale student whose small portrait he had left unfinished, he told the man, "I have carried it with me ever since, and over Europe, and thought a hundred times that I would wash it out and put the ivory to some other use. . . . This memorial of our former intimacy is still in my possession."[24] It is a

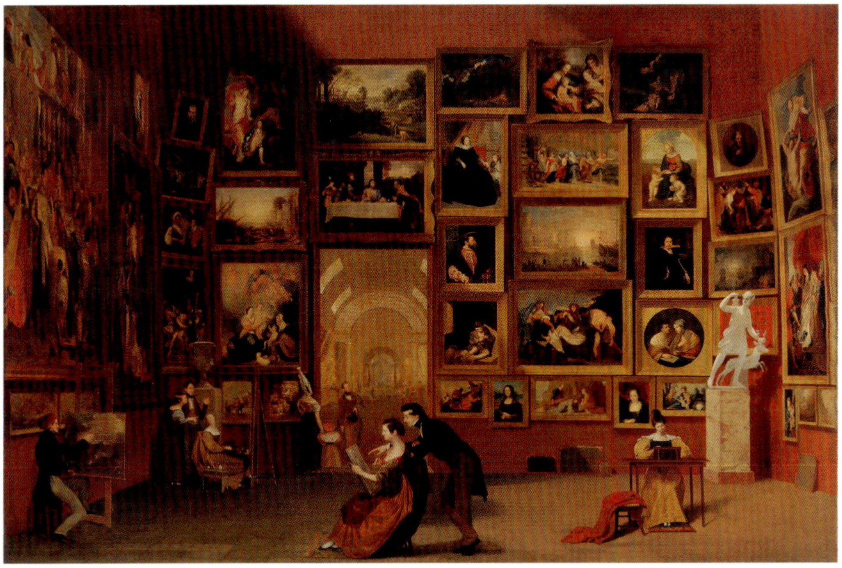

Fig. 5. Samuel F. B. Morse, *Gallery of the Louvre*, 1831–33. Oil on canvas. Terra Foundation for American Art, Chicago

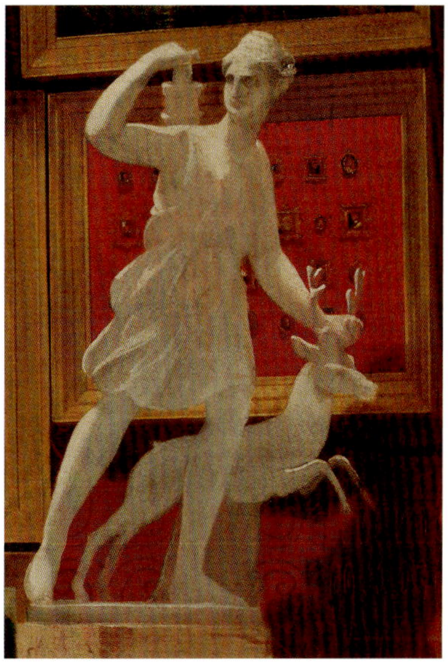

Fig. 6. Detail of fig. 5

remarkable statement, suggesting that the token was much more, a relic—not so erasable after all—of Morse's own life. In the artist's deeply self-referential *Gallery of the Louvre*, the framed miniature portraits bear witness to his youthful beginnings.

Morse had proximate cause to reflect on those early experiences with art as he prepared to complete the masterpiece of his maturity. During the last week of December 1832, his first teacher, Thomas Gimbrede, aged fifty-one, died suddenly at West Point, where he had been a professor of drawing since 1819.[25] William Dunlap, the indefatigable chronicler of American artists and vice president of the National Academy as of 1832, could summon no kind words for Gimbrede, of whom he wrote in 1834 that "it must have required uncommon talents . . . to teach that which he did not know."[26] Dunlap could be harsh about artists he felt had done little to advance the cause of American art or, in his estimation, had even done harm, as an inferior instructor might. Morse, the Academy's president and (in his own mind, certainly) the nation's chief educator in matters of art, was, under the circumstances, kinder, even grateful. In *Gallery of the Louvre*, among "the most splendid . . . collection of works of art in the world," jewel of the city where Gimbrede had trained as an artist, Morse tucked a memento that paid quiet tribute to the miniaturist who had nudged him into his career.[27]

1. Samuel was eleven when Jedidiah sent one of his drawings to the boy's paternal grandfather, noting, "He is self-taught—has had no instructions"; Jedidiah Morse to Deacon Jedidiah Morse, Sr., October 5, 1802, box 3 (Correspondence January 1800–December 1805), Morse Family Papers (MS 358), Yale University Library, Manuscripts and Archives. At fourteen, Morse was drawing and had

"painted a few pictures"; entries for January 28–31 and February 2, 1805, Diaries and Notebooks 1793–1844, Samuel F. B. Morse Papers, Library of Congress.

2. For extended consideration, see Susan Rather, *The American School: Artists and Status in the Late Colonial and Early National Era* (New Haven and London: Yale University Press for the Paul Mellon Centre for Studies in British Art, 2016).
3. Morse to his parents, June 25, 1810, General Correspondence and Related Documents, Morse Papers, Library of Congress. At the start of a notable career in 1818, Charles Fraser typically charged fifty dollars for a miniature; Charles Fraser's Book of Records, Gibbes Museum of Art, Charleston, SC.
4. Sir Martin Archer Shee, *Rhymes on Art; or, the Remonstrance of a Painter* (London, 1805), 30–31.
5. The miniature entered the Academy's collection in 1900 by sale from Samuel F. B. Morse II, the artist's grandson, a transaction documented in correspondence with Frederick Dielman, NAD Secretary, NAD object file.
6. Savage's double portrait appears in Arlene Katz Nichols, *The American Vasari: William Dunlap and His World*, exh. cat. (New York: Hirschl and Adler Galleries, 1999).
7. For Hancock's miniature, see Robin Jaffee Frank, *Love and Loss: American Portrait and Mourning Miniatures* (New Haven: Yale University Press, 2000), 81–88.
8. Robert Dossie, *The Handmaid to the Arts*, 2 vols. (London, 1758), 1:135–40. Claude Boutet, *The Art of Painting in Miniature . . .* (London, 1739). For American evidence of these texts, see Janice G. Schimmelman, *Books on Art in Early America* (New Castle, DE: Oak Knoll Press, 2007), 28–29, 58–67.
9. *Connecticut Herald* (New Haven), November 11, 1806; April 28 and May 12, 1807.
10. Morse to his parents, June 7, 18, and 30, 1807, General Correspondence and Related Documents, Morse Papers, Library of Congress. Morse was still studying with Value in early December.
11. Carrie Rebora Barratt and Lori Zabar, *American Portrait Miniatures in the Metropolitan Museum of Art*, exh. cat. (New York: Metropolitan Museum of Art; New Haven: Yale University Press, 2010), 106, where "[Autumn]" appears as an alternate for "Aetat," although this seems unlikely in conjunction with the number 25; I have not seen the inscription myself. Gimbrede's other, signed miniature was sold at Bonhams, London, on November 21, 2007.
12. Curators have reasonably proposed that a man holding a large miniature in a work attributed to Samuel L. Waldo might be Gimbrede, of whom Waldo exhibited a portrait at the American Academy of the Fine Arts in 1817; see John Caldwell, Oswaldo Rodriguez Roque, and Dale T. Johnson, *A Catalogue of Artists Born before 1815*, vol. 1 of Kathleen Luhrs, ed., *American Paintings in the Metropolitan Museum of Art* (New York: Metropolitan Museum of Art; Princeton: Princeton University Press, 1994), 320–21. Whether it is Gimbrede's younger self in the miniature remains open to question, not least because physiognomic matching is tricky when different hands, mediums, and dimensions are concerned.
13. Tony Halliday, *Facing the Public: Portraiture in the Aftermath of the French Revolution* (Manchester, UK: Manchester University Press, 1999), 26–47, 123–39; Amy Freund, *Portraiture and Politics in Revolutionary France* (University Park: Pennsylvania State University Press, 2014), 26–27.
14. "R. Letton, Taker of Profile Likenesses," *Connecticut Journal* (New Haven), May 12, 1807.
15. Gimbrede announced a "Drawing Academy" and "Likenesses in three or four different styles" in the *Newport Mercury*, November 21, 1807.
16. Morse to his parents, August 1809, General Correspondence and Related Documents, Morse Papers, Library of Congress.
17. Morse's son Edward, born in 1857, remembered West's portrait as having hung in the library of the family's home in New York City; Edward Morse to C. K. Johnson, May 28, 1923, NAD object file.
18. Greg Smith, "Watercolourists and Watercolours at the Royal Academy, 1780–1836," in David Solkin, ed., *Art on the Line: The Royal Academy Exhibitions at Somerset House, 1780–1836* (New Haven and London: Yale University Press for the Paul Mellon Centre for Studies in British Art and the Courtauld Institute Gallery, 2001), 193–96. Public display of miniatures altered their appearance and meaning, as Marcia Pointon observes in an essay exploring the interplay of miniatures and their containers when intended for private consumption; see "'Surrounded with Brilliants': Miniature Portraits in Eighteenth-Century England," *Art Bulletin* 83, no. 1 (March 2001): 48–71.

19. *Catalogue of Pictures by the Late Sir Joshua Reynolds* (London: British Institution for Promoting the Fine Arts in the United Kingdom, 1813).

20. Morse to his parents, March 25, 1812, General Correspondence and Related Documents, Morse Papers, Library of Congress.

21. John Galt, *The Life and Studies of Benjamin West, Esq., President of the Royal Academy in London, prior to his Arrival in England, compiled from materials furnished by himself* (London, 1816). For Williams, West, Galt, and the impact of the biography, see Rather, *American School*, 51–87, 207–33.

22. Morse's painting has been the subject of extensive scholarly inquiry, most recently in Peter John Brownlee, ed., *Samuel F. B. Morse's "Gallery of the Louvre" and the Art of Invention* (Chicago: Terra Foundation for American Art; New Haven: Yale University Press, 2014). Efforts to identify the figures began in David Tatham, "Samuel F. B. Morse's *Gallery of the Louvre*: The Figures in the Foreground," *American Art Journal* 13, no. 4 (Fall 1981): 38–48.

23. See Wendy Bellion, "The Sculpture Club," in Brownlee, *Morse's "Gallery of the Louvre" and the Art of Invention*, 95.

24. Joseph M. Dulles, in a letter of October 16, 1872, recalling a conversation with Morse in Charleston, probably between 1818 and 1821, when Morse was active there; see Samuel Iranaeus Prime, *The Life of Samuel F. B. Morse, LL.D., Inventor of the Electro-Magnetic Recording Telegraph* (New York: D. Appleton, 1875), 26–27.

25. Morse's correspondence of 1825–32 poignantly exposes his sensitivity to premature death. He may have discussed Gimbrede's with the artist Charles Robert Leslie, who succeeded Gimbrede at West Point and had been a close friend of Morse's since their early days in London.

26. William Dunlap, *A History of the Rise and Progress of the Arts of Design in the United States*, 3 vols. (New York: Dover, 1969; first published 1834), 2:255.

27. Samuel F. B. Morse, *Descriptive Catalogue of the Pictures, Thirty-Seven in Number, from the Most Celebrated Masters, Copied into the "Gallery of the Louvre"* (New York, 1833), 3.

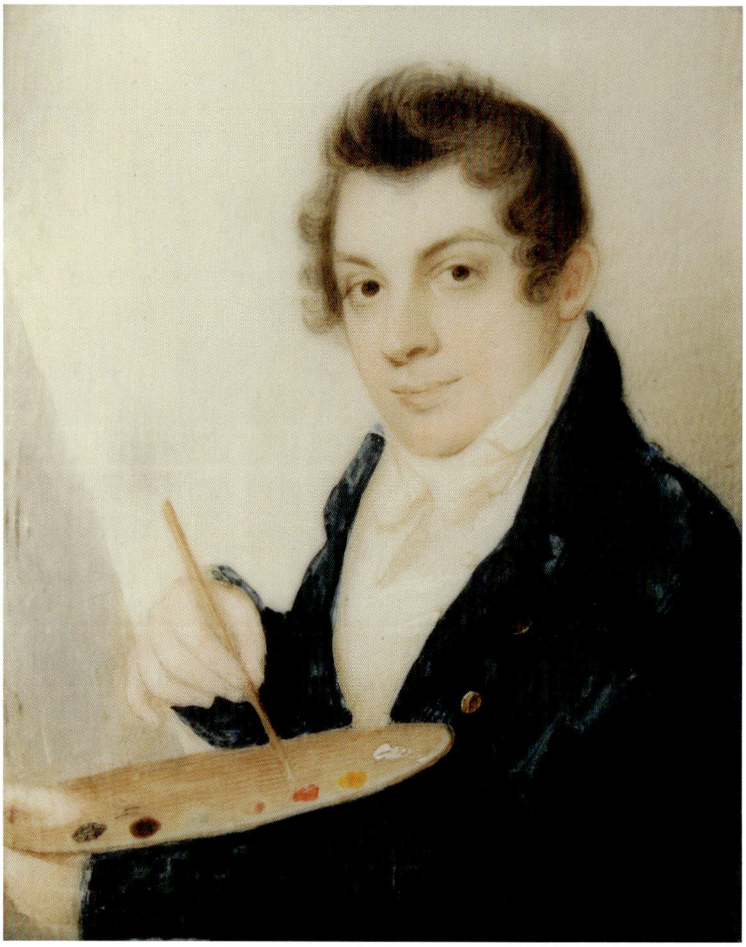

Samuel F. B. Morse, *Self-Portrait*, ca. 1809. Watercolor on ivory, 3 ¼ × 2 ⅝ in. (8.3 × 6.7 cm)

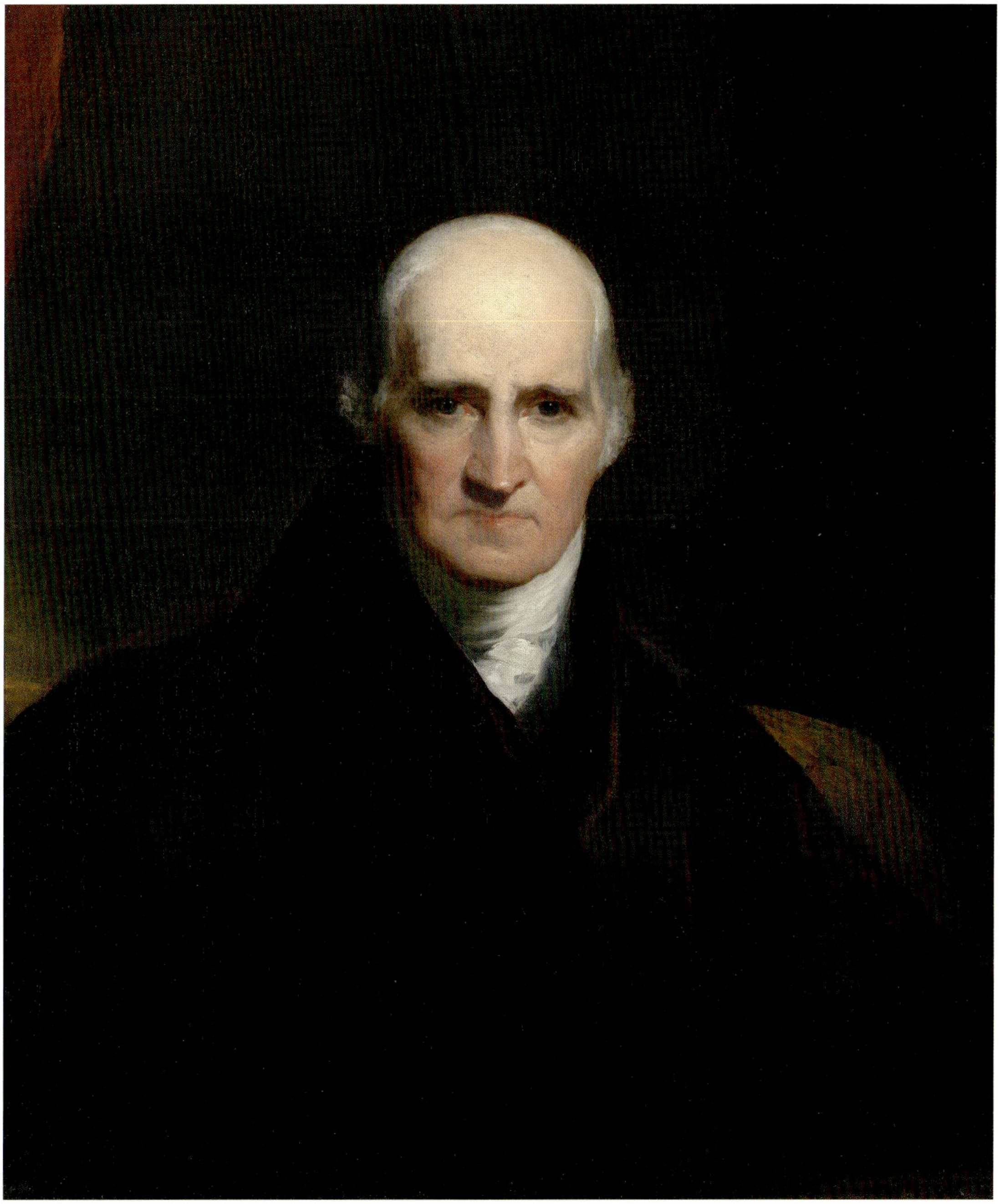

Samuel F. B. Morse, *Benjamin West*, ca. 1811. Oil on canvas, 30 ¼ × 25 ⅜ in. (76.8 × 64.5 cm)

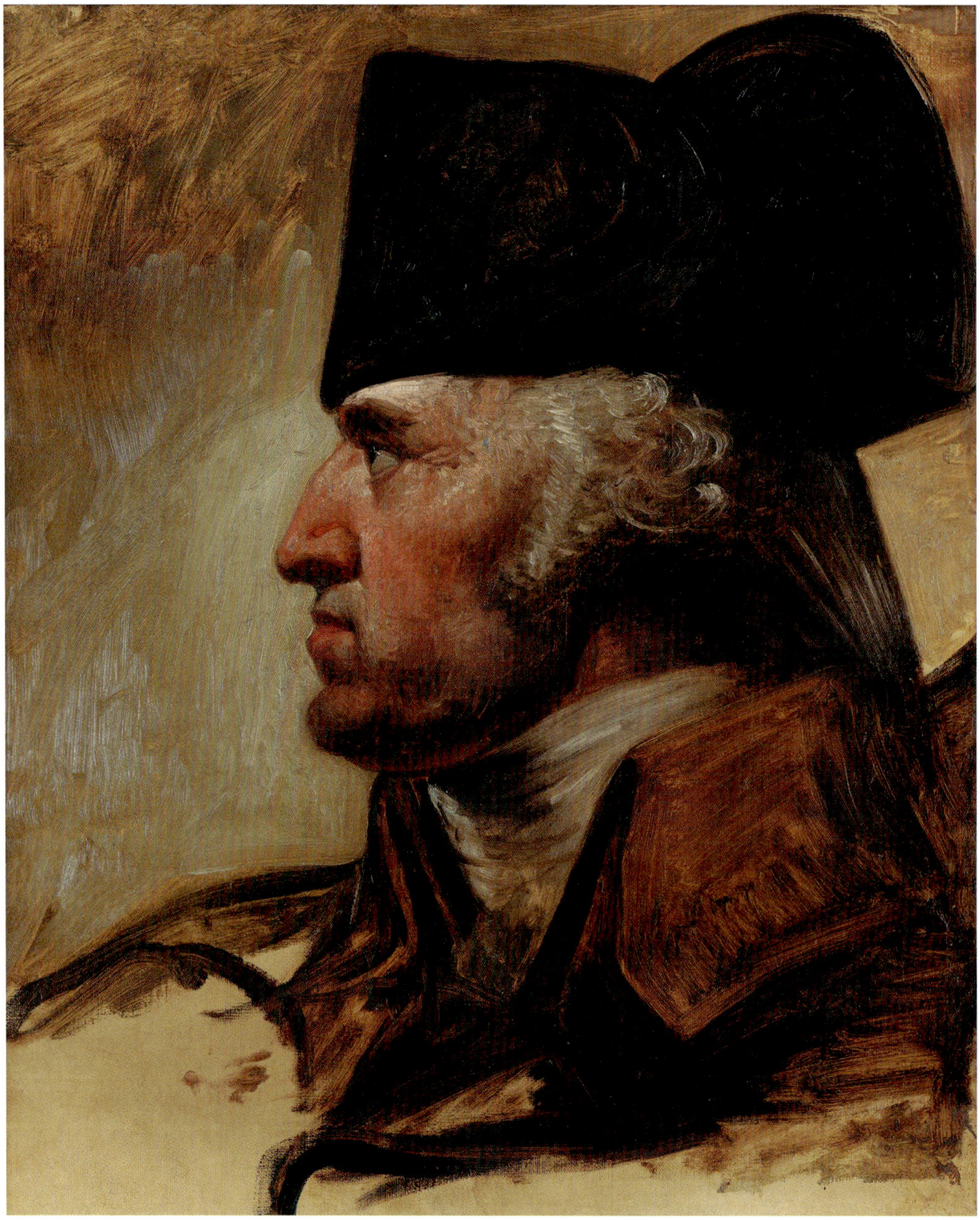

Emanuel Leutze, *George Washington, Study for "Washington Crossing the Delaware,"* ca. 1850. Oil on canvas, 21 × 17 in. (53.3 × 43.2 cm)

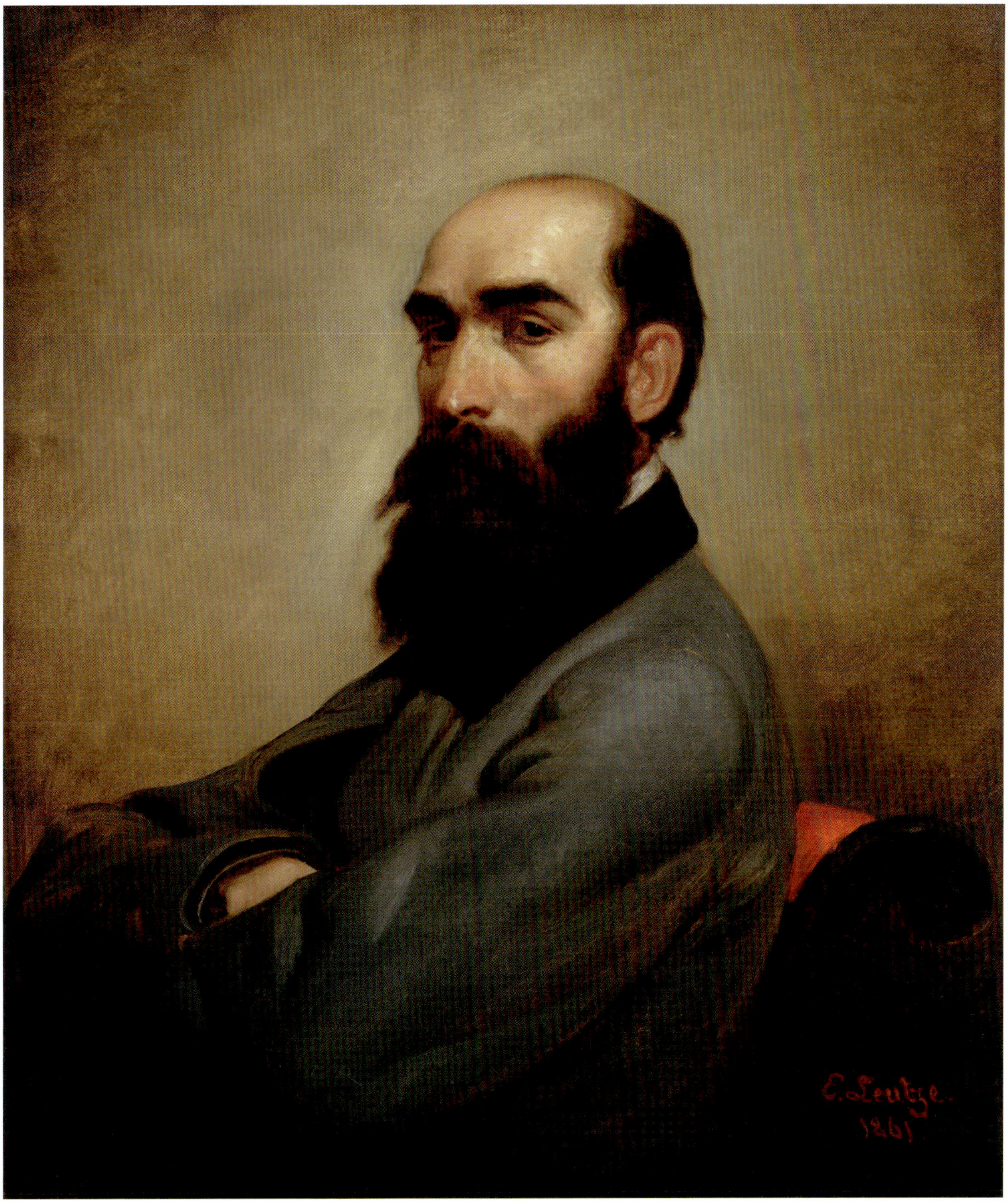

Emanuel Leutze, *Worthington Whittredge*, 1861. Oil on canvas, 30 × 24⅝ in. (76.2 × 62.5 cm)

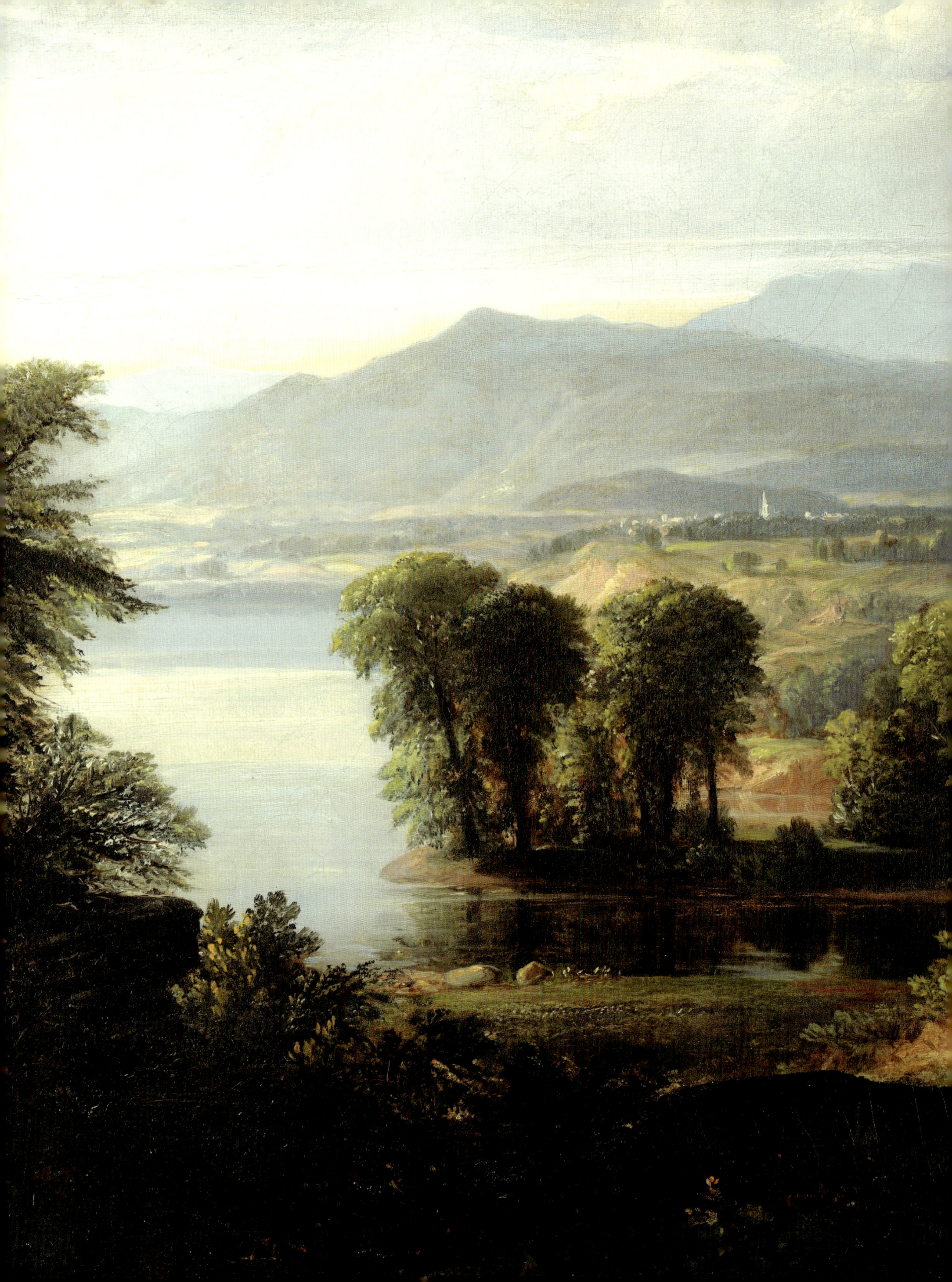

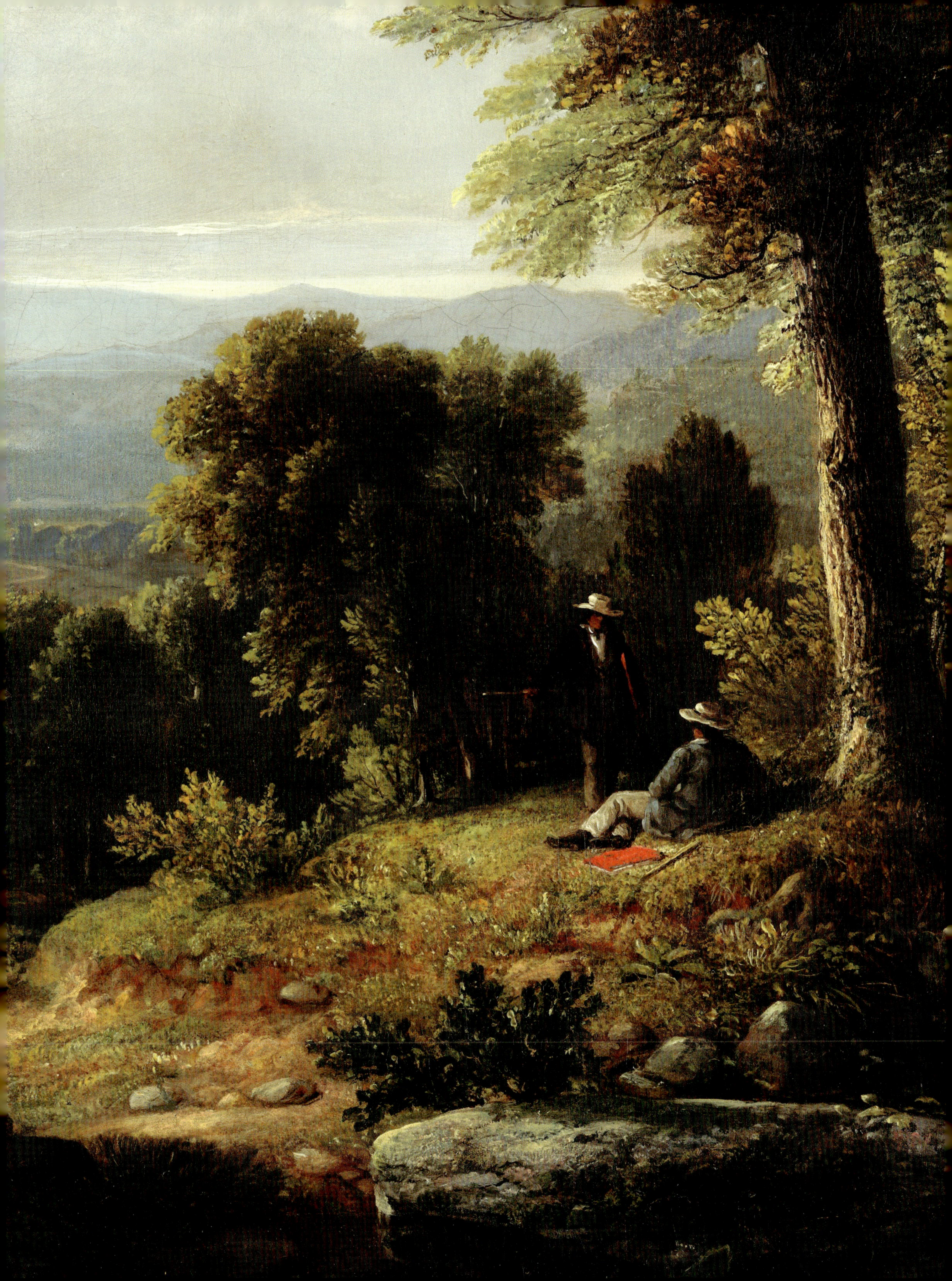

A NATION ON DISPLAY: ALBERT BIERSTADT, FREDERIC EDWIN CHURCH, AND ASHER B. DURAND

ELIZABETH A. SPEAR

As a category of images, landscapes are particularly given to what might be called "spectacularization." Beginning with the Irish painter Robert Barker's 1787 invention of the panorama—initially, a cylindrical room in which a continuous, 360-degree landscape painting was installed—and continuing through the succeeding century in devices such as the stereograph, artist-entrepreneurs sought to replicate the visual sensation of encountering grand and distant vistas of the kind previously available only to wilderness explorers and hot-air balloonists. Such experiences held consistent appeal for audiences who happily paid a modest fee in exchange for a brush with the sublime.

Nearly contemporary with the birth of the panorama was the emergence of another innovation in artistic display: the "single picture" or "great picture" exhibition, first undertaken in England by John Singleton Copley and Benjamin West as a means of promoting their work. In the beginning, the term had no particular connection to the landscape genre, indicating simply the idea of publicly exhibiting a single, often large-scale painting and charging a per-person viewing fee. By the early nineteenth century, American painters such as John Trumbull, Rembrandt Peale, William Dunlap, and Samuel F. B. Morse were also turning to the format to offset the costs of their more ambitious paintings.[1] In addition to single-picture exhibitions, trained artists often opened panoramas, moving panoramas, or dioramas in the hope of subsidizing other, less lucrative artistic pursuits, including traditional gallery exhibitions.[2] From the time of its founding, the National Academy of Design provided a crucial venue for artists of both generations of the Hudson River School to build audiences for and test critical responses to work they might later exhibit in more grandiose fashion.

Thomas Cole was the first artist to truly marry conventional easel painting with the spectacular qualities of panoramic display. Like many of his contemporaries, Cole had exhibited his paintings in single-picture shows and even considered making his own panorama.[3] Instead of the latter, beginning with his five-panel cycle *The Course of Empire* (1833–36; New-York Historical Society), he translated the monumentality and narrative structure of the panorama to a flat canvas. For contemporary viewers, the scale of the installation, in combination with its "serial" format, recalled the experience of viewing a panorama.[4] An 1833 diagram of Cole's planned design for the painting cycle indicates that he intended it, when complete, to be installed and read in three horizontal columns, progressing from top to bottom, then left to right. The artist's close friend and fellow Academician Asher B. Durand was undoubtedly working under Cole's influence when he executed his 1840 pairing *The Morning of Life* and *The Evening of Life*, now in the Academy's collection.[5]

Though an engraver by training and trade, Durand had been a talented portraitist from early in his career. A self-portrait, which he likely executed by 1835 and donated to the Academy sometime between 1843 and 1852 (p. 52), may have been among the examples that impressed Luman Reed, the patron of Cole's *The Course of Empire*, sufficiently for him to commission from Durand, in 1835, portraits of all seven US presidents to date.[6] Reed's patronage allowed Durand to give up his engraving business and pursue painting seriously for the first time in his career. He continued to concentrate on portraiture throughout the mid-1830s before dedicating himself to landscape painting around 1837. Following Cole's untimely death in 1848, Durand—by then, president of the Academy—famously memorialized his friend by depicting him with William Cullen Bryant, the Academy's first professor of mythology and history, in his 1849 canvas *Kindred Spirits* (Crystal Bridges Museum of American Art, Bentonville, AR). The following year, he revisited the theme of artistic fellowship in nature with his *Landscape* (p. 53). In it, two men with sketchbooks converse in a landscape evocative of the upper Hudson, one standing and gesturing with a maulstick as his reclining protégé absorbs the lesson. For Durand and his circle, Cole's death meant the loss not only of a friend but of the leading American landscape artist, and although critics teased the question of whether Durand could fill his slightly younger compatriot's shoes, it was generally understood that he would assume the mantle of leader in the wake of Cole's passing. Durand was undoubtedly still grappling with the loss and its consequences for his own place in the art world when he painted *Landscape*, and the work, with its two deliberately unidentifiable figures perhaps serving as stand-ins for any two painters, may be read as a rumination on the relationship between student and teacher and the bonds of friendship that develop between artists.[7]

In light of Cole's enduring fascination with the panoramic, it should perhaps come as no surprise that the artist who ultimately took the spectacularization of landscape painting to its furthest

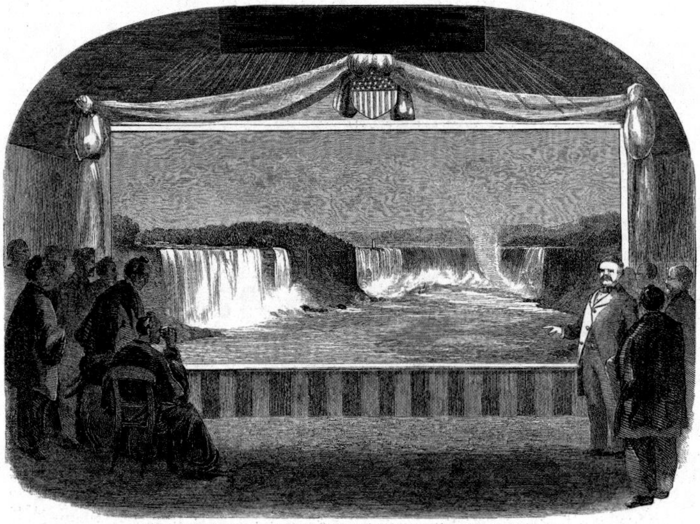

Fig. 1. *Mr. Thorpe's Niagara*, engraving published in *Harper's Weekly*, July 7, 1860

extreme was his sole pupil, Frederic Edwin Church. The painting that is now most closely associated with the single-picture tradition in American art, *The Heart of the Andes* (1859; Metropolitan Museum of Art, New York), resulted from Church's interest in the writings of the German naturalist Alexander von Humboldt, particularly in his multivolume treatise *Cosmos: A Sketch of a Physical Description of the Universe*, which details, among a great many other topics, Humboldt's study of the ecology of South America.[8] In 1853, Church traveled with his friend Cyrus Field to Colombia and Ecuador to retrace the explorations Humboldt had made half a century earlier. From the trip, Church produced volumes of notes and drawings that he would later use to compose modest oil sketches and full-scale exhibition pieces. Among these was *Scene among the Andes* (p. 57). Following what would become a familiar theme in Church's South American works, it depicts a lone figure making an arduous journey—possibly a pilgrimage—along a rugged path, set against a backdrop of lush Andean wilderness.[9] The success of Church's most ambitious canvas in this series, his 1855 *The Andes of Ecuador* (Reynolda House Museum of American Art, Winston-Salem, NC), contributed to his decision to return to South America two years later.

In the spring of 1857, Church completed and began exhibiting his large painting *Niagara* (Corcoran Collection, National Gallery of Art, Washington, DC). With a height-to-width ratio of less than one to two and lacking a foreground as well as the vertical framing elements of the classical landscape format, *Niagara* made a clear break with earlier easel-based American landscape painting.[10] Touring as a single-picture exhibition throughout the United States and England, the work was met with enormous popular and critical acclaim, securing Church's reputation as the leading painter of the

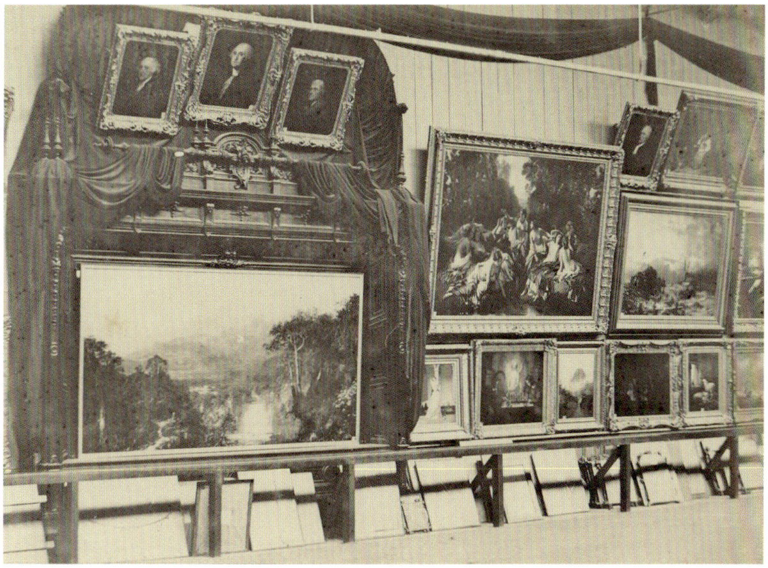

Fig. 2. Mathew Brady, *Recollections of the Art Exhibition, Metropolitan Fair, New York*, 1864

American landscape. When he exhibited *The Andes of Ecuador* at the Academy's annual exhibition that same year, it would be the last time he participated in one of its group exhibitions. Thereafter, he focused on promoting individual paintings by capitalizing on the showman-like display techniques of the single-picture format.[11] Fortunately for Church, his gamble paid off; scarcely two weeks after its public debut at the Tenth Street Studio Building on April 29, 1859, *The Heart of the Andes* became the most expensive American landscape painting sold to that point, commanding a price of ten thousand dollars.[12]

By this time, artists had begun adopting more openly stagy practices in mounting these exhibitions. Church and others achieved dramatic and sophisticated lighting effects through the use of drapery, skylights, and gas jets. An 1860 *Harper's Weekly* engraving seems to illustrate such techniques at work in the display of Thomas Bangs Thorpe's *Niagara As It Is* (fig. 1). The visitors' animated reactions to the spectacle and use of optical instruments to heighten their viewing experience were typical of single-picture exhibitions, as was the generally sensational atmosphere. The same was certainly the case for the debut of *The Heart of the Andes*, and Church went a step further, commissioning a massive, dark walnut frame for the painting. This decision, in combination with the availability of two descriptive booklets for sale at the entrance to the exhibition, may have aggravated the mild controversy over the artist's use of gas lighting; although critical responses to the painting were generally positive, there remained some critics who objected to any practices they perceived as deceptive as well as any whiff of self-promotion, dismissing such actions as "puffery."[13]

Following the success of *The Heart of the Andes*, it was clear that any landscape painter who wished to compete with Church must devise an equally impressive spectacle. Although his *Lake*

Lucerne of the previous year had already won him critical success and election to the Academy as an Honorary Member, it was likely with just such intentions that Albert Bierstadt headed westward from Saint Joseph, Missouri, with Frederick W. Lander's expedition in the spring of 1859. The official purpose of the expedition was to establish a shorter, safer overland alternative to the Oregon Trail; however, Bierstadt was one of three artists who had received permission to accompany the surveying party.[14] His *On the Sweetwater near the Devil's Gate* (p. 59) depicts a stretch of the Sweetwater River near a 370-foot-tall granite ridge that forms part of the Devil's Gate, a natural gorge in present-day Wyoming and a well-known landmark along the trail. While scholars have long believed that Bierstadt and his fellow artists turned back prematurely, never reaching the Rocky Mountains, a series of sketches and letters by Bierstadt and his fellow artist Henry Hitchings suggests that was not the case; therefore, it is possible that this scene was, in fact, sketched from nature.[15]

After returning east, Bierstadt spent the next three years setting the stage for a rivalry with Church by slowly building interest in his large-scale Western landscapes. His strategy proved effective, and when he finally presented his *Rocky Mountains, Lander's Peak* (1863; Metropolitan Museum of Art) at the 1864 Metropolitan Sanitary Fair in New York, where it was hung directly opposite *The Heart of the Andes*, critics had already been comparing the two works for over a year.[16] In addition to the painting itself, Bierstadt mounted an additional public spectacle, which he branded "Bierstadt's Indian Department." Just steps away from the fair's fine art gallery, a troupe of nineteen dancers from the Onondaga and Cayuga tribes portrayed the Shoshone figures shown in the painting in a live reenactment of its foreground, performing dances while surrounded by various Native American artifacts.[17] Meanwhile, the presentation of *The Heart of the Andes* had also been augmented on the occasion of the fair; underscoring the event's pro-Union theme, portraits of George Washington, John Adams, and Thomas Jefferson topped Church's massive frame and draperies (fig. 2).

While their association with mass audiences and unconcealed profit motive have often led critics and art historians to dismiss panoramas and related inventions as lowbrow "amusements," the pursuit of the same moment of wonder inspired by an all-encompassing view—and, indeed, of the attendant profits—is behind the work of many masters of the Hudson River School, and their canny spectacularization of the genre played an integral role in establishing it as the unofficial national art form. Through their early formal innovations of the panoramic mode of easel painting, Cole, Church, and Bierstadt helped to define "the American landscape," paving the way for the monumental views of the American West that Bierstadt and Thomas Moran would produce throughout the latter decades of the century.[18]

1. Kevin J. Avery, "The Panorama and Its Manifestation in American Landscape Painting, 1795–1870" (PhD diss., Columbia University, 1995), xiii. On Trumbull's single-picture exhibitions at the American Academy of the Fine Arts, see Kenneth John Myers, "The Public Display of Art in New York City, 1664–1914," in David B. Dearinger, ed., *Rave Reviews: American Art and Its Critics, 1826–1925*, exh. cat. (New York: National Academy of Design, 2000), 36.
2. Likely the most famous example is that of John Vanderlyn and his panorama enterprise in New York City, called the Rotunda, which opened in 1818. On the panorama and related art forms, see Stephan Oettermann, *The Panorama: History of a Mass Medium*, trans. Deborah Lucas Schneider (New York: Zone Books, 1997), and John-Roch Bouiller and Laurence Madeline, *J'aime les panoramas: S'approprier le monde*, exh. cat. (Paris: Flammarion, 2015).
3 Ellwood C. Parry III, *The Art of Thomas Cole: Ambition and Imagination* (Newark: University of Delaware Press, 1988), 124–25.
4. On "serial landscape," see Avery, "Panorama and Its Manifestation," 73–79, 407.
5. Durand was accused of exactly this when he exhibited them at the Academy's annual exhibition of 1840. See Barbara Dayer Gallati, "'A Year of Toilsome Exile': Asher B. Durand's European Sojourn," in Linda S. Ferber, ed., *Kindred Spirits: Asher B. Durand and the American Landscape*, exh. cat. (New York: Brooklyn Museum, 2007), and Katherine Manthorne, "Asher Brown Durand," in Barbara Novak, ed., *Next to Nature: Landscape Paintings from the National Academy of Design*, exh. cat. (New York: Oxford University Press, 1980), 38–41.
6. Gallati, "'Year of Toilsome Exile,'" 130.
7. Jonathan P. Harding points out that although the painting's first owner was likely James A. Suydam, a younger artist who almost certainly knew Durand, we cannot assume that Durand intended their specific relationship as its subject. See his entry in David B. Dearinger, ed., *Paintings and Sculpture in the Collection of the National Academy of Design, 1826–1925* (New York: Hudson Hills Press, 2004), 172.
8. Church was deeply influenced by the second volume of *Cosmos*, which he likely read after it was first published in English in 1849.
9. The painting is based on an 1853 sketch titled *Recollection of the Scenery on the Road from Fusagasuga to Pandi* (Cooper Hewitt, Smithsonian Design Museum, New York). See Pablo Navas Sanz de Santamaria, *The Journey of Frederic Edwin Church through Colombia and Ecuador, April–October 1853*, trans. Jimmy Weiskopf (Bogota: Villegas Asociados S.A. in association with Universidad de los Andes; Washington, DC: Thomas Greg and Sons, 2008), 81–82.
10. Kevin J. Avery, *Church's Great Picture: The Heart of the Andes*, exh. cat. (New York: Metropolitan Museum of Art, 1993).
11. For precedents and potential influences on Church's decision, see Gerald L. Carr, *Frederic Edwin Church: The Icebergs* (Dallas: Dallas Museum of Fine Arts, 1980), 27.
12. See Avery, *Church's Great Picture*, 34.
13. Ibid., 35–39. See also Avery, "'The Heart of the Andes' Exhibited: Frederic E. Church's Window on the Equatorial World," *American Art Journal* 18, no. 1 (1986).
14. See Nancy K. Anderson, Linda S. Ferber, and Helena Wright, *Albert Bierstadt: Art and Enterprise*, exh. cat. (New York: Brooklyn Museum; Hudson Hills Press, 1990).
15. Jourdan Moore Houston and Alan Fraser Houston, "The 1859 Lander Expedition Revisited: 'Worthy Relics' Tell New Tales of a Wind River Wagon Road," *Montana: The Magazine of Western History* 49, no. 2 (1999).
16. Gordon Hendricks, *Albert Bierstadt: Painter of the American West* (New York: H. N. Abrams, 1974), 63–90.
17. *A Record of the Metropolitan Fair in Aid of the United States Sanitary Commission, Held at New York, in April, 1864* (New York: Hurd and Houghton, 1867), 52–53.
18. See Joni Kinsey, *Thomas Moran and the Surveying of the American West* (Washington, DC: Smithsonian Institution Press, 1992), and Angela Miller, "Albert Bierstadt, Landscape Aesthetics, and the Meanings of the West in the Civil War Era," *Art Institute of Chicago Museum Studies* 27, no. 1 (2001): 40–59. The term "panoramic mode" comes from Alan Wallach's essay "Some Further Thoughts on the Panoramic Mode in Hudson River School Landscape Painting," in Phillip Earenfight and Nancy Siegel, eds., *Within the Landscape: Essays on Nineteenth-Century American Art and Culture* (Carlisle, PA: Trout Gallery, Dickinson College, 2005).

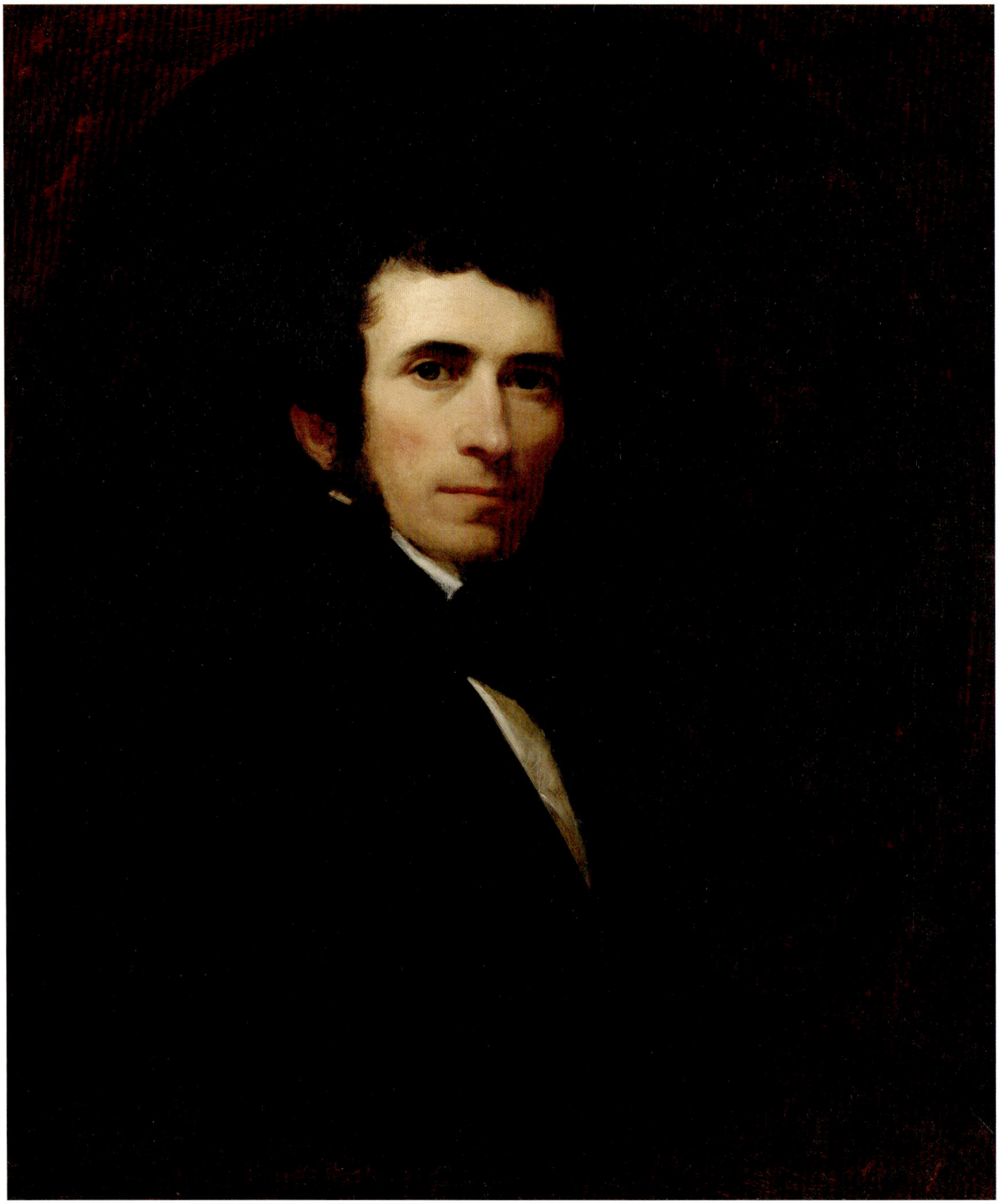

Asher B. Durand, *Self-Portrait*, ca. 1835. Oil on canvas, 30 ⅛ × 25 ¼ in. (76.5 × 64.1 cm)

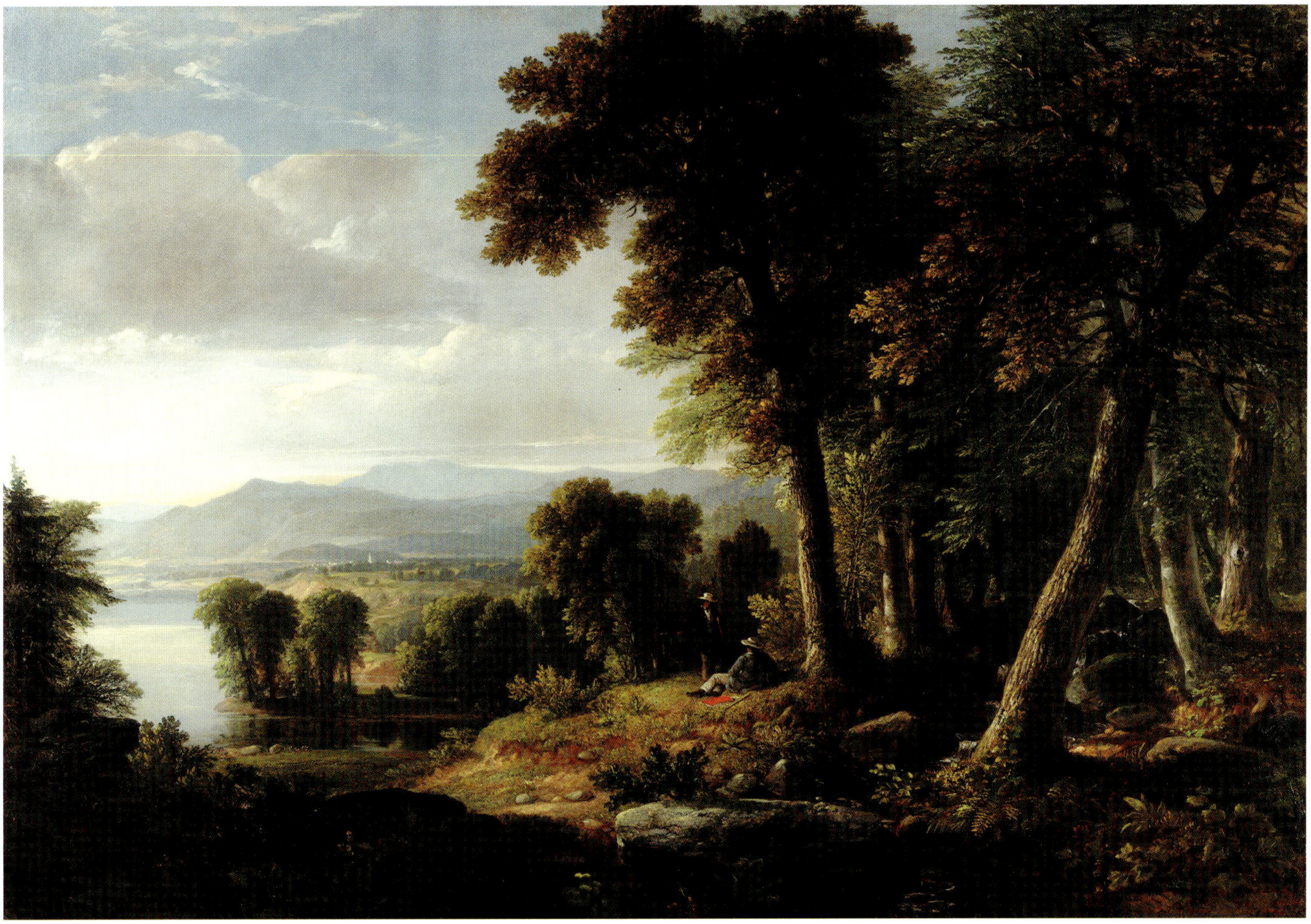

Asher B. Durand, *Landscape*, 1850. Oil on canvas, 27 ¼ × 38 ½ in. (69.2 × 97.8 cm)

STEPHEN WESTFALL ON JOHN FREDERICK KENSETT

The Bash-Bish is not the sort of painting that immediately comes to mind when considering the oeuvre of John Frederick Kensett. The artist's Luminism was more often expressed in placid horizontals of Lake George and Long Island Sound, which reflect afternoon light as if in a sort of bowl, anticipating the gloaming meadows of Inness and, more remotely, the sun-drenched, Divisionist waters of Seurat. Kensett's Lake George paintings, in particular, look back to Caspar David Friedrich's still expanses while posing as more direct transcriptions of place, and therefore as more modern. Kensett may fall to one side of the Hudson River School by virtue of the relatively intimate sizes of his works, yet, through his connection to those painters, he links to an even broader tradition of quietude—all of which contributes to the exceptionalism of Kensett's paintings of the Bash-Bish Falls, located on the border between New York and Massachusetts. These are seemingly the noisiest paintings he ever made. To be sure, he also painted Niagara Falls and a seascape or two with roiling surf. But the Niagara works push the falls back into at least the middle distance, and both they and the surf paintings imply a steady drone or rhythmic pulse. *The Bash-Bish*, by contrast, has a closer vantage point, and the falls begin to push against the picture plane, their "sound" registering as a more irregular cacophony of water falling in two asymmetrical streams. We come upon the scene as if stumbling into a sacred place, but there are no faeries or nymphs, just nature itself, presenting a prospect that approaches the miraculous in its confluence of light and shadow; near and far; rocks, pool, waterfall, forest, and mountain; earth, air, fire (light), and water.

I once heard the contemporary English painter John Walker say that all landscape paintings have something going on in them that is making a sound. I'm not sure that's entirely true, but it's true often enough that once you start looking for it, you find that it dimensionalizes a picture by supplying a sonic referent for the projected scale of the viewer's body, to go along with the visual clues. *The Bash-Bish* is not the only painting Kensett made of these falls, but it is one of the wildest, with deep shadows in the foreground and a reaching tumble of trees along the tops of the rocks, largely obscuring the misty violet ridge of the Berkshire hills in the background. Even though the painting is vertical, the falls themselves are presented more horizontally than in some of Kensett's other paintings of the site. A canvas owned by the Museum of Fine Arts, Boston (*Bash-Bish Falls, Massachusetts*, 1855), is similar to the National Academy's painting, but drawn farther back, with a wider view. I'm partial to the Academy's painting because, as noted above, the scene is closer to the picture plane so that the "wide stance" contrapposto of the split falls more closely evokes the human body, intensifying the viewer's sense that his own gaze, whether looking at a painting that portrays a space or at an actual landscape, is also something *embodied*: to consciously look at something is to take one's own measure in relation to it. And I never forget that paintings are bodies, too.

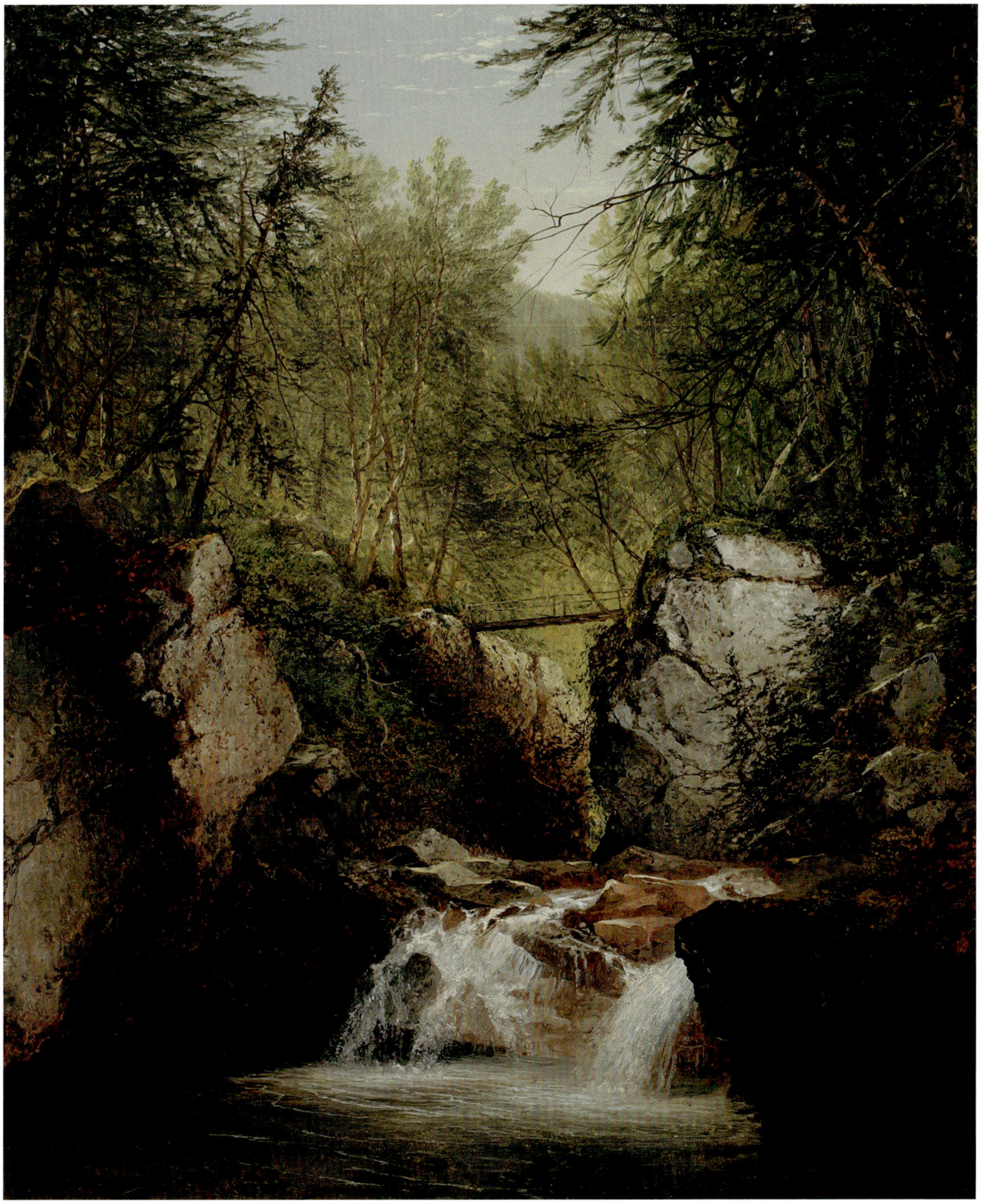

John Frederick Kensett, *The Bash-Bish*, 1855. Oil on canvas, 36 ⅛ × 29 in. (91.8 × 73.7 cm)

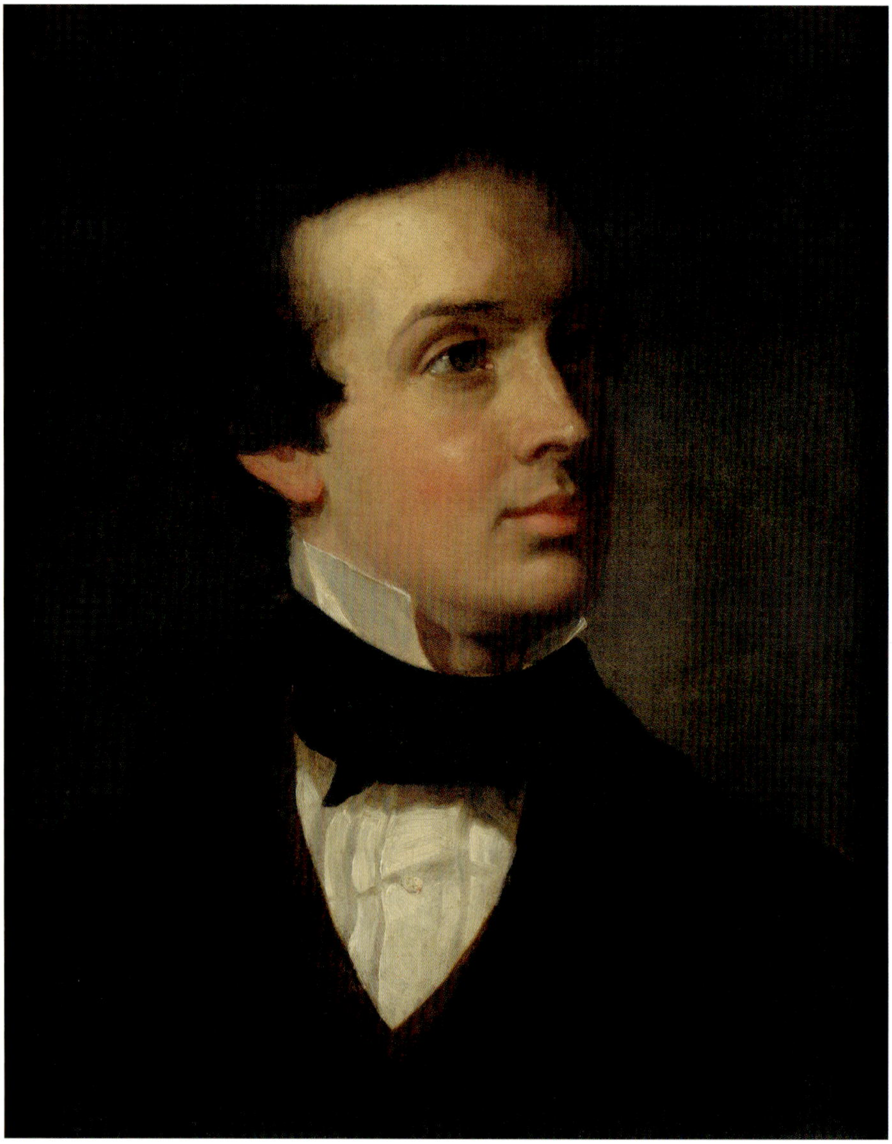

Edward Harrison May, *Frederic Edwin Church*, n.d. Oil on canvas, 19⅞ × 15⅞ in. (50.5 × 40.3 cm)

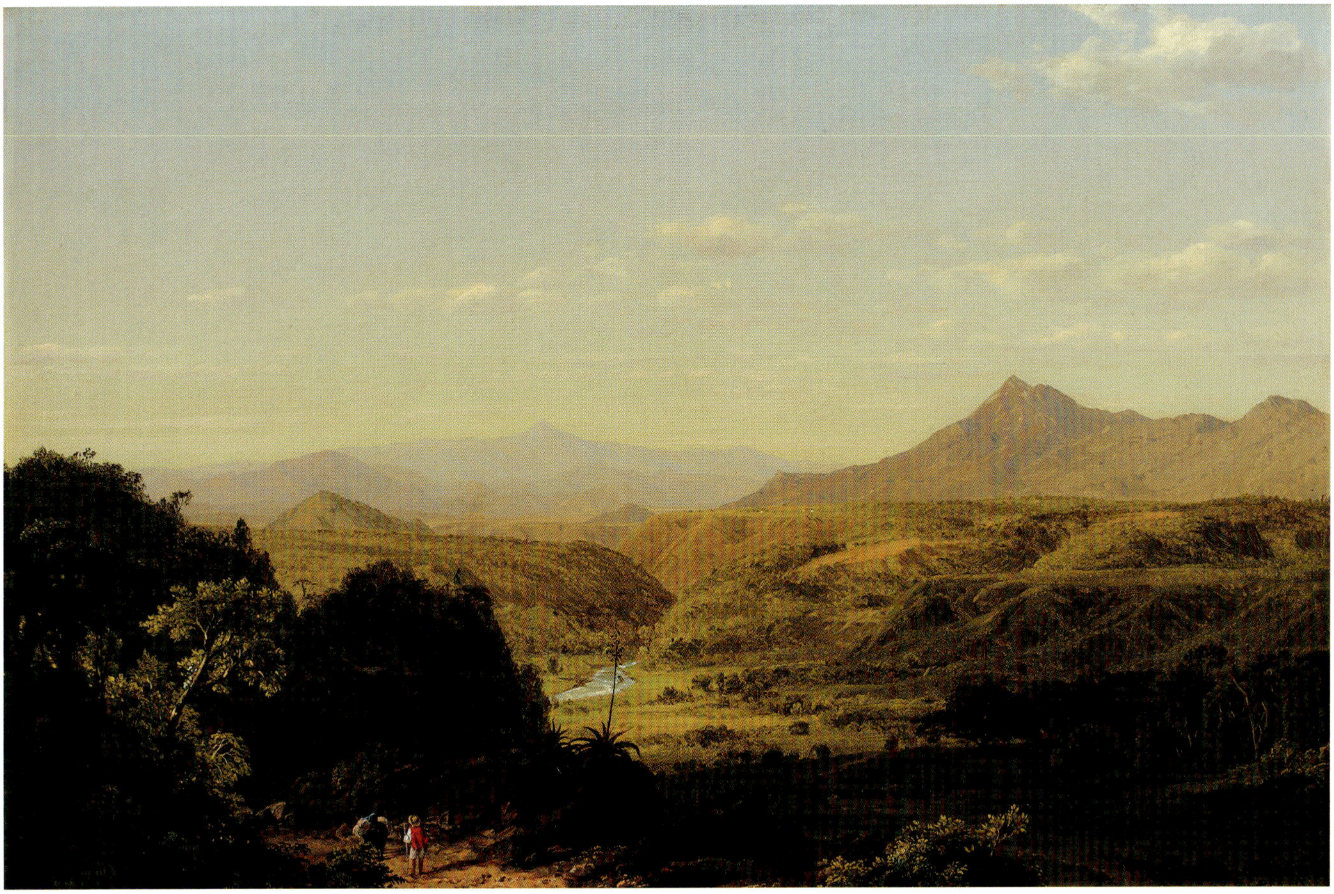

Frederic Edwin Church, *Scene among the Andes*, 1854. Oil on canvas, 15 ⅞ × 24 in. (40.3 × 61 cm)

JAUNE QUICK-TO-SEE SMITH ON ALBERT BIERSTADT

In Hudson River School paintings, what you see is not what you get. For the most part, these artists were paid extraordinary sums of money to show that North America was a utopia, a nirvana, an empyrean paradise filled with peace, serenity, and zero suffering. Nothing could have been further from the truth. The wealth that paid for the pictures likely came from exploitation of land and resources, and there was no end in sight as wagon trains, entrepreneurs, and the Corps of Engineers moved westward in the expansion known as Manifest Destiny, which meant that the perpetrators' god empowered them to do so.

If Native Americans did appear in the tranquil land, they were considered symbiotic and in harmony with the universe. In his paintings, Albert Bierstadt conveyed the idea that Indians and deer were interchangeable wild things, and he was not alone. Today, the Bureau of Land Management still conducts business with tribal nations alongside managing the national parks and wild animals.

Devil's Gate was a fur-trading post in the central part of Wyoming, a stop on the well-worn route for settlers of the Oregon Trail seeking their fortune in the western part of the continent. This painting, like so many others, is not an exact replica of Devil's Gate or Independence Rock. The artist made a habit of combining certain natural elements—rocks, trees, mountains, fluffy clouds, and a few grazing deer on a lake or a river—which he would juggle around to create a more-than-respectable landscape. He loved the theatrical more than accuracy. His fame and fortune did not rely on the realistic aspect of his paintings but rather on the stage lighting and special effects he created, overblown dioramas of landscapes that never existed.

At the time of Bierstadt's painting, America was, and still is today, a land of contrasts, of good and evil, the sublime and the violent, the land of the free and the land of the enslaved and oppressed. His lavish landscapes took no note of the beginning of the industrial era or its pollutants and waste. The world's largest genocide was taking place on the Native population as well as a massive pillaging of the land. There is virtually no mention of this in the writings about the Hudson River School, because that history has been written by the conquerors in the Great Invasion (my term).

By the time Bierstadt painted *On the Sweetwater near the Devil's Gate*, my people were incarcerated at Fort Missoula in present-day Montana, held as prisoners while our land was being stolen from under our feet. It's likely that my tribe, the Confederated Salish and Kootenai Nation, had hunted buffalo in the area of Devil's Gate, but we had to sign away the northwest section of Wyoming, part of Idaho, a piece of Canada, and half of Montana in the Hellgate Treaty of 1855. Of course, Bierstadt's painting is uninhabited save for a couple of grazing deer. My great-grandparents, grandparents, great-aunts, and great-uncles were all imprisoned at the fort, ravaged by smallpox and starved by the wormy beef and moldy flour rationed to my family. Yes, Bierstadt was painting the sublime while this tragedy was going on. It's a miracle that I am here to write this.

One more thing. Bierstadt was welcomed as an Honorary Member of the National Academy of Design in 1858, yet no Native American artist was nominated until 153 years later, when I became the first Native Academician.

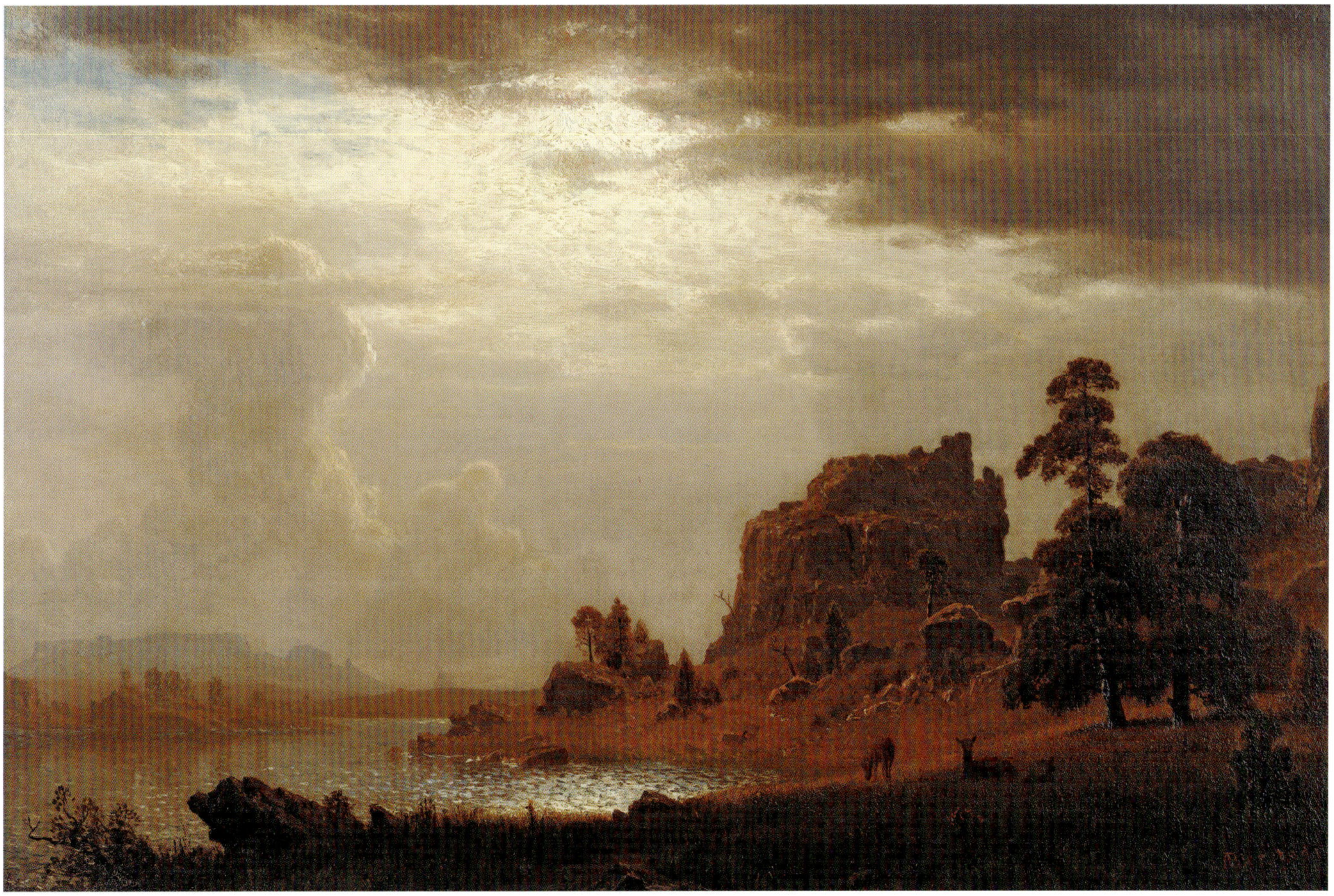

Albert Bierstadt, *On the Sweetwater near the Devil's Gate*, 1860. Oil on millboard, 12 ¼ × 18 in. (31.1 × 45.7 cm)

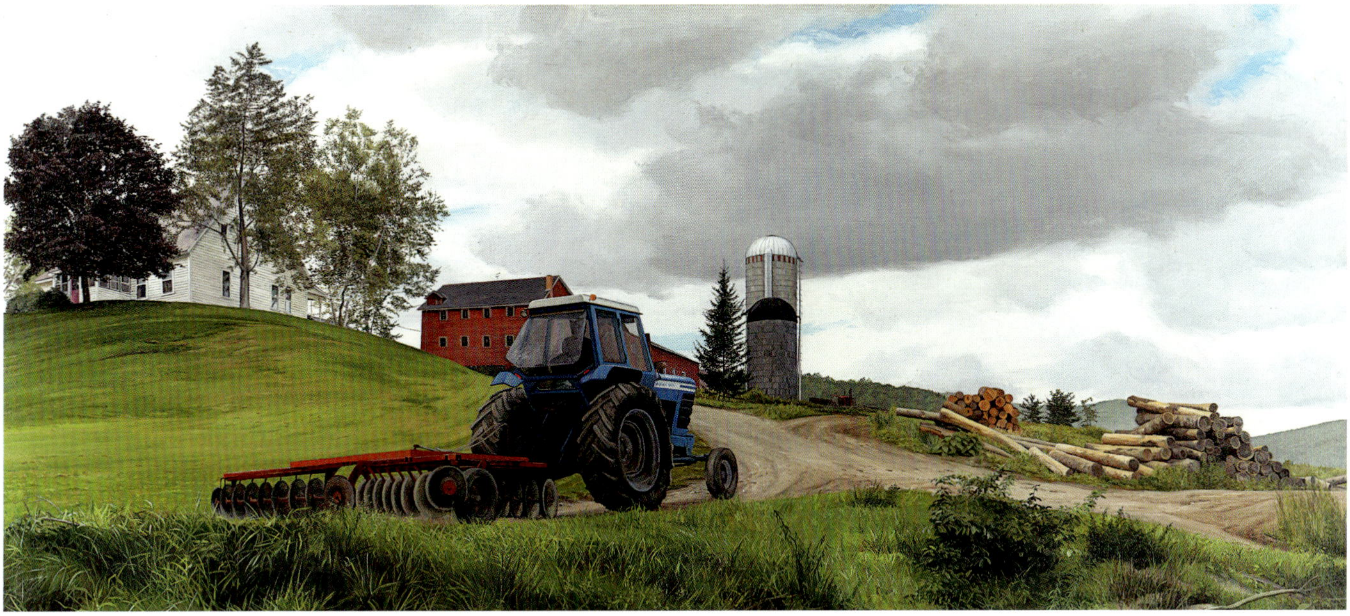

Altoon Sultan, *Tractor and Disc Harrow, Pawlett, Vermont*, 1987. Oil on canvas, 22 × 48 in. (55.9 × 121.9 cm)

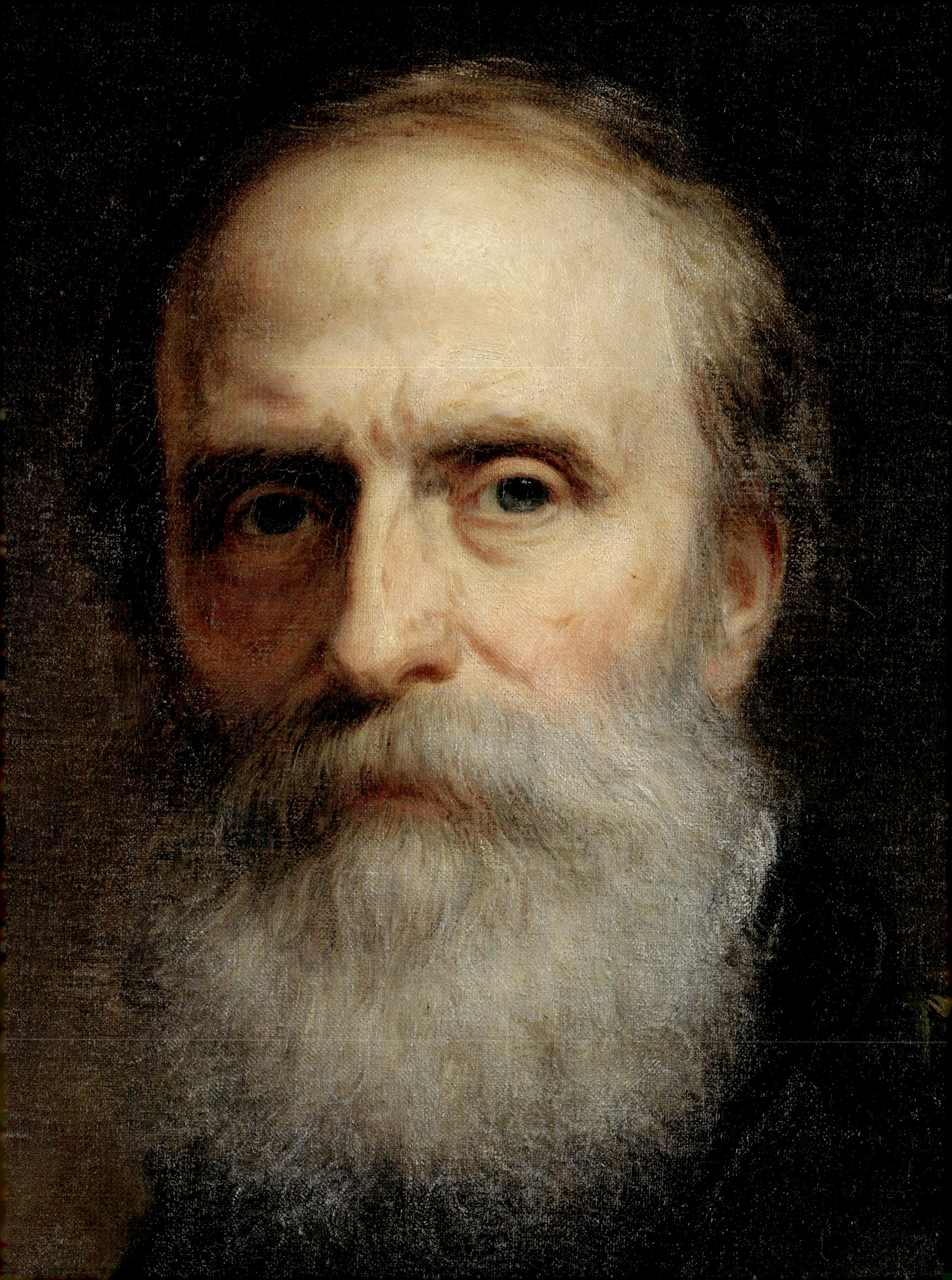

AWAKENED DREAM: IMAGES OF READING AND BEHOLDING IN THE WORK OF DANIEL HUNTINGTON AND HIS CONTEMPORARIES

KENNETH HALTMAN

Images of reading and beholding in the art of Daniel Huntington represent parallel expressions of an equally absorptive experience of inwardness—states of reverie not just visual but sensuous and tactile, serving to invite a vicarious response, though one ultimately frustrated and disappointing because unfulfillably contingent. Such structurally mediated access to a source of evident pleasure within picture space, at once available yet not, informs the viewer's own experience accordingly.

Huntington's *The Fair Student* (p. 70), for instance, depicts an elegant young woman comfortably seated at a small, richly polished wood table, reading. She cradles a gathering of pages between the middle and index fingers of her left hand, above which the open page toward which she gazes magically floats. She holds herself effortlessly erect yet drifts forward, resting her right cheek weightlessly against the folded fingers of her right hand, which gracefully emerges from a silk sleeve trimmed with lace. Light pours in from an unseen casement behind her, softly illuminating the text she studies and rendering an elaborately carved candlestick just beyond unnecessary for that purpose. The candlestick does serve thematically, however, in its reach toward a Dutch portrait of a man holding a wax-sealed letter that hangs beyond the reader on the wall of the library, linking one text illegible to the viewer to another. But unlike that public performance of identity, the woman's state of seductively rapt engagement is one (however much we are drawn to admire the flush in her cheeks and fairness of her skin, shown off against the sumptuous green velvet of her dress) from which we find ourselves emphatically excluded. From her fingers literally *in* the quarto pages—a performance of intimacy at the picture plane, the book's red-tinted headband and green bookmark echoing the colors of her head scarf, rosy cheeks, and dress—to the hand on which she rests her head, the woman's reading forms a closed circuit of reverie inspired by a text that seems less printed than drawn upon the sheet, soft-edged if not calligraphic, stanzaic and illegible.

Huntington's title might offer a clue. While he liked to refer to the painting, executed in London, somewhat more neutrally as *Girl Reading*, the work's original owner, the painter James Augustus Suydam of New York, appears to have preferred the current title, in which both *Fair* and *Student* signify in multiple and punning ways, involving the young woman's complexion perhaps more than her judiciousness but offering as well a gentle critique of her dreaminess and detachment as a student of letters, of her state of sensuous, as much as intellectual, engagement in the act of reading (or beholding).

In a self-portrait painted over three decades later (p. 71), in 1891, the year he retired from his second term as president of the National Academy of Design, Huntington returned to this theme, with the many structural similarities—the figure again represented seated, in three-quarter profile, similarly oriented in space in a subdued interior and associated with an open book—outweighed, in a typical Victorian gendered opposition, by one key difference, which we might term, after the art historian Michael Fried, "theatricality" versus "absorption." While the beholder's gaze is invited to play freely over the vividly colored figure of the young woman who is, in this respect, passively absorbed in her reading, less aware or, arguably, unaware of being seen, Huntington looks up to confront the viewer, his elaborate facial hair a cloud of softening that calls attention to his sharp nose and gaze, so salient by contrast with those of his earlier sitter. He leans forward, one hand and one forearm on the tabletop before him, stable and solid, while the fair student's touch, like her clothing and skin, comes across as relatively yielding, delicate, and soft. While she appears wholly engrossed, his concern, however spiritualized by the image of the supplicant Magdalen before him (and enhanced by the bareness of the room, by its mistily dreamlike evanescence), seems far more worldly, presenting for posterity the sign of his devotion to the arts in the form of the print he lifts into view, from which he may draw inspiration and to which he does obliquely call attention yet to which he, at this moment, pays *no* attention whatsoever, in dramatic contrast to the unidentified student's intensity of focus.

The association of inwardness with femininity in *The Fair Student* brings to mind a very strange and charming interpretation of the theme of reading by Huntington's exact contemporary Eastman Johnson. In *The Art Lover* (fig. 1), a chubby, curly haired, rosy-cheeked Dutch girl pores over a bound folio half propped on one knee, half resting on a worn, leather-covered footrest, opened to a print, or perhaps a painting, featuring brown earth and blue sky. Johnson has represented the girl's absorption as an act of delectation as much haptic as optical. Her downturned eyes escape our view; her hands, to which Johnson paid particular attention—holding the book open, caressing the sheet just below the image, the shadows of her fingertips playing over its surface, delicate and eager—suggest something

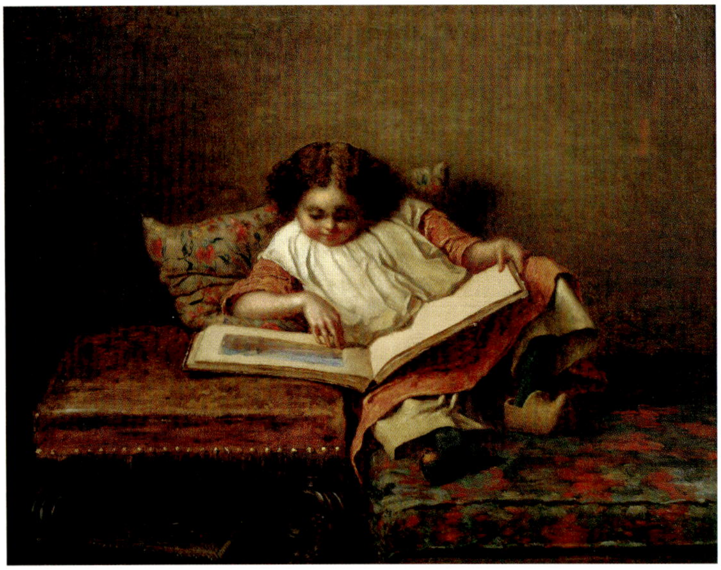

Fig. 1. Eastman Johnson, *The Art Lover*, 1859. Oil on canvas. National Academy of Design, New York

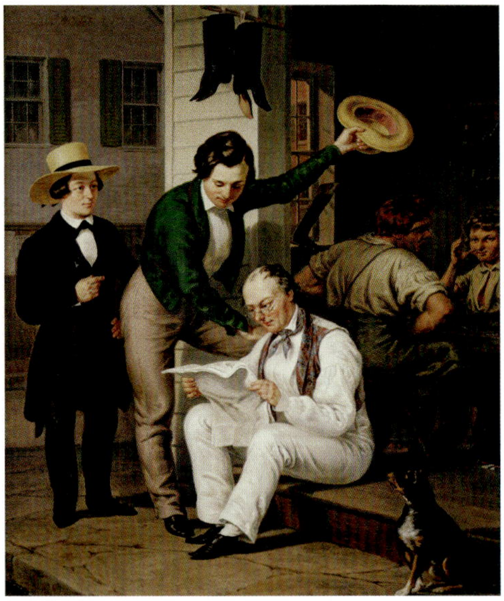

Fig. 2. Christian Mayr, *Reading the News*, 1844. Oil on canvas. National Academy of Design, New York

sensuous in her immersion, an experience in which the viewer is encouraged to participate by an equally sensuous decor of flowered pillows and upholstery and a softly mottled wall surface in the same palette, framing and surrounding her. The girl leans into the distant world represented on the page with a quiet smile of private pleasure, as if aspiring to float forward above the various openings (the gutter of the book, the gap between the uneven surfaces on which her body rests) that yawn before her, an art lover for whom loving art is both to ponder and to dream. Echoed by the strong middle part in her hair, the divides over which she leans suggest the impact on her thoughts of what she beholds, just as the volume she peruses echoes in form both the landscape through which her mind's eye wanders and the larger image through which we, too, find our way, the apparent weightlessness of her experience a visual metaphor, familiar from Huntington, for a style of private, feminized, bibliophilic reflection.

This gendered inflection becomes even more apparent when we compare these two works with a slightly earlier genre painting on a related theme but set in the public sphere, without a woman in sight: Christian Mayr's *Reading the News* (fig. 2). The news reader in question—a working man beyond middle age, reasonably prosperous, to judge from his appearance and attire as well as his location (like that of his establishment) one step up from a stone-paved sidewalk and another from the street, seated, as he is, in white pants on the thus freshly swept, perhaps washed, doorstep to the business—holds his lips conspicuously closed, suggesting that he reads to himself, not aloud, a simultaneous opening onto and closure to the world to which those around him variously respond. Although numerous details make the presence of allegory obvious—the pointing gesture of the standing figure to the left, balanced and echoed by the dog that looks on in the right foreground, framing the central vignette; the theatrical gesture of the dapper gentleman in the green jacket, doffing his hat; the pair of boots dangling above their heads—two opposing readings suggest themselves.

The two workers seated in the shop interior conduct no work because of their master's distraction, a social critique of the power of newsprint and its comedic effects: customers kept waiting by an artisan with his mind elsewhere; business neglected. The cobbler clutches his paper before him with two hands, gingerly yet possessively, its content indiscernible to the viewer, although its form, corresponding morphologically and spatially to his own, folding where he does, its whiteness matching his own, suggests commensurability with his interests. Spectacles further amplify his absorption. His customers, however, are annoyed. They've come for their shoes. The laborers within, hands free—still more interestingly, perhaps, feet bare—manifestly labor not.

But there is something more going on here than the representation of reading as a feminized, introspective interruption of the capitalist enterprise, a counternarrative enabled by the ambiguity of Mayr's title, which would more conventionally have served to describe a public reading (one thinks of Richard Caton Woodville's 1848 *War News from Mexico*, presently in the collection of the Crystal Bridges Museum of Art, Bentonville, AR) rather than simply reading in public. The cobbler may or may not be reading aloud, but it is as if he were. Virtually everyone in picture space, representing a range of urban classes, seems engaged in the gerundial activity, from the affluent customer in green, who waves his hat as if to inquire if the shop is open for business but whose eye has been caught by the words on the page, to the nonlaboring laborers, one of whom cups a hand to an ear while the other turns his head, and thus his own ear, in the news reader's direction. Even the dog, whose gaze aligns with that of the first man in line, stares at the rumpled paper, sensing something serious in the air. In this sense, Mayr's image represents a prototypically masculine mode of engagement, less a warning about possible threats to production than a graphic acknowledgment of a style of public absorption that it, too, as a painting—like Huntington's *Self-Portrait*, like the news itself—demands, serious enough to require labor to decipher, its decipherment its own reward.

Other images in the National Academy's collection concerned with reading as a style of self-fashioning follow—even when they might at first appear to diverge from—much the same pattern. In Thomas Hovenden's *The Revised Version* (fig. 3), a bearded, elderly farmer, absorbed in a recent retranslation of the Bible from the original Greek and Hebrew (the English Revised Version, issued over the course of the 1880s and 1890s, beginning with the New Testament in 1881), plants his feet on a floral rug, stabilizing his rocking chair's movement much as his reading serves to stabilize his circumstances as a widower at work on a "revised version" of his own life, a project glossed and explained by a cracked, framed picture of the departed on the wall beside him, similarly reading.

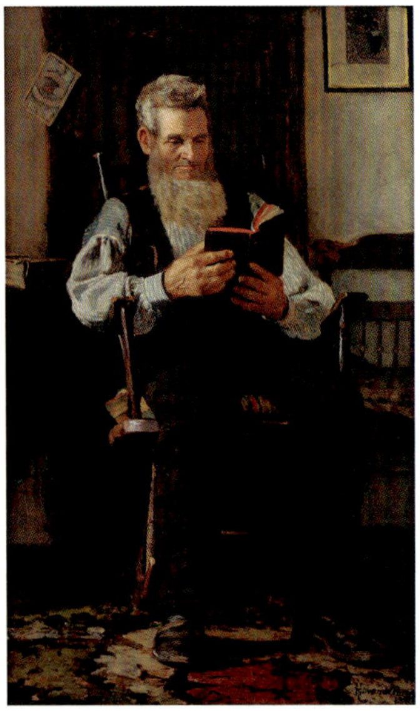

Fig. 3. Thomas Hovenden, *The Revised Version*, 1881. Oil on canvas. National Academy of Design, New York

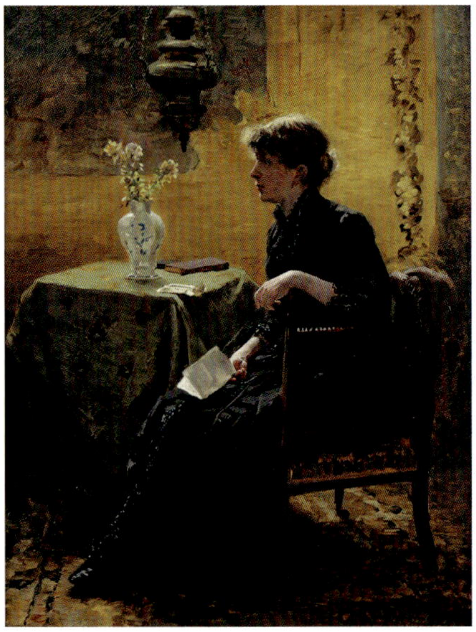

Fig. 4. Hamilton Hamilton, *Lady in Black*, 1889. Oil on canvas. National Academy of Design, New York

Here, significantly, in what would otherwise be a feminized expression of privacy and solitude, of retirement, social condition trumps gender in a display of acquiescence to a higher power.

In an upper-class expression of this theme of communion with an absent other through the written word, Hamilton Hamilton's lovely *Lady in Black* (fig. 4) represents a recent widow looking up from a letter just torn from its envelope with a gaze nonetheless entirely inward, still wholly absorbed, in the Friedian sense, in her thoughts, a golden-hued dream of romantic feeling darkened only, if at all, by her clothing and the title's insistence on mourning.

What all these images share is a strategy of redirection. The attention and interest of the viewer, offered a glimpse of an illegible text within picture space, are displaced into consideration of the painting in which that sub- or metatext appears, thrown back on the question of what the image we *can* see has to tell us about reading and beholding as related acts of imagination: an artistic self-consciousness represented in gendered modes by the relatively arid conceptual space of masculine performance in Huntington's self-portrait or the urban street in Mayr; by the introspective, feminized spaces of affective indulgence in Huntington's earlier image of a young woman in the throes of literary engagement, Johnson's figure of ekphrastic reverie (further sentimentalized by a reiterative floral design), Hovenden's softening of a bear of a man reading to manage his bereavement, or Hamilton's epistolary portrait of a woman dreaming her own desires, her own loss.

BIBLIOGRAPHICAL NOTE:

On the change in title of Huntington's *The Fair Student*, see Wendy Greenhouse, catalogue entry for the work, in David B. Dearinger, ed., *Paintings and Sculpture in the Collection of the National Academy of Design, 1826–1925* (New York: Hudson Hills Press, 2004), 295. The terms I have chosen to differentiate these arguably gendered modes of represented reading have their origin in Michael Fried, *Absorption and Theatricality: Painting and Beholder in the Age of Diderot* (Chicago: University of Chicago Press, 1976). Huntington acknowledged the thematic equivalence of reading and beholding in his introduction to *A General View of the Fine Arts, Critical and Historical* (New York: A. S. Barnes, 1851), 13, describing that text, at least, as "arranged, lively, and picturesque," with "colours vivid and truthful." I am indebted to typically astute essays by John Davis on both Hovenden's *The Revised Version* and Hamilton's *Lady in Black* in Dearinger, *Paintings and Sculpture*, 247–48, 283–84. In addition to those mentioned in this essay, the NAD's collection includes numerous scenes of reading and beholding; see, for example, the exhibition catalogue *From All Walks of Life: Paintings of the Figure from the National Academy of Design*, exh. cat. (New York: National Academy of Design, 1979). *The Old Version* [or] *Sunday Afternoon*, the companion piece to Hovenden's *The Revised Version*, also of 1881, is in the collection of the Fine Arts Museums of San Francisco.

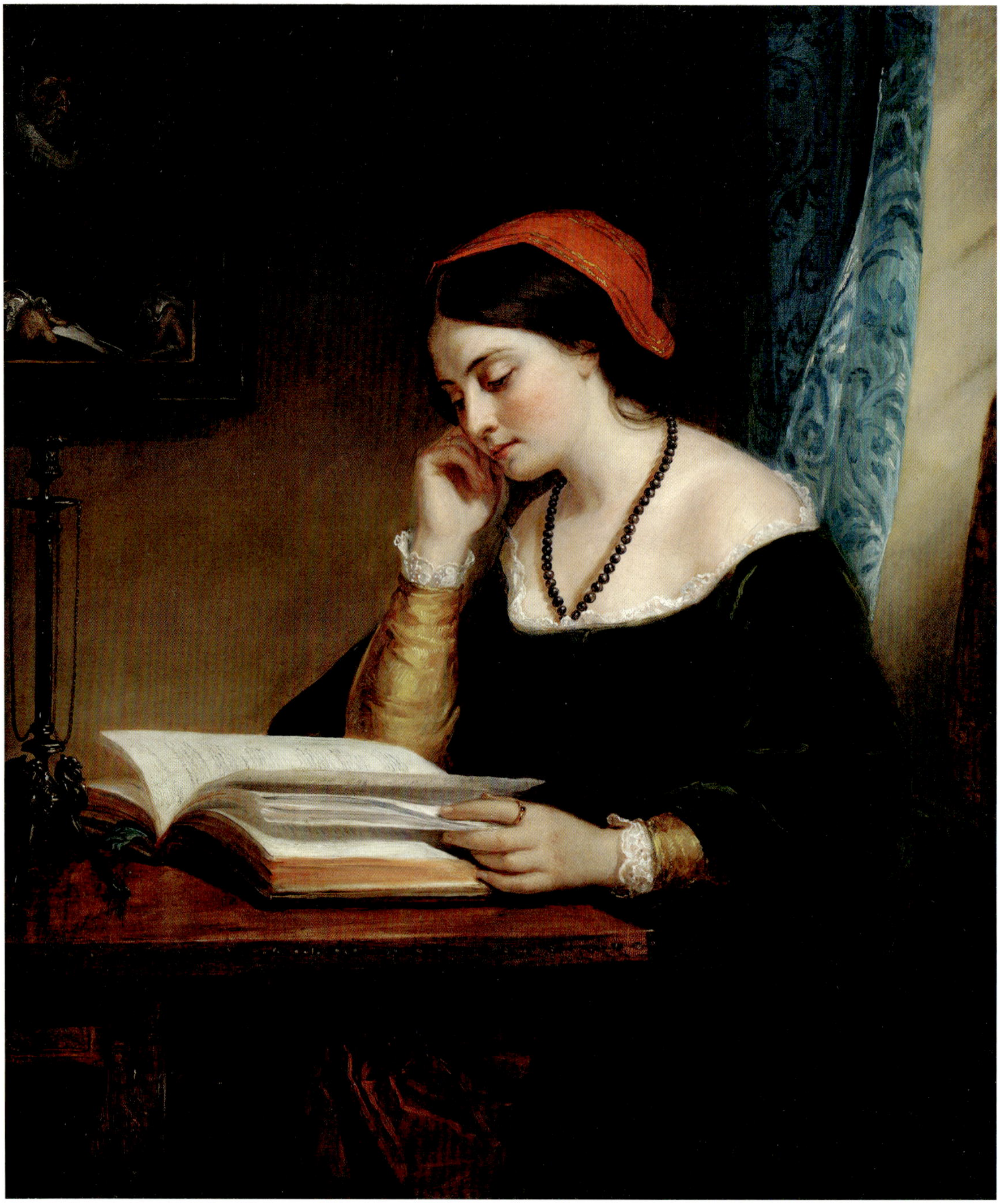

Daniel Huntington, *The Fair Student* [or] *Girl Reading*, 1858. Oil on canvas, 30 × 25 in. (76.2 × 63.5 cm)

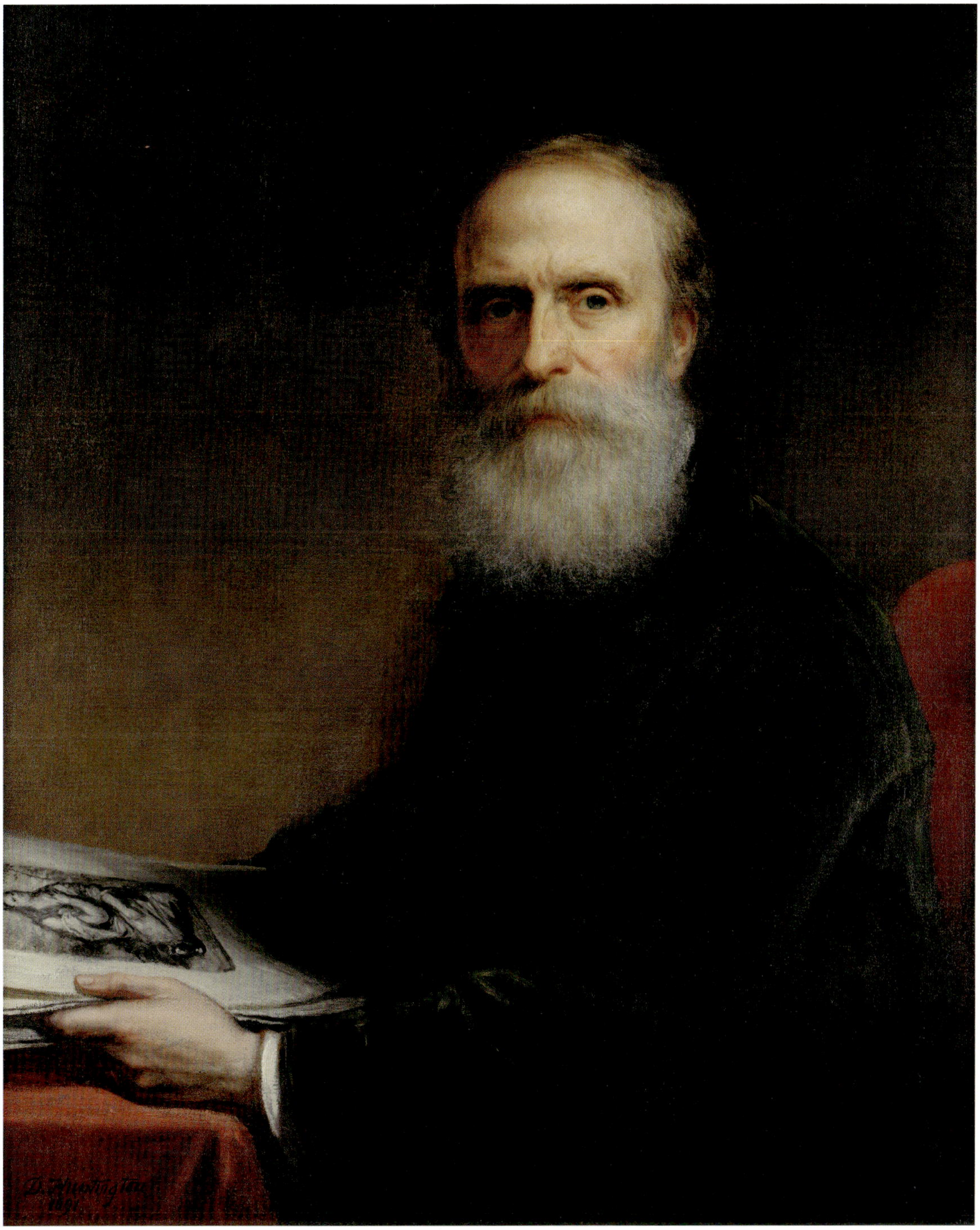

Daniel Huntington, *Self-Portrait*, 1891. Oil on canvas, 36 ⅛ × 29 in. (91.8 × 73.7 cm)

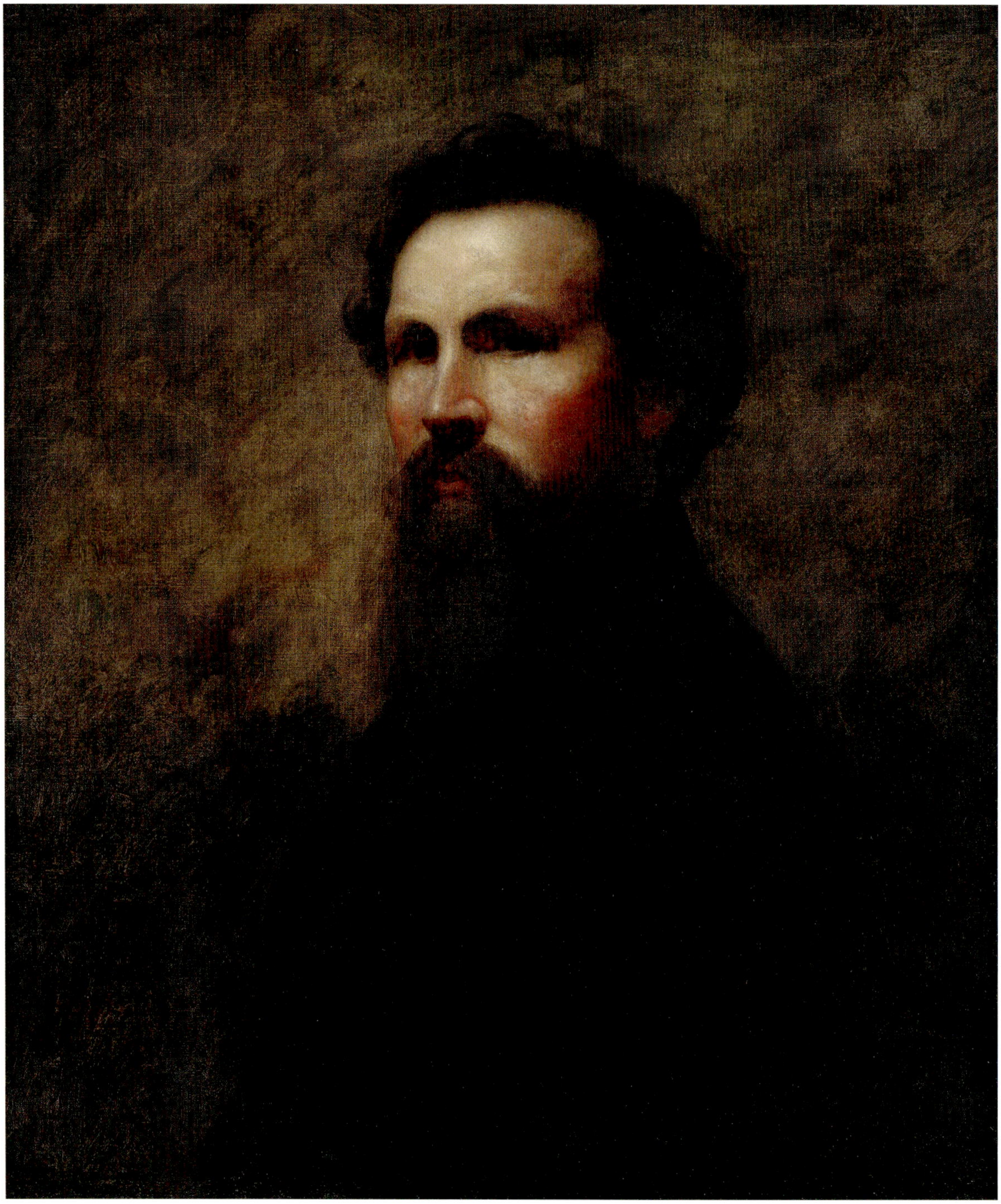

Eastman Johnson, *Self-Portrait*, ca. 1859–60. Oil on canvas, 30⅜ × 25 in. (77.2 × 63.5 cm)

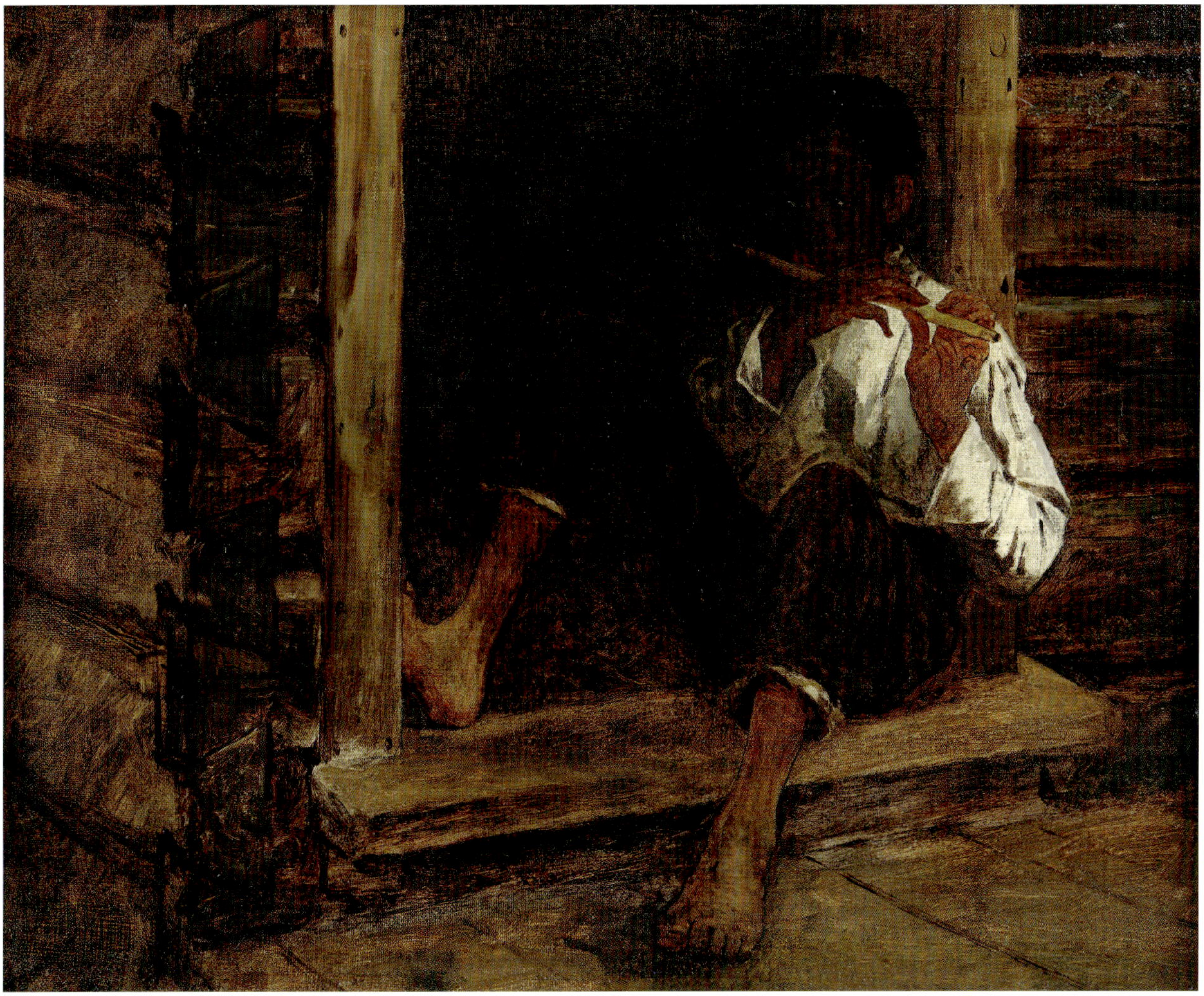

Eastman Johnson, *Negro Boy*, ca. 1860–61. Oil on canvas, 14 × 17 in. (35.6 × 43.2 cm)

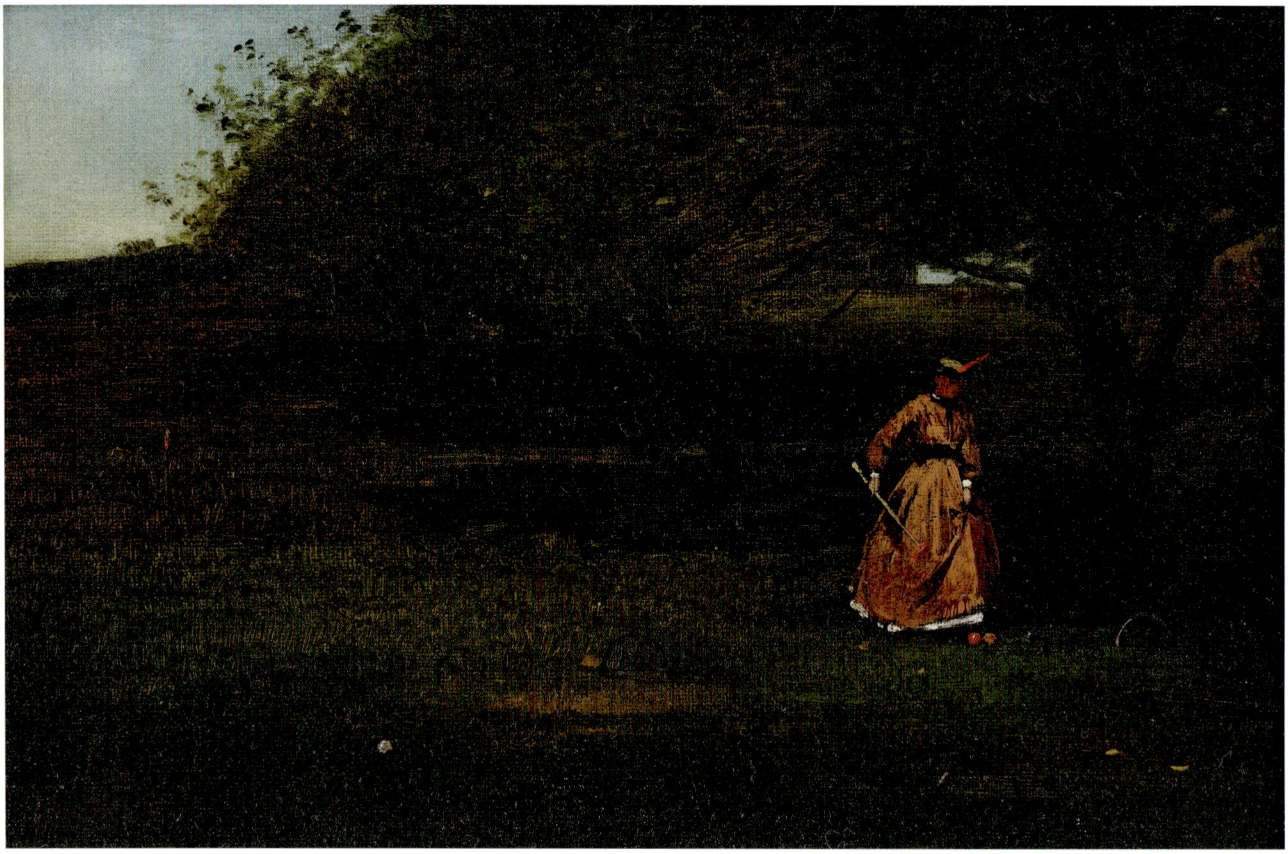

Winslow Homer, *Croquet Player*, ca. 1865. Oil on canvas, 8 ⅛ × 12 ⅛ in. (20.6 × 30.8 cm)

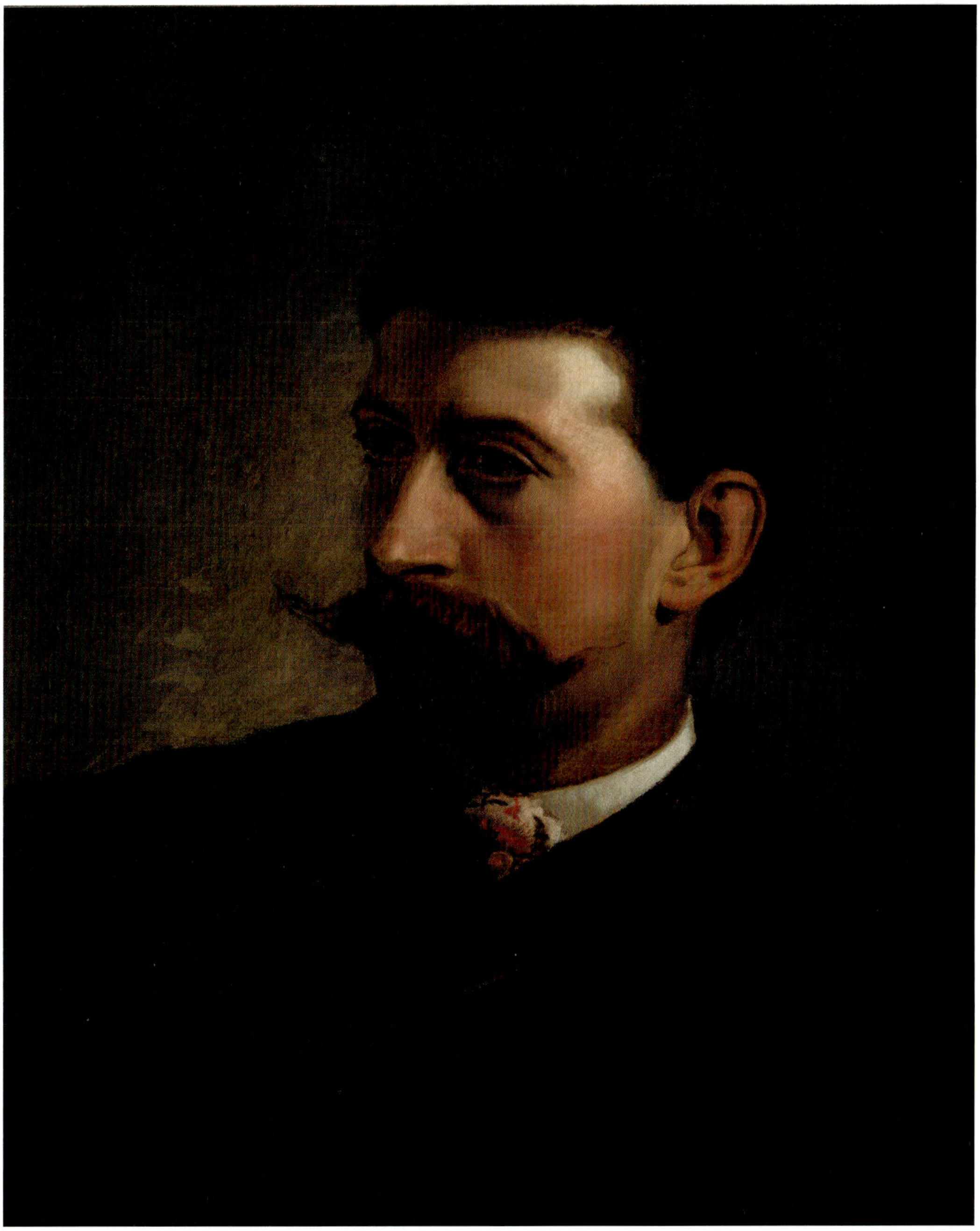

Oliver Ingraham Lay, *Winslow Homer*, 1865. Oil on canvas, 20 ⅛ × 16 ⅛ in. (51.1 × 41 cm)

ANTHONY PANZERA ON GEORGE INNESS

George Inness's *Landscape*, executed in oil on paper, appears to have been an *ébauche*, or sketch, but has all the stability and structure of a finished composition. Dominated by two enormous trees, the painting is divided almost in half between sky and land, with the lower half further divided into three horizontal bands.

The first band, a loosely painted scrub brush, runs across the foreground and ambles around the right side of a pond, which makes up the second band. A fallen tree trunk, partially submerged, draws our attention to a lone fisherman casting his line into the water. His body and movement are carefully outlined against the reflection of the brilliant white sky in the pond. The left side of the top band consists of a series of horizontal fields edged by trees in the distance, along with a few small white houses and what appears to be a manor house. At the far right is a sizable hill (cut off by the edge of the painting) that moves downward at a 45-degree angle. All of these elements—the horizontal activity of the distant landscape on the left, the dramatic slope of the hill on the right, and the angle of the fishing pole—direct our attention to the two magnificent trees in the center.

Inness carefully orchestrated this effect through the quality of his brushstrokes and the clarity of his colors. An imprimatura of burnt sienna and yellow ochre applied as an undercoat is visible around all the trees, particularly the two largest ones, defining their shapes. The leaves of the tree closest to the viewer (an oak) are made up of loosely applied but carefully positioned brushstrokes of chromium oxide green that allow portions of the imprimatura to show through. The tree behind it (a maple) was created with daubs of viridian green. Inness tempered the intensity of his colors by working wet-on-wet, which also helped to define the dark hollows in the foliage and indicate the direction of the sunlight. The overall effect was realized through a soft, painterly, emotive approach, as opposed to a controlled application of specific painted details. Inness explained his approach in a letter: "Several years before I went to Europe . . . I had begun to see that elabourateness [*sic*] in detail did not gain me meaning. . . . I could not sustain it everywhere and produce the sense of spaces and distances and with them that subjective mystery of nature with which wherever I went I was filled."[1]

While his paintings were grounded in the same lessons and traditions as those of his Hudson River School colleagues, Inness set himself apart, delving deeper into his own theories of art and theology. He drew strength from his belief in the divine significance found in Nature and adhered to the mystical teachings of Emanuel Swedenborg. During the 1870s and 1880s, in the visionary paintings of his late career, his brushstroke became an expressive tool and his color dissolved into ephemeral atmosphere. His spatial preoccupation was now with "organic and non-spatial space." Even his figures now existed in a world of ambiguity, vagueness, and dissolving boundaries.

When Inness died in August 1894, his body was laid in state at the National Academy of Design, and his eulogy was delivered by Rev. Dr. J. C. Agar, his spiritual advisor, who said, "To him all Nature was symbolic—full of spiritual meaning. He prized nothing in Nature that did not stand for something. That was the true secret of his theory of art."

1. Adrienne Baxter Bell, *George Inness and the Visionary Landscape* (New York: George Braziller, 2003), 19. The citation refers to a letter written by George Inness, Sr., to Ripley Hitchcock, March 23, 1884, in George Inness, Jr., *Life, Art, and Letters of George Inness* (New York: Century, 1917), 119.

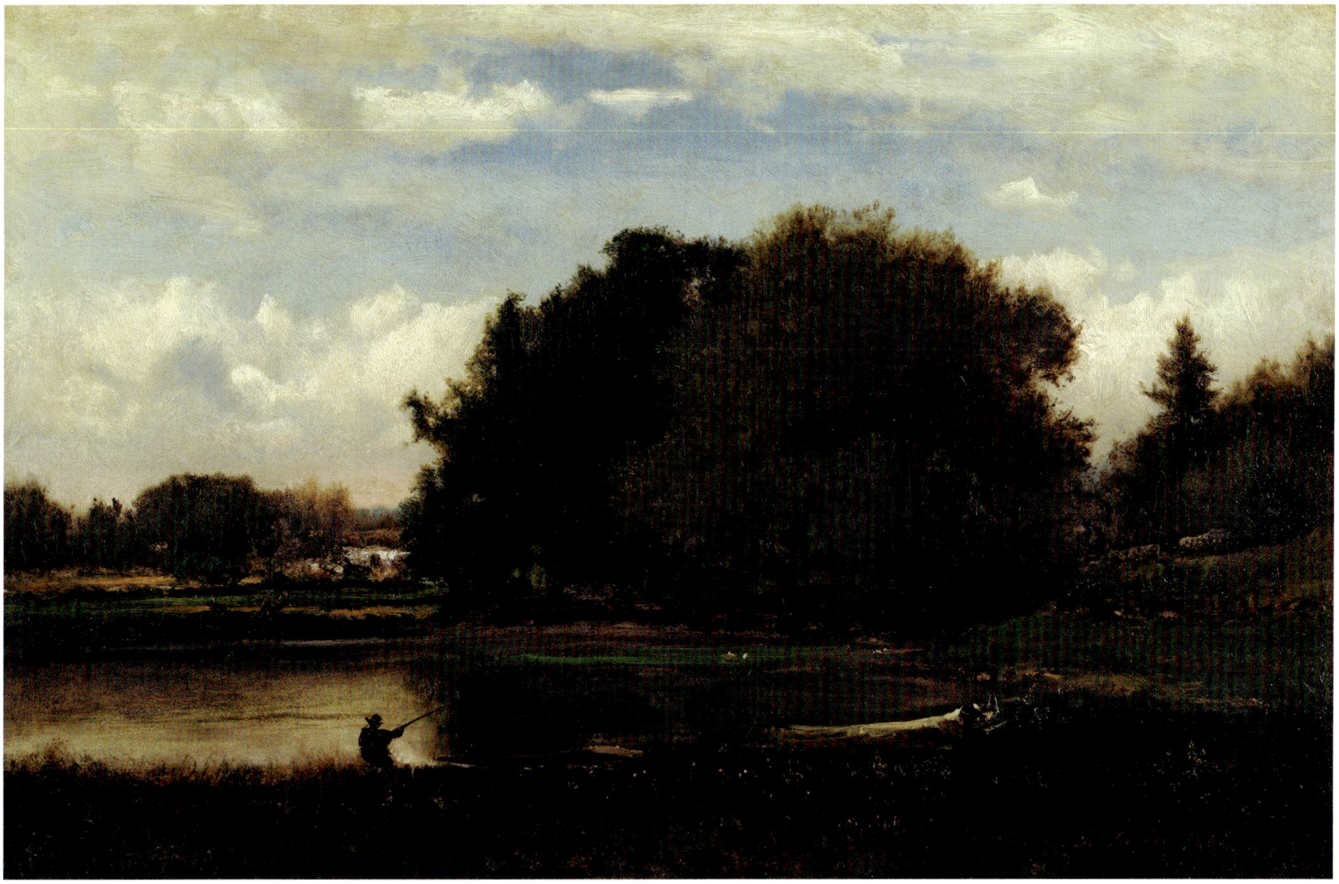

George Inness, *Landscape*, 1860. Oil on paper, mounted on wood panel, 16 ¼ × 24 in. (41.3 × 61 cm)

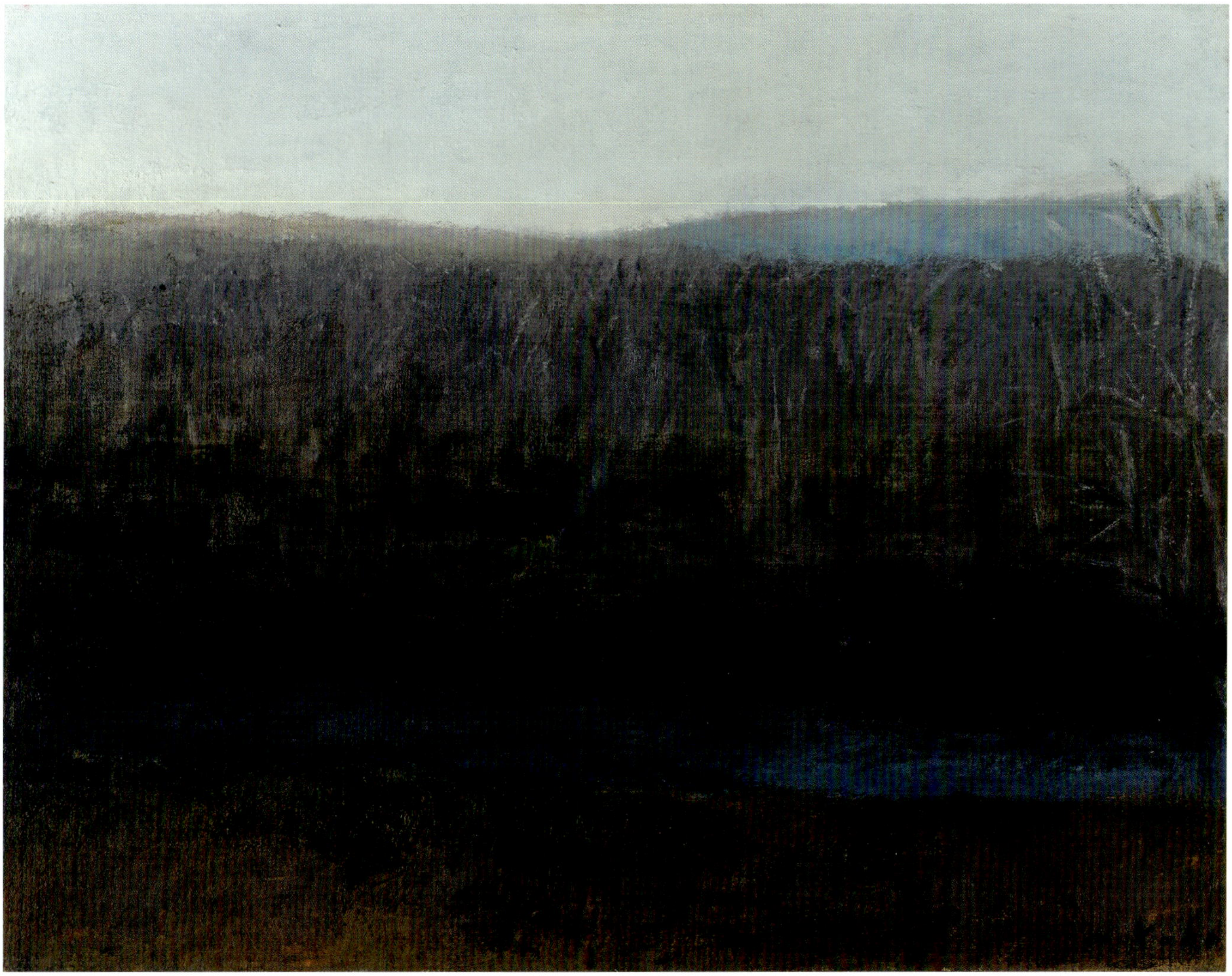

Wolf Kahn, *Pond in November*, 1977. Oil on canvas, 29 × 36 in. (73.7 × 91.4 cm)

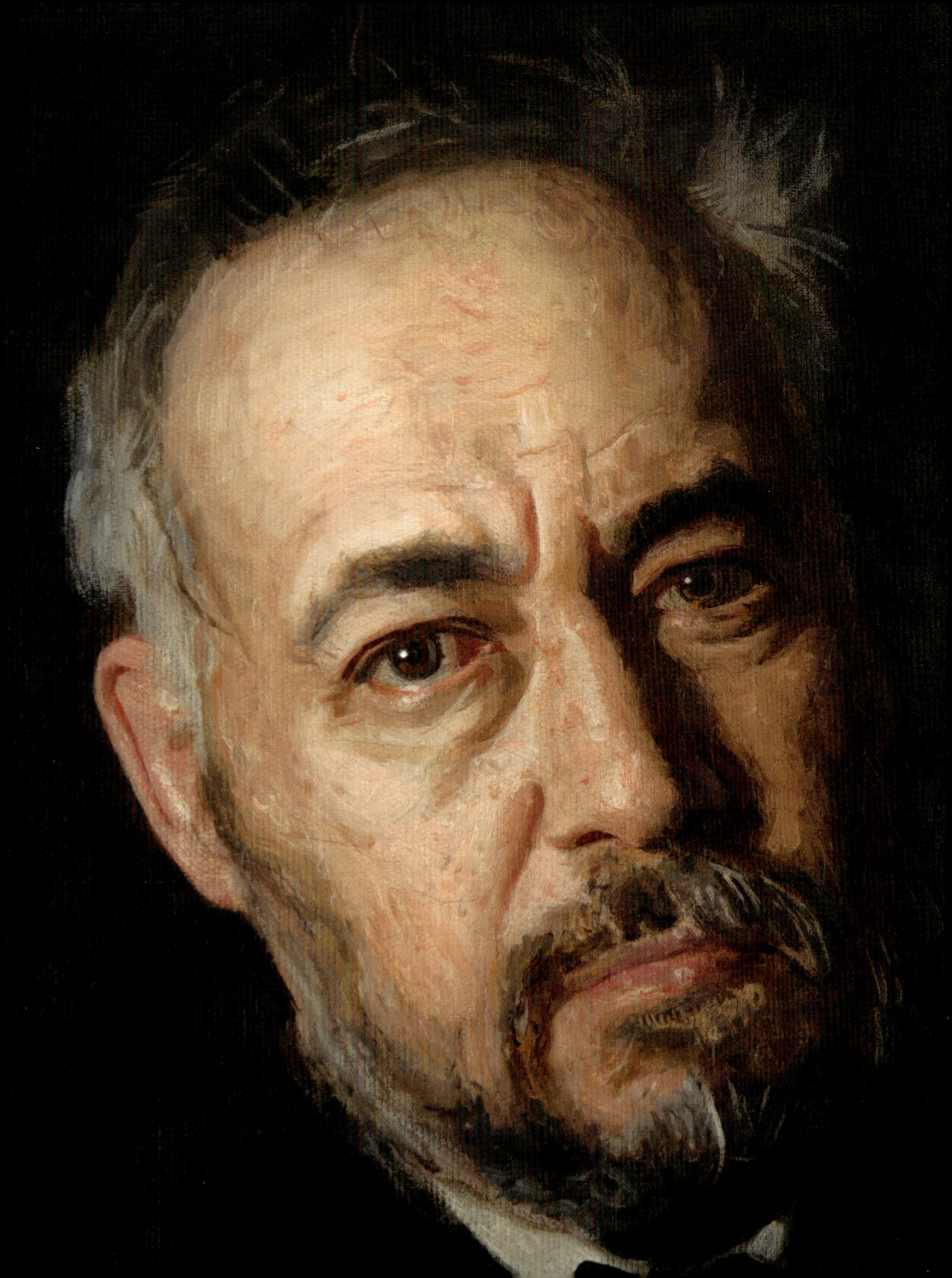

ARTISTIC FRIENDSHIP IN THE GILDED AGE: WILLIAM MERRITT CHASE, THOMAS EAKINS, AND HENRY OSSAWA TANNER

AKELA REASON

American artists of the late nineteenth-century Gilded Age were, in many ways, members of an elite fraternity: they exhibited in the same places, joined the same associations, and led the academies that trained subsequent generations of artists in the United States.[1] In this milieu, painters with such different temperaments and careers as Thomas Eakins and William Merritt Chase became not only colleagues but friends. This unlikely friendship was based on mutual respect and rooted in the artists' shared European training, interest in depicting the human figure, and dedication to teaching. As the profession of painter matured in the United States, Eakins, Chase, and comparable figures helped to shape it for the next generation, whose members would find that they could train at home just as well as in Europe and still find professional success.[2]

Following the American Civil War, European academies became a mecca for young artists seeking professional training, drawing an international community of students. Eakins and Chase were among the Americans who benefited from this education, although they chose different paths: Eakins entered the École des Beaux-Arts in Paris, and Chase, the Akademie der Bildenden Künste in Munich. Each artist was shaped in significant ways by his training, adopting methods of painting in keeping with the techniques of his masters. Eakins maintained a deep commitment to the study of the human body, including knowledge of muscles and bones achieved through both lectures and dissection, while Chase initially adhered to the old master style that was a hallmark of the German Realists. Upon their return to the United States, both men expanded on their training and developed their own styles, sometimes sharply independent of the ideals they had absorbed in the European academies. At the same time, they began to alter American institutions to conform more closely with the training they had received abroad. Although Eakins has been most closely associated with his hometown of Philadelphia and the Pennsylvania Academy of the Fine Arts (PAFA), he also taught at the National Academy of Design and, more frequently, at some of the same institutions as Chase, including the Art Students League and the Brooklyn Art Association. And Chase eventually accepted a teaching appointment at the PAFA in Philadelphia, where he made regular visits to Eakins's home. It is difficult to imagine the two men side by side, enjoying one another's company, but apparently, they did so.[3]

Thomas Eakins lacked the gentlemanly polish of William Merritt Chase. While Chase fashioned his public image as a dapper bon vivant, Eakins seemed almost willfully negligent in his appearance, once reportedly greeting a distinguished female visitor to his studio "in an old pair of trousers and an *undershirt*."[4] These tendencies were apparent even during Eakins's student days in Paris. The muralist and one-time NAD president Edwin Howland Blashfield, who, like Eakins, studied with Léon Bonnat, recalled that "the joy of his young life was the flouting of conventions, and an unbounded iconoclasm when he was in 'society' which was as rarely as he could contrive."[5] The shunning of social mores and polite conventions that Blashfield found "picturesque" and bohemian during their student days, however, later made securing portrait commissions difficult for Eakins—he was more than rough around the edges and definitely not a flatterer. In contrast, the convivial Chase was known for his fastidious attire, appearing the gentleman in both manners and looks. Putting such matters of personal deportment aside, visitors also noticed considerable differences in the two artists' working spaces. While Chase maintained a prominent atelier in New York's Tenth Street Studio Building, carefully decorated with objects displaying his cosmopolitan taste, Eakins worked primarily in a prosaic studio space built at the top of his father's private residence. The critic Mariana Van Rensselaer, upon visiting there in 1881, marveled at Eakins's "untidy" appearance, finding that "his home and surroundings and family were decidedly of the *lower* middle-class."[6] Although the two artists became friends, Eakins seemed to revel in the distinctions between them, famously distinguishing their working environments with the declaration that "Chase's studio is an atelier; this is a workshop."[7]

These superficial differences also suggest the opposing characters of the two men. Chase courted recognition from the fine arts establishment of critics, patrons, and peers. Although he, like Eakins, sometimes struggled to obtain portrait commissions, he achieved a measure of professional success that eluded Eakins. Chase was both a joiner and a leader in ways Eakins was not; he was, for example, a founding member of the Society of American Artists (SAA), the Tile Club, and the Society of Painters in Pastel. Chase became president of the SAA and was named a National Academician a full decade before Eakins. Stylistically, the two men's works also had little in common. Chase mostly eschewed the dark tones of his training in Munich to become a full-blown Impressionist, lightening his palette and painting landscapes *en plein air*. In his figure paintings, he demonstrated a special talent for depicting

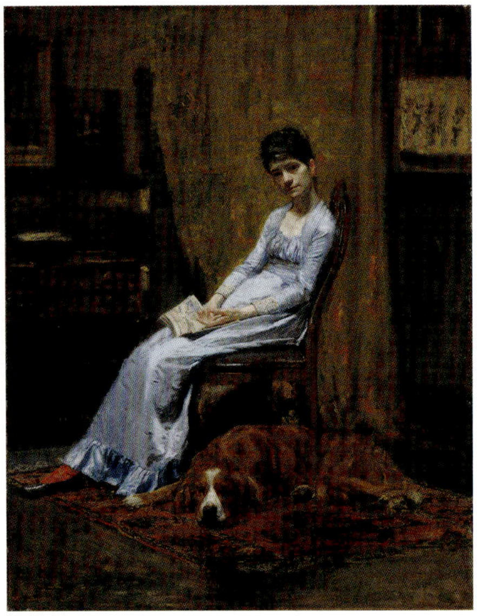

Fig. 1. Thomas Eakins, *The Artist's Wife and His Setter Dog*, ca. 1884–89. Oil on canvas. Metropolitan Museum of Art, New York

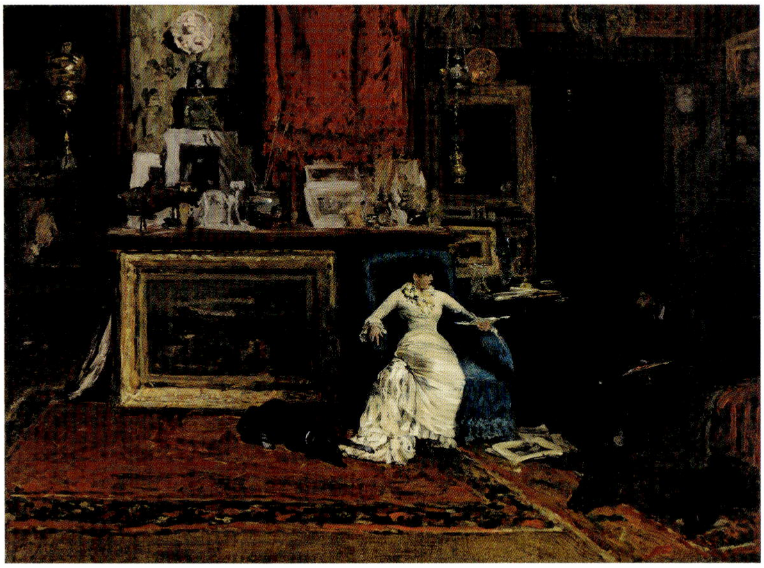

Fig. 2. William Merritt Chase, *The Tenth Street Studio*, 1880. Oil on canvas. Saint Louis Art Museum

attractive young women, often sumptuously attired. *The Young Orphan* (p. 92), also exhibited under the titles *An Idle Moment* and *Portrait*, displays the influence of James McNeill Whistler's famous 1871 composition *Arrangement in Grey and Black, No. 1 (Portrait of the Artist's Mother)* (Musée d'Orsay, Paris); however, as the curator and art historian Barbara Dayer Gallati has noted, Chase turned that painting on its head by replacing its gray harmonies with bold terracotta reds.[8] Indeed, Chase's work is both coloristically and texturally lush. The viewer is brought close to the languid sitter, likely a resident of the Protestant Half-Orphan Asylum, located near the artist's studio on Tenth Street, yet the brushwork and the rough weave of the canvas leave her features slightly blurred, as if somewhat out of focus. Eakins, too, tried his hand at the Whistlerian composition but with dramatically different results. *The Artist's Wife and His Setter Dog* (fig. 1) shows Susan Macdowell Eakins, also an artist, similarly positioned in a chair but seeming small and weary by contrast to Whistler's more formidable mother and Chase's dreamy orphan. Here, by showing his wife in "artistic" dress with a constellation of bric-a-brac and artwork behind her, Eakins was also attempting a studio picture in the manner of Chase's numerous paintings of his Tenth Street studio (fig. 2).[9] This is the most Chase-like of Eakins's works, while remaining thoroughly an Eakins.

Eakins surely knew Chase at the time he painted this portrait of Susan, as he participated in exhibitions organized by the SAA, over which Chase presided in 1880 and then again from 1885 to 1895. In 1879, on behalf of the SAA, Chase visited Philadelphia in an effort to resolve a conflict over the installation of an exhibition at the PAFA, where Eakins was teaching. One of the points of tension was over the placement within the exhibition of Eakins's 1875 painting *Portrait of Dr. Samuel D. Gross (The Gross Clinic)* (Philadelphia Museum of Art). Although the issue was not resolved in Eakins's favor, the mere acceptance of the painting by the SAA demonstrated a bold commitment to the controversial picture. Eakins later gave Chase two of his paintings (*Sailing* of 1875 and *Arcadia* of ca. 1883, now in the Philadelphia Museum of Art and Metropolitan Museum of Art, New York, respectively), and around 1899, when Chase was teaching at the PAFA, the two men painted each other's portraits. Eakins's picture of Chase (fig. 3), inscribed "To My Friend William M. Chase," shows the dapper artist in profile, with a flower in his lapel. Art historians have noted that the portrait captures Chase's confidence in his own professional stature.[10] Chase's portrait of Eakins was, according to the latter's student Samuel Murray, likely destroyed by Susan Eakins after her husband's death, for unknown reasons.[11]

The self-portrait Eakins painted for the National Academy of Design after he was made an Associate and then, nine days later, an Academician (p. 89) contrasts sharply with his portrayal of Chase. As in many of Eakins's later portraits, it depicts not only the sitter's physical attributes but also the emotional wear and tear of life—something Chase was sometimes criticized for not capturing.[12] In the case of Eakins's self-portrait, the curator Darryl Sewell has suggested that he "shows himself as a vulnerable being, capable of deep emotion."[13] The art historian Sarah Burns has argued that Eakins portrayed himself as a careworn victim with "brimming eyes," conveying the toll of a career he sometimes felt was marred by "misunderstanding, persecution, and neglect."[14] Other scholars have suggested that his appearance exhibits a sense of defiance or even an ironic insouciance at the belated honors bestowed upon him by the National Academy. What each of these interpretations expresses, at its heart, is that the self-portrait, like many of Eakins's best works of this period, overflows with humanity. His self-portrait may be favorably compared with those of Rembrandt. Both artists portrayed their own aging flesh with a poignant sense of mortality. While Eakins did not often depict himself in formal self-portraits, as Rembrandt did, the pathos of the seventeenth-century Dutch master's later self-representations (fig. 4) is also evident in Eakins's work, along with striking tonal similarities. This is not to suggest that Eakins intended to copy Rembrandt but, rather, that he undertook his official self-portrait mindful of the long tradition of artistic self-representation, and perhaps even with a degree of solemnity about the implications of the task.[15]

In spite of the loss of Chase's portrait of Eakins, the exchange of portraits between the two artists highlights one aspect of the artistic friendships forged during this period. Such portraits were frequently exchanged as gifts, and some were even undertaken as exhibition works.[16] While much has been made of Eakins's interest in depicting members of the clergy in the early years of the twentieth century, he also made numerous paintings of his students and peers.[17] Around the time of

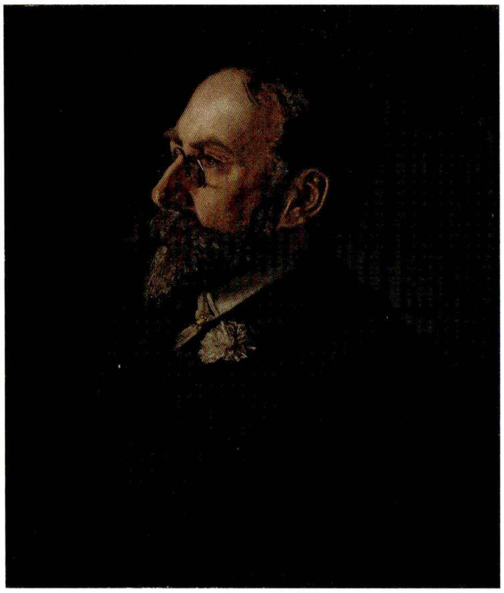

Fig. 3. Thomas Eakins, *Portrait of William Merritt Chase*, ca. 1899. Oil on canvas. Hirshhorn Museum and Sculpture Garden, Smithsonian Institution, Washington, DC

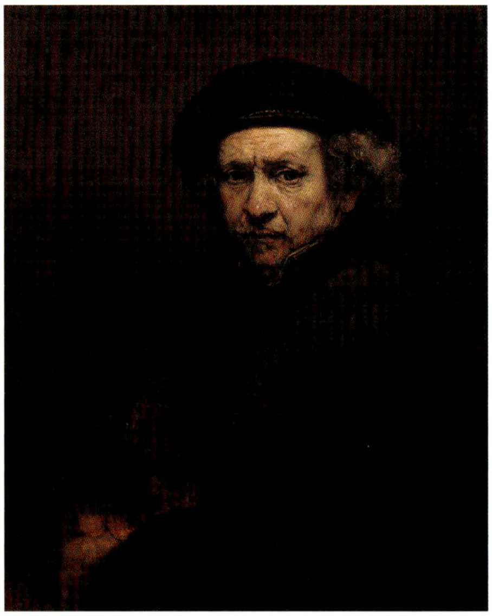

Fig. 4. Rembrandt van Rijn, *Self-Portrait*, 1659. Oil on canvas. National Gallery of Art, Washington, DC

his self-portrait, Eakins painted his African American student Henry Ossawa Tanner (fig. 5); it is one of his most sensitive portraits. Unlike in the artist's self-portrait, Tanner does not meet the viewer's gaze but appears lost in thought. The strength of the image is especially noteworthy when compared with a more formal example, such as Eakins's portrait of the landscapist Edward W. Redfield (fig. 6), in which the sitter sits more stiffly and betrays much less interiority. Although Tanner trained for a period under Eakins, there is little remaining besides the portrait and a handful of brief written accounts to suggest the depth of their relationship.[18] Although it is composed very differently, the portrait shares some of the strengths of Eakins's depiction of Chase in its suggestion of collegial respect. Tanner is shown as a thoughtful professional, an equal in the markedly unequal society of the pre-civil-rights era. While Tanner was among those who benefited from the professionalization of the American art academies under artists such as Chase and Eakins, he found that the United States was far from hospitable to him as an artist because of his race, and in 1891, he moved to France, where he found greater success.

Eakins's influence is not at all apparent in Tanner's mature works, such as *The Miraculous Haul of Fishes* (p. 99), which are more indebted to modern European artistic movements such as Impressionism and Symbolism. By the 1890s, Tanner, the son of a bishop in the African Methodist Episcopal Church, had begun to specialize in religious paintings. *The Miraculous Haul of Fishes* reflects his interest in biblical subject matter and, in the lighter, blue-green-purple palette and broad brushwork, his connection to the expatriate milieu. The artist's early talent for religious imagery had been noted not by Eakins but by Chase, who reportedly admired Tanner's 1896 painting *Daniel in the Lions' Den* (location unknown) and "spoke of it in a public address to his students and privately praised it very often."[19]

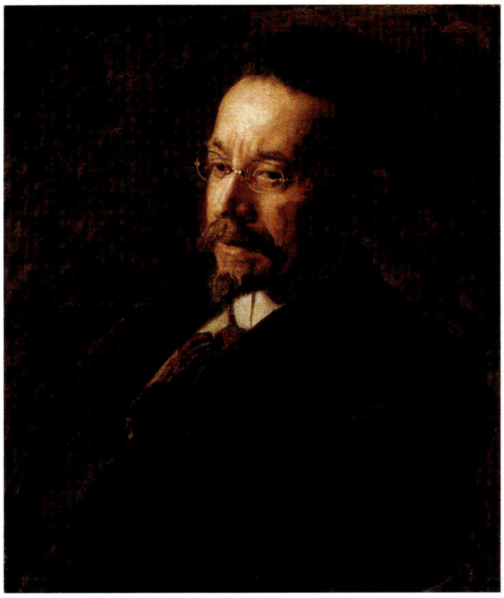

Fig. 5. Thomas Eakins, *Portrait of Henry O. Tanner*, ca. 1897. Oil on canvas. Hyde Collection, Glens Falls, NY

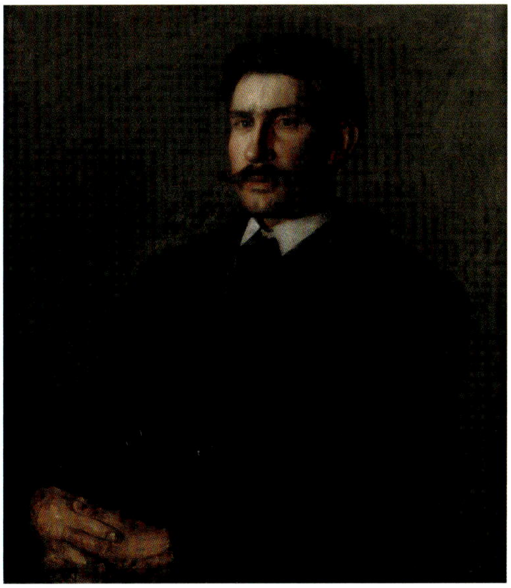

Fig. 6. Thomas Eakins, *Edward W. Redfield*, n.d. Oil on canvas. National Academy of Design, New York

Chase was not Tanner's only admirer; from his position in France, Tanner received many American artists who sought his fellowship and advice. Among them were African American artists who found his life and work inspiring.[20] But in the less racialized climate of France, Tanner also crossed paths with many other well-known American and European artists, including Richard E. Miller, the American Impressionist and fellow Academician who painted Tanner's diploma portrait (p. 98). In the latter work, Tanner appears far less introspective than in Eakins's rendering, yet the teal blue background and paint handling relate more closely to Tanner's own work than do the brown tones of Eakins's painting, tying the likeness stylistically to the sitter's oeuvre in ways not often seen in portraiture.

These few instances of artistic friendship drawn from the collection of the National Academy are merely suggestive of the many social relationships between artists of the Gilded Age. The three artists discussed here, though engaged in very different careers, were bound together by their training and embrace of European painting practices, yet many American artists found community through the countless new clubs and exhibition venues that were being established during this period. The Academy's former practice of requiring Associates to submit portraits offers a rich field to mine for these tight social networks, providing nearly limitless connections worthy of deeper exploration.

1. In the period under discussion, the vast majority of professional artists were white men, educated in the great artistic academies of Europe, which, by and large, barred women from attendance. Although women were able to train in professional schools and in ateliers, few became professional artists. On the training of women artists in Paris during this period, see Laurence Madeline, *Women Artists in Paris, 1850–1900*, exh. cat. (New York: American Federation of Arts; New Haven: Yale University Press, 2017). See also Kirsten Swinth, *Painting Professionals: Women Artists and the Development of Modern American Art, 1870–1930* (Chapel Hill: University

of North Carolina Press, 2001), and Laura R. Prieto, *At Home in the Studio: The Professionalization of Women Artists in America* (Cambridge, MA: Harvard University Press, 2001).

2. On the role of fraternalism in American society, see Jason Andrew Kaufman, *For the Common Good: American Civic Life and the Golden Age of Fraternity* (New York: Oxford University Press, 2002).
3. Lloyd Goodrich, *Thomas Eakins* (Washington, DC: National Gallery of Art; Cambridge, MA: Harvard University Press, 1982), 2:220–21.
4. Ibid., 72.
5. "Reminiscences of Paris Life," Edwin Howland Blashfield Papers, New-York Historical Society.
6. Mariana Van Rensselaer to Sylvester R. Koehler, June 12, 1881, Sylvester R. Koehler Papers, Archives of American Art, Smithsonian Institution, Washington, DC.
7. Goodrich, *Thomas Eakins*, 2:8. For a detailed examination of artists of the period, Chase's self-fashioning, and his extraordinary studio, see Sarah Burns, *Inventing the Modern Artist: Art and Culture in Gilded Age America* (New Haven: Yale University Press, 1996).
8. Barbara Dayer Gallati, *William Merritt Chase* (New York: Harry N. Abrams, 1995), 31–34. An insightful assessment of the painting can be found in Bruce Weber and Sarah Kate Gillespie, *Chase Inside and Out: The Aesthetic Interiors of William Merritt Chase* (New York: Berry-Hill Galleries, 2005), 40–43; see also Ronald G. Pisano et al., *William Merritt Chase: The Complete Catalogue of Known and Documented Work by William Merritt Chase*, vol. 2, *Portraits in Oil* (New Haven: Yale University Press, 2006), 53–54. For a recent study of Chase's career, see Elsa Smithgall et al., *William Merritt Chase: A Modern Master* (New Haven: Yale University Press, 2016).
9. On Eakins's *The Artist's Wife and His Setter Dog*, see Akela Reason, *Thomas Eakins and the Uses of History* (Philadelphia: University of Pennsylvania Press, 2010), 70–80. Another work by Eakins that seems relevant to Chase's painting is the portrait called *An Actress* (1903; Philadelphia Museum of Art), executed during the period when Eakins and Chase were socializing in Philadelphia. However, the removal of glazes from this work makes comparison difficult, as the reds Eakins used now read as hot pinks throughout most of the gown, causing the sitter's skin tones to appear ashen in contrast.
10. John Wilmerding, ed., *Thomas Eakins* (Washington, DC: Smithsonian Institution Press, 1993), 141.
11. Goodrich, *Thomas Eakins*, 2:220–21. Goodrich obtained this information from a 1930 interview with Murray.
12. On the criticism of Chase, see Jeremiah William McCarthy and Diana Thompson's introduction to this volume, p. 17n4.
13. Wilmerding, *Thomas Eakins*, 156.
14. Sarah Burns, "Ordering the Artist's Body: Thomas Eakins's Acts of Self-Portrayal," *American Art* 19, no. 1 (Spring 2005): 101. For "misunderstanding," etc., see Thomas Eakins to Harrison Morris, April 23, 1894, Pennsylvania Academy of the Fine Arts Archives.
15. Although Eakins painted few true self-portraits, he did include himself in several genre paintings and in his two great paintings of surgery, *The Gross Clinic* (Philadelphia Museum of Art) and *The Agnew Clinic* (Penn Art Collection, University of Pennsylvania). The literature on Rembrandt is enormous, but one helpful study of his numerous self-portraits is Christopher White and Quentin Buvelo, eds., *Rembrandt by Himself* (London: National Gallery, 1999).
16. Chase, for example, painted and exhibited a large picture of his pupil Dora Wheeler in 1882–83.
17. See, for example, Kristen Schwain, *Signs of Grace: Religion and American Art in the Gilded Age* (Ithaca, NY: Cornell University Press, 2008), 13–41.
18. Tanner recalled his experience at the PAFA under Eakins in H. O. Tanner, "The Story of an Artist's Life, Part I," *World's Work* 18, no. 2 (June 1909): 11,663.
19. Anna O. Marley, ed., *Henry Ossawa Tanner: Modern Spirit*, exh. cat. (Philadelphia: Pennsylvania Academy of the Fine Arts; Berkeley: University of California Press, 2012), 26.
20. Ibid., 85.

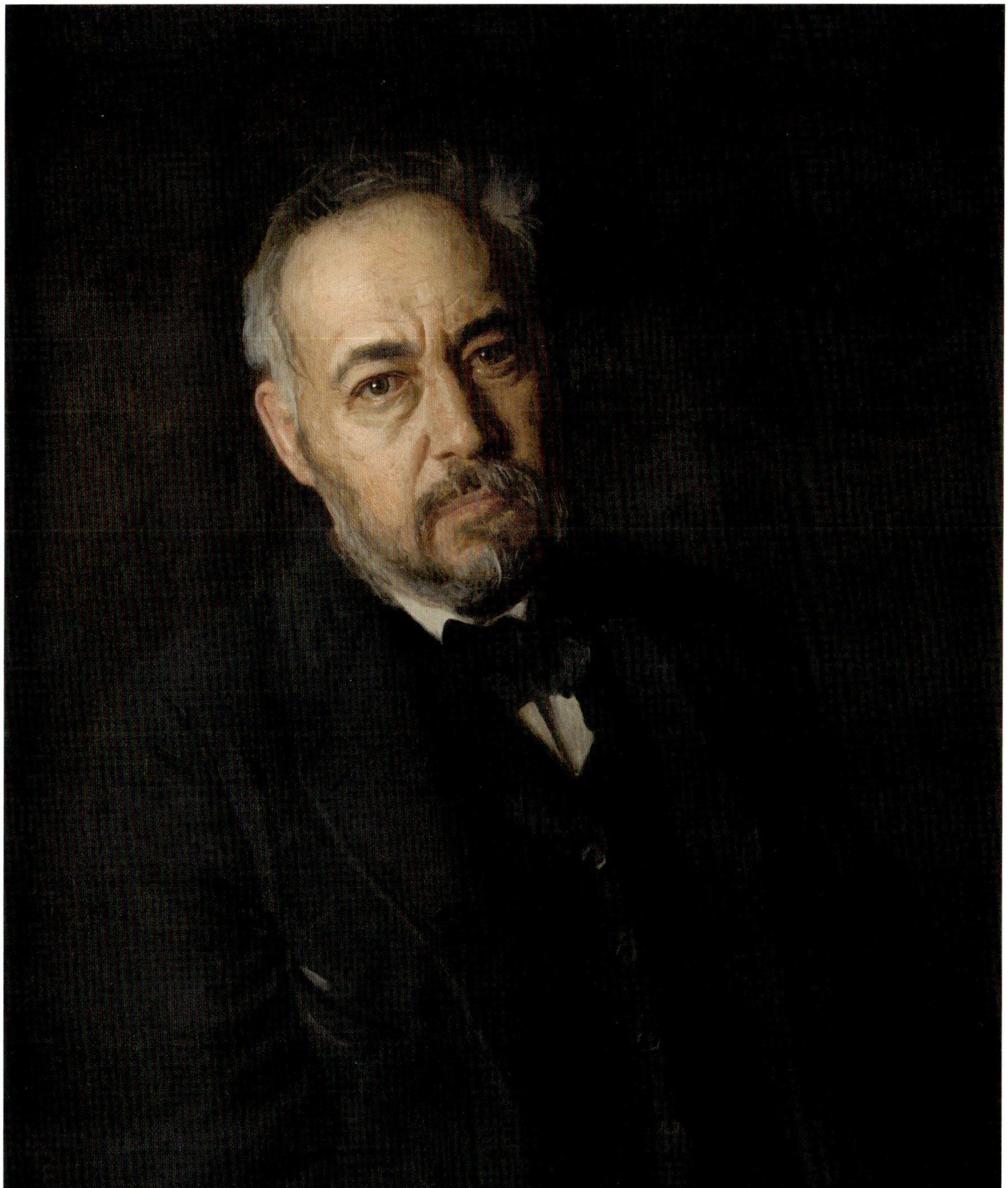

Thomas Eakins, *Self-Portrait*, 1902. Oil on canvas, 30 × 25 in. (76.2 × 63.5 cm)

ROBERT KUSHNER ON CECILIA BEAUX

So confident. So proud. So beautiful. I have always been struck by the bold assertiveness of this self-portrait. Cecilia Beaux depicts herself as an artist at the height of her powers. Eyes steely blue and observant. Lips pursed, maybe a hint of a bemused smile, but no display of the teeth and mirth we would see today. She is saying: I am handsome, young, educated, and refined, but most of all I am a professional.

Beaux was a talented painter from the start. As a single woman from an old family but with a distinct lack of fortune, she made her way in her professional life as a portraitist, one of the best of her era. Society portraiture is today a vanished art. But Beaux had perceived a need: both newly minted millionaires and well-to-do scions of aristocratic families were seeking a contemporary read on the ancestral claims that commissioned portraits offered. She filled that niche with a panache both traditional and new—brighter chroma, brilliant brushwork, and psychological immediacy. Her self-portrait is an advertisement. She is declaring: others may be able to depict stout, successful businessmen, but come to me for sympathetic views of men, women, and children. Beaux gazes self-assuredly into the distance, into the light that illuminates her face, the world of patrons finding their way to her in her studio.

The technique here is fast and accurate—the paint itself intentionally thin, only one very lean layer; the colors and tones absolutely correct, no possibility of retouching, correcting, overpainting. Then, as we glance down from the solidity of the face, the striped bodice dissolves into a frenzy of brushstrokes barely coalescing into recognizable form. Almost an abstract painting, her clothing flattens the form of her shoulders, barely discernible amid the thicket of wide brushstrokes. The beige of the raw canvas becomes part of the shading. There are spots of red, a slash of ochre, a sliver of pure black, even some wayward phthalo blue. Who knew there could be such color harmony in a blue-and-white-striped fabric? There is no décolletage, no jewels—symbols of female allure reserved for wealthy patrons. Rather, she is prim, neat, proper, and ready to work. Center front is a bow (could bow equal Beaux?). All of this is painted wet-on-wet.

What a bravura performance.

Truth to tell, Cecilia Beaux was my wife's great-great-aunt, and we lived for two summers (1975 and 1976) in the artist's beloved shore house, Green Alley, outside Gloucester, Massachusetts. It was a charming house, just large enough for a single owner and three servants. Each room was small, slightly rustic, oddly Mediterranean—all in all, an aestheticized New England fairy tale. A wood-paneled dining room facing the sea, a half-round staircase, a morning loggia for coffee, an afternoon loggia overlooking the harbor for libations, a master bedroom with its own grassy terrace, all designed by Beaux herself. But at the heart of the compound was a large, detached studio with a huge north-facing window, designed to capture the light necessary for portrait painting. Art making was at the core of the whole operation. By the time we stayed there, the house was empty, no furnishings left. But Beaux's presence was still strong and her tastes evident: the green tiles and stones she had selected for the small fireplace, the by-then defunct artificial stream that once greeted guests, the lack of window screens (she claimed that mosquitos never bit her), the carefully considered views from each room, the puritanical bathroom and tub. The environments of her life and work embodied elegance and practicality in equal measure.

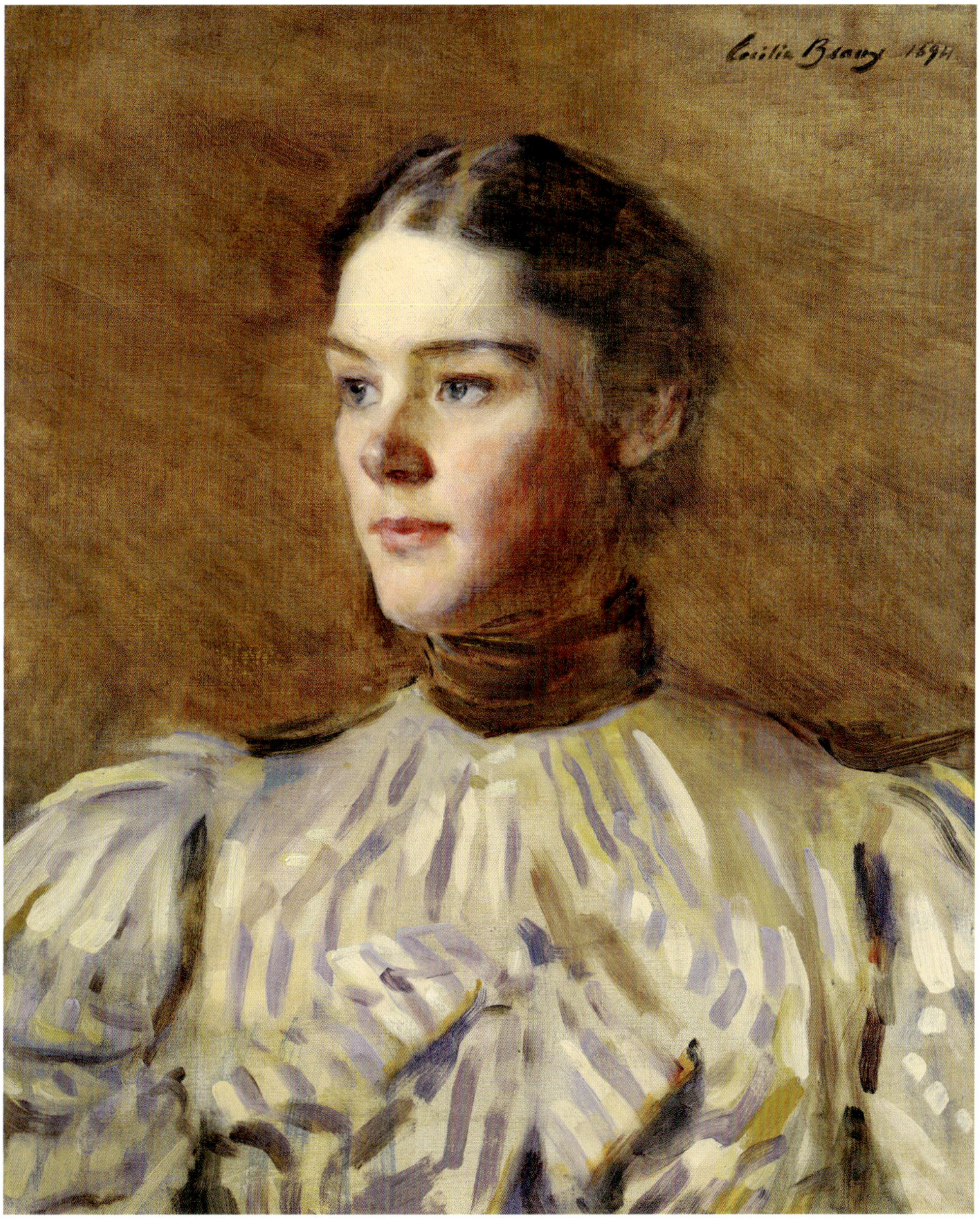

Cecilia Beaux, *Self-Portrait*, 1894. Oil on canvas, 25 × 20 in. (63.5 × 50.8 cm)

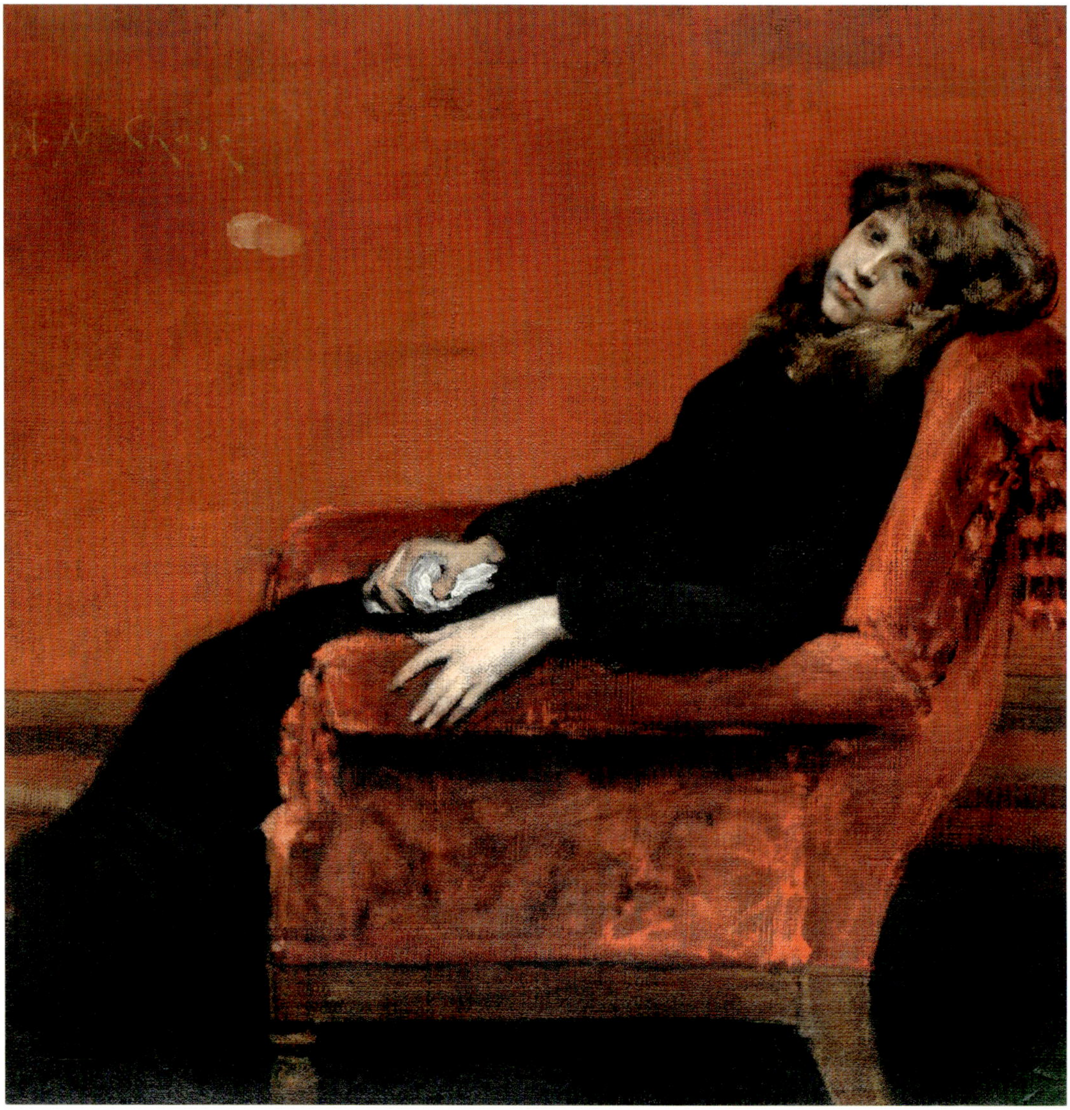

William Merritt Chase, *The Young Orphan* [or] *An Idle Moment* [or] *Portrait*, 1884. Oil on canvas, 44 × 42 in. (111.8 × 106.7 cm)

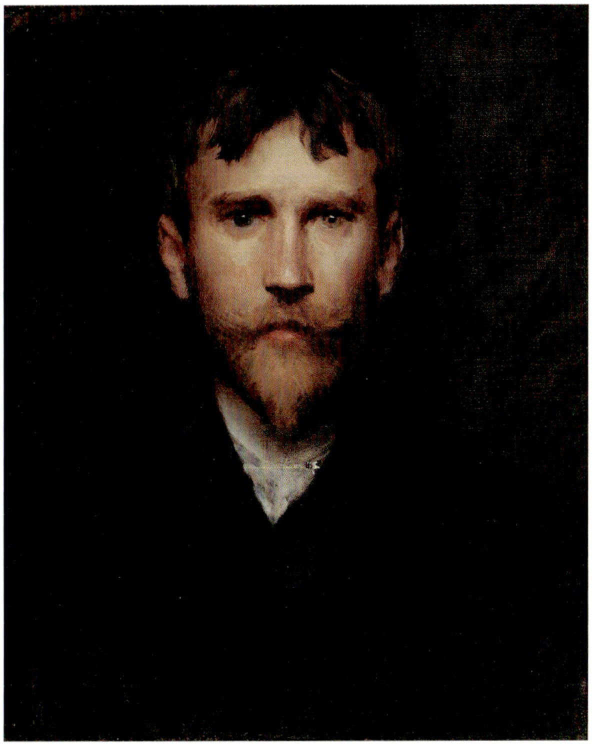

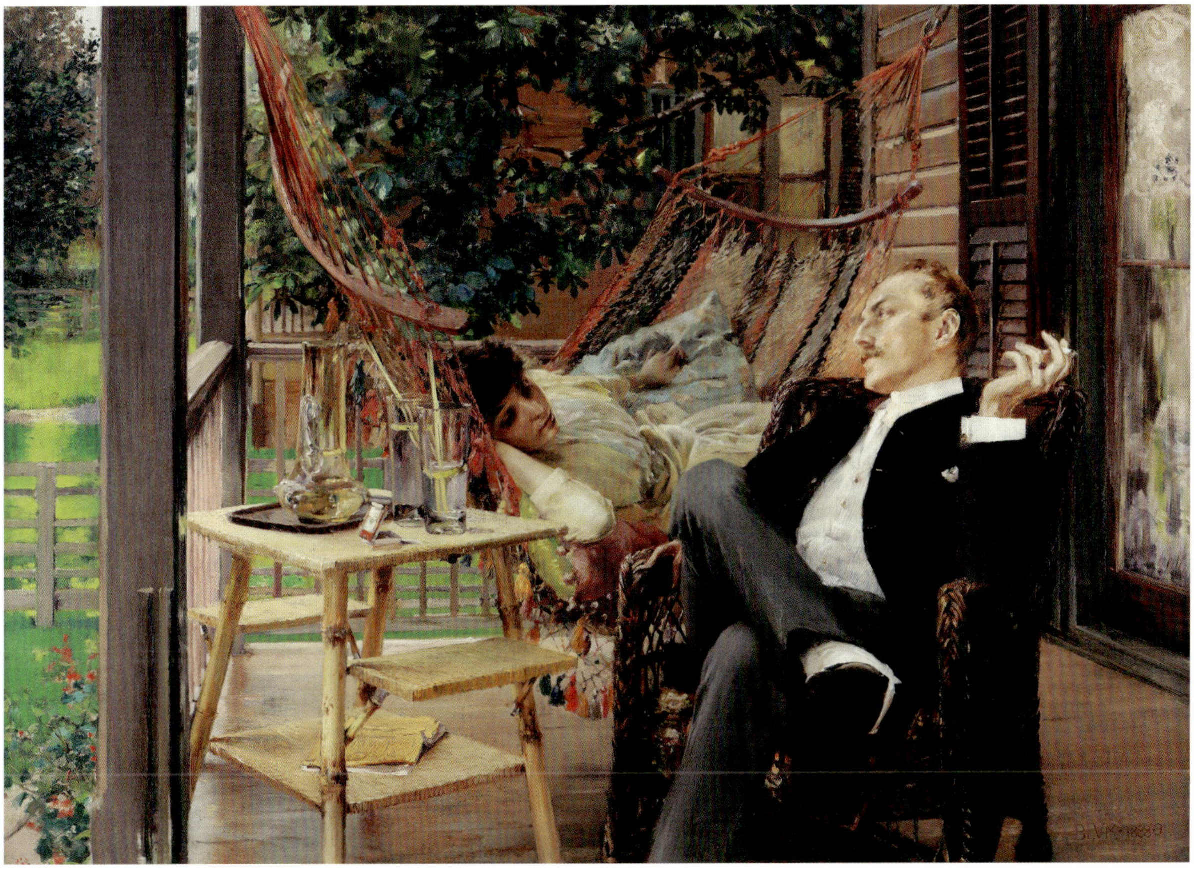

Top: William Merritt Chase, *Robert Blum*, 1888. Oil on canvas, 21⅛ × 17⅛ in. (53.7 × 43.5 cm)
Bottom: Robert Frederick Blum, *Two Idlers*, 1888–89. Oil on canvas, 29 × 40 in. (73.7 × 101.6 cm)

Painted representations of palettes make me very happy. Artists can besmirch their carefully rendered images with blobs of gooey color as if the canvas were an actual palette. Paint becomes a representation of itself as well as a reminder of the messy, undifferentiated origins of the crafted picture. Paint is both in the image and falling out of it.

In William J. Whittemore's portrait of Charles Courtney Curran, a palette tips into the picture like an extension of Curran's body. His thumb lies across it to secure a collection of brushes ready for their turn at the brown canvas he is working on. One of the brushes almost seems to be touching the marble base of a nearby sculpture, as if it were independently painting a loose, atmospheric abstraction. Curran is looking at his canvas, and his gaze is carried to its destination along the leg of the naked female sculpture squatting beside him. He steadies his hand with a maulstick as he brushes the surface of the painting, but that same hand overlaps the flexed foot of the sculpture to complete a circuit that connects eye to hand, hand to brush, brush to palette. This is a story about vision tangled with bodies. Curran peers through spectacles but also though art history, embodied as a naked woman. Her head has been cropped out of the picture, but a bust in the upper left corner and part of a naked torso at the top center stand in for the parts we cannot see. Curran's lower parts are cropped out of the picture, too, and it looks as if Whittemore may have been staging an all-too-familiar gendered pair: the carnality of a naked woman and the well-dressed civility of an accomplished man.

I like thinking, though, that the painting makes a complete body out of dispersed, heterogeneous parts, a complicated body constrained and subdivided by guardrails, pedestals, canvas edges, bowler hats, and neckties. My intuition is that Whittemore and Curran were committed traditionalists, not in the business of questioning social or aesthetic conventions. But some works of art have the power to break free of their makers' intentions. Was Whittemore picturing Curran like Balzac's Frenhoffer, an artist whose ambition and practiced skill have led him to make a sticky monochrome, the observable world collapsed into fecal shadow? Or was he perhaps portraying Curran making a portrait of his palette, a blank space of potential waiting for wet colors to be squeezed out and smeared across it?

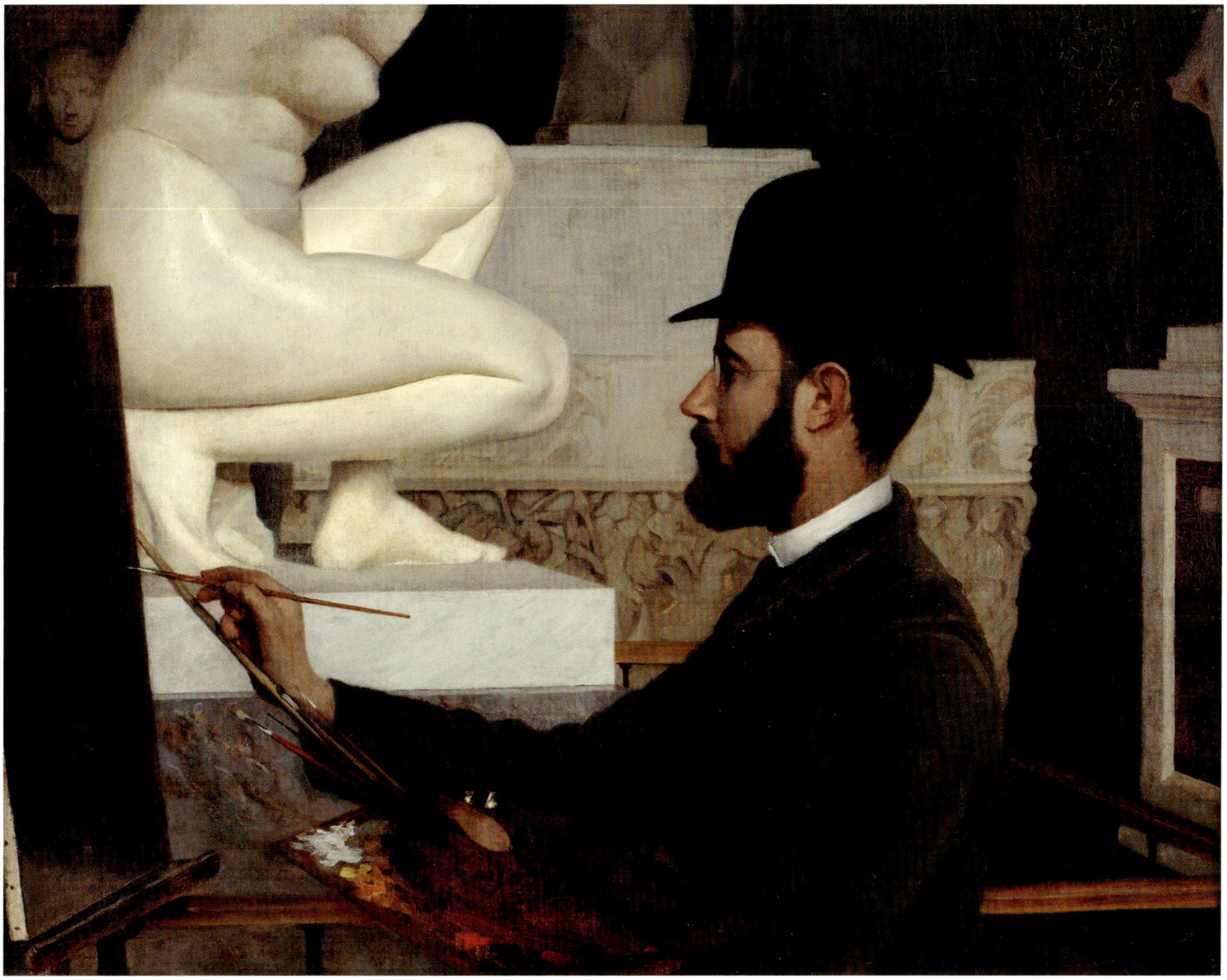

William J. Whittemore, *Charles Courtney Curran*, 1888–89. Oil on canvas, 17 × 21 in. (43.2 × 53.3 cm)

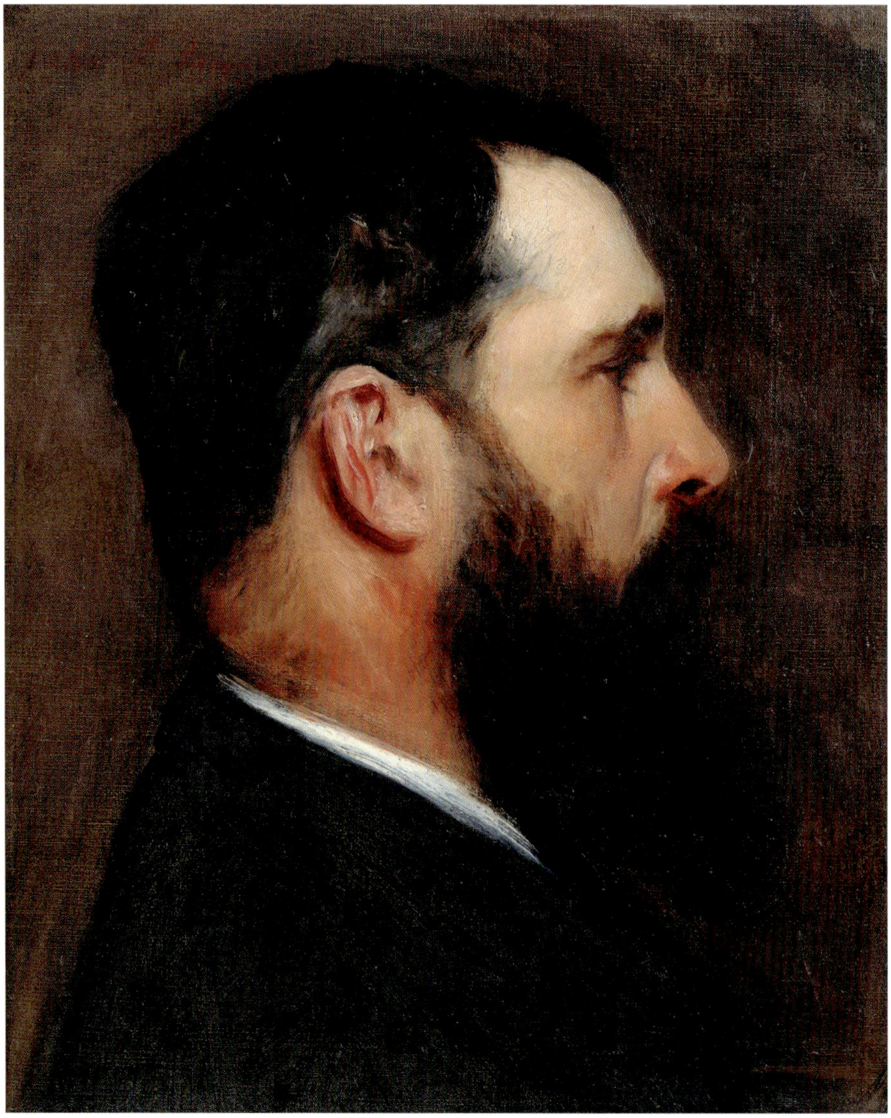

John Singer Sargent, *Claude Monet*, ca. 1887. Oil on canvas, 16 × 13 in. (40.6 × 33 cm)

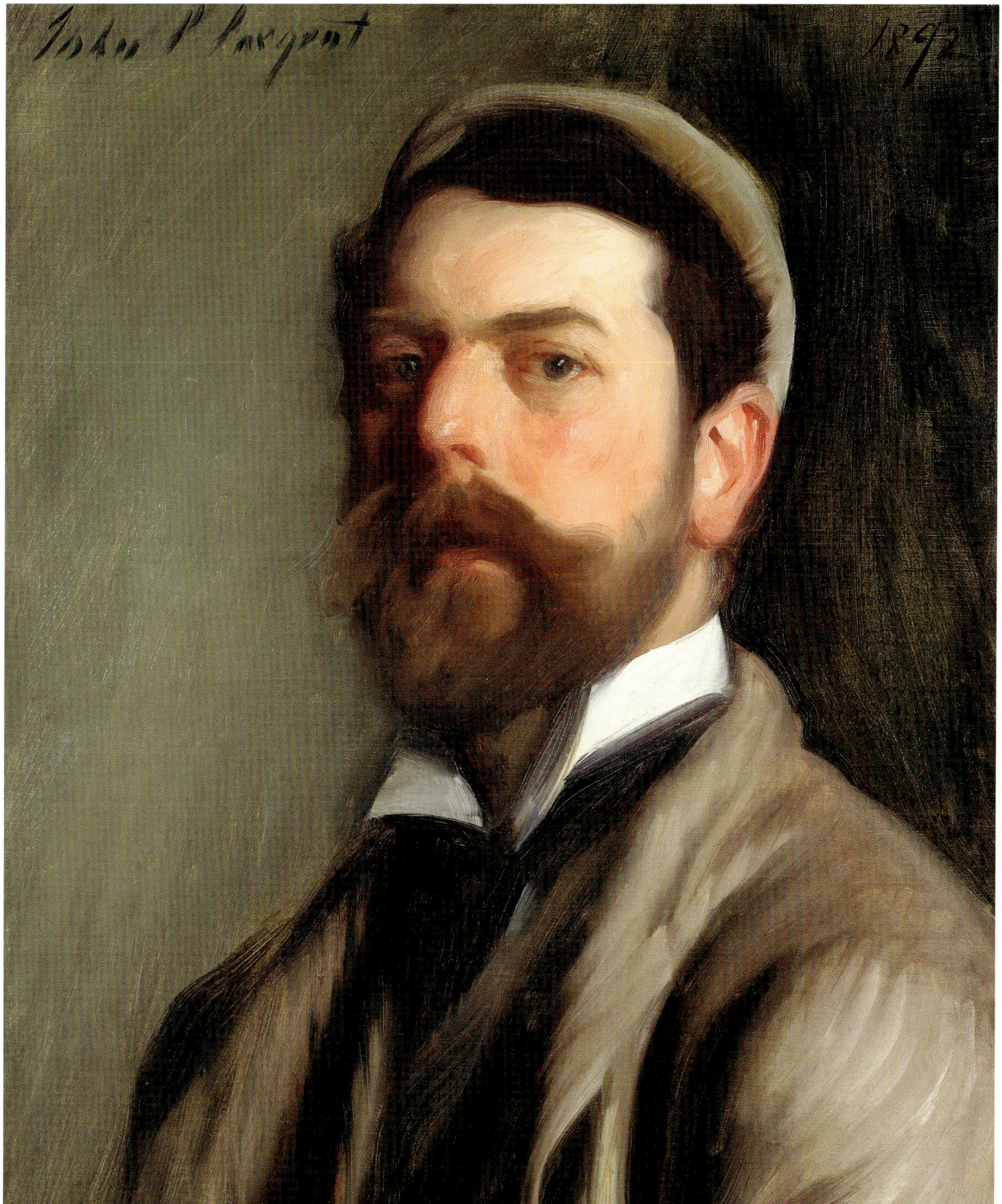

John Singer Sargent, *Self-Portrait*, 1892. Oil on canvas, 21 × 17 in. (53.5 × 43.2 cm)

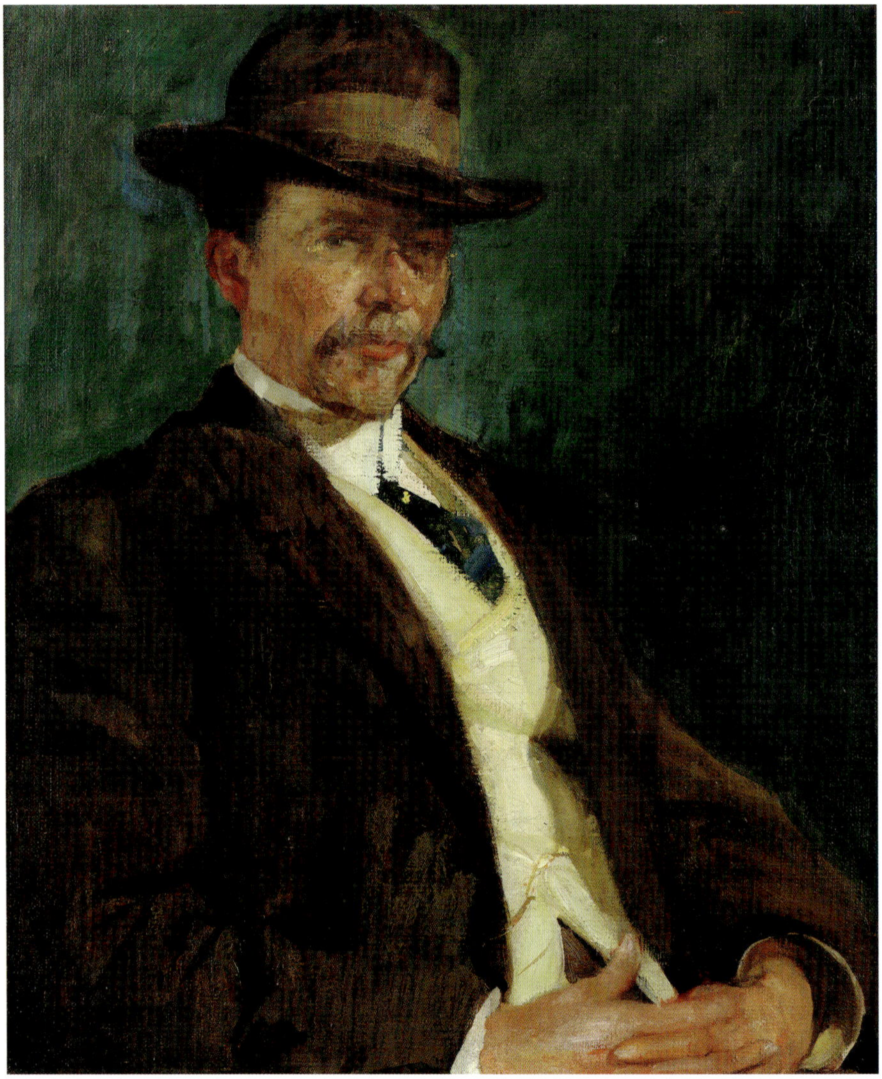

Richard E. Miller, *Henry Ossawa Tanner*, n.d. Oil on canvas, 30 × 25 in. (76.2 × 63.5 cm)

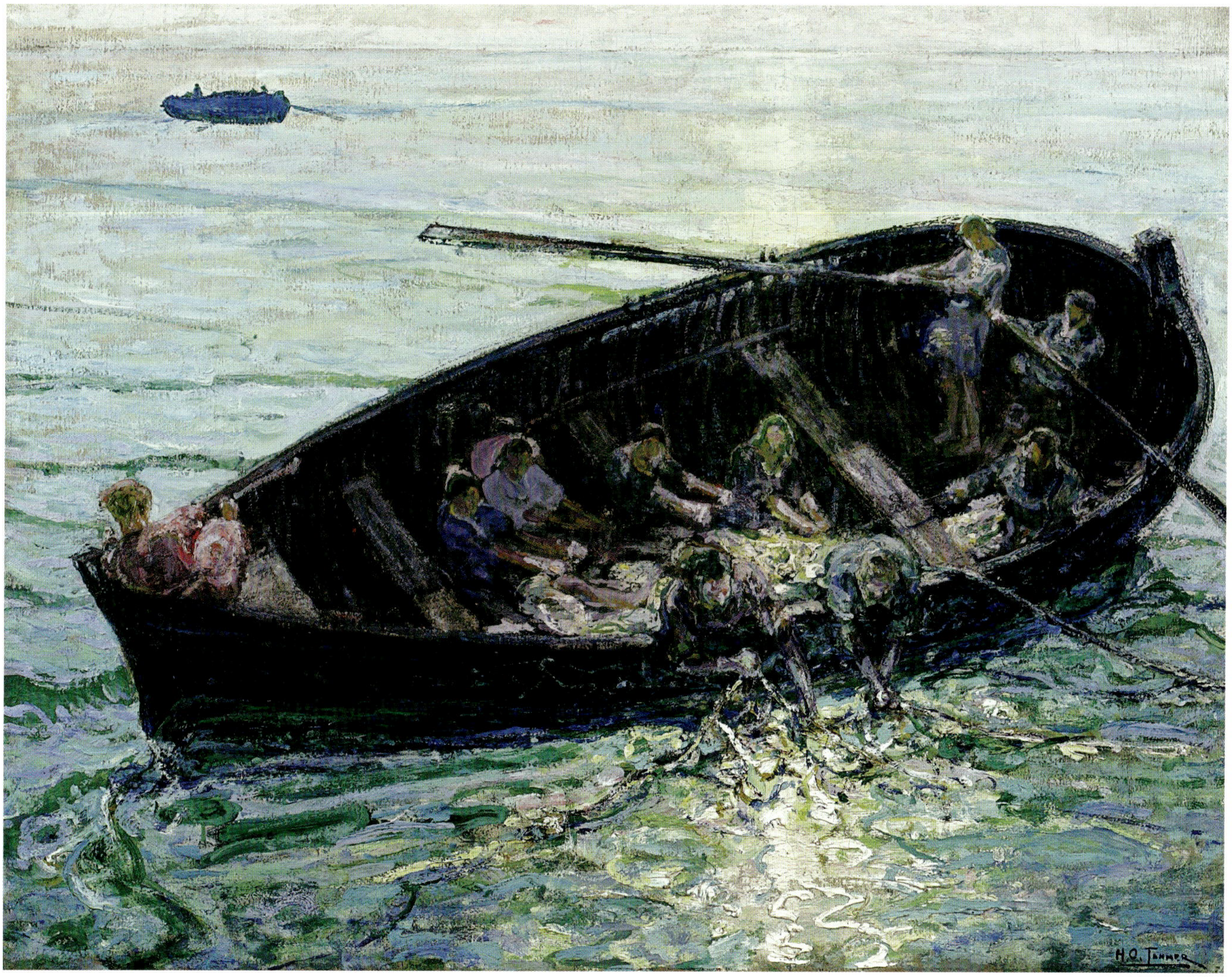

Henry Ossawa Tanner, *The Miraculous Haul of Fishes*, ca. 1913–14. Oil on canvas, 38 × 47 ½ in. (96.5 × 120.7 cm)

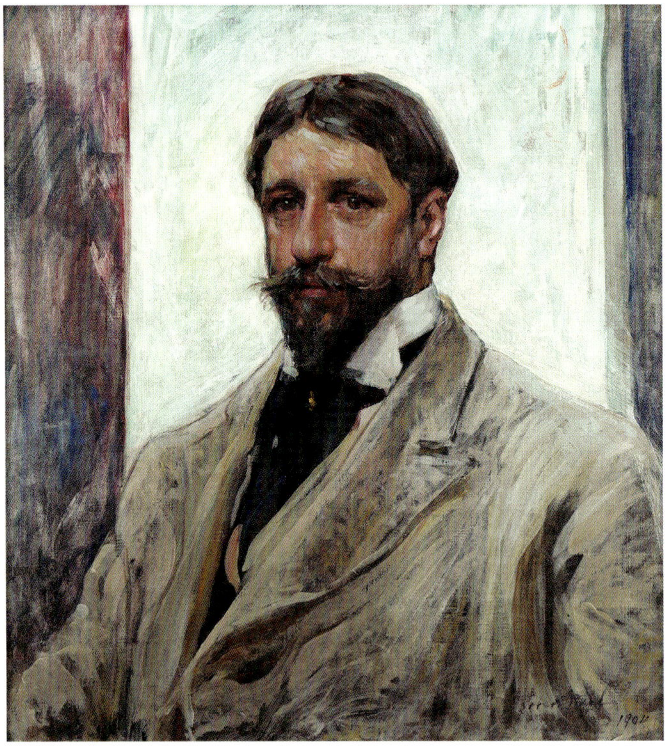

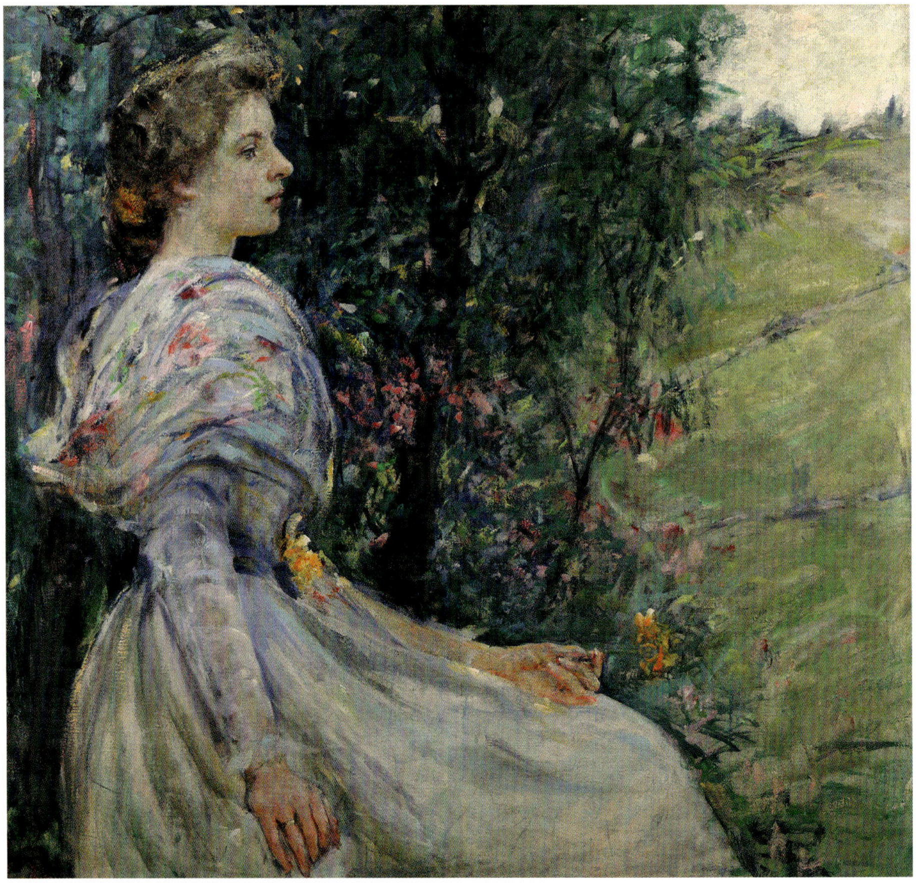

Top: Robert Reid, *Self-Portrait*, 1904. Oil on canvas, 27 ½ × 24 ⅝ in. (69.9 × 62.5 cm)
Bottom: Robert Reid, *Daffodils*, n.d. Oil on canvas, 42 × 44 in. (106.7 × 111.8 cm)

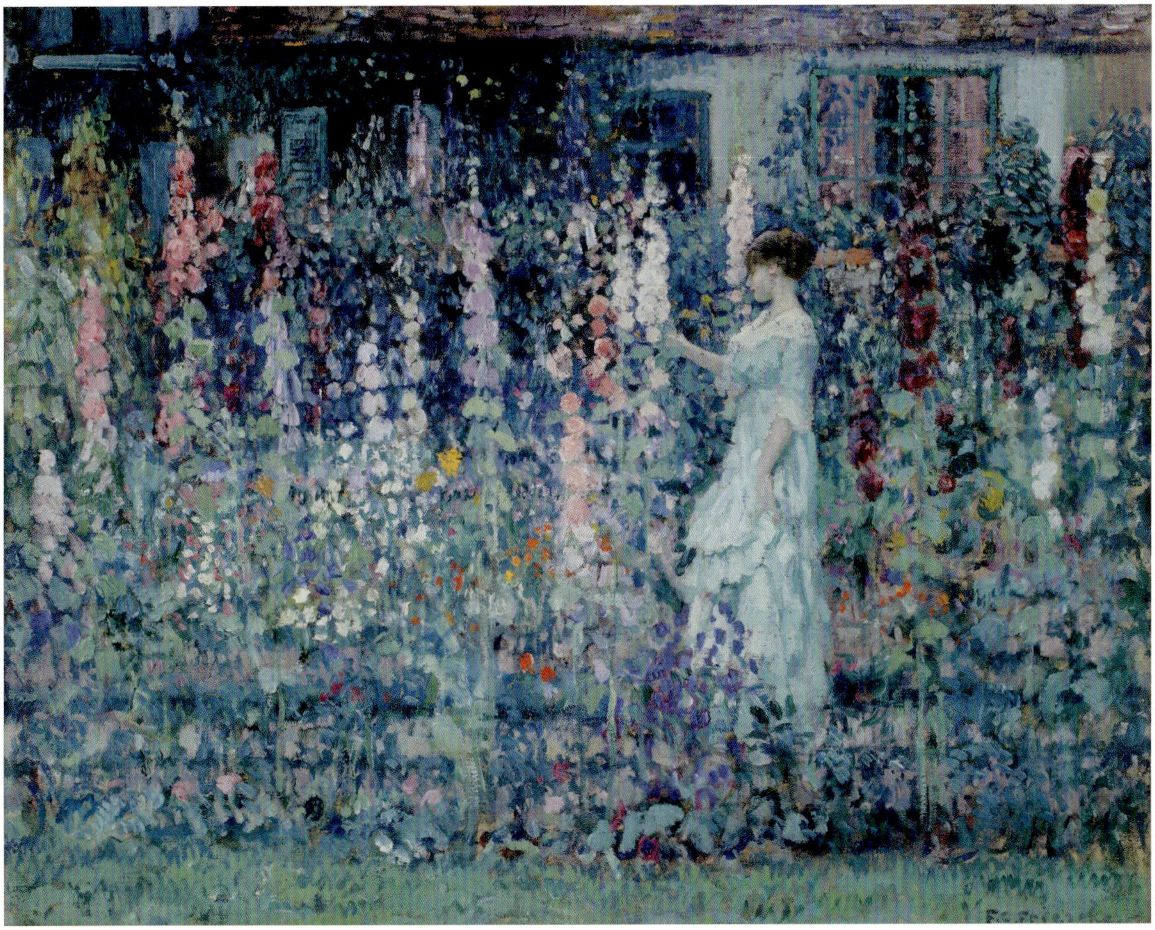

Frederick Carl Frieseke, *Hollyhocks*, by 1911. Oil on canvas, 25 ½ × 32 in. (64.8 × 81.3 cm)

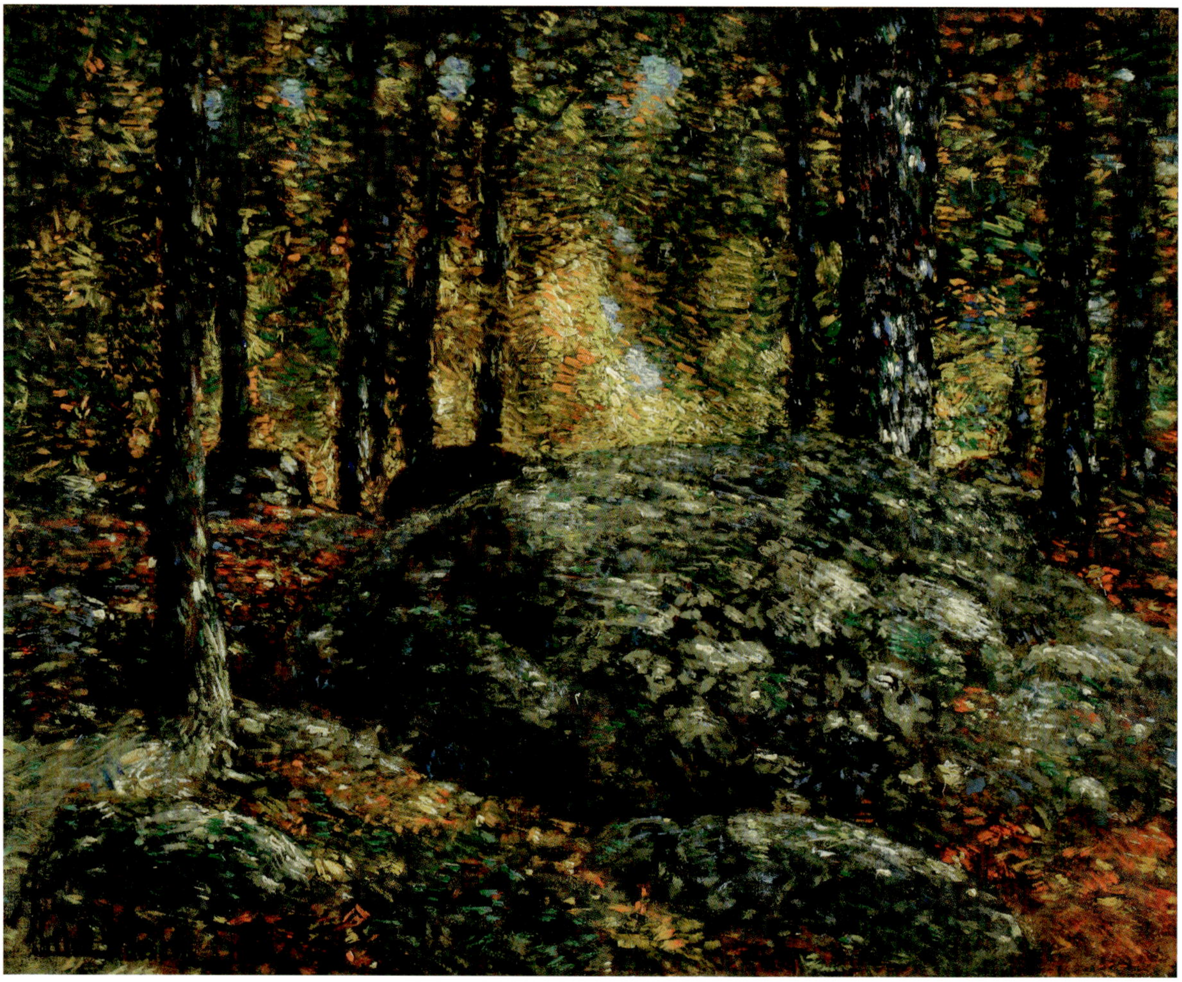

Childe Hassam, *The Jewel Box, Old Lyme*, 1906. Oil on canvas, 20 × 24 in. (50.8 × 61 cm)

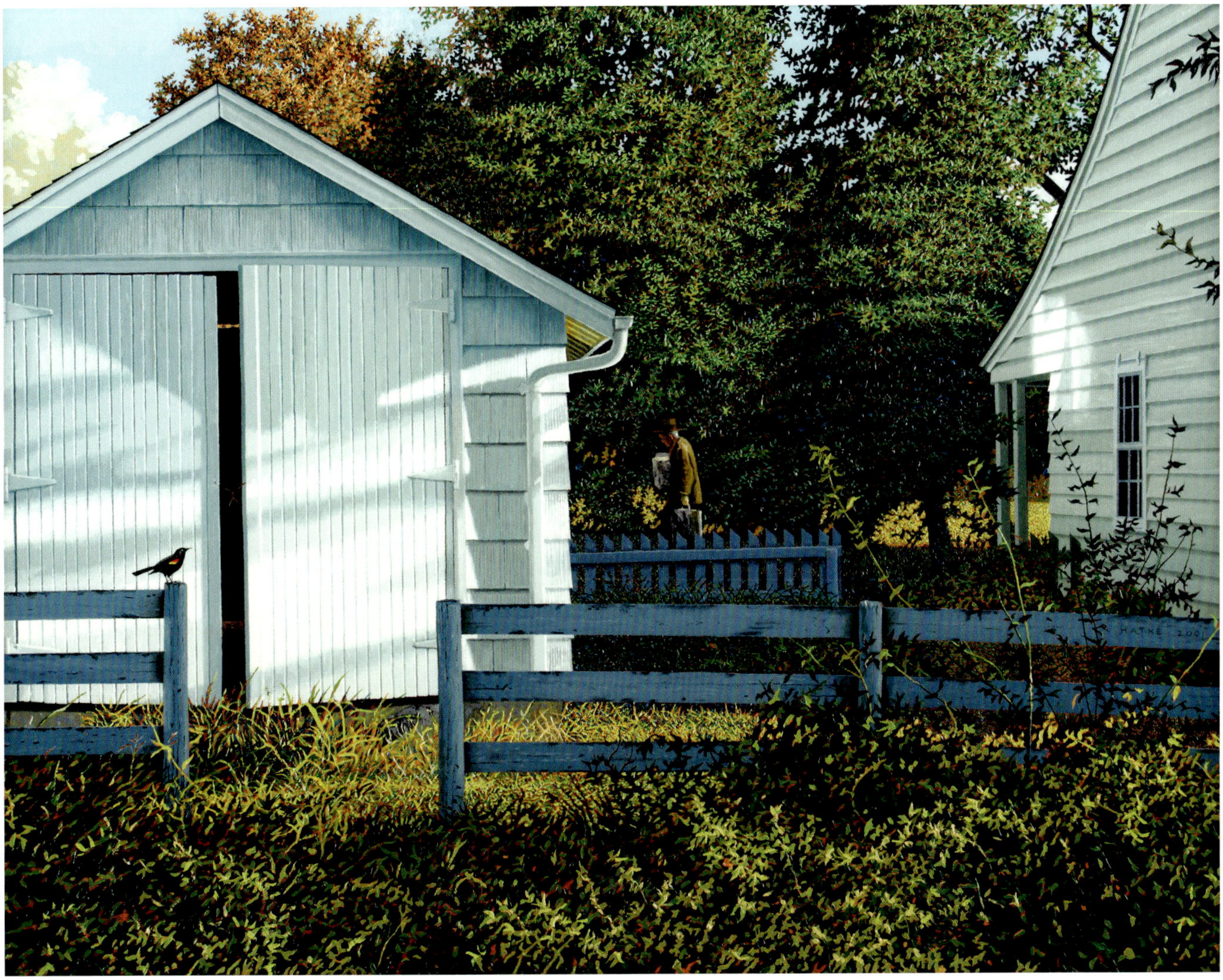

Walter Hatke, *Provider*, 2001. Oil on linen, 24 × 29¾ in. (61 × 75.6 cm)

MAXFIELD PARRISH, A.N.A.

By KENYON COX · 1905 ·

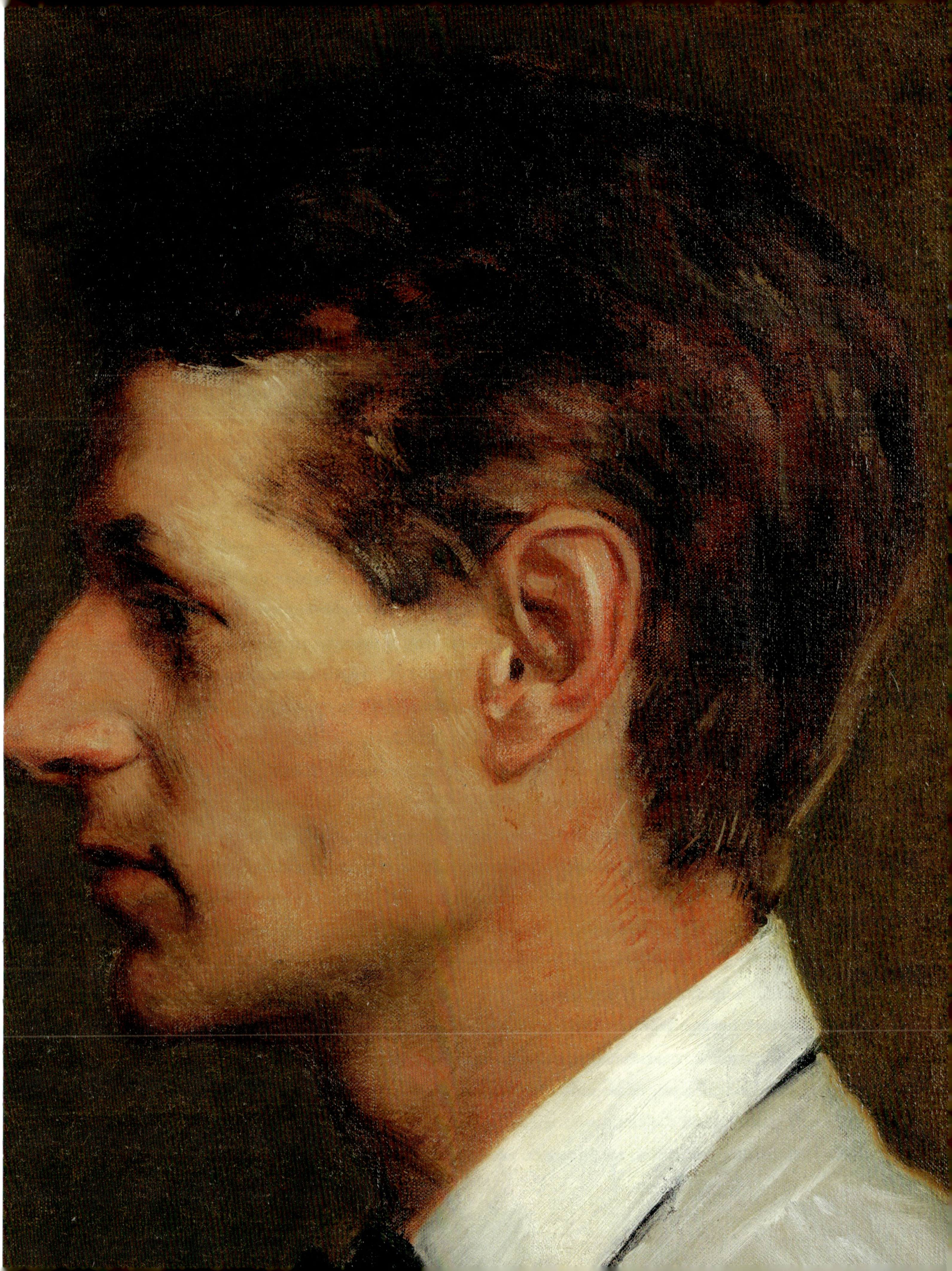

JOHN MOORE ON MAXFIELD PARRISH

The most familiar artist to me, growing up in a working-class family in Saint Louis, was certainly Maxfield Parrish, whose calendars or posters would have been found above the refrigerators in the kitchens of my childhood. Parrish's work, and that of the artist Hal Foster, whose *Prince Valiant* covered the full-page frontispiece of the Sunday comics section of the *St. Louis Post-Dispatch*, originally (and, I think, indelibly) forged my idea of the appropriate form for visual art. Both artists, with their detail-oriented, carefully researched, realistic renderings, touched viewers in the most direct way. Parrish was the best-known American artist of his time, and *Prince Valiant* is still running as a comic strip today.

The National Academy of Design's painting *Saint Valentine* was commissioned as a cover for *Life* magazine and based on a photographic self-portrait by Parrish. With his dark hair styled in a pageboy, Parrish's saint could very well have been a prototype for Prince Valiant. While the two artists' realistic impulse was similar, Hal Foster's linear, graphic style could never be mistaken for Parrish's near-photographic illusion. The source materials for the latter's art, in addition to scale models of imaginary locales, were usually photographs taken by the artist of himself or his favorite model. Parrish lost no sleep over the idea that using a photographic source might be "cheating," nor did he worry too much about any bias toward fine art versus illustration, a distinction that has lost much of its certainty.

Despite his celebrated illusionism, however, the primacy of imagination was the driving force in Parrish's work, as is evident in his statement "People need outlets for their imagination. They need windows for their minds. Artists provide them."[1] His imaginative feats were brought to life by his masterful synthesis of superb drawing skill, approaching caricature; his Pre-Raphaelite sensibility; a technicolor palette influenced by the time he had spent in the southwestern United States while in his twenties; and an emphasis on geometric compositional structures. Most of these elements are evident in *Saint Valentine*.

Later in his career, Parrish shifted his priorities to landscape, a move foreshadowed by the stunning forty-nine-foot-long mural he designed for the foyer of the Curtis Publishing Company's headquarters in Philadelphia, executed in Favrile glass by Louis Comfort Tiffany in 1914–16. *The Dream Garden* is a lush, romantic, make-believe masterpiece. A decade earlier, St. Valentine, the patron saint of romance, is looking up, surely dreaming of that garden and the imaginary landscapes its creator would increasingly produce in the years to come.

1. Maxfield Parrish, quoted in Lawrence Cutler and Judith Guffman Cutler, *Maxfield Parrish: A Retrospective* (San Francisco: Pomegranate Artbooks, 1995), 15.

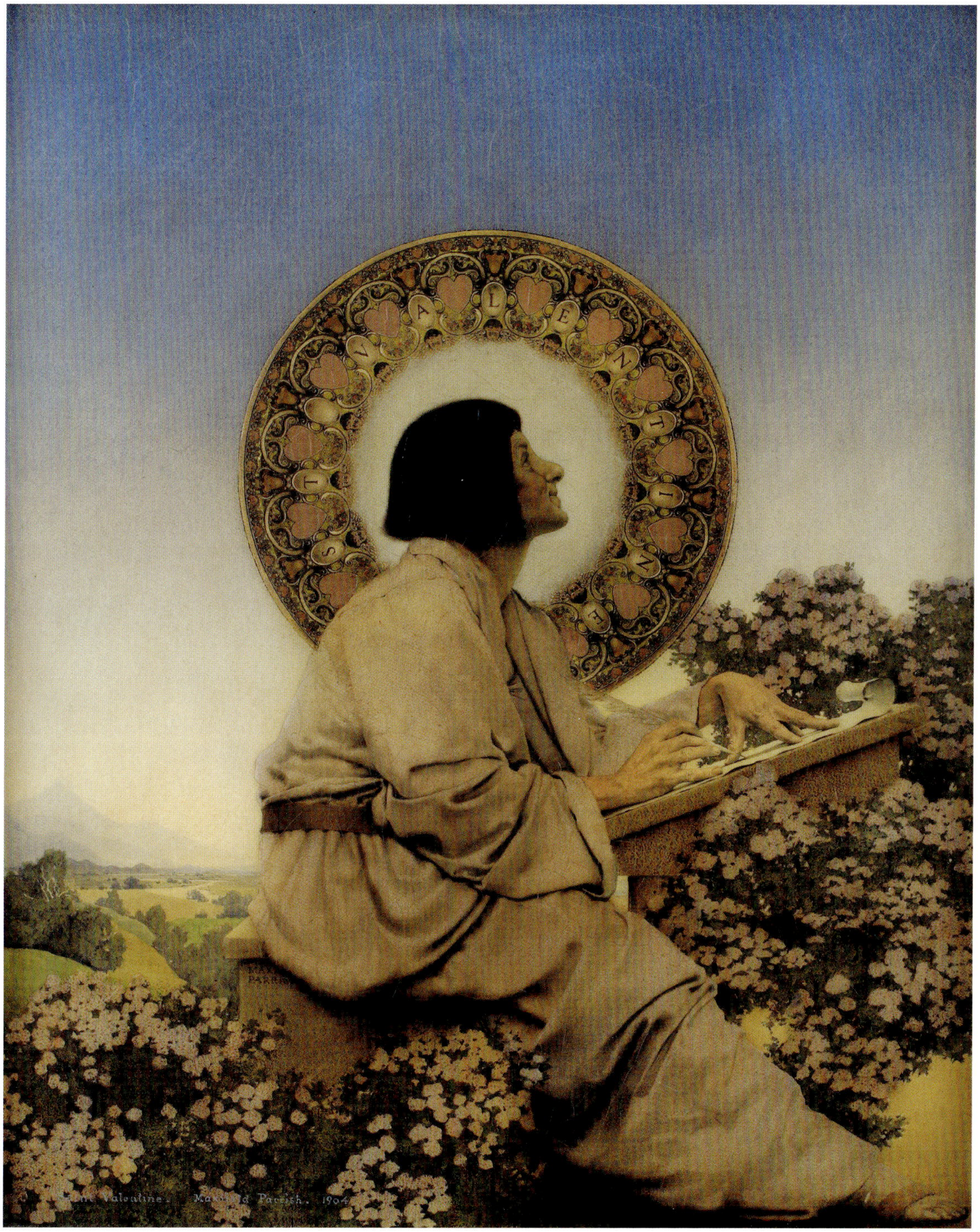

Maxfield Parrish, *Saint Valentine*, 1904. Tempera on gessoed panel, 20 × 15¾ in. (50.8 × 40 cm)

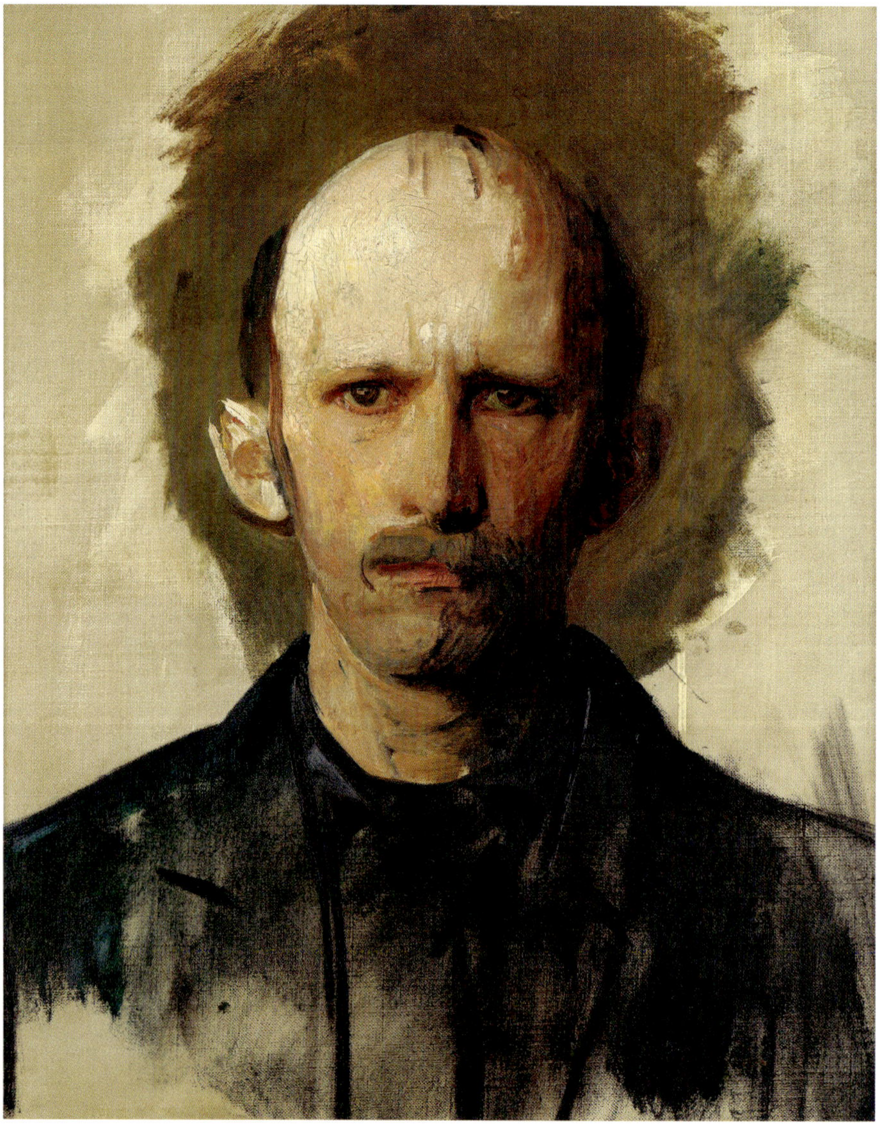

George Of, *Abbot* [*sic*] *H. Thayer*, n.d. Oil on canvas, 20 × 16 in. (50.8 × 40.6 cm)

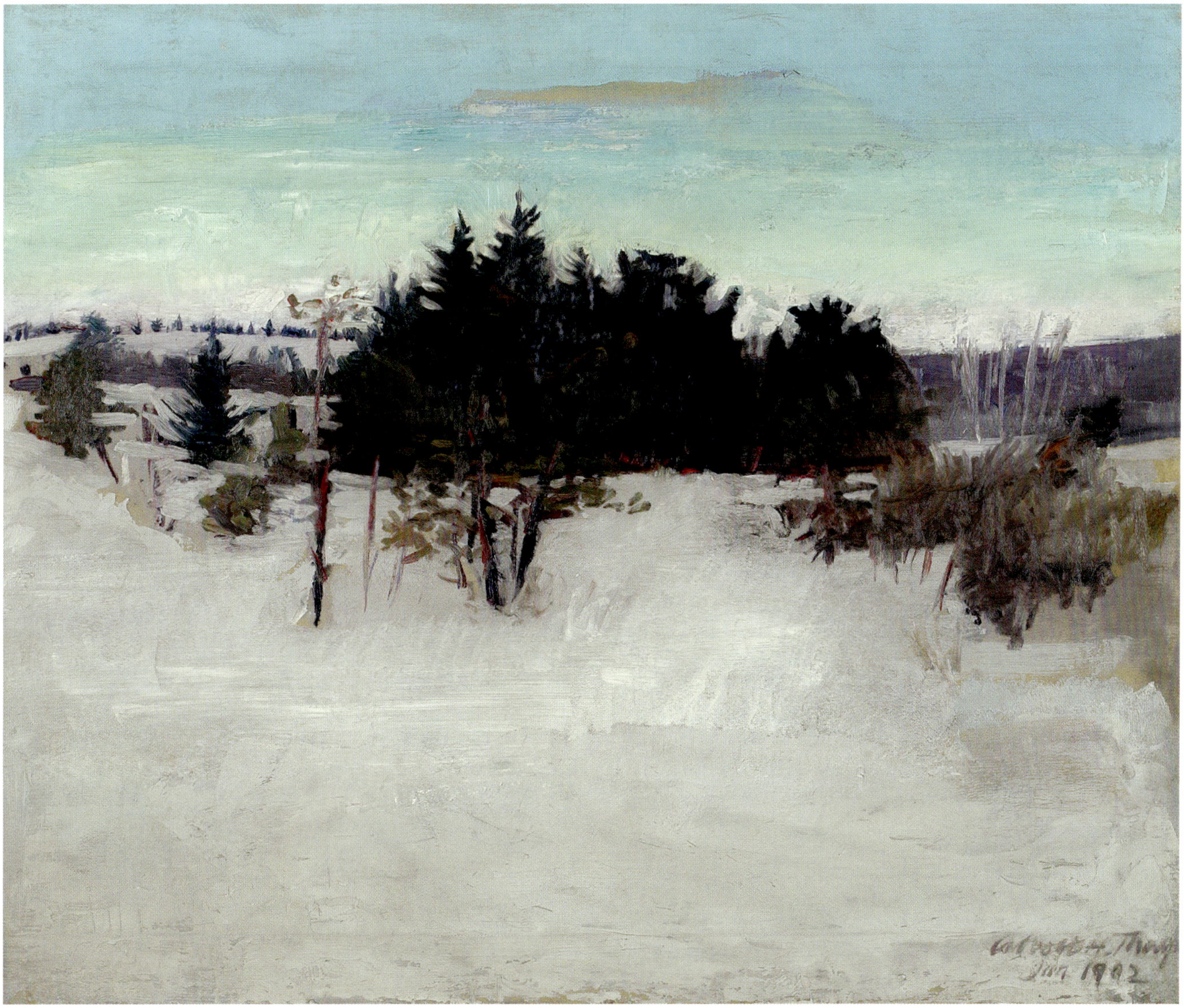

Abbott H. Thayer, *Winter Landscape*, 1902. Oil on canvas, 29⅜ × 34⅞ in. (74.6 × 88.6 cm)

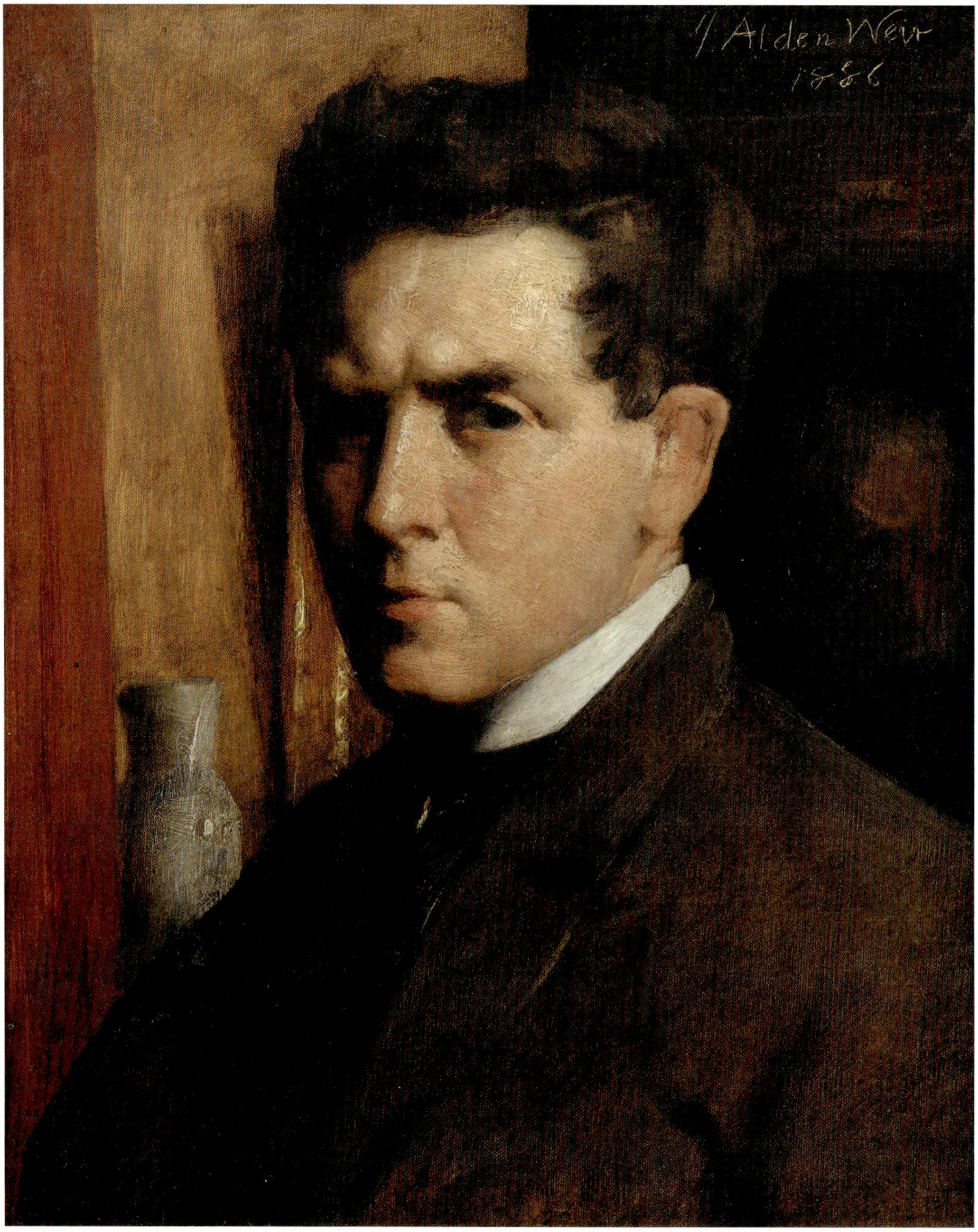

J. Alden Weir, *Self-Portrait*, 1886. Oil on canvas, 21 × 17 in. (53.3 × 43.2 cm)

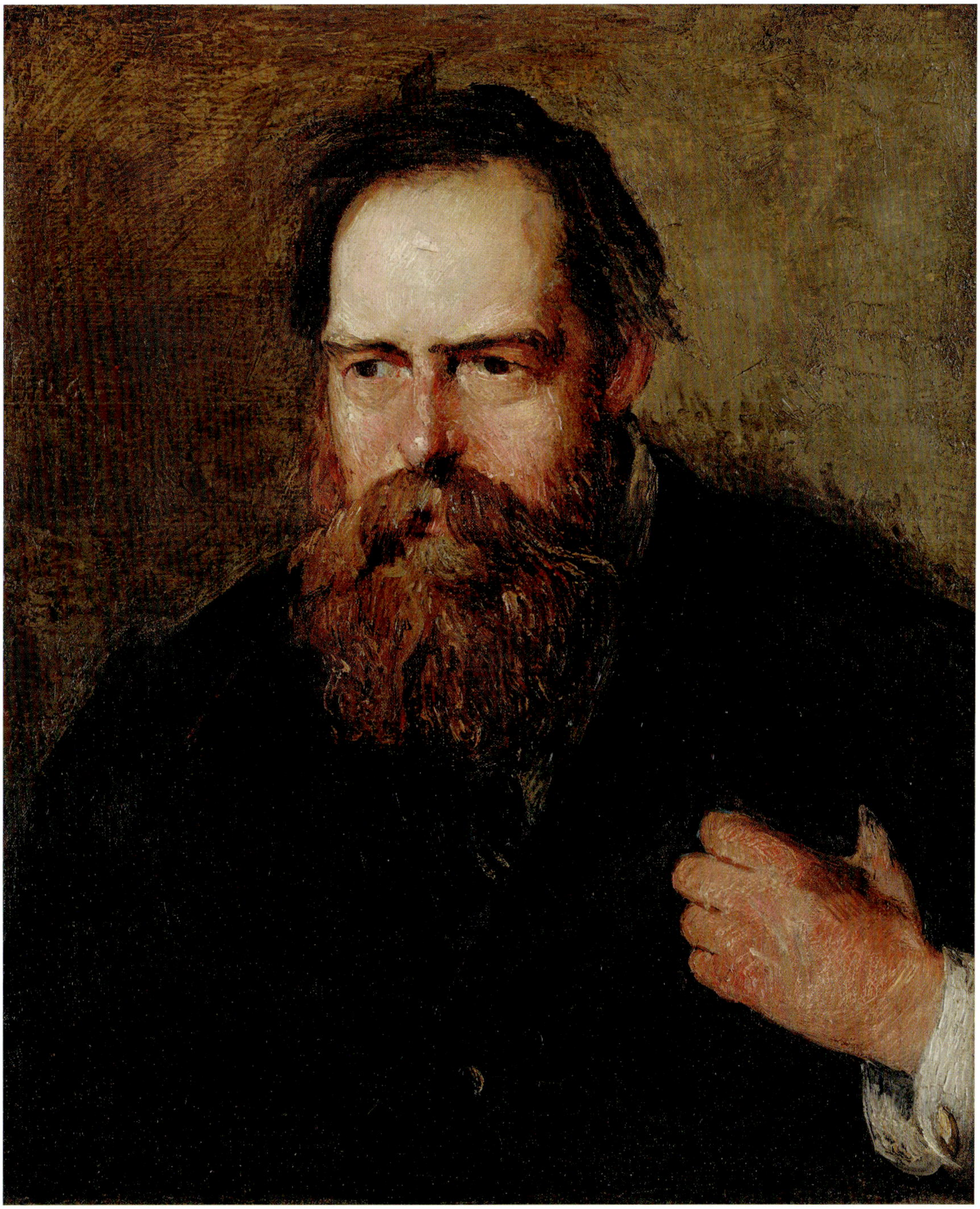

J. Alden Weir, *Albert Pinkham Ryder*, 1902–3. Oil on canvas, 24 × 20 in. (61 × 50.8 cm)

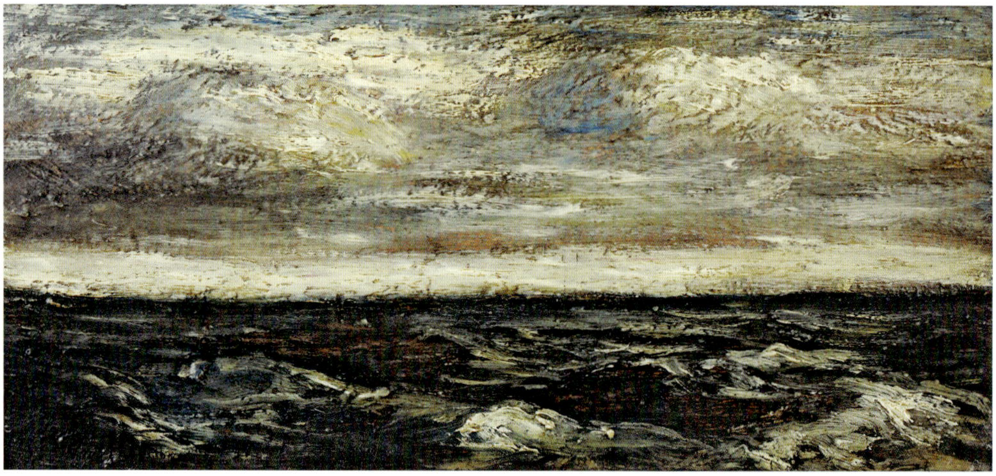

Albert Pinkham Ryder, *Marine*, 1907. Oil on wood panel, 8 ⅝ × 17 ¾ in. (21.9 × 45.1 cm)

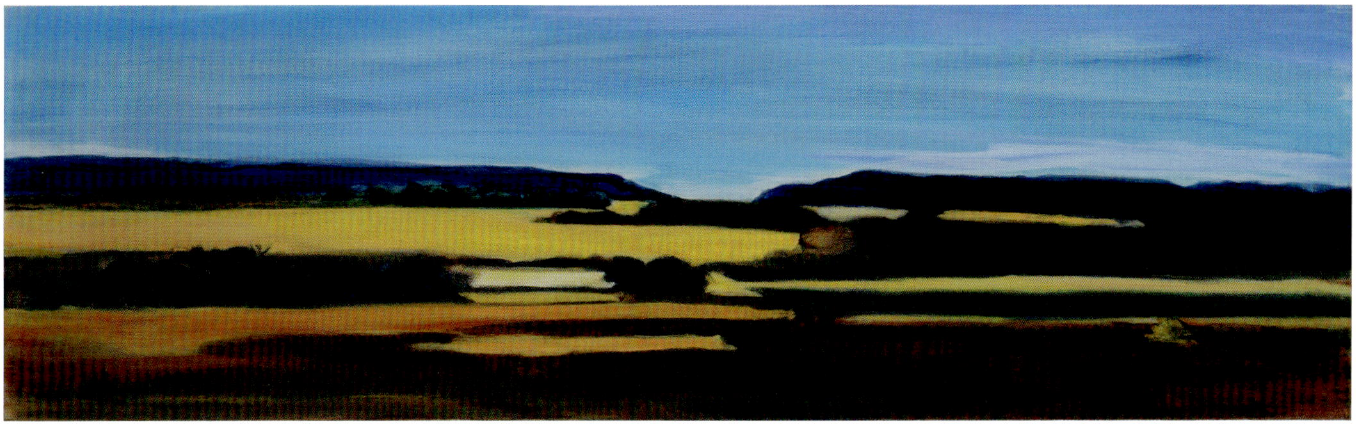

Albert Kresch, *North of Taos, N.M.*, 2005. Oil on canvas, 14 ½ × 46 ½ in. (36.8 × 118.1 cm)

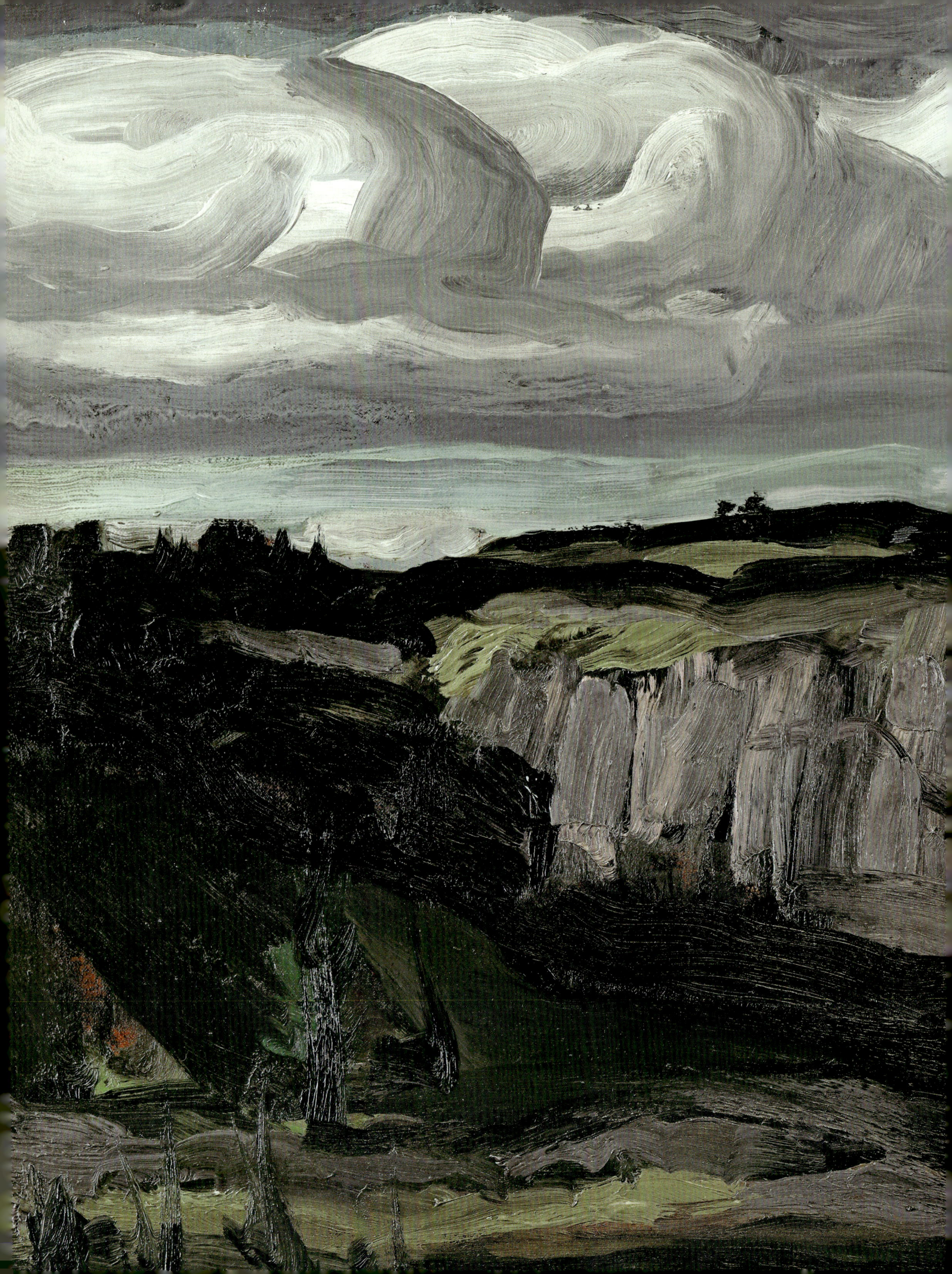

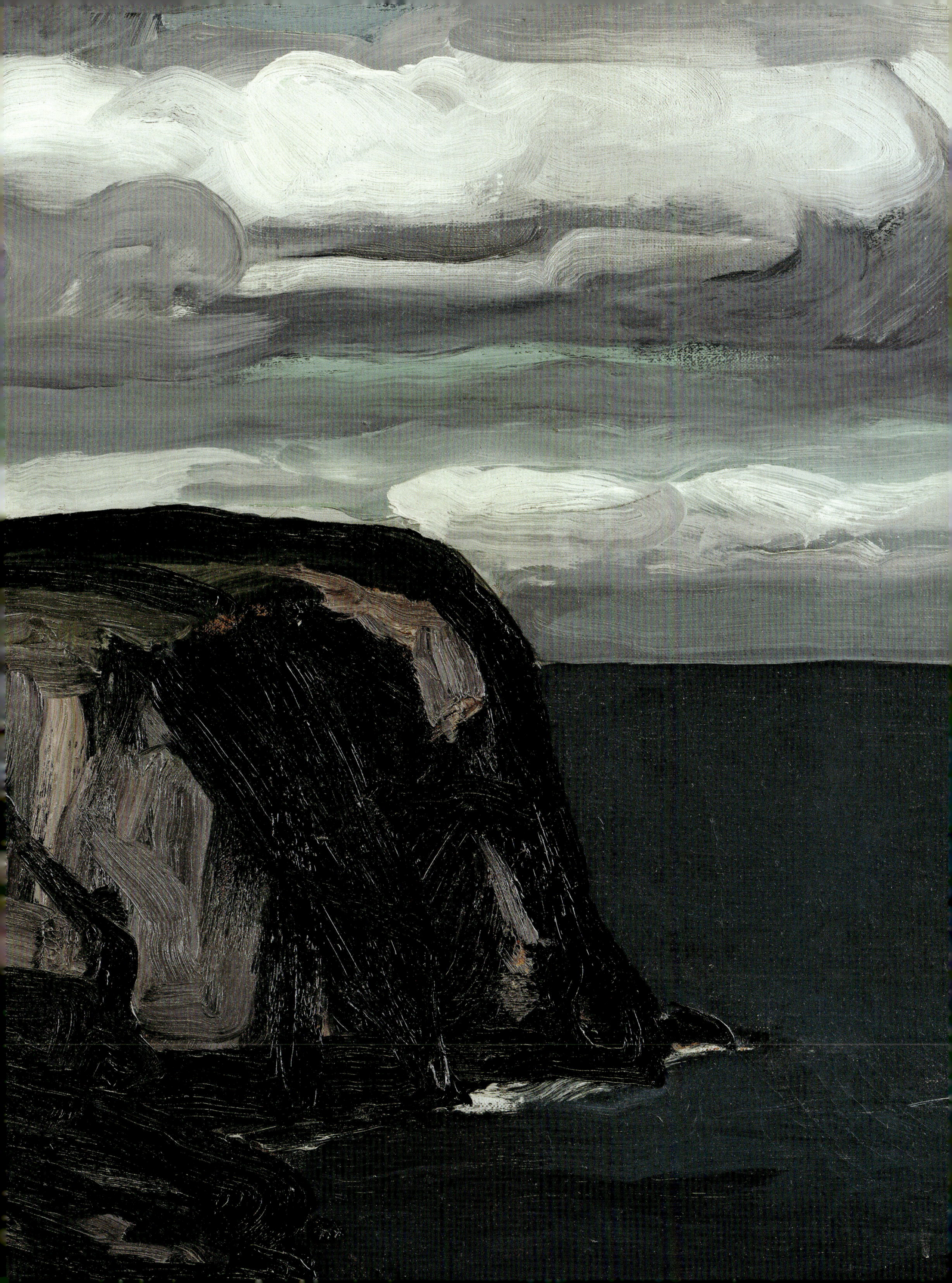

PLACE AND PAINTING ON MONHEGAN ISLAND: GEORGE BELLOWS, ROBERT HENRI, AND REUBEN TAM

KIMIA SHAHI

> I looked at a snapshot of the Maine coastal islands. And in the golden moment when I faced myself and my world in that picture I came to see how hugely important place was for me—as before, as ever.
>
> —Reuben Tam

George Bellows spent July and August of 1911 on Monhegan Island, fifteen miles off the coast of Maine. Alongside Robert Henri, his friend and former teacher, Bellows "tramped" Monhegan's "wild places," sketching and painting the diverse topography: remote coastline, rocky cliffs, dense forests, and chilly ocean waters. Bellows found the island "endless in its wonderful variety," and the summer proved productive: on Monhegan, he completed at least thirty plein-air panel studies and, in a shared makeshift studio, twelve larger canvases.[1] Back in New York in September, Bellows produced four more large oil paintings based on Monhegan, including *Three Rollers* (p. 132), the canvas he selected as his diploma work in 1913.[2]

Thirty years later, the Hawaiian-born painter Reuben Tam found similar inspiration on Monhegan. Over decades spent visiting and living on the island, he produced works that express intimate relationships with the surf and scenery through personal topographies of pigment and gesture, such as *Monhegan Night* and *Monhegan Landform* (pp. 134–35). For Tam, as for Bellows and Henri, painting on Monhegan led to a powerful connection to place that inflected the rest of his career. The landscape acted for all three artists as, in Henri's words, "a medium for ideas," providing a vital means of articulating new ways of seeing in relation to experience, memory, and the practice of painting.[3]

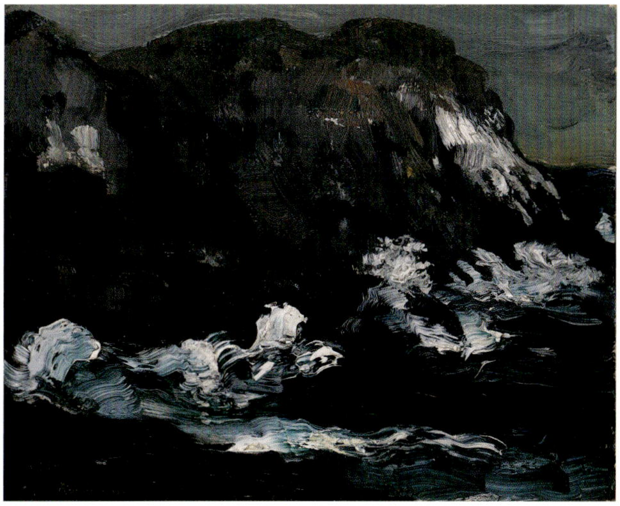

Fig. 1. Robert Henri, *Monhegan Island*, 1903. Oil on wood panel. Farnsworth Art Museum, Rockland, ME

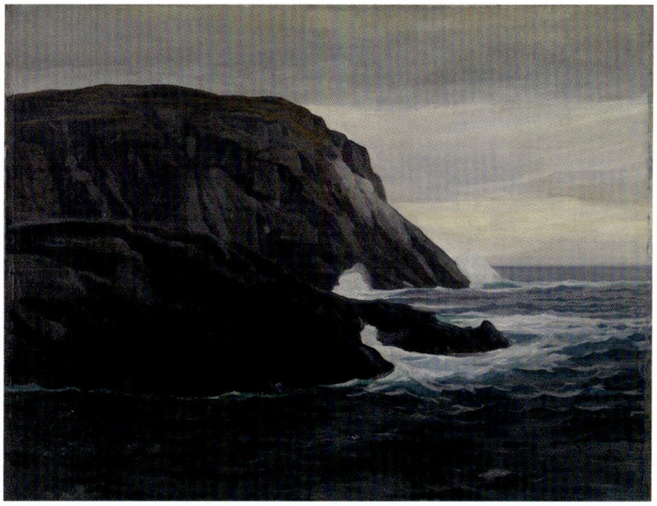

Fig. 2. Rockwell Kent, *Blackhead, Monhegan*, ca. 1909. Oil on canvas. Colby College Museum of Art, Waterville, ME

Robert Henri had first visited Monhegan in the summer of 1903. In small oil studies such as *Monhegan Island* (fig. 1), his loose, wet-on-wet brushwork captures the surf's churning tension and powerful rhythm. In its technical spontaneity and emotional energy, *Monhegan Island* resonates with Henri's characterization of art as the product of an individual's subjective perception of the world, a principle he imparted to his students: "The various details in a landscape painting mean nothing to us if they do not express some mood of nature as felt by the artist."[4] He encouraged his students to visit the island and the Maine coast, where he hoped they would be moved by dramatic and rugged scenery similar to that which had inspired Winslow Homer, of whose celebrated marine paintings he declared: "You are made to feel the force of the sea, the resistance of the rock; the whole thing is an integrity of nature."[5]

The first of Henri's students to heed his teacher's call was Rockwell Kent, who moved to Monhegan in 1905 and lived there sporadically for the next six years, producing paintings that garnered considerable artistic and critical attention in New York.[6] It is likely that Kent's attraction to the island and the strength of the paintings he made there had a significant influence on Bellows; together, work by these artists helped to cement an enduring art-historical association between the Maine coast and a recognizably modern, formally innovative strand of American painting, to which Tam's work was also indebted.[7] Kent's painting *Blackhead, Monhegan* (fig. 2) shares with Henri's *Monhegan Island* and Bellows's *Three Rollers* its relatively square format, thick paint, muted colors, and gestural brushwork. With Henri's painting in particular, *Blackhead, Monhegan* also shares its close attention to the dark Atlantic water and the surf's backlash against the rocks. However, Kent's application of paint is less energetic than the others', and the cleaner lines and more measured proportions of his composition are closer to *Three Rollers* than to Henri's picture. Like *Three Rollers*, Kent's painting focuses on the rugged contours of Monhegan's Black Head promontory and includes three visible bands of clouds that parallel a spare horizon line.[8] These multiple comparisons establish Kent's Monhegan paintings as an important link between Henri's precedent and Bellows's work and suggest that, by representing himself in the collection of the National Academy of Design with *Three Rollers*, Bellows was amplifying his connections to Henri and to others in Henri's circle.

Three Rollers presents a view across the pine-dotted cliffs of Black Head. The outer contours of the rocky coastline are delineated in weighty black paint against an inky gray sea and tumultuous sky, while the uneven terrain stretching away from the foreground undulates with the energy of thick brushstrokes, echoing the clouds above. Although the painting's title denotes the presence of "rollers," definable as "long, heavy waves which roll in upon a coast, as after a storm," the water appears calm.[9] The only disruption in the otherwise smooth surface is a lone strip of horizontal white—the front edge of a cresting wave. The three long bands of cloud above approximate the titular "rollers" much more closely than does this thin white line, which is easily the most delicate passage in the composition. Registered with the economy of a single brushstroke, the solitary wave configures *Three Rollers* as a landscape scaled not only to recognizable dictates of depth and perspective but also to the instance of painterly gesture, establishing a formal connection between Bellows's experience of place and the process of painting.[10]

The first work Bellows submitted to the Academy, prior to *Three Rollers*, was a portrait of himself painted by Henri (p. 133). Considered together, the two pictures offer insight into both artists' ideas about the nature of painting and illuminate a shared conceptual framework underpinning the genres of portraiture and landscape. In Henri's portrait, the three-quarter view, dynamic contrasts, and direct brushwork convey his sitter's vitality and presence, giving form to his own belief that "an artist must first of all respond to his subject, he must be filled with emotion toward that subject and then he must make his technique so sincere, so translucent that it may be forgotten, the value of the subject shining through it."[11] Bellows, too, considered paintings to be "human documents." It is probable that both he and his mentor would have understood *Three Rollers* not only as a representation of a place but, more importantly, as "an arrangement or ordering of forces with the motive of stimulating the emotions and the receptivity of the mind to aesthetic impression and creation"—Bellows's definition of the essential nature of a work of art.[12] Viewed side by side and in the context of the two artists' teachings and writings, Bellows's diploma works literalize Henri's call to his students

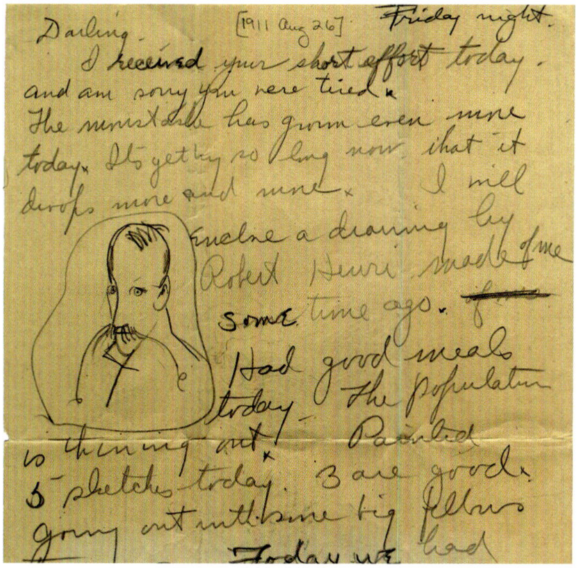
Darling. [1911 Aug 26] Friday night.
I received your short effort today.
and am sorry you were tired.
The mustache has grown even more
today. Its getting so long now that it
drops more and more. I will
Enclose a drawing by
Robert Henri made of me
some time ago.
Had good meals
today. The population
is thinning out. Painted
5 sketches today. 3 are good.
going out with some big fellows
Today we had

Fig. 3. Detail of letter from George Bellows to Emma Bellows dated August 26, 1911

> . . . to take things of certain constructive values and build with them a special thing, your unique vision of nature, the thing you caught in an instant look of a face or the formation of a moment in the sky, [making] it possible to state not only that face, that landscape, but make your statement of them as they were when they were most beautiful to you.[13]

Like Henri, Bellows believed that the process of working from memory was crucial to an artist's ability to harness his own emotions and subjectivity in the making of a painting. On Monhegan, he focused on recording his experiences in sketches that provided material for future works as well as in numerous letters to his wife, Emma. These letters attest to the island's profound effect on his psyche and chronicle the days he spent traversing the landscape, which prompted an equivalent inward exploration. The artist also documented his changing physical appearance in verbal descriptions and quick self-portraits. One letter even mentions "a drawing by Robert Henri . . . of me" alongside a caricature-like pencil sketch of himself, perhaps hinting at the painted portrait Henri would complete later that year (fig. 3).[14] Like his daily habit of making sketches, Bellows's processes of remembering and recording in his letters reveal how he endeavored to describe and transmit his experiences on Monhegan across space and time. In works such as *Three Rollers*, the artist continued to develop and explore these memories in paint.

A letter to Emma dated August 12 offers some insight into how he conceived the relationship between his firsthand observations and his artistic practice: "I've painted seven little beauts all of which will make beautiful big canvases if I succeed in enlarging the idea in size. The Island is only a mile wide and two miles long, but it looks as large as the Rocky Mountains. It's three times as high as Montauk and all black and gray rock. Beautiful pine forests and wonderful varieties of all kinds."[15] Here, Bellows seems to have been interested in scale as a means of understanding his relationship to his work and to Monhegan: preparatory sketches required "enlarging" in both size and idea, and the small island recalled the vastly larger Rocky Mountains. Yet, as he and Henri knew, the workings of memory necessary to create a painting such as *Three Rollers* were more complex than merely enlarging an initial idea after the fact. Amid Bellows's efforts to articulate his various and mixed impressions of the island, the geographical slippage between Monhegan and the Rockies evokes Henri's later musings about the elusive nature of place, time, and experience in relation to one another and to art making: "Somehow times, places, things overlapped. Memories carried into each other. . . . We have strange ways of seeing. If we only knew—then we could tell. If we knew what we saw, we could paint it."[16]

It seems from his correspondence with Emma that Bellows struggled similarly with time and memory on Monhegan. In one letter, he described Monhegan as "an eternal subject" and, in another, worried about never having adequate time to paint all that he had seen.[17] Missing Emma intensely, he envisioned walking the shore with her as a kind of dream in which the couple both exceeded and embodied the vastness of rock and sea: "We two and the great sea and the mighty rocks. greater than the sea and we two greater than the rocks and the sea Four eternities."[18] In another instance, he exclaimed, "I'm living in the future again," further suggesting that disorientation and dislocation were essential components of his attempts to remember, understand, and, eventually, paint the island as both a topographical and an emotional terrain.[19]

Bellows's written accounts of Monhegan, as well as his relationship to Henri and to Henri's teachings, chart a complex experience of place and time that inflected *Three Rollers*' form and content. The curator Michael Quick has observed that the painting's passages of unusually thick brushstrokes mimic "the character of oil sketches that have been enlarged rather than reinterpreted," implying that the artist scaled the painting up from an initial study while carefully maintaining the proportion between the smaller study's brushstrokes and its overall composition.[20] *Three Rollers* bears a strong resemblance to *Blackhead, Evening Gray* (fig. 4), an oil study from that summer with a similar palette and composition, down to the spiny evergreen in the foreground. Absent from the study, however, are the rolling clouds and distant breaker that anchor *Three Rollers* in time while contributing to the curiously disorienting relationship between water and sky. These differences, along with the obvious disparities in size and finish, indicate that although *Three Rollers* might retain the appearance of an on-the-spot sketch on account of its thick and energetic brushwork, it does so in a way that visibly

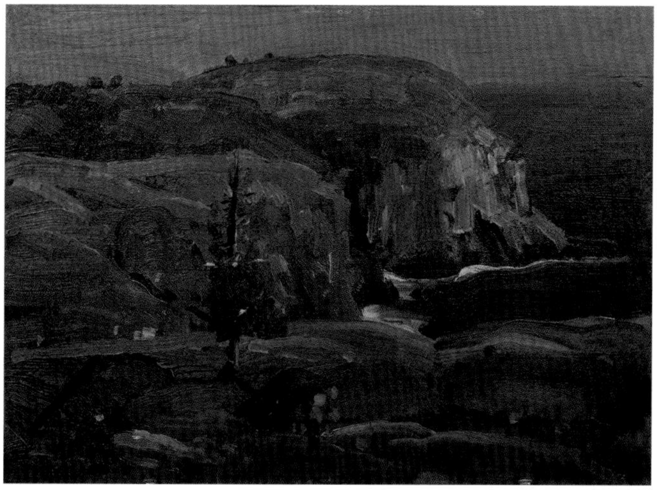

Fig. 4. George Bellows, *Blackhead, Evening Gray*, 1911. Oil on wood panel. Lauren Rogers Museum of Art, Laurel, MS

departs from the artist's initial impressions in both size and idea, thereby encoding the painting's belatedness in the very aspects meant to register its immediacy and spontaneity.[21]

Ultimately, in content and composition, *Three Rollers* draws on certain conventions of the landscape genre rooted in Romantic ideas about the sublime power of nature. In particular, its focus on the ocean, sky, and conspicuous geological features conjures associations with awe-inspiring natural forces working at a scale far beyond that of human life or history.[22] Moreover, the painting's composition, based on the golden ratio, indicates Bellows's engagement with universal aesthetic principles that transcend the specifics of a given location or subject.[23] The convergence of these various approaches in *Three Rollers* reflects the artist's evolving attitude about the relationship between art and nature, which he eventually articulated in writing. Defining nature as "the mode, partly known and mostly unknown, in which all things take place," Bellows critiqued the dictum that art must "follow nature" as premised on the false assumption that the two are separate in the first place. Rather, he argued, "all the acts of life are the reordering, recognized or not, of phenomena, and the search for a finer reordering" under "laws of nature which are always in operation."[24] Even as *Three Rollers* relays an encounter between artist and place, it also advances an approach to art making as both analogous to, and inseparable from, the ordering "forces" of nature that sometimes exceed the bounds of human comprehension.

Like *Three Rollers*, Reuben Tam's *Monhegan Night* and *Monhegan Landform* (pp. 134–35) are anchored in convergences of sea, sky, and land that are tactile as well as topographical. Both pictures are largely gray, white, and black, a palette Tam associated with "the confluence of Atlantic wind and ocean currents and the weathering of rocky promontories."[25] The artist's identification of these characteristics so closely with Monhegan underscores his engagement with the geological and atmospheric forces continually at work in shaping the island. Like *Monhegan Landform*'s slow crawl across the surface and edges of a coastal promontory, Tam pursued a deepening understanding of the island through the material process of painting. Their surfaces alive with the artist's searching brushwork, these paintings balance on the edge of abstraction but remain grounded in Tam's rigorous study of, and emotional closeness to, Monhegan's land and water.

Tam shared with Bellows and Henri the notion that landscape is not just a subject but also a generative medium. His work was animated by his concern that "painting + vision + way of seeing the land + the sea . . . have some objective, communicable value to others."[26] While Bellows foregrounded the personal impact of Monhegan's rugged topography and powerful sea by enlarging *Three Rollers*' sketch-like brushwork to monumental proportions, Tam defined his practice in ongoing exchange with the topographies he encountered such that geography itself became the means by which he understood his approach to painting, and vice versa. He wrote in his diary: "I can mark the nebulous passage of days + nights only by the completion of a new picture. It is like arriving on an island . . . and I am then able to look back and survey the vague stretch of waters I have traversed."[27] Tam's "pursuit of place" as a landscape painter began in and around his birthplace of Kaua'i before leading him to coasts farther afield.[28] His way of moving through the world was at once locally specific and rooted in the experience of home: "Each place has its own geomorphology, and I look upon these landscapes as variations of the earth's crust, with the Hawaiian Islands providing the basic vocabulary of landforms through which other earth structures can be perceived and understood."[29]

Although the bulk of his career as a successful artist and teacher centered on New York, Tam's private writings, published poetry, and works of art are all characterized by what he called an "abiding sense of place" formed around "stretches of rocks + sea found, explored, loved, understood + painted."[30] Part of Tam's trajectory from "Hawaii to Monhegan—birthplace + home," *Monhegan Night* and *Monhegan Landform* exemplify his innovative approach to landscape, born of this "sense of place" and of self.[31] Departing from convention, when elected to the Academy as an Associate, the artist submitted *Monhegan Landform* in lieu of the specified portrait, and it was accepted by the governing council. This rather extraordinary fact attests to the depth of Tam's connection to Monhegan and builds on similar connections embedded in Bellows's diploma portrait, evoking both artists' understanding of works of art as documents of their makers' inner lives and experiences.

While *Three Rollers* employs compositional conventions in productive tension with more spontaneous modes of facture, Tam, in his Monhegan pictures, departed much more radically from illusionistic representation. "Rather than transfer the values of a landscape to traditionally prescribed forms, he transfers the form to meet the heavy demand of new experience," the critic Edward Deverill

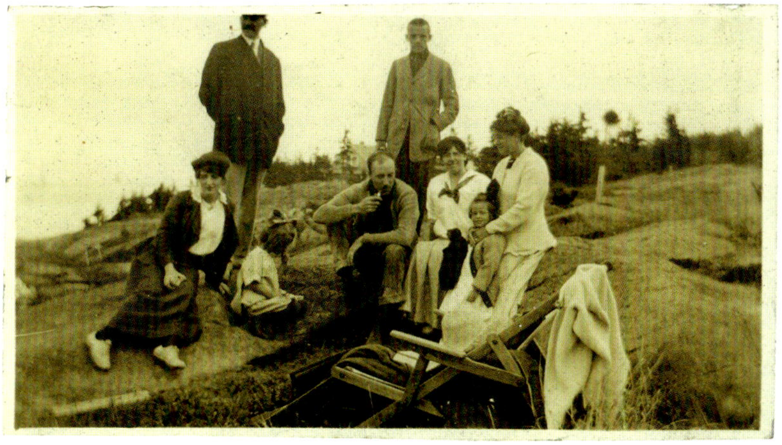

Fig. 5. George Bellows, Randall Davey, and Robert Henri with friends on Monhegan Island, 1911

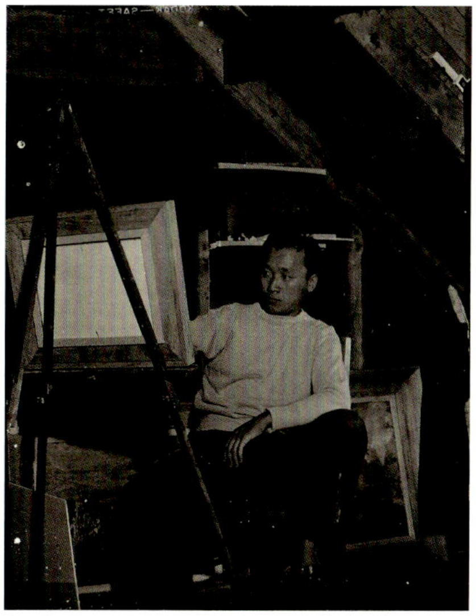

Fig. 6. Reuben Tam in his studio on Monhegan Island, ca. 1951

wrote.[32] For example, although *Monhegan Night* is recognizable as a "landscape form," the painting's shifting slabs of gray, punctuated by fissures of brighter blue and white, evoke a sense of tectonic and temporal movement that links the act of painting to the formation of the land itself. Although different in tone and focus, *Monhegan Landform* is similarly dynamic, with loose passages of paint tightening and converging along a rocky coastline silhouetted against "the vastness of oceanic space."[33] These attributes contribute to what contemporaries deemed "metaphysical" in Tam's work. In the words of another critic: "The painter transcends nature as seen by the waking retina. He triturates and distills it into something that is at once a substance and a light, a compound that is an essence, something curiously and insistently tactile . . . known only to the inner eye."[34] This interpretation recalls Tam's vision of a constantly unfolding interaction with the perpetually relational world around him. What the artist called "the Spirit of Place" was, for him, always oriented to "awareness of land as dynamic presence, ephemeral entity, omnipotent, mystical, and beautiful." His perception of that presence changed continually according to "distance" across space, "the passage of night into day," and the vastness of "geologic time."[35]

Like Bellows and Henri before him (fig. 5), Tam moved productively between New York and the Maine coast, his work shaped by the interchange between new ideas developed in "the art center of the world" and deeply personal revelations experienced on Monhegan's remote shoreline (fig. 6).[36] Notwithstanding his considerable success during his lifetime and acquaintance with artists such as William Baziotes, Max Beckmann, and Georgia O'Keeffe, Tam occupies a much less prominent place in histories of American modernism than either Henri or Bellows.[37] Yet his innovations in landscape painting, and the complex conceptual vocabulary he formulated therein, demonstrate the great need for, and promise of, additional scholarship on his work. Further, considering Tam, Bellows, and Henri in the context of their shared attraction to Monhegan Island affirms the importance of landscape and marine painting as arenas for formal experimentation and individual expression in twentieth-century American art. Alongside examples by Henri, *Three Rollers*, *Monhegan Landform*, and *Monhegan Night* illuminate the ways in which the island offered what Bellows called "illimitable experience,"[38] prompting Tam, in turn, to seek out metaphysical meanings in the particularities of topography, tides, and painting itself. In these works, Monhegan emerges as both a specific place and a terrain of artistic possibility, perhaps best summarized in Tam's own words: "I dream of Monhegan—I feel there I shall find identification with reality."[39]

Epigraph: Reuben Tam, diary for 1947–48 (entry dated April 3, 1948), box 5, folder 7, Reuben Tam Papers, Archives of American Art, Smithsonian Institution, Washington, DC.

1. George Bellows to Emma Bellows, August 15, 1911, box 1, folder 3, and undated letter, box 1, folder 4, George Wesley Bellows Papers, Amherst College Archives and Special Collections, Amherst College Library. For the numbers of works, see Sarah Cash, "Life at Sea, 1911–1917," in Charles Brock et al., *George Bellows*, exh. cat. (Washington, DC: National Gallery of Art, 2012), 160. Nearing the end of his visit to Monhegan, Bellows noted "12 pictures and 30 panels now, in 3 weeks. Not mentioning what I scraped out." George Bellows to Emma Bellows, August 28, 1911, box 1, folder 4, Bellows Papers.
2. David B. Dearinger, ed., *Paintings and Sculpture in the Collection of the National Academy of Design, 1826–1925* (New York: Hudson Hills Press, 2004), 39.
3. Robert Henri, "Letter of Criticism," in *The Art Spirit*, comp. Margary Ryerson (Philadelphia: J. B. Lippincott, 1960), 117. The phrase "ways of seeing" appears frequently in Tam's writings; see, for example, Reuben Tam, diary for 1947–48 (entry dated April 2, 1948), box 5, folder 7, Tam Papers.
4. Henri, "Letter of Criticism," 118. On the centrality of the artist's subjectivity in the work of Henri's circle, see David Corbett, "Decreation and Undoing: George Bellows's Excavation Paintings, 1907–1909," *Art History* 40, no. 4 (September 2017): 838–55, and Rachael Ziady DeLue, "Diagnosing Pictures: Sadakichi Hartmann and the Science of Seeing, circa 1900," *American Art* 21, no. 2 (Summer 2007): 42–69, esp. pp. 60 and 65.
5. Robert Henri, quoted in Jessica F. Nicoll, *The Allure of the Maine Coast: Robert Henri and His Circle, 1903–1918*, exh. cat. (Portland, ME: Portland Museum of Art, 1995), 9. Nicoll also notes that Henri eventually purchased land on Monhegan, although on his trip with Bellows and Randall Davey in 1911, the three artists stayed at Monhegan House, a local summer hotel (pp. 10, 17).
6. Kent wrote a great deal about his life and work on Monhegan in his autobiography, *It's Me, O Lord!* (New York: Dodd, Mead, 1955). When Kent first showed his Monhegan paintings in New York in 1907, critics such as Guy Pène du Bois praised their "economy, precision, dignity and force," as quoted in Bruce Robertson, "Perils of the Sea," in William H. Truettner and Roger B. Stein, eds., *Picturing Old New England: Image and Memory*, exh. cat. (Washington, DC: National Museum of American Art, Smithsonian Institution; New Haven: Yale University Press, 1999), 148. Robertson notes that these works and others that followed were compared favorably to Winslow Homer's in the press, a possible motivating factor for Bellows in planning his own visit. See also Bruce Robertson, *Reckoning with Winslow Homer: His Late Paintings and Their Influence* (Cleveland, OH: Cleveland Museum of Art, 1990). Kent was made a National Academician in 1966, in the category of graphic arts. While he did not submit a diploma work then, he had submitted a diploma portrait in 1948: *Das Ding an Sich*, a 1936 lithograph depicting his head.
7. Robertson, "Perils of the Sea," 148. Tam was an admirer of Kent; see Tam, diary for 1947–48 (entry dated April 3, 1948), Tam Papers.
8. The spelling of the promontory's name varies. On present-day maps, it is typically rendered as two words.
9. "Roller," in *Webster's New International Dictionary of the English Language* (Springfield, MA: G. and C. Merriam, 1910), 1844.
10. Similarly, see Franklin Kelly, "So Clean and Cold: Bellows and the Sea," in Michael Quick et al., *The Paintings of George Bellows*, exh. cat.

(Fort Worth, TX: Amon Carter Museum; Los Angeles: Los Angeles County Museum of Art; New York: H. N. Abrams, 1992), 149.

11. Robert Henri, "My People," *Craftsman* 27, no. 5 (February 1915): 462. On Henri's "direct" style of paint application, see Michael Quick, "The Ashcan School," in *Artists by Themselves: Artists' Portraits from the National Academy of Design*, exh. cat. (New York: National Academy of Design, 1983), 133. Bellows's diploma portrait of the sculptor Paul H. Manship is similar in color and composition to Henri's portrait of Bellows and further reflects the senior artist's influence on his former pupil.
12. George Bellows, quoted in Emma S. Bellows, comp., *The Paintings of George Bellows* (New York: Alfred A. Knopf, 1929), ix–x.
13. Henri, "Letter of Criticism," 118; Henri, "Letter to the Class, Art Students' League, 1915," in *Art Spirit*, 27, 31.
14. It is not clear from the letter whether it was Henri or Bellows who made the sketch included in the text or whether the "enclosed" drawing was something different. George Bellows to Emma Bellows, August 26, 1911, box 1, folder 4, Bellows Papers. For other examples of self-portraiture in Bellows's letters, see George Bellows to Emma Bellows, August 17, 1911 (of his face), and August 18, 1911 (of a hand), box 1, folder 3, Bellows Papers.
15. George Bellows to Emma Bellows, August 12, 1911, box 1, folder 3, Bellows Papers; quoted in Charles H. Morgan, *George Bellows, Painter of America* (1965; repr., Millwood, NY: Kraus Reprint, 1979), 135–36.
16. Henri, "Letter to the Class," 33.
17. George Bellows to Emma Bellows, August 18, 1911, box 1, folder 3, Bellows Papers. "My head is full of millions of great pictures which I will never have time to paint": George Bellows to Emma Bellows, August 21, 1911, box 1, folder 4, Bellows Papers.
18. Punctuation and capitalization per original. George Bellows to Emma Bellows, August 15, 1911, box 1, folder 3, Bellows Papers.
19. Sarah Newman makes a similar point in "Working Life: Pennsylvania Station Excavation, 1907–1909," in Brock, *George Bellows*, 87–88.
20. Michael Quick, "Technique and Theory: The Evolution of George Bellows's Painting Style" in Quick et al., *Paintings of George Bellows*, 34.
21. This contrasts notably with Robert Henri's choice, in 1903, to exhibit his plein-air studies of Monhegan as finished paintings.
22. On similar themes in Bellows's Monhegan paintings, see David Corbett, "The World Is Terrible and It Is Not There at All: George Bellows on Monhegan Island," in Alexander Nemerov, ed., *Experience*, Terra Foundation Essays 4 (Chicago: Terra Foundation for American Art, 2017).
23. Quick, "Technique and Theory," 34.
24. George Bellows, quoted in E. Bellows, *Paintings of George Bellows*, ix–x.
25. Tam, autobiographical essay dated December 15, 1975, box 5, folder 10, Tam Papers.
26. Tam, diary for 1947–48 (entry dated April 2, 1948), Tam Papers.
27. Ibid. (entry dated March 11, 1948).
28. Tam, autobiographical essay.
29. Ibid.
30. Ibid.
31. Tam, diary for 1947–48 (entry dated April 3, 1948), Tam Papers.
32. Edward Deverill, "Reuben Tam's One Man Show: 20 Oil Paintings on Exhibit at the Art Academy for Two Weeks from March 18th," *Hawaii Sentinel*, March 20, 1941.
33. Tam, autobiographical essay.
34. Martin James, "Reuben Tam, Metaphysical Painter" [review of exhibition of oils at Downtown Gallery, 43 East 51st Street, New York, January 23–February 10, 1945], box 5, folder 16, Tam Papers. The artist Isamu Doi is also quoted discussing Tam's "metaphysics" in "At the Honolulu Academy of Arts: Reuben Tam," *Honolulu Star-Bulletin*, March 22, 1941.
35. Tam, autobiographical essay; Maude Riley, "Tam of Hawaii," *Art Digest*, February 1, 1945, collected in scrapbook 2 (of 2) for 1945–47, box 7, folder 18, Tam Papers.
36. Tam, autobiographical essay.
37. Margo Machida makes this important observation in "New Critical Directions: Transnationalism and Diaspora in Asian American Art," in "Cross-Cultural Issues in Art from the Nineteenth Century to the Present," special issue, *Source: Notes in the History of Art* 21, no. 3 (Spring 2012): 26.
38. George Bellows, quoted in E. Bellows, *Paintings of George Bellows*, xi.
39. Tam, diary for 1947–48 (entry dated March 22, 1948), Tam Papers.

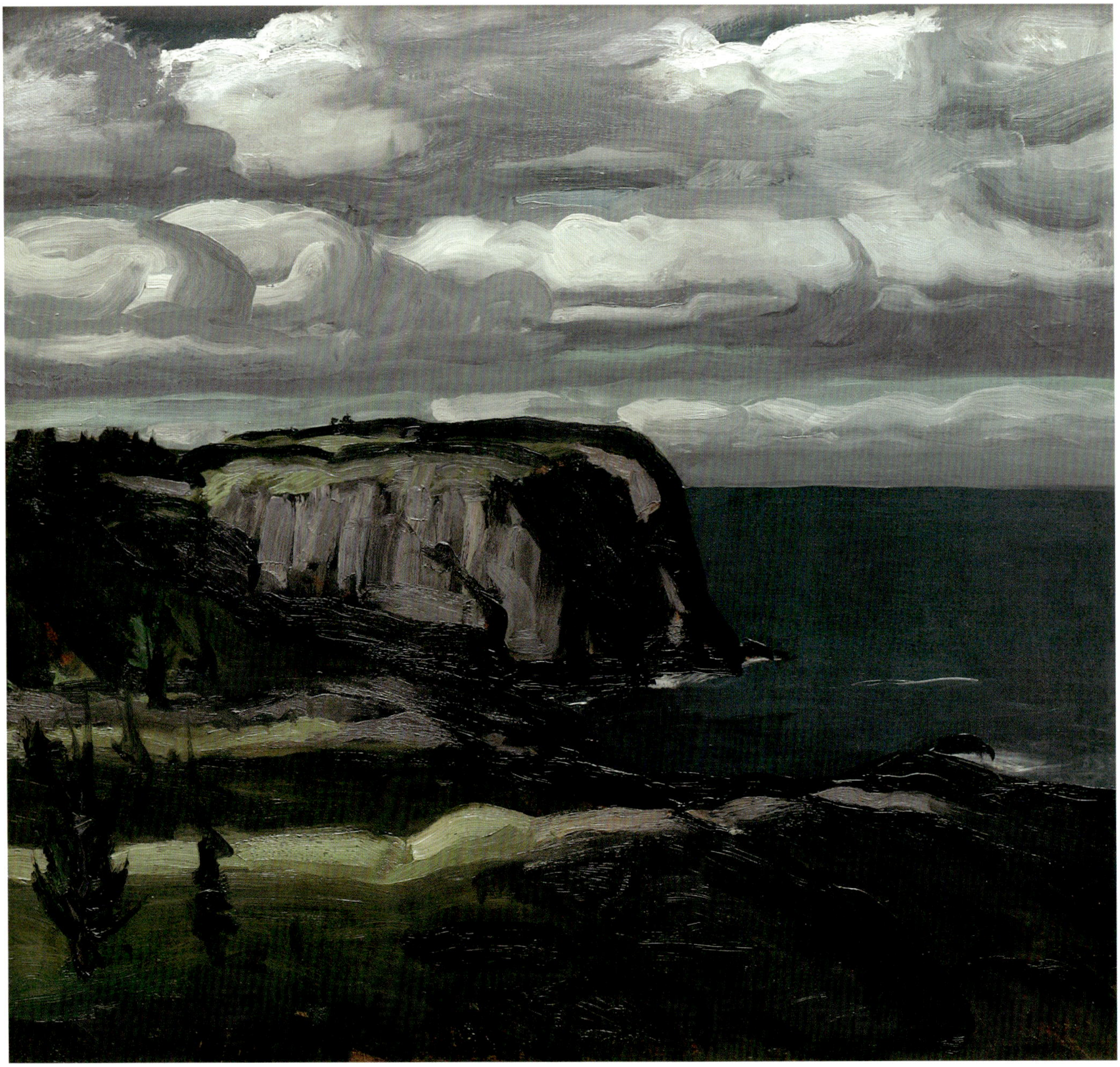

George Bellows, *Three Rollers*, 1911. Oil on canvas, 39 5/8 × 41 3/4 in. (100.6 × 106 cm)

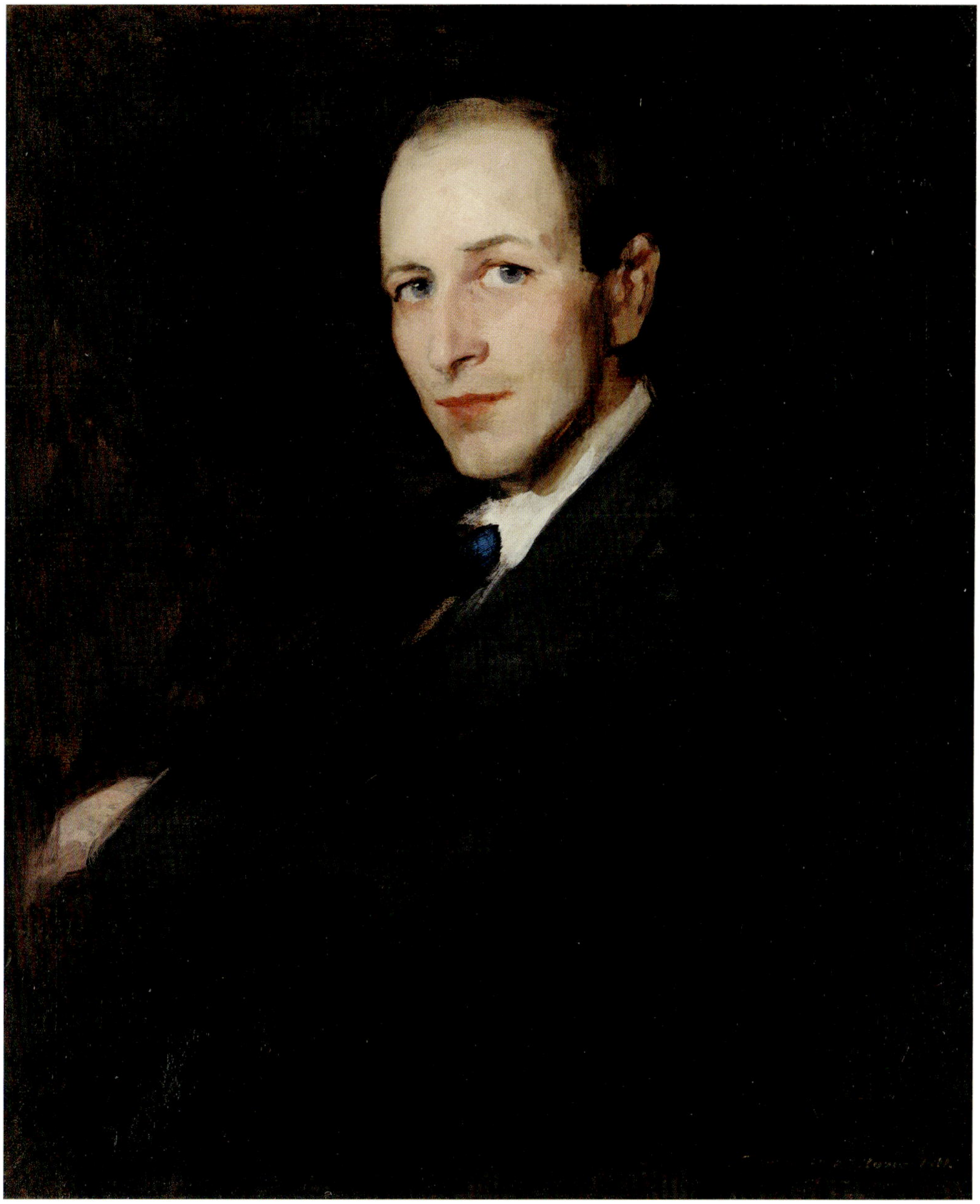

Robert Henri, *George Wesley Bellows*, 1911. Oil on canvas, 32 × 25⅞ in. (81.3 × 65.7 cm)

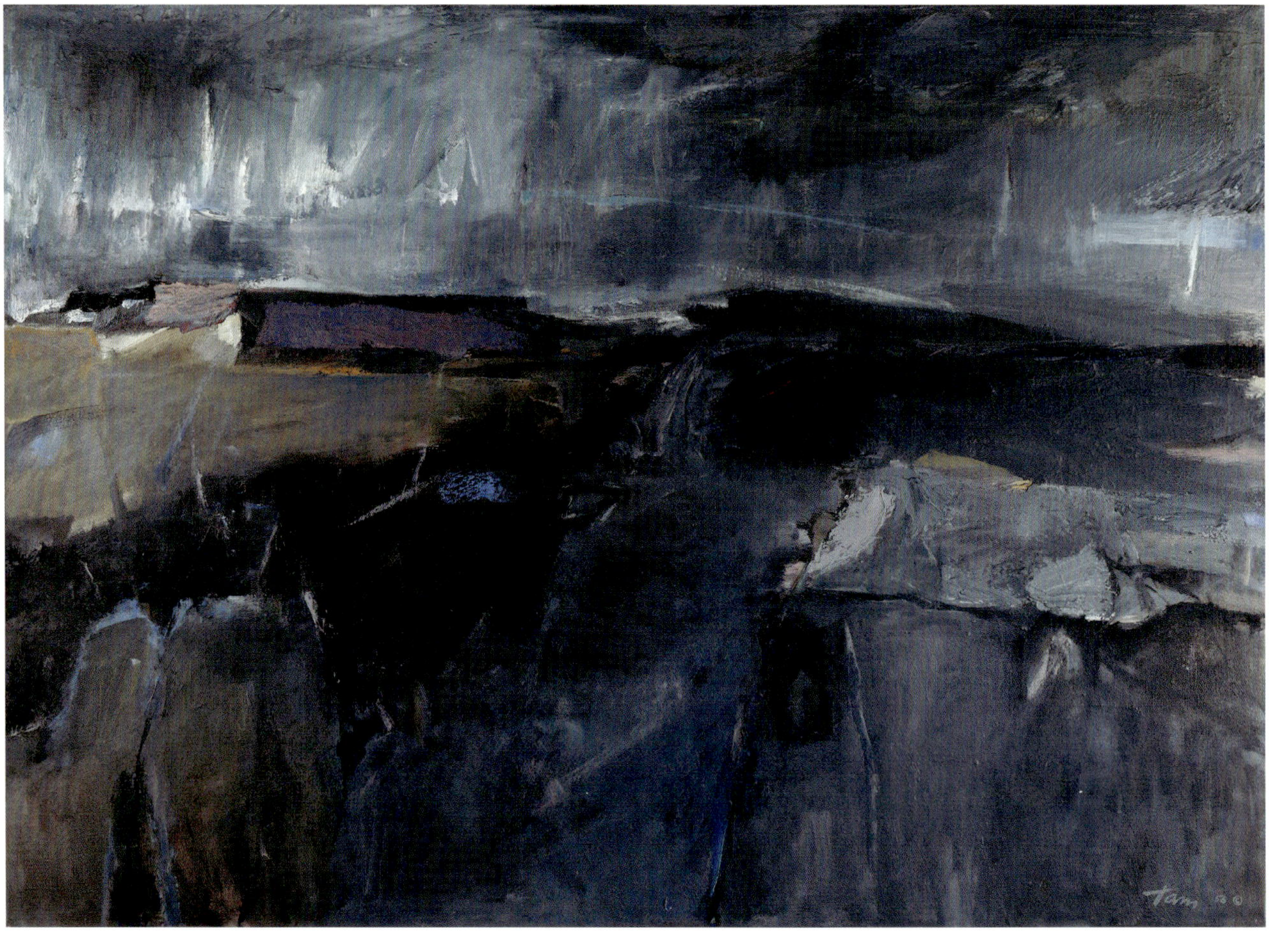

Reuben Tam, *Monhegan Night*, 1956. Oil on canvas, 34 × 46 in. (86.4 × 116.8 cm)

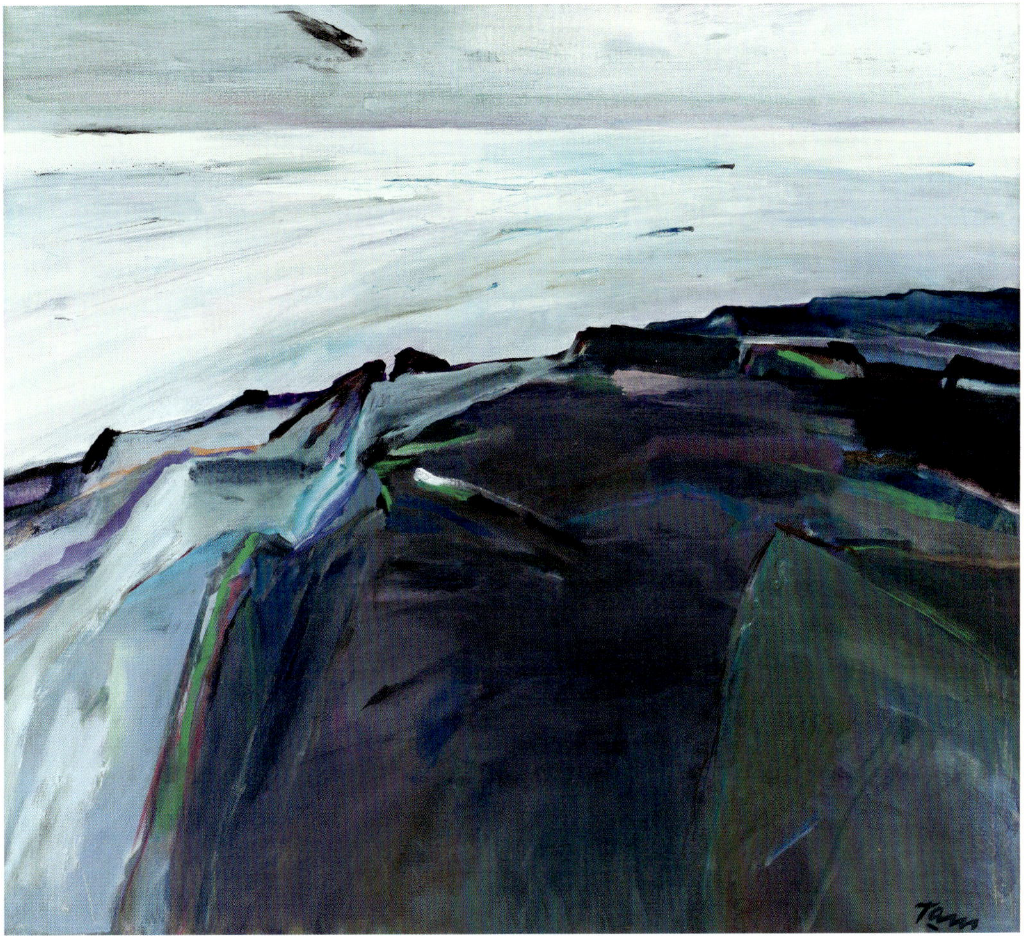

Reuben Tam, *Monhegan Landform*, 1974. Oil on canvas, 36 × 30 in. (91.4 × 76.2 cm)

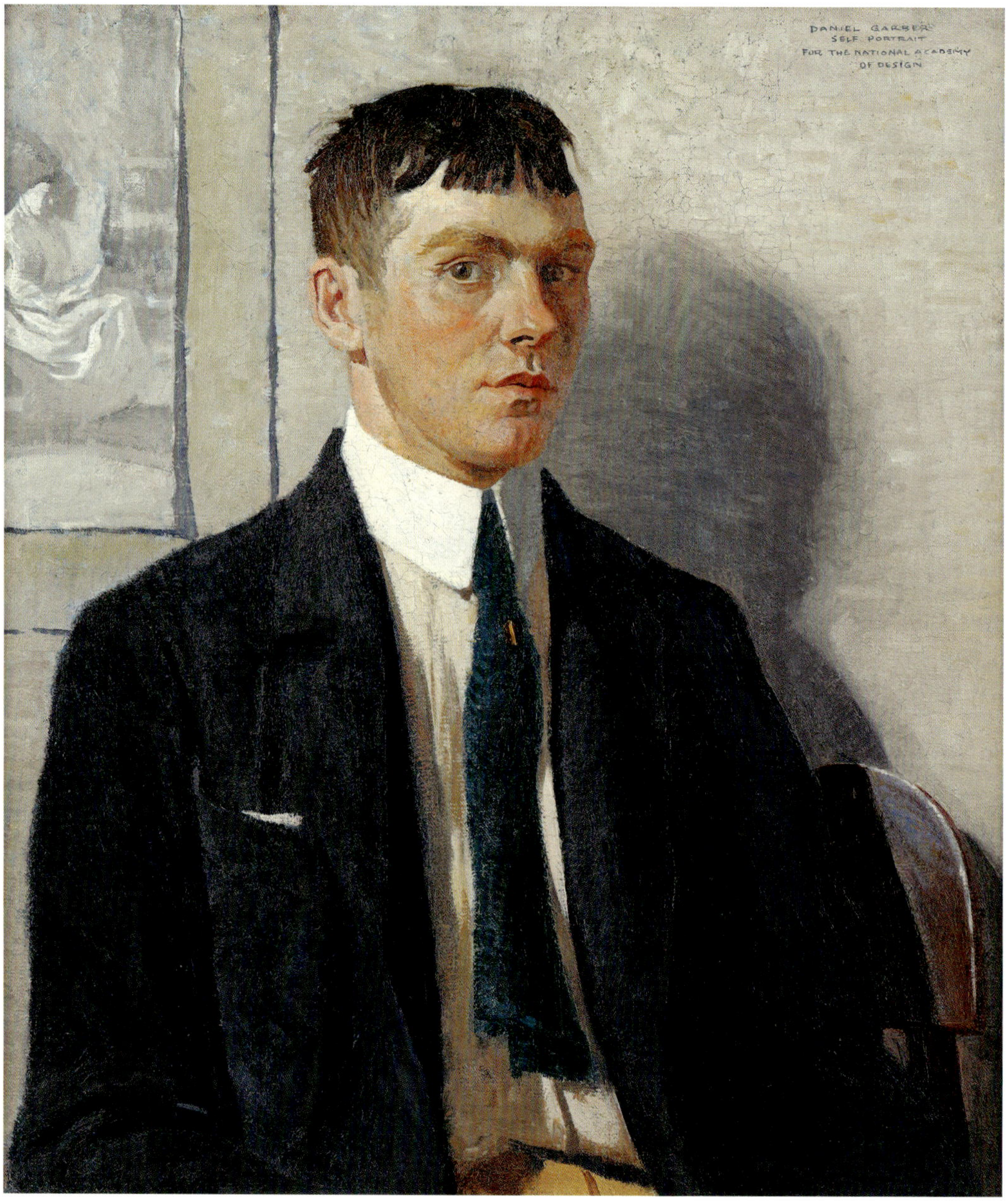

Daniel Garber, *Self-Portrait*, ca. 1911. Oil on canvas, 30 × 25 ¼ in. (76.2 × 64.1 cm)

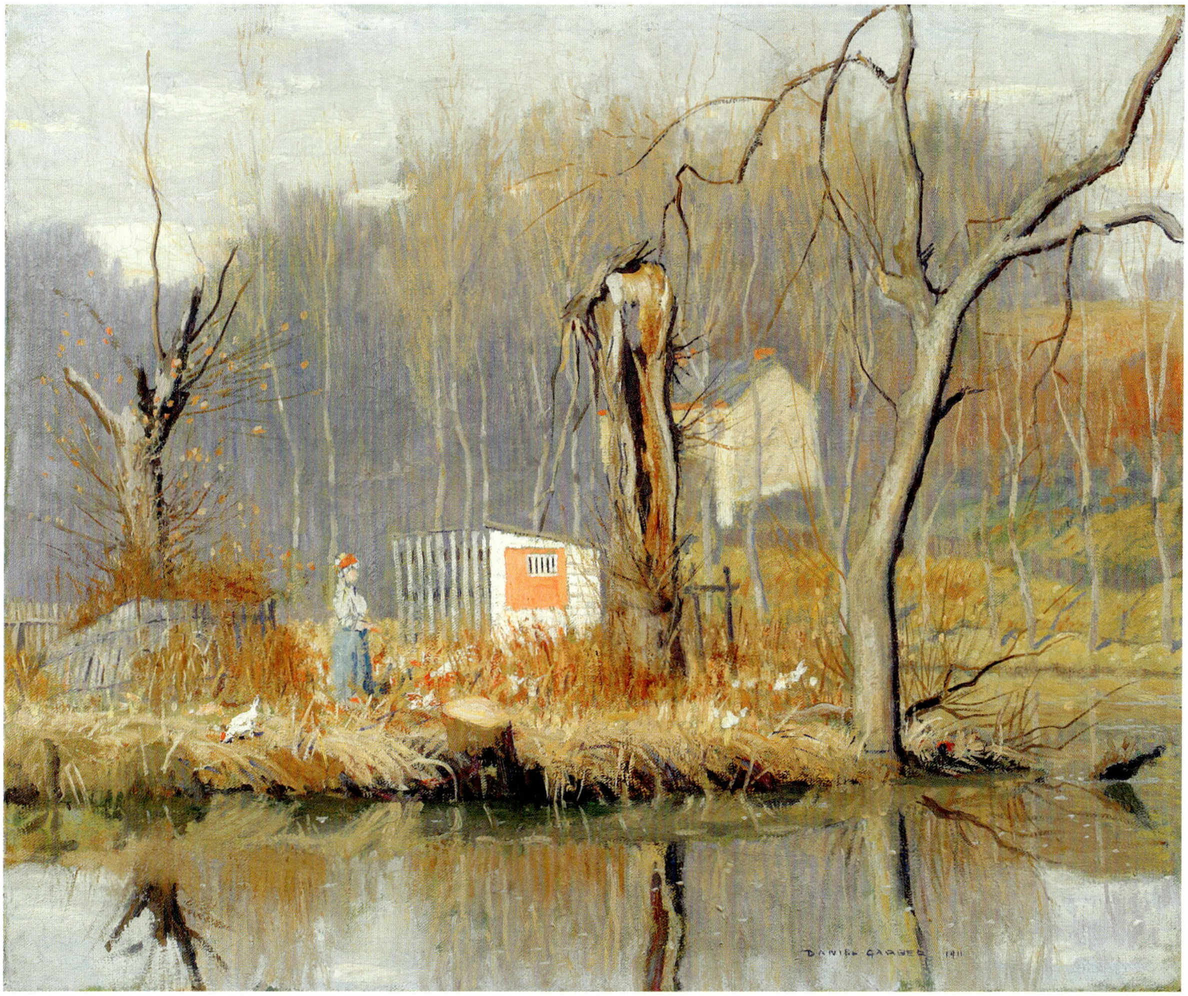

Daniel Garber, *By Addingham*, 1911. Oil on canvas, 25 ¼ × 30 ⅛ in. (64.1 × 76.5 cm)

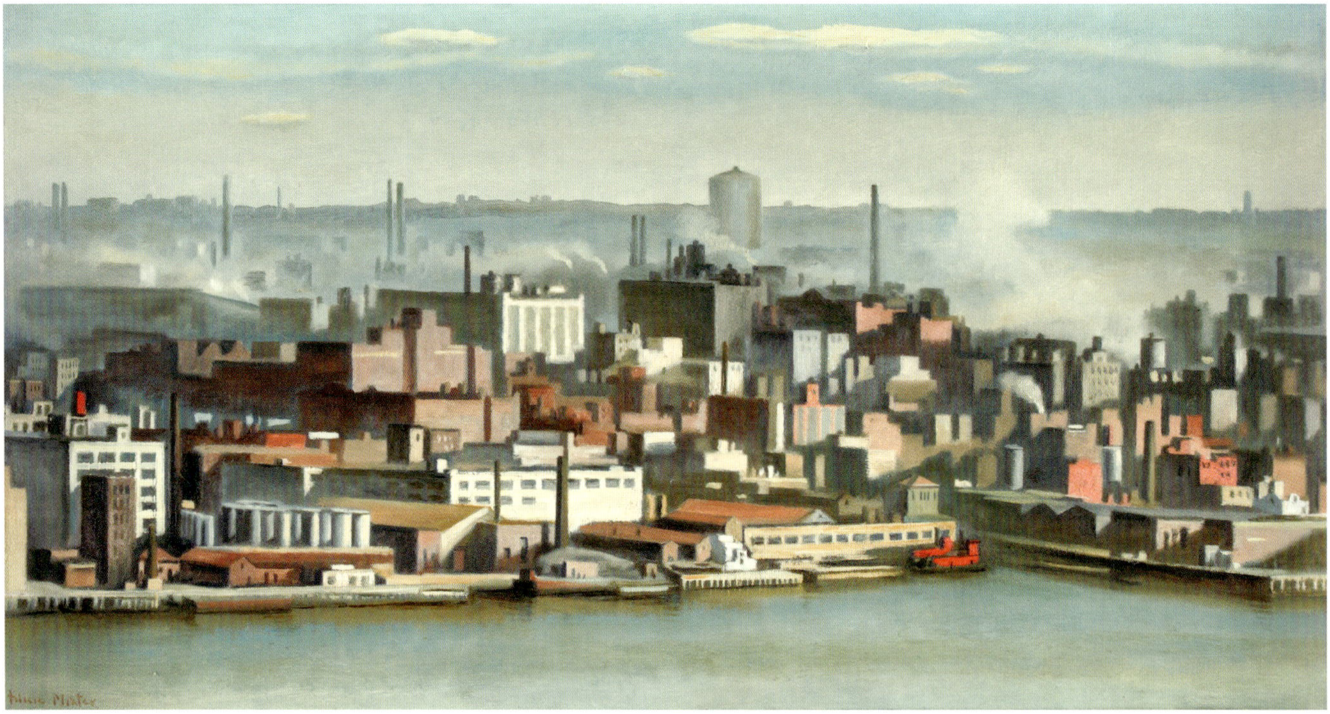

Felicie Waldo Howell Mixter, *City Waterfront*, between 1934 and 1946. Oil on canvas, 16 × 30 in. (40.6 × 76.2 cm)

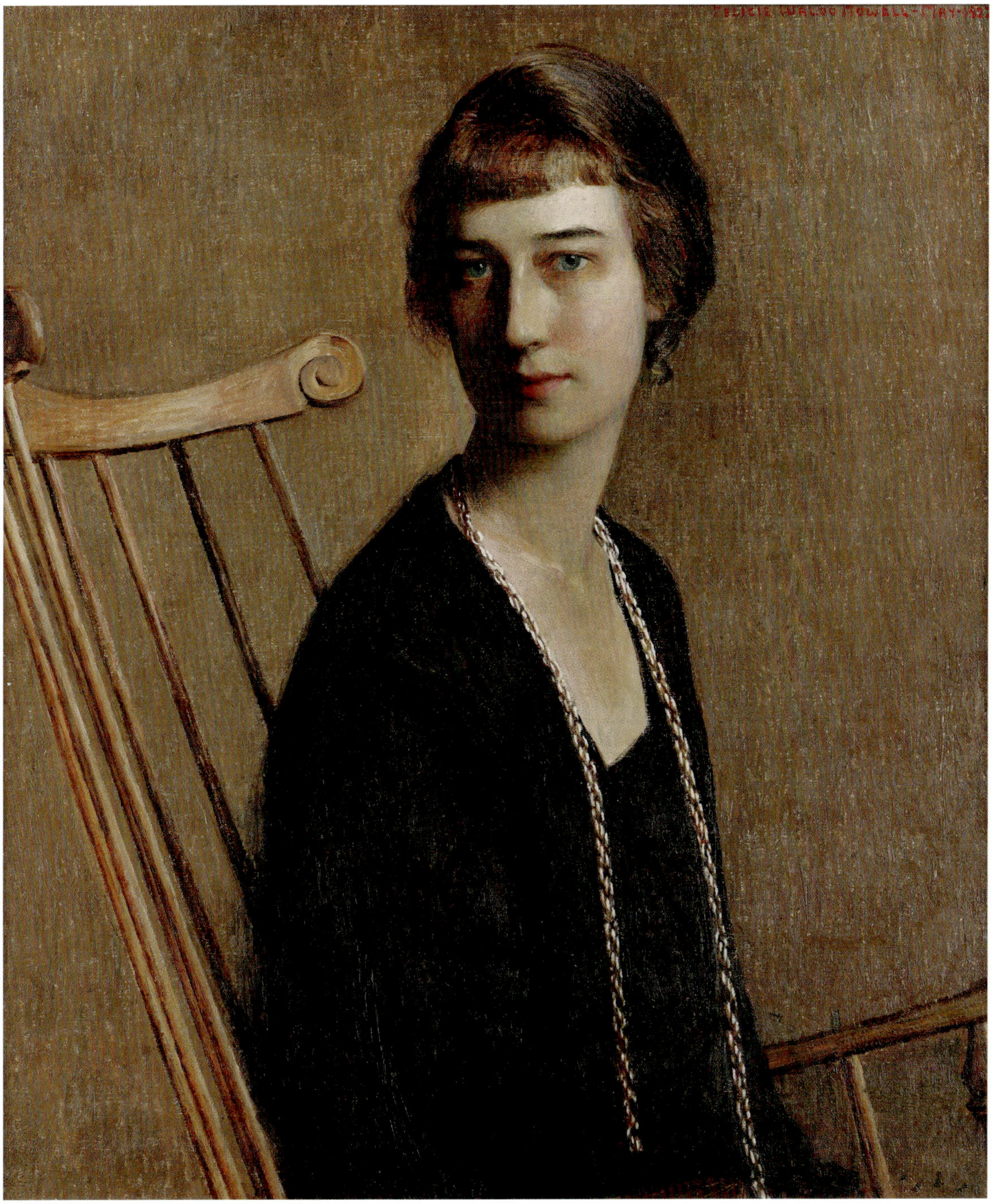

Felicie Waldo Howell Mixter, *Self-Portrait*, 1922. Oil on canvas, 30 × 25 in. (76.2 × 63.5 cm)

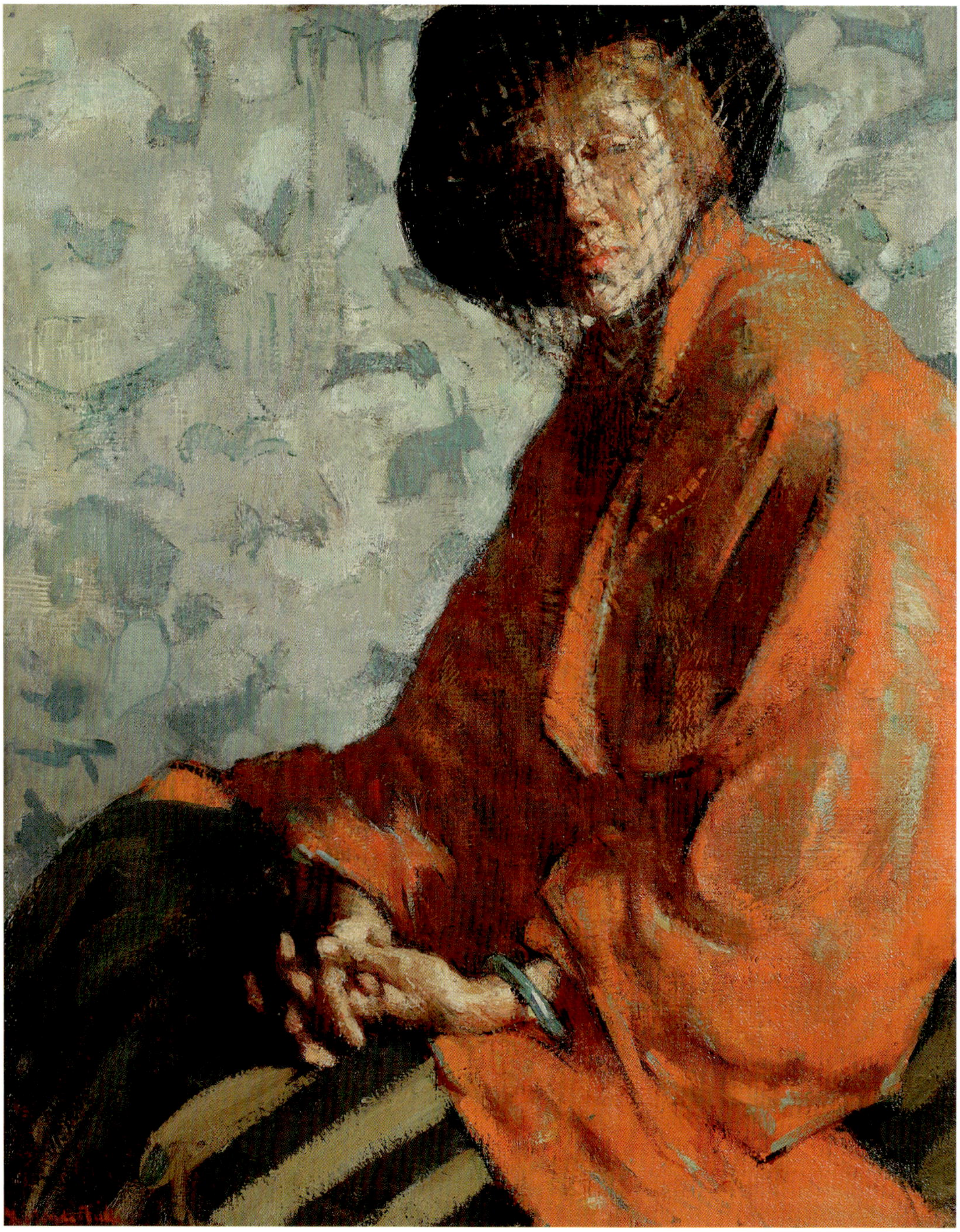

Gertrude Fiske, *Jade*, ca. 1918. Oil on canvas, 29¾ × 23¾ in. (75.6 × 60.3 cm)

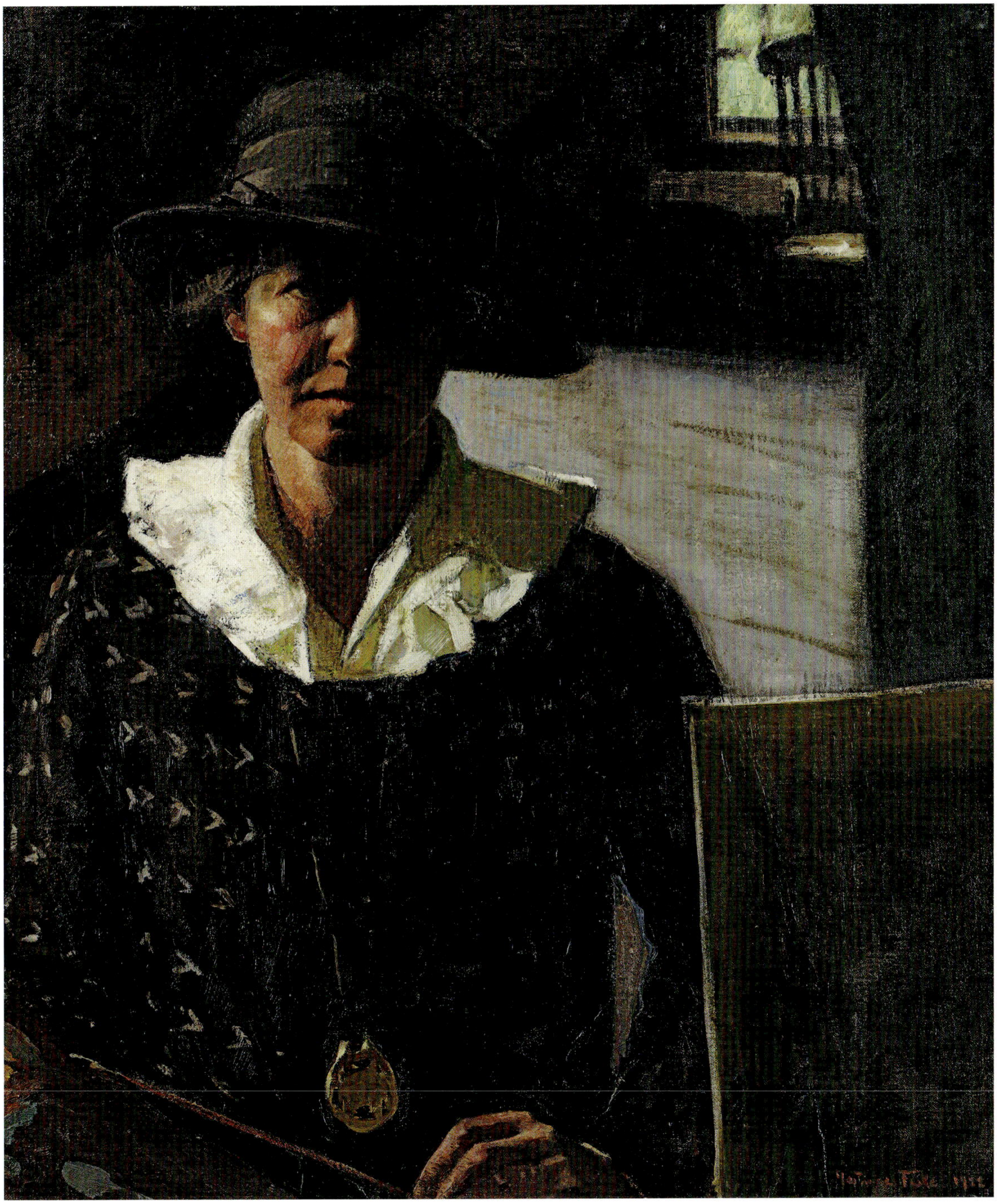

Gertrude Fiske, *Self-Portrait*, 1922. Oil on canvas, 30 ½ × 25 ¼ in. (77.5 × 64.1 cm)

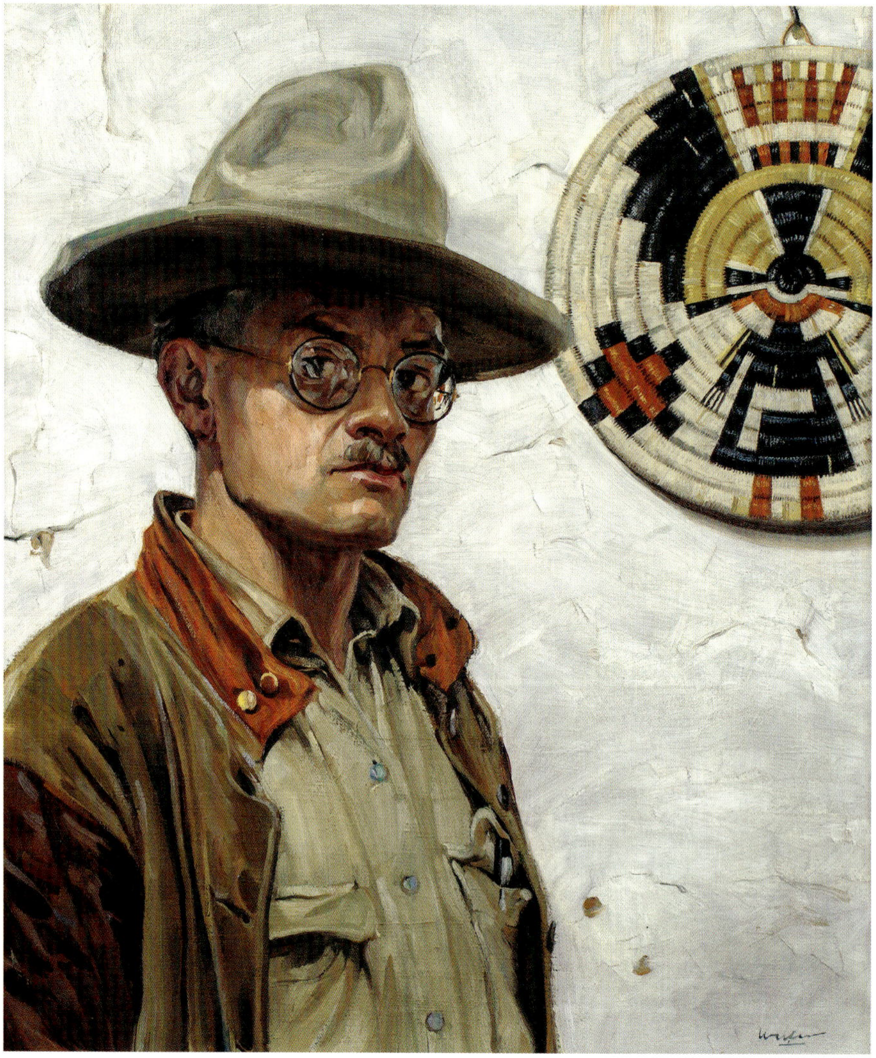

Walter Ufer, *Self-Portrait*, n.d. Oil on canvas, 30 ¼ × 25 in. (76.8 × 63.5 cm)

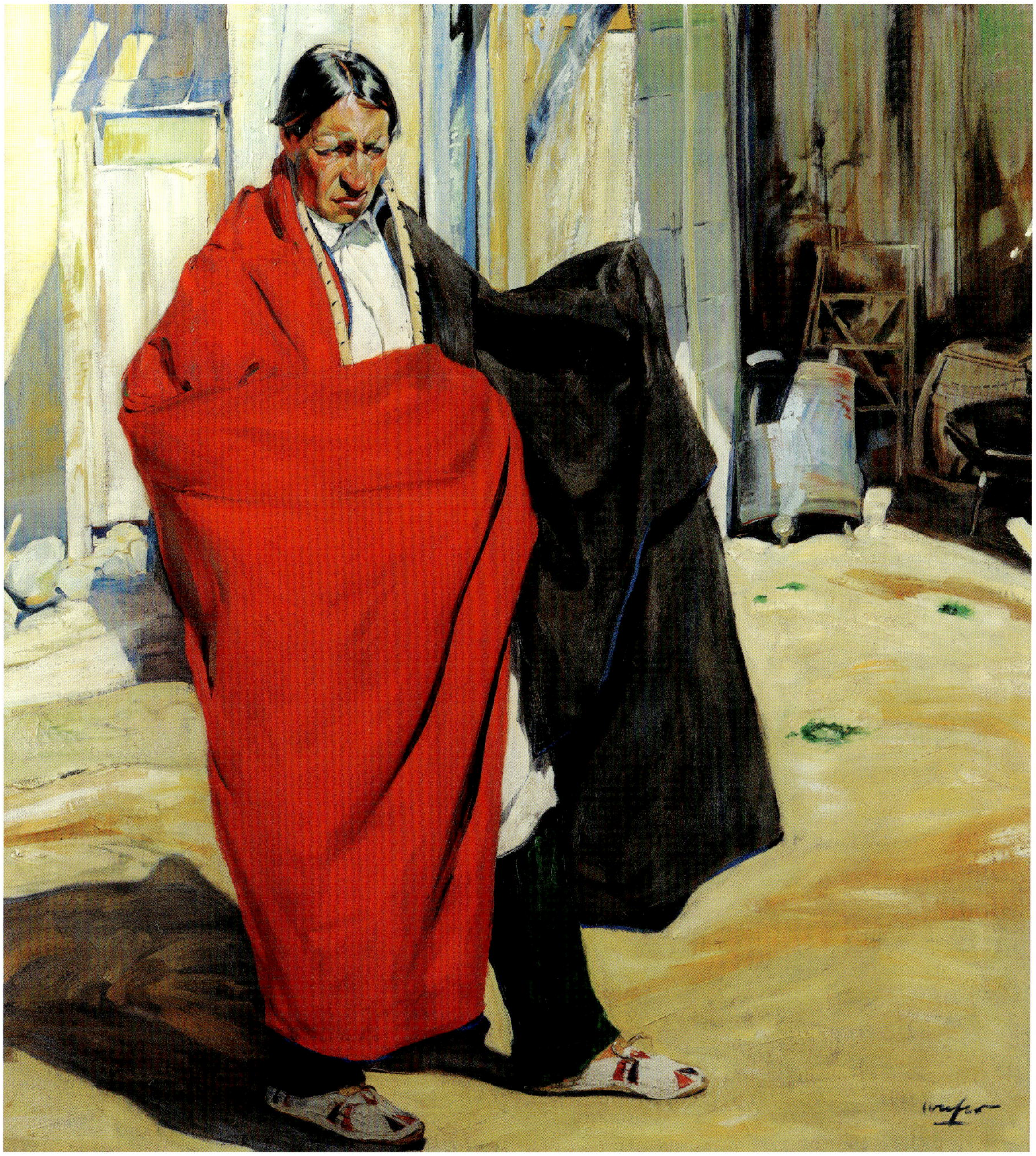

Walter Ufer, *Jim*, 1918. Oil on canvas, 40 ⅛ × 36 ¼ in. (101.9 × 92.1 cm)

LESLIE WAYNE ON ERNEST L. BLUMENSCHEIN

The first time I saw a reproduction of this painting, I immediately felt empathy and longing. Blumenschein captured the visceral, three-dimensional sense of *being there*—of feeling the power of the weather in those towering clouds, the billowing mountains on the move, the sun framing the contours of every tree and bush with its golden glow, the glassy flatness of the lake and the rolling scruffiness of the hills around it. The little cabin nestled in the foreground can hardly compete with the grandeur of its surroundings. It's a fugue of forms and colors singing their hymn to the glory of nature without the slightest need for an audience.

And yet, if you look hard, you'll see what appears to be a couple standing at the edge of their balcony, oddly outsized to the dimensions of their home, yet tiny compared to the view they are taking in. (They are porch posts.) It's a strange depiction. Perhaps Blumenschein was suggesting that we are large and important in our own homes, masters of our domain, but insignificant in the greater scheme of things.

I feel as if I could be standing there. For many years, I painted landscapes *en plein air*. It's an extremely challenging thing to do. One is in constant battle with the elements—the changing light, the shifting shadows, the insects, and the wind, always the wind. But it's that very challenge that, when successfully translated into the painting, is glorious and tangible. As an artist, you feel a tremendous sense of accomplishment, and the painting, a reminder of the many sensations with which you did battle, is also a record of the hours and days you spent communing with the great outdoors.

When I look at *The Lake*, another artist immediately comes to mind: Lawren Harris, the great landscape painter and founding member of the Canadian Group of Seven. Harris's works had a similar muscularity, although they became more stripped down and stylized as he got older. I think Blumenschein and Harris could have been close colleagues had they known each other, but they were born eleven years apart and in different countries—Blumenschein in Pennsylvania in 1874, Harris in Canada in 1885. Interestingly, they both studied music, specifically the violin (Blumenschein's father was director of the Ohio Philharmonic Orchestra, and music was an integral part of his childhood). So, it's not surprising that the two artists' landscapes share a kind of symphonic sensibility.

Ultimately, however, they were very different men. Harris was to the manor born, while Blumenschein had to work for a living. After moving to New York in 1909 with his new wife, Mary Shepard Greene—a very successful artist in her own right (p. 147)—he taught painting at the Pratt Institute and illustration at the Art Students League and worked as a freelance book and magazine illustrator. He discovered the American West while on assignment in Arizona and New Mexico and fell in love with the landscape and the Native American residents, whom he painted for years. He made many sketching trips to Taos after that and, in 1915, became a founding member of the Taos Society of Artists. Four years later, at the age of forty-five, Blumenschein moved permanently to Taos with his family in tow and devoted himself thereafter to painting full time.

The Lake is a generic title, and perhaps the scene is an amalgam of many sketches the artist had made over time. But one thing is certain: the painting vibrates with the energy and passion of an individual who was deeply connected to the natural world and made that world the focus of his art and life.

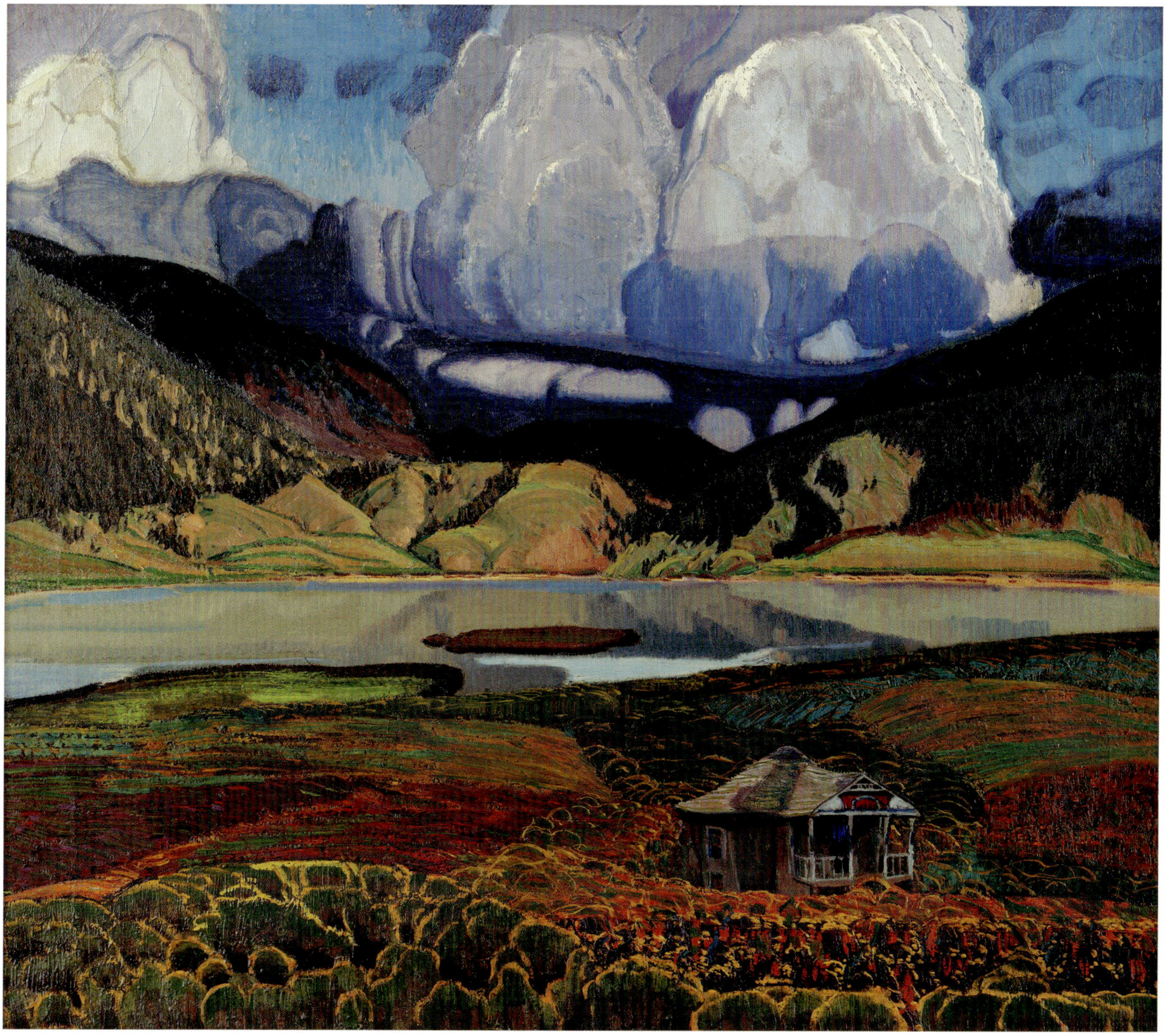

Ernest L. Blumenschein, *The Lake*, ca. 1923. Oil on canvas, 24 ⅛ × 27 in. (61.3 × 68.6 cm)

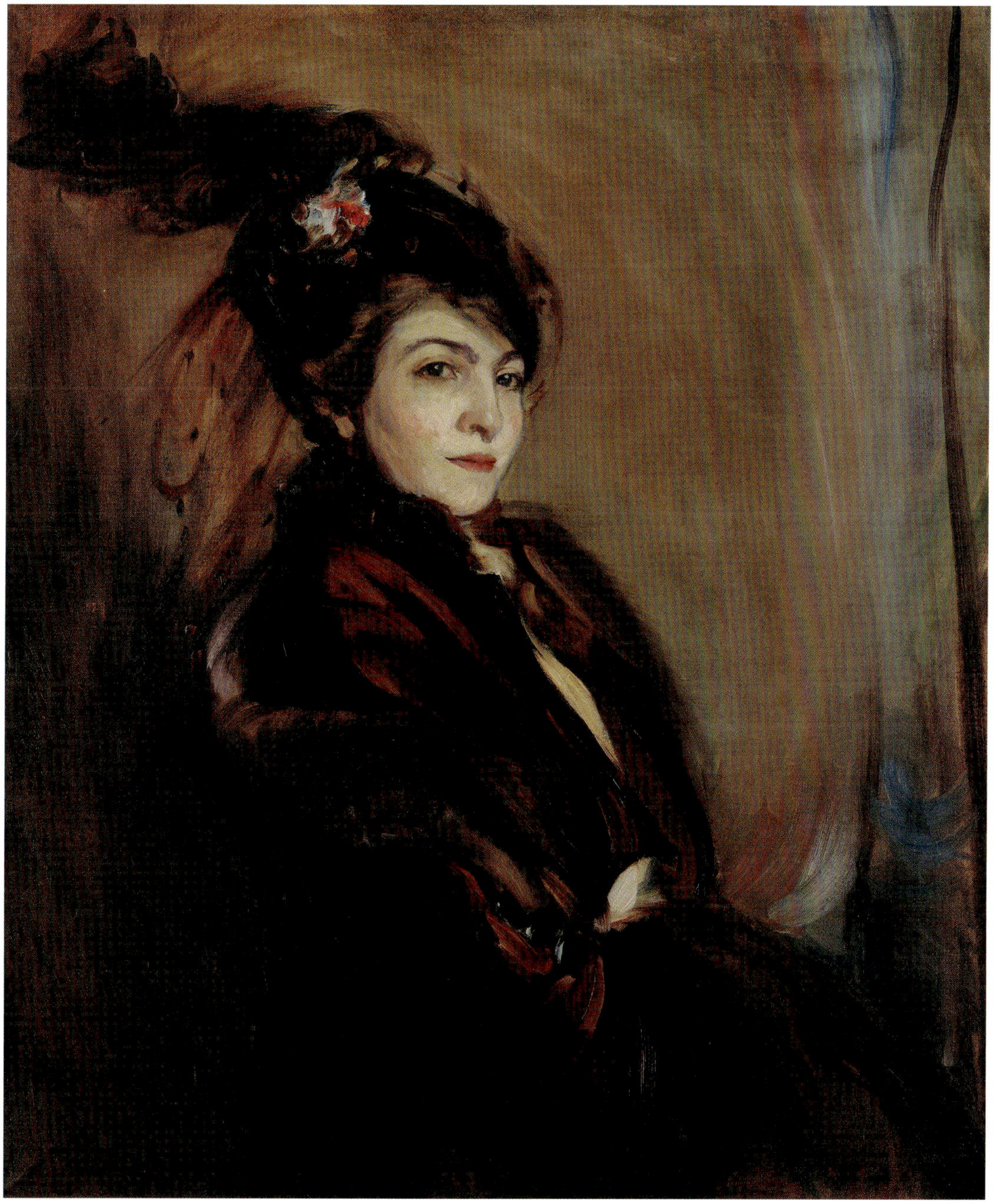

Mary Shepard Greene Blumenschein, *Self-Portrait*, 1915. Oil on canvas, 30 × 25 in. (76.2 × 63.5 cm)

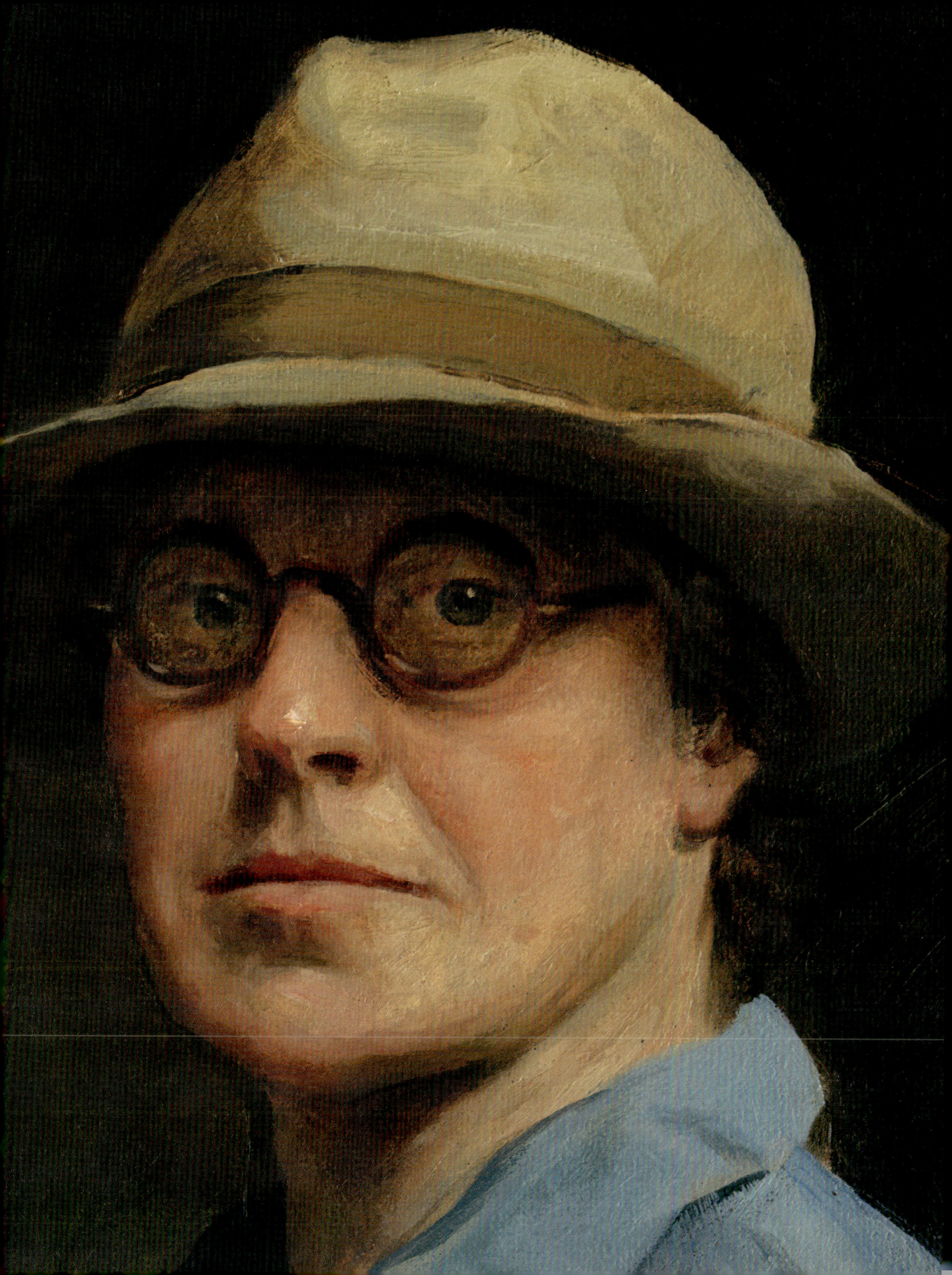

PAST AND PRESENT IN THE 1920S: ELLEN EMMET RAND

JONATHAN FREDERICK WALZ

"Every age contains contradictions," the curator Barbara Haskell has avowed, "but none more so than the twenties."[1] In the United States, the florescence of the Harlem Renaissance took place during a resurgence of the Ku Klux Klan, and the development of a pervasive consumer culture was concurrent with the onset of Prohibition. The country expressed a reinvigorated isolationism, passing strict anti-immigration laws in 1924, but simultaneously enjoyed a newfound role on the world stage, demonstrated in accomplishments such as the first transatlantic telephone conversation and Charles Lindbergh's solo intercontinental flight from New York to Paris, both in 1927. Ellen Emmet Rand, one of the country's first professional woman portraitists, had a front-row seat to the decade's social changes.

Today, despite the valiant recuperative efforts of feminist art historians, Rand remains overshadowed by her more famous cousins: the author Henry James; the intellectual William James; and the painter Lydia Emmet Field. Yet Rand's current reputation belies the stature she enjoyed during her lifetime. Following in the footsteps of Mary Cassatt and Cecilia Beaux, Rand, Field, and their cousin Rosina Emmet Sherwood all became successful artists. Rand, in particular, like John Singer Sargent (pp. 96–97), documented the transatlantic culture of the period, producing more than eight hundred likenesses of public personages, artists, and socialites in both America and Europe.[2]

Having begun to draw as a young girl, Rand (nicknamed "Bay") received early encouragement from her family, who sent her, at the age of twelve, to study with Dennis Miller Bunker in Boston. Further training followed with William Merritt Chase, Kenyon Cox, and Robert Reid in New York and Frederick MacMonnies in Paris. After securing a bronze medal for portraiture at the 1900

Exposition universelle in Paris, the artist returned to New York, and in 1911, she married William Blanchard Rand. Because her husband lost most of his inheritance as a result of the 1929 stock market crash and the ensuing Great Depression, Rand actively sought portrait commissions for the rest of her career.[3] A 1954 *Time* review of a posthumous exhibition noted that the artist had earned the staggering sum of $74,000 in 1930, when the average net income was $4,887.01.[4] Her artistic talent and social connections led to many commissions, including the first portrait for which President Franklin Delano Roosevelt sat following his 1932 election.

Rand was named an Associate of the National Academy of Design in 1926, at the age of fifty, and advanced to Academician in 1934. For the artist's diploma portrait (p. 155), Rand depicted herself against a plain and somber background, recalling Velázquez and Manet, frequent artistic sources in the early twentieth century. Unlike late nineteenth-century ateliers filled with bric-a-brac and fancy costumes, Rand's studio is the locus of sober work, not a place for entertainment (as opposed, for example, to several images from the hand of her teacher Chase, such as *The Tenth Street Studio*; see fig. 2 on p. 84). Her blue smock signifies serious (if quasi-genteel) manual labor and contrasts strongly with the bespoke outfits usually worn by her high-society subjects. Period photographs confirm that the artist favored her right hand (fig. 1); therefore, the portrait denies the use of a mirror in its creation, as Rand's dominant arm should appear closer to, rather than farther from, the picture plane.

In the current cultural moment, as scholars have theorized the performative nature of gender and transgender community members have inhabited every possible subject position along the spectrum of feminine and masculine, the artist's self-presentation in this work may seem like "no big deal." But the battered fedora Rand wears, her hidden hairstyle, her broad frame, and the erect brushes thrust through the hole in the palette all convey a startlingly modern masculinity for the 1920s. As a professional artist who practiced portraiture grounded in naturalistic transcription and physiognomic recognition, Rand possessed a profound understanding of posing, agency, and identity construction as well as of what the art historian David Peters Corbett calls "facingness": "To face and to be faced are complex experiences. The face is both our self-image and the point where that image becomes vulnerable and has to be negotiated. . . . To face something or someone and to be faced in turn is . . . to be intimately forced to confront questions of knowledge and interpretation, resistance and openness."[5]

Rand's self-representation, like Luigi Lucioni's handsome *William Whitehead* (p. 163), also participates in what the art historian Teresa A. Carbone has identified as "the new portrait form of choice" in the 1920s: the close-up. "Bound up in the new photographic aesthetic that straddled the borders separating 'serious' art, advertising, and the movies," close-ups, she writes, "implied a deeper level of contact with the individual, a means through which one reached the 'reticence and reserve'

JUDITH SHEA ON ELLEN EMMET RAND

From my first glimpse of Ellen Emmet Rand's *Self-Portrait,* it seemed iconic somehow, in spite of its modest size, but also very real. In a blue smock, with Bauhaus-like glasses and a fedora worn low over the eyes, under which she hides her hair, the artist looks out at us, a woman of her time. The hat reminds me of a Hopper self-portrait of 1925–30 in the collection of the Whitney Museum of American Art, New York, in which he wears a similar one, if a bit more propped up on his head. A more interesting difference is that Hopper painted himself smiling as if for a camera, while Rand did not. She is working on her portrait in earnest, looking directly at the mirror, which translates to looking directly out at the viewer. It's more of an encounter than a greeting. And she leaves it as such. The large palette in the foreground takes up a full third of the composition, and she holds it tight to her body, anchored by a fistful of brushes. The palette's placement makes a natural allusion to a shield and sword, and Rand turns her head to look out at us over its edge.

Because of how she's dressed and her serious demeanor, the portrayal is decidedly mannish and no-nonsense. Perhaps Rand was simply portraying herself at work, making this self-portrait to complete the requirements of being elected to membership in the National Academy of Design. The image is practical, straightforward, without any room for detailed autobiography. She wasn't trying to look attractive. She wasn't in her best clothes, or even in street clothes. This is how she looked in the studio, painting. On the other hand, Rand was a seasoned and sought-after portraitist, so her choices, or instincts, of how to portray herself were surely well considered. Did she look like this when she spent two days in the White House painting Franklin Delano Roosevelt? Perhaps she did. That was 1935—no video exists. She depicted the president reading and annotating correspondence. She also painted FDR's secretary of war, Henry Stimson, as well as Teddy Roosevelt's secretary of state, John Milton Hay (who had been a personal secretary to Lincoln).

In her portrayals of two renowned artists, Augustus Saint-Gaudens and her teacher, Frederick MacMonnies, the former is shown seated, in profile, wearing formal dress, while the latter is shown from behind, sitting at his easel. Both of them, and many others Rand painted, probably took the lead in determining how they wanted to appear, presumably starting with what they wore for their sittings. By choosing to portray herself at work, Rand told us how *she* wanted to be seen. She placed herself in her professional context, as she had done with her successful sitters. More importantly, knowing that this was to be part of the National Academy's collection, she had it convey how she wanted to be remembered in history. Everything she wanted us to know about her is right there. In fact, everything in Rand's self-portrait is attached to her physically: smock, glasses, hat, paint, palette, brushes. There is no background or foreground. There is no setting. There are no symbolic details lodged in the periphery. No coded narrative in the textiles, out the window, or on a table. In its formal self-sufficiency, it is more like a statue than a painting. Self-contained. Solid.

And so, in this quietly powerful image, Ellen Emmet Rand offered us a prototype of a strong successful female artist in early twentieth-century America. It is a great lineage.

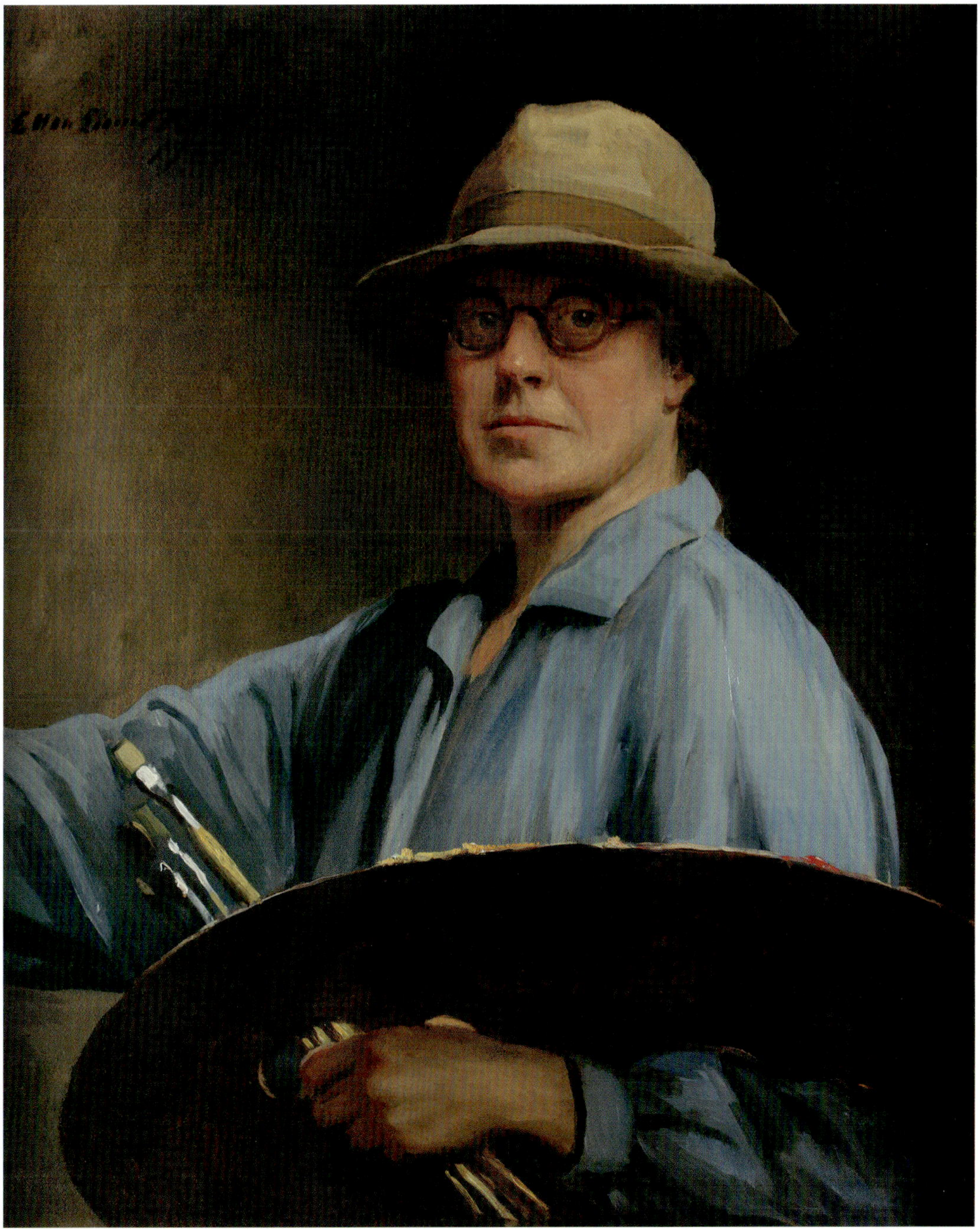

Ellen Emmet Rand, *Self-Portrait*, 1927. Oil on composition board, 30 × 24 in. (76.2 × 61 cm)

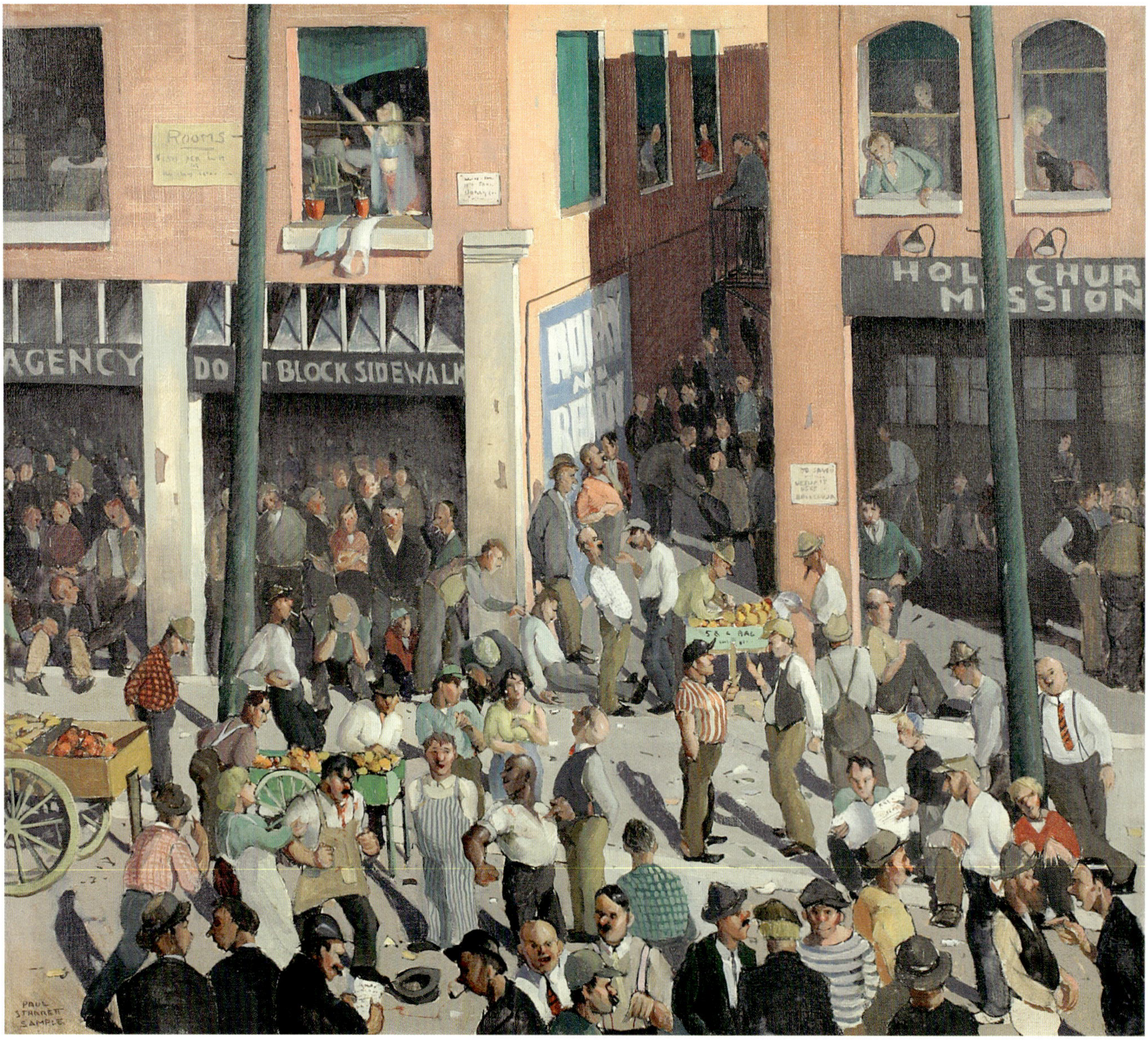

Paul Sample, *Unemployment*, 1931. Oil on canvas, 36 × 40 in. (91.4 × 101.6 cm)

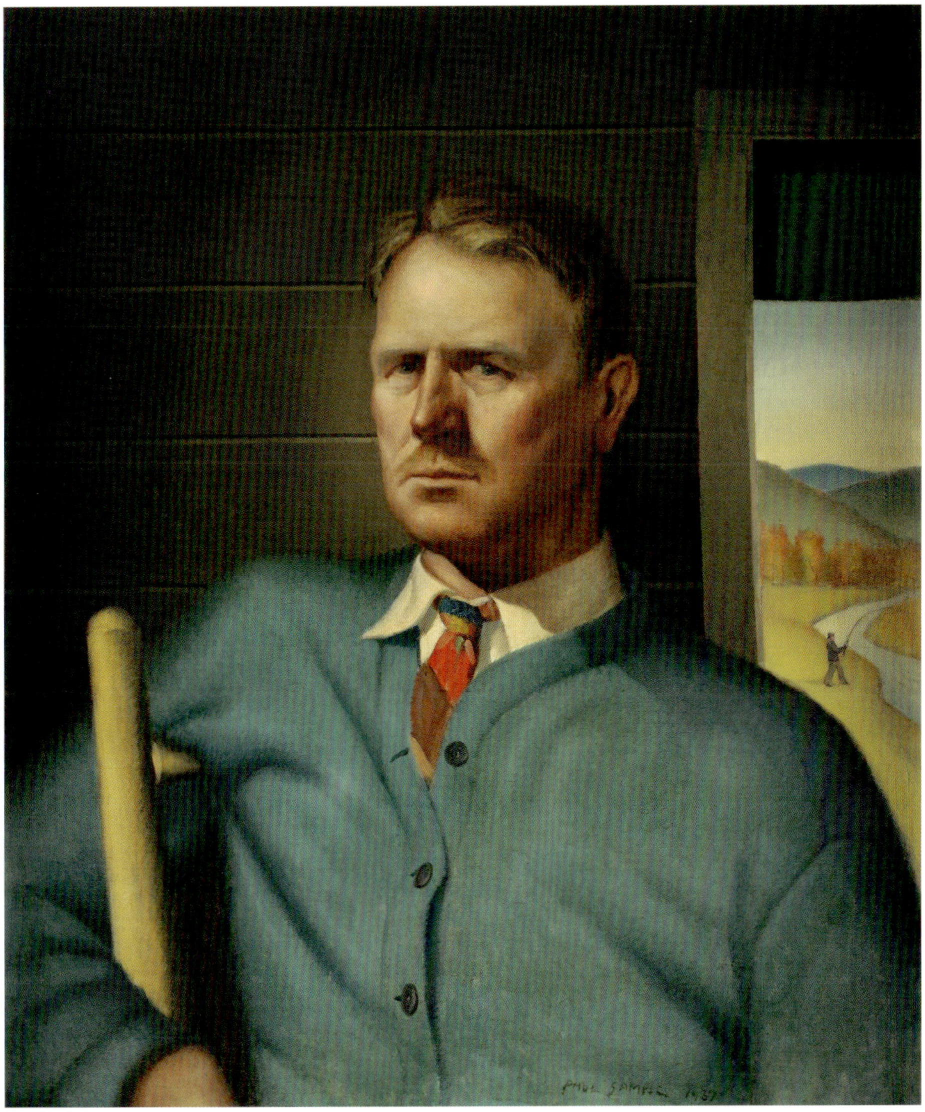

Paul Sample, *Self-Portrait*, 1937. Oil on canvas, 30 × 25 in. (76.2 × 63.5 cm)

GLENN GOLDBERG ON PETER HURD

I was not familiar with Peter Hurd before this painting, *Evening in the Sierras*, struck me with its calmness, its depiction of a vast open space, and the artist's overall handling of paint. The work feels accessible, friendly, and welcoming in its demeanor. Somehow, it is fitting that it was created in the natural material of egg tempera on a wood panel. The image instantly made me think that I would like to drive down that long country road to the house at the foot of the mountain and embrace the solitude. In the distance is a blue pickup truck that appears to be in motion, just arriving at the house, as a great deal of dust is being kicked up behind it. It is still light out, so one might guess that it is early evening. Such a tranquil domestic scene in rural America is most appealing to this lifelong resident of New York City. The painting is an invitation.

I found myself wanting to learn something about this heretofore unfamiliar artist. Hurd studied privately with N. C. Wyeth (pp. 160–61), the well-known American Realist painter and book illustrator, father of Andrew (p. 7) and Henriette and grandfather of Jamie, also an Academician. As it happens, Hurd married Henriette, and the couple had three children together. Hurd and all the Wyeths painted portraits, still lifes, and landscapes throughout their lifetimes.

Looking further back, I learned that Hurd attended military school as a boy in Roswell, New Mexico. He enrolled at West Point but, having always loved art and painting, decided to leave halfway through to attend the Pennsylvania Academy of the Fine Arts in Philadelphia. That decision was quite radical, especially for the early 1920s. This is the story of a person who had an inner desire to do something, followed his dream, and ended up not only living the rest of his life as an artist but also finding his wife and family in the process. There is a "lived happily ever after" spirit to this decision, which is instructive as an example of following one's passion and calling.

Hurd ultimately chose to return to the rural area of his upbringing. In the 1930s, he and Henriette moved to forty acres in San Patricio, New Mexico, which later grew into a 2,200-acre ranch. Hurd spent his life ranching and painting the landscape and the people living in his midst in rural New Mexico. *Evening in the Sierras* holds and delivers the spirit of the Great American West.

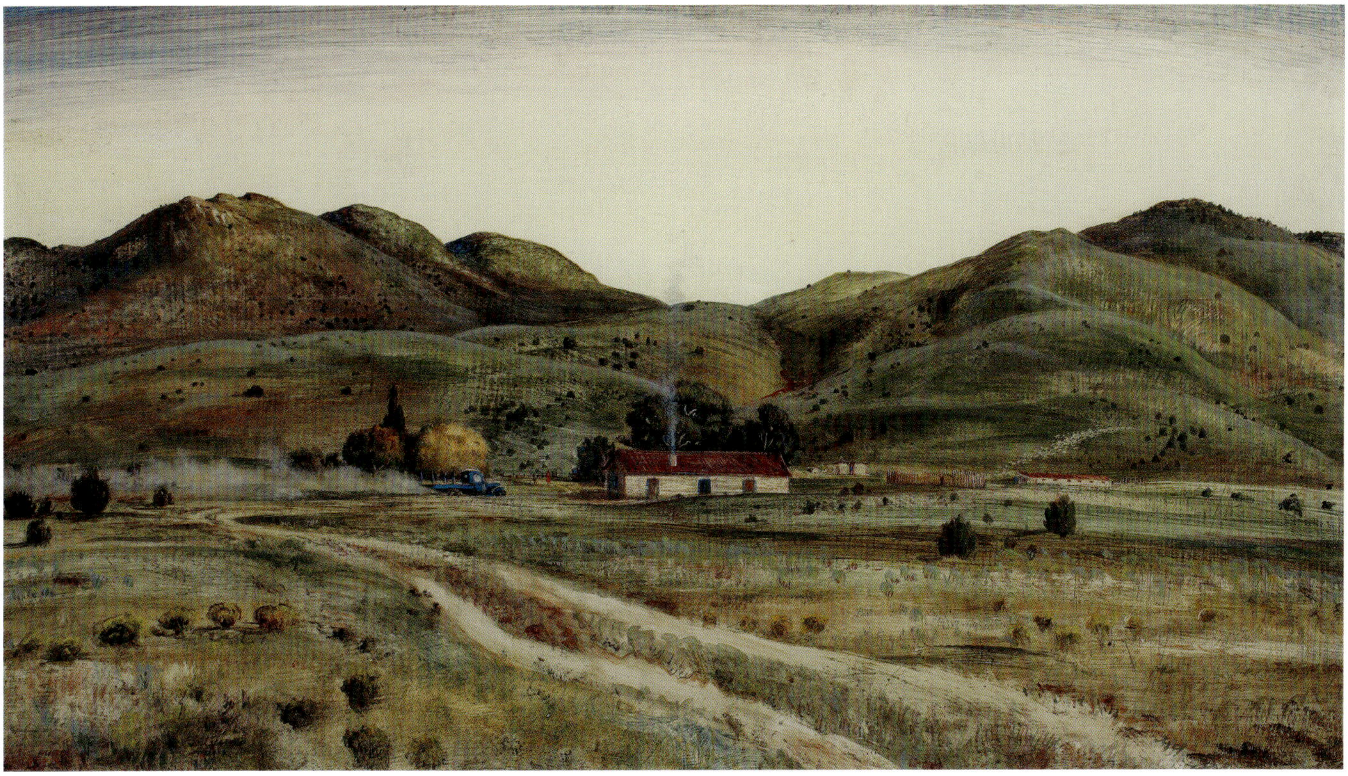

Peter Hurd, *Evening in the Sierras*, 1938–39. Egg tempera on gessoed panel, 24 ¼ × 42 in. (61.6 × 106.7 cm)

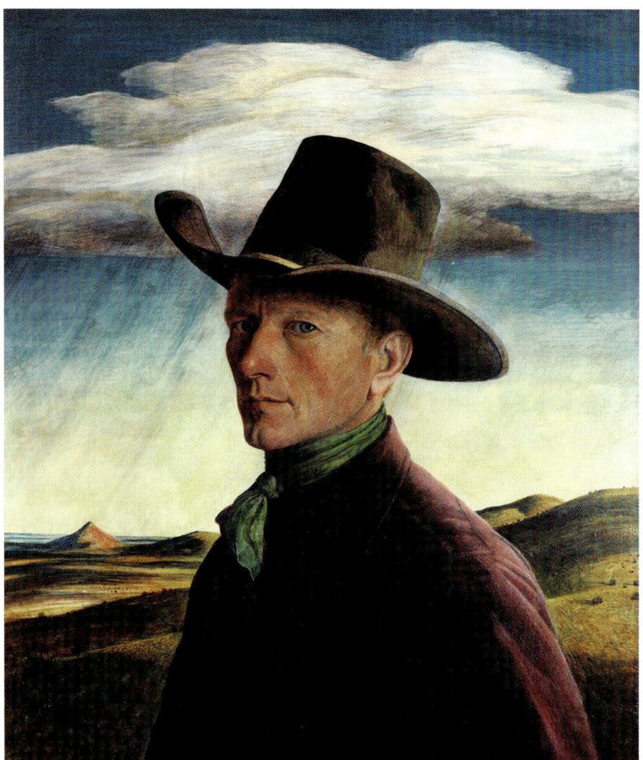

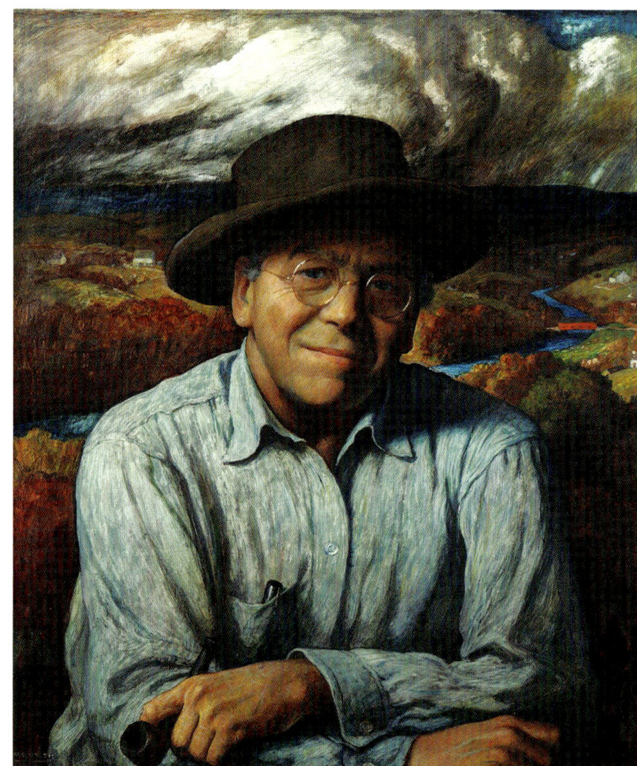

Left: Peter Hurd, *Self-Portrait*, 1941. Oil on wood panel, 29 × 24 in. (73.7 × 61 cm)
Right: N. C. Wyeth, *Self-Portrait*, 1940. Egg tempera on gessoed panel, 32 ¾ × 27 ½ in. (83.2 × 69.9 cm)

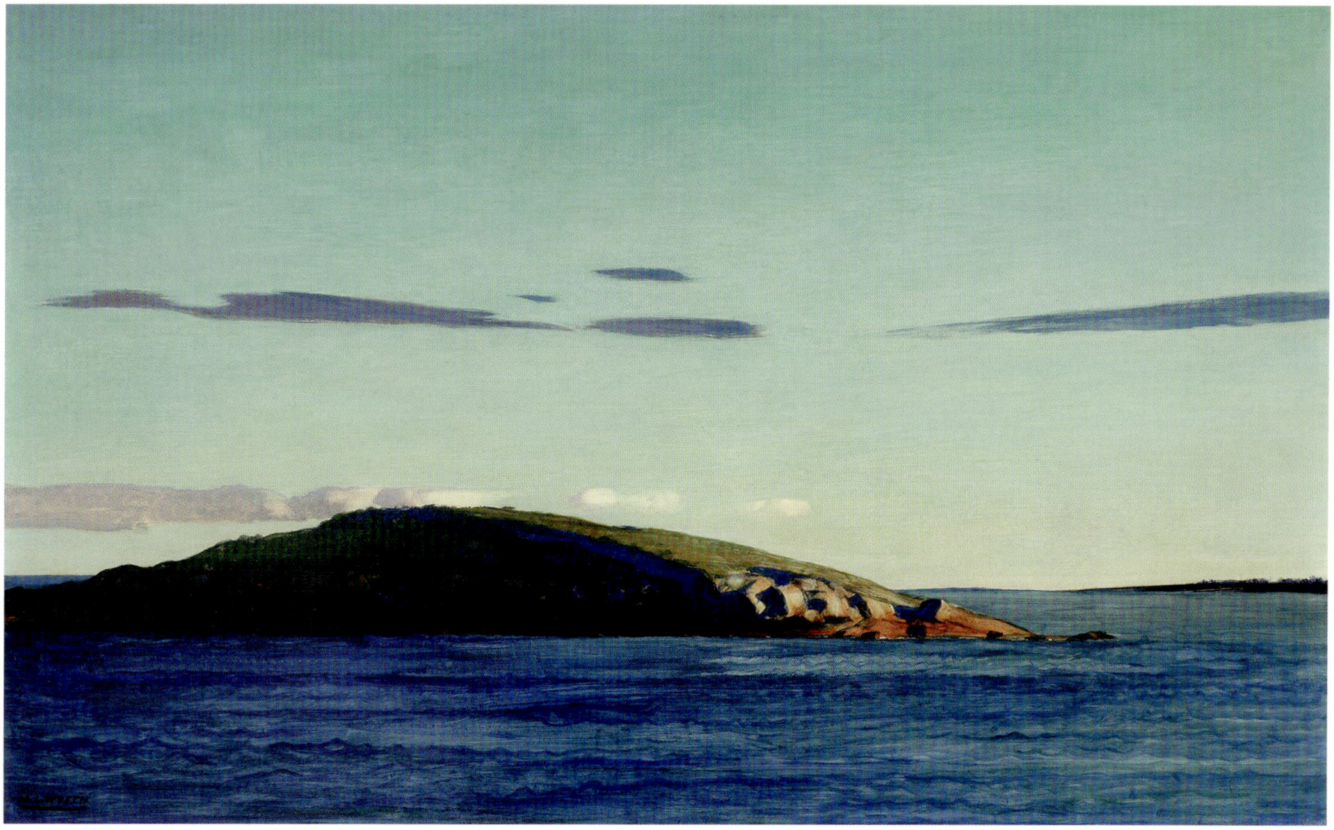

N. C. Wyeth, *Blubber Island, Maine*, 1938. Oil on gessoed panel, 25 × 40 in. (63.5 × 101.6 cm)

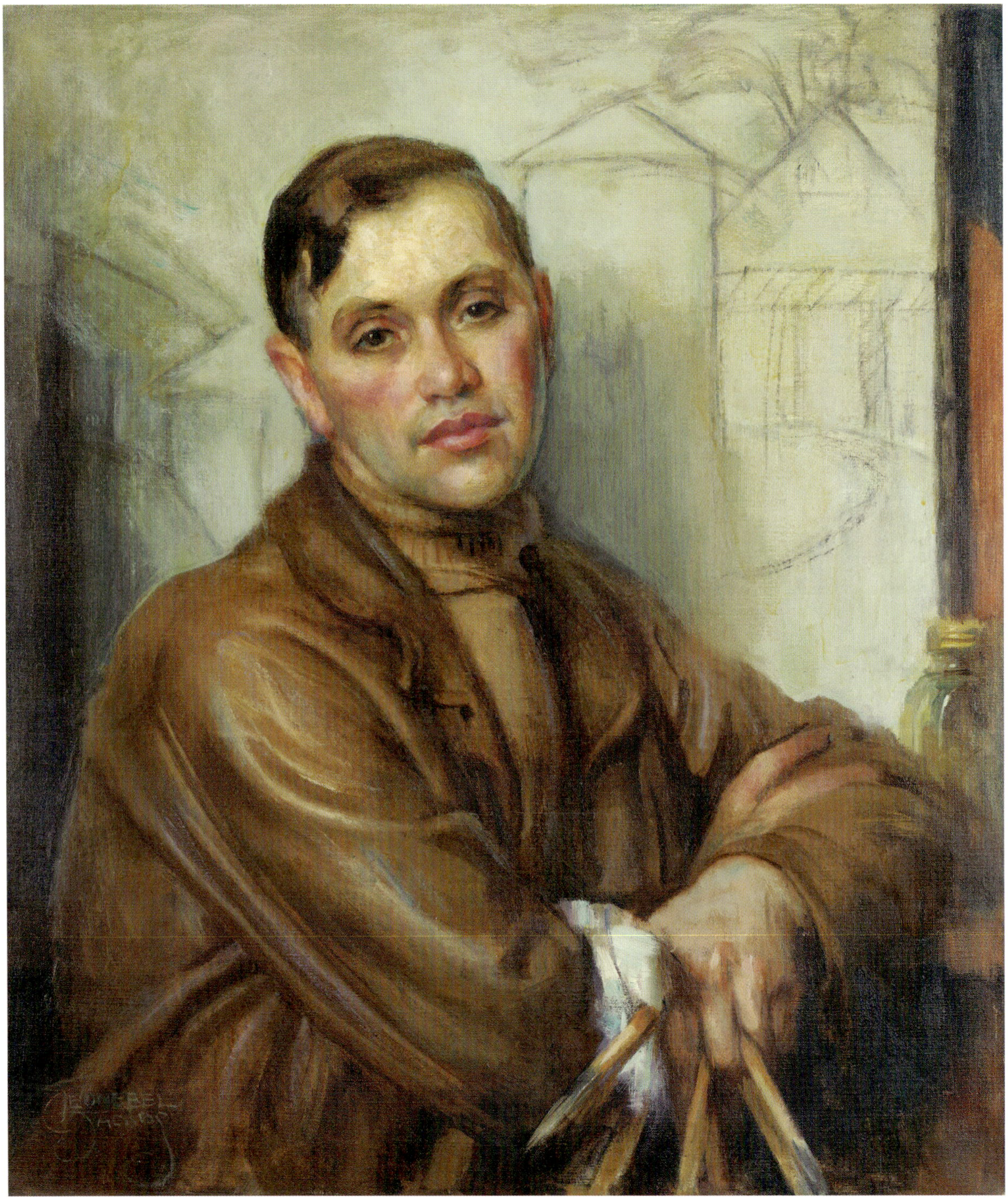

Leonebel Jacobs, *Luigi Lucioni*, 1938. Oil on canvas, 30 × 24⅞ in. (76.2 × 63.2 cm)

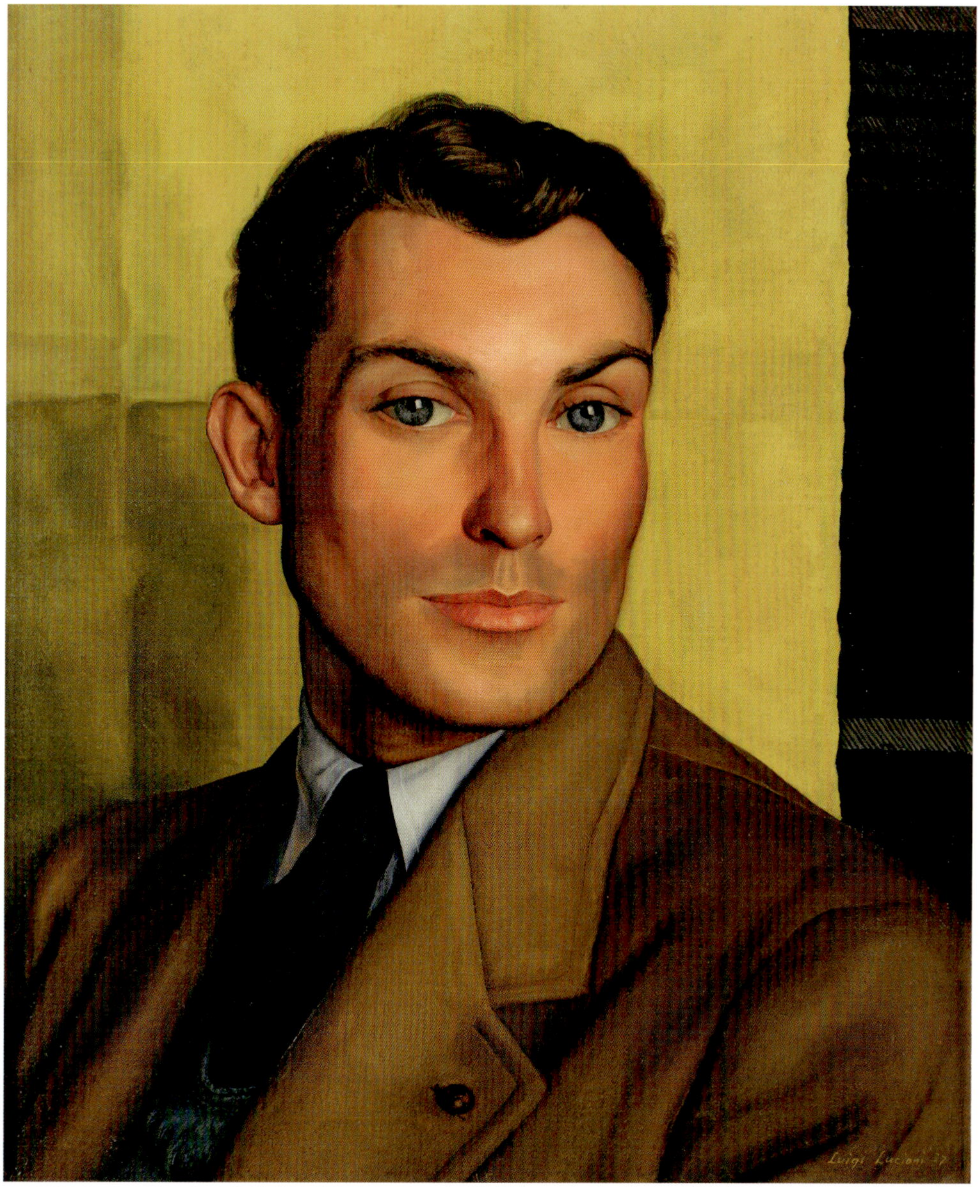

Luigi Lucioni, *William Whitehead*, 1937. Oil on canvas, 17 × 14¼ in. (43.2 × 36.2 cm)

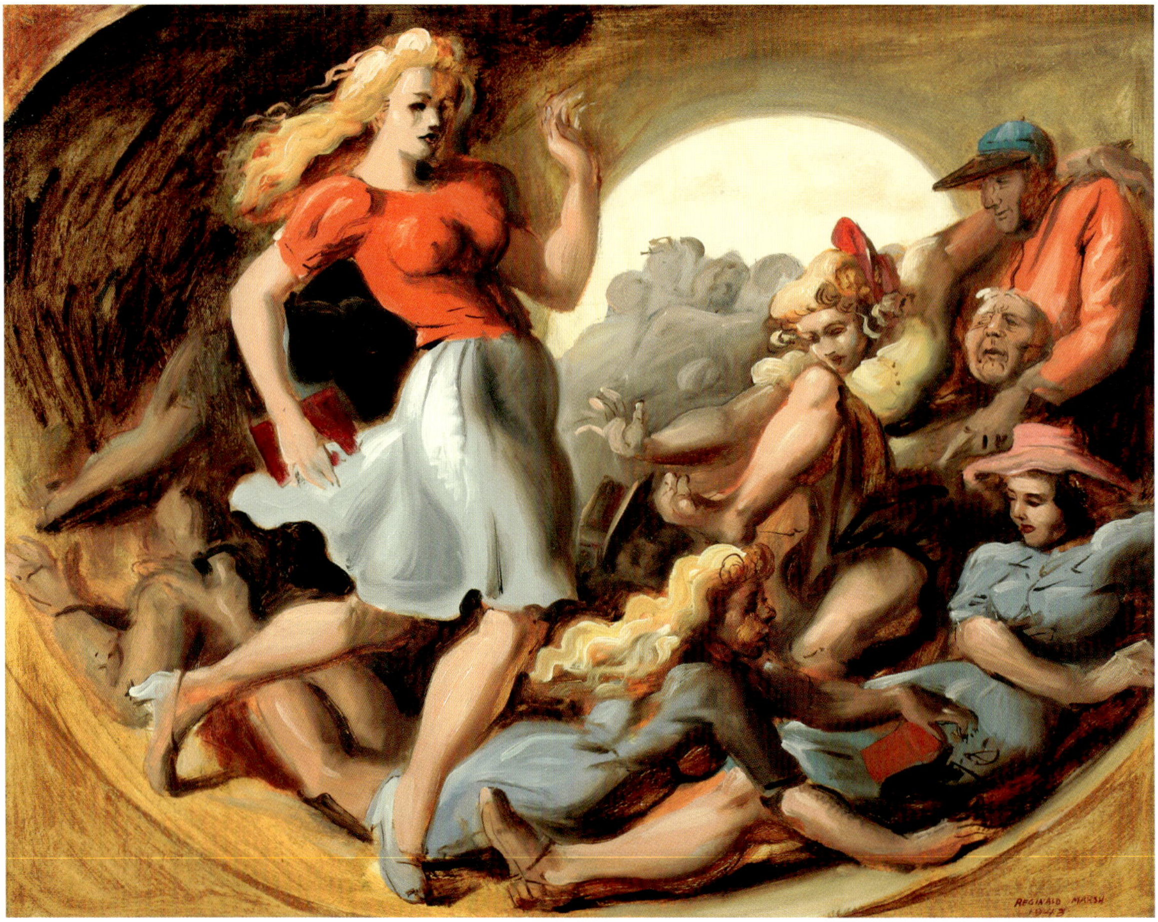

Reginald Marsh, *Barrel of Fun*, 1943. Oil on composition board, 24 × 29¾ in. (61 × 75.6 cm)

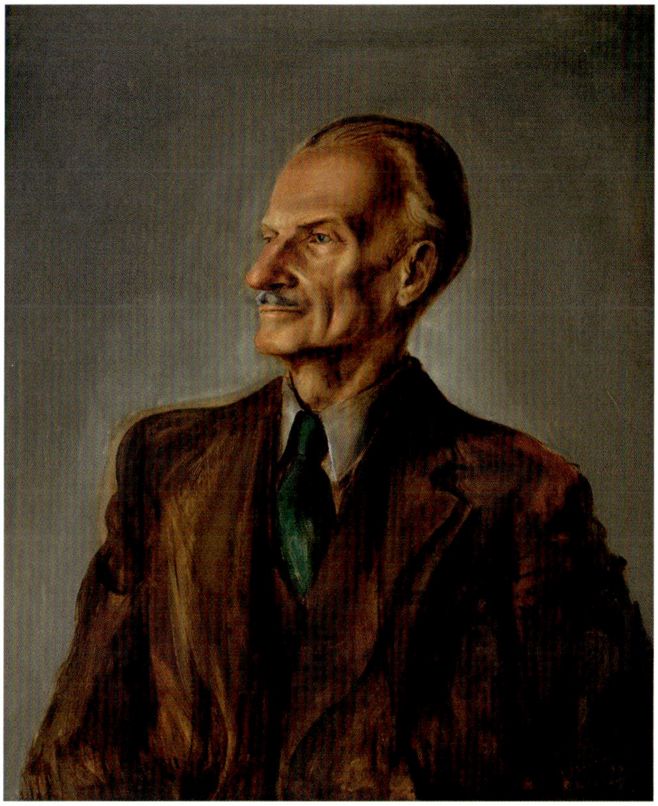 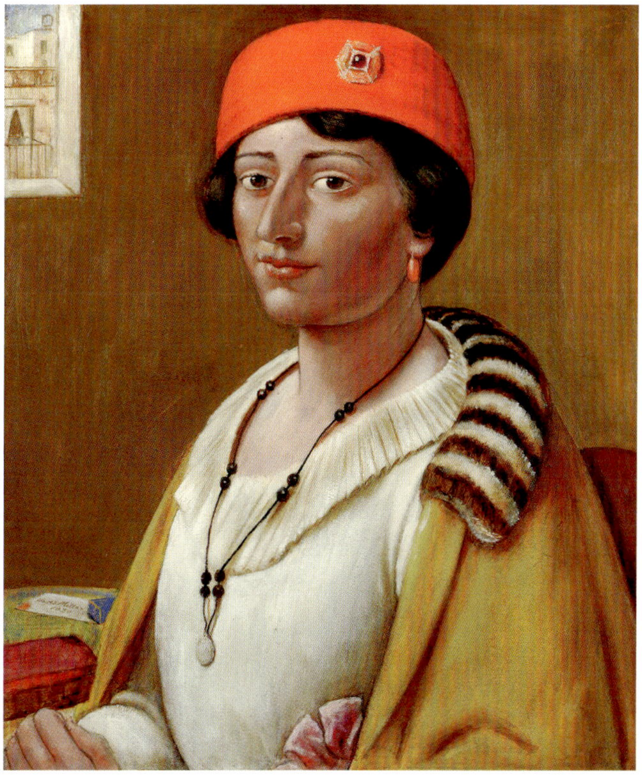

Left: Reginald Marsh, *Kenneth Hayes Miller*, 1943. Oil on canvas, 30⅛ × 25¼ in. (76.5 × 64.1 cm)
Right: Kenneth Hayes Miller, *Red Turban*, 1930. Oil on wood panel, 24 × 20 in. (61 × 50.8 cm)

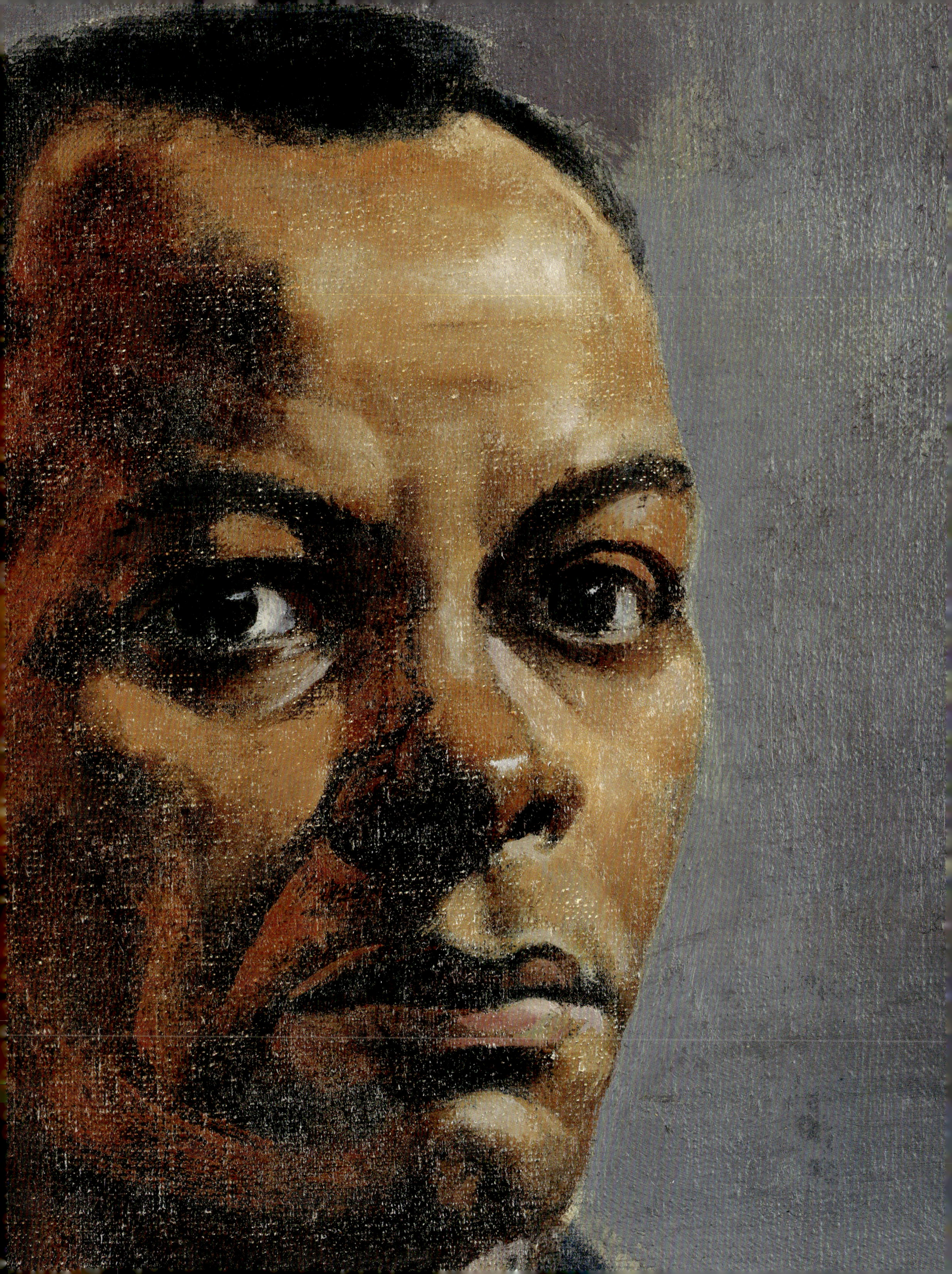

BEYOND THE SURFACE: HUGHIE LEE-SMITH

ALONA COOPER WILSON

When Hughie Lee-Smith received the title of National Academician in 1967, he considered it the most significant accomplishment of his career. "It's rather odd the way I view it," he stated the following year, "because this is one of my—well you might say, childhood dreams. . . . It represented to me or for me a sort of life-long dream come true. I am very happy indeed to be a member of the Academy."[1] Lee-Smith was fifty-two years old and only the second African American artist to achieve the prestigious membership.[2] As was required, he submitted two paintings, the first of which was a self-portrait, and the second, a landscape.

Portraiture has long been important to our understanding of humanity. It is intimate, emotive, and, at its best, expressive of the inner feelings of a fellow human. Lee-Smith's diploma portrait (p. 172) presents the artist as a self-assured, serious man accompanied by neither professional attributes nor symbols. Simply dressed, he wears a blazer, dress shirt, and necktie, the last slightly off-center from the collar as if the artist had turned his head quickly to see or hear what is just outside the picture frame. His attentive, piercing gaze is accentuated by his highly arched eyebrows. In another self-portrait completed during this period (fig. 1), Lee-Smith's expression appears defiant rather than inquisitive; tightly cropped, the singular focus is on his gaze. In both portraits, Lee-Smith honored the tradition of academic portraiture, yet at the same time, with his open, forthright gaze, the artist may have intended to challenge established concepts of African American racial identity and social confidence.[3]

Over the course of his career, Lee-Smith received numerous portrait commissions. As in his self-portraits, he evoked his sitters' psychological states in a manner similar to nineteenth-century

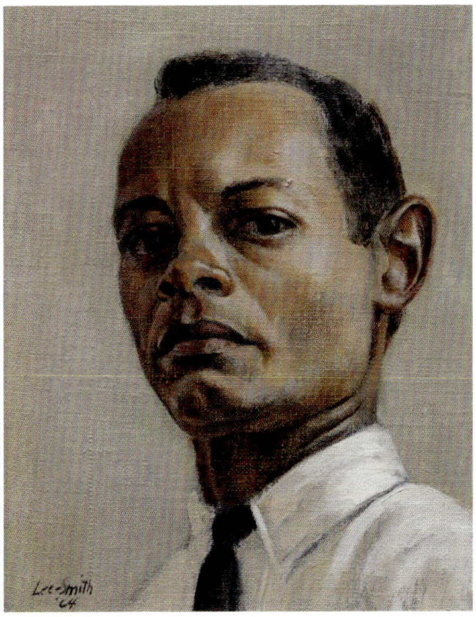

Fig. 1. Hughie Lee-Smith, *Self-Portrait*, 1964. Oil on canvas. Detroit Institute of Arts

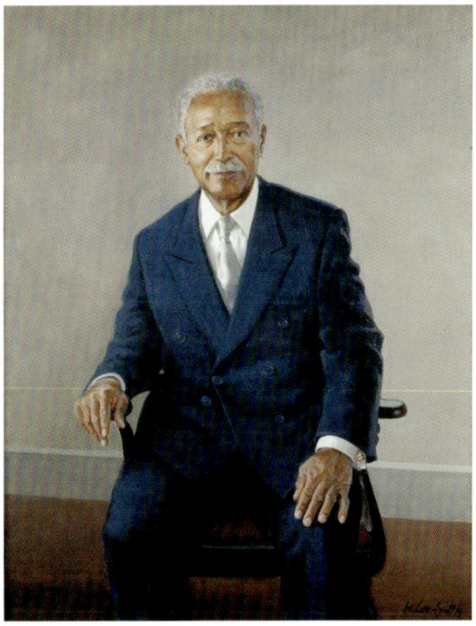

Fig. 2 Hughie Lee-Smith, *Mayor David Dinkins*, 1994. Oil on canvas. Collection of the Public Design Commission of the City of New York

portraits by such artists as Thomas Eakins.[4] Lee-Smith painted easily with his subjects sitting before him or from memory in his studio, using sketches and photographs. In 1959, he completed a striking full-length portrait of the stage actor Ira Frederick Aldridge for Howard University in Washington, DC.[5] Also in 1959, he received a commission from the Hotel Gotham in Detroit for several portraits of African American professional men.[6] The paintings, which included one of Norman O. Houston, then president of Golden State Mutual Life Insurance, an African American–owned company with its corporate office in Los Angeles, were hung in the hotel lobby.[7] In the last decade of Lee-Smith's life, he received an important commission to paint David Dinkins, former mayor of New York City.[8] In the three-quarter-length portrait (fig. 2), Dinkins is seated, and the focus is on his playful blue eyes gazing out at the viewer. The softly curling gray hair and gnarled fingers contribute to the impression of an aging man still attentive and engaged. Handsomely dressed, he appears dignified, confident that his image will be rendered successfully by Lee-Smith, a renowned painter whose race is the same as his own.

While his portraits are significant in form and number, landscapes are equally important in Lee-Smith's oeuvre, and the artist submitted *The Bridge* (p. 173) to the National Academy as his diploma work. In it, the sky serves as a backdrop to the tall grasses in the foreground, glistening and swaying in a gentle breeze. Only a fragment of the solidly built bridge is visible, and fissures mark the aging structure, perhaps a reminder of man's presence. Lee-Smith had observed nature closely from the shores of the Great Lakes and smaller bodies of water in Cleveland, Chicago, and Detroit—Midwestern cities where he lived, worked, and developed his artistic techniques and teaching skills. In

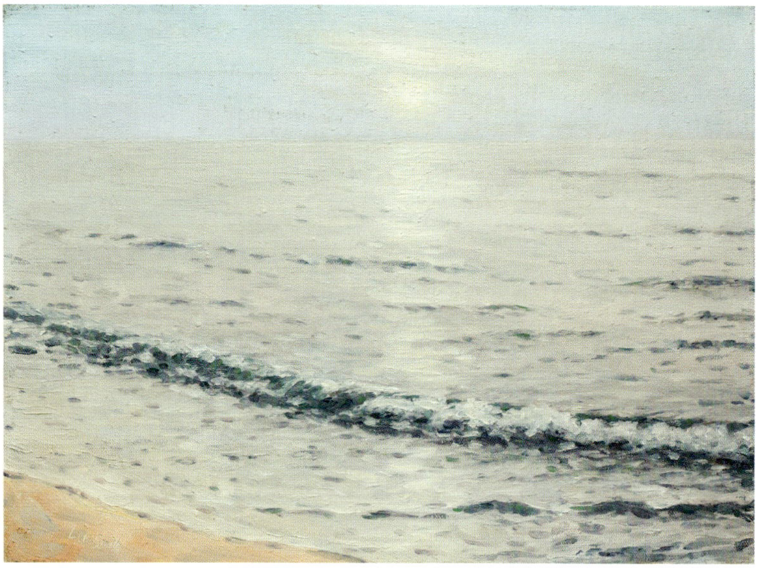

Fig. 3. Hughie Lee-Smith, *Sunrise over Lake Erie*, ca. 1950. Oil on canvas. Detroit Institute of Arts

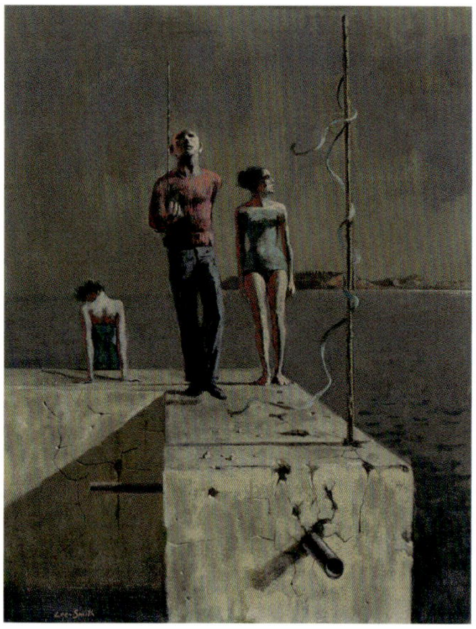

Fig. 4. Hughie Lee-Smith, *The Juggler #1*, ca. 1964. Oil on canvas. Museum of Fine Arts, Boston

Sunrise over Lake Erie (fig. 3), painted in the same period as *The Bridge*, the viewer's gaze is guided to a small corner of the canvas where a sliver of beach gives way to the water. The sun dances lightly atop the waves, emitting a feeling of endless warmth. Such works infuse nature with quietude. However, Lee-Smith's renderings of these tranquil settings as well as his sensitive portraits coincided with the nation's tumultuous twentieth-century history of race relations and civil disobedience, and *The Bridge*, in particular, may have served as a metaphor for transitions in the artist's personal life or for the visible fractures in America's political landscape.

Indeed, the National Academy's highest honor had been awarded to Lee-Smith at a time when the African American fight for civil rights escalated from peaceful demonstrations to violent street actions and the tragic deaths of national leaders.[9] As early as the 1950s, Lee-Smith had recorded the displacement of Detroit's urban poor, Eastern European immigrants as well as generations of impoverished Southerners who had traveled north seeking work. By the mid-1960s, he had become known both for those works and for his enigmatic images of figures engaged in mysterious, disconnected narratives. These paintings, which often incorporate motifs such as balloons, ribbons, water, and walls—termed "insistent symbols" by the artist—are not easily interpreted or classified but have often been discussed in relation to art-historical movements such as Surrealism and metaphysical or magical realism.[10] In *The Juggler #1* (fig. 4), for example, the figures lack individual characteristics, and the scene is dark and ambiguous—perhaps a reflection of a society in the midst of structural and social changes of which the outcome is unknown. The artist sometimes described his life experiences through a lens of established conditions or unchangeable facts determined by his race and profession.

Lee-Smith contended that such circumstances fostered feelings of isolation because artists often require seclusion and contemplation to work and because his experience as an African American distanced him from the majority of society. As he expressed it in 1968, "I would say that I somehow deal with alienation as a factor in human life today . . . an alienation from the main stream [*sic*] of American life."[11] Writing nearly three decades later, Lee-Smith stated what he hoped to express about the human condition through his art: "In essence, my aim is to evoke, through the manipulation of figural imagery, a fresh new insight into the nature of objective reality—beyond the surface."[12]

While Lee-Smith's portraits and landscapes affirm his adherence to the academic traditions of those two genres as well as his technical mastery, his intellectual breadth and artistic contributions are best seen in the works infused with his unique, complex symbolic imagery. There, we see the private, inner landscapes this gifted artist had to continually negotiate in an America challenged and divided by race and class.

1. Hughie Lee-Smith, transcript of 1968 interview by Carroll Greene, Jr., Oral History Project, Archives of American Art, Smithsonian Institution, Washington, DC, 60–61. Patricia Lee-Smith, the artist's widow, wrote that her husband enjoyed his long, active membership and service as a National Academician; letter dated June 26, 1999, NAD artist file.
2. In 1927, Henry Ossawa Tanner became the first African American National Academician. As Tanner's portrait was painted by Richard E. Miller (p. 98), Hughie Lee-Smith's self-portrait was the first by an African American artist to enter the collection.
3. For discussions of the visual image of African Americans in the first half of the twentieth century, see Alain L. Locke's *The New Negro: An Interpretation* (1925) and *The Negro in Art* (1940); Locke promoted Lee-Smith's work from the late 1930s on. See also James A. Porter's seminal book, *Modern Negro Art* (1943); throughout his life, Porter was a mentor to Lee-Smith.
4. On Eakins's portraits, see Akela Reason's essay in this volume, pp. 82–88.
5. The portrait was hung in the lobby of Howard's newly built Ira Aldridge Theater. The building's African American architects were Hilyard R. Robinson and Paul R. Williams.
6. John J. White and his partner, Irving Roane, both African American, purchased the stately Hotel Gotham from Alfred Hartz in 1943. The building became an elite showcase for African American life. See David Maraniss, *Once in a Great City: A Detroit Story* (New York: Simon and Schuster, 2015), 1–16, and Ernest H. Borden, *Detroit's Paradise Valley* (Charleston, SC: Arcadia, 2003).
7. Golden State's headquarters were designed by Paul R. Williams (see n. 5), and the lobby also held commissioned murals by Hale Woodruff and Charles Alston.
8. David Firestone, "Ceremonial Moment Mellows the Mayors," *New York Times*, October 28, 1995.
9. To express frustration about social and political injustice and respond to events such as the bombing of the 16th Street Baptist Church in 1963 and the murder of three civil rights workers in 1964—James Chaney, Andrew Goodman, and Michael Schwerner—violent street protests took place in many American cities during the 1960s. Notable figures were assassinated during this period—Malcolm X in 1965 and Martin Luther King, Jr., and Robert F. Kennedy in 1968—and legislation such as the Civil Rights Act (1964), Voting Rights Act (1965), and Fair Housing Act (1968) was passed to begin to rectify previous inequities.
10. Carol Wald, "The Metaphysical World of Hughie Lee-Smith," *American Artist* 42, no. 435 (October 1978): 51.
11. Lee-Smith, 1968 interview by Greene, 48–49.
12. Hughie Lee-Smith, "Artist Statement" (1997), Exhibition Files, June Kelley Gallery, New York.

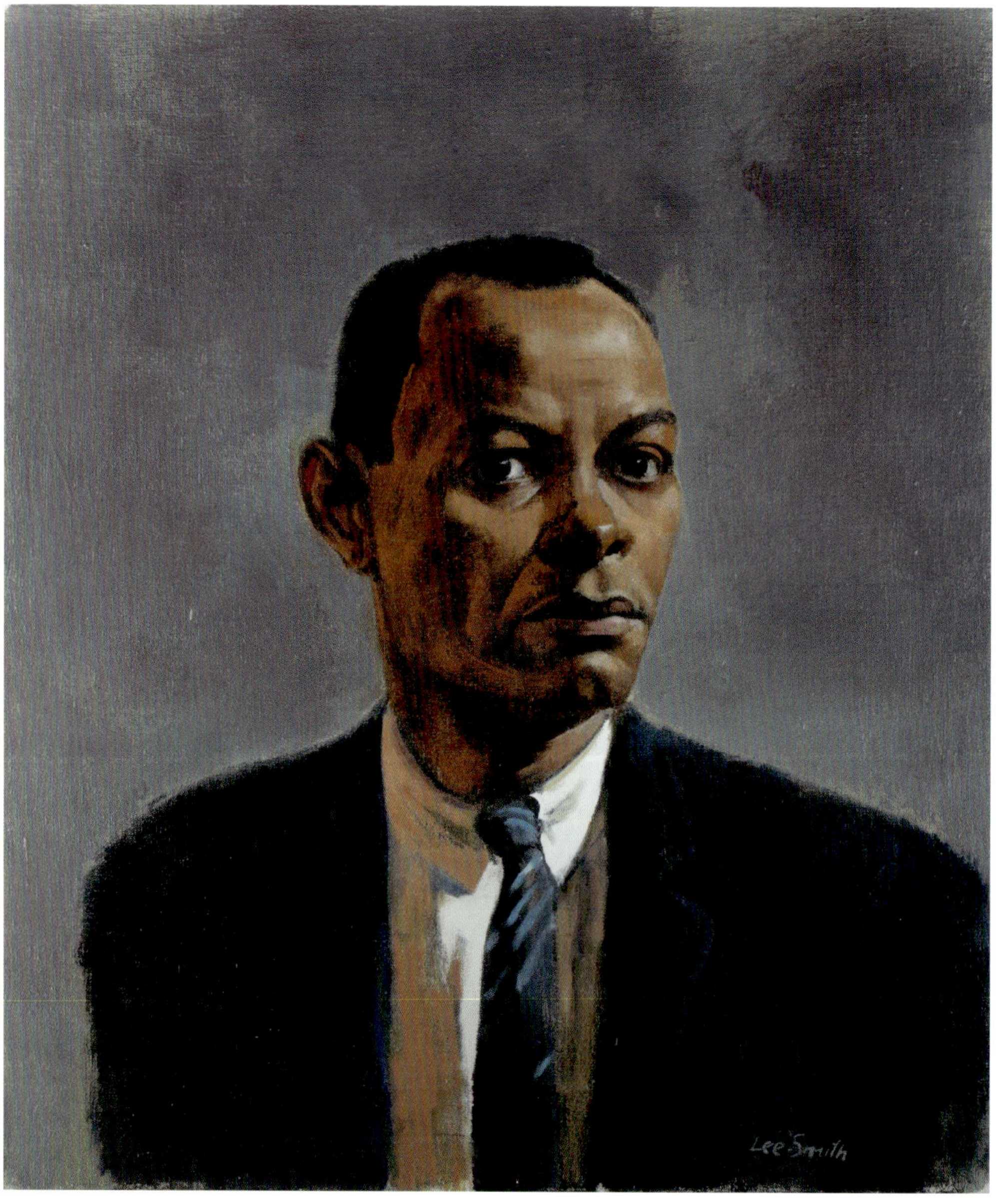

Hughie Lee-Smith, *Self-Portrait*, 1964. Oil on canvas, 24 × 20 in. (61 × 50.8 cm)

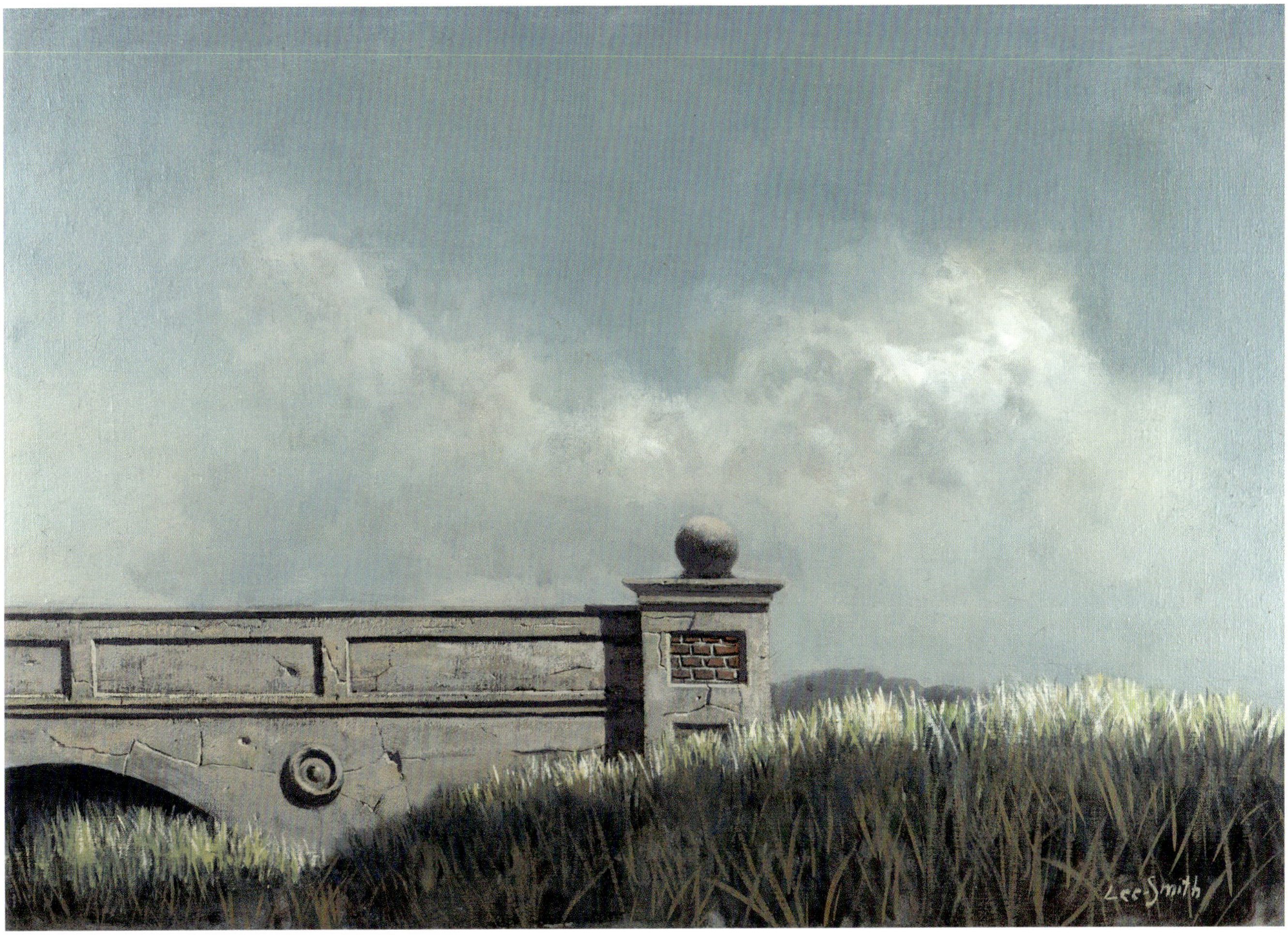

Hughie Lee-Smith, *The Bridge*, before 1968. Oil on canvas, 25 ⅞ × 36 in. (65.7 × 91.4 cm)

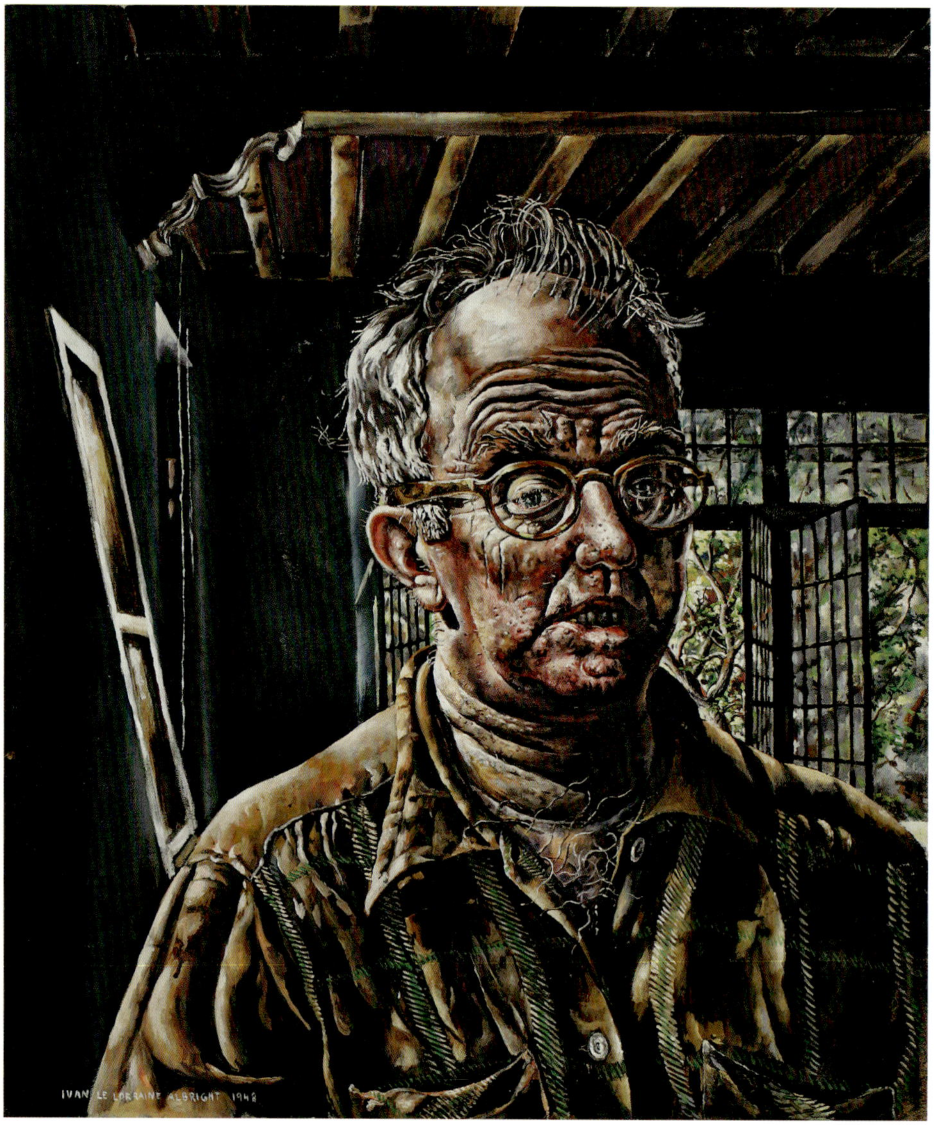

Ivan Albright, *Self-Portrait*, 1948. Oil on canvas, 24 × 20 in. (61 × 50.8 cm)

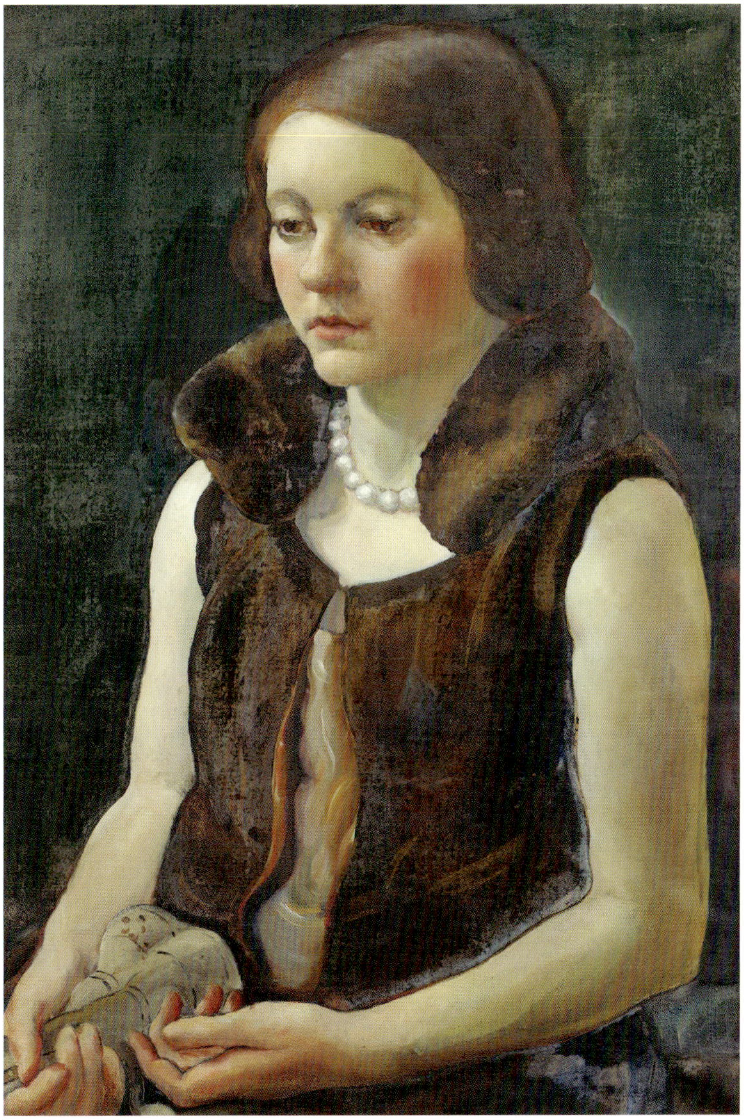

Ivan Albright, *Fur Collar* [or] *The Baskerville Portrait*, 1925–26. Oil on canvas, 30 × 20 in. (76.2 × 50.8 cm)

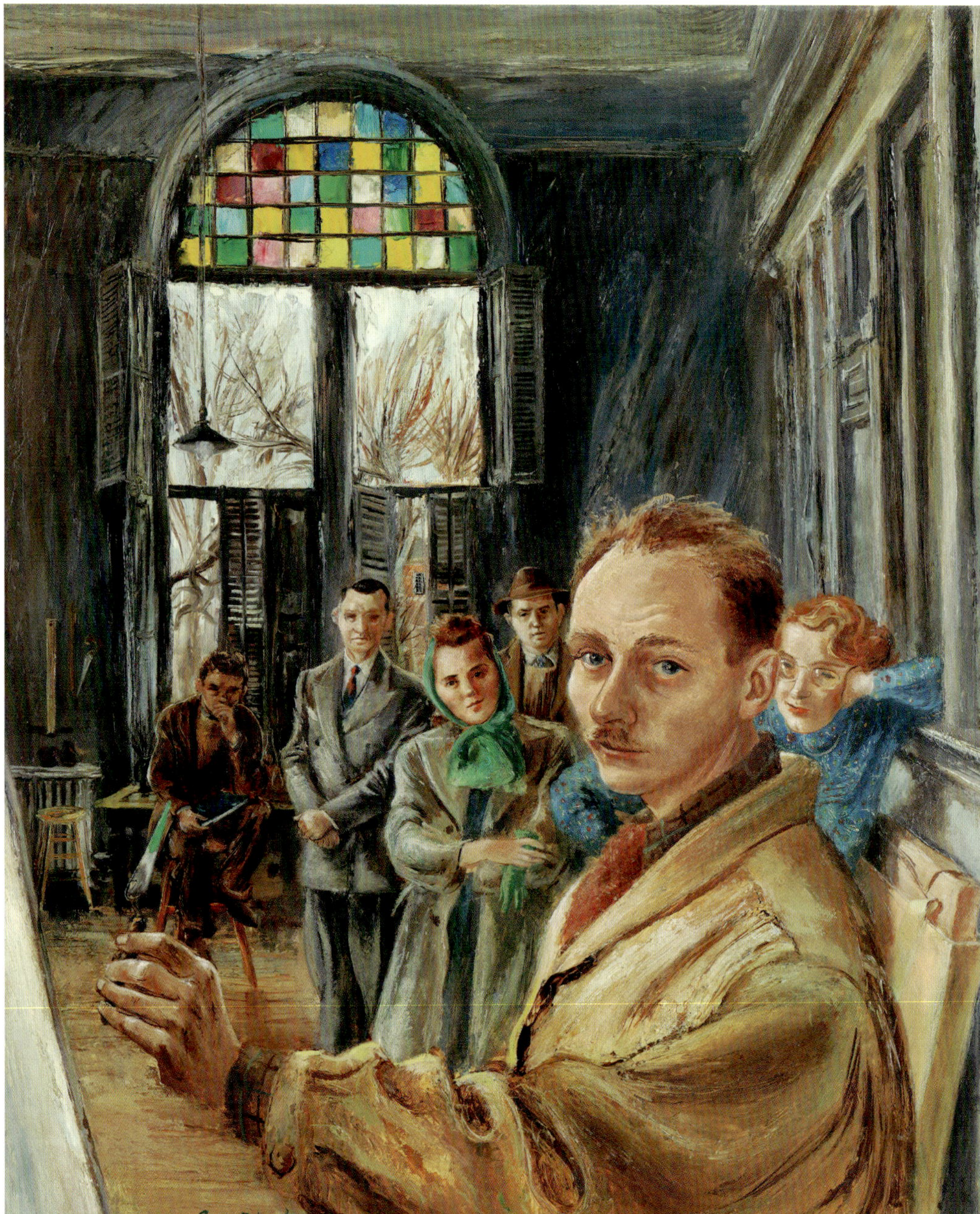

Aaron Bohrod, *Artist in Residence: Self-Portrait*, 1943. Oil on canvas, 26 × 21 ⅛ in. (66 × 53.7 cm)

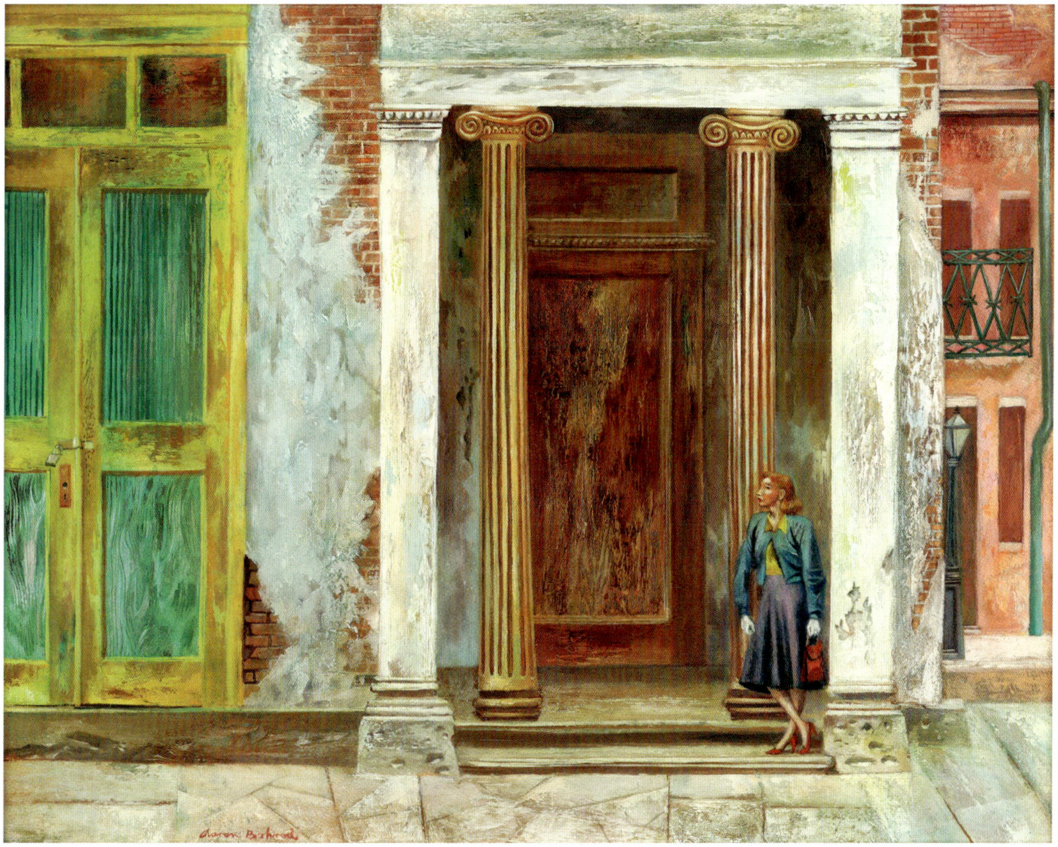

Aaron Bohrod, *Façade, New Orleans*, n.d. Oil on canvas, 16 × 19¾ in. (40.6 × 50.2 cm)

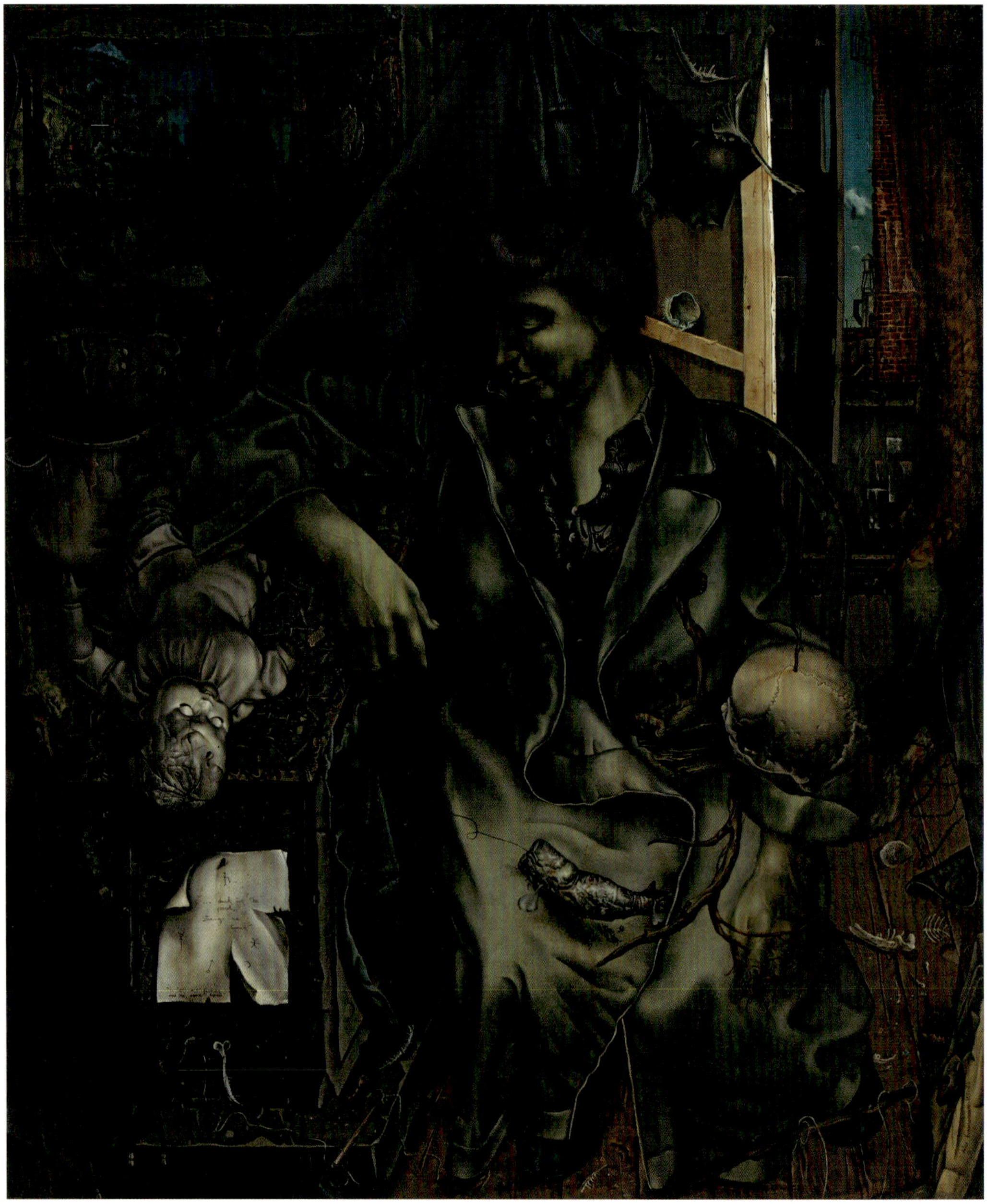

Jules Kirschenbaum, *Dark in the Forest*, 1951–52. Oil on canvas, 36 × 29¾ in. (91.4 × 75.6 cm)

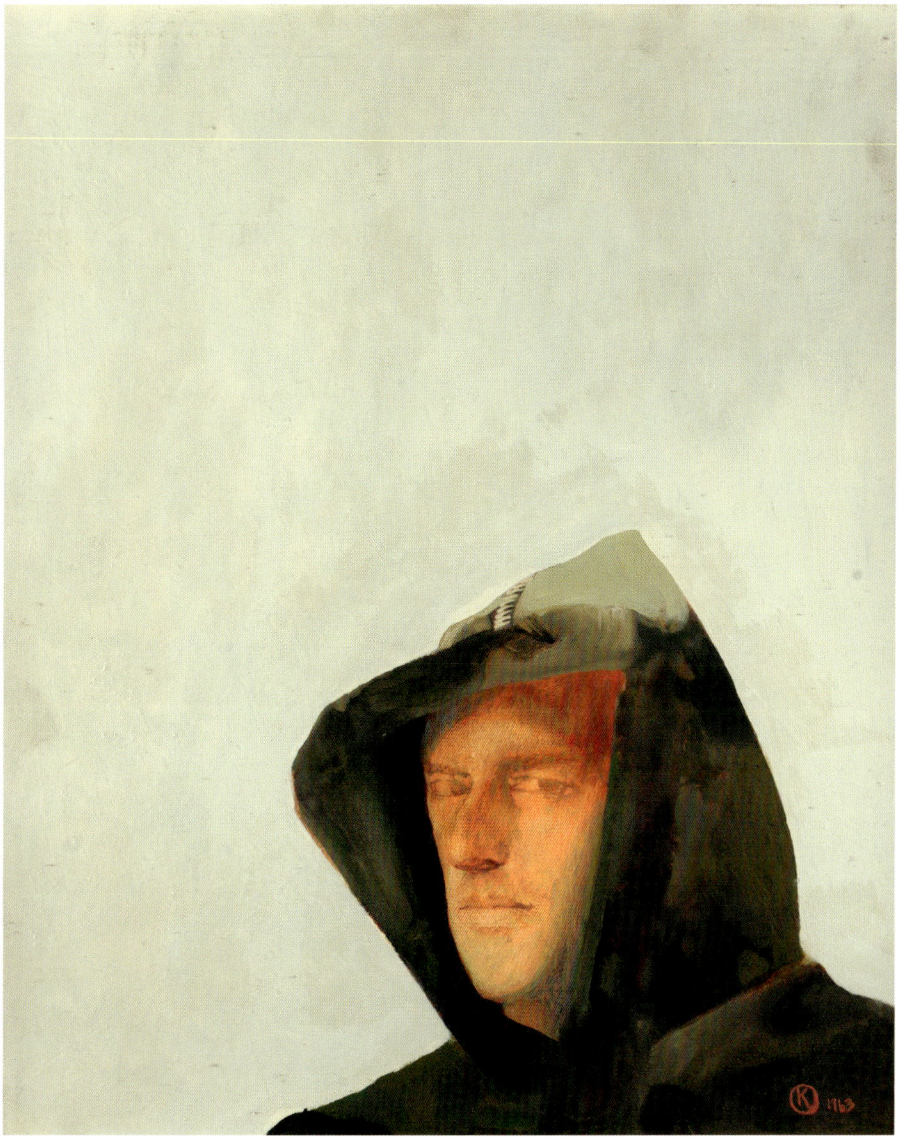

Jules Kirschenbaum, *Self-Portrait*, 1963. Oil on Masonite, 23¾ × 19⅞ in. (60.3 × 50.5 cm)

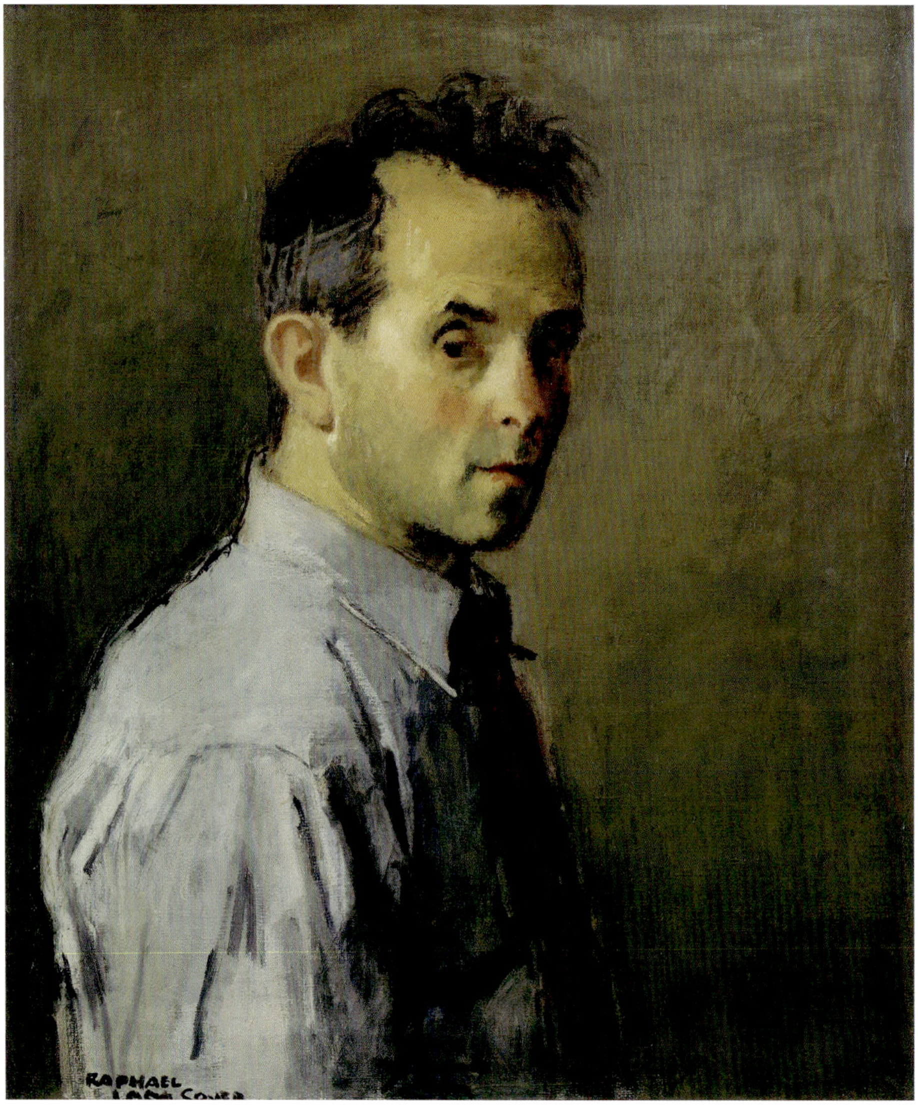

Raphael Soyer, *Self-Portrait*, 1950. Oil on canvas, 24 ½ × 20 ⅛ in. (62.2 × 51.1 cm)

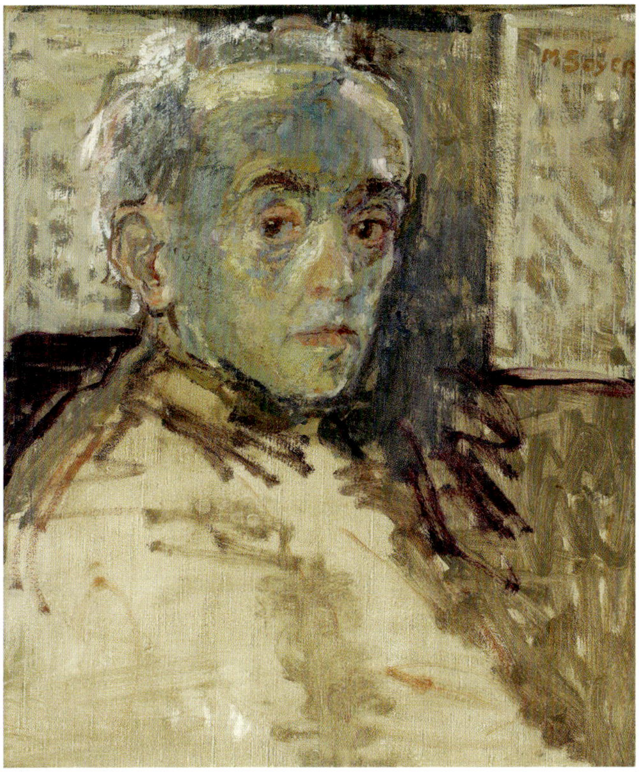

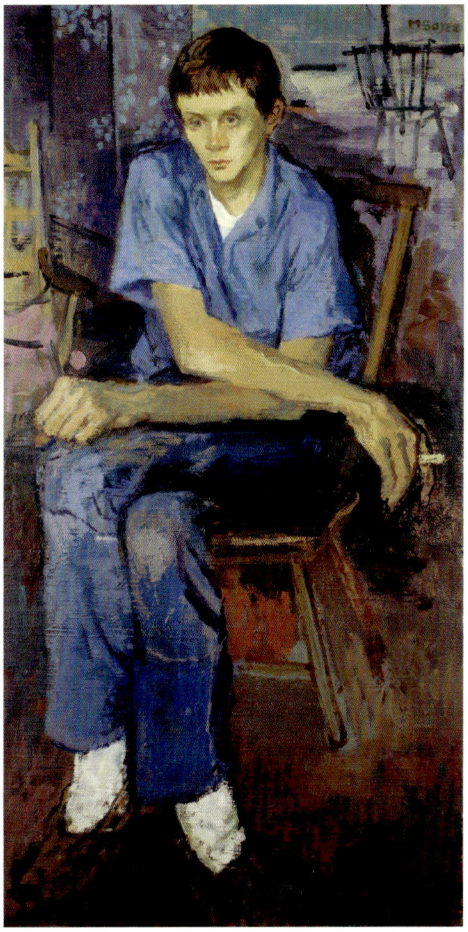

Left: Moses Soyer, *Self-Portrait*, n.d. Oil on canvas, 24 × 20 in. (61 × 50.8 cm)
Right: Moses Soyer, *Felix* [Nussbaum], ca. 1930. Oil on canvas, 40 × 20 in. (101.6 × 50.8 cm)

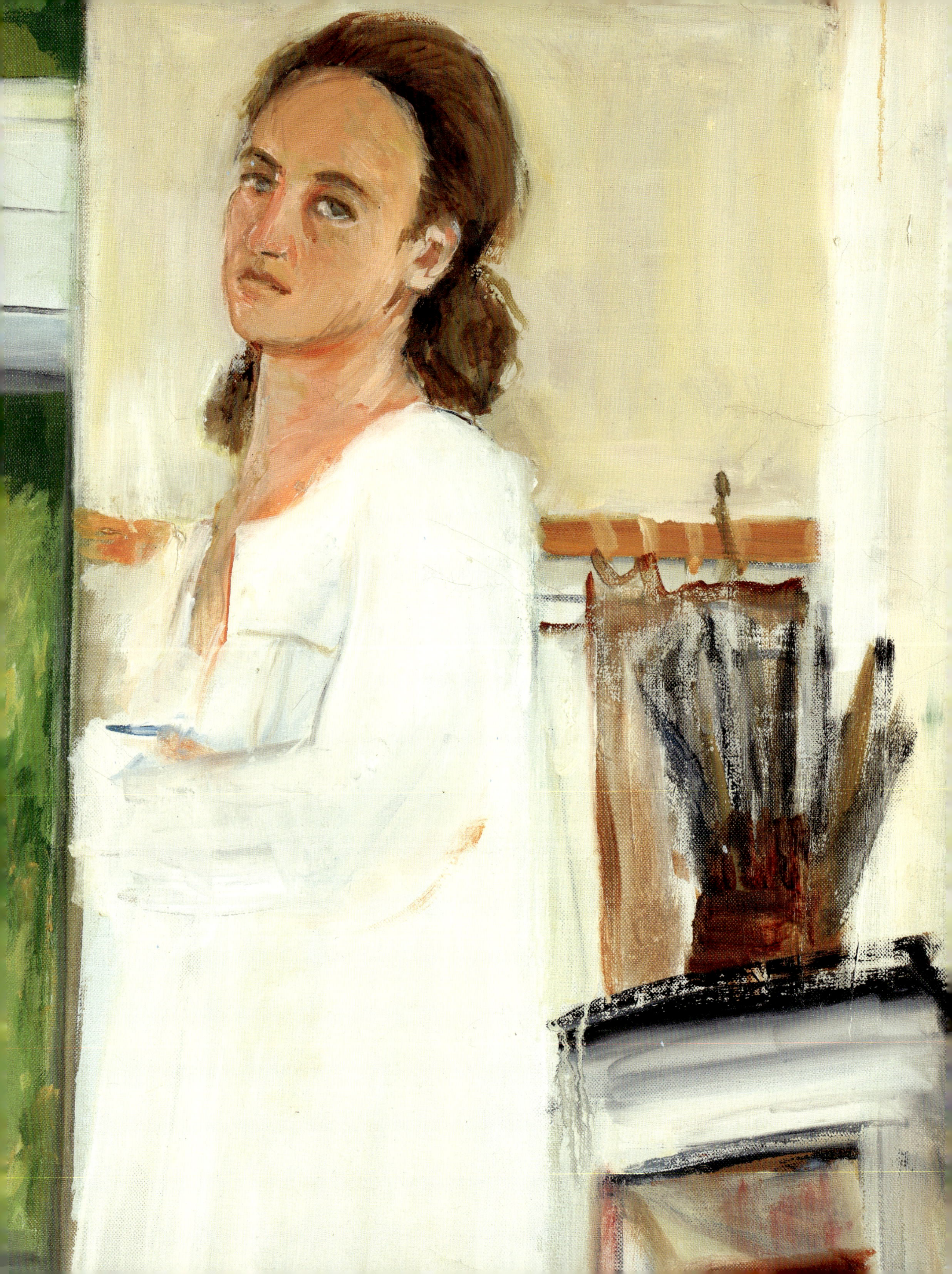

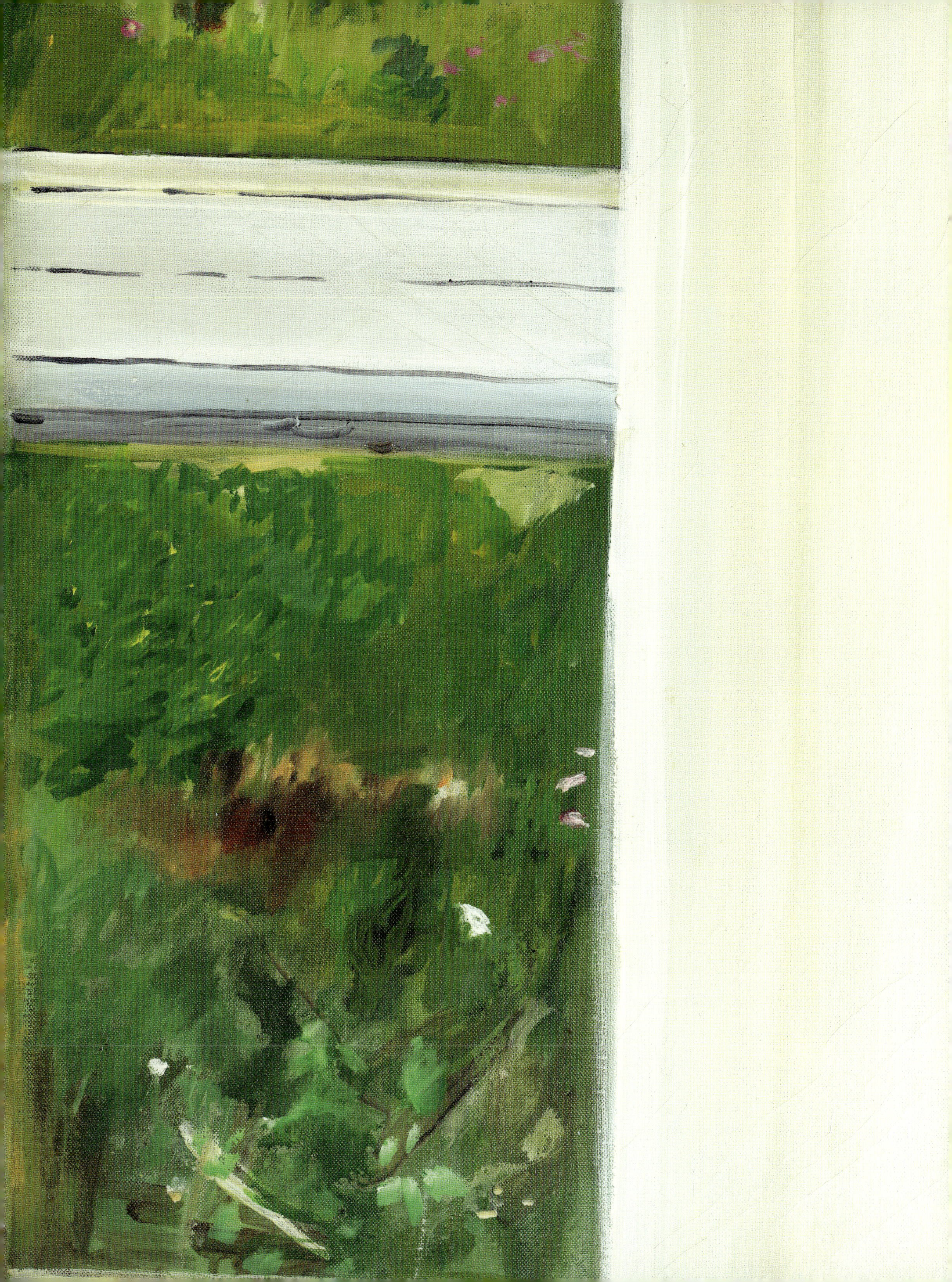

SELF-PORTRAITURE IN A TIME OF OUTRAGE: JANE FREILICHER

ALEXANDER NEMEROV

Does a self-portrait really even show a self at all? Consider the case of Jane Freilicher's *Self-Portrait in a Mirror* (p. 197), which the artist submitted to the National Academy of Design upon her election as an Associate in 1980.

The painting shows the artist's reflection in a rectangular mirror propped on a blue chair in her studio at Water Mill, Long Island, in New York's Hamptons. Although both her hands disappear at the left edge of the mirror, we understand that Freilicher—clad in a loose-fitting white dress or smock, her thick hair tied back and swept over her shoulder—is standing at an easel and painting a picture, an act portrayed in her reflection. A pot of paintbrushes sits on the table at her side, the brushes rising up like the steeply climbing table itself, its underside visible. Expanses of green meadow appear outside the cruciform window frame against which the mirror leans. A curtain hangs at the right.

What is unfolding here? Freilicher was a painter of "what there is there," as her friend the poet John Ashbery observed.[1] She did not freight her pictures with weighty existential statements preordained for the purpose. She liked to paint ideas even less than she liked to paint realistic pictures—that is, paintings that look just like what they show. She sought instead to take the humble givens of a situation—the patterns of light and objects in a room, for example—and slowly discover their hidden rhymes and implicit questions. Wresting structure from unpromising everyday things, Freilicher aimed to make "a stable ensemble [out] of a stubbornly flaccid jungle of original details," in the approving words of the critic Peter Schjeldahl, writing in 1971, the year *Self-Portrait in a Mirror* was painted.[2] That same decade, Ashbery noted Freilicher's wish "to reinstate that higher naturalness

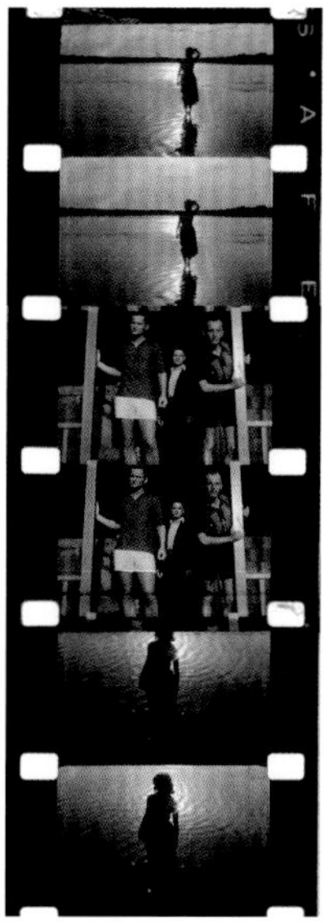

Fig. 1. Frames from *Presenting Jane*, 1953

which can only become visible with a little artifice."[3] Art makes life, revealing the "there" that is there. How does this approach concern the reflection in the mirror?

The reflection is not exactly synonymous with Freilicher herself. The artist presumably stood on the studio floor, whereas the legless reflection floats on the chair. As flat as the mirror, the reflection leagues with the window frame and the curtain, and even with the field behind it, more than it does with the artist, whose "actual" presence we never see. All told, the reflection stares back at the painter as a subtly different being—related to the artist, indeed indebted to her for its very existence—and yet, somehow, *not* her. What would it mean to call that being Freilicher's "muse?"

Back in 1952, when she was twenty-eight years old, Freilicher made a short film with her friends Ashbery, Frank O'Hara, and James Schuyler. All were brilliant poets in the making, and all were about Freilicher's age (she was born in 1924, Ashbery in 1927, O'Hara in 1926, and Schuyler in 1923). The closeness of the four was remarkable in those years—their "badinage" at parties was so arcane and superior, recalled O'Hara's long-time roommate, Joe Lesueur, that he felt excluded by their "campy, dry, superior wit," the banter that made them seem like "a high school clique . . . the smartest kids in school, which I'm sure they all once were." At the center was Freilicher, with her "subdued, astringent personality" that kept the camp from "becoming insufferably precious."[4] She was definitely the muse, as the film—called *Presenting Jane*—makes clear.

In the film, Jane walks on water (fig. 1). Weightless, she stands in great curvy beauty and walks slowly forward, gesturing languidly, graciously, the sun shaping her silhouette as the three young gay men look on, awestruck. Filmed in the Hamptons and only recently rediscovered by Ashbery's

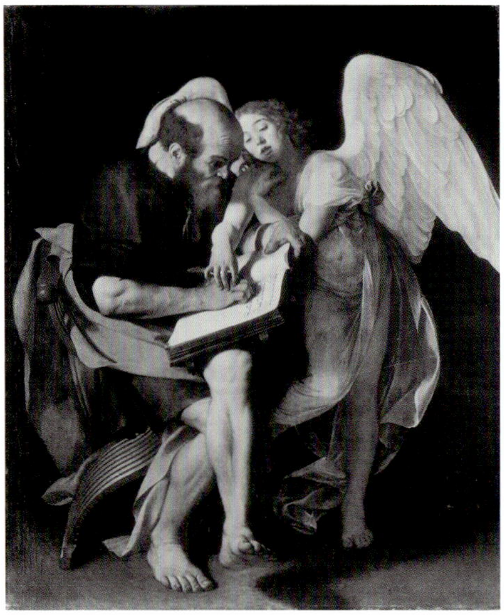

Fig. 2. Caravaggio, *Saint Matthew and the Angel*, 1602. Oil on canvas (destroyed)

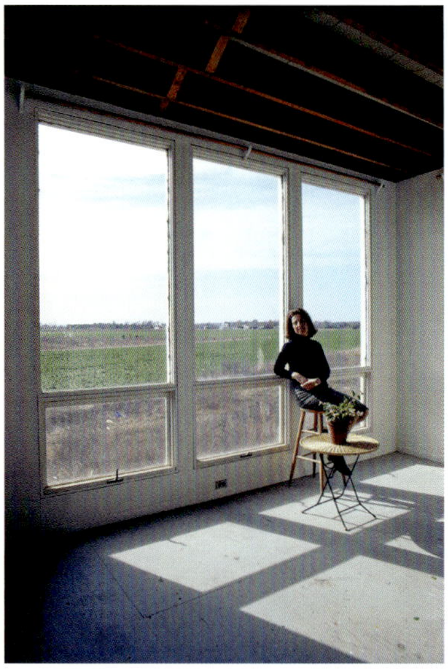

Fig. 3. Jane Freilicher in her studio in Water Mill, Long Island, ca. 1970

biographer, Karen Roffman, *Presenting Jane* portrays Freilicher as an otherworldly being, a visionary priestess, whom her disciples help ashore.[5]

Years passed. Freilicher married the artist and businessman Joseph Hazan in 1957, and the couple built their house at Water Mill in 1960. The "Freilicher Mystique," as Lesueur called it, gradually declined, for O'Hara at least, who complained to Lesueur that the married Freilicher "cares more about her new refrigerator than she does about her painting."[6] But back in 1952, she had floated, walking on water (thanks to a plank submerged two inches beneath the surface by the film's director, Harrison Starr). And she was still floating in 1971, to judge by *Self-Portrait in a Mirror*, only now just for herself.

What does it mean to be a solitary muse? The person in the mirror is not the artist herself but —in a subtle and important difference—the figure who appears to the artist as she paints. Contrast this solitude with images of a muse who assists someone else, as in Caravaggio's portrayal of the angel guiding Saint Matthew's hand as the evangelist writes his Gospel (fig. 2). Freilicher's reflection is akin to that angel, except smooth of surface, unruffled and without wings, and not nearly so insinuating or overfamiliar, not like that flirty Roman angel who dips into the bald man's book to guide the shaping of individual letters. Instead, against her backdrop of Long Island meadow, Freilicher's muse looks on from a distance, plaintively, attentively, at the person whose art she makes possible. The mirror, set atop the chair, becomes the prop for this presiding genius who attends on creative acts. It is all so different from the Freilicher we see in a photograph taken in that same studio around 1970 (fig. 3)—a photograph that shows how large the windows actually were and that gives us, conventionally, the artist posing as herself. By contrast, in the painting, we see not Freilicher herself but the being who attends as she paints. Only Freilicher inspires herself. Gone are the youthful days when she fretted neurotically to her poet friends about her sources, her debt to dead painters, the styles the dead men demanded of her. By 1971, those lessons have been internalized, not lost and not drowned but suspended in the form of her own muse, her own self that—in appearing to her—cancels out the person she otherwise was. The spirit of oneself travels from afar; it walks on water.

In another painting in the Academy's collection, Wyatt Eaton's *The Artist in His Studio* (p. 195), we see a version of the gender politics of inspiration that Freilicher transcended. It shows an artist, possibly Eaton himself, staring Pygmalion-like at a painting of a beautiful, white-clad young woman. Having created her, the dark-clad artist is now wistful, pensive, a little dejected. His legs awkwardly crossed, his hands tense, he stares across a distance at a figure hopelessly remote—a figure whose own pensive stare registers that reticence, that withdrawal. The muse floats on, caught in her separate world, tantalizing the brooding painter into nervous and restive contortions. Falling in love with this passive being, suffering her virginal defiance as the white music of his bachelor pad, he accepts that frustration, desire, and longing are the artist's lot—all objectified in that wraith of remoteness he calls his muse. In the melodrama of himself, he imagines that he must quaff this teetotaling elixir and be poisoned by its purity if he and his art are to be called to higher things. Freilicher's painting, by contrast, empties the studio of the man and allows the muse to appear without flux or volatility, passionless. It is just the artist alone with this being who has floated in from the fields, an angel in the guise of herself who attends curiously on the act of creation.

Not that Freilicher was exactly a feminist. In January 1971, the cover of *ARTnews* featured a detail of the Metropolitan Museum of Art's *Marie Joséphine Charlotte du Val d'Ognes*, a portrait then attributed to Constance Marie Charpentier, a student of Jacques Louis David's (figs. 4, 5). The painting was an apt choice for the cover of a special issue devoted to "Women's Liberation, Women Artists and Art History" featuring Linda Nochlin's legendary article "Why Have There Been No Great Women Artists?" Nochlin, born in 1931 and, like Freilicher, a native of Brooklyn, saw things differently than the artist did. Focusing on large-scale institutional and social ideologies that informed the very questions a person could ask, let alone the social relations those questions might address, Nochlin saw the idea of greatness as itself misleading. Accounts of creative genius, she argued, stress the "apparently miraculous, non-determined and a-social nature of artistic achievement." Noting that "this semi-religious conception of the artist's role [had been] elevated to hagiography in the 19th century," she pointed out the ways artists and critics elevated art into a "substitute religion, the last bulwark of Higher Values in a materialistic world." It was a good thing, Nochlin observed, that "now no serious contemporary art historian takes such obvious fairy tales at their face value."[7]

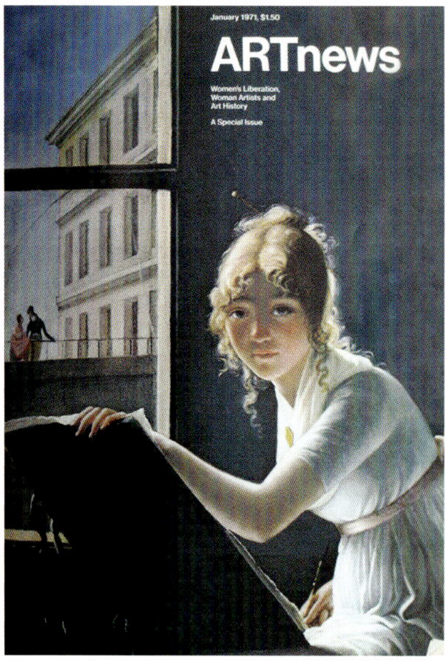

Fig. 4. Cover of *ARTnews*, January 1971

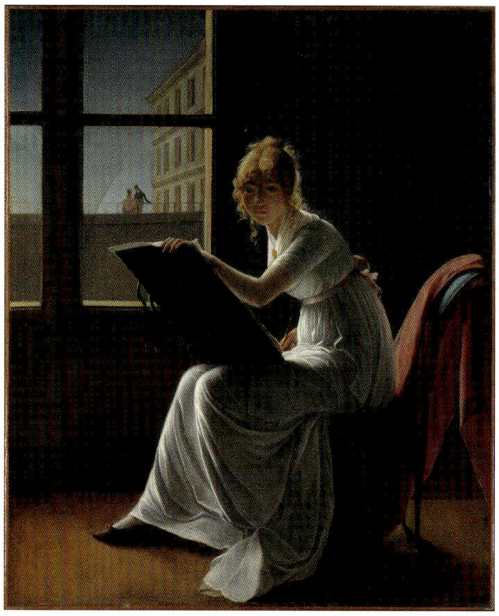

Fig. 5. Marie Denise Villers, *Marie Joséphine Charlotte du Val d'Ognes*, 1801. Oil on canvas. Metropolitan Museum of Art, New York

Freilicher did take such fairy tales at face value, albeit in a specific way. She saw her solitude as a portrait of the mystery of the world, of the fact that its meadows and bays and flowers were themselves comparable solitudes in search of a person who, sensing their own mad mixture of banality and mystery, might give them the artistic form they could not portray for themselves. Ashbery described Freilicher's wish to inject "not her own note but that of things," her aim to show "each element's poignant desire to make its own point, to put itself across, to be accepted on its own terms, to restore the primitive calm that the world presumably had before anyone had looked at it."[8] Such a pursuit is a mystical vocation. It does not admit of social constructions and determinations. It is a kind of calling, and although it can always be called a dream or a delusion, it is a powerfully enabling fantasy whose effects include, not least, the production of an autonomous relation to the world and one's own mind. "I've always had faith in this kind of artistic moment or whatever it is," Freilicher told an interviewer in 1987, describing such a moment as "some little experience which is not really connected in any way to any greater meaning or movement."[9]

In such artistic moments, a person's genius appears. That genius comes from nowhere but is at home in ordinary surroundings. It is among the phenomena of the world, like a potted plant or a kitchen table, a gardenia or a clock tower. It is part of "what there is there." Otherworldliness is among the givens of time and space; it appears like other things, as part of the material world from which it floats free. Whereas Nochlin approved of Gustave Courbet's statement "I have never seen an angel; show me an angel, and I'll paint one," Freilicher, herself an admirer of Courbet, again felt differently. For her, genius or soul or muse *does* appear. It does so, however, not as freedom incarnate,

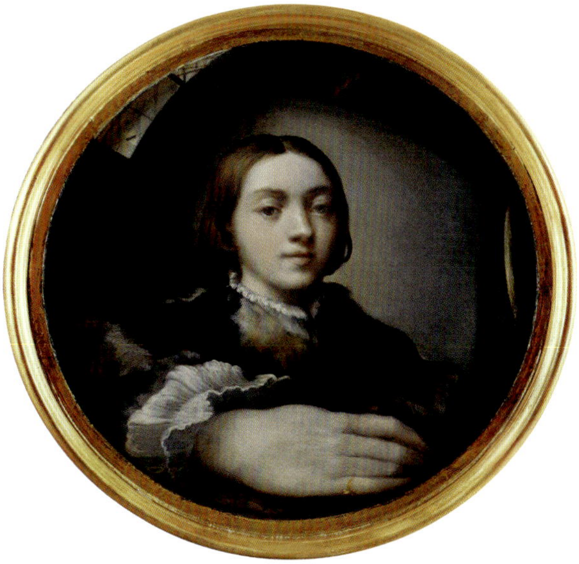

Fig. 6. Parmigianino, *Self-Portrait in a Convex Mirror*, ca. 1524. Oil on wood panel. Kunsthistorisches Museum, Vienna

not as Lord-swept wings thrumming among the seraphim and cherubim, but in drastic localities and denominations. These the artist accepts, sadly but gratefully, as proof of her higher life, her consciousness sucked out into the stars, even if the heavens have now flown down, unexalted, manifesting only as the homely realizations of one's creative existence. Ashbery put this well in his most famous poem, "Self-Portrait in a Convex Mirror" (1974), a meditation on Parmigianino's famous painting (fig. 6):

> The soul has to stay where it is,
> Even though restless, hearing raindrops at the pane,
> The sighing of autumn leaves thrashed by the wind,
> Longing to be free, outside, but it must stay
> Posing in this place. It must move
> As little as possible. This is what the portrait says.

Ashbery acknowledged that

> The secret is too plain. The pity of it smarts,
> Makes hot tears spurt: that the soul is not a soul,
> Has no secret, is small, and it fits
> Its hollow perfectly: its room, our moments of attention.[10]

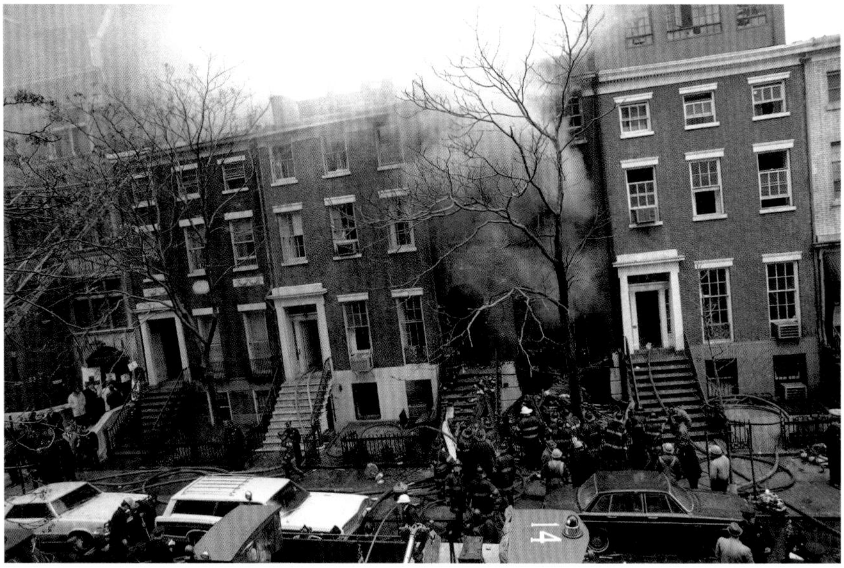

Fig. 7. View of West 11th Street, New York City, March 6, 1970

Freilicher, who recognized the affinity between her vision and Ashbery's, likewise fit her soul into her room. Mirror-bound, perched on a chair, the genius of the white summer smock accepts her limitations. Unlike the young woman in the Metropolitan's painting, now attributed to Marie Denise Villers (another of David's students), her creative body does not glow in folds of moonlight, mused and amused in channels of cosmic simplicity. Freilicher's creativity comes precisely from *somewhere*, a given situation, a random arrangement that happens to be hers. But emerging there, stuck in place, the Madonna of the mirror asserts its metaphysical freedom. That freedom is not a woman's liberation. "I was very aware of it," Freilicher recalled in 1987 of the feminist movement, "and obviously it's something to think about, [but] I don't think it affected my work really."[11] Instead, hers is a more private form of independence.

That independence is even more notable if we consider another aspect of *Self-Portrait in a Mirror*. On March 6, 1970, about a year and a half before Freilicher painted the picture, a bomb exploded in the Greenwich Village town house next to the one she and Hazan owned (fig. 7). The bomb went off around noon in the basement of the house at 18 West 11th Street as two members of the radical group the Weather Underground were assembling it, killing the two of them (Diana Oughton and Terry Robbins) and a third Weatherman, Theodore Gold, who was crushed by debris upstairs when the house collapsed. The bomb, destined for a dance in the officers' club at Fort Dix, New Jersey, that night, was made of dynamite and nails inserted into a one-foot length of water pipe. Neither Oughton nor Robbins had any experience with explosives; the bomb blew up in their hands. Police later found fifty-seven sticks of dynamite on the premises, along with a 37mm antitank shell dating from World War I. The owner of the house was a vacationing former Young and Rubicam vice president whose daughter, Cathlyn Wilkerson, also a member of the Weather Underground, survived the blast (she was on an upper floor at the time).

The home of Freilicher and Hazan at 16 West 11th Street was severely damaged. "A hole was blown in the basement wall, and part of the ceiling on the top floor collapsed," according to a *New York Times* article published the next day. Erroneously attributing ownership of the town house to the actor Dustin Hoffman (actually Freilicher and Hazan's tenant), the article featured a photograph of Hoffman walking stunned on the street outside and noted that the actor was seen carrying several paintings and a Tiffany lampshade "before the police prevented him from re-entering the building."[12]

Whether or not Freilicher and Hazan themselves were present in the house is unclear—an extensive oral history with Freilicher conducted in 1987 makes no mention of the explosion—but one can guess at her attitude toward the young terrorists.[13] A longtime reader of *Commentary* and the *Partisan Review*, Freilicher would likely have agreed with the influential critic Irving Howe (a mainstay of those Leftist publications), who castigated the "New Left" terrorists in a *Times* op-ed published several weeks after the blast. "Deciding whom to smite, [the terrorist] replaces God," Howe wrote. "Choosing whom to punish, he replaces the justice (be it good or bad) of society. And since the conflicts of social classes must be bent to his will, he replaces history, too." Acknowledging that social problems in the United States were dire—"There is plenty of reason for dismay and disgust at the state of American society"—Howe insisted that "it does not follow that if you feel the country to be in a desperate condition you should necessarily start throwing bombs."[14]

Like Howe, Freilicher grew up in a working-class, Leftist household, and she may well have agreed when the critic noted that "a large percentage of the New Left young are children of the middle class and rich."[15] Whereas Freilicher came from Flatbush, a section of Brooklyn well known, according to the painter, as a "hotbed for Communism, Stalinism," the terrorists seemed to have less real-world experience of social inequality.[16] On the contrary, felt Howe, they were inexperienced and idealistic, leading them "to the delirium of terrorist fantasy."

Freilicher understood that delirium from early on. One of her two older brothers was a "wild Trotskyite," exposing her "to all the venality of the Stalinist machinations as a child." Even back then, she recalled, "I was very contemptuous of Stalin. About 25 years later, it [the contempt] began to be the accepted wisdom."[17] In 1970, her town house damaged by a modern-day act of political radicalism, Freilicher may have been as dismayed as James Merrill, the poet who grew up at 18 West 11th Street back in the 1930s, when it was the home of his father, Charles Merrill, a cofounder of Merrill Lynch. Although Flatbush and Merrill Lynch were two different worlds, Freilicher may have nodded when Merrill, apostrophizing the terrorists, asked them in a poem published in 1972: "The point / Was anger, brother? Love? Dear premises / Vainly exploded, vainly dwelt upon."[18]

Even so, Freilicher's *Self-Portrait in a Mirror*, painted the year after the explosion, ventures none of these questions. As vainly as the terrorists promoted their causes, we look for reverberations of the blast. In the muteness of the Water Mill studio, there is not even a discernible "after-quiet," to use Herman Melville's term for the silence of postbellum Civil War battlefields.[19] All we see in the muse's face is the same sad gaze she may always have worn. At most, the gaze may just perceptibly register the chaos. As Freilicher said in 1987, "As you sort of look around the world which seems more and more crazy, chaotic and terrible things happening, you find somehow that there is some cry you want to make." But you cannot, because

> Social realism is a kind of parody of that feeling. It doesn't really express the enormousness of the pain that everybody feels. . . . There is so much that one is faced with nowadays; a sort of violence or general madness it seems to me. That while it may have existed, in a sense 35 years ago, it somehow seems more of an issue now. Things are flying apart even more now.[20]

Disasters reckon with us, throw all into tumult, but some calm angel emerges unscathed from the clamor and smoke. In *Self-Portrait in a Mirror*, Freilicher's alter ego is momentary but enduring. No specific crisis—even the walls of one's home crashing down—affects the impersonal attendance of this imaginary entity. Summoned by the act of painting, the figure appears as if by magic in the mirror, the likeness of a being whose calm is not only the soul of the moment but a fiction of creative forces that cannot be touched. Deep in the steady face is the likeness of Raphael's Madonnas, denizens of the Renaissance paintings Freilicher so admired (fig. 8). Her muse shares their tilt of the head, their soft and sad expression. No blast shatters her glass.

There is a difference, however. Freilicher's Madonna is Our Lady of Not Knowing. She is adrift in a world where the verities have been lost, as the painter well understood. "The artist is a free agent but without any fixed position," she wrote in notes for an undated lecture. The artist is even "a social parasite except in his own eyes, [those of] his fellow artists and those who still retain the idea that life without art would be less than human." This aloneness is a historical condition: "The increasing secularization of life cost the artist both the economic and philosophic protection of the church—the patronage of the great royal houses withered away with the growth of democracy."[21] Even the making of a painting portrays this uncertainty, as Freilicher noted in 1987: "Because I create the painting as I go along without having any preconception, at each moment it's like a decision, and it's sort of

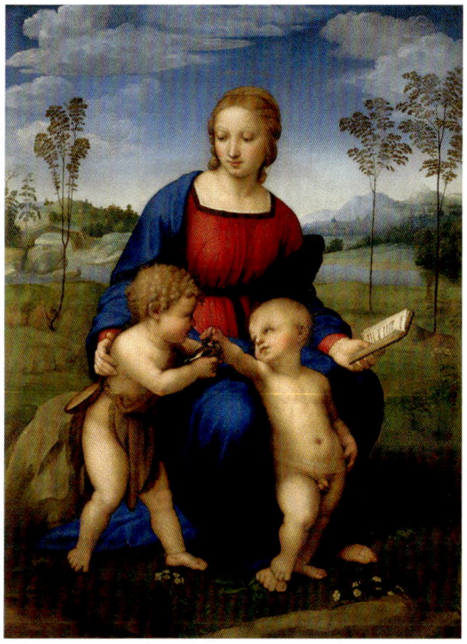

Fig. 8. Raphael, *Madonna of the Goldfinch*, before February 1506. Oil on wood panel. Galleria degli Uffizi, Florence

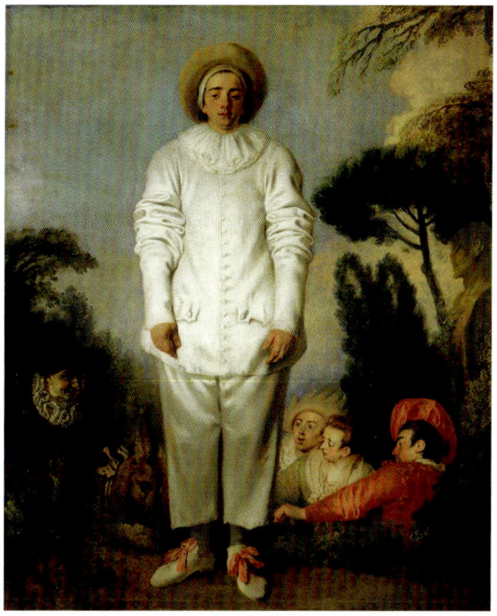

Fig. 9. Jean-Antoine Watteau, *Pierrot*, formerly known as *Gilles*, ca. 1718–19. Oil on canvas. Musée du Louvre, Paris

exhausting, because you're really going on nerve . . . you have nothing to guide you." The artist floats, unmoored, an emissary from another time, cut adrift from the old musings, the old beliefs, the sureties of church and crown. Shades of Watteau's Pierrot, that modern archetype of sadness and isolation, flicker across the white-clad painter of Water Mill (fig. 9).

In one sense, this freedom of aloneness is pleasurable, as in Ashbery's poem "No Way of Knowing," published in the same volume as "Self-Portrait in a Convex Mirror." There, Ashbery contrasts a poet's and painter's lovely fugues to the scars that knowledge makes on the surface of the world.[22] Facts and mastery make the world operate efficiently, but they also constitute a heartless tide carrying the broken fragments of lived experience along with it. The artist and poet, by contrast, wonder if there could be one moment, one place—a lover's embrace—that would afford a greater knowledge than all the knowledge that is cheap, rampant, and demeaning. Ashbery hoped so: "Surely that would solve everything."

But he admitted that the muse offered no such consolation. Instead, it glided into the study and the studio as only the perfection of a question, not the delivery of an answer. One's genius proved to be, at last, the royal waif, the lovely Other, whose news is that there is no news, not even from the strange world whence she comes. Freilicher may have sensed the same thing. Perceiving her ally in *Self-Portrait in a Mirror*, maybe she saw nothing but "no way of knowing."

What does "no way of knowing" tell us? It rhymes reason and randomness so that every sight is never quite itself. In it, the "real" world is transformed, shuddered into deflections and gains, enriched by the mind but always so that the mind withdraws, content with the scene it has made and, in so making, has lost its claim upon. Nothing ever quite becomes a brushstroke or a field. Likewise, the grasses of the meadow look sufficiently like and unlike the sprig of paintbrushes in a jar to both make and dissolve the analogies between them. The underside of the table is the belly of a nude. The mind, allowed to roam, creates what it will, trading its capacities of invention for the recognition that nothing it creates can ever be known.

That is why the goddess of not-knowing presides over her empty field, amorous without embrace, adrift in her mirror. Against the facts, she holds out, taking a lonely place. "Usually, now that I think about it, she wore a look of disappointment, as if nothing in the world ever pleased her," recalled Lesueur of Freilicher. Why was that? Maybe it was because the world—having been scrutinized as something without order, without structure, without any inevitability except that which the artist could bestow upon it—returned the favor upon the person who saw it so. Resenting having been recognized for its randomness, the world gazed back at the artist who so wisely judged it and deemed her, likewise, a being who merely exists, who merely floats. The secret of the wavering branches and the rustling grasses, once looked into, is that there is no secret, not of them, and not of oneself.

1. John Ashbery, "Jane Freilicher at Fischbach" [review], *Art in America*, May–June 1975, in which Ashbery quotes the poet Kenneth Koch.
2. Peter Schjeldahl, "Urban Pastorals," *ARTnews* 69, no. 10 (February 1971): 60.
3. Ashbery, "Freilicher at Fischbach."
4. Joe Lesueur, *Digressions on Some Poems by Frank O'Hara* (New York: Farrar, Straus and Giroux, 2003), 126–27.
5. Karen Roffman, *The Songs We Know Best: John Ashbery's Early Life* (New York: Farrar, Straus and Giroux, 2017), 206–10.
6. Lesueur, *Digressions*, 127–28.
7. Linda Nochlin, "Why Have There Been No Great Women Artists?" *ARTnews* 69, no. 9 (January 1971).
8. Ashbery, "Freilicher at Fischbach."
9. Barbara Shikler, oral history interview with Jane Freilicher, August 4–5, 1987, 41, Jane Freilicher Papers, Archives of American Art, Smithsonian Institution, Washington, DC.
10. John Ashbery, "Self-Portrait in a Convex Mirror," in *Self-Portrait in a Convex Mirror* (New York: Penguin, 1976), 68.
11. Shikler, interview with Freilicher, 73.
12. Douglas Robinson, "Townhouse Razed by Blast and Fire; Man's Body Found," *New York Times*, March 7, 1970.
13. Shikler, interview with Freilicher.
14. Irving Howe, "Political Terrorism: Hysteria on the Left," *New York Times Magazine*, April 12, 1970, 113.
15. Ibid.
16. Shikler, interview with Freilicher, 65.
17. Ibid., 66.
18. James Merrill, "18 West 11th Street," *New York Review of Books*, June 29, 1972.
19. Herman Melville, "An Uninscribed Monument on One of the Battle-Fields of the Wilderness," in *Battle-Pieces, and Aspects of the War* (New York: Harper and Brothers, 1866).
20. Shikler, interview with Freilicher, 59.
21. Jane Freilicher, lecture (MS Am 3029), box 7, Jane Freilicher Additional Papers, Houghton Library, Harvard University; reprinted in Nathan Kernan et al., *Jane Freilicher: '50s New York*, exh. cat. (New York: Paul Kasmin Gallery, 2018), n.p.
22. Ashbery, "No Way of Knowing," in *Self-Portrait in a Convex Mirror*, 54–56.

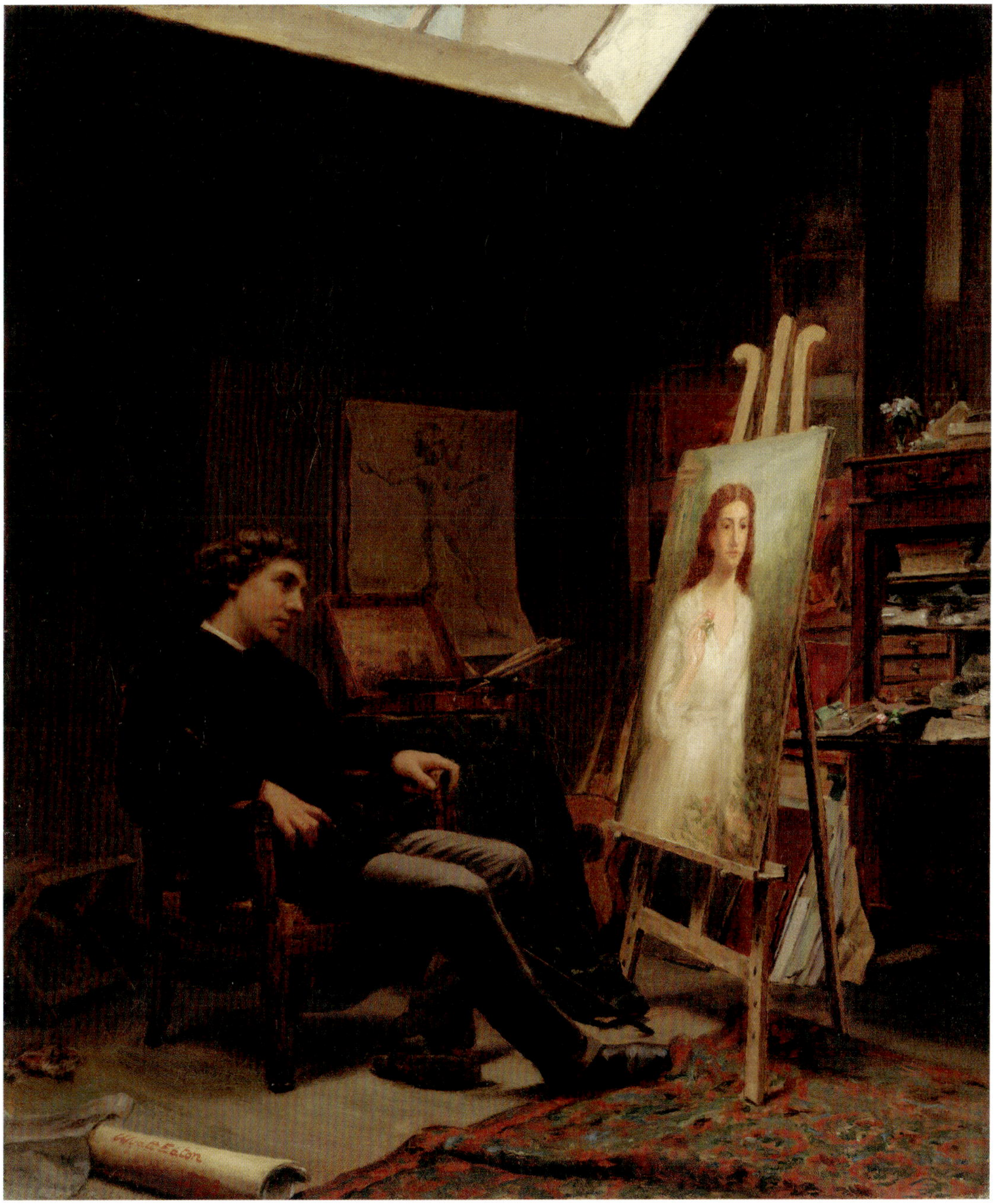

Wyatt Eaton, *The Artist in His Studio*, 1873. Oil on canvas, 24 ⅛ × 19 ¾ in. (61.3 × 50.2 cm)

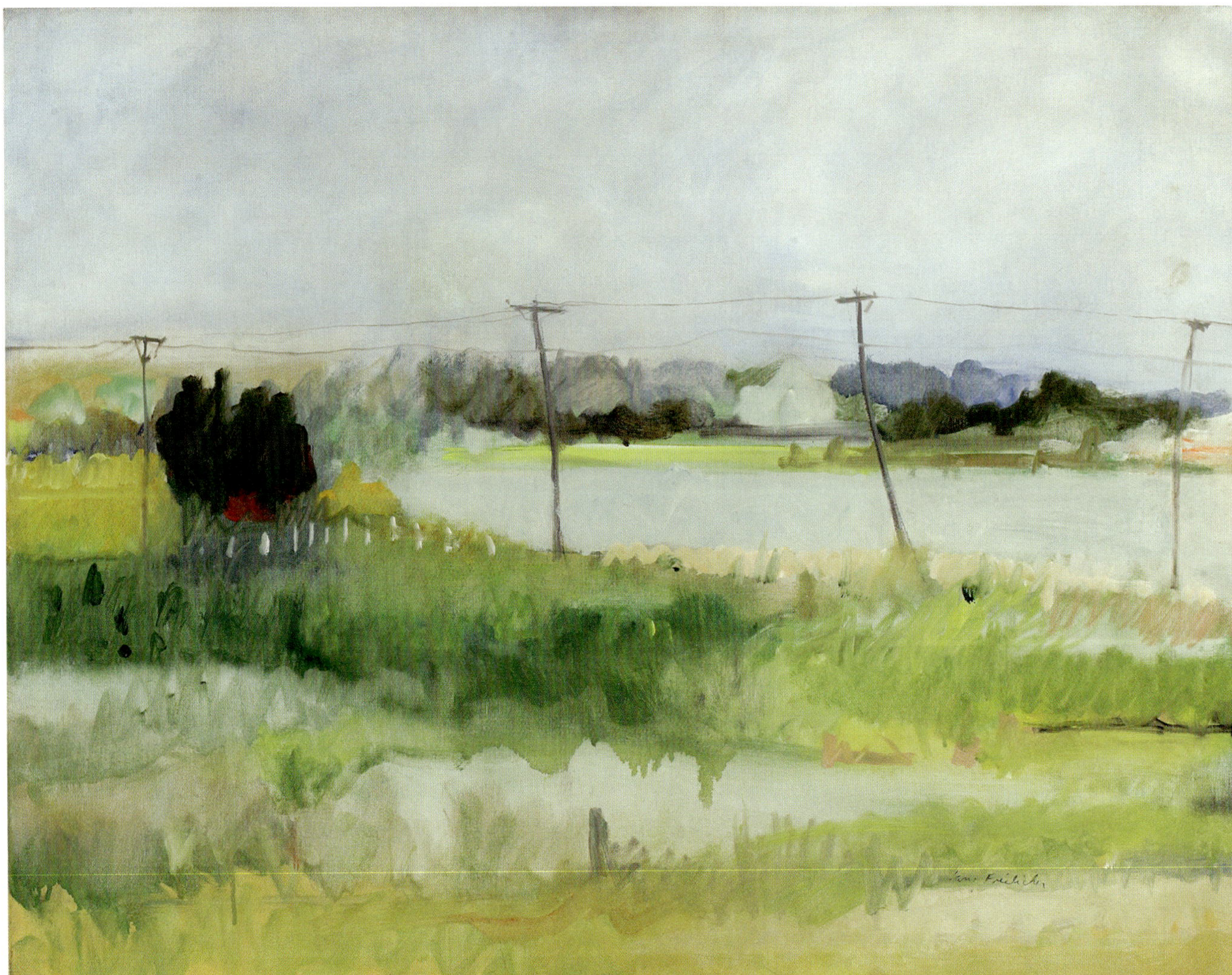

Jane Freilicher, *Telephone Poles*, 1963. Oil on canvas, 32 × 40 ½ in. (81.3 × 102.9 cm)

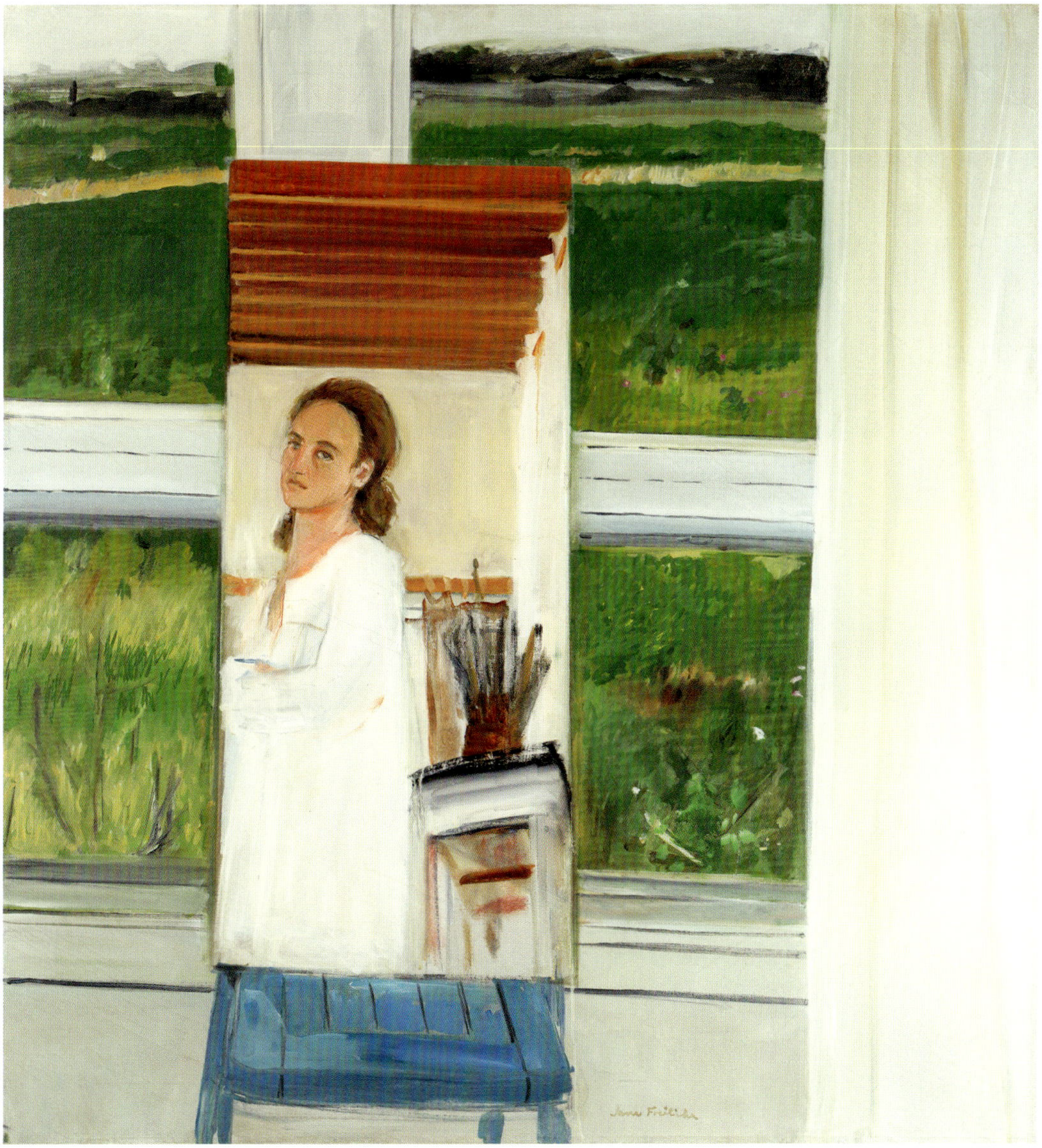

Jane Freilicher, *Self-Portrait in a Mirror*, 1971. Oil on linen, 42 × 38 in. (106.7 × 96.5 cm)

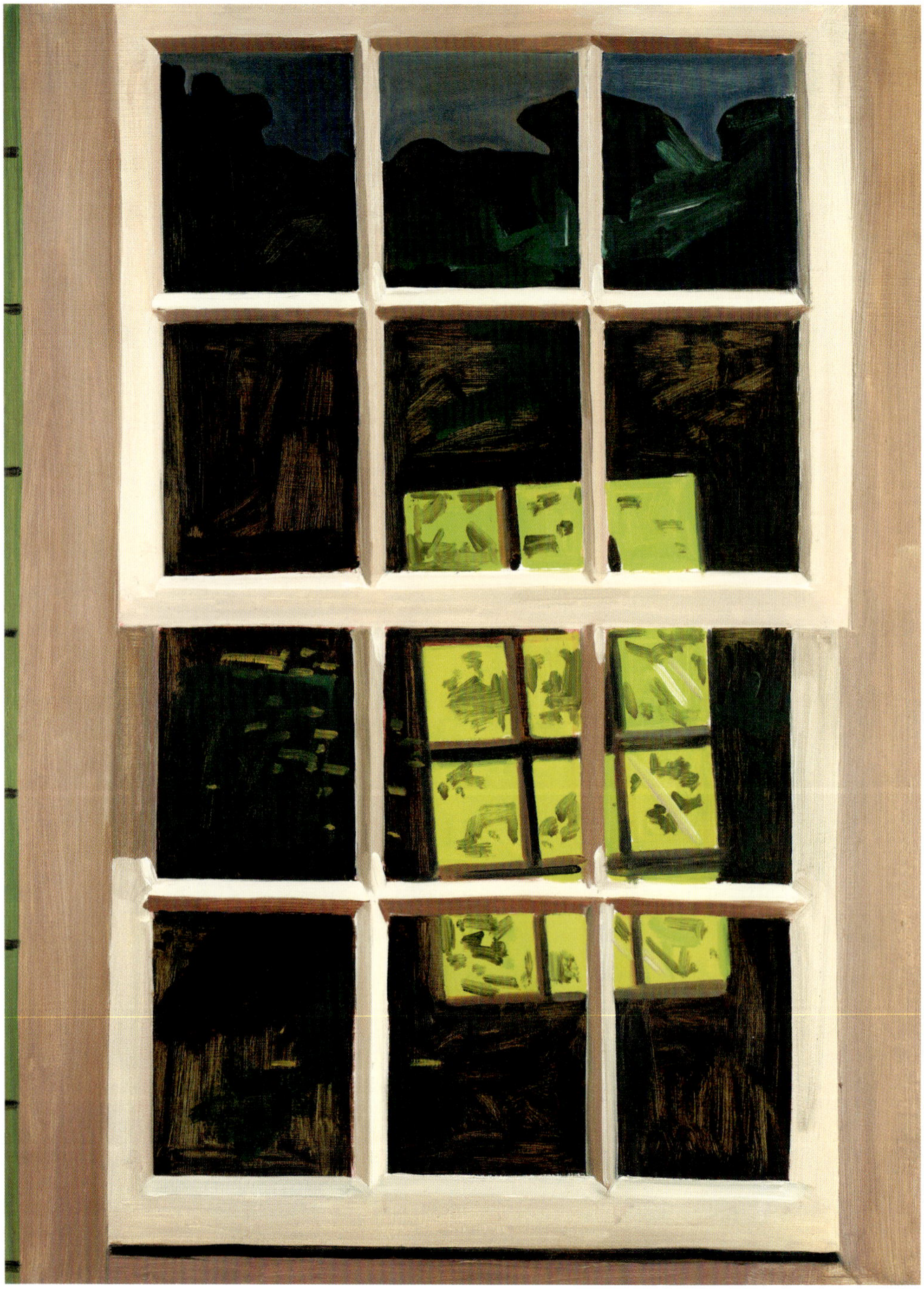

Lois Dodd, *View through Chicken House*, 1971. Oil on Masonite, 28 × 20 in. (71.1 × 50.8 cm)

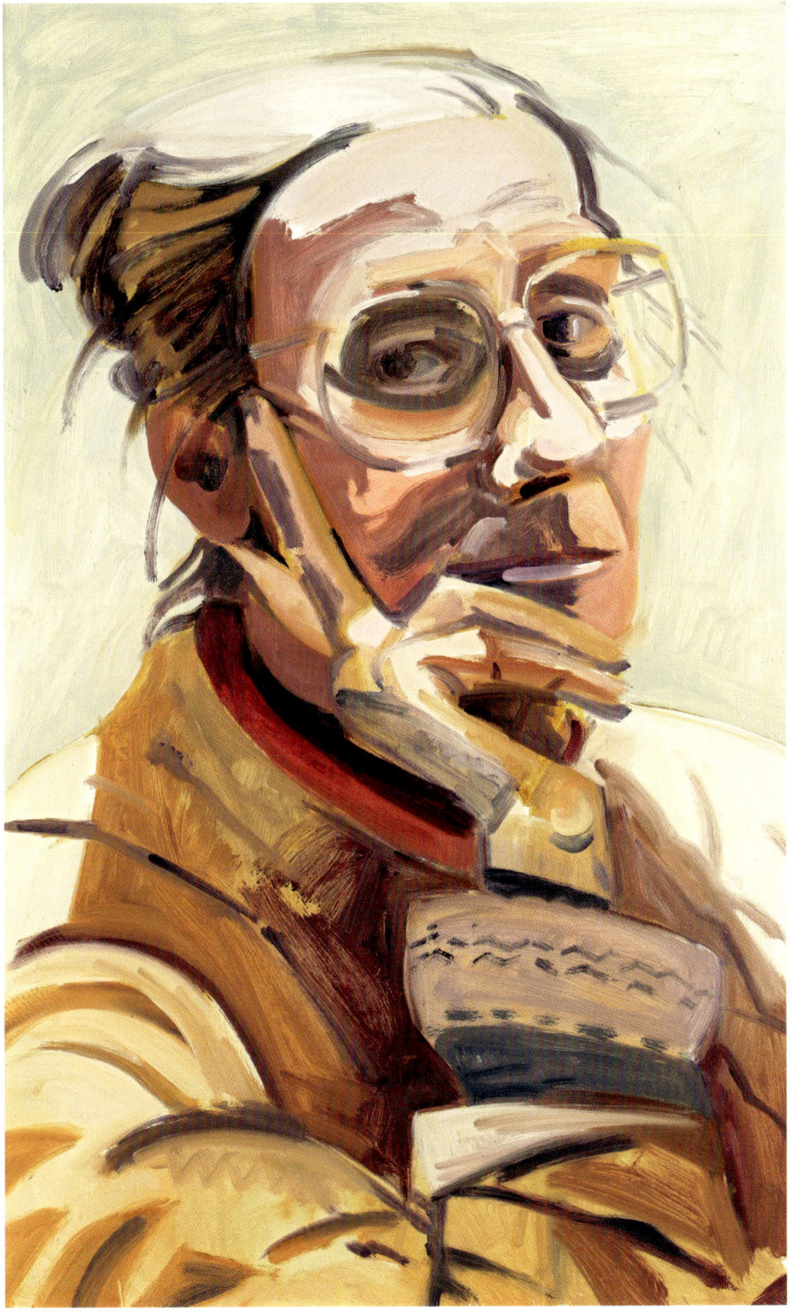

Lois Dodd, *Self-Portrait*, 1984. Oil on composition board, 20 × 12 in. (50.8 × 30.5 cm)

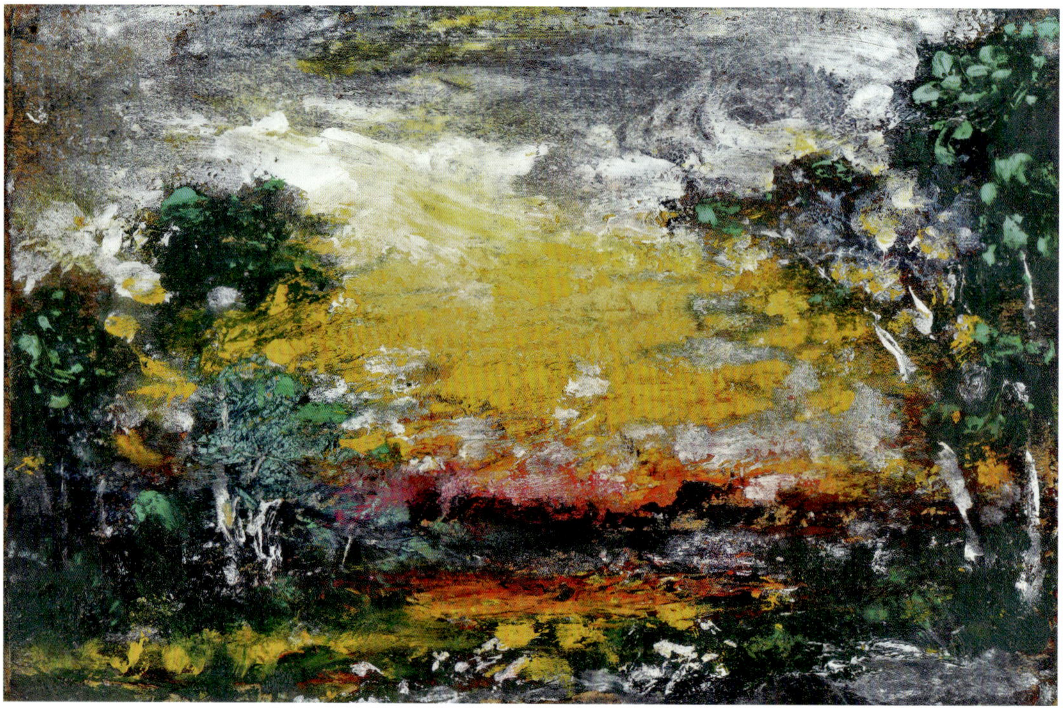

Ralph Albert Blakelock, *Sunset*, 1916. Oil on cardboard, 3 ½ × 5 ½ in. (8.9 × 14 cm)

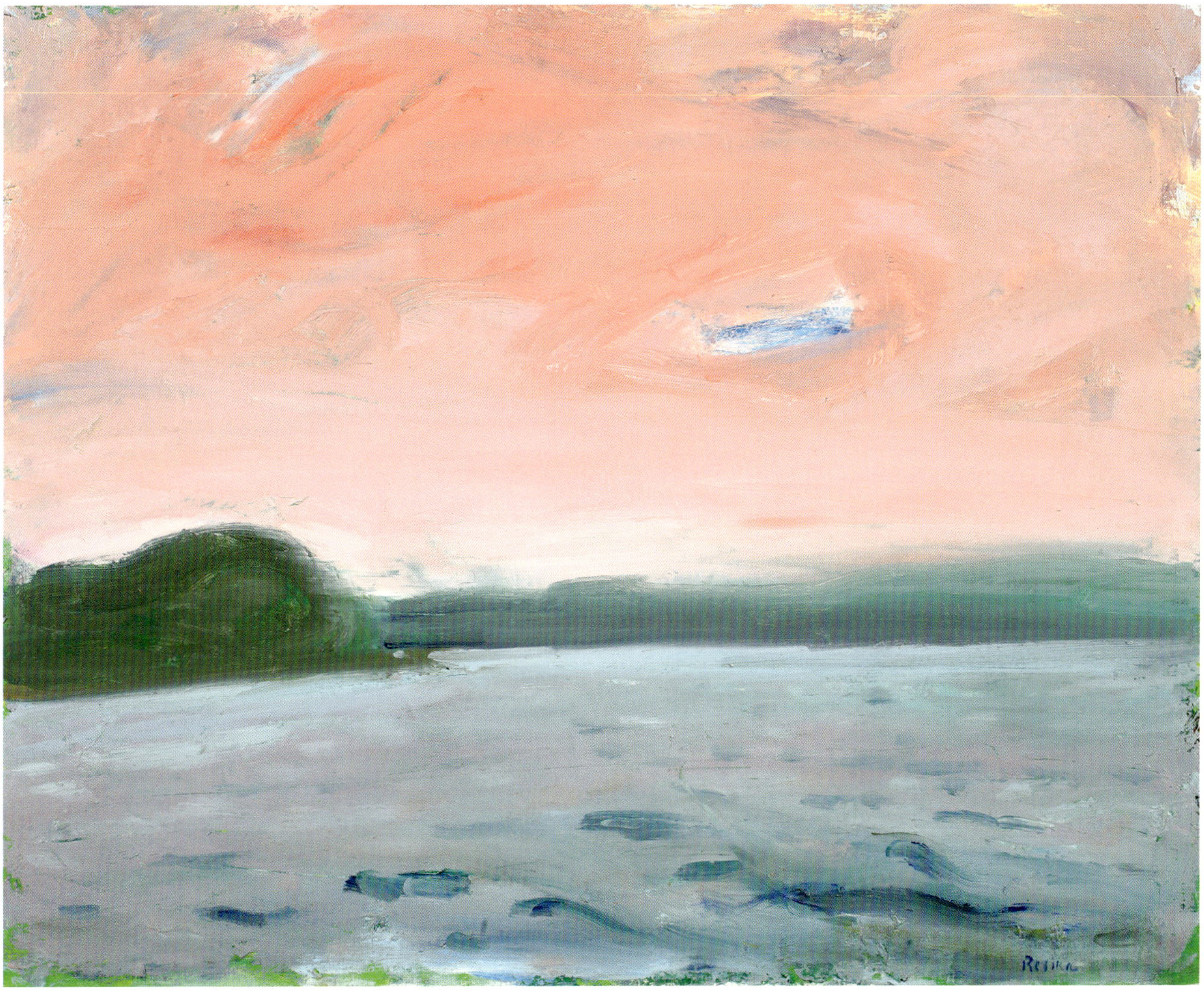

Paul Resika, *The End of the Hurricane*, 1979. Oil on canvas, 24 × 29 in. (61 × 73.7 cm)

BARBARA GROSSMAN ON GRETNA CAMPBELL

Gretna Campbell—a woman who painted, taught masterfully, and raised a family—was a mentor of mine, although she never knew that. I admired her and thought, as a young woman, If she can do it, so can I. Of course, the most impressive part of this is that she was an extraordinary artist.

When we met, I was part of a drawing group that got together once a week. Gretna loved to draw and did so with keen observation, purpose, and feeling. The figure was of interest, but I believe that landscape was the apex of painting for her. She spent as much time as she could outdoors. In the summer, she and her husband, the painter and educator Louis Finkelstein, lived on Cranberry Island, Maine, where her subject was often the land and its relation to the sea. The vast and the intimate.

In the fall, winter, and spring, Gretna worked in the Delaware Water Gap region in New Jersey. Those are the pictures I know best. Gretna prided herself on painting in all seasons and evoked each time of year in the work: the icy blue light of a snow-covered field, or a jumble of weeds and vines in the height of summer. Or the blush of early color that spring whispered to her eyes. She tackled the intensity of fall, which was so difficult but part of the challenge she happily took on.

Garden in Brazil is a bit of an exception, as she painted it while on a trip abroad with her husband. It is still Gretna's voice that is seen and felt in this vibrant and expressive picture. The dynamic between the man-made structures and the natural forms is totally abstract, yet it is a strong and believable cohesiveness. We are enveloped in a complete sense of place. The spaces between the small increments, such as the tree trunks and branches, the wild growth of plants on the ground, are a foil for the expansive space between the sky and the floor plane. There is an overarching understanding of planar space within the seeming fragmentation.

We are viewing this particular place not through a window but through the intraspatial experience of modernist painting. Gretna admired Bonnard, Constable, and, always, Rembrandt. She was trained at Cooper Union, where the emphasis during her years of training was Cubism. De Kooning was a living force, too, which, I believe, gave her certain permissions, such as the exuberant use of paint. The life-affirming energy and passion of the Abstract Expressionism of the 1950s went along with that. This painting is a powerful example of the forces of twentieth-century modernism that Gretna held dear. The colors are driven by the perception of light and nature—they are particular to the situation. They are real within the boundaries of the canvas because they are equivalents of the experience, not imitations.

Gretna's work is complicated. She had her personal sources, which she drew upon at will . . . no single interest overrode another. All the ideas played in her head and in her work, and thus her voice is unique. To prepare for her plein-air days in the winter months, Gretna would bake a couple of potatoes which she then put in her pockets to use as hand warmers. After several hours, when the potatoes began to lose their heat, she ate them for lunch!

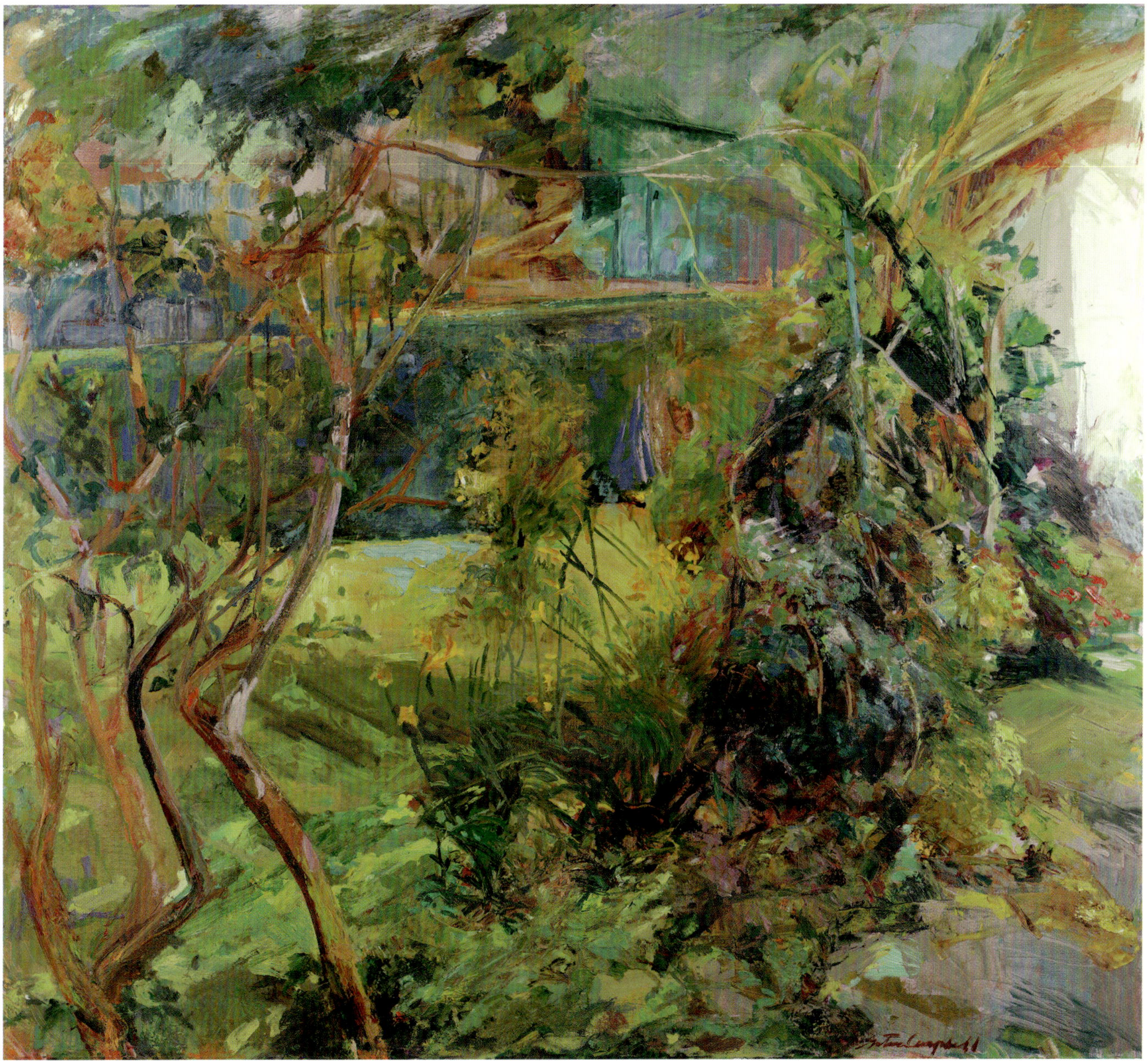

Gretna Campbell, *Garden in Brazil*, 1983. Oil on canvas, 54 × 58 in. (137.2 × 147.3 cm)

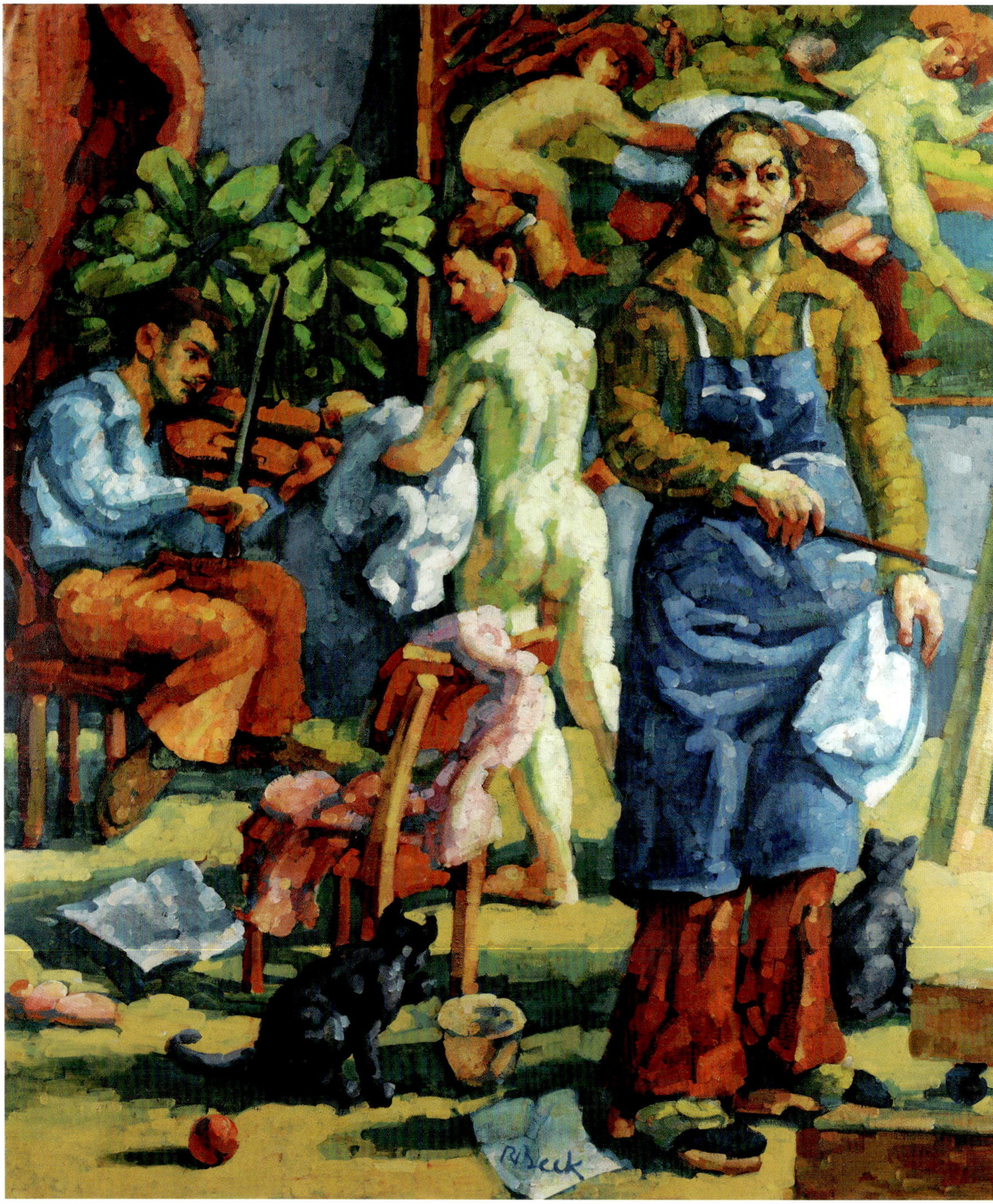

Rosemarie Beck, *Self-Portrait*, 1975. Oil on linen, 60 × 50 in. (152.4 × 127 cm)

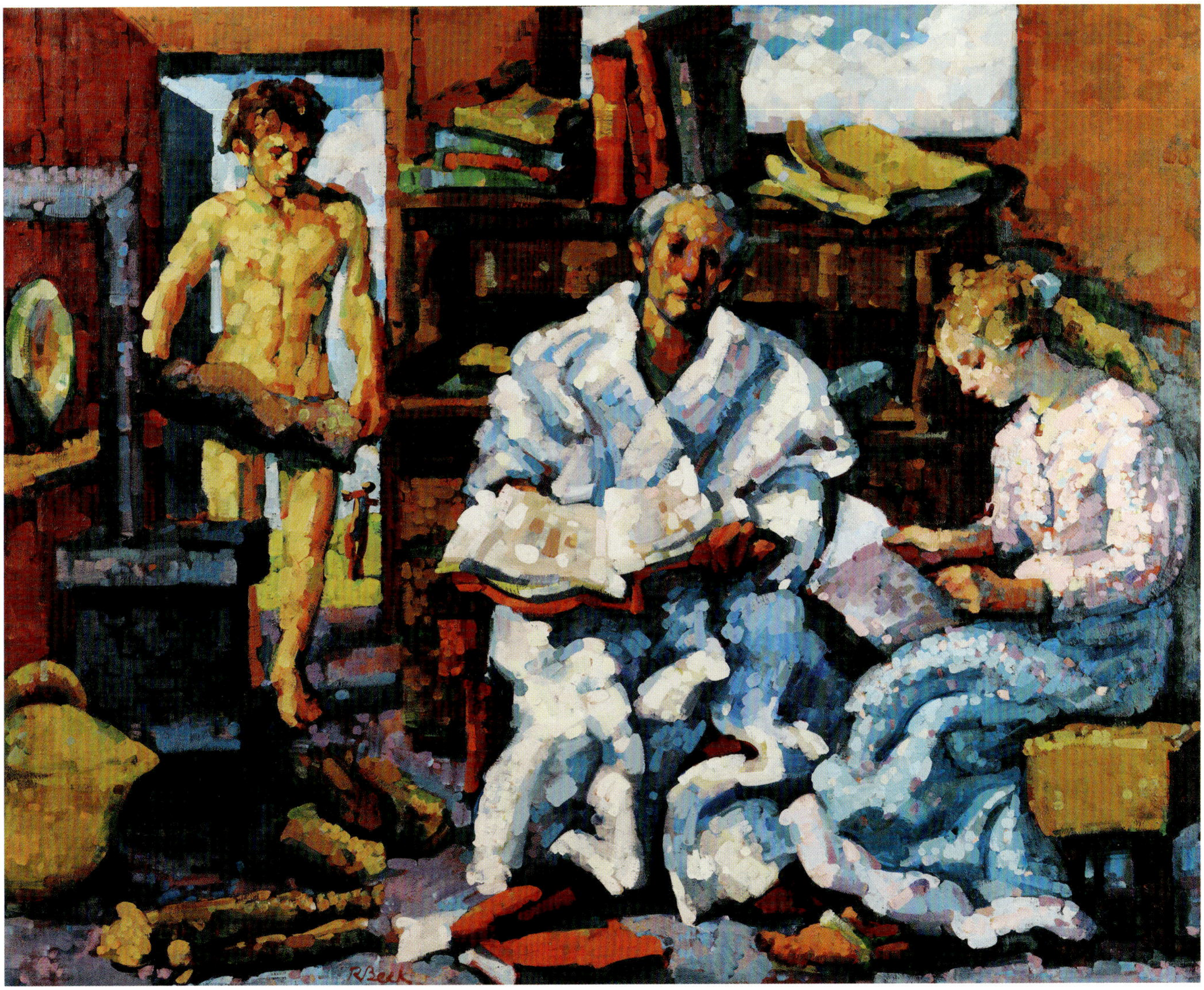

Rosemarie Beck, *The Tempest: Prospero, Miranda, Ferdinand*, 1976. Oil on linen, 49½ × 60 in. (125.7 × 152.4 cm)

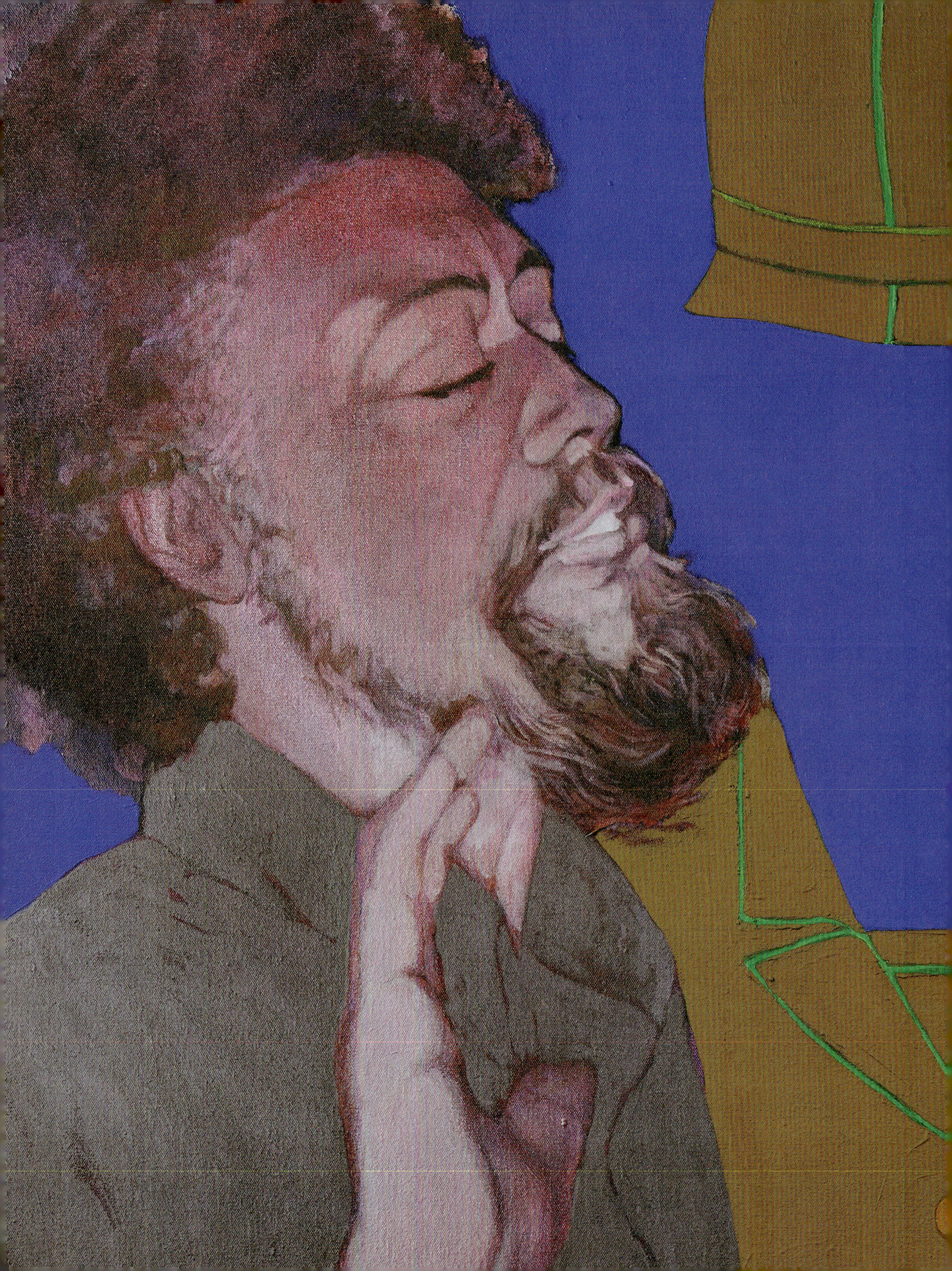

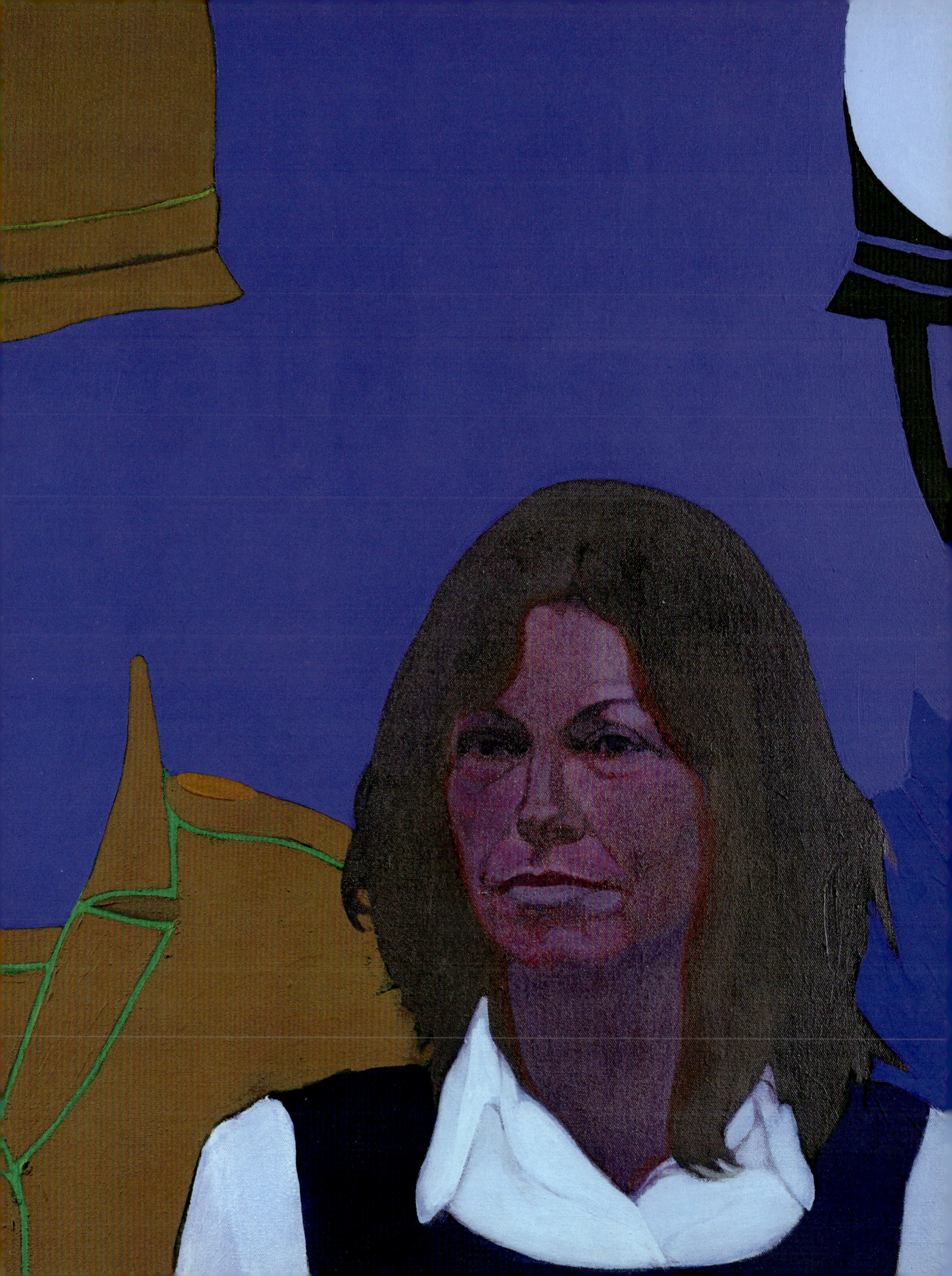

THE SUBJECT IS POLITICS: BENNY ANDREWS AND MAY STEVENS

PATRICIA HILLS

During the heady, protest-filled years of the late 1960s and 1970s, the lives of May Stevens and Benny Andrews crossed on many levels—geographic, political, aesthetic, and personal. Both artists had come from working-class backgrounds: she, from Quincy, Massachusetts; he, from Plainview, Georgia. Both had spent time in their early twenties outside New York: she, in Paris with her husband, Rudolf Baranik, studying art from 1948 to 1951; and he, stationed in California and Alaska with the United States Air Force from 1950 to 1954.[1] Once established in New York, in the early 1960s, both became part of the ferment of activity in Lower Manhattan focused on issues of war and incarceration, sexism and racism. Not surprisingly, as figurative artists who shared convictions about the uses and abuses of power and who questioned what it meant to be a contemporary American, they became good friends.

Stevens's painting *Benny Andrews, the Artist, and Big Daddy Paper Doll* (p. 217), which she submitted to the National Academy of Design as her diploma work in 2004, incorporates many of the themes and motifs that also engaged Andrews. The painting has three spatial layers, each keyed to part of the title. Andrews, in the foreground, is the main subject. With one hand raised, eyes shut, and lips pursed, he seems ready to make a conversational point during a visit to Stevens's studio. Indeed, in the mid-1970s, Stevens methodically took photographs of visitors posed casually in her studio, later using many of the photographs as sources for paintings.[2] Stevens stands stiffly in the middle distance, studying Andrews's face. Behind her, in the third spatial register, are two of her larger-than-life "paper doll" uniforms, a soldier and a policeman—imagery she had established in 1968 with the first work in the series, *Big Daddy Paper Doll* (fig. 1).

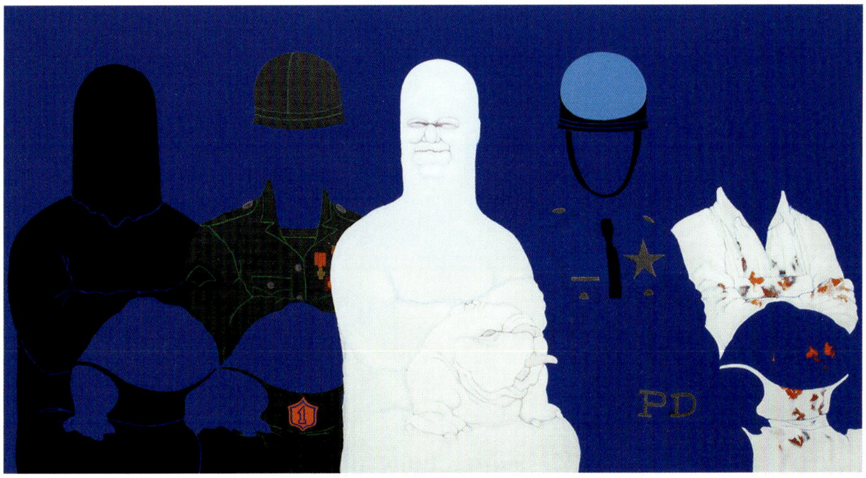

Fig. 1. May Stevens, *Big Daddy Paper Doll*, 1968. Acrylic on canvas. Hood Museum of Art, Dartmouth College, Hanover, NH

Stevens had developed the iconography that led to these "paper dolls" over the course of the 1960s, when she and Baranik were drawn to the area south of Houston Street soon known as SoHo, then becoming the favored location for artists, galleries, and the antiwar movement.[3] They joined with the author Grace Paley, who was active in the War Resisters League, and others in the group Artists and Writers Protest to demonstrate against the war in Vietnam. In late January and early February of 1967, they participated in Angry Arts Week and lent works to the exhibition *Collage of Indignation*, held at New York University's Loeb Student Center.[4] By the early 1970s, Baranik was becoming well known for his antiwar *Napalm Elegies* paintings and activism in groups such as Artists Meeting for Cultural Change, and Stevens, for her *Big Daddy* pictures and involvement with the feminist movement. In 1976, she was a founding member of the Heresies Collective, which published *Heresies: A Feminist Publication on Art and Politics*, to which, in the early years, Stevens contributed her writing and organizational skills.[5]

It is fitting that Andrews stands near the soldier and policeman in Stevens's diploma work for, in real life, he had performed a combination of just those two roles, serving as a military policeman during the Korean War. Years after his military service, he became stridently antiwar in his art, depicting the pathos and humiliations of the soldiers he considered to be pawns to a hawkish American government. For example, his *Wounded Sgt. (Sergeant)* (fig. 2) depicts a sergeant grasping his chest, wounded spiritually as much as physically—a scene no doubt triggered by the artist's intimate knowledge of soldiers' experiences. It is also a work with strong visual affinities to Baranik's 1967 poster for Angry Arts Week, which shows a bandaged child whose face has been burned and scarred by the chemical agent Napalm.

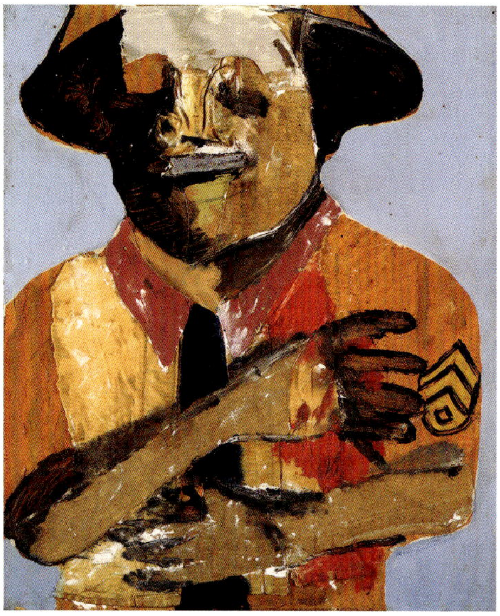

Fig. 2. Benny Andrews, *Wounded Sgt. (Sergeant)*, 1970. Oil and collage on board. Museum of Fine Arts, Boston

During these years, in addition to protesting the war, Andrews was becoming an antiracism activist. In 1959, he had moved to Greenwich Village and become active in antiwar exhibitions, and in 1969, he cofounded the Black Emergency Cultural Coalition (BECC) to protest the Metropolitan Museum of Art's failure to include Harlem residents and Black artists in the planning of its exhibition *Harlem on My Mind: The Cultural Capital of Black America, 1900–1968.* Andrews's active teaching career, beginning in 1968 at Queens College of the City University of New York, included developing programs to teach art to underprivileged children. In 1972, he edited, along with Baranik, *Attica Book*, a compilation of artists' responses, in prose and visual images, to the notorious 1971 shootings of inmates by police officers and members of the National Guard at the Attica Correctional Facility, a maximum-security New York State prison.[6] He later invited Baranik to join him in teaching art to (mostly Black) prisoners at the Rikers Island Correctional Facility in New York City.[7]

Returning to *Benny Andrews, the Artist, and Big Daddy Paper Doll*: in her composition, Stevens placed herself to the right of Andrews in front of an empty space on the canvas—the place where, typically in the series, the naked figure of a smirking, bald, white man is located. That figure, missing here, was based on her own father, who stood for all the things she opposed. Even though he had, in her younger days, encouraged her artistic career, she now saw him as racist, anti-Catholic, anti-Semitic, anticommunist, and disrespectful to Stevens's mother, Alice. In her pictures of him, he often holds in his lap a bulldog, symbol of stubborn aggression. In the diploma work, one can see the partial silhouette of a bulldog in front of both the soldier and the policeman.

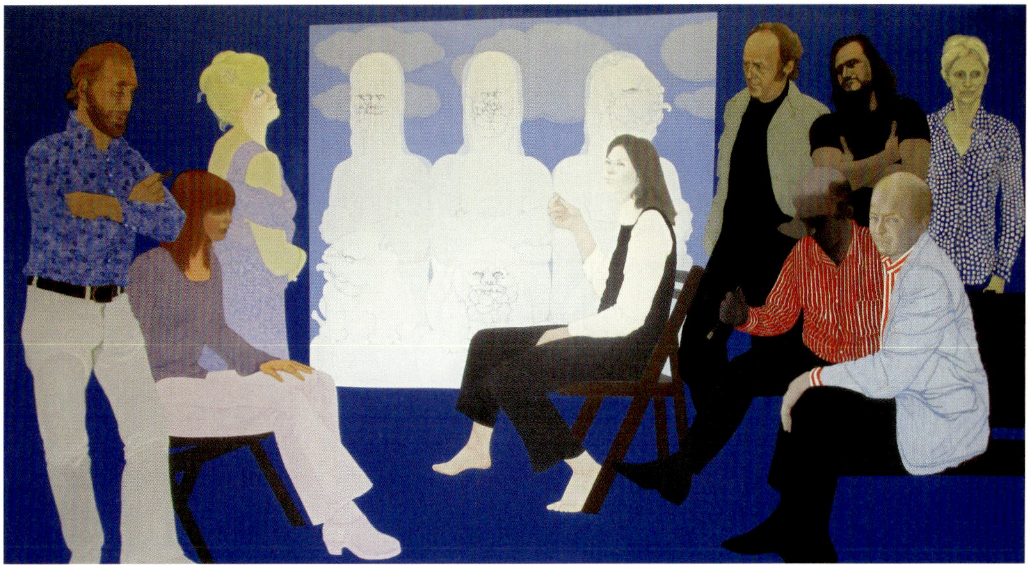

Fig. 3. May Stevens, *The Artist's Studio (After Courbet)*, 1974. Acrylic on canvas. Collection of the University of Missouri–St. Louis

In the history of Western art, images of visitors to an artist's studio, such as that of Andrews in Stevens's studio, inevitably recall Gustave Courbet's large, ambitious *The Painter's Studio: A Real Allegory Summing Up Seven Years of My Artistic and Moral Life* (1854–55; Musée d'Orsay, Paris). Because it was rejected by the art jury of the 1855 Exposition universelle in Paris, Courbet showed it independently in a temporary exhibition. In the painting, the artist brought together representations of people from everyday life, allegorical figures, and cultural personages, many of whom were his friends. In a "manifesto" accompanying the independent exhibition, Courbet wrote: "To know in order to be able to create, that was my idea. To be in a position to translate the customs, the ideas, the appearance of my epoch, according to my own estimation; to be not only a painter, but a man as well; in short, to create living art—this is my goal."[8]

To Courbet, Realist painting was a political act—a declaration that an artist's experiences counted and that one's art should be of one's own time. Therefore, he depicted himself in the process of painting, in the surround of his experiences. Stevens's response was similar, as she wrote in her induction questionnaire for the National Academy: "To be an artist means being open to and responsible to the world around you."[9] Thus, in her painting, she linked Andrews to the context of the contemporary art world they both knew so well, with its emphases on feminism and antiracism.

But Stevens, whose feminist convictions were intensifying, had already made an homage to Courbet with her painting *The Artist's Studio (After Courbet)* (fig. 3), in which she seated her painted image in front of her 1973 painting *Metamorphosis* (a work, now unlocated, that depicts the transformation of Big Daddy's phallic male head into that of a bulldog and, conversely, the bulldog's

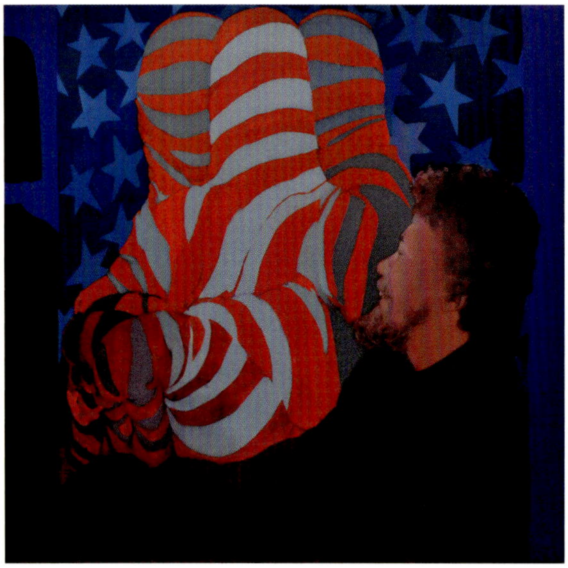

Fig. 4. May Stevens, *Benny and the Flag*, 1976. Acrylic on canvas. Collection of the artist

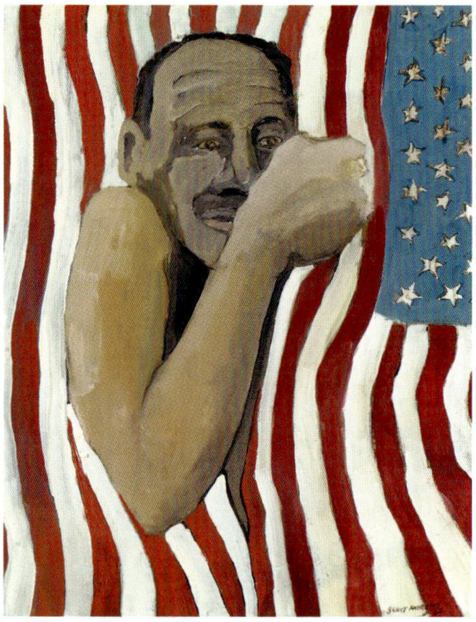

Fig. 5. Benny Andrews, *Flag Day*, 1968. Oil on canvas. Art Institute of Chicago

transformation into a lap version of Big Daddy). Only twelve feet wide, compared to Courbet's almost twenty-foot-wide painting, Stevens's group portrait is necessarily more limited in the number of its figures; there are nine in total. The artist wears the same simple white shirt and black vest seen in her later painting with Andrews. She looks in the direction of the three painters at the left: Arnold Belkin, Felicity Rainnie, and Sylvia Sleigh. Standing behind Stevens to the right are Baranik, the critic Joachim Neugroschel, and the artist Nancy Spero; seated are the artist Leon Golub and the critic Lawrence Alloway. Alloway, married to Sleigh, was one of the early champions of the feminist art movement in New York, and Stevens placed him in a position of honor—at the lower right-hand corner, where the poet Charles Baudelaire sits in Courbet's painting. This work marked the beginning of her series of "history" paintings, although she was still to finish more variations on the Big Daddy theme.[10]

In 1976, Stevens also included a portrait of Andrews in another painting, *Benny and the Flag* (fig. 4). Andrews sits in profile in front of an image of Stevens's recently painted *Dark Flag* (Whitney Museum of American Art, New York), which depicts a tripled Big Daddy with his bulldog on his lap, all tightly swaddled in the red and white stripes of an American flag; behind the bulging lump of their massed figures, white stars on blue fill in the background. Stevens must have relished the irony of the racist Big Daddies being smothered by their own patriotic flags while an amused Black man, Benny Andrews, smiles in front.[11] He, however, may have been thinking of *Flag Day*, his own painting of eight years earlier (fig. 5), which depicts the head and bare right shoulder and arm of a Black man emerging from an open slit in an excessively striped version of the American flag, hanging like a curtain across the picture plane. This man, desperately grasping a couple of the flag's stripes as if they

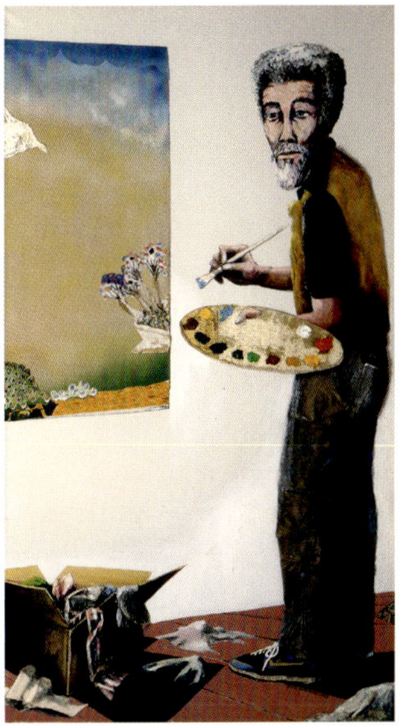

Fig. 6. Benny Andrews, *Portrait of a Collagist*, 1989. Oil and collage on canvas. Detroit Institute of Arts

were the vertical bars of a prison cell, seems to look furtively into the distance as he plans his escape. Stevens may well have known Andrews's *Flag Day*.[12]

For his own National Academy diploma presentation, Andrews submitted *Collagist, Self-Portrait* (p. 219), a work in both collage and oils. In it, he gazes down at a worktable, where he has been using his large scissors to cut vermillion-and-white-striped fabric into pieces. Behind him, an empty stretched canvas stands on an easel. Five years earlier, he had created a similar subject, *Portrait of a Collagist* (fig. 6), depicting himself standing in front of an almost completed lyrical landscape, typical of his late style. Artists' supplies spill out of a box at the lower left. Although calling himself a collagist in the title, he instead holds a brush and a palette as he turns to face us. The collage elements, pieces of painted canvas affixed to the picture within the picture, seem relatively minor.

Andrews may have been brooding about this 1989 painting in 1999, when he presented his 1994 work to the Academy. He provided the following information on his induction questionnaire: "This is a self portrait of me working with collage. I wanted to depict . . . working with collage beyond it being a medium but also as part of the painting's subject."[13] The implication is that he was now identifying with the *process* of collage, a process that generally required working on a flat surface. To his colleagues at the National Academy, most of whom were painters, he wanted to emphasize that collage meant a different way of thinking about art: not the imitation of the natural world but a comment on the cultural world of making art. In the late 1960s, the art historian Leo Steinberg had recognized "a radically new orientation, in which the painted surface is no longer the analogue of a visual experience of nature but of operational processes."[14] Steinberg credited Robert Rauschenberg with introducing the "flatbed or work-surface picture plane as the foundation of an artistic language that would deal with a different order of experience."[15] Whether or not Andrews had read Steinberg is immaterial; Rauschenberg's breakthrough paralleled the shift from elite thinking about the nature of art to the reality of everyday creativity. As Rauschenberg said in 1959, "Painting relates to both art and life. Neither can be made. (I try to act in that gap between the two.)"[16]

Indeed, the reality of everyday materials preoccupied Andrews. His strongest political paintings had often included collage—specifically, layers of ripped and shaped canvas pasted over other layers of canvas. Andrews was not alone in realizing the possibilities of collage beyond its historical roots in early Cubism. Rudolf Baranik, after the first few canvases of his *Napalm Elegies* series, also began to work with patches of ripped and jaggedly cut canvas, to which he affixed photostats to evoke the travails of war and the death of innocents, as in his *Napalm Elegy Diptych* of 1971 (Western Michigan University, Kalamazoo). Of his use of collage in these paintings, Baranik remarked, "I would like to make a separation between my works so described and the so-called collage aesthetic. Some of the qualities found in traditional collage, an emphasis on materiality, textural juxtapositions and pointed origin of source, do not exist in my collages. On the contrary, expressive illusionism is aimed for as strongly as in the paintings."[17] In Andrews's *Wounded Sgt. (Sergeant)* (fig. 2), the pieces of canvas splayed over the soldier's face accentuate his mournful pathos, as if his whole face were covered with bandages. Here, too, Andrews was using collage to express tactile illusion—to represent the layers of skin over deep flesh and bone.

Andrews's insistence on being thought of as a collagist also acknowledged his own past. He would have recalled his own cultural heritage, his years of growing up in the South, when poor families used newspapers and pictures from magazines to paper the walls of their homes as part of a culture of "making do." In 1990, he had told an interviewer, "I didn't want to lose my sense of rawness. Where I am from, the people are very austere. We have big hands. We have ruddy faces. We wear rough fabrics. We actually used the burlap bagging sacks that seed came in to make our shirts. These are my textures."[18] The "we" would have included the artist's father, George Andrews, a former sharecropper and, after his retirement, self-taught artist.[19] Known as the "Dot Man," George covered simple wood furniture with rows of dots and, in his flatly painted, accomplished portraits, filled the negative spaces with decorative dot patterns. For both father and son, theirs was a culture of "making do"—early on, by necessity, and later, because of the satisfaction of living simply.[20]

By 1994, Andrews had mellowed. In the intervening years since the 1970s, he had served a stint as director of visual arts for the National Endowment for the Arts (1982–84) and resumed teaching at Queens College, until his retirement in 1997. Beginning in 1999, he began illustrating books for children and involved himself in educational programs for youth. Indeed, *Collagist, Self-Portrait* shows a seemingly calm, not visibly militant, artist at his worktable, focused on the painted scissors that cut the painted cloth. As an image, the artist turns his back on the vertical blank canvas behind him; but in terms of the two-dimensional composition, his head and shoulders have been placed to fill that blank canvas. While not hammering home a critique about "America," the striped cloth hints at the stripes of the American flag, thus functioning symbolically as the "American" material with which the artist has chosen to work.

The works submitted by Stevens and Andrews were appropriate, though uncompromising, diploma portraits for the august National Academy of Design. However, self-portraits are also avatars—imaginative beings that perform in the way their creators would like to see their real selves performing. Stevens's self-portrait reflected her commitment to living as an artist in the gap between her politically inflected art and the activism she and her lifelong comrades had pursued. Andrews's self-portrait projected his increasingly urgent conviction that his identity as an artist came from his mastery of craft while simultaneously acknowledging the power of his memories to recall the rural, working-class traditions of "making do." And that, in itself, not only was a political act but also tapped into the wellspring of his, and our, humanity.

The author would like to thank halley k. harrisburg, Director, Michael Rosenfeld Gallery, and Bridget Casey of Ryan/Lee Gallery for facilitating the acquisition of images for reproduction and Jeremiah William McCarthy and Diana Thompson, as well as Zoë Samels, for making available for examination original works of art in the collections of the National Academy of Design and the Museum of Fine Arts, Boston, respectively.

1. For Stevens, see Patricia Hills and Phyllis Rose, *May Stevens* (San Francisco: Pomegranate Art Books, 2005). For Andrews, see J. Richard Grubar, *American Icons: From Madison to Manhattan; The Art of Benny Andrews, 1948–1997*, exh. cat. (Augusta, GA: Morris Museum of Art, 1997), and the website of the Benny Andrews Estate, http://www.bennyandrews.com/biography.
2. Stevens took several such photographs of me in early 1978, when I was pregnant, and used them for her 1978 painting *Mysteries and Politics* (San Francisco Museum of Modern Art).
3. By 1968, Stevens and Baranik had moved into two lofts in an artists' cooperative building at 97 Wooster Street.
4. For the anti–Vietnam War movement in the arts, see Matthew Israel, *Kill for Peace: American Artists against the Vietnam War* (Austin: University of Texas Press, 2013).
5. By the time the journal folded, in 1993, the collective had an entirely different roster of women artists and writers.
6. *Attica Book*, a joint project of the Black Emergency Cultural Coalition and Artists and Writers Protest, contained poetry by prisoners and reproductions of paintings, drawings, and collages by forty-eight artists, including Carl Andre, Andrews, Baranik, Romare Bearden, Antonio Frasconi, Jacob Lawrence, Robert Morris, Alice Neel, Faith Ringgold, Nancy Spero, and Stevens.
7. See Hills and Rose, *Stevens*, 33. The website of the Benny Andrews Estate notes that he began teaching prisoners at the Manhattan Detention Complex, informally known as the Tombs; later, he received an award for this work.
8. Gustave Courbet, quoted in Linda Nochlin, ed., *Realism and Tradition in Art, 1848–1900* (Englewood Cliffs, NJ: Prentice-Hall, 1966), 33–34, translated from Gustave Courbet, *Exhibition et vente de 40 tableaux et 4 dessins de l'oeuvre de M. Gustave Courbet, avenue Montaigne* (Paris, 1855), n.p.
9. May Stevens, "Questionnaire" (ca. 2004), NAD artist file.
10. See Patricia Hills, "May Stevens: Painting History as Lived Feminist Experience," in Patricia M. Burnham and Lucretia Hoover Giese, eds., *Redefining American History Painting* (New York: Cambridge University Press, 1995), 310–30, 383–87.

11. Stevens painted a third painting of Andrews with his first wife, Mary Ellen Jones Smith Andrews (location unknown).

12. Jasper Johns, Faith Ringgold, and others had used American flags in their art to comment or protest; in 1976, flags became especially evident in popular culture because of the country's bicentennial celebrations.

13. Benny Andrews, "Questionnaire" (ca. 1999), NAD artist file.

14. Leo Steinberg, *Other Criteria: Confrontations with Twentieth-Century Art* (New York: Oxford University Press, 1972), 84. I am grateful to Jeremiah William McCarthy for reminding me to mention Steinberg's concept of the "flatbed picture plane," of which I have been very much aware since the late 1960s, when I was a student of Steinberg's.

15. Ibid., 85.

16. Robert Rauschenberg, "Artist's Statement," in Dorothy C. Miller, ed., *Sixteen Americans*, exh. cat. (New York: Museum of Modern Art, 1959), 58.

17. Rudolf Baranik, quoted in Jonathan Green, ed., *Rudolf Baranik: Elegies; Sleep—Napalm—Night Sky*, exh. cat. (Columbus: Ohio State University Gallery of Fine Art, 1987), 81.

18. Benny Andrews, quoted in Judd Tully, "A Collage of Painterly Roots," in Patricia P. Bladon, *Folk: The Art of Benny and George Andrews*, exh. cat. (Memphis, TN: Memphis Brooks Museum of Art, 1990).

19. For George Andrews, see Bladon, *Folk*, and J. Richard Grubar, *The Dot Man: George Andrews of Madison, Georgia*, exh. cat. (Augusta, GA: Morris Museum of Art, 1994).

20. For cutout newspapers and magazines used as wallpaper as a component of the collage sensibility, see Patricia Hills, "Cultural Legacies and the Transformation of the Cubist Collage Aesthetic by Romare Bearden, Jacob Lawrence, and Other African-American Artists," in Ruth Fine and Jacqueline Francis, eds., *Romare Bearden, American Modernist*, Studies in the History of Art 71 (New Haven: Yale University Press, 2011), 223–47.

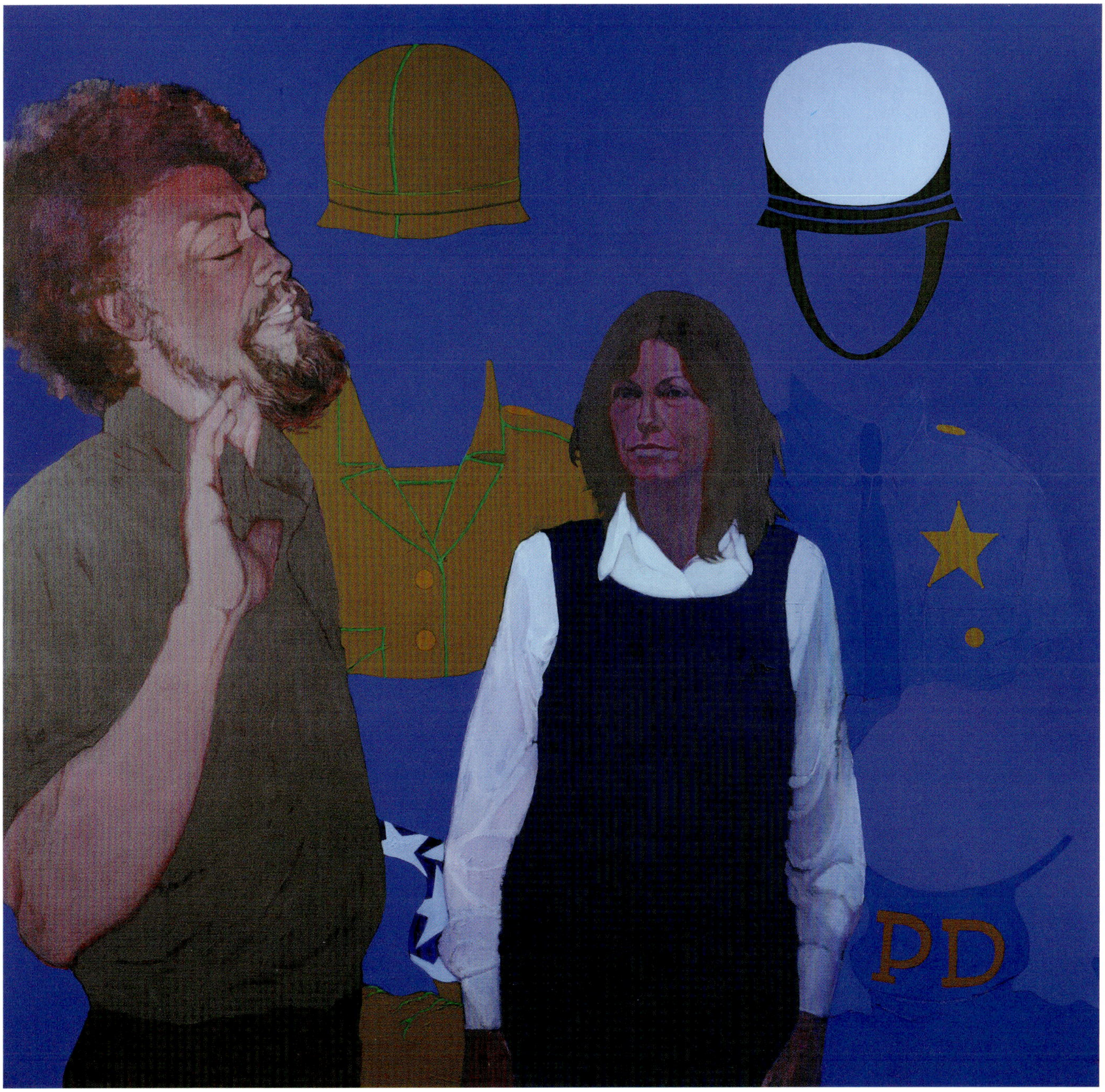

May Stevens, *Benny Andrews, the Artist, and Big Daddy Paper Doll*, 1976. Acrylic on canvas, 60 ¼ × 60 ¼ in. (153 × 153 cm)

FRED WILSON ON BENNY ANDREWS

I met Benny years ago, when I was a very young artist exhibiting at an alternative gallery in SoHo. I was thrilled to make his acquaintance: Andrews's work was well known in Black circles at the time, and I was well aware of his leadership in the historic protest against the *Harlem on My Mind* exhibition held at the Metropolitan Museum of Art in 1969. The museum had organized an exhibition about Harlem but chosen to leave Black artists out completely (except for the photographer James VanDerZee—and his works were photographic reproductions, not the originals). I was taking classes in the Metropolitan's high-school program when this was going on, and the protest was an education in how museums create meaning and artists can reveal bias. Benny was a thoughtful and congenial presence in the art world, but he was always ready to challenge the policies and presumptions of the self-satisfied, self-congratulatory, and flat-out racially ignorant art world of his time.

In his paintings, Andrews paired texture and meaning in ways that leapt from the canvas. His works often had political content, whether subtle or strident; in either case, the satire was always pointedly clear. The events of the late 1960s and early 1970s produced an urgent need for social commentary in art, just as there is now. Throughout his career, Andrews's work revealed social injustice wherever he found it. The image of the American flag appears in many of his canvases—a symbol of all this country purports to be when, so often, it falls short.

Collagist, Self-Portrait depicts the artist with scissors in hand, cutting fabric. Behind him is a blank canvas, which could be the intended destination of the fabric he is cutting—he is, after all, identified in the title as a collagist. The slant of the canvas creates the illusion of depth, and the crumpled fabric protruding from the surface adds a three-dimensional element. In my opinion, the reddish-striped fabric slyly represents the American flag. Andrews shows himself metaphorically refashioning it (and, by extension, America) into something representative, useful, and relevant to all. The intensity of his gaze indicates the importance of his project—a redesigning of what it means to be American.

In addition to the social commentary, this is a self-portrait of the artist at work. Looking closely, one realizes that it is not only America that is being re-created. Benny's face is constructed from many pieces of fabric and many brushstrokes. Perhaps, through the act of making art, Benny was re-creating himself. The artist's process in creating the work reverberates between the activity and the image. Andrews's painting of himself cutting cloth is a soundless version of Robert Morris's 1961 work *Box with the Sound of Its Own Making* (Metropolitan Museum of Art, New York); it could have been titled *Painting with the Image of Its Own Making.*

Now that I am as gray as Benny was when I knew him, I admire this work more than ever. Making and remaking oneself and revealing to the world all that you see that is unspoken or unjust is one of the greatest contributions an artist can make.

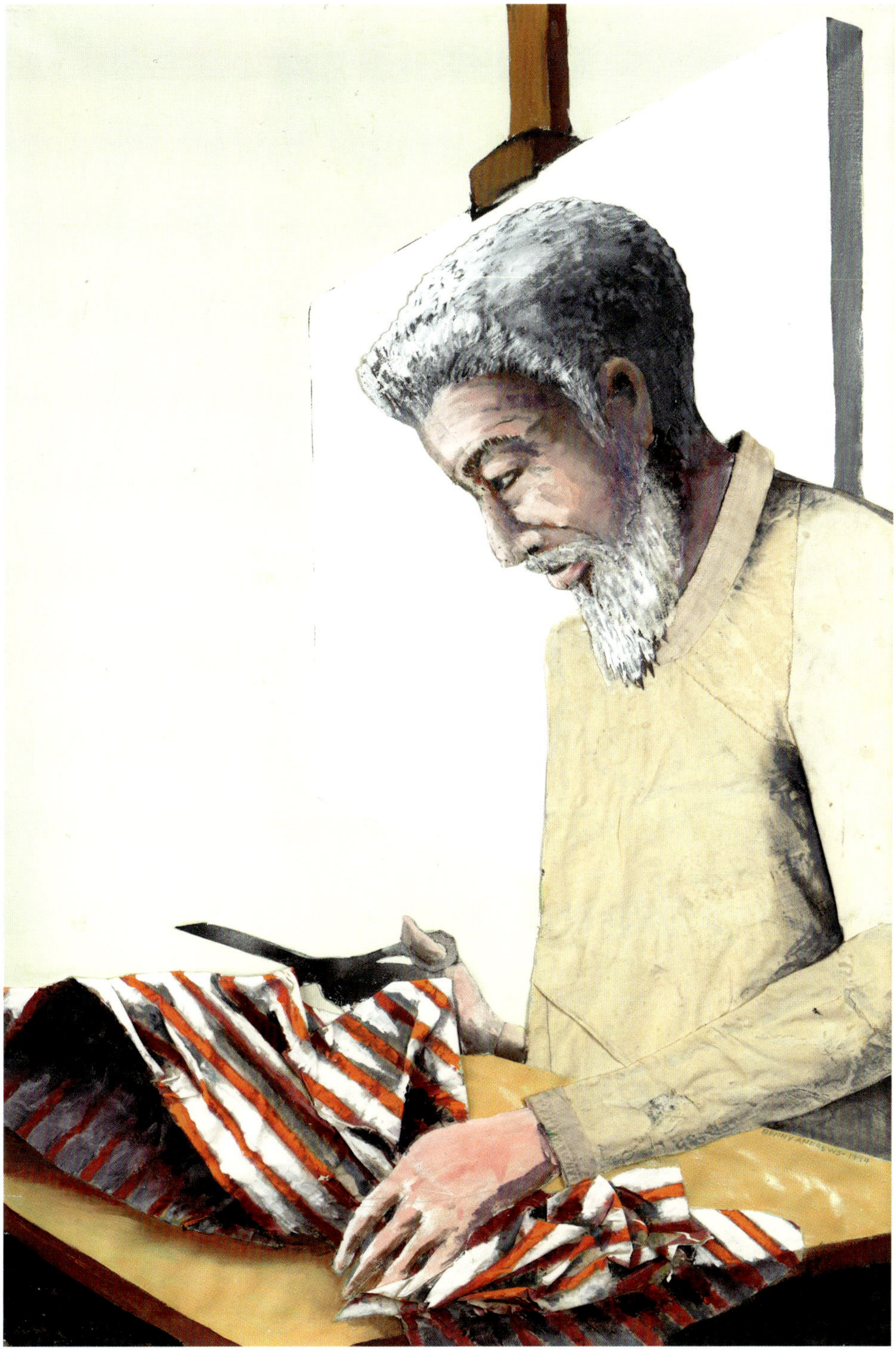

Benny Andrews, *Collagist, Self-Portrait*, 1994. Oil and collage on canvas, 36 × 24 in. (91.4 × 61 cm)

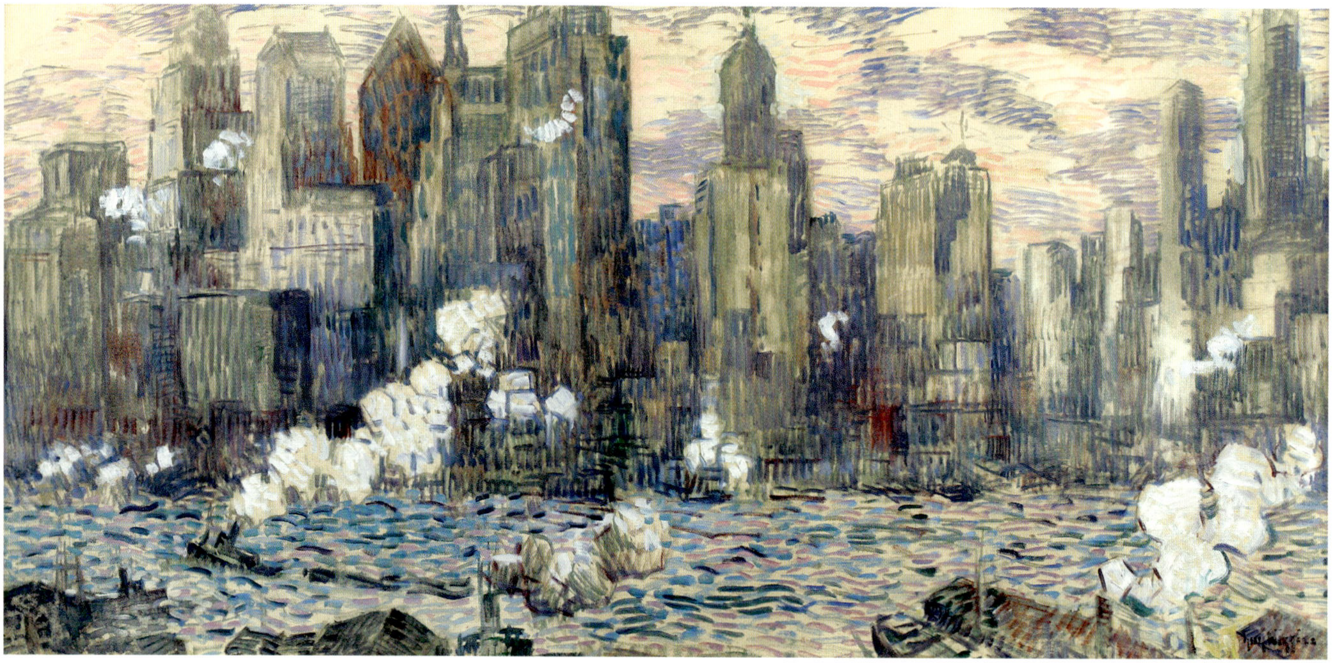

Guy C. Wiggins, *Manhattan*, 1929. Oil on canvas, 30 × 60 in. (76.2 × 152.4 cm)

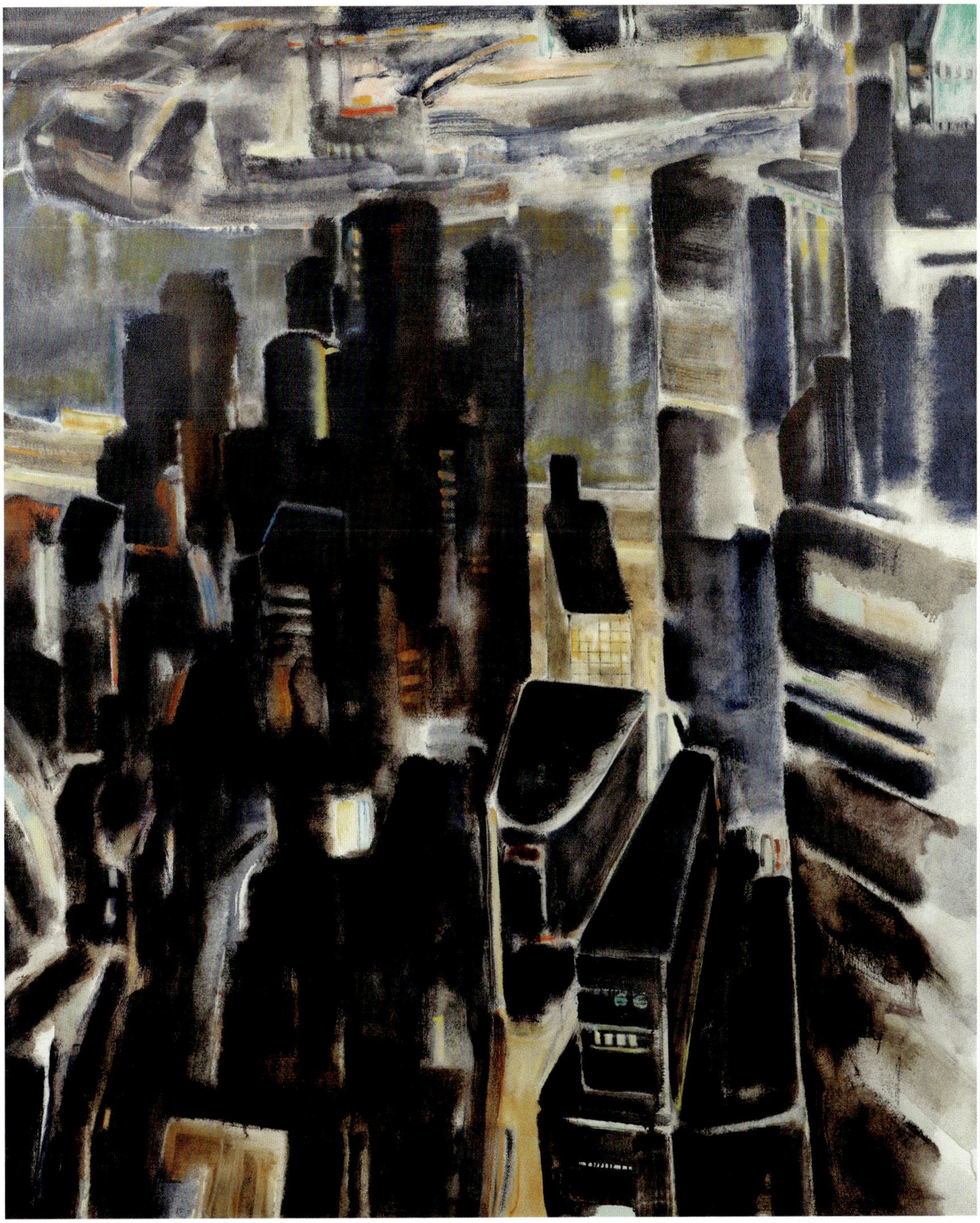

Jacqueline Gourevitch, *Night: WTC Looking East*, 2000–2001. Oil on canvas, 50 × 40 in. (127 × 101.6 cm)

WALTER CHATHAM ON RICHARD ESTES

"We affirm that the world's magnificence has been enriched by a new beauty: the beauty of speed. A racing car whose hood is adorned with great pipes, like serpents of explosive breath—a roaring car that seems to run on grapeshot is more beautiful than The Victory of Samoth-race." This remarkable passage, written by Filippo Tommaso Marinetti, a founder of Italian Futurism, and first published on February 20, 1909, in the Paris newspaper *Le Figaro*, reflects the obsession with speed and movement inspired by the automobile at its inception. By the time Richard Estes painted *NYC Parking Lot*, in 1969, a different aesthetic had taken hold—a movement known as photorealism. Estes was a founding member of that movement, which sought an aesthetic expression of its time in the mostly manufactured objects and buildings that make up our cities.

A strong influence on Estes's work was Edgar Degas, the master of the "captured moment"—the flash of a dancer, the glint of light off a racehorse at speed, motion captured as if by a camera. Following Degas's example, the formal composition and stasis of traditional art gave way to more informal, off-balance compositions in which the aesthetic of the photograph and its apparent "objectivity" seized the viewer's attention.

Like a closely cropped photograph, Estes's *NYC Parking Lot* is filled to capacity with cars, with not an inch to spare. Because the artist deliberately condensed and clogged the picture, its abstract qualities dominate. The "objects" are relative, their wholeness implied rather than spelled out. The congestion and anxiety of the city are fully expressed in the way the cars are almost touching, but beyond the discomfort this provokes in the viewer is a liberating, almost dizzying experience. The reflective surfaces of the cars in the foreground show the surrounding buildings and the sky as highly distorted images—similar to what you would see if the cars were in motion and the buildings and sky appeared to be rushing by.

Having established this congested, ambiguous, hyperdistorted composition, Estes then dove deep into the beauty of his models—their slick, shiny paint, lavish chrome trim, and voluptuous forms are avatars for their absent owners. Degas and his contemporaries treated fabrics and interiors in a similar fashion, using them to express the essence of humanity. Estes pulled this off in his *NYC Parking Lot*. At first glance, the picture appears to show an unremarkable jumble of empty cars. But they could just as easily be a crowd of commuters squeezed into uncomfortable proximity. They maintain their individuality and dignity despite it all. The TLC Estes lavished on these beauties ennobles them and the banal space they occupy. This is "street art" at its finest: transforming ordinary moments into joyful, transcendent aesthetic experiences.

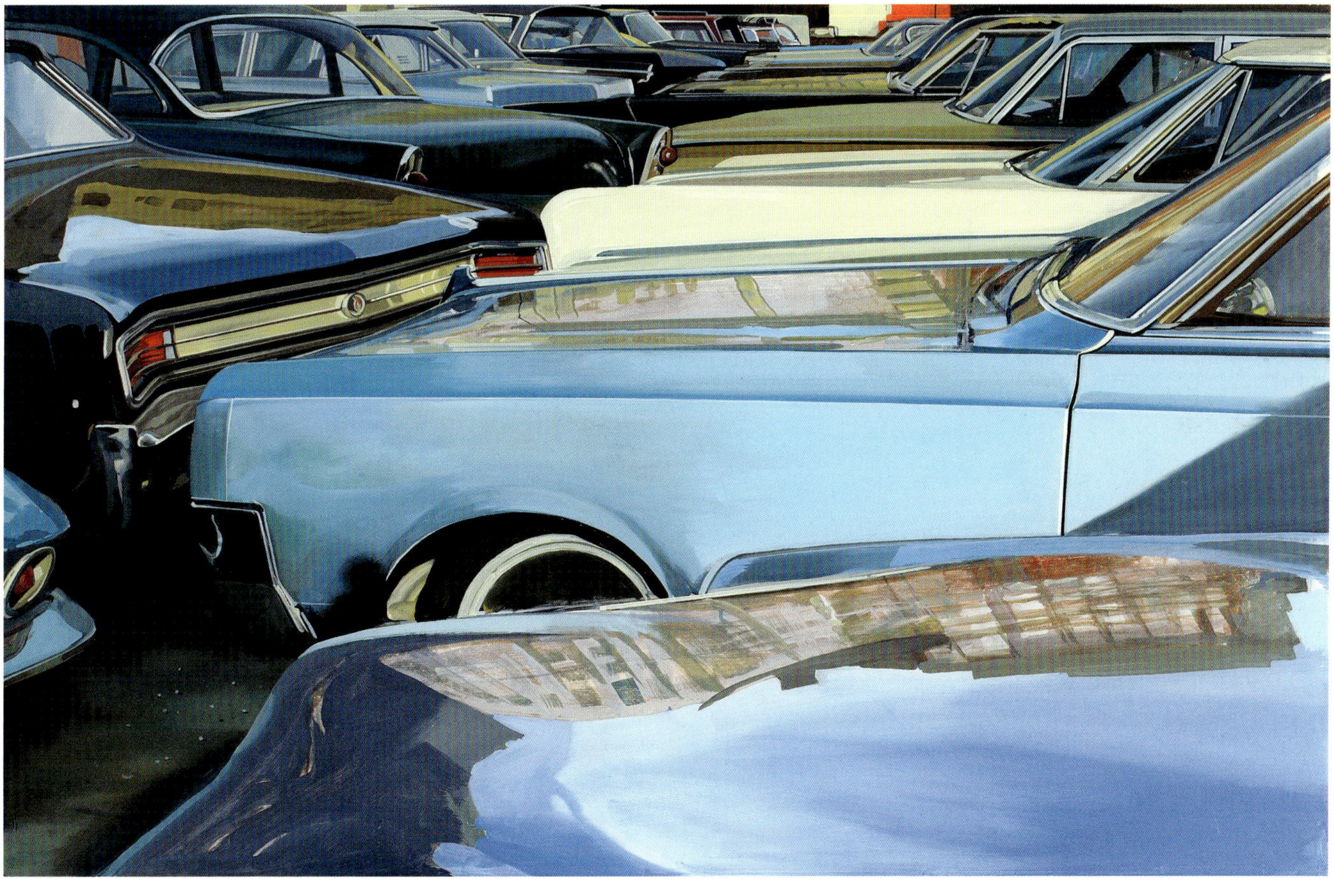

Richard Estes, *NYC Parking Lot*, 1969. Oil on Masonite, 23¾ × 36 in. (60.3 × 91.4 cm)

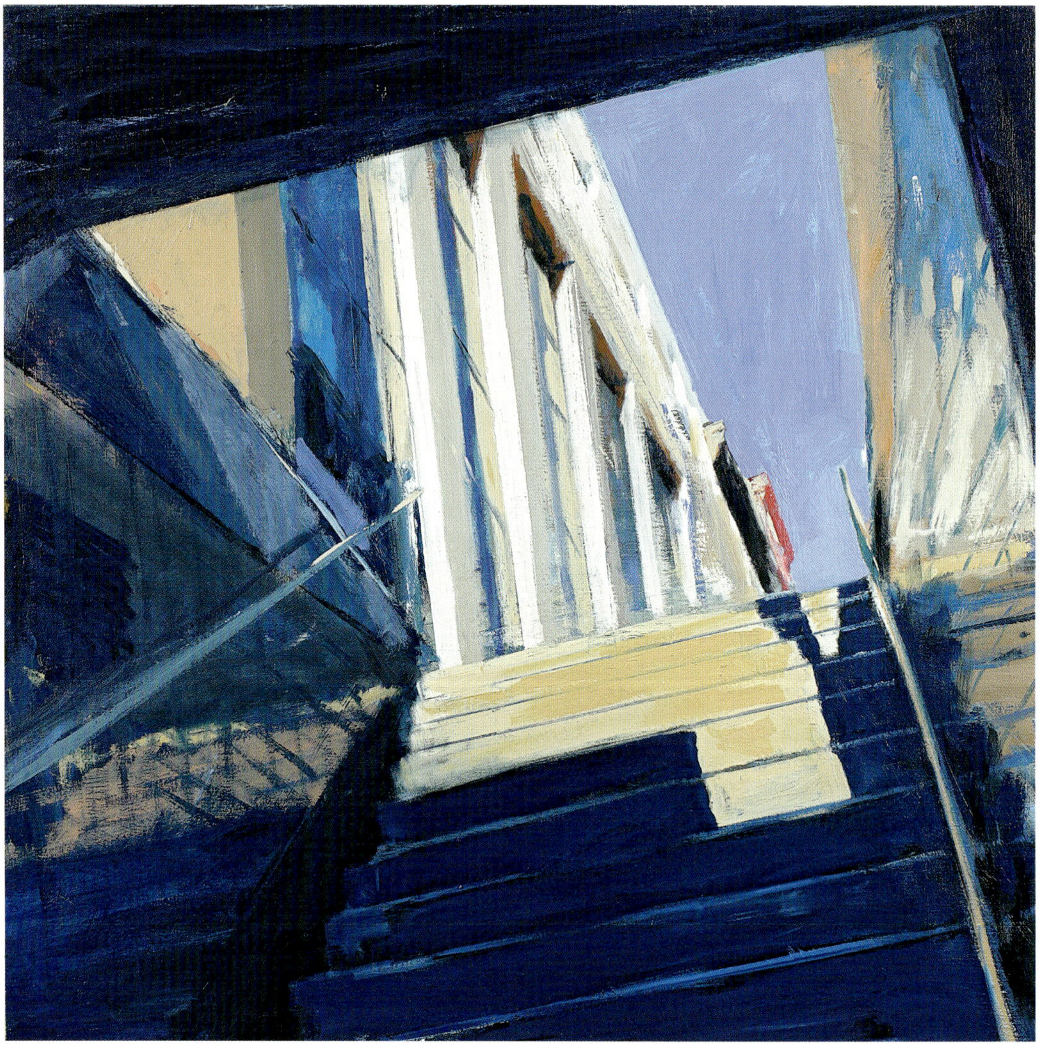

David Kapp, *Coming out of the Subway*, 1998. Oil on linen, 50 ¼ × 50 ¼ in. (127.6 × 127.6 cm)

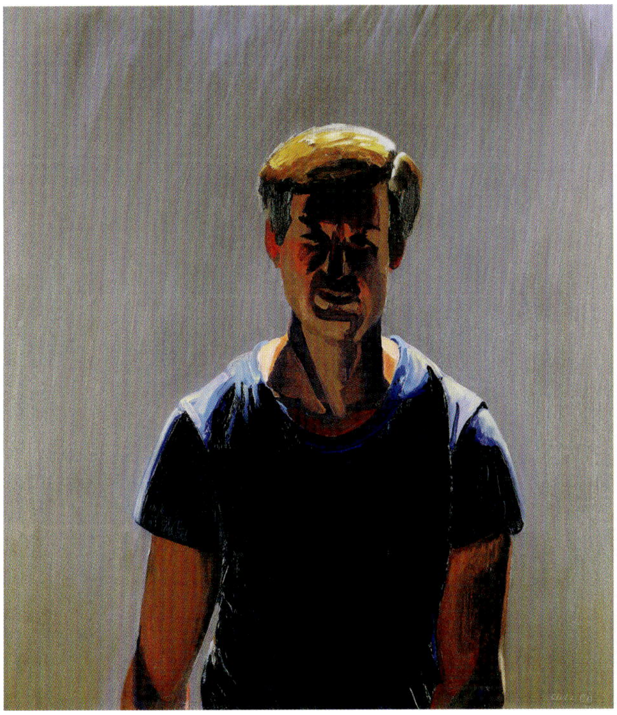

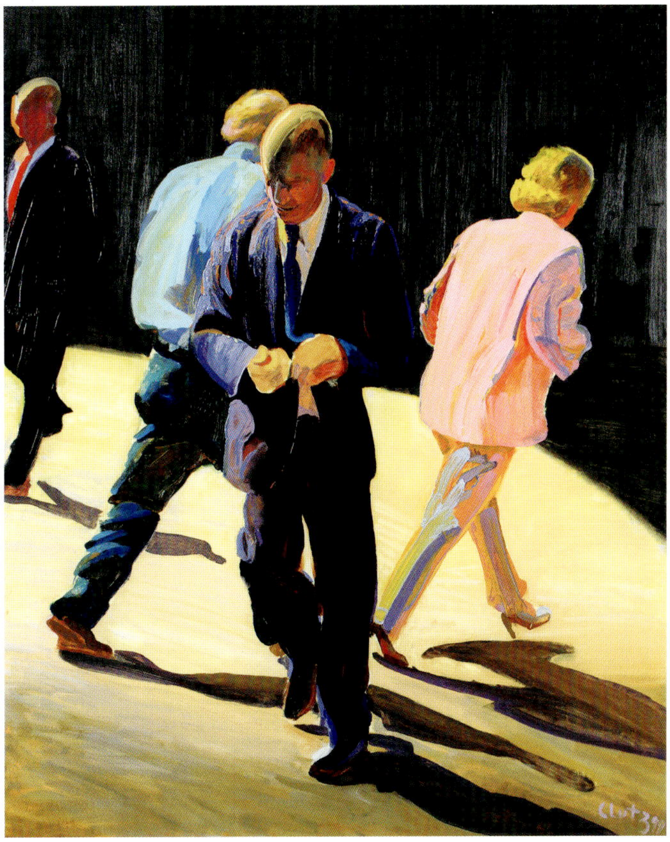

Left: William Clutz, *Self-Portrait (Walking)*, 1980. Oil on canvas, 35 ⅛ × 30 ¼ in. (89.2 × 76.8 cm)
Right: William Clutz, *Autumn Street*, 1999. Oil on canvas, 50 × 40 in. (127 × 101.6 cm)

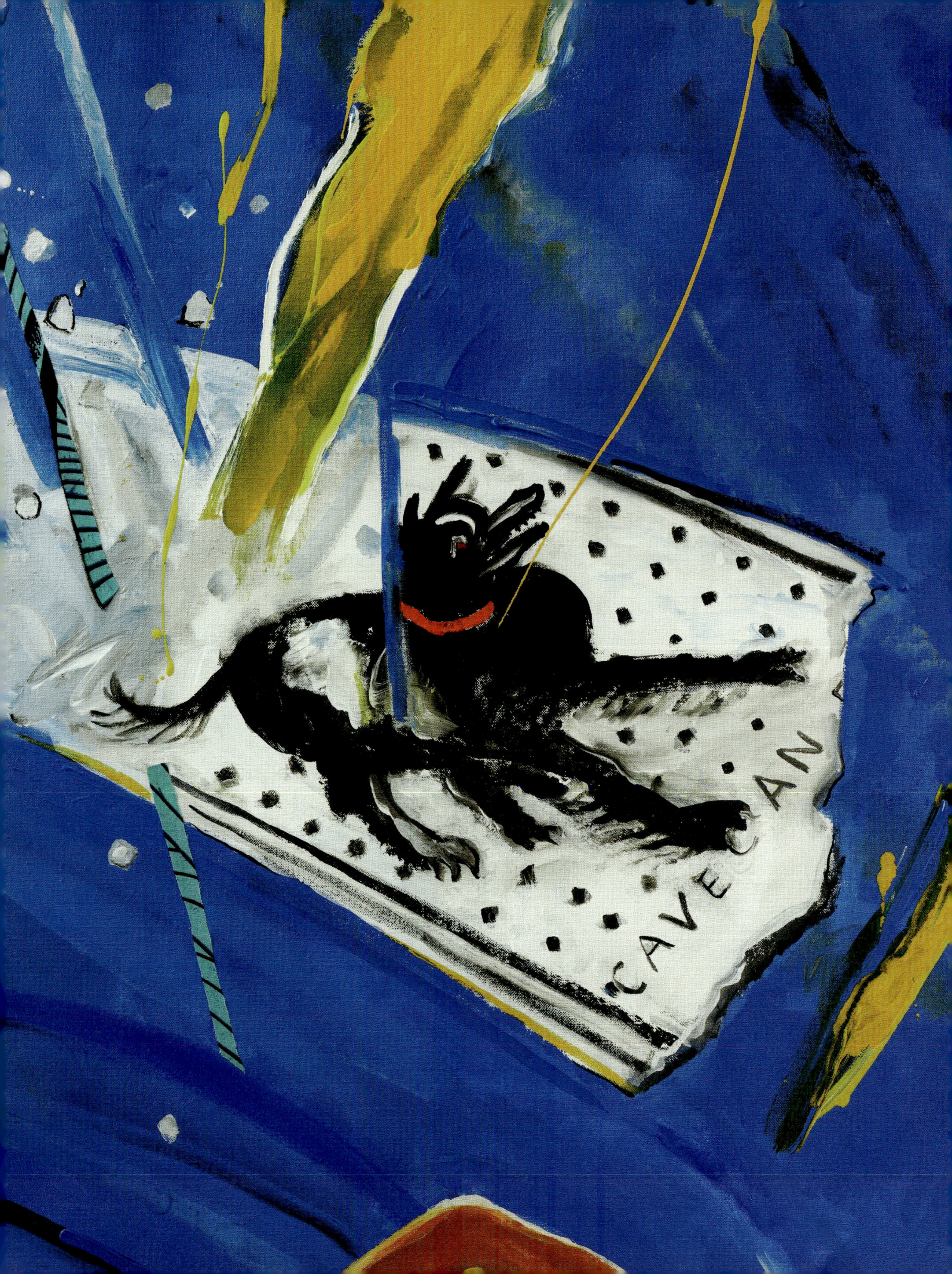
CAVE CAN

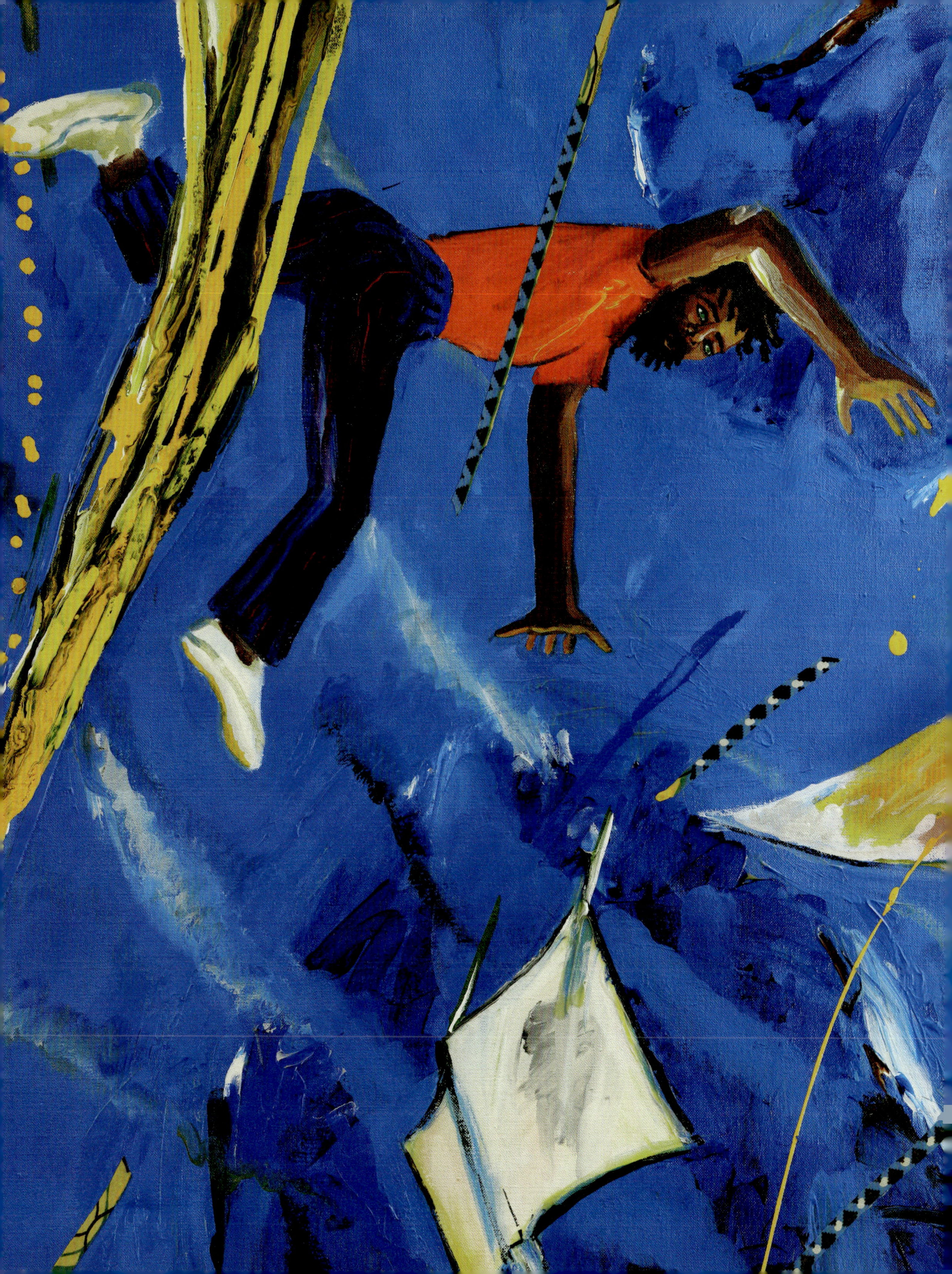

TO PAINT A FIGURE

JEREMIAH WILLIAM MCCARTHY

> The particular question—here
> The particular answer to the particular question
> Is not in point—the question is in point.
> —Wallace Stevens, "The Ultimate Poem Is Abstract"

Upon surveying the paintings collection of the National Academy of Design, one is struck by the overwhelming impression that representational fidelity—the desire to lay bare, in recognizable visual form, the human experience of the world—is at the center of American artists' concerns, and has been for nearly two hundred years. If this painterly concern itself can be said to have a history, then the practice of working from life surely represents one of its longest unbroken traditions. And if we put aside for a moment the question of why a painter might depict the human form—that is to say, all the motivations that spur painters to do so in the first place—the questions of *how* one paints a figure and what exactly *constitutes* a figure, of how an individual acquires both the technical facility and the conceptual vocabulary to render the living body in pigment, might at first appear so self-evident that they are rarely even asked.

The National Academy was founded with the belief that access to the human figure, originally through casts of ancient statuary (fig. 1) and, later, through the living nude (fig. 2), is the cornerstone of the arts of design, and although the world faced by contemporary painters may be infinitely different from the one inhabited by artists of the past, much of the academic training surrounding the human figure has endured, and certain figural leitmotifs appear.[1] The text that follows will explore

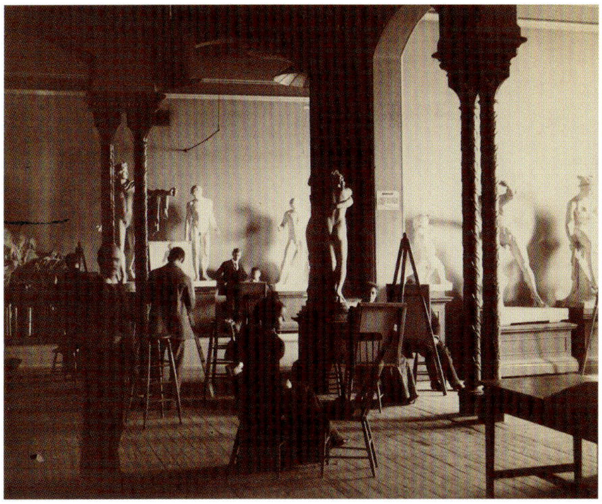

Fig. 1. Antique class of the NAD, Fourth Avenue and 23rd Street, ca. 1895

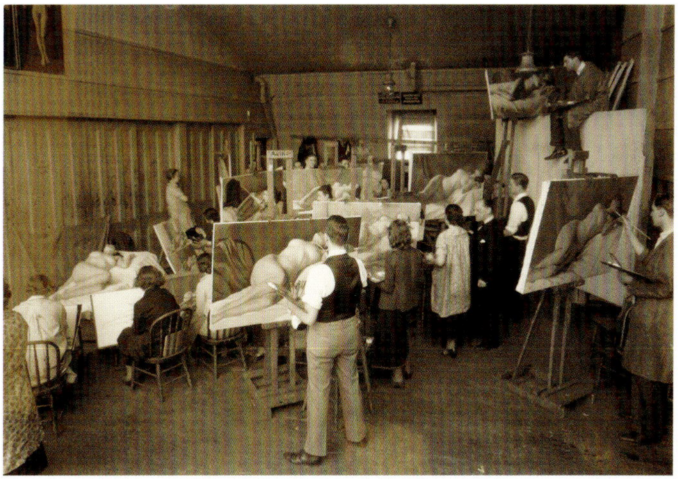

Fig. 2. Leon Kroll's life class of the NAD, Amsterdam Avenue and West 109th Street, ca. 1930

those themes and questions too often taken for granted, but it will not attempt to explain away painting, for as we all know, paintings unfold slowly for both their makers and their viewers, their meanings as provisional as they may be profound. As Fairfield Porter put it, "So far as it has merit, a painting is a fact, arbitrary and individual."[2] Nevertheless, we will proceed in the hope that, by turning our attention to the figure that is created through painting, we may begin to understand what painted figures have to say about the world.

Our discussion cuts across a familiar narrative of American art. Listen to how the eminent art critic Mariana Van Rensselaer told the story in the introduction to her sumptuously illustrated *Book of American Figure Painters* in 1886:

> When I say that such a book could not well have been given us even a very few years ago, I do not merely refer to the quality of its pages. I speak also of the nature of their subject-matter, the character of the aspirations they reveal. For in the very earliest days of our art, portraiture was all in all to us; and in the period next succeeding, landscape attracted almost every brush. . . . And, quickly following to profit by the opening thus secured, came the new band of native artists preaching a new artistic gospel.[3]

This new gospel of the figure graces the volume in lavish, full-page photogravures of paintings and drawings by "forty of the leading American artists." There are names well known today, such as William Merritt Chase, Thomas Eakins, and Eastman Johnson, as well as important artists largely consigned to history, such as Frederick Arthur Bridgeman, Kenyon Cox, and Thomas Waterman Wood.[4] In Van Rensselaer's eyes, these "new men" had occasioned nothing short of the first truly national art form: figure painting "bound together by . . . common artistic value."[5] Yet while her selection of then-contemporary art certainly constituted new directions for American figure painting, Van Rensselaer deliberately understated figuration's vital role in earlier periods in favor of that nationalistic claim. This simplified evolution of American art—from portrait to landscape to figure—ignored paintings and careers that are not easily interpreted by art historians to this day.[6]

Consider George Henry Hall's *A Dead Rabbit* of 1858 (p. 245). The painting meets you, almost life-sized. It depicts with exceptional care nearly three-quarters of an Irish gang member or, more specifically, of his body, as his face is partially obscured from view. Backed against a masonry wall, he stands frozen, brick in hand, while a riotous fire rages beyond the wall's edge, just barely visible. When Hall submitted this picture to the Academy as his diploma work in 1882—to replace his 1868 submission of a still life—he was making a specific claim before his peers: that the human figure is, for an artist, the most interesting, ambitious, and engaging subject of all, and that although an artist must seek out lengthy training in both anatomy and the depiction of the human form, painting becomes art only by surpassing slavish recording. This insight was born of Hall's stint at the Düsseldorf Akademie, where he attended classes in 1849 and was likely taught, at one point, by Emanuel Leutze (pp. 42–43).[7]

In 1850, Hall reflected on his year of study in a letter to Andrew Warner, then corresponding secretary of the American Art-Union in New York:

> Let me tell you in a few words what I think are the characteristics of that school. Good composition, accurate drawing, and faithful and elaborate finish; but a lack of invention, and an entire want of originality. . . . The mind is wearied with the exactness of the picture. In color they are dry. . . . Flesh has the same texture as the ground and the rocks—they paint with clay and brick dust. . . . It is a hackneyed remark that the artist must be true to himself; let it not be forgotten, do not urge him into paths where no forms of life or beauty meet his eye, where the air, soft and healthful perhaps for others, gives *him* no invigorating impulse, where he may stumble at strange obstacles,—but let him quietly seek his own way, humble and obscure [as] it may be, perhaps contemptible, but he will reach his goal at last. . . . I shall go on painting the same unpopular and perhaps ridiculous subjects; with the same style of color and execution, improving, of course, as much as is in my power.[8]

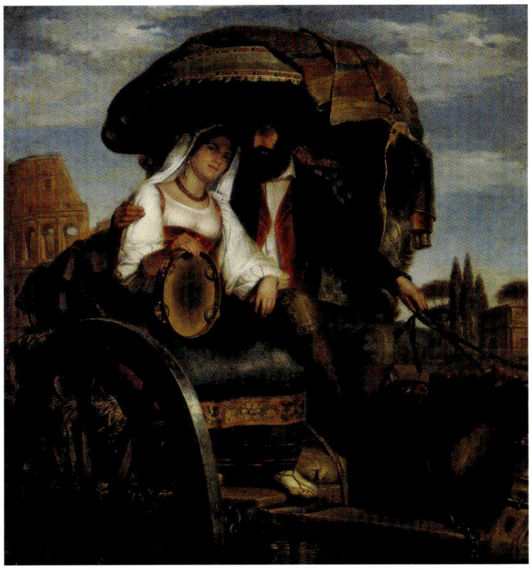

Fig. 3. George Henry Hall, *Roman Wine Cart*, 1851. Oil on canvas. Museum of Fine Arts, Boston

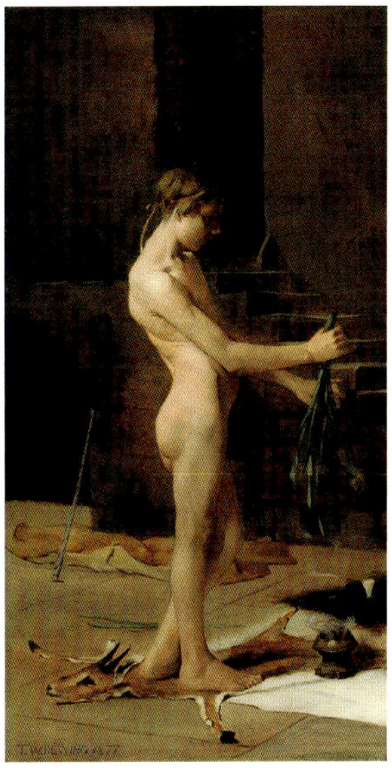

Fig. 4. Thomas Wilmer Dewing, *The Sorcerer's Slave*, 1877. Oil on canvas. National Academy of Design, New York

Months later, Hall would paint one such "perhaps ridiculous" subject, *Roman Wine Cart* (fig. 3), which he exhibited at the National Academy in 1853. Depicting a pair of *pifferari*—Italian musician-peasants of a type Hall had no doubt seen during the time he spent in that country after Düsseldorf—leaving the city, as the *pifferari* were forced to do after the Christmas holidays, the work humanizes two individuals more typically viewed, through the lens of the time, as completely foreign and otherworldly. "O, the *eyes* of these people! . . . You lose yourself in the vain efforts to read a soul life within them . . . eyes into which an angel might look, and lose heaven, believing he saw it there—eyes into which a little child might look, and dream of a hell of which he had never heard," reads a traveler's account published the following year.[9] However unpopular works such as *Roman Wine Cart* may have been with some of the day's critics, and however much Hall's foregrounding of the couple's dignity and the specificity of their plight diverged from his peers' more picturesque genre treatments, the painting was still understandable within such a frame of expectations.

This was not the case with *A Dead Rabbit*, a work that combines myriad conventions into a single image, surpassing the limits imposed by each: it is no genre scene or "fancy" picture, but it is drawn from the life of the underclass; no still life, yet it bears the name of one; no history painting, though it depicts the previous year's infamous gang uprising and conflates it with religious imagery; no standard *académie* (fig. 4), though it foregrounds anatomy and physiognomy and bears the following documentary inscription on the back: "Study of an Irishman . . . 3 afternoons work."[10] Simply put, outside any easily comprehensible category for figure painting as it was, there was no fitting context for *A Dead Rabbit* at the time it was painted *other* than the framework offered by the

National Academy.[11] Within the Academy's collection, the painting would have been viewed by Hall's fellow Academicians as a summary of his previous training as well as a statement of his independence from such influence—a thoroughly original take on flesh and figure, built from "brick dust."

The impulse to reconcile direct observation of the human body with the elevated and intellectually rigorous demands of painting, with its attendant connotations of mythology, literature, and history, is evident in the work of Elihu Vedder, whom Hall befriended when living in Italy once again, from 1883 to 1887. While Vedder's interpretations of Greek mythology and his illustrations for the *Rubáiyát of Omar Khayyam* are well known for their visionary quality and speculative play, working from life was fundamental to the artist's practice, and many of his most dreamlike compositions were the result of extensive figure studies and on-site sketching. Take his diploma work for the Academy *Jane Jackson* (p. 247), a tondo variation on the familiar *tête d'expression* prototype inherited from the Académie royale de peinture et de sculpture in Paris.[12] The idea that an individual's interior life could manifest itself on his or her face had been codified in the theories of René Descartes and in schematic depictions by the French academy's founder, Charles Le Brun. Later, fatigued by students' rote repackaging of Le Brun's faces, which were widely available in engravings, instructors introduced the Prix Caylus, a competition that tasked students with drawing "expression" directly from the faces of live models.[13] Uniting this practice with the specificity of portraiture, Vedder's painting moved the novelist Herman Melville to call its subject "Sibylline, yet benign" in a poem he dedicated to the work after seeing it in the National Academy's annual exhibition of 1865.[14]

The Academy's tondo marks a turning point in Vedder's career, from the intimate scale and mood of earlier days—evident, for example, in his rare and brooding portrait of the landscapist Andrew W. Warren (p. 246)—to the artist's mature, almost epic style, as the sitter, Jane Jackson, became the inspiration for a suite of works devoted to the subject of the Cumaean Sibyl, including the large-scale work now in Detroit (fig. 5).

> I had my studio in the old Gibson Building on Broadway; I used to pass frequently a near corner, where an old negro woman sold peanuts. Her meekly bowed head and a look of patient endurance and resignation touched my heart and we became friends. She had been a slave down South, and had at that time a son, a fine tall fellow, she said, fighting in the Union Army. I finally persuaded her to sit to me and made a drawing of her head and also had her photograph taken. Having been elected associate of the National Academy, according to custom I had to send in a painting to the permanent collection, so I sent in this study of her head and called it simply by her name—which was Jane Jackson. Time went on and I found myself in a mood. As I always try to

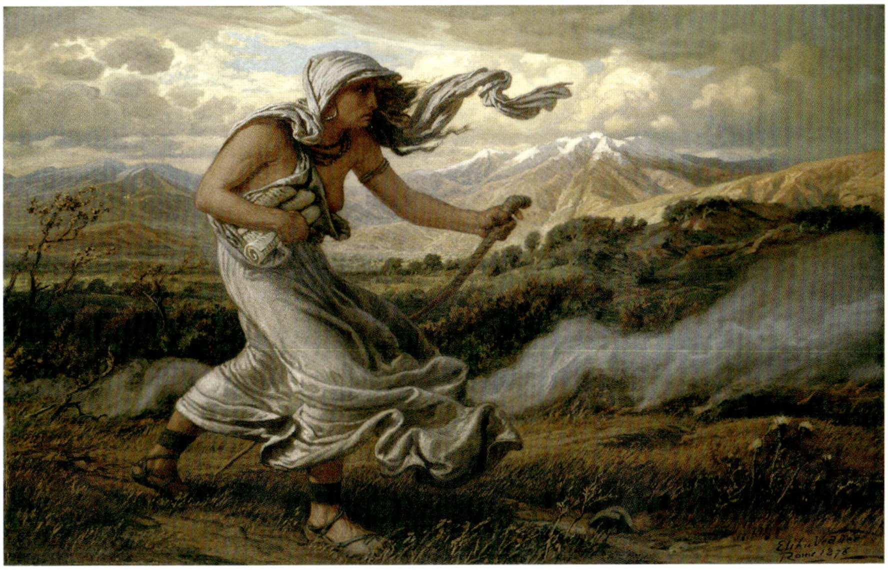

Fig. 5. Elihu Vedder, *The Cumaean Sibyl*, 1876. Oil on canvas. Detroit Institute of Arts

> embody my moods in some picture, this mood found its resting-place in the picture of "The Cum[a]ean Sibyl." Thus this fly—or rather this bee in my bonnet—was finally preserved in amber-varnish, and thus Jane Jackson became the Cum[a]ean Sibyl.[15]

Vedder's recollection offers insight into a painter's practice, putting words to something that often eludes outright definition: the idea that inspiration may not happen all at once but can, like a nagging "bee in a bonnet," be understood only in retrospect, because, by definition, if one is inspired, one is lost in the unselfawareness of creativity. Painting begins when a painter knows where she or he wants to go, but the painter's openness to what unfolds in the act of painting may mean that the original course shifts to a different destination midway through the journey, or that randomness and happenstance interfere to carve out new inroads into familiar territory. The story of Jackson's transition from flesh-and-blood woman to painted prophetess also suggests that, in answering the question of how to paint a figure, a painter may figure out a new direction for painting.

In Vedder's case, this resulted in an expansion of his frame of reference into the landscape, where, as the art historian Jane Dillenberger so eloquently suggested with respect to his work, "life, death, and destiny have coalesced."[16] By the 1860s, however, the relationship between figure and landscape had already been a subject of investigation by American painters for some time. For example, in 1836—the year of Vedder's birth—Thomas Cole had laid out one of the most persuasive and influential theorizations of this topic in his "Essay on American Scenery."[17] In the artist's formulation, mountains were "garbed" by dense forests and picturesque woods; bodies of water were as expressive as "the eye in

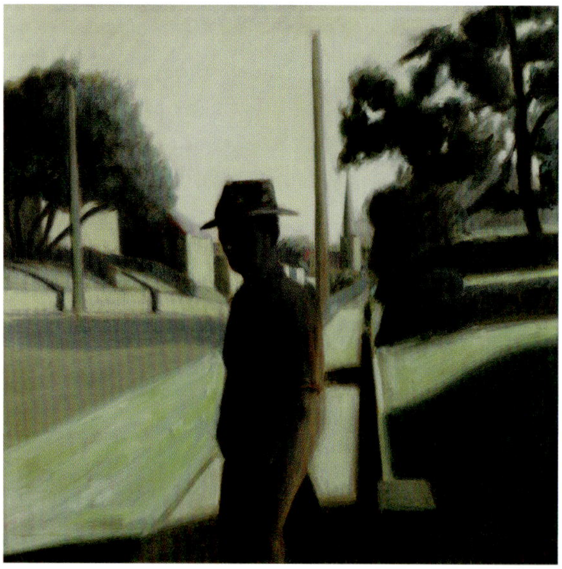

Fig. 6. Robert Kipniss, *Self-Portrait: Petersburg, Virginia*, 1957. Oil on canvas. National Academy of Design, New York

the human countenance"; waterfalls cried out "the voice of the landscape"; and trees acted "like men, differing wildly in character." Cole conceived the very landscape itself as a figure with a soul in need of unclothing by "a lonely traveler" searching for signs of divine presence.[18] The essay expresses a central ambiguity: a painter can adumbrate the contours of the celestial in nature only in relation to his body and through the organizing metaphor of the figure. This tension animates much of Cole's oeuvre, as he consistently pictured the immensity of the landscape in relation to the figure, and both figure and history painting remained important touchstones for the artist from the beginning to the end of his short career, even as his landscapes secured his place as the father of the Hudson River School.[19]

Expanding on this idea, the trope of a solitary figure set into the landscape appears in numerous works in the Academy's collection: from the contemplative modes of Frederic Edwin Church (p. 57) and George Inness (p. 77), through the impressionisms of Frederick Carl Frieseke (p. 101), Karl Anderson, and Daniel Garber (p. 137), to Robert Kipniss's brooding wartime self-portrait (fig. 6) and Walter Hatke's *Provider* (p. 103). While in the work of Cole and other Hudson River School painters—especially that of his great friend Asher B. Durand (p. 53)—the figure in nature typically bespoke a tempered transcendentalism, the landscape continued to provide, in these later paintings, a powerful organizing principle for the figure, allowing artists to conceptualize the move from a studio-based practice of life painting to one that pictured the figure's relationship to—both its isolation from and its engagement with, more broadly—the world outside.[20] In their focus on the singular figure's absorption in its surroundings, such images also registered the idea that any representation of the landscape is a work of the mind as much as it is a topographical account or objective experience

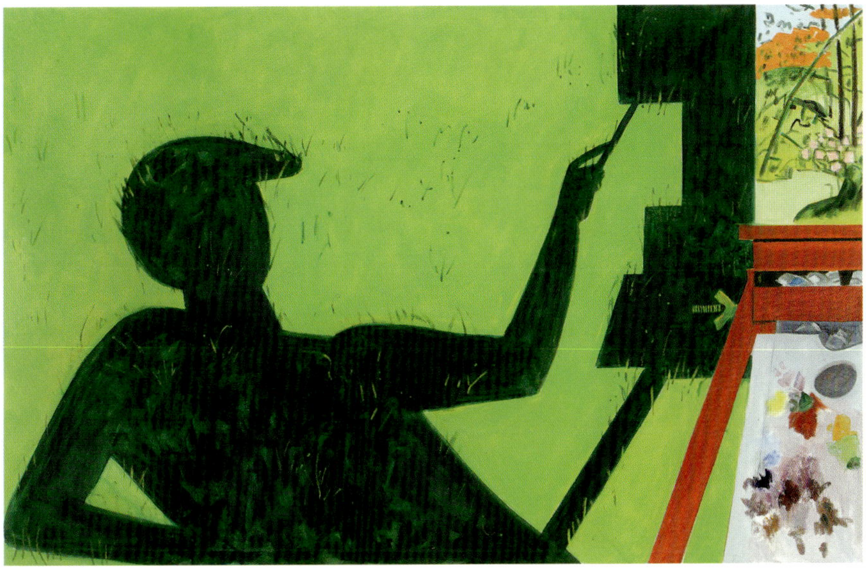

Fig. 7. Lois Dodd, *Shadow of Painter Painting "September Light,"* 2009. Oil on linen. Private collection

of place. In the words of Henry David Thoreau, "It is in vain to dream of a wildness distant from ourselves. . . . I shall never find in the wilds . . . any greater wildness . . . than I import into it."[21]

A more recent interpretation of the figure-in-the-landscape idiom is Lois Dodd's *Shadow of Painter Painting "September Light"* (fig. 7), a work that—by offering the artist's absence as a figure—operates very differently from the bravura directness of her Academy self-portrait (p. 199). Dodd came of age in the wake of Abstract Expressionism, and her brilliance in the former work is to suggest, in the most unassuming and gentle painterly manner possible, that although abstraction categorically poses a challenge to the representation of both the figure and the landscape by prohibiting realism's visual cues in both their veristic and their imagined varieties, easel painting always demands—*prefigures*, even—the human being at the edge of the canvas, whether painter or viewer. Throughout her career, Dodd has probed this contention in paintings that employ reflections in windowpanes (p. 198) and shadows, both serving as visual metaphors for the presence of the figure's absence within the landscape of modernism.

Another long-standing preoccupation of figure painters has been the nude, and we can trace this unfolding in the work of three Academicians for whom the subject was or has been a chief painterly concern: Kenyon Cox, Isabel Bishop, and Philip Pearlstein. Cox's *A Blonde* (p. 249), the earliest of the three paintings, aimed to translate the idealized language of the past into the vernacular of the present. Like many artists of his generation, Cox had traveled to Paris to further his art, eventually finding a mentor in Jean-Léon Gérôme—a teacher as well, we should note, of Thomas Eakins (p. 89), for whom the nude also occupied pride of place, albeit with very different aims. As Cox and Eakins returned stateside along with other students from Gérôme's atelier, such as George

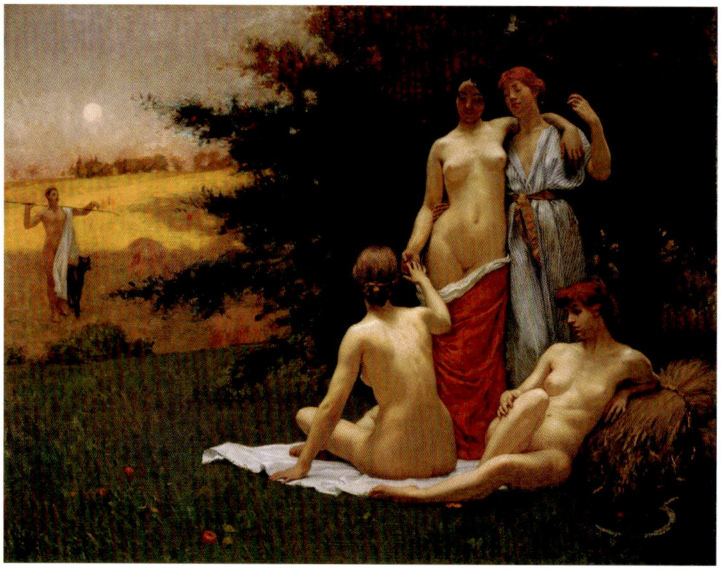

Fig. 8. Kenyon Cox, *An Eclogue*, 1890. Oil on canvas. Smithsonian American Art Museum, Washington, DC

de Forest Brush, Wyatt Eaton (p. 195), and J. Alden Weir (pp. 116–17), they brought with them an awareness of European precedent as well as the ambition to say something novel in paint about the figure and, more specifically, the nude. All five of these artists were chosen for Van Rensselaer's compendium, the book with which this discussion opened, and moving through the volume, a reader witnesses the efflorescence of the artists' differing styles at the turn of the century.

We approach Cox's figure from behind; with the bare wall, rumpled fabric, and pillow, there are just enough visual data to create the plastic space against which the figure is defined. Whereas the nude was a frequent subject for Cox, previous works, such as *An Eclogue* (fig. 8), overtly reference classical ideals. With *A Blonde* and the large-scale works Cox made in the same series, viewers and critics of the day were presented with a woman's corporeality, free from any trappings of allegory or the halcyon past.[22] The sole of a foot is ever-so-slightly unclean; the flesh folds and fingernails shine idiosyncratically; buttocks dimple under pressure; hairs dapple the nape below a chignon; and a backbone segments beneath strained skin. While many found Cox's nudes vulgar, some even going so far as iconoclastic attacks, the artist believed that by extracting details from the "multiplicity of the real" and combining them with the ideal—for example, in the marble-like expanses of the skin and the expressionless face of *A Blonde*—art offered the potential for public edification.[23]

"Should [artists'] treatment of [the nude] be 'realistic' or 'idealistic'? My answer is—both," Cox proffered in a treatise on the subject.[24] For him, this was the unspoken magic of painting: the ability of an image made by human hands to appear so natural or realistic, so viscous or tactile, so sumptuous or disturbing—or any other words that seem only to skim the surface of painting's ability—that for a moment, enchanted by alchemy, the viewer accesses the mind that invented the picture. Whereas modernism would aim to unmask this ideological function of realism, Cox, in 1891, could still believe in the ability to communicate powerful ideals through accessible imagery and could see modern abstraction, in contrast, as an elevation of the individual experience at the expense of the social order. And although his near-hysterical criticism of the 1913 Armory Show—with its triumvirate of nude manifestos in paint, Marcel Duchamp's *Nude Descending a Staircase (No. 2)*, Robert Henri's *Figure in Motion*, and Henri Matisse's *Blue Nude*—is well known, Cox descended into this unyielding orthodoxy only late in life, fearing that modernism would give rise to the uncoupling of artists from the public.[25]

With Isabel Bishop's *Nude Study* (p. 248), we immediately feel the weight of tradition that engaged Cox forty-three years earlier, yet here, there is no overtly moralizing tone, no didactic resolve. A student of Kenneth Hayes Miller (p. 165), himself a former student of Cox, Bishop struggled internally for decades to break free of her teacher's traditional methods and classicizing vision while maintaining her relationship to the history of art. Eventually, she accomplished this through her choice of subject matter, which focused on the lived reality of individuals, usually women absorbed in unselfconscious tasks such as bathing, picking their teeth, removing a stocking, or ascending subway steps. With her studio located on the top floor of a timeworn office building at Broadway and 17th Street, Bishop often called models in from Union Square—working girls, personable hobos, café patrons—in order to work from life, as was the case with *Nude Study*, whose subject was a tailor's daughter with aspirations of becoming a dancer.[26] In 1974, John I. H. Baur, then director of the Whitney Museum of American Art, admitted that "in some mysterious manner which I do not really understand [Bishop's works] carry forward the great tradition of North-European, seventeenth-century figure painting. Beyond argument is their monumental existence—in terms of both humanity and art."[27] Bishop achieved this monumentality through a laborious process of numerous quick sketches, preliminary to polished drawings; multiple states of etchings and aquatints; photostat enlargements for canvas; and, finally, the heavily worked painting. This perpetual, ever-changing working method allowed the artist to quarrel with an idea and its forms over time, as the painting stage alone took months—in some cases, years—to complete.

There is a paradox evident in *Nude Study* that runs through all of Bishop's works (nearly all of which involve the figure). The inwardly focused moments of life she chose to depict are the most evanescent and hard to sustain, yet paint is a timeless and static mode of address. How to represent transient, transformative sensations, such as movement or fleeting introspection, on a flat, still surface without flattening out the roundness of experience? Bishop's answer was to unite the world around her with the visual topoi of art history—in this case, the pregnant moments of life pithily summed up by Rubens, Rembrandt, and Fragonard. She called this operation "the metaphor" in numerous interviews, implying something like a visual form in which the past and the present are collapsed.[28]

Throughout much of her career, Bishop kept a piece of paper taped to her easel dotted with six painterly aphorisms. One reads, "To understand a form plastically is to comprehend its inner character and its position in nature." The list culminates in a question: "Is it so?"[29] This searching quality—a modest yet unyielding quest to discover what figure painting can accomplish, how it affirms life, and what it can preserve of it—characterizes Bishop's artistic production.

Three decades after Bishop's nude, when Pop art appeared to have fully parsed the dialectic between the signs of high and mass culture, Philip Pearlstein was espousing an aesthetic position with his *Nude Torso* (p. 251) simply by dint of its representing a studio nude, regardless of its painterly style. "It seems madness on the part of any painter educated in the twentieth-century modes of picture-making to take as his subject the naked human figure, conceived as a self-contained entity possessed of its own dignity, existing in an inhabitable space, viewed from a single vantage point," Pearlstein had written in *ARTnews* the previous summer.[30] He offered this apologia at a time when major museums were starting to acknowledge the role of the figure in contemporary art but seemed to be getting the interpretation completely wrong. It is no coincidence that Pearlstein's article followed the mounting of two such exhibitions at the Museum of Modern Art, 1959's *New Images of Man* and 1962's *Recent Painting U.S.A.: The Figure*.

Although the checklist of the former exhibition was a formidable convocation of European and American painters and sculptors—from Bacon, Dubuffet, and Giacometti to the Academicians Richard Diebenkorn, James McGarrell (pp. 254–55), and Leonard Baskin—Pearlstein saw nothing of his current pictorial project in the existential framework layered onto the show by its curator, Peter Selz.[31] That bleak outlook, steeped in Cold War unease, was summed up by the Christian theologian Paul Tillich in his prefatory note to *New Images of Man*: "In the development of art since the beginning of our century the negative emphasis in the expression of the fight for humanity by far prevails. This is also true of the works presented in this exhibition with their distortions."[32] While both exhibitions ostensibly took the figure as their subject, the abstraction that had dominated the previous decade was their real theoretical context. In the words of Alfred H. Barr, Jr., in *Recent Painting U.S.A.*, "These human figures were painted in a period (a glorious period in American art) when the painted surface often functioned in virtual and even dogmatic independence of any represented image. Some of these pictures suggest uncertainty as to whether a painting in the 1960s can or cannot, should or should not, live by paint alone."[33] This point of view was anathema to Pearlstein and other Academicians such as Rosemarie Beck (pp. 204–5), Jane Freilicher (pp. 196–97), Alex Katz, Louisa Matthíasdóttir (p. 273), and Wayne Thiebaud (p. 272)—some of whom, like William Clutz (p. 225), happened to be included in *Recent Painting U.S.A.*—who were working in different ways to acknowledge the integrity of the figure in the perceived world *as well as* the space of the canvas.

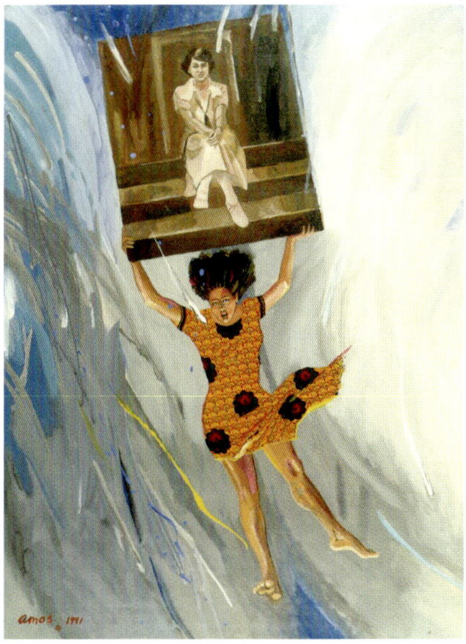

Fig. 9. Emma Amos, *Will You Forget Me? (Falling Series)*, 1991. Acrylic on linen with African fabric. Private collection

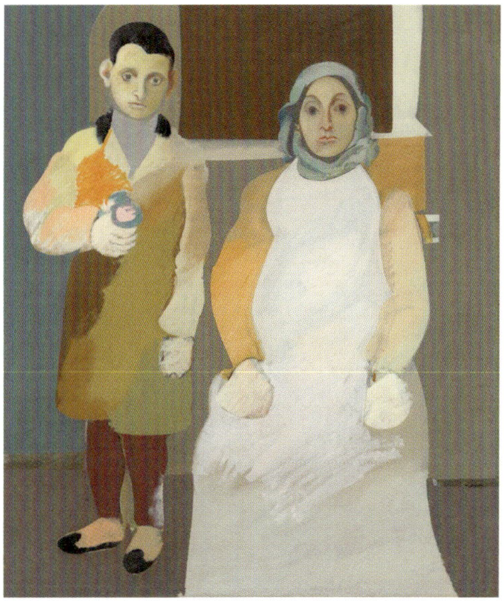

Fig. 10. Arshile Gorky, *The Artist and His Mother*, ca. 1926–36. Oil on canvas. Whitney Museum of American Art, New York

Returning to Pearlstein's *Nude Torso*, we see a female figure standing against a bare wall, blazingly lit up as if by dentist's lamps. Tripartite shadows cast a landscape of modeled forms in various directions. Although this is no lived body but a rhetorical figure cast from purely pictorial concerns, it can only have resulted from an artist's working from life. In its combination of intensely scrutinized detail; horizontal orientation, which repudiates the body's verticality; and completely anonymous subject, *Nude Torso* asks us to consider a startling question: at what point is the figure created in art more important than its human referent? It is interesting that Pearlstein's insight was born at the same time as the dematerialized practices of conceptualism were just beginning to question the nature of the physical manifestations of the institution called "Art" and the human body as a coherent and stable entity.

This brief discussion of the figure will end with two paintings, Emma Amos's *Giza and Faith* (p. 243) and W. Lee Savage's *Endangered Bobby* (p. 252). The first work, part of the artist's *Falling* series, portrays Amos in a blue-black expanse. All around her, the world of things is unmoored; several book-kites, strips of African cloth, a misplaced jellyfish, and even paint itself appear to drop down, or float up, in a delicate choreography. A red-collared dog hovers on a field of white and black tesserae bearing half the Latin inscription CAVE CANEM, or "beware of dog," which Amos appropriated from the foyer mosaic of the House of the Tragic Poet in Pompeii. A redoubtable portrait of the artist's peer Faith Ringgold appears at the far right, and a border of textile eyes collaged across the bottom of the canvas invokes painting's apotropaic magic. In the upper register, another tumbling body mirrors Amos's own; he is Giza Daniels-Endesha, Amos's recently departed former student and friend, whose life was cut short when he was just shy of thirty years old.[34] In another autobiographical work of the same year, *Will You Forget Me?* (fig. 9), Amos falls through the air holding a sepia-toned photograph taken in her late mother's college years. Painting, Amos seems to be saying, is a way of picturing both what history elides and what slips from memory. Painting is all that lasts.

W. Lee Savage would likely have agreed. *Endangered Bobby* depicts the artist's first cousin, the titular Bobby Kelly, clad in blue stripes.[35] He stands up straight, with the clumsy nonchalance of boyhood, while his proud grandfather pulls him close. Collaged onto the canvas is a faded photograph that depicts, from left to right, the artist, known as Lee; his older brother, John; and Lon, his twin brother. By the time Savage made this work, the adult Bobby Kelly had taken his own life, a fact that irrevocably changes any attempt to make sense of the painting. There is a studied reticence to the picture that recalls Arshile Gorky's searching meditation on loss, *The Artist and His Mother* (fig. 10)—an element of control visible in much of Savage's work.[36] Passages just barely limned abut deep, sculpted space, and forms trail off beyond canvases' edges; faces fade from focus or are vividly detailed, yet they withhold expression. *Endangered Bobby* is an intellectually suggestive memorial that offers no easy takeaway.

Look again at *Giza and Faith*. Perhaps Amos is not falling at all. Perhaps she is standing in the black passage at the painting's left side, conjuring all that is before her as she waves her arms from side to side, her fingers creating the brushstrokes underneath. Much like *Endangered Bobby*, this work is an attempt to picture the senseless. And now, we have returned to the question with which this discussion began—the one kept momentarily at bay—of *why* a painter might paint the figure. "'Like' and 'like' and 'like'—but what is the thing that lies beneath the semblance of the thing?" Virginia Woolf famously penned. "The structure is now visible; what is inchoate is here stated."[37] For the figure is never a form without content: its representations both fall short of and exceed the terms of experience.

Epigraph: Wallace Stevens, "The Ultimate Poem Is Abstract," in *The Collected Poems of Wallace Stevens* (London: Faber and Faber, 1984), 429–30. I would like to thank Will Clutz, James McGarrell, and Michael Neumeister for their stimulating conversation and Katrina for her endless encouragement.

1. The first session of the National Academy School was held on November 15, 1826, in the Old Almshouse at City Hall Park in Lower Manhattan; under the supervision of two Academicians, twenty male students sketched plaster casts of antique sculpture by candlelight. Female students were admitted to these classes as early as 1831. Life classes for advanced male students began in the fall of 1837 but for female students not until 1871, although women were frequent contributors to the annual exhibitions and had always been allowed membership in the Academy. On May 2, 1827, Rosalba Peale was named an Honorary Member, and Ann Hall, Emily Maverick, Maria Ann Maverick, Frances Platt Townsend Lupton, and Julia Fulton were all named Associates.
2. Fairfield Porter, artist's statement, *Recent Works by Fairfield Porter* (New York: Hirschl and Adler Galleries, 1974), n.p.
3. Mariana G[riswold] Van Rensselaer, introduction to *Book of American Figure Painters* (Philadelphia: J. B. Lippincott, 1886), n.p.
4. Only six of the forty artists included in Van Rensselaer's book were not (or did not become) National Academicians; the endpapers were designed by George W. Maynard (ANA 1881, NA 1885). All the included works were made within a year of the book's publication, and peppered between the plates are selections of lyrical poetry, mainly seventeenth-century British.

5. Van Rensselaer, introduction, n.p. Five years earlier, she had used the term "new men" to describe this group of artists in "The New York Art Season," *Atlantic Monthly* 48, no. 286 (August 1881): 193.

6. A similar dismissal of the accomplishments of figure painters before the Civil War as "all pretty shallow" and "uncritical" can be found in *The History of American Painting* by the Academician Samuel Isham (New York: Macmillan, 1905), 291. Selected earlier examples of ambitious figure painting include the history paintings displayed at the American Academy of the Fine Arts and the Pennsylvania Academy of the Fine Arts from the end of the 1820s on and at the National Academy's annual exhibitions beginning in the early 1840s; Washington Allston's lyrical figures of the first quarter of the century and, later, those of his acolyte Thomas Buchanan Read; the historical and religious pictures painted by Robert Walter Weir and Thomas P. Rossiter during the 1840s and 1850s; and the literary and genre experiments of some painters during this period, including Henry Inman and William Sidney Mount. See Carrie Rebora, "History Painting at the American Academy of Fine Arts," in Patricia M. Burnham and Lucretia Hoover Giese, eds., *Redefining American History Painting* (New York: Cambridge University Press, 1995), 229–41; Anna Wells Rutledge, ed., *Cumulative Record of Exhibition Catalogues: The Pennsylvania Academy of the Fine Arts, 1807–1870; The Society of Artists, 1800–1814; The Artists' Fund Society, 1835–1845* (Philadelphia: American Philosophical Society, 1955); Mary Bartlett Cowdrey, ed., *National Academy of Design Exhibition Record, 1826–1860*, 2 vols. (New York: New-York Historical Society, 1943); Elizabeth Johns, "Washington Allston: Method, Imagination, and Reality," *Winterthur Portfolio: A Journal of American Material Culture* 12 (1977): 11–15; Clara Erskine Clement, "Early Religious Painting in America," *New England Magazine* 9, no. 4 (December 1894): 387–402; Kent Ahrens, "Religious Paintings of Robert Walter Weir," *Antiques* 103, no. 4 (April 1973): 744–49; Henry T. Tuckerman, "Weir," in *Book of the Artists* (New York: G. P. Putnam and Son, 1867), 203–15; Elizabeth Johns, *American Genre Painting: The Politics of Everyday Life* (New Haven: Yale University Press, 1991), 24–59; and William H. Gerdts, "Henry Inman: Genre Painter," *American Art Journal* 9, no. 1 (May 1977): 26–48. That, in some cases, ambition outmatched ability does not mean that this work should be ignored.

7. Hall left behind little personal information, but before he died he wrote an autobiographical sketch; a copy can be found in the George Washington Stevens Papers (1910–11), Archives of American Art, Smithsonian Institution, Washington, DC.

8. George Henry Hall to Andrew Warner, October 28, 1850, reel 6, letter 241, BV American Art-Union, New-York Historical Society Museum and Library. Hall's letters to Warren frequently reference the inadequacy of an artistic training that emphasizes drawing and exactitude over color and imagination.

9. Grace Greenwood, *Haps and Mishaps of a Tour in Europe* (Boston: Ticknor, Reed, and Fields, 1854), 191–92.

10. The full inscription reads: "Study of an Irishman / Painted 1858 a la prima / 3 afternoons work / 805 Broadway, N.Y. City / Presented 1882."

11. For important interpretations of *A Dead Rabbit*, see Ross Barrett, *Rendering Violence: Riots, Strikes, and Upheaval in Nineteenth-Century American Art* (Oakland: University of California Press, 2014), 75–103, and Joshua Brown and Patricia Hill's exchange in *American Art (Smithsonian American Art Museum)* 17, no. 2 (Summer 2003): 4–12.

12. Another variation is Frank Duveneck's exceptional *Head of an Italian Woman* (1887; NAD, New York). On Duveneck's influence on figure painters from 1878 on, see Lewis Henry Meakin, "Duveneck, a Teacher of Artists," *Arts and Decoration* 1, no. 9 (July 1911): 382–84.

13. On the history of the theory of the passions, see Thomas Kirchner, *L'expression des passions* (Mainz: Philipp von Zabern, 1991). On Charles Le Brun more specifically, see Jennifer Montagu, *The Expression of the Passions* (New Haven: Yale University Press, 1994).

14. Herman Melville, "Formerly a Slave," in *Battle-Pieces, and Aspects of the War* (New York: Harper and Brothers, 1866), 154.

15. Elihu Vedder, *The Digressions of V. Written for His Own Fun and That of His Friends* (Boston: Houghton Mifflin, 1911), 238–39.

16. Jane Dillenberger, "Between Faith and Doubt: Subjects for Meditation," in Joshua C. Taylor, Jane Dillenberger, and Richard Murray, *Perceptions and Evocations: The Art of Elihu Vedder*, exh. cat. (Washington, DC: Smithsonian Institution, 1979), 126.

17. Thomas Cole, "Essay on American Scenery," *American Monthly Magazine* 7, no. 1 (January 1836): 1–12, first delivered as a lecture before the American Lyceum Society in New York on May 8, 1835.

18. Ibid., 5–6, 8–9, 7. William Cullen Bryant employed similar language nearly twenty years after Cole's death in an address delivered at the opening of the National Academy's new building in 1865: "Here, we said, is a young man who does not paint nature at second hand. . . . Here is the physiognomy of our own woods and fields." See William Cullen Bryant, "The Academy of Design," in Parke Godwin, ed., *Prose Writings of William Cullen Bryant* (New York: D. Appleton, 1884), 2:232.

19. See Ellwood C. Parry III, "Thomas Cole and the Problem of Figure Painting," *American Art Journal* 4, no. 1 (Spring 1972): 66–86.

20. Although it is beyond the scope of the present essay, a parallel visual trope would be the nude set into the landscape, beginning with one of its earliest examples, John Vanderlyn's *Ariadne Asleep on the Island of Naxos* (1809–14; Pennsylvania Academy of the Fine Arts), and including examples as diverse as Asher B. Durand's subsequent copies across media; Kenneth Hayes Miller's submission to the 1913 Armory Show, *Recumbent Figure* (ca. 1910–11; Columbus Museum of Art); Leon Kroll's variations on the theme; Horace Pippin's *Lady of the Lake* (1936; Metropolitan Museum of Art); Edwin Dickinson's abstract *Nude Figure, Marie* (1939; Collection Gilbert and Ruth Scharf); and, more recently, Neil Welliver's *Girl with Striped Washcloth* (1971; Whitney Museum of American Art) and *Reflections* (1973; private coll.) as well as Joan Semmel's *Intimacy-Autonomy* (1974; Brooklyn Museum) and *Beachbody* (1985; artist's coll.).
21. Henry David Thoreau, *The Writings of Henry David Thoreau*, vol. 9, *Journal, August 16, 1856–August 7, 1857*, edited by Bradford Torrey (Boston: Houghton Mifflin, 1906), 43.
22. See Cox's *Brune* (1888; Georgia Museum of Art, Athens) and *Nude on a Yellow Couch* (1889; NAD).
23. In January 1910, Cox's *The Girl with Red Hair* of 1890, which is described as closely resembling *A Blonde*, was found slashed and stuffed behind a radiator in the room used for the women's life class at the Art Students League; see *American Art News* 8, no. 14 (January 15, 1910): 1. The phrase "multiplicity of the real" is used by Kenyon Cox in "What Is Painting?" pt. 1, "Painting as an Art of Imitation," *Art World* 1, no. 1 (October 1916): 32.
24. Will H. Low and Kenyon Cox, "The Nude in Art," *Scribner's Magazine* 12, no. 6 (December 1892): 748.
25. Kenyon Cox, "The Modern Spirit in Art: Some Reflections Inspired by the Recent International Exhibition," *Harper's Weekly*, March 15, 1913, 10; Kenyon Cox, "Artist and Public," *Scribner's Magazine* 55, no. 4 (April 1914): 512–20.
26. Therese Lichtenstein, "Isabel Bishop," in *From All Walks of Life: Paintings of the Figure from the National Academy of Design*, exh. cat. (New York: National Academy of Design, 1979), 24.
27. John I. H. Baur, foreword to *Isabel Bishop*, exh. cat. (Tucson: University of Arizona Museum of Art, 1974), 10.
28. Bishop often employed the term "metaphor" but was reticent to define it; the fullest definition can be found in Dorothy Seckler, "Bishop Paints a Picture," *ARTnews* 50, no. 7 (November 1951): 38–41, 63–64. Although the author's understanding of Bishop's art differs from my own, Charlene Cline Marsh's "Isabel Bishop, the Nude, a Means to an End: The Quest for Pictorial Mobility in Art" (master's thesis, Southern Methodist University, 1991) is a valuable resource, as it is based on interviews with the artist. I am grateful to Kathryn Johnston for making it available to me.
29. A copy of the list can be found in the artist's file, NAD Archives.
30. Philip Pearlstein, "Figure Paintings Today Are Not Made in Heaven," *ARTnews* 61, no. 4 (Summer 1962): 39.
31. Also relevant is the critical panning of the curator Norman Geske's thematic exhibition *The Figurative Tradition in Recent American Art* (1968), which represented the United States at the 34th Venice Biennale and included many of the Academicians under discussion; see, for example, Grace Glueck, "The Razzle Dazzle Lost Its Pizzazz," *New York Times*, June 30, 1968.
32. Paul Tillich, "A Prefatory Note," in Peter Selz, *New Images of Man* (New York: Museum of Modern Art, 1959), 10. While the show received many positive reviews, New York–based artists were particularly hostile to its premise; see, for example, Manny Farber, "New Images of (Ugh) Man," *ARTnews* 58, no. 6 (October 1959): 38–39, 58, and Fairfield Porter, "New Images of Man," *Nation*, October 17, 1959, reprinted in Rackstraw Downes, ed., *Fairfield Porter: Art in Its Own Terms: Selected Criticism, 1935–1975* (Boston: MFA Publications, 2008), 59–61. On the exhibition's intellectual context, see Patricia Hills, "The 'New-Image-of-Man' Sensibility," in Patricia Hills and Roberta K. Tarbell, *The Figurative Tradition and the Whitney Museum of American Art: Paintings and Sculpture from the Permanent Collection*, exh. cat. (New York: Whitney Museum of American Art; Newark: University of Delaware Press, 1980), 129–34; and Jed Perl, "The Representational Impulse: Painting in New York, 1960–1985," *New Criterion*, April 1, 1985, 20–33.
33. Alfred H. Barr, Jr., introduction to *Recent Painting U.S.A.: The Figure* (New York: Museum of Modern Art, 1962), n.p.
34. Natalia de Campos and jc lenochan kindly provided me with information on this work.
35. I am grateful to Karen, Kate, and Pete Savage for discussing their recollections with me.
36. Gorky briefly enrolled at the Academy in 1925 and took life classes with Charles Hawthorne. See Michael R. Taylor, "Learning from 'Papa Cézanne': Arshile Gorky and the (Self-) Invention of the Modern Artist," in Joseph Rishel and Katherine Sachs, eds., *Cézanne and Beyond*, exh. cat. (Philadelphia: Philadelphia Museum of Art; New Haven: Yale University Press, 2009), 558n21.
37. Rhoda's words in the wake of Percival's death in Virginia Woolf's *The Waves* (London: Hogarth Press, 1960), 116.

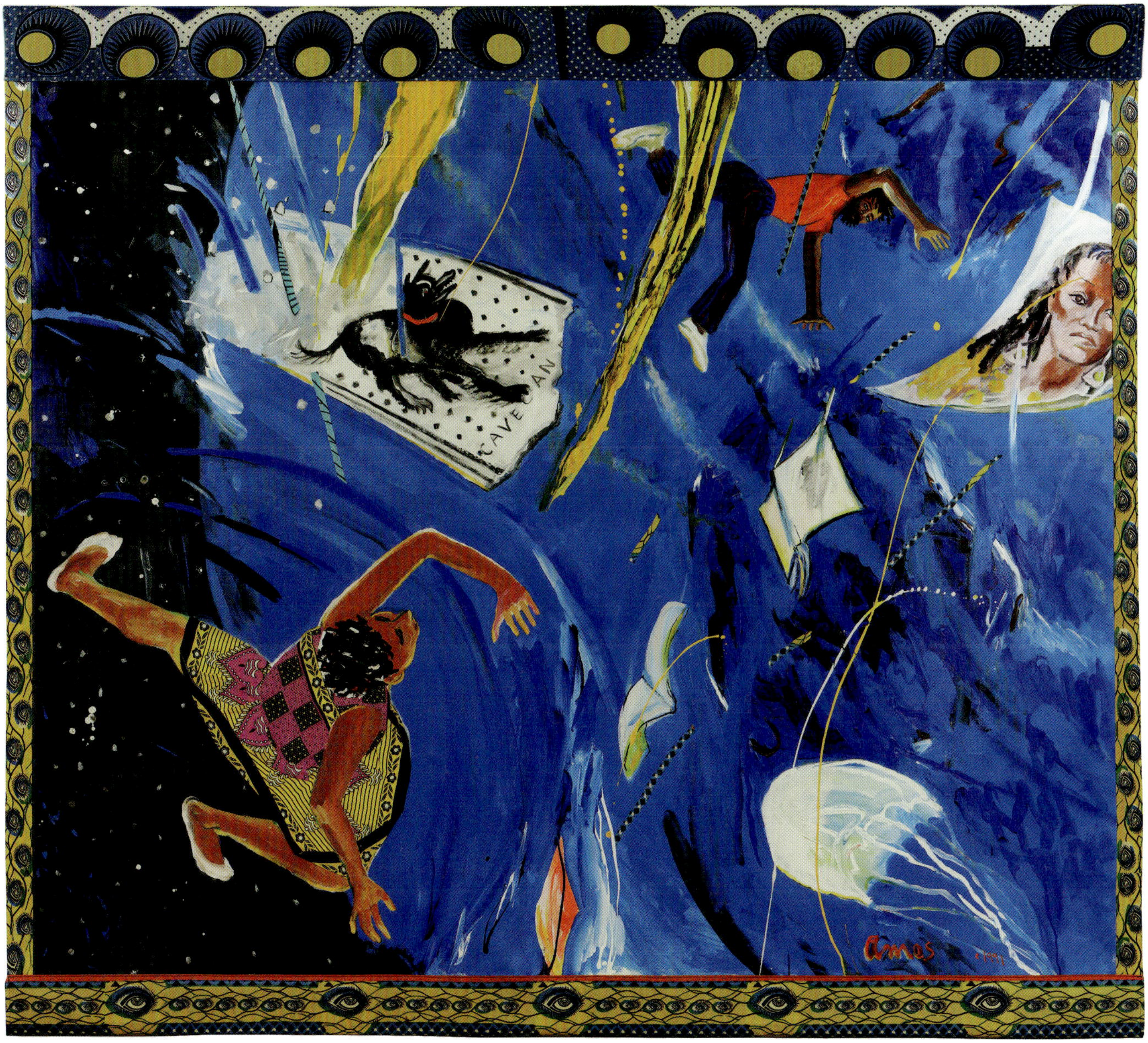

Emma Amos, *Giza and Faith*, 1991. Acrylic on *kanga* cloth and African fabric, 78 × 84 in. (198.1 × 213.4 cm)

CATHERINE OPIE ON GEORGE HENRY HALL

He stands against a wall, a beautiful darkness that seeps into brown shadows. This is a portrait about staring at the male body. It shows a man who most likely works outside, his face ruddy, the flesh turning creamy below the neck. Near the fleshy nipple above the rib cage, a bruise on the same plane as the nipple appears from his armpit. In this portrait I gaze upon the body more than the face; perhaps that is why I picked it, forever interested in what flesh reveals to us. I stare at my bad computer printout, wanting the actual scale of the painting and to see the way the artist handled the paint on the canvas. I am aware of the white cloth tied at the waist, which I presume is his shirt tied loosely. One hand holds what I thought at first was a book; I now believe it is a brick, a brick with a chip, as hard and vulnerable as his body. The thumb rests lightly as he holds the brick. I think of August Sander's photographs and how they reveal to the viewer his subjects' professions. *A Dead Rabbit* suggests something outside the frame that we don't see, the brick as weapon or as work. The portrait asks more questions than it reveals, especially with the title.

Thank you, Google: Dead Rabbit was a notorious street gang in New York, and George Henry Hall made the portrait in 1858. I then think of the wintry days of my Ohio youth, in the basement watching old movies about the Bowery Boys, the accents thick, which resonated a masculinity of fearless desire in the immigrant's life, with the ever-present kind priest who leads the boys out of becoming thugs. It is the tenderness and vulnerability of flesh that the artist portrays in the portrait, which allows a question to be raised as to the subject's identity and character. If he, the subject, looked back at us with eyes on fire and brick posed to be thrown, we, the audience, would read "thug"; behind him in the distance a rabbit on a spike would be present in the true narrative and intention of creating a history painting. The read would be easy and descriptive. Instead, we gaze upon the flesh and the sideways look of the subject with empathy. That is the quality I appreciate and the attraction I have to this particular portrait and, most likely, the reason I chose to commune with it.

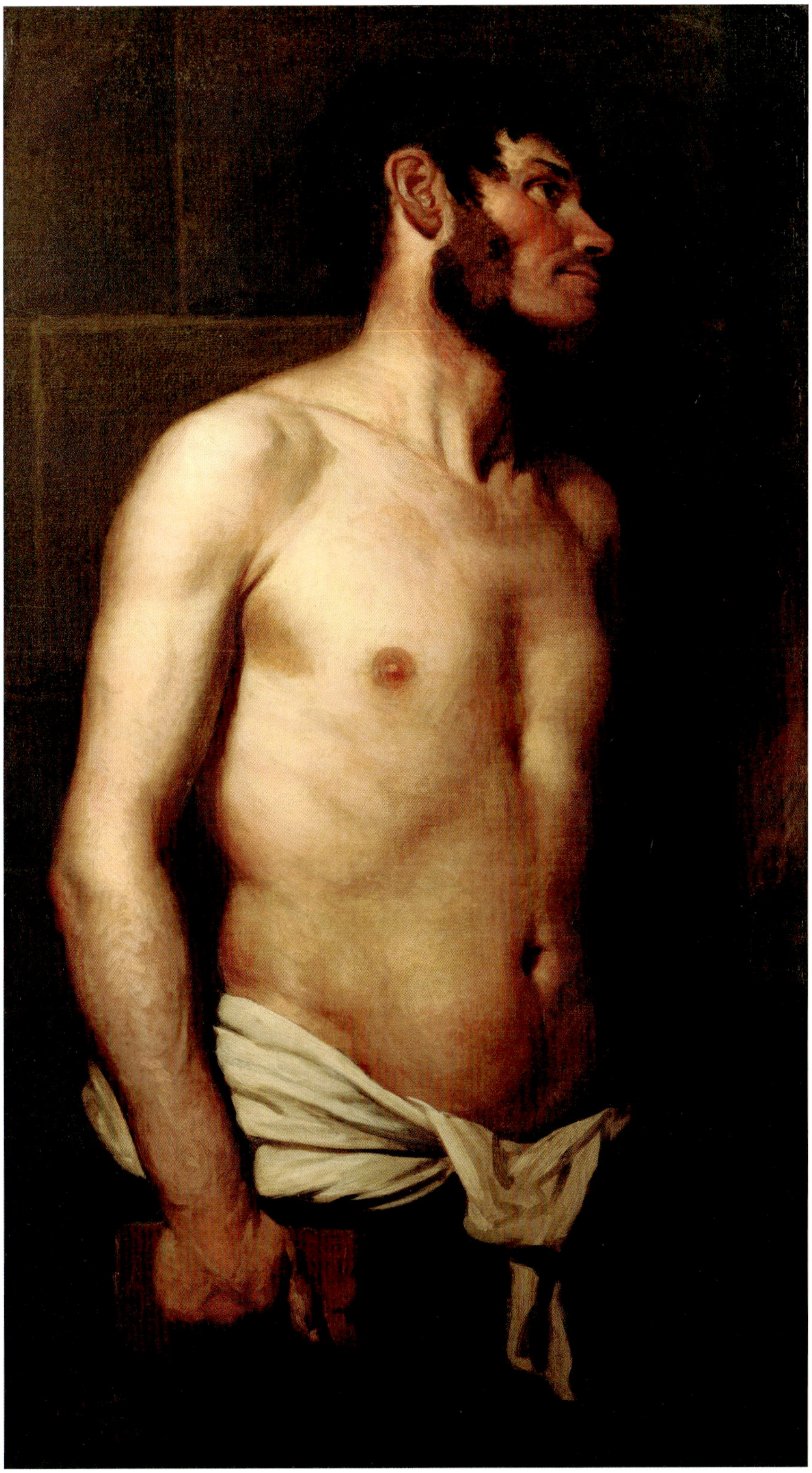

George Henry Hall, *A Dead Rabbit*, 1858. Oil on canvas, 43 ¼ × 24 in. (109.9 × 61 cm)

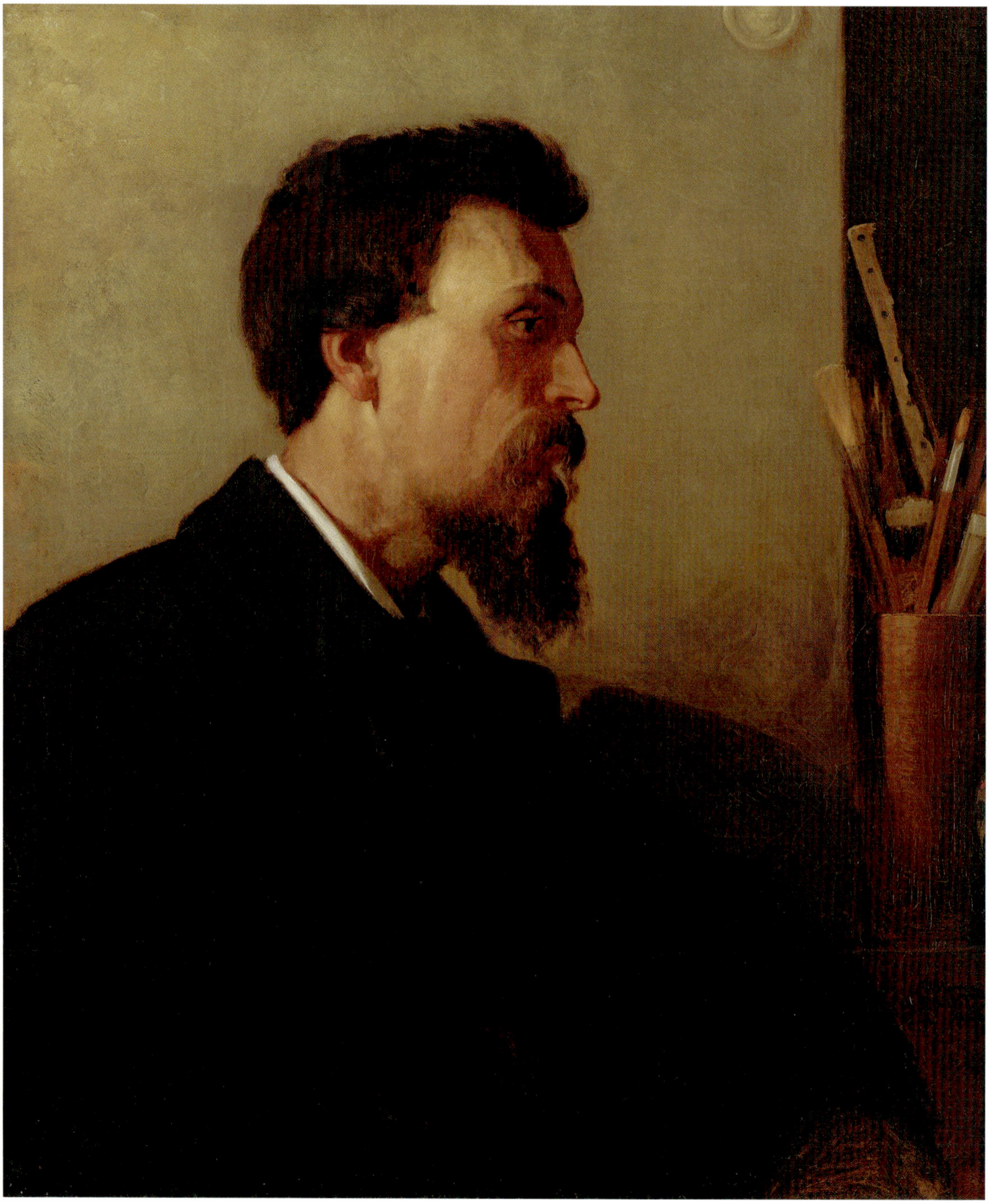

Elihu Vedder, *Andrew W. Warren*, 1864. Oil on canvas, 30 × 25 in. (76.2 × 63.5 cm)

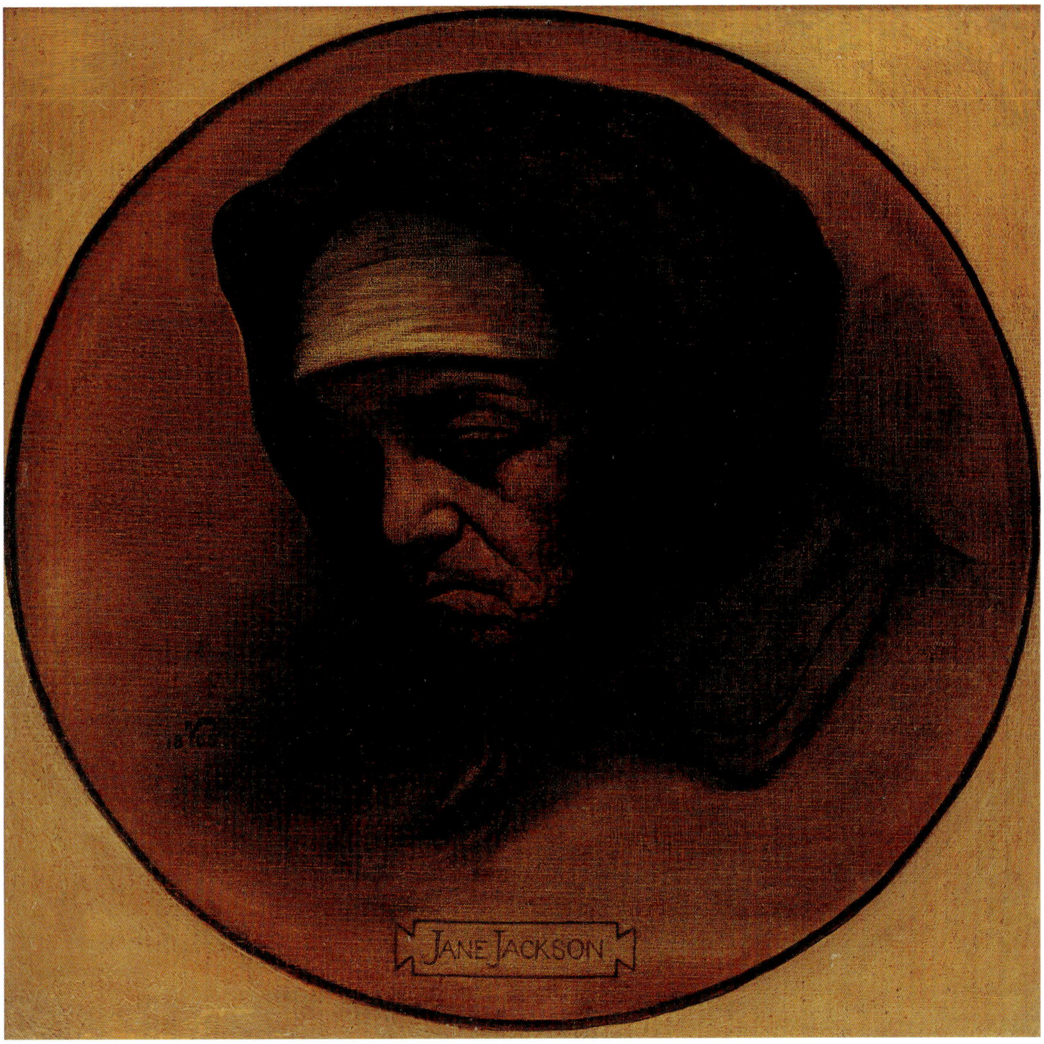

Elihu Vedder, *Jane Jackson*, 1865. Oil on canvas, 18 × 18 in. (45.7 × 45.7 cm)

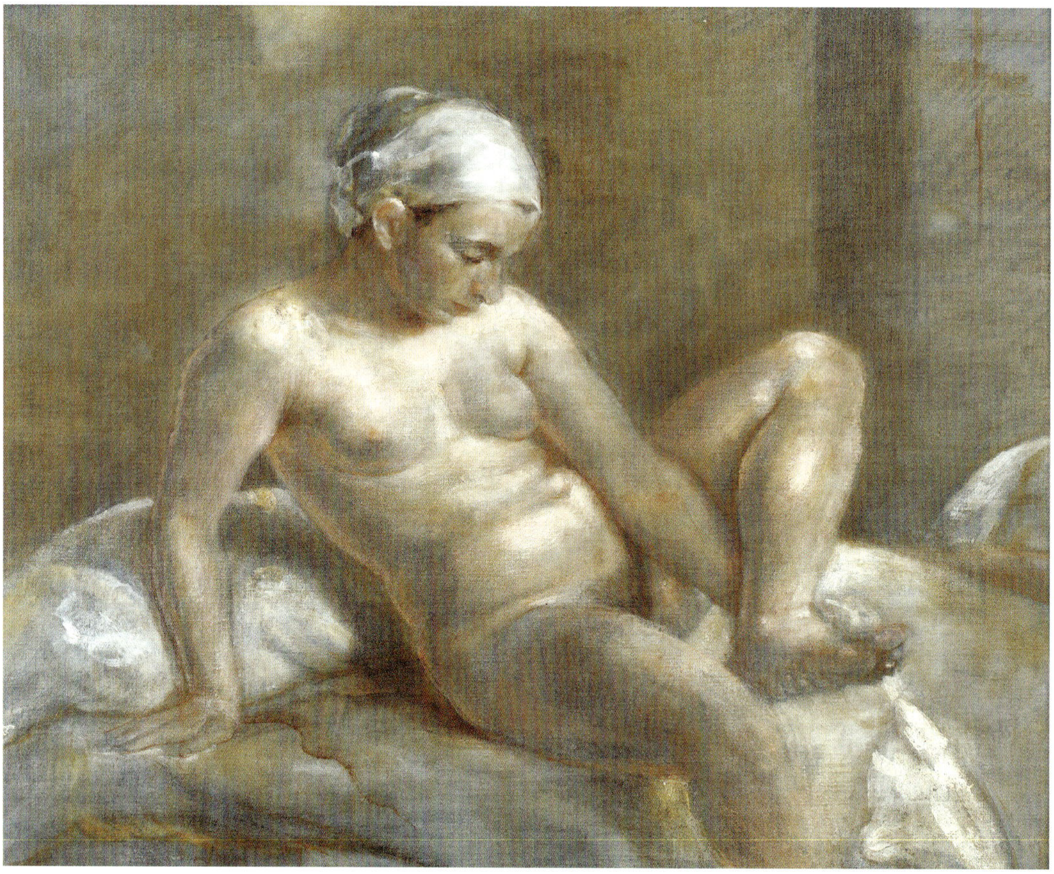

Isabel Bishop, *Nude Study*, 1934. Oil on canvas, 15 × 18 in. (38.1 × 45.7 cm)

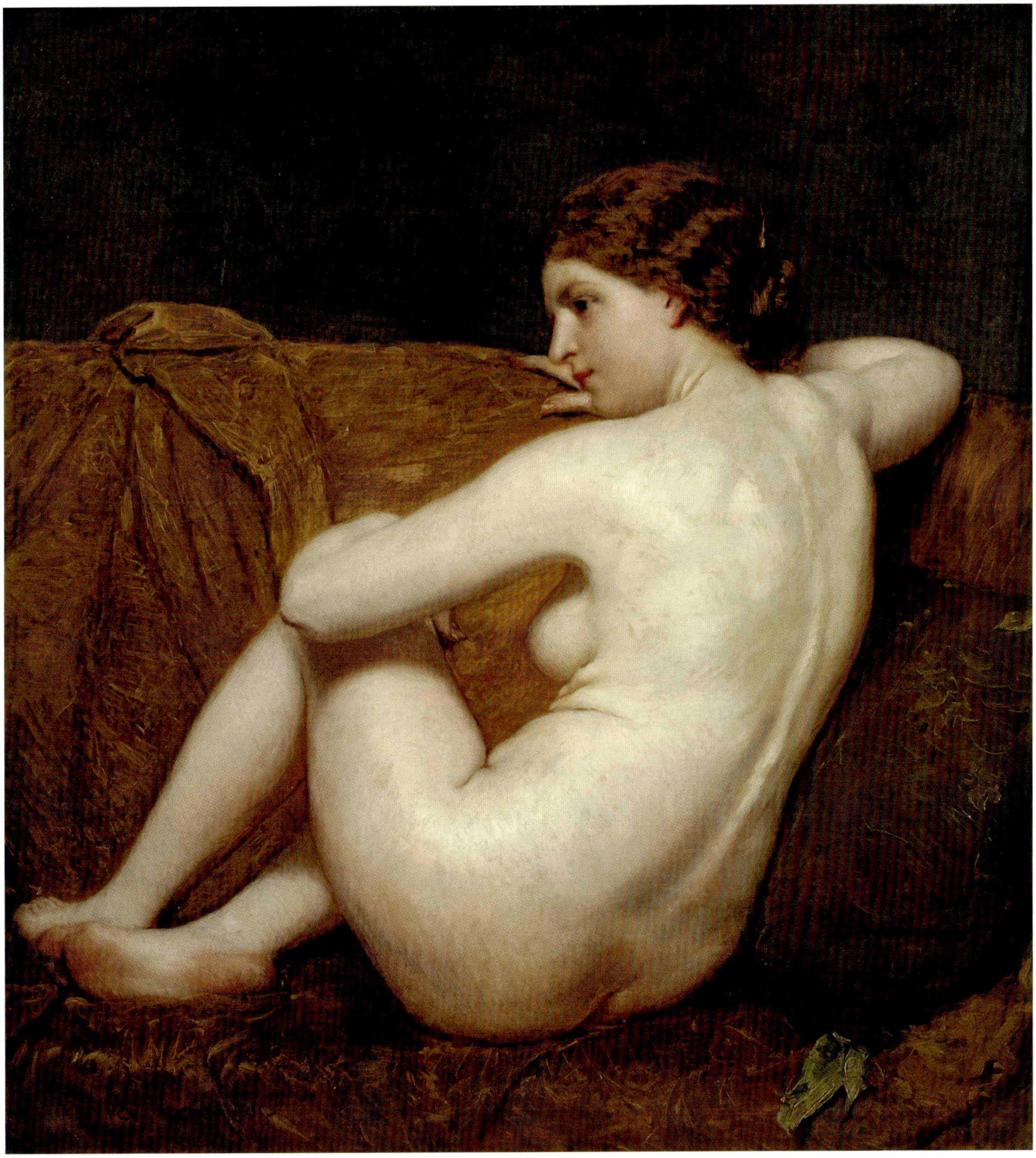

Kenyon Cox, *A Blonde*, 1891. Oil on canvas, 41 × 36 in. (104.1 × 91.4 cm)

ALEXI WORTH ON PHILIP PEARLSTEIN

We expect "naked lady" pictures to be ingratiating. Not this one. Think of the smooth simplicity of a Greek statue or the taut planes of fashion photography, and it's clear at once that this is something different: an ordinary woman, neither idealized nor beautified. Her bony, overlit body is too complicated to be voluptuous. And yet, this is not a picture of expressive ugliness. There are no distortions, no grotesque details, nothing that calls to mind the hairy harpies painted by Grosz or Dix or Neel. Neither seductive nor moralizing, Pearlstein's depiction delivers something we don't expect: impartiality. The paint handling is poker-calm. Look at those greenish triple shadows on the wall, and then at the overlapping shadows under the model's left breast, all rendered with egalitarian precision, as if "wall" and "breast" were equally interesting. Except for a few rare pockets of reflected light, the palette is almost drab.

Impartiality? Drabness? I love this painting, but I can't blame viewers who initially feel disappointed by it. Because, of course, the image *intends* to disappoint. Even if you don't love it, you can feel its purposefulness. Inspired by Pearlstein, the critic John Perreault once published a "New Realist" manifesto as a list of prohibitions. In the tough-minded art of the future, there would be:

> No stories; no allegories; no symbols.
> No hidden meanings; no obvious meanings.
> No philosophy, religion, or psychology.
> No jokes; no political content; no illustration.
> No fantasy or imagination; no dreams; no poetry.[1]

Almost crazy, isn't it? But it captures the extremity of Pearlstein's premise. Pictures like this one shrug off all our expectations of pictorial freedom, all the things that make art "artful." Back in the early 1960s, this kind of radical intransigence was very much in the air. In a similar anti-explanatory spirit, the young Frank Stella famously declared about his reductive pinstripe paintings, "What you see is what you see." Meanwhile, Donald Judd coined the aggressively neutral phrase "specific objects" to describe his sculptures, making clear that they should not be associated with the traditional categories of European art. Pearlstein's nude is a "specific object." It's Judd-like in its uncompromising bluntness. But Pearlstein was no Minimalist. Instead, beginning with nudes such as this one, his art proposed something simultaneously conservative and radical, at once Eurocentric and Yankee-plain. By reviving the most old-fashioned subject of all—the nude—while stripping away its metaphorical associations, he devised a paradoxical style, an antifigurative figuration.

Any nude triggers memories of past art: Venuses and courtesans, mythological gardens, come-hitherish glances. Involuntarily recalling all of that, we get this. An austere, factual body. Nothing else. No flavorings, no sweeteners, no captions. To me, Pearlstein's empiricism gives the human body a strange, compelling dignity, and even makes it seem (impossibly!) *new*. Looking at this torso, right at eye level, I feel like an art student on the first day of life class. I'm absorbed and calm, buoyed by the optical Adderall of bright light.

One final note: for Pearlstein fans, there's a special charge in thinking that this is one of the earliest paintings made in his mature style. After *Nude Torso* came more refined, multifigure compositions, the bodies within them ever more sculptural, more overtly beautiful, despite their matter-of-factness. In 1963, that was all in the future. Here, we see only a single woman leaning against a wall, the Eve of Planet Pearlstein.

1. John Perreault, *Philip Pearlstein: Drawings and Watercolors* (New York: Harry N. Abrams, 1982), 199.

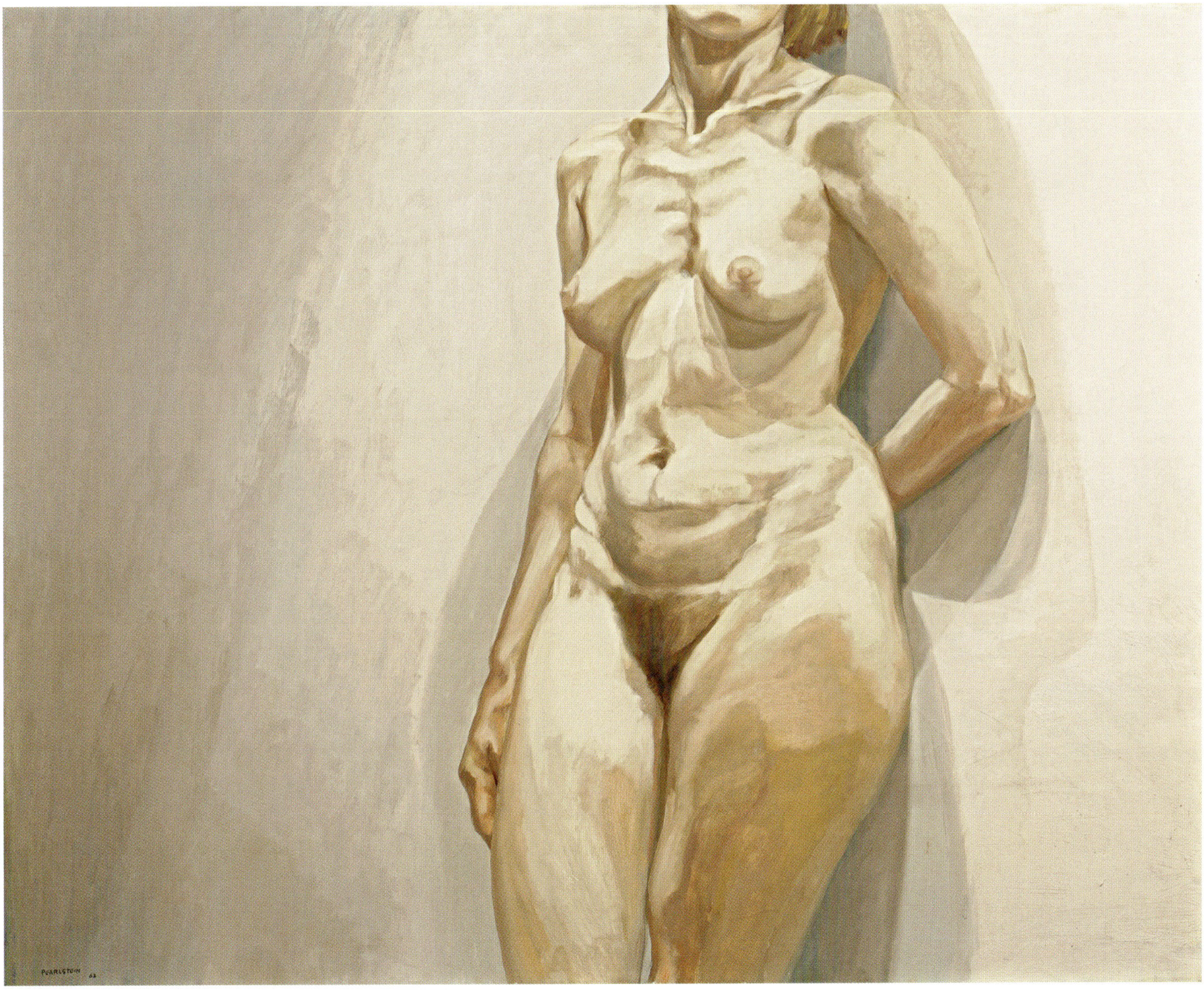

Philip Pearlstein, *Nude Torso*, 1963. Oil on canvas, 36 × 44 in. (91.4 × 111.8 cm)

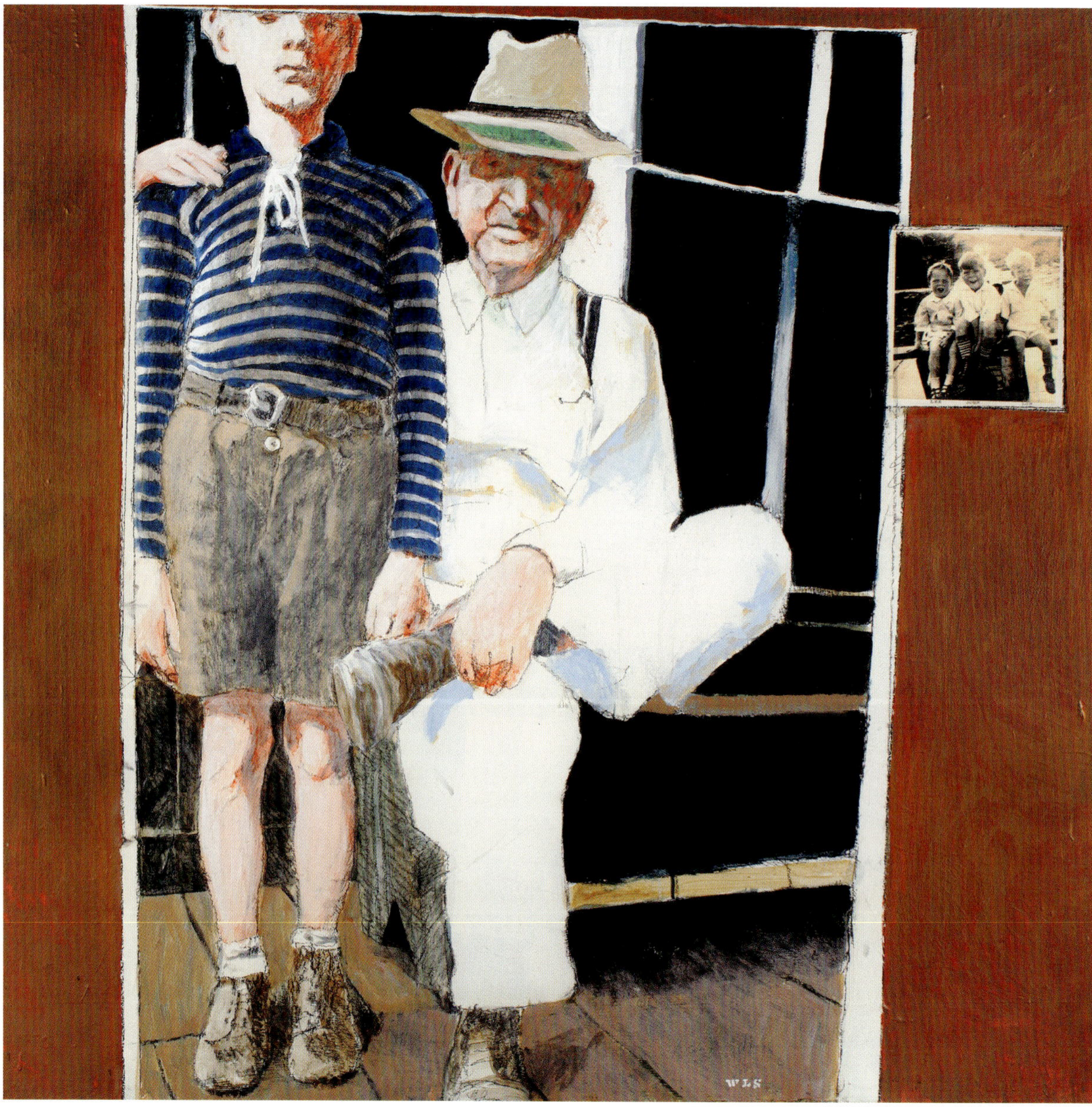

W. Lee Savage, *Endangered Bobby*, 1992. Acrylic and mixed media on canvas, 54 × 54 in. (137.2 × 137.2 cm)

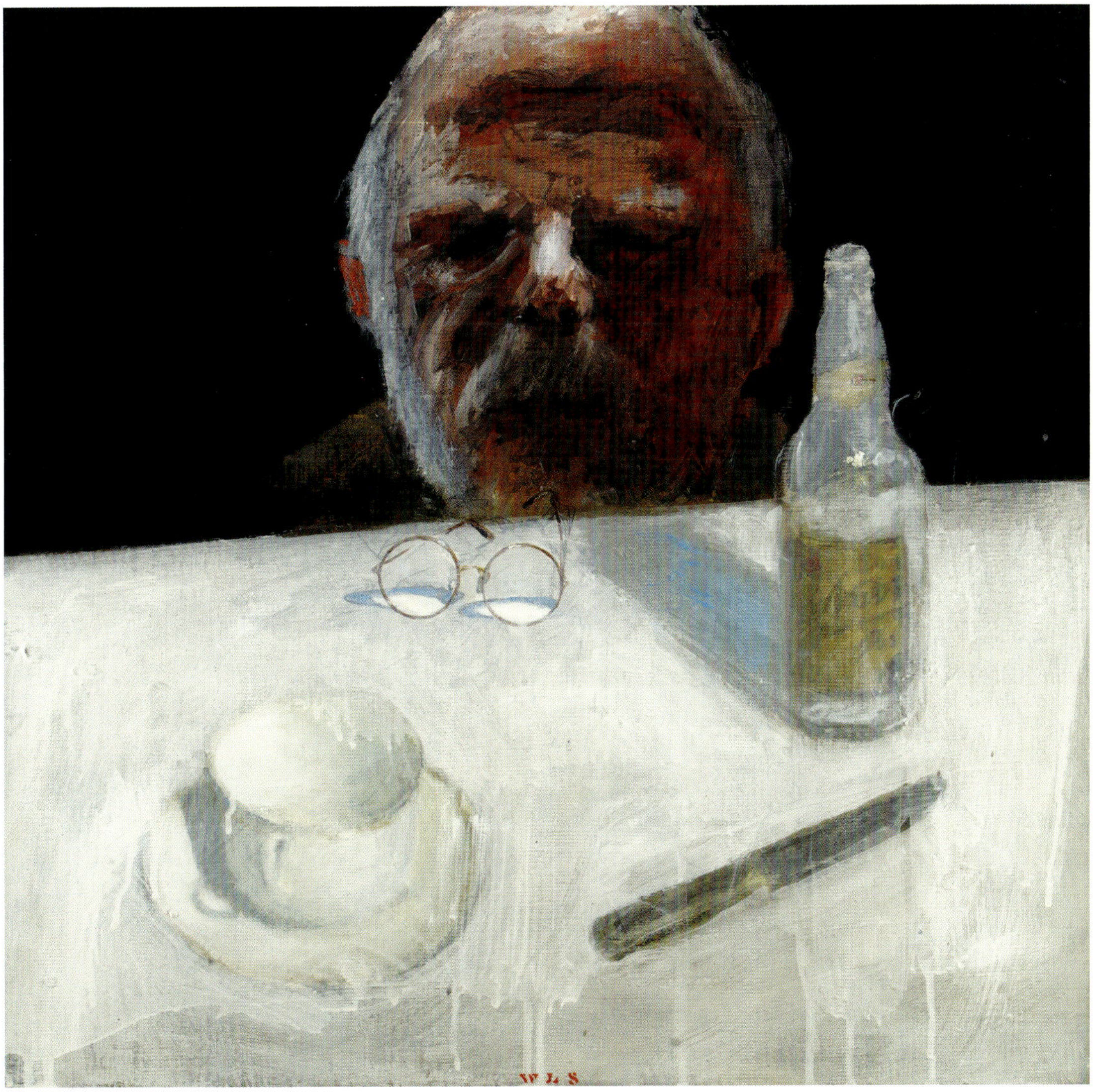

W. Lee Savage, *Self-Portrait with Cup and Narragansett Beer*, 1988. Acrylic on board, 25 × 25 in. (63.5 × 63.5 cm)

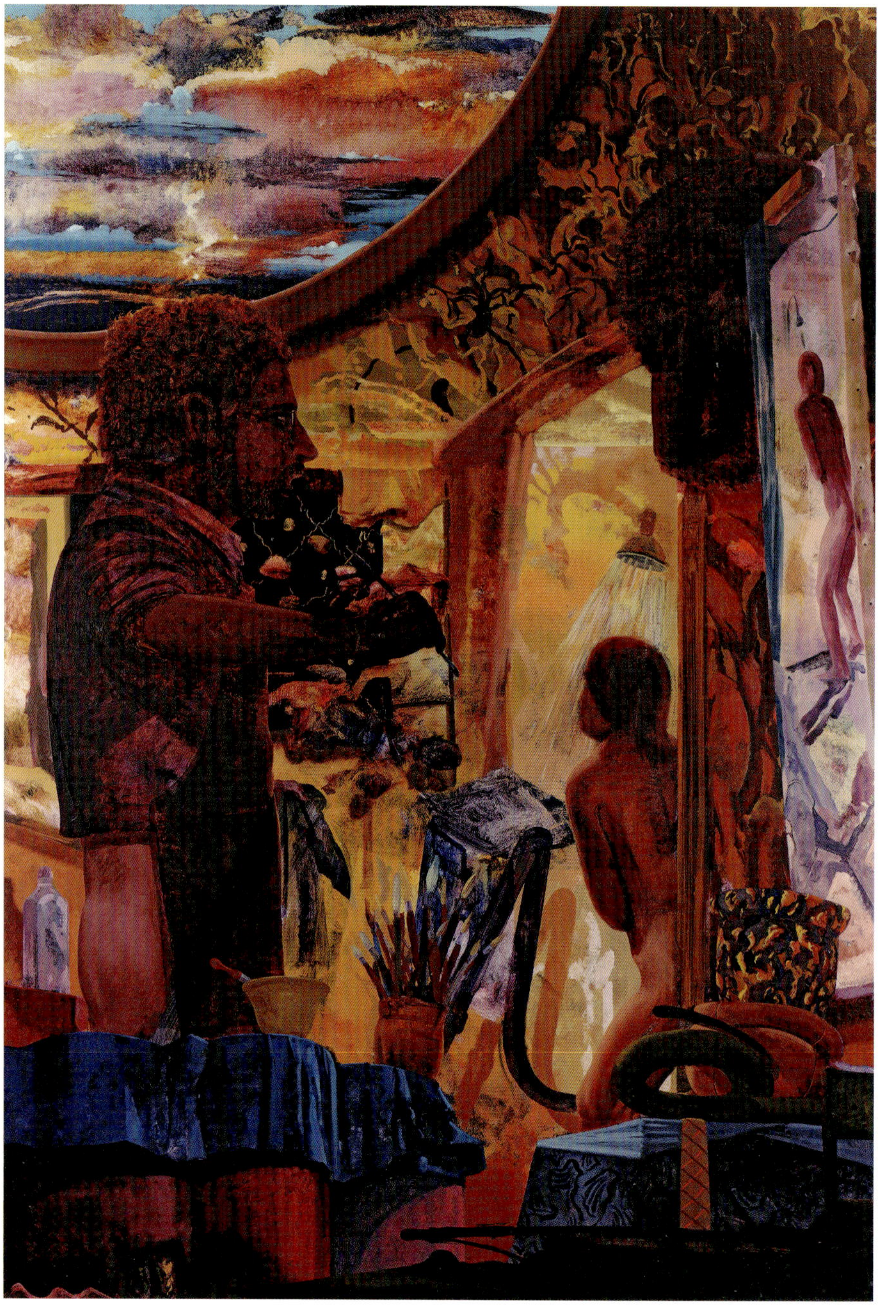

James McGarrell, *Bison Self-Portrait*, 1987. Oil on canvas, 80 × 52 in. (203.2 × 132.1 cm)

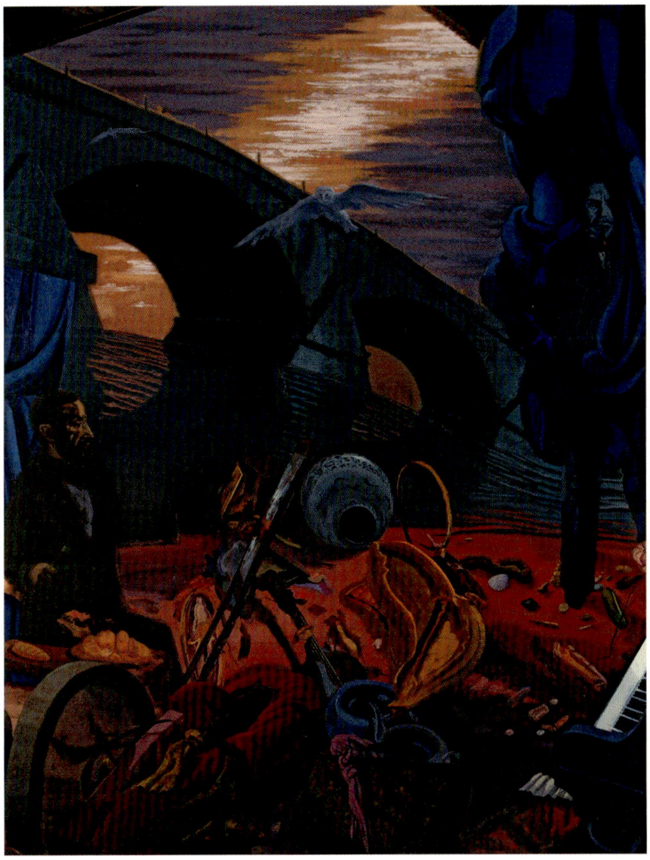

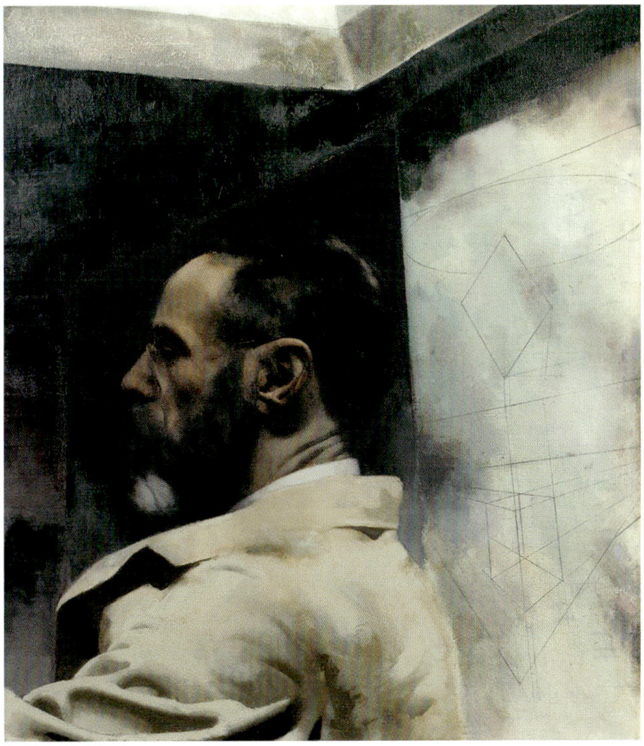

Left: James McGarrell, *The Painter, Young and Old (Edwin Dickinson)*, 1992. Oil on canvas, 80 × 60 in. (203.2 × 152.4 cm)
Right: Edwin Dickinson, *Self-Portrait*, 1949. Oil on canvas, 23 × 20 ⅛ in. (58.4 × 51.1 cm)

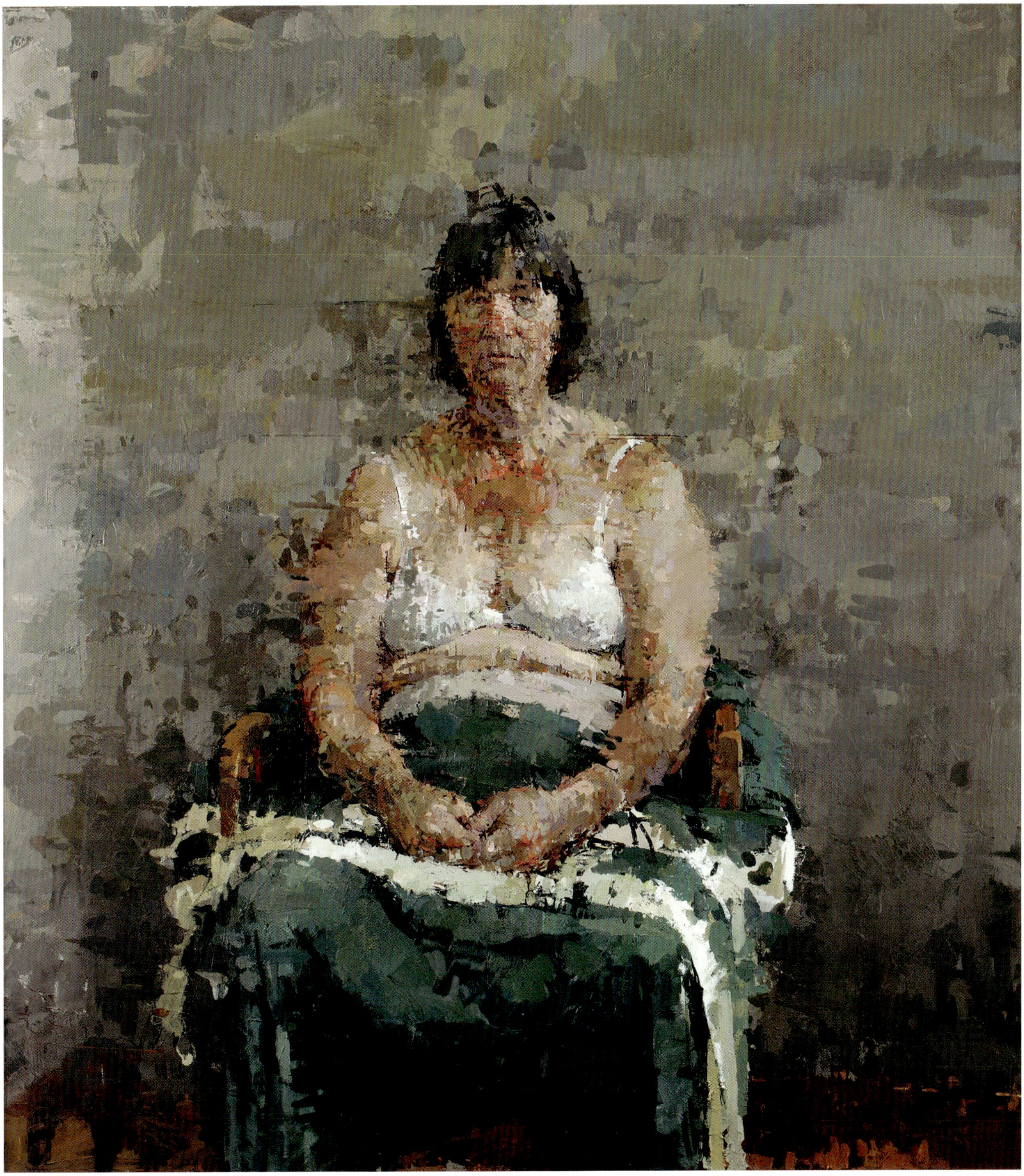

Ann Gale, *Babs with Ribbons*, 2007. Oil on canvas, 48 × 42 in. (121.9 × 106.7 cm)

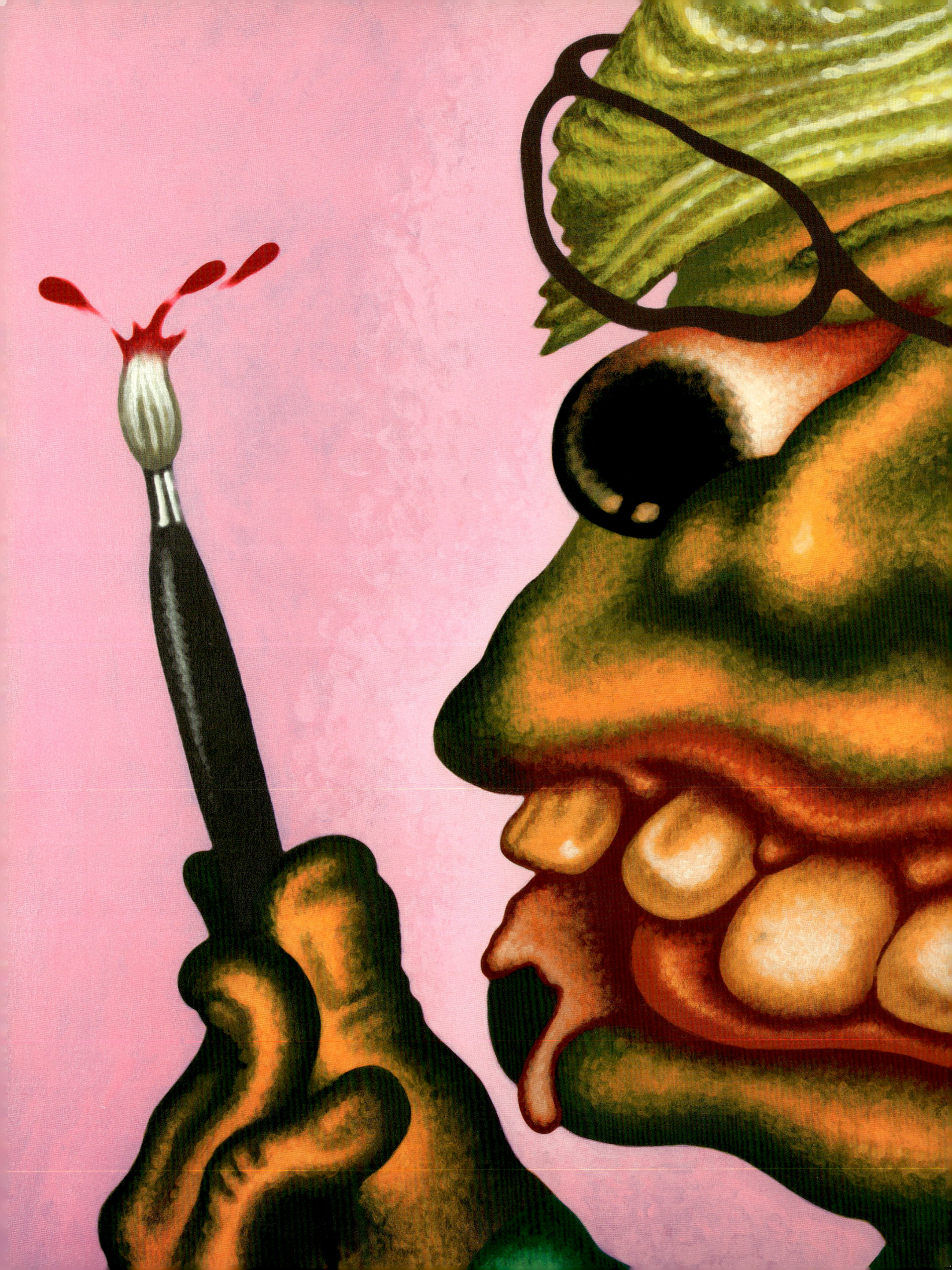

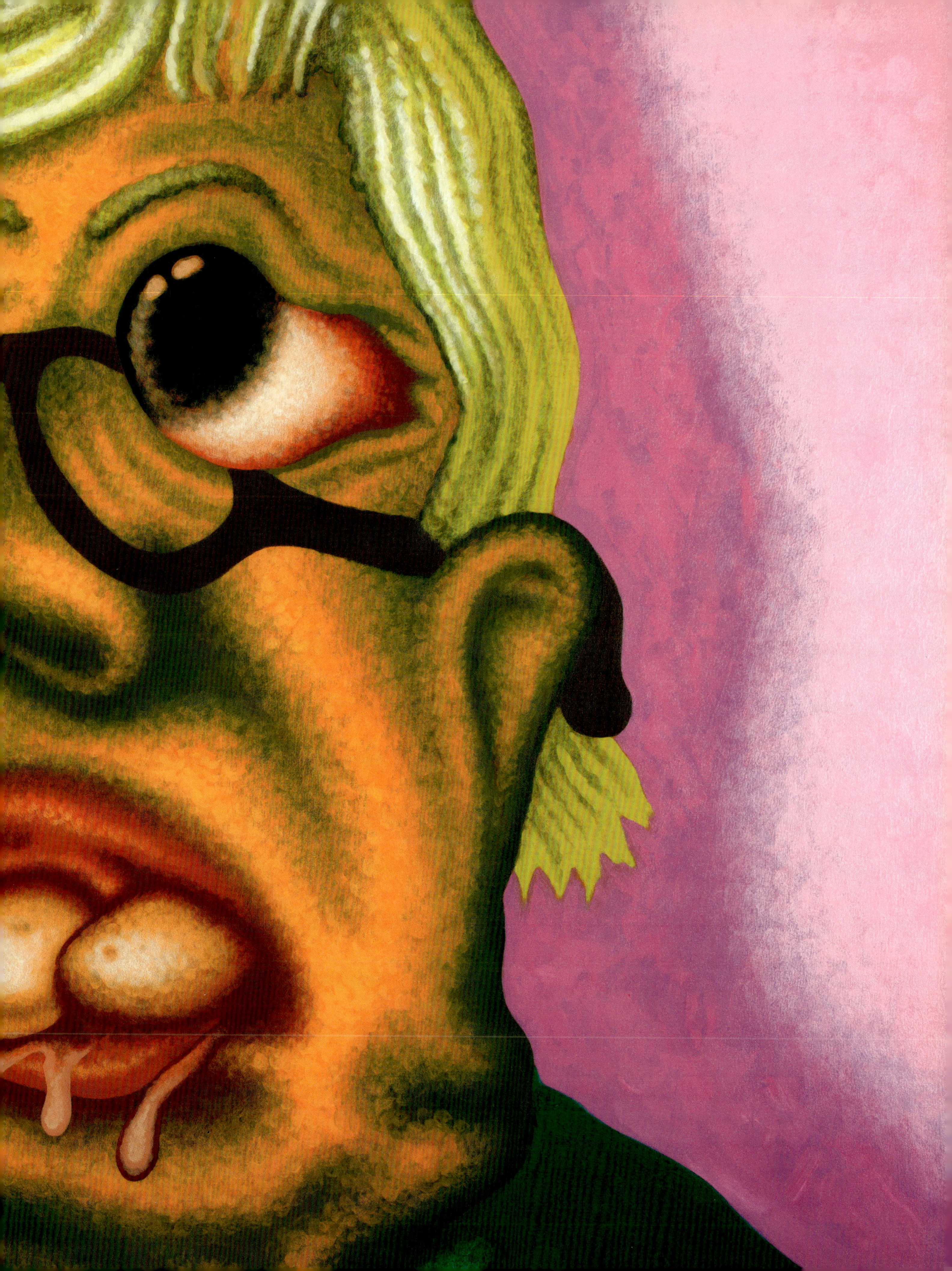

FOUR AMERICANS: DAVID DIAO, LOUISA MATTHÍASDÓTTIR, PETER SAUL, AND JAUNE QUICK-TO-SEE SMITH

JARRETT EARNEST

> There are many ways of making kinds of men and women. In each way of making kinds of them there is a different system of finding them resembling. Sometime there will be here every way there can be of seeing kinds of men and women. Sometime there will be then a complete history of each one. Every one always is repeating the whole of them and so sometime some one who sees them will have a complete history of every one. Sometime some one will know all the ways there are for people to be resembling, some one sometime then will have a completed history of every one.
> —Gertrude Stein, *The Making of Americans*

I

"My main focus is to preserve the Indian culture," Jaune Quick-to-See Smith told the curator Susan Zwinger in 1986, "and I am as interested in preserving traditional art as I am in preserving contemporary art."[1] A member of the Confederated Salish and Kootenai Tribes of the Flathead Nation in Montana, Smith emerged in the 1970s as a major voice in contemporary Native American culture, as an artist, an activist, and a curator. Her multimedia paintings blend broad cultural references drawn from ancient and modern art with Native American imagery and contemporary politics. One of the clearest distillations of her ongoing project is 1995's *Celebrate 40,000 Years of American Art* (fig. 1), which presents a "succinct comment on colonial thinking," as the artist has put it.[2] The print is a very large collograph, made from a low-relief collage—of

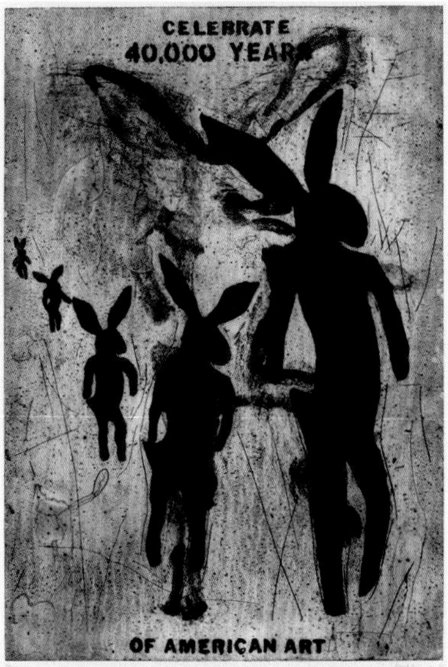

Fig. 1. Jaune Quick-to-See Smith, *Celebrate 40,000 Years of American Art*, 1995. Collograph. Whitney Museum of American Art, New York

papers, pastes, and relatively flat objects—laid out on a PVC plastic sheet into which the artist also carved. The plate was then inked and run through a press to produce an image of diaphanous gray washes, dense with scratches and textures. Slanting in from the left side is a diagonal of five walking figures with rabbit ears, ascending in size. The last figure, on the far right, stands almost the entire height of the slightly over six-foot-tall paper.

Smith has said that she borrowed the motif of a standing rabbit from the famous petroglyphs in Peterborough, Ontario, an important site where hundreds of images were carved into crystalline limestone thousands of years ago. There has been much conjecture over the meaning of the rabbit-eared image found there and its connection to the horned figures encountered at the same location. One interpretation associates it with the character of Nanabozho, also called Nanabush, in Ojibwe mythology, a culture-hero trickster figure who sometimes takes the form of the "Great Hare," an important intermediary between the Great Spirit and mankind.[3] "I was looking for an icon," Smith explained upon the work's inclusion in the Whitney Museum of American Art's exhibition *An Incomplete History of Protest*; she then free-associated a number of rabbits that might come to mind: "Jeff Koons, Barry Flanagan, Watership Down, Easter Bunny, Harvey, Playboy Rabbit, March Hare, White Rabbit, Peter Rabbit, Thumper, Bugs Bunny, Velveteen Rabbit, Roger Rabbit, Miffy, Peter Cottontail. And so then I decided, that's a good icon."[4]

At the top of the sheet are the words CELEBRATE 40,000 YEARS, with the line completed at the bottom: OF AMERICAN ART. This is both an invitation and a provocation. Made just after the quincentennial of Christopher Columbus's arrival in the Americas, the print proposes European

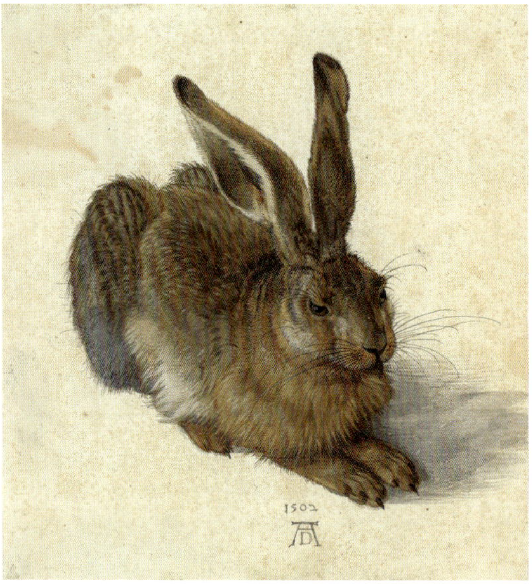

Fig. 2. Albrecht Dürer, *Young Hare*, 1502. Watercolor and gouache, heightened with white gouache. Albertina, Vienna

history as a mere eightieth of cultural life on the continent. "In educational institutions in this country, reference is often made to the age of [the] Americas as being two hundred or five hundred years, but because we still live under the aegis of colonial thinking, it's never taken into consideration that some of the world's greatest cultures and cities were here in the Americas for thousands of years—and are still here."[5]

Smith's *Snake Dance* (p. 271), given to the National Academy of Design upon her election in 2011, shows a tangle of looping, dark umber lines symbolizing the snakes of the titular Hopi ceremony but also the movements of the dance itself and the clouds that gather as a result, delivering the prayed-for rain. All kinds of things are collaged onto the canvas: a Bronx subway map, swatches of colored fabric, bits of text that slide in diagonals down the right side. The trickster rabbit figure appears here, too, as a simple brushwork interpretation of Albrecht Dürer's famous watercolor *Young Hare* of 1502 (fig. 2) and an outline of Bugs Bunny's feet taken from a children's coloring book. When we triangulate these two rabbits with the walking figures of the earlier print, we get a fuller sense of the visual and cultural context Smith is claiming for herself, citing ancient indigenous art, European masterpieces, and Saturday morning cartoons to forge an idiom saturated with the world and its histories in the broadest sense. Describing *Snake Dance*, the artist has said, "I nearly always do research for each painting, though it might not show or might not ever come to light, it is part of my process. In a way I was painting a diary of my life."[6]

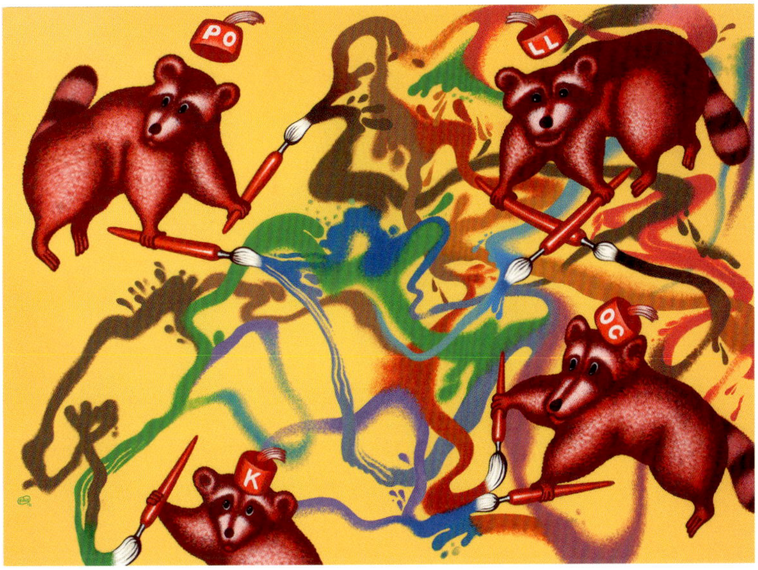

Fig. 3. Peter Saul, *Raccoons Paint a Picture*, 2011. Acrylic on canvas. Collection of the artist

II

"The only articles I don't like are the ones that say, 'He tried to be a Pop artist and failed to make the grade,'" Peter Saul told me—"which is kind of true, but I don't like it."[7] Saul started out in the early 1960s showing brushy, cartoony expressionism alongside such artists as Andy Warhol and Roy Lichtenstein but soon distinguished himself by depicting important cultural events in large multifigure compositions, "history paintings" of a sort—the most prestigious genre of the eighteenth and nineteenth centuries, which had all but disappeared with modernism. During the Vietnam War, Saul painted acid-colored orgies of death in works such as *Vietnam* (1966) and *Typical Saigon* (1968), showing wobbly figures with large breasts labeled COMMY or INNOCENT VIRGIN being crucified by hulking American GIs in sadomasochistic rituals. In hot pink, neon yellow, and lime green, bodies are stretched around these pictures like taffy. Over the past half century, the artist has developed this approach—blending the allover composition and scale of Abstract Expressionism with the imagery of underground comix—into a particularly warped view of human civilization as slow-motion massacre, interpreting events as varied as those referenced in *Custer's Last Stand* (1974), *Fall of Constantinople (1453 A.D.)* (2004), and *Bush at Abu Ghraib* (2006).

The title of Saul's 2011 canvas *Raccoons Paint a Picture* (fig. 3) is a riff on the "Paints a Picture" series published in midcentury *ARTnews*, which followed the step-by-step process of making a single work in an artist's studio. The most famous installment, Thomas B. Hess's "De Kooning Paints a Picture" (1953), is a classic of art criticism, detailing the formal and existential heroics of making *Woman I* (1950–52;

Museum of Modern Art, New York). In Saul's six-by-eight-foot painting, four fluffy red raccoons scurry at the corners of a squash-colored canvas. Each holds a paintbrush or two in its dainty paws, joyfully trailing serpentine splashes of green, orange, blue, sienna, coral, and lavender. All the raccoons wear little red fezzes complete with tassels and emblazoned with the white letters PO, LL, OC, and K—thereby reenacting the famous Hans Namuth photographs of Jackson Pollock at work, slinging his now-famous "skeins" of paint. In the rhetoric of *ARTnews*, Pollock was a mythic figure who galvanized what has come to be known as postwar abstraction—a tormented "American genius." By contrast, the raccoons seem to be saying, "Not only is this easy—it's fun, too!" Saul insists that "the ability to use cute animals in modern art is not common." When I suggest that the raccoons might be surrogates for himself as the maker of the painting, Saul says, "Close enough! Maybe my self-portrait is a cute animal, too!"

He is referring to the self-portrait he made in 2013 for his election into the National Academy, his only to date (p. 277). The painting shows the artist from the shoulders up against a pink background, a subtle spotlight encircling his oversized head, casting a deep rose shadow on the wall behind. The volumes are shaded in Saul's typical manner of overlapping circular swirls, and the resulting texture is like flattened lamb's fur. The face itself looks like melting putty, with Saul's signature protuberant eyes, red around the stems and dewy at the bulbous black iris, reaching in opposite directions around his lopsided spectacles. The mouth reveals oversized, caramelized teeth, with gums as red as raw hamburger. Salmon-colored drool drips down onto the artist's lower lip and chin. On the left side of the canvas, he raises a paintbrush spurting three red drops from its tip. That red may have been used to paint the artist's own mouth and eyes in this picture; certainly, it is related to the blood that has flowed through his paintings for decades. Unlike the carefree and lighthearted raccoons, here the painter is an anguished cretin. "He certainly shows plenty of anxiety," Saul says, laughing. "Just because *Citizen Kane* is the greatest movie in the world doesn't mean you want to watch it every night of your life. Once you experience Cézanne, you're free to look at bad stuff. I'm volunteering my art to be that bad stuff."

III

"The reason I paint is because I want to paint what I see," Louisa Matthíasdóttir once told her friend the poet Mark Strand. "But to paint what I see I must build from color. I try to paint what I see. I don't do shapes and colors without seeing them in nature. Either it looks like a landscape or it doesn't. That's all."[8] Whether depicting a sheep-strewn Icelandic hillside or a kitchen still life, Matthíasdóttir's paintings are lucid patchworks of color, usually executed in one go. Their geometry is pronounced; the shapes carved out by her broad brushwork are simplified but not generic.

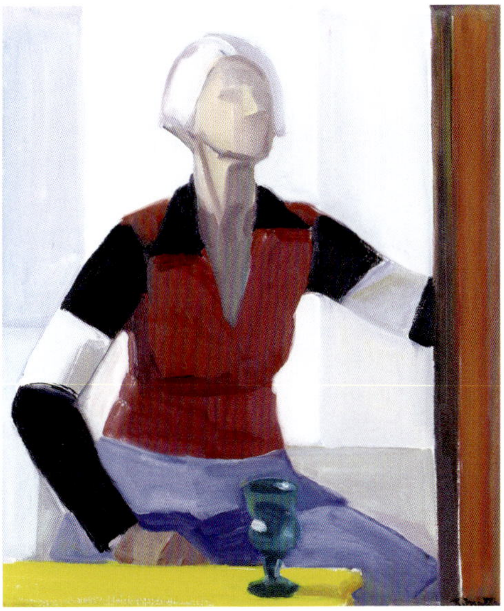

Fig. 4. Louisa Matthíasdóttir, *Self-Portrait with Yellow Table*, 1981. Oil on canvas. Smithsonian American Art Museum, Washington, DC

When Matthíasdóttir emigrated to the United States in 1942, she studied with the German-born American painter Hans Hofmann, famous for the "push and pull" dynamics of his vibrating rectangles. Hofmann taught both abstract and representational painters, stressing formal elements such as "color *as color*," which creates light and space in a painting. An inspiring, permissive figure, he opened the floodgates of midcentury American art with his nonlinear view of art history: "There is in reality no such thing as modern art. Art is carried on up and down in immense cycles through centuries and civilizations."[9] As a representational painter who continued to work from life throughout the reign of Abstract Expressionism, Matthíasdóttir, along with her husband, the painter and Academician Leland Bell, took Hofmann's views to heart, marrying the formal imperatives of abstract painting with plausible depictions of the observed world.

The background of the National Academy's *Self-Portrait in Overalls* (p. 273) is a cool, dirty cream that shifts gently from a blue to a yellow cast across the painting, flooding the image with light. The artist's deep ultramarine jumpsuit looks faceted, sliced out of the bright space, which shimmers around her silhouette in muted pinks, oranges, and purples. Her technique of cutting the pale background in to correct the body's outline, blending the overpainted color into the ground, produced an edge that feels both stable and fluid, as though it is moving very slightly—almost breathing. This is a life-sized, full-length portrait, at a scale that lends the picture the gravity of a living presence. Looking in the mirror, Matthíasdóttir holds a brush in her reflected right hand, her arm extending toward the edge of the painting; her left arm is bent at the same angle as in her earlier *Self-Portrait with Yellow Table* (fig. 4), this time with hand tucked into pocket. But unlike in palette knife. "I spend a lot of time getting rid of the texture of the canvas. . . . When the surface has no texture left, that is when I begin with color. It is very tedious, time-consuming work, but it has become part of the process." The image inserted in a smaller, off-center blue-green rectangle shows Diao sitting in a modernist chair à la Marcel Breuer, nonchalantly lifting one arm parallel to Lee's, which towers over him in the background at a much larger scale. "Of course, every aspect of my work is animated against claiming any kind of subjectivity, whether it is a brushstroke or my own image. But I guess I can't deny it is a self-portrait—there it is, staring at me. But it does play tongue in cheek, in who is being portrayed, me or Bruce Lee. . . . There is a dichotomy between his animus, his kind of male gesturing, and my equanimity."

What can these four prose sketches, focusing on a couple of works apiece by four different artists, add up to? Certainly not a single story, not even about each artist. They all fit at odd angles to any smooth account of modern and contemporary American art. Take, for example, Jaune Quick-to-See Smith, who is tirelessly reminding the art world of its narrow colonial perspective, creating found-object collages that recall Robert Rauschenberg in the same breath as they do indigenous textiles. Or Peter Saul, who stages both history and painting as a violent *Raft of the Medusa* scenario, signaling desperately to contemporary culture for their rescue. Or Louisa Matthíasdóttir, who painted landscapes, portraits, and still lifes throughout the entire sequence of Abstract Expressionism, Pop, and conceptualism, which were supposed to render such production obsolete. And David Diao, whose work is as much a mockery of the legacies of modernist painting as it is an homage, all the while refusing to leave behind the arduous work of painting itself for conceptualism's cool embrace. These artists, as different as they are in form, sensibility, and intention, constitute a kind of "art history and its discontents."

And still, as different as they all are, there are resonances. You could compare Saul's and Smith's use of anthropomorphized animals, or Saul's and Diao's engagements with the legacy of Jackson Pollock. Of course, the selection process for works in the National Academy's collection was long focused on self-portraits, so you could compare these artists through the lens of self-presentation, seeing Matthíasdóttir, Saul, and Diao within a several-thousand-year-old lineage and including Smith's *Snake Dance*, which she has called a "diary of my life."[12] What this shows is that "mainstream" American art history, for a long time, meant a very narrow band of white Anglo-Saxon men living in and around New York City. What happens with the introduction of any kind of *difference*—Diao and Matthíasdóttir are both immigrants; Smith and Diao, people of color; Matthíasdóttir and Smith, women—is that the edifice of that history implodes, and you're left wondering what kind of generalizations—social, historical, discursive—can be used to knit together a history that more closely resembles such a wide array of facts scattered across the American landscape.

While these artists each have their individual visions, they're not *outsiders*; all were elected to the National Academy, which is based in New York, and have been acclaimed by their peers and publics. But their publics are not necessarily made up of the same people, which is why we now have to talk about contemporary art *worlds*—plural. The Americas are an incredibly heterogeneous place, stretching over two continents and comprising more than a billion people, of which the United States is just a cross section. Even within our national borders, we have yet to find a model, in criticism or history, to account for that profound plurality of artistic lineages and values. It gets reduced to either "dominant" or "minority" narratives rather than accommodating the reality that we're all in it together, and it's all happening all the time. In this sense, "history" is simply a story, or set of stories, always shifting according to the needs of those telling it. All attempts at understanding the texture or tenor of an age rub against the limits of those stories, finessing the ragged edges into new stories. Perhaps the first step will be to abandon storytelling where everything flows, leaving lots of loose ends and open spaces—something more like a kaleidoscope, where every slight turn reshuffles the shards into another gorgeous picture.

Epigraph: Gertrude Stein, *The Making of Americans: Being a History of a Family's Progress* (Normal, IL: Dalkey Archive Press, 1995; first published 1925), 290.

1. Jaune Quick-to-See Smith, quoted in Susan Zwinger, "Viewpoint: An Interview with Artist Jaune Quick-to-See Smith," *El Palacio* 92, no. 1 (Summer/Fall 1986): 53.
2. Jaune Quick-to-See Smith, "Celebrate 40,000 Years of American Art," *Frontiers: A Journal of Women Studies* 23, no. 2 (2002): 154–55.
3. Joan M. Vastokas and Romas K. Vastokas, *Sacred Art of the Algonkians: A Study of the Peterborough Petroglyphs* (Peterborough, Ontario: Mansard Press, 1973), 74.
4. Audio guide for *An Incomplete History of Protest* exhibition, Whitney Museum of American Art, New York, August 18, 2017–August 27, 2018, https://whitney.org/WatchAndListen/AudioGuides/1867?stop=13.
5. Smith, "Celebrate," 154–55.
6. Jaune Quick-to-See Smith, "Questionnaire" (2012), NAD artist file.
7. All quotations by Peter Saul are from a conversation with the author, June 2018.
8. Louisa Matthíasdóttir, quoted in Mark Strand, *Art of the Real: Nine American Figurative Painters* (New York: C. N. Potter, 1983), 161.
9. Hans Hofmann, quoted in Helmut Friedel and Tina Dickey, *Hans Hofmann* (New York: Hudson Hills Press, 1998), 91.
10. Strand, *Art of the Real*, 161.
11. All quotations by David Diao are from a conversation with the author, June 2018.
12. Smith, "Questionnaire."

JOYCE KOZLOFF ON JAUNE QUICK-TO-SEE SMITH

Snake Dance is a fierce, elegiac, tribal, global, sophisticated, rough, tender, manic, subdued, calligraphic, painterly, rhythmic, decorative, expressionistic, ebullient work that evokes the ritual the artist herself has described as follows:

> In August about twenty years ago, my artist friends Linda Lomahaftewa (Hopi and Choctaw) and Karita Coffey (Comanche) invited me to the Snake Dance at Hopi in Arizona. For several days before the dances, the men and boys had gathered snakes—whip snakes, bullsnakes, racers, and rattlesnakes. As the men danced through the afternoon, they reached into pouches hanging from their belts and brought out snakes, which they draped around their necks, coiled on their arms, and hung from their mouths. Toward the end, they laid them on the ground. Snakes crawled in all directions while the afternoon thunderheads gathered over us, bringing much-needed rain.[1]

This is not a dance for wimps! The participants are men, but the manikin-like figure at the center of Jaune Quick-to-See Smith's work is androgynous, so the artist may be posing a question about Native culture, about who performs such dances and why. The central personage is anchored into a tightly organized, frontal structure overlaid with geometric strokes that suggest scaffolding on a building. When the viewer moves closer, sketched and collaged traces of other stories emerge from the background.

> Snakes are considered the traditional guardians of springs. The summer I worked on this painting, we were experiencing severe drought in New Mexico and I remembered the Snake Dance as I worked, making my own call to water. I found multiple images of coiled snakes and, in the end, loosely appropriated a Celtic one.

The Celtic snakes have become a bold, dynamic, free-floating black line at the top of the painting, perhaps its most prominent element, yet the figure beneath keeps asserting itself. The artist's varied treatments of the individual parts of the image evoke bark or flesh, water or fire. People expect the Native American symbolism, but do they also recognize Smith's European references, I wonder?

> I added rectangular land patches to my painting as symbolic of my life in the desert, collecting old Indian seeds that grow in this climate. As in this painting, I sometimes use a rabbit to represent Tricksterism. The most noted is Br'er Rabbit, who is claimed by the Southeastern tribes and also by African Americans. I changed Standing Rabbit to Dürer's sitting rabbit as an observer.

Loose drips of ochre and sienna form the central section, like a massive tree trunk, while playful, Polke-like blue and white dots bring us back up to the surface. Who would have imagined Dürer's rabbit in this context, peering out at us quizzically? Smith may have begun with the Hopi snake dance, but it led her to roam across time and space. And that is how *Snake Dance* retains its mystery while incorporating the many languages of art making.

1. All quotations by Jaune Quick-to-See Smith are from an e-mail correspondence with the author, May 2018.

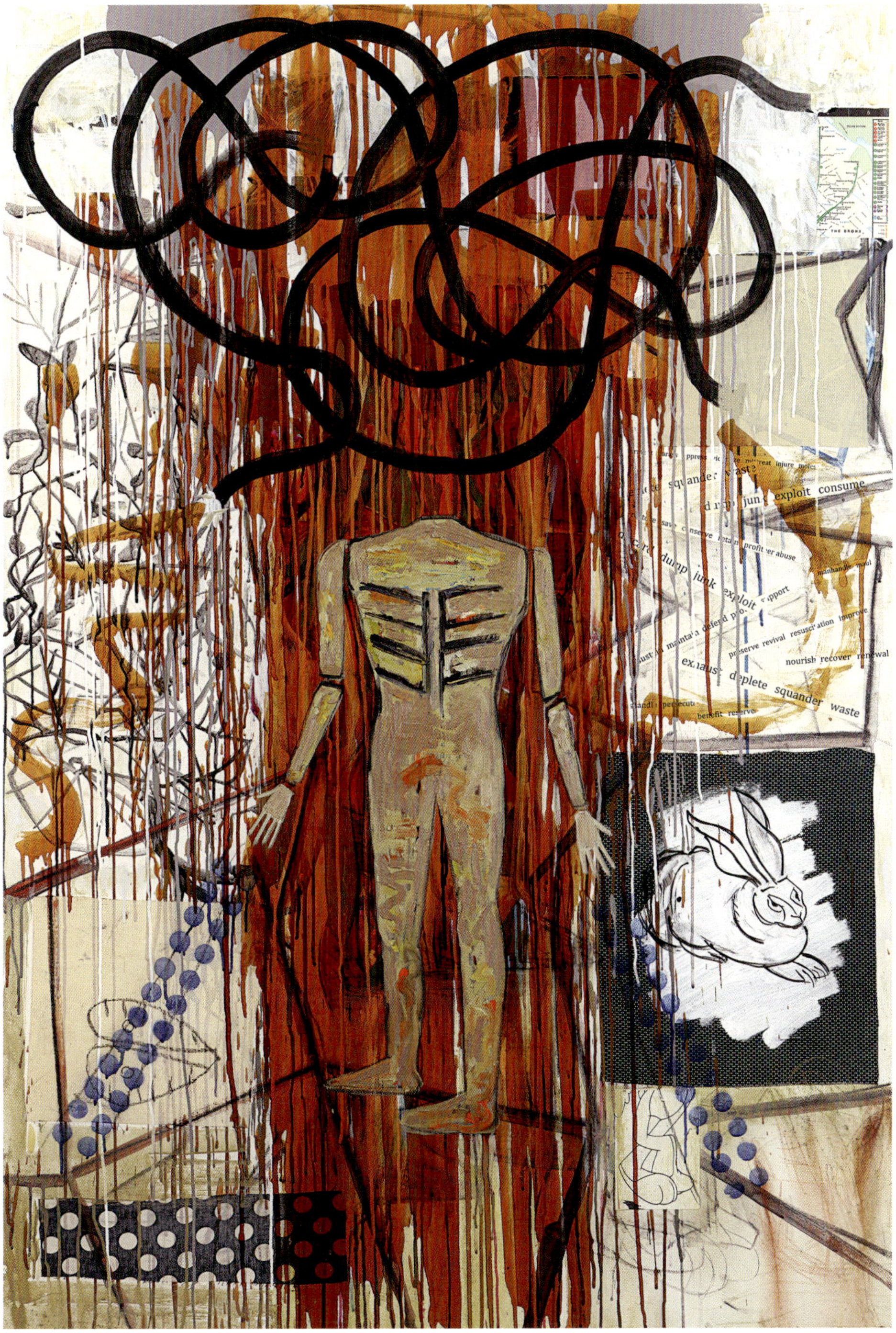

Jaune Quick-to-See Smith, *Snake Dance*, 2011. Oil, collage, and mixed media on canvas, 72 × 48 in. (182.9 × 121.9 cm)

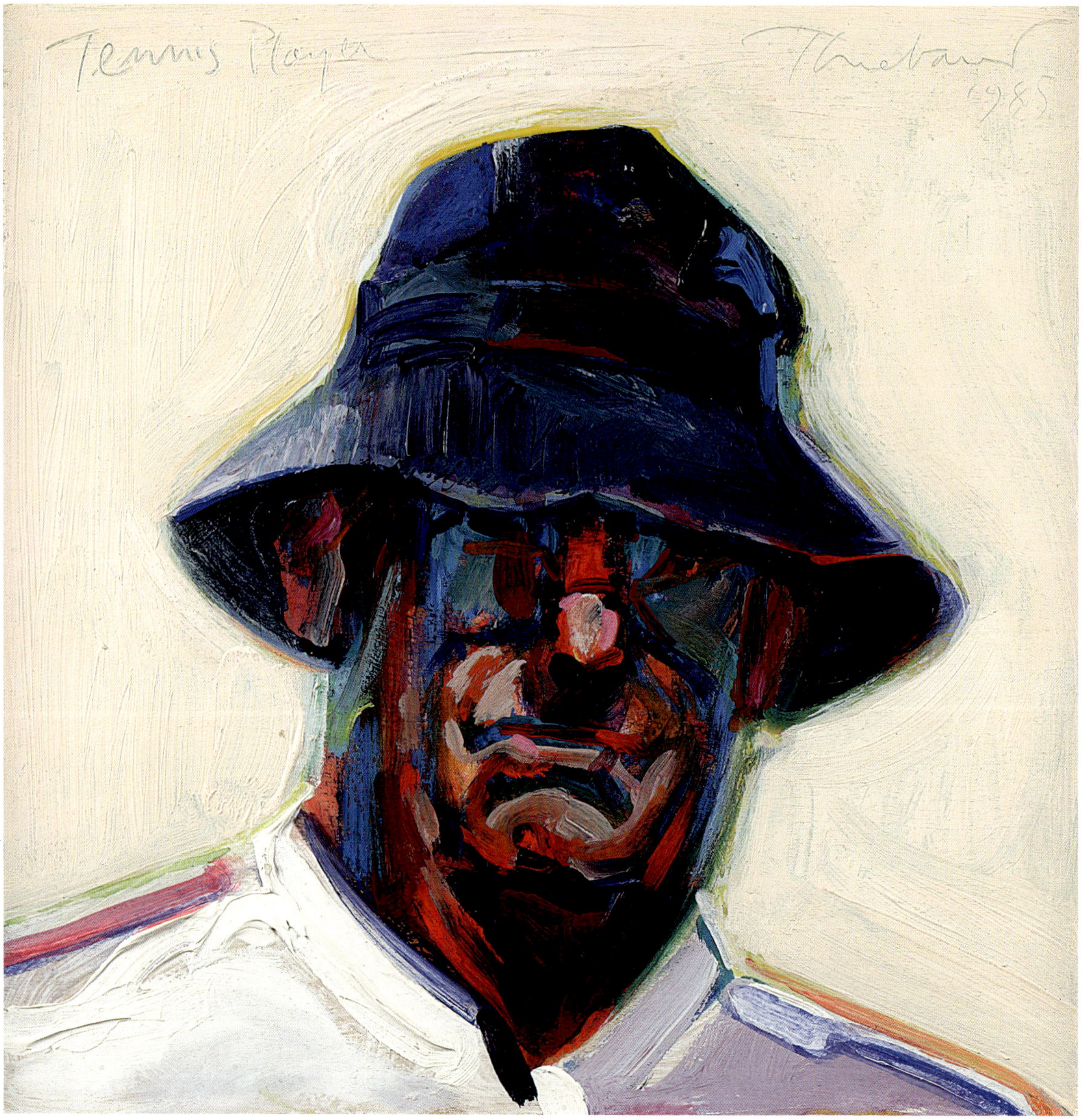

Wayne Thiebaud, *Tennis Player (Self-Portrait)*, 1985. Oil on plywood panel, 12 × 11⅝ in. (30.5 × 29.5 cm)

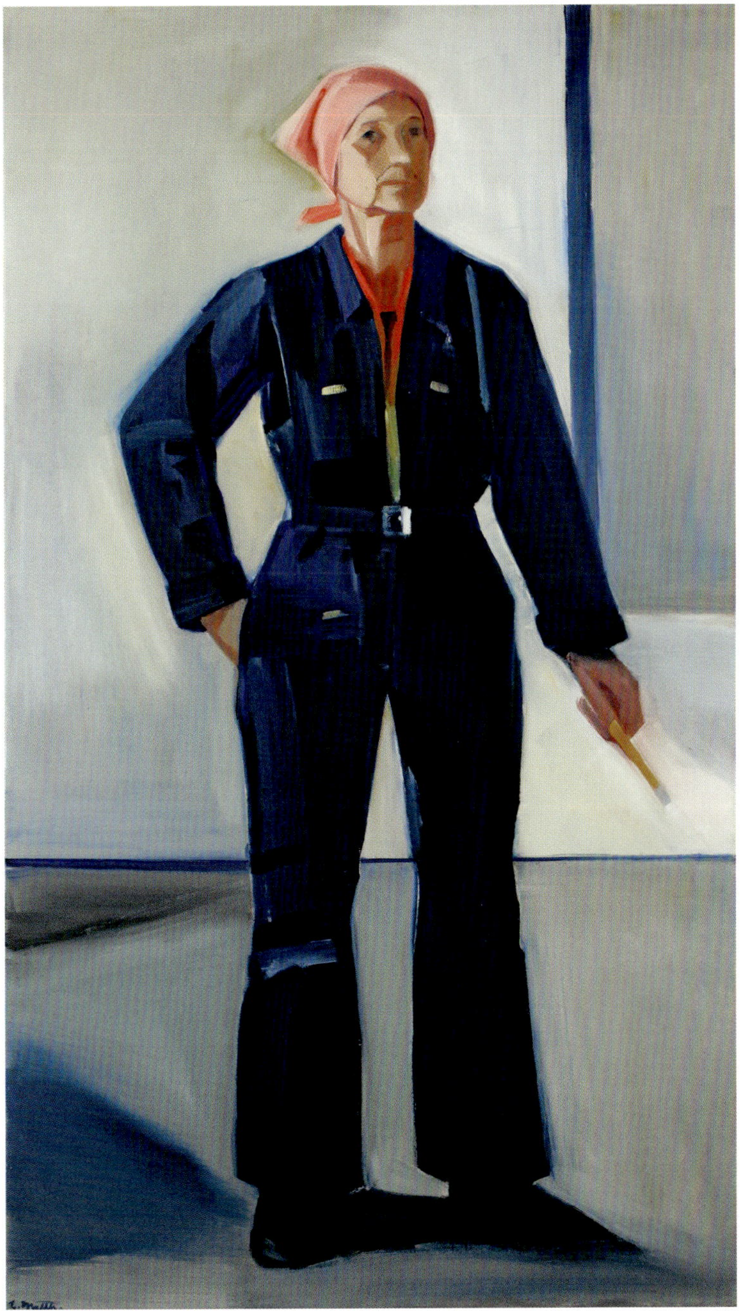

Louisa Matthíasdóttir, *Self-Portrait in Overalls*, ca. 1985. Oil on canvas, 68 × 38 in. (172.7 × 96.5 cm)

MIRA SCHOR ON DAVID DIAO

In 1991, David Diao gave an artist's talk at Hunter College of the City University of New York and showed so many slides and went into such detail about the history of his work that, at one point, he'd been speaking for over an hour and had barely reached the 1980s! In fact, the talk was fascinating, and I was inspired by Diao's having figured out how to address critical themes with appropriated imagery from the history of modernism, including language, in paintings that were also formally beautiful. Sometime during the talk, I determined to follow a new way of representing language myself, one that would be appropriational and theoretical as opposed to the personal approach I had taken during the 1970s. Simply, I envisioned how I would paint the alphabet—and, in fact, I soon started work on a group of paintings that repeat the letter *a*. I became a member of the David Diao Fan Club and eventually wrote the essay "'The Bitter Tea of General Yen': Paintings by David Diao."

Diao has said, "Very early on I understood art-making as critique: to move forward is to critique."[1] But in the 1980s, when he began the phase of his work to which *Bruce and Me* belongs, there were very polarized and carefully policed views about which artistic media were acceptable for a critical practice, and painting was not one of them. Thus, Diao's work has been a touchstone for artists looking for models of painters who are as committed to text-based philosophical investigation, political critique, and conceptual rigor as to the material and formal conditions of the medium of painting.

The critic Raphael Rubinstein has used the term "self-historicization" to describe Diao's ongoing analysis of the process of art-historical canon formation and reflection on the particulars of individual artists' careers, including his own.[2] In addition to these concerns, *Bruce and Me* examines constructions of masculinity and race that have been created mostly by and for the white Western imaginary. The painting incorporates a screenprint of a detail of a photograph taken in Diao's studio in 1997 by the Magnum photographer Thomas Hoepker. In the photograph, the seated artist is partially veiled by a large transparency of an iconic image of Bruce Lee that hung in the studio; in the detail, the figures of Lee and Diao seem to merge, or one seems to grow out of the other. The double portrait is an overlay, a merging, an emanation that plays out two narratives, or stereotypes, of Chinese masculinity—Diao, the aristocratic aesthete dedicated to the hermetic pursuit of art and philosophy, and his alter ego, Bruce Lee, the bare-chested, ferocious warrior.

There is a dry, sly humor to Diao's representations of art history and the rituals of an artist's career. His approach is always enigmatic and subtle: he never tips his hand as to his opinion. In *Bruce and Me*, the screenprint is set onto or into a field of hot pink—the color that has been, in the twentieth and twenty-first centuries, the overdetermined code of hyperfeminity. With indexical traces of palette-knife marks visible up close, marking a surface that is nevertheless characteristically smooth and radiant, the pink field embodies the duality of critique and visual pleasure that makes Diao's work so distinctive.

1. David Diao, interviewed in Matthew Deleget, "David Diao," *Bomb*, no. 133 (Fall 2015): 51.
2. Raphael Rubinstein, "Total Service Artists," *Art in America* 103, no. 9 (October 2015): 110–25.

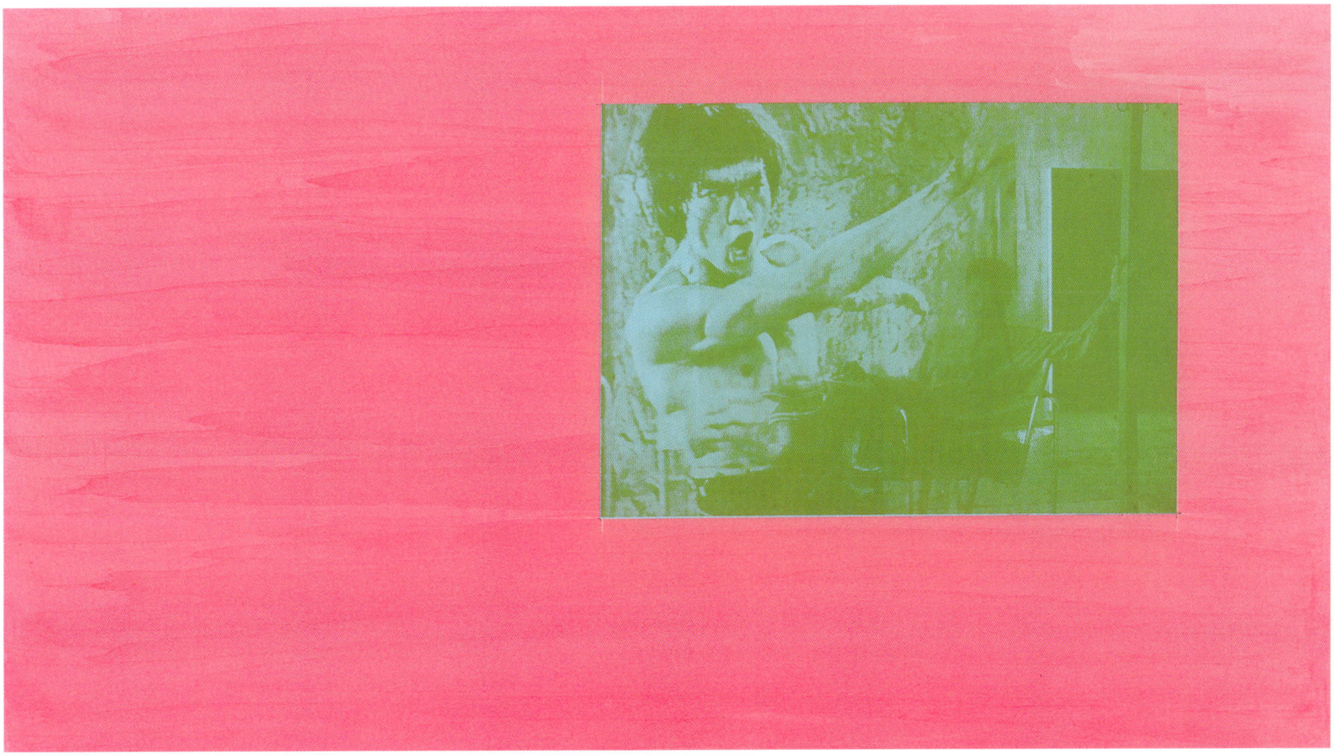

David Diao, *Bruce and Me*, 2000. Acrylic and silkscreen on canvas, 24 × 42 in. (61 × 106.7 cm)

TOM BURCKHARDT ON PETER SAUL

Peter Saul is the nicest bastard I've ever met. In 1986 I was a participant at the Skowhegan School of Painting and Sculpture and Peter was one of the resident faculty. I have a vivid memory of him convening a meeting and accusing all of us of being "a bunch of yuppies." Of course many were outraged, exactly the reaction he had hoped for. I remember his studio critiques by the metaphor of rolling a grenade into a room and getting out before he got splattered. But he was, and is, also one of the sweetest people in person. He just doesn't like the rules of consensus as demarcated by the art world. His paintings have always had a savage and funny anger against all sacred cows, but this hasn't led him to spare himself. This self-portrait is a perfect example of his self-lacerating attack. What on earth would lead anyone to depict himself like this, glasses askew, like he just ran into a wall? Eyeballs drift independently of each other, and potato teeth push past slobbering gums. He holds a bloody paintbrush aloft like some lame torch of liberty, just utterly pathetic. There are never any heroes in Peter's paintings, and so we are all one with original sin, meatbags, blobs of stipple. Although on first impression it might seem that he is awash in judgment, a painting like this refutes that impression and reveals him to be a low-expectation humanist.

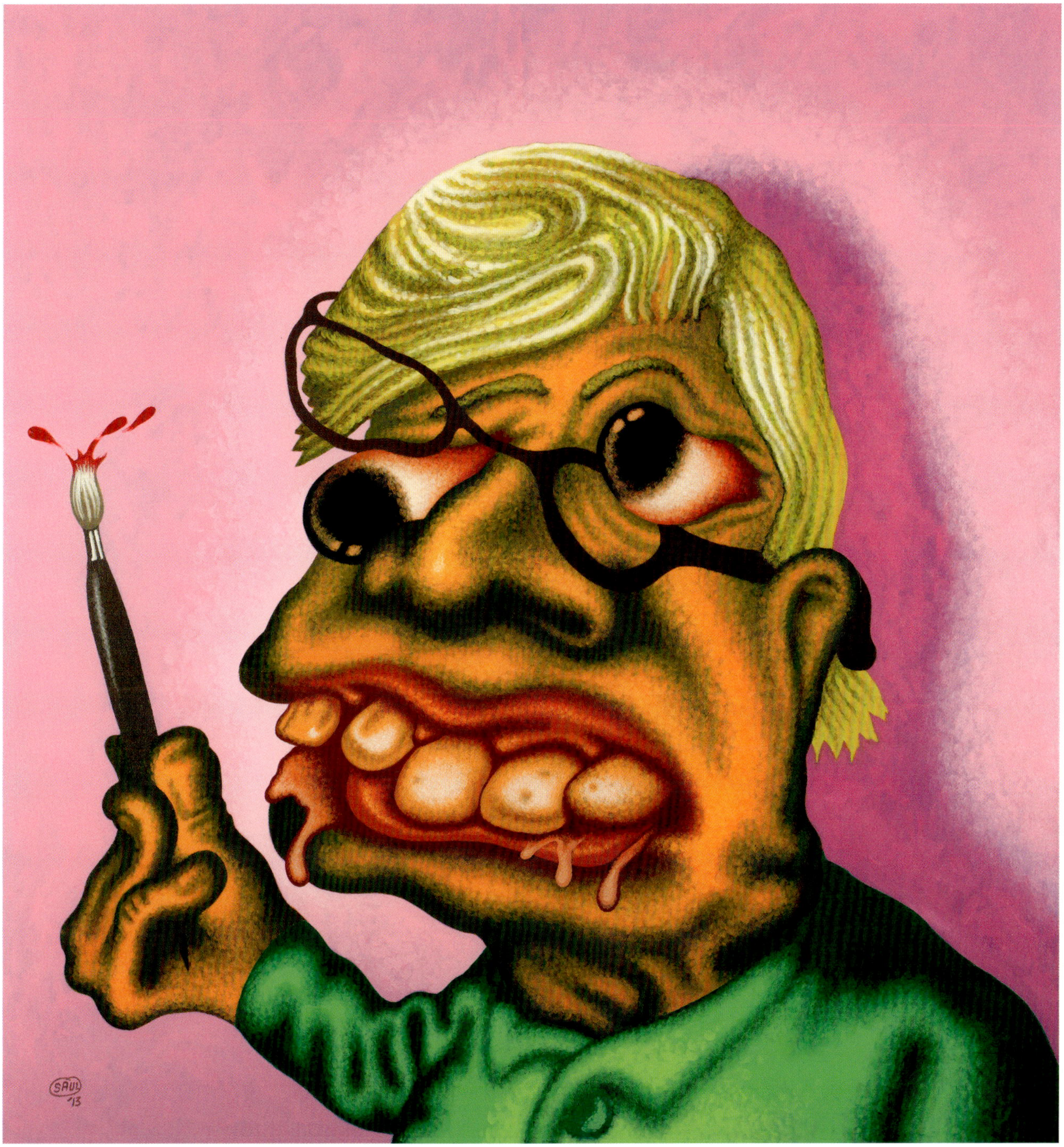

Peter Saul, *Self-Portrait*, 2013. Acrylic on canvas, 60 × 55 in. (152.4 × 139.7 cm)

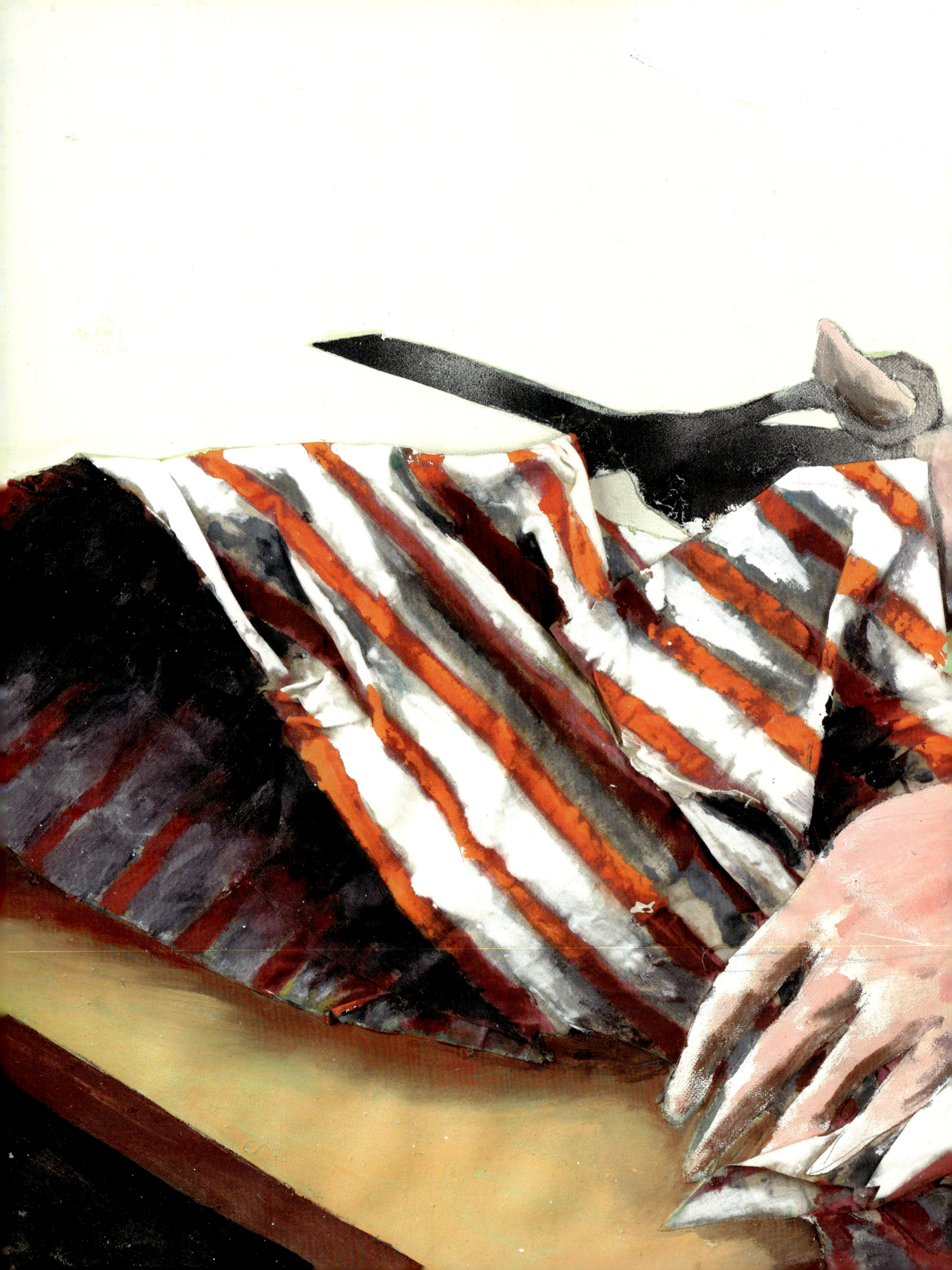

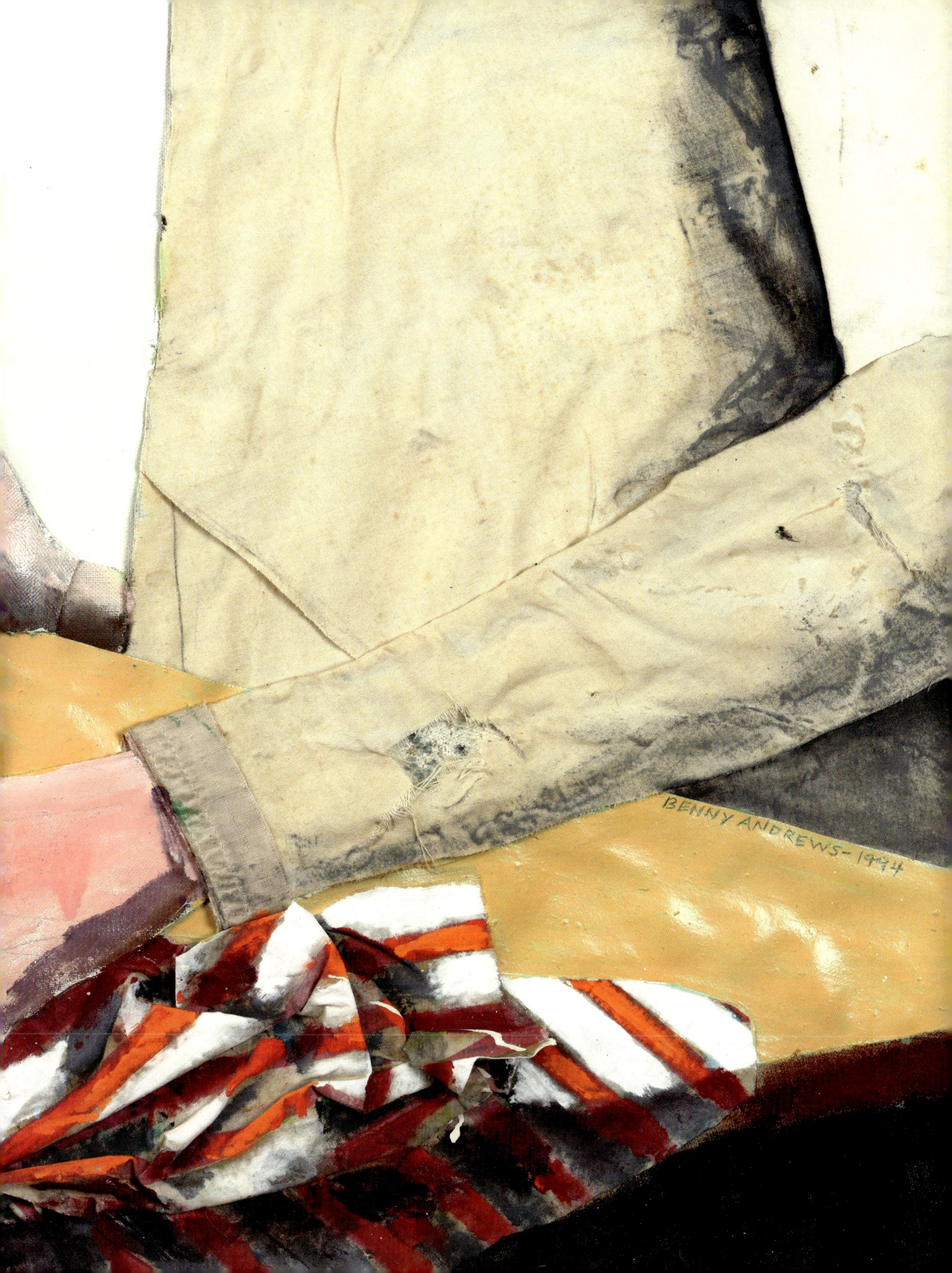
BENNY ANDREWS

CATALOGUE AND SELECTED BIBLIOGRAPHY

JEREMIAH WILLIAM MCCARTHY
WITH PAVLA BERGHEN-WOLF

All paintings are in the collection of the National Academy of Design, New York. A star ★ denotes works included in the traveling exhibition *For America: Paintings from the National Academy of Design*. Short bibliographies provide selected authoritative sources for the Academician and, whenever possible, a sampling of his or her voice.

The following abbreviations are used throughout:

ANA	Associate National Academician
HM	Honorary Member
NA	National Academician
PNAD	President of the NAD
FNAD	Founder of the NAD

From 1829 to 1863, professional artists who did not reside in the City of New York, patrons of the arts, and other distinguished amateurs and professionals were eligible to be elected as Honorary Members.

In 1994, the Associate class of membership was eliminated.

Ivan Albright
ANA 1942; NA 1950
North Harvey, IL 1897–1983 Woodstock, VT

Fur Collar [or] *The Baskerville Portrait*, 1925–26
Oil on canvas, 30 × 20 in. (76.2 × 50.8 cm)
NA diploma presentation, October 9, 1951

★ *Self-Portrait*, 1948
Oil on canvas, 24 × 20 in. (61 × 50.8 cm)
ANA diploma presentation, May 2, 1949

Oehler, Sarah Kelly, ed. *Ivan Albright Paintings at the Art Institute of Chicago*. With essays by Sarah Burns, Kelly Keegan, John P. Murphy, and Sarah Kelly Oehler. Chicago: Art Institute of Chicago, forthcoming 2019.

Rossen, Susan F., ed. *Ivan Albright*. Chicago: Art Institute of Chicago, 1997. Exh. cat.

Croydon, Michael. *Ivan Albright*. New York: Abbeville Press, 1978.

Sweet, Frederick A., and Jean Dubuffet. *Ivan Albright: A Retrospective Exhibition*. Chicago: Art Institute of Chicago; New York: Whitney Museum of American Art, 1964. Exh. cat.

Kuh, Katherine. "Ivan Albright." In *The Artist's Voice: Talks with Seventeen Artists*, 23–37. New York: Harper and Row, 1962.

John White Alexander
ANA 1901; NA 1902; PNAD 1909–15
Allegheny, PA 1856–1915 New York City

Mrs. Thomas Hastings, 1901
Oil on canvas, 47 ½ × 35 ½ in. (120.7 × 90.2 cm)
Gift of The Helen and Thomas Hastings Fund, Inc., 1958

Goley, Mary Anne. *John White Alexander: An American Artist in the Gilded Age*. London: Philip Wilson, 2018.

Moore, Sarah J. *John White Alexander and the Construction of National Identity: Cosmopolitan American Art, 1880–1915*. Newark: University of Delaware Press, 2003.

Alexander, John W. "The Need of a National Academy, and Its Value to the Growth of Art in America." *Craftsman* 17, no. 6 (March 1910): 607–18.

Brinton, Christian. "The Art of John W. Alexander." *Munsey's Magazine* 39, no. 6 (September 1908): 744–55.

Emma Amos
NA 2006
Born Atlanta, GA 1938

* *Giza and Faith*, 1991
Acrylic on *kanga* cloth and African fabric, 78 × 84 in. (198.1 × 213.4 cm)
NA diploma presentation, March 19, 2008

Martin, Courtney J., and Emma Amos. "The Spiral Group: A Conversation of Emma Amos and Courtney J. Martin." In Ellie Tweedy, ed., *Romare Bearden and the Modernist Tradition: Essays from the Romare Bearden Foundation Symposium in Chicago, 2007*, 85–92. New York: Romare Bearden Foundation, 2008.

Patton, Sharon. "Emma Amos: Art Matters." *Nka: Journal of Contemporary African Art*, no. 16/17 (Fall/Winter 2002): 40–47.

Amos, Emma. "Measuring Content." In Jo Anna Isaak, ed., *Looking Forward, Looking Black*, 38–39. Geneva, NY: Hobart and William Smith Colleges Press, 1999.

Gouma-Peterson, Thalia, and Kathleen McManus Zurko. *Emma Amos: Paintings and Prints, 1982–92; An Exhibition*. Wooster, OH: College of Wooster Art Museum, 1993. Exh. cat.

Benny Andrews
NA 1997
Plainview, GA 1930–2006 New York City

* *Collagist, Self-Portrait*, 1994
Oil and collage on canvas, 36 × 24 in. (91.4 × 61 cm)
NA diploma presentation, September 15, 1999

Rosenfeld, Michael, Jonathan P. Binstock, and Lowery Stokes Sims. *African American Art: 200 Years; 40 Distinctive Voices Reveal the Breadth of Nineteenth and Twentieth Century Art*. New York: Michael Rosenfeld Gallery, 2008. Exh. cat.

Gruber, Richard J. *American Icons: From Madison to Manhattan; The Art of Benny Andrews, 1948–1997*. Augusta, GA: Morris Museum of Art, 1997. Exh. cat.

Thompson, Mildred. "Portrait of Benny Andrews with an Interview by Mildred Thompson." *Art Papers*, July/August 1988.

Andrews, Benny. "On Understanding Black Art." *New York Times*, June 27, 1970.

Will Barnet
ANA 1974; NA 1982
Beverly, MA 1911–2012 New York City

* *Self-Portrait*, 1981
Oil on canvas, 31 ⅛ × 45 ½ in. (79.1 × 115.6 cm)
ANA diploma presentation, April 6, 1981

Barnet, Peter, Gail Stavitsky, Anne Betty Weinshenker, and M. Teresa Lapid Rodriguez. *Will Barnet*. Montclair, NJ: George Segal Gallery, Montclair State University, 2010. Exh. cat.

Doty, Robert M., and Will Barnet. *Will Barnet*. New York: H. N. Abrams, 1984.

Wooden, Howard E. *Will Barnet: Paintings and Prints, 1932–1982*. Wichita, KS: Wichita Art Museum, 1983. Exh. cat.

Seckler, Dorothy. "Will Barnet Makes a Lithograph." *ARTnews* 51, no. 2 (April 1952): 38–40, 62–64.

Cecilia Beaux
ANA 1894; NA 1902
Philadelphia 1855–1942 Gloucester, MA

* *Self-Portrait*, 1894
Oil on canvas, 25 × 20 in. (63.5 × 50.8 cm)
ANA diploma presentation, May 13, 1895

Yount, Sylvia. *Cecilia Beaux: American Figure Painter*. Atlanta, GA: High Museum of Art; Berkeley: University of California Press, 2007. Exh. cat.

Burns, Sarah. "The 'Earnest, Untiring Worker' and the Magician of the Brush: Gender Politics in the Criticism of Cecilia Beaux and John Singer Sargent." *Oxford Art Journal* 15, no. 1 (1992): 36–53.

Drinker, Henry S., and Royal Cortissoz. *The Paintings and Drawings of Cecilia Beaux*. Philadelphia: Pennsylvania Academy of the Fine Arts, 1955.

Beaux, Cecilia. *Background with Figures: Autobiography of Cecilia Beaux*. Boston: Houghton Mifflin, 1930.

Rosemarie Beck
ANA 1980; NA 1982
Westchester County, NY 1923–2003 New York City

* *Self-Portrait*, 1975
Oil on linen, 60 × 50 in. (152.4 × 127 cm)
ANA diploma presentation, January 12, 1981

The Tempest: Prospero, Miranda, Ferdinand, 1976
Oil on linen, 49 ½ × 60 in. (125.7 × 152.4 cm)
NA diploma presentation, October 4, 1982

Beck, Rosemarie. *Rosemarie Beck: Letters to a Young Painter and Other Writings*. Edited by Eric Sutphin. Chicago: Soberscove Press, 2018.

Taylor, Sue, ed. *Lyric Truth: Paintings, Drawings, and Embroideries*. Portland, OR: College of the Arts, Portland State University, 2015. Exh. cat.

Sawin, Martica. "Rosemarie Beck: Never Form, but Forming." In Diane Fitch and Glen Cebulash, eds., *Rosemarie Beck: Paintings, 1965–2001*, 4–7. Dayton, OH: Wright State University, 2002. Exh. cat.

Salzberg, Joel. "The Rhythms of Friendship in the Life of Art: The Correspondence of Bernard Malamud and Rosemarie Beck." *Salmagundi*, no. 116/117 (Fall/Winter 1997): 61–124.

George Bellows
ANA 1909; NA 1913
Columbus, OH 1882–1925 New York City

* *Three Rollers*, 1911
Oil on canvas, 39 ⅝ × 41 ¾ in. (100.6 × 106 cm)
NA diploma presentation, December 1, 1913

Brock, Charles, Sean Wilentz, Marianne Doezema, David Peters Corbett, Sarah Newman, Carol Troyen, David Park Curry, Sarah Cash, Melissa Wolfe, Robert Conway, Mark Cole, and Glenn C. Peck. *George Bellows*. Washington DC: National Gallery of Art, 2012. Exh. cat.

Quick, Michael, Jane Myers, Marianne Doezema, and Franklin Kelly. *The Paintings of George Bellows*. With an introduction by John Wilmerding. Fort Worth, TX: Amon Carter Museum; New York: Harry N. Abrams, 1992. Exh. cat.

Adams, Philip R., et al. *George Wesley Bellows: Paintings, Drawings, and Prints.* Columbus, OH: Columbus Museum of Art, 1979. Exh. cat.

Morgan, Charles W. *George Bellows: Painter of America.* New York: Reynal, 1965.

Albert Bierstadt
HM 1858; NA 1860
Solingen, Germany 1830–1902
New York City

* *On the Sweetwater near the Devil's Gate*, 1860
Oil on millboard, 12¼ × 18 in. (31.1 × 45.7 cm)
NA diploma presentation, December 17, 1860

Anderson, Nancy K., and Linda S. Ferber. *Albert Bierstadt: Art and Enterprise.* New York: Brooklyn Museum; Hudson Hills Press, 1990. Exh. cat.

Howat, John K. *American Paradise: The World of the Hudson River School.* New York: Metropolitan Museum of Art, 1987. Exh. cat.

Baigell, Matthew. *Albert Bierstadt.* New York: Watson-Guptill, 1981.

Hendricks, Gordon. *Albert Bierstadt: Painter of the American West.* New York: H. N. Abrams, 1974.

Isabel Bishop
ANA 1940; NA 1941
Cincinnati, OH 1902–1988 New York City

* *Nude Study*, 1934
Oil on canvas, 15 × 18 in. (38.1 × 45.7 cm)
NA diploma presentation, February 17, 1942

Nemser, Cindy. "Conversations with Isabel Bishop." *Feminist Art Journal* 5, no. 1 (Spring 1976): 14–20.

Lunde, Karl. *Isabel Bishop.* New York: H. N. Abrams, 1975.

Seckler, Dorothy. "Bishop Paints a Picture." *ARTnews* 50, no. 7 (November 1951): 38–41, 63–64.

Marsh, Reginald. Foreword to *Isabel Bishop.* New York: Midtown Galleries, 1932. Exh. cat.

Ralph Albert Blakelock
ANA 1913; NA 1916
New York City 1847–1919 Elizabethtown, NY

Sunset, 1916
Oil on cardboard, 3½ × 5½ in. (8.9 × 14 cm)
NA diploma presentation, November 13, 1916

Geske, Norman A. *Beyond Madness: The Art of Ralph Blakelock, 1847–1919.* Lincoln: University of Nebraska Press, 2007.

Davidson, Abraham A. *Ralph Albert Blakelock.* University Park: Pennsylvania State University Press, 1996.

Goodrich, Lloyd. *Ralph Albert Blakelock Centenary Exhibition.* New York: Whitney Museum of American Art, 1947. Exh. cat.

Morton, Frederick W. "Work of Ralph A. Blakelock." *Brush and Pencil* 9, no. 5 (February 1902): 257–69.

Edwin Howland Blashfield
ANA 1882; NA 1888; PNAD 1920–26
New York City 1848–1936 Cape Cod, MA

Saint Michael, n.d.
Oil on canvas, 30⅛ × 22 in. (76.5 × 55.9 cm)
NA diploma presentation, October 4, 1889

Weiner, Mina Rieur, and Anne Day. *Edwin Howland Blashfield: Master American Muralist.* Classical America Series in Art and Architecture. New York: Institute of Classical Architecture and Classical America; W. W. Norton, 2009.

Cortissoz, Royal. *The Works of Edwin Howland Blashfield.* New York: Charles Scribner's Sons, 1937.

Blashfield, Edwin Howland. *Mural Painting in America: The Scammon Lectures, Delivered at the Art Institute of Chicago, March, 1912 and Since Greatly Enlarged.* New York: Charles Scribner's Sons, 1913.

Saint-Gaudens, Homer. "Edwin Howland Blashfield." *International Studio* 35, no. 139 (September 1908): 69–78.

Robert Frederick Blum
ANA 1888; NA 1893
Cincinnati, OH 1857–1903 New York City

* *Two Idlers*, 1888–89
Oil on canvas, 29 × 40 in. (73.7 × 101.6 cm)
NA diploma presentation, March 26, 1894

Burke, Doreen Bolger. "Robert Blum, 1857–1903." In *A Catalogue of Works by Artists Born between 1846 and 1864*, 301–5. Vol. 3 of *American Paintings in the Metropolitan Museum of Art.* Edited by Kathleen Luhrs, assisted by Carrie Rebora and Patricia R. Winders. New York: Metropolitan Museum of Art; Princeton: Princeton University Press, 1980.

Boyle, Richard J. *Robert F. Blum, 1857–1903.* Cincinnati, OH: Cincinnati Art Museum, 1966.

Caffin, Charles H. "Robert Frederick Blum." *American Studio Talk*, December 1903, 176–92.

Blum, Robert. "An Artist in Japan." *Scribner's Magazine* 13, no. 5 (May 1893): 399–414.

Ernest L. Blumenschein
ANA 1910; NA 1927
Pittsburgh, PA 1874–1960 Albuquerque, NM

* *The Lake*, ca. 1923
Oil on canvas, 24⅛ × 27 in. (61.3 × 68.6 cm)
NA diploma presentation, October 18, 1927

Scott, Sascha T. *A Strange Mixture: The Art and Politics of Painting Pueblo Indians.* The Charles M. Russell Center Series on Art and Photography of the American West 16. Norman: University of Oklahoma Press, 2015.

Hassrick, Peter H., and Elizabeth J. Cunningham. *In Contemporary Rhythm: The Art of Ernest L. Blumenschein.* The Charles M. Russell Center Series on Art and Photography of the American West 2. Norman: University of Oklahoma Press, 2008.

Cook, Howard. "Ernest L. Blumenschein: The Artist and His Environment." *New Mexico Quarterly Review* 19, no. 1 (Spring 1949): 18–24.

Blumenschein, Ernest L. "The Painting for To-morrow." *Century Magazine* 87, no. 6 (April 1914): 844–50.

Mary Shepard Greene Blumenschein
ANA 1913
New York City 1869–1958 Santa Fe, NM

★ *Self-Portrait*, 1915
Oil on canvas, 30 × 25 in. (76.2 × 63.5 cm)
ANA diploma presentation, March 1, 1915

McCarthy, Jeremiah William. "Mary Shepard Greene Blumenschein." In Laurence Madeline, *Women Artists in Paris, 1850–1900*, 255. New York: American Federation of Arts; New Haven: Yale University Press, 2017. Exh. cat.

Blumenschein, Helen. *Recuerdos: Early Days of the Blumenschein Family*. Silver City, NY: Tecolote Press, 1979.

The Blumenscheins of Taos. Flagstaff: Museum of Northern Arizona, 1979. Exh. cat.

Trenton, Patricia. *Picturesque Images from Taos and Santa Fe*. Denver, CO: Denver Art Museum, 1974. Exh. cat.

Aaron Bohrod
ANA 1951; NA 1953
Chicago 1907–1992 Madison, WI

★ *Artist in Residence: Self-Portrait*, 1943
Oil on canvas, 26 × 21 ⅛ in. (66 × 53.7 cm)
ANA diploma presentation, December 3, 1951

★ *Façade, New Orleans*, n.d.
Oil on canvas, 16 × 19 ¾ in. (40.6 × 50.2 cm)
NA diploma presentation, April 5, 1954

Cozzolino, Robert. "Aaron Bohrod at 100." *Wisconsin People and Ideas*, Fall 2007, 29–36.

Nordland, Gerald. "Aaron Bohrod." In Rosalie A. Goldstein et al., *Leaders in Wisconsin Art, 1936–1981: John Steuart Curry, Aaron Bohrod, John Wilde*, 25–29. Milwaukee: Milwaukee Art Museum, 1982. Exh. cat.

Bohrod, Aaron. *Aaron Bohrod: Master of Trompe l'Oeil*. New York: Danenberg and Roman Galleries, 1971. Exh. cat.

Bohrod, Aaron. "Aaron Bohrod on Art." *New York Herald Tribune Magazine*, November 17, 1957, 9.

Ferdinand Thomas Lee Boyle
ANA 1849
Ringwood, England 1820–1906 New York City

★ *Eliza Greatorex*, 1869
Oil on canvas, 30 × 25 ¼ in. (76.2 × 64.1 cm)
ANA diploma portrait, date unknown

Quick, Michael. "Ferdinand Thomas Lee Boyle." In *Artists by Themselves: Artists' Portraits from the National Academy of Design*, 64–65. New York: National Academy of Design, 1983. Exh. cat.

Styles, Henry R., ed. *History of Kings County, Including the City of Brooklyn*, 1147–48. New York: W. W. Munsell, 1884.

"Our Artists and Their Works." *Brooklyn Monthly* 1, no. 5 (November 1877): 1–2.

Ferdinand Thomas Lee Boyle artist accounts, Manuscripts and Archives Division, New York Public Library.

Gretna Campbell
ANA 1987
New York City 1922–1987

★ *Garden in Brazil*, 1983
Oil on canvas, 54 × 58 in. (137.2 × 147.3 cm)
Posthumous ANA diploma presentation, December 2, 1987

Sawin, Martica. *Gretna Campbell: Paintings from Great Cranberry Island*, Ellsworth, ME: Courthouse Gallery Fine Art, 2016. Exh. cat.

Turner, Norman. "Thinking of Gretna Campbell." *Transfer*, no. 5 (1990): 17–25.

Finkelstein, Louis. *Gretna Campbell, Early and Late*. New York: New York Studio School, 1987. Exh. cat.

Goodrich, Lloyd, Senator J. William Fulbright, and Donald J. Shank. *Fulbright Painters*. New York: Institute of International Education, 1958. Exh. cat.

William Merritt Chase
ANA 1888; NA 1890
Williamsburg, IN 1849–1916 New York City

★ *The Young Orphan* [or] *An Idle Moment* [or] *Portrait*, 1884
Oil on canvas, 44 × 42 in. (111.8 × 106.7 cm)
NA diploma presentation, November 24, 1890

★ *Robert Blum*, 1888
Oil on canvas, 21 ⅛ × 17 ⅛ in. (53.7 × 43.5 cm)
ANA diploma presentation, March 18, 1889

Smithgall, Elsa, Erica E. Hirshler, Katherine M. Bourguignon, John Davis, and Giovanna Ginex. *William Merritt Chase: A Modern Master*. Washington, DC: Phillips Collection, 2016. Exh. cat.

Pisano, Ronald G. *Complete Catalogue of Known and Documented Work by William Merritt Chase (1849–1916)*. 4 vols. New Haven: Yale University Press, 2006–10.

Cikovsky, Nicolai, Jr. "William Merritt Chase's Tenth Street Studio." *Archives of American Art Journal* 16, no. 2 (1976): 2–14.

Chase, William Merritt. "The Import of Art: An Interview with Walter Pach." *Outlook*, June 25, 1910, 441–45.

Jones, Jessie. "Blum and Chase Teaching Contrasted by a Member of the Art Students League Who Studied under Both Masters." *Art Amateur* 35, no. 5 (October 1896): 91.

Frederic Edwin Church
ANA 1848; NA 1849
Hartford, CT 1826–1900 New York City

★ *Scene among the Andes*, 1854
Oil on canvas, 15 ⅞ × 24 in. (40.3 × 61 cm)
Bequest of James A. Suydam, 1865

Raab, Jennifer. *Frederic Church: The Art and Science of Detail*. New Haven: Yale University Press, 2015.

Carr, Gerald L. *Frederic Edwin Church: Catalogue Raisonné of Works of Art at Olana State Historic Site*. 2 vols. Cambridge: Cambridge University Press, 1994.

Kelly, Franklin, Stephen J. Gould, and James Ryan. *Frederic Edwin Church*. Washington, DC: National Gallery of Art, 1989. Exh. cat.

Huntington, David C. *The Landscapes of Frederic Edwin Church: Vision of an American Era.* New York: George Braziller, 1966.

William Clutz
NA 2005
Born Gettysburg, PA 1933

★ *Self-Portrait (Walking)*, 1980
Oil on canvas, 35 ⅛ × 30 ¼ in. (89.2 × 76.8 cm)
Gift of the artist, September 23, 2009

★ *Autumn Street*, 1999
Oil on canvas, 50 × 40 in. (127 × 101.6 cm)
NA diploma presentation, May 17, 2006

Egan, Shannon. *William Clutz: Crossings.* Gettysburg, PA: Schmucker Art Gallery, Gettysburg College, 2016. Exh. cat.

Fahnstock, Andrea Henderson. *William Clutz: Five Decades of New York Streets.* New York: Katharina Rich Perlow Gallery, 2002. Exh. cat.

Woods, Jean. *William Clutz: Retrospective.* Hagerstown, MD: Washington County Museum of Fine Arts, 1991. Exh. cat.

Mangan, Doreen. "William Clutz Captures the Soul of a City." *American Artist* 42, no. 427 (February 1978): 36–41, 91–92.

Kenyon Cox
ANA 1900; NA 1903
Warren, OH 1856–1919 New York City

★ *A Blonde*, 1891
Oil on canvas, 41 × 36 in. (104.1 × 91.4 cm)
NA diploma presentation, June 1, 1903

★ *Maxfield Parrish*, 1905
Oil on canvas, 30 × 25 in. (76.2 × 63.5 cm)
ANA diploma presentation, December 5, 1905

Morgan, H. Wayne. *Kenyon Cox, 1856–1919: A Life in American Art.* Kent, OH: Kent State University Press, 1994.

Morgan, H. Wayne. "Kenyon Cox: Traditionalist Painter and Critic." In *Keepers of Culture: The Art-Thought of Kenyon Cox, Royal Cortissoz, and Frank Jewett Mather, Jr.*, 15–60. Kent, OH: Kent State University Press, 1989.

Cox, Kenyon. *The Classic Point of View.* New York: Charles Scribner's Sons, 1912. Reprint, New York: Norton, 1980.

Smith, Minna C. "The Work of Kenyon Cox." *International Studio* 32, no. 125 (July 1907): 3–12.

John Steuart Curry
ANA 1937; NA 1943
Dunavant, KS 1897–1946 Madison, WI

★ *Belgian Stallions*, 1938
Oil on wood panel, 30 × 25 ½ in. (76.2 × 64.8 cm)
NA diploma presentation, October 4, 1943

Junker, Patricia A. *John Steuart Curry: Inventing the Middle West.* New York: Hudson Hills Press, 1998. Exh. cat.

Kendall, M. Sue. *Rethinking Regionalism: John Steuart Curry and the Kansas Mural Controversy.* New Directions in American Art. Washington, DC: Smithsonian Institution Press, 1986.

Czestochowski, Joseph S. *John Steuart Curry and Grant Wood: A Portrait of Rural America.* Cedar Rapids, MO: Cedar Rapids Art Association; Columbia: University of Missouri Press, 1981.

Schmeckebier, Laurence Eli. *John Steuart Curry's Pageant of America.* New York: American Artists Group, 1943.

David Diao
NA 2012
Born Chengdu, China 1943

★ *Bruce and Me*, 2000
Acrylic and silkscreen on canvas, 24 × 42 in. (61 × 106.7 cm)
NA diploma presentation, February 6, 2013

Tinari, Philip. *David Diao.* New York: Prestel, 2018.

Diao, David, and Matthew Deleget. "David Diao." *BOMB*, no. 133 (Fall 2015): 48–57.

Anderson, Paul A. "David Diao: Critical Painting and the Racial Sublime." *Third Text* 9, no. 33 (Winter 1995): 41–50.

Ferguson, Bruce. "From Vision to Text: A Re-Action." In *David Diao.* Saint-Étienne, France: Musée d'art moderne Saint-Étienne, 1989. Exh. cat.

Edwin Dickinson
ANA 1948; NA 1950
Seneca Falls, NY 1891–1978 Wellfleet, MA

Self-Portrait, 1949
Oil on canvas, 23 × 20 ⅛ in. (58.4 × 51.1 cm)
ANA diploma presentation, November 7, 1949

Berlind, Robert. "Edwin Dickinson: Waking Visions." *Art in America* 91, no. 2 (February 2003): 88–95.

Dreishpoon, Douglas, ed. *Edwin Dickinson: Dreams and Realities.* Buffalo, NY: Albright-Knox Art Gallery; New York: Hudson Hills Press, 2003. Exh. cat.

Ward, John L. *Edwin Dickinson: A Critical History of His Paintings.* Newark: University of Delaware Press, 2003.

Goodrich, Lloyd. *Edwin Dickinson.* New York: Whitney Museum of American Art, 1965. Exh. cat.

Lois Dodd
ANA 1987; NA 1989
Born Montclair, NJ 1927

★ *View through Chicken House*, 1971
Oil on Masonite, 28 × 20 in. (71.1 × 50.8 cm)
Gift of Lois Dodd, 2004

Self-Portrait, 1984
Oil on composition board, 20 × 12 in. (50.8 × 30.5 cm)
ANA diploma presentation, March 2, 1988

Hirsch, Faye. *Lois Dodd.* Contemporary Painters Series. London: Lund Humphries, 2017.

Packard, Andrea, and Barry Schwabsky. *Lois Dodd: Windows and Reflections.* Swarthmore, PA: List Gallery, Swarthmore College, 2016. Exh. cat.

O'Brien, Barbara, John Yau, and Alison Ferris. *Lois Dodd: Catching the Light.* Kansas City, MO: Kemper Museum of Contemporary Art, 2012. Exh. cat.

Prescott, Theodore. "In Plain Sight: The Art of Lois Dodd." *American Arts Quarterly* 28, no. 4 (Fall 2011): 42–48.

Asher B. Durand
FNAD 1826; PNAD 1845–61
Maplewood, NJ 1796–1886

★ *Self-Portrait*, ca. 1835
Oil on canvas, 30 ⅛ × 25 ¼ in. (76.5 × 64.1 cm)
Gift of the artist, between 1843 and 1852

★ *Landscape*, 1850
Oil on canvas, 27 ¼ × 38 ½ in. (69.2 × 97.8 cm)
Bequest of James A. Suydam, 1865

Ferber, Linda S., Barbara Dayer Gallati, Marilyn S. Kushner, and Barbara Novak. *The American Landscapes of Asher B. Durand (1796–1886)*. New York: New-York Historical Society; Madrid: Fundación Juan March, 2010. Exh. cat.

Sweet, Frederick A. "Asher B. Durand, Pioneer American Landscape Painter." *Art Quarterly* 8, no. 2 (Spring 1945): 141–60.

Durand, John. *The Life and Times of A. B. Durand*. New York: Charles Scribner's Sons, 1894.

Durand, Asher B. "Letters on Landscape Painting." *Crayon* 1, nos. 1, 3, 5, 7, 10, 14, 18, 23; 2, no. 2 (January–July 1855).

Thomas Eakins
ANA 1902; NA 1902
Philadelphia 1844–1916

★ *Self-Portrait*, 1902
Oil on canvas, 30 × 25 in. (76.2 × 63.5 cm)
ANA diploma presentation, May 5, 1902

Reason, Akela. *Thomas Eakins and the Uses of History*. Philadelphia: University of Pennsylvania Press, 2010.

Burns, Sarah. "Ordering the Artist's Body: Thomas Eakins's Act of Self-Portrayal." *American Art* 19, no. 1 (Spring 2005): 82–107.

Sewell, Darrel. *Thomas Eakins*. Philadelphia: Philadelphia Museum of Art; New Haven: Yale University Press, 2001. Exh. cat.

Goodrich, Lloyd. *Thomas Eakins*. The Ailsa Mellon Bruce Studies in American Art. 2 vols. Cambridge, MA: Harvard University Press for the National Gallery of Art, 1982.

Bregler, Charles. "Thomas Eakins as a Teacher." Pts. 1 and 2. *Arts* 17, no. 6 (March 1931): 378–86; 18, no. 1 (October 1931): 29–42.

Wyatt Eaton
Nominated 1875 and 1878
Phillipsburg, Quebec 1849–1896
Middletown, RI

★ *The Artist in His Studio*, 1873
Oil on canvas, 24 ⅛ × 19 ¾ in. (61.3 × 50.2 cm)
Gift of John Elderkin, May 14, 1902

Lowrey, Carol. "Eaton, Wyatt." In *Dictionary of Canadian Biography*, vol. 12. Quebec: University of Toronto/Université Laval, 1990.

Hellman, George S. "Wyatt Eaton." *Art World* 3, no. 3 (December 1917): 204–9.

Eaton, Charlotte. "Wyatt Eaton, Painter." *Canadian Magazine*, December 1908, 145–52.

Eaton, Wyatt. "Recollections of Jean-François Millet." *Century Magazine* 38 [n.s., 16], no. 1 (May 1889): 90–104.

Richard Estes
ANA 1971; NA 1984
Born Kewanee, IL 1932

★ *NYC Parking Lot*, 1969
Oil on Masonite, 23 ¾ × 36 in. (60.3 × 91.4 cm)
NA diploma presentation, January 7, 1987

Sims, Patterson, Jessica May, and Helen Ferrulli. *Richard Estes' Realism*. Portland, ME: Portland Museum of Art, 2014. Exh. cat.

Parmiggiani, Sandro, and Guillermo Solana. *Richard Estes: The Sensuousness of the Real*. Milan: Skira, 2008. Exh. cat.

Wilmerding, John. *Richard Estes*. New York: Rizzoli, 2006.

Meisel, Louis K., and John Perreault. *Richard Estes: The Complete Paintings, 1966–1985*. New York: H. N. Abrams, 1986.

Gertrude Fiske
ANA 1922; NA 1930
Boston 1879–1961 Weston, MA

★ *Jade*, ca. 1918
Oil on canvas, 29 ¾ × 23 ¾ in. (75.6 × 60.3 cm)
NA diploma presentation, October 6, 1930

★ *Self-Portrait*, 1922
Oil on canvas, 30 ½ × 25 ¼ in. (77.5 × 64.1 cm)
ANA diploma presentation, May 7, 1923

McCartney, Lainey. *Gertrude Fiske: American Master*. Portsmouth, NH: Portsmouth Marine Society Press, 2018. Exh. cat.

Hirshler, Erica E., Janet L. Comey, and Ellen E. Roberts. *A Studio of Her Own: Women Artists in Boston, 1870–1940*. Boston: MFA Publications, 2001. Exh. cat.

Aten, Carol Walker. *Gertrude Fiske*. Boston: Vose Galleries, 1987. Exh. cat.

Fairbrother, Trevor J., Theodore E. Stebbins, Jr., William L. Vance, and Erica E. Hirshler. *The Bostonians: Painters of an Elegant Age*. Boston: Museum of Fine Arts, 1986. Exh. cat.

Jane Freilicher
ANA 1980; NA 1982
New York City 1924–2014

★ *Telephone Poles*, 1963
Oil on canvas, 32 × 40 ½ in. (81.3 × 102.9 cm)
NA diploma presentation, November 1, 1982

★ *Self-Portrait in a Mirror*, 1971
Oil on linen, 42 × 38 in. (106.7 × 96.5 cm)
ANA diploma presentation, April 6, 1981

Schuyler, James. "The Painting of Jane Freilicher." In Jed Perl, ed., *Art in America, 1945–1970: Writings from the Age of Abstract Expressionism, Pop Art and Minimalism*, 503–8. New York: Library of America, 2014.

Kertess, Klaus. *Jane Freilicher*. New York: H. N. Abrams, 2004.

Doty, Robert, ed. *Jane Freilicher: Paintings*. New York: Taplinger for Currier Gallery of Art, 1986. Exh. cat.

Ashbery, John. "On Jane Freilicher." In Daniel Halpern, ed., *Writers on Artists*, 323–28. San Francisco: North Point Press, 1985.

Porter, Fairfield. "Jane Freilicher Paints a Picture." *ARTnews* 55, no. 5 (September 1956): 46–49, 65–66.

Frederick Carl Frieseke
ANA 1912; NA 1914
Owosso, MI 1874–1939 Mesnil-sur-Blangy, France

★ *Hollyhocks*, by 1911
Oil on canvas, 25 ½ × 32 in. (64.8 × 81.3 cm)
NA diploma presentation, November 2, 1914

Kilmer, Nicholas, and Linda McWhorter. *Frederick Carl Frieseke: The Evolution of an American Impressionist*. Savannah, GA: Telfair Museum of Art; Princeton: Princeton University Press, 2001. Exh. cat.

Frieseke, Frederick C., and Nicholas Kilmer. *Uneventful Reminiscences: A Childhood in Florida*. New York: Hollis Taggart Galleries, 2000. Exh. cat.

Taylor, E. A. "The Paintings of F. C. Frieseke." *International Studio* 53, no. 212 (October 1914): 259–67.

MacChesney, Clara T. "Frieseke Tells Some of the Secrets of His Art." *New York Times*, June 7, 1914.

Ann Gale
NA 2010
Born Baltimore, MD 1966

★ *Babs with Ribbons*, 2007
Oil on canvas, 48 × 42 in. (121.9 × 106.7 cm)
NA diploma presentation, February 12, 2014

Malcolm, Frances. *Ann Gale*. San Francisco: Dolby Chadwick Gallery, 2012. Exh. cat.

Selz, Peter. *Heads*. San Francisco: Dolby Chadwick Gallery, 2011. Exh. cat.

Gately, Jennifer A. *APEX: Ann Gale*. Portland, OR: Portland Art Museum, 2007. Exh. cat.

Nixon, Bruce. "Eye of the Beholder: Recent Paintings." In Ann Gale, *Ann Gale: Recent Paintings*. San Francisco: Hackett-Freedman Gallery, 2004. Exh. cat.

Daniel Garber
ANA 1910; NA 1913
North Manchester, IN 1880–1958 Lumberville, PA

★ *By Addingham*, 1911
Oil on canvas, 25 ¼ × 30 ⅛ in. (64.1 × 76.5 cm)
NA diploma presentation, April 6, 1914

★ *Self-Portrait*, ca. 1911
Oil on canvas, 30 × 25 ¼ in. (76.2 × 64.1 cm)
ANA diploma presentation, May 11, 1911

Peterson, Brian H., ed. *Pennsylvania Impressionism*. Doylestown, PA: James A. Michener Art Museum; Philadelphia: University of Pennsylvania Press, 2002.

Folk, Thomas. *The Pennsylvania School of Landscape Painting*. Allentown, PA: Allentown Art Museum, 1984. Exh. cat.

Foster, Kathleen. *Daniel Garber, 1880–1958*. Philadelphia: Pennsylvania Academy of the Fine Arts, 1980. Exh. cat.

Breck, Bayard. "Daniel Garber, A Modern American Master." *Art and Life* 11, no. 9 (March 1920): 493–97.

Jacqueline Gourevitch
NA 2011
Born Paris, France 1933

★ *Night: WTC Looking East*, 2000–2001
Oil on canvas, 50 × 40 in. (127 × 101.6 cm)
NA diploma presentation, March 7, 2012

Ratcliff, Carter. *SITE/SIGHT*. Saugerties, NY: Cross Contemporary Art, 2017. Exh. cat.

Buhmann, Stephanie, ed. "Jacqueline Gourevitch." In *New York Studio Conversations: Seventeen Women Talk about Art*, 153–61. Berlin: The Green Box, 2016.

Paoletti, John T. "Activated and Tenacious: The Art of Jacqueline Gourevitch." *Arts Magazine*, November 1982, 132–35.

Cate, Philip Dennis. *Skying*. New Brunswick, NJ: Rutgers University Museum, 1972. Exh. cat.

George Henry Hall
ANA 1853–55, 1863; NA 1868
Boston 1825–1913 New York City

★ *A Dead Rabbit*, 1858
Oil on canvas, 43 ¼ × 24 in. (109.9 × 61 cm)
NA diploma exchange presentation, April 3, 1882
Original NA diploma presentation, 1868

Barrett, Ross. "Riot, Rowdying, and Reform: George Henry Hall and the Picturing of Midcentury Urban Upheaval." In *Rendering Violence: Riots, Strikes, and Upheaval in Nineteenth-Century American Art*, 75–103. Oakland: University of California Press, 2014.

Boone, Mary Elizabeth. "George Henry Hall, *Costumbrismo*, and the Vogue for Murillo." In *Vistas de España: American Views of Art and Life in Spain, 1860–1914*, 37–59. New Haven: Yale University Press, 2007.

Carbone, Teresa A., Barbara Dayer Gallati, and Linda S. Ferber. "George Henry Hall." In *Artists Born by 1876*, 583–85. Vol. 2 of *American Paintings in the Brooklyn Museum*. New York: Brooklyn Museum, 2006.

Favretti, Margaret. "George Henry Hall." In Kenneth Myers, *The Catskills: Painters, Writers, and Tourists in the Mountains, 1820–1895*, 138–40. Yonkers, NY: Hudson River Museum of Westchester, 1987. Exh. cat.

Childe Hassam
ANA 1902; NA 1906
Dorchester, MA 1859–1935 East Hampton, NY

★ *The Jewel Box, Old Lyme*, 1906
Oil on canvas, 20 × 24 in. (50.8 × 61 cm)
NA diploma presentation, January 7, 1907

Weinberg, H. Barbara. *Childe Hassam: American Impressionist*. New York: Metropolitan Museum of Art, 2004. Exh. cat.

Buckley, Charles E. *Childe Hassam: A Retrospective Exhibition*. Washington, DC: Corcoran Gallery of Art, 1965. Exh. cat.

Adams, Adeline. *Childe Hassam*. New York: American Academy and Institute of Arts and Letters, 1938.

Ives, A. E. "Talks with Artists: Mr. Childe Hassam on Painting Street Scenes." *Art Amateur* 27 (October 1892): 116–17.

Walter Hatke
NA 2003
Born Topeka, KS 1948

* *Provider*, 2001
Oil on linen, 24 × 29 ¾ in. (61 × 75.6 cm)
Gift of the artist, May 9, 2012

Seligman, Rachel, ed. *Walter Hatke: Recent Work*. Schenectady, NY: Mandeville Gallery, Union College, 2005. Exh. cat.

Young, Christopher R. *New Horizons in American Realism*. Flint, MI: Flint Institute of Art, 1991. Exh. cat.

Lambert, Don. "Walter Hatke." *American Artist* 46, no. 483 (October 1982): 52–57.

Filstrup, E. Christian. "The Alphabet of Things in Walter Hatke's Art." *World Order* 12, no. 1 (Fall 1977): 20–28.

Robert Henri
ANA 1905; NA 1906
Cincinnati, OH 1865–1929 New York City

* *George Wesley Bellows*, 1911
Oil on canvas, 32 × 25 ⅞ in. (81.3 × 65.7 cm)
ANA diploma presentation, December 4, 1911

Leeds, Valerie Ann. *Robert Henri: The Painted Spirit*. New York: Gerald Peters Gallery, 2005. Exh. cat.

Milroy, Elizabeth. *Painters of a New Century: The Eight and American Art*. Milwaukee: Milwaukee Art Museum, 1991. Exh. cat.

Perlman, Bennard B. *Robert Henri: His Life and Art*. New York: Dover, 1991.

Henri, Robert. *The Art Spirit*. Compiled by Margery Ryerson. Philadelphia: J. B. Lippincott, 1923.

Henri, Robert. "My People." *Craftsman* 27, no. 5 (February 1915): 459–69.

Winslow Homer
ANA 1864; NA 1865
Boston 1836–1910 Prouts Neck, ME

* *Croquet Player*, ca. 1865
Oil on canvas, 8 ⅛ × 12 ⅛ in. (20.6 × 30.8 cm)
NA diploma presentation, May 7, 1866

Conrads, Margaret C. *Winslow Homer and the Critics: Forging a National Art in the 1870s*. Kansas City, MO: Nelson-Atkins Museum of Art; Princeton: Princeton University Press, 2001. Exh. cat.

Burns, Sarah. "Being Big: Winslow Homer and the American Business Spirit." In *Inventing the Modern Artist: Art and Culture in Gilded Age America*, 187–217. New Haven: Yale University Press, 1996.

Cikovsky, Nicolai, Jr., ed. *Winslow Homer: A Symposium*. Studies in the History of Art 26/Symposium Papers 11. Washington, DC: National Gallery of Art, 1990.

Hendricks, Gordon. *The Life and Work of Winslow Homer.* New York: H. N. Abrams, 1979.

Goodrich, Lloyd. *Winslow Homer*. New York: Macmillan, 1944.

Daniel Huntington
ANA 1839; NA 1840; PNAD 1862–69, 1876–91
New York City 1816–1906

* *The Fair Student* [or] *Girl Reading*, 1858
Oil on canvas, 30 × 25 in. (76.2 × 63.5 cm)
Bequest of James A. Suydam, 1865

* *Self-Portrait*, 1891
Oil on canvas, 36 ⅛ × 29 in. (91.8 × 73.7 cm)
ANA diploma exchange presentation, March 13, 1893

Greenhouse, Wendy. "Daniel Huntington and the Ideal of Christian Art." *Winterthur Portfolio* 31, no. 2/3 (Summer/Fall 1996): 103–40.

Gerdts, William H. "Daniel Huntington's Mercy Dream: A Pilgrimage through Bunyanesque Imagery." *Winterthur Portfolio* 14, no. 2 (Summer 1979): 172–93.

Benjamin, S. G. W. "Daniel Huntington, President of the National Academy of Design." *American Art Review* 2, pt. 2 (1881): 1–6, 223–28.

Townley, D[aniel] O'C[onnell]. "Living American Artists: Daniel Huntington, Ex-President N.A.D." *Scribner's Monthly* 2, no. 1 (May 1871): 44–49.

Peter Hurd
ANA 1941; NA 1942
Roswell, NM 1904–1984

* *Evening in the Sierras*, 1938–39
Egg tempera on gessoed panel, 24 ¼ × 42 in. (61.6 × 106.7 cm)
NA diploma presentation, February 3, 1947

Self-Portrait, 1941
Oil on wood panel, 29 × 24 in. (73.7 × 61 cm)
ANA diploma presentation, March 2, 1942

Hurd, Peter. *My Land Is the Southwest: Peter Hurd Letters and Journals*. Edited by Robert Metzger. College Station: Texas A&M University Press, 1983.

Horton, Tonia L., and James K. Ballinger. *Peter Hurd: Insight to a Painter.* Phoenix: Phoenix Art Museum, 1983. Exh. cat.

Meyer, S. "Peter Hurd." *American Artist* 39, no. 391 (February 1975): 46–51, 100–104.

Horgan, Paul. *Peter Hurd: A Portrait Sketch from Life*. Fort Worth, TX: Amon Carter Museum of Western Art; Austin: University of Texas Press, 1965. Exh. cat.

George Inness
ANA 1853; NA 1868
Newburgh, NY 1825–1894 Bridge of Allan, Scotland

* *Landscape*, 1860
Oil on paper, mounted on wood panel, 16 ¼ × 24 in. (41.3 × 61 cm)
NA diploma presentation, May 3, 1869

Quick, Michael. *George Inness: A Catalogue Raisonné*. New Brunswick, NJ: Rutgers University Press, 2007.

Baxter, Adrienne, ed. *George Inness: Writings and Reflections on Art and Philosophy*. New York: George Braziller, 2006.

DeLue, Rachael Ziady. *George Inness and the Science of Landscape*. Chicago: University of Chicago Press, 2004.

Cikovsky, Nicolai, Jr., and Michael Quick. *George Inness*. Los Angeles: Los Angeles County Museum of Art, 1985. Exh. cat.

Ernest L. Ipsen
ANA 1913; NA 1924
Malden, MA 1869–1951 Miami, FL

Edwin H. Blashfield, 1925
Oil on canvas, 60 ¼ × 38 in. (153 × 96.5 cm)
NA diploma exchange presentation, April 5, 1926
Original NA diploma presentation, October 18, 1924

Lowrey, Carol. "Ernest L. Ipsen." In *A Legacy of Art: Paintings and Sculpture by Artist Life Members of the National Arts Club*, 132–33. New York: National Arts Club, 2007.

"Ernest Ipsen Dies; Portrait Painter." *New York Times*, November 4, 1951.

Leonebel Jacobs
Tacoma, WA 1884–1967 Manchester, VT

Luigi Lucioni, 1938
Oil on canvas, 30 × 24 ⅞ in. (76.2 × 63.2 cm)
ANA diploma presentation, March 7, 1938

Jacobs, Leonebel. *Portraits of Thirty Authors.* New York: Charles Scribner's Sons, 1937.

Leonebel Jacobs Printed Materials, n.d. Microfilm. Archives of American Art, Smithsonian Institution, Washington, DC.

Leonebel Jacobs Papers, 1930s–1960s. Coll 402, Special Collections and University Archives, University of Oregon Libraries, Eugene.

Eastman Johnson
ANA 1859; NA 1860
Lovell, ME 1824–1906 New York City

* *Self-Portrait*, ca. 1859–60
Oil on canvas, 30 ⅜ × 25 in. (77.2 × 63.5 cm)
ANA diploma presentation, date unknown

* *Negro Boy*, ca. 1860–61
Oil on canvas, 14 × 17 in. (35.6 × 43.2 cm)
NA diploma presentation, May 6, 1861

Carbone, Teresa A., and Patricia Hills. *Eastman Johnson: Painting America.* New York: Brooklyn Museum; Rizzoli, 1999. Exh. cat.

Ames, Kenneth. "Eastman Johnson: The Failure of a Successful Artist." *Art Journal* 29, no. 2 (Winter 1969–70): 174–83.

Baur, John I. H. *Eastman Johnson, 1824–1906: An American Genre Painter.* New York: Brooklyn Institute of Arts and Sciences, Brooklyn Museum, 1940. Exh. cat.

Walton, William. "Eastman Johnson, Painter." *Scribner's Magazine* 40, no. 2 (August 1906): 263–74.

Wolf Kahn
ANA 1979; NA 1980
Born Stuttgart, Germany 1927

Pond in November, 1977
Oil on canvas, 29 × 36 in. (73.7 × 91.4 cm)
Gift of Donald S. Crook, accepted as ANA diploma presentation, February 4, 1980

Spring, Justin. *Wolf Kahn*. 2nd ed. New York: Harry N. Abrams, 2011.

Kahn, Wolf, and John Updike. *Wolf Kahn's America: An Artist's Travels*. New York: Harry N. Abrams, 2003.

Berlind, Robert. "Beyond Easy Pleasures." *Art in America* 91, no. 10 (October 2003): 120–23.

Kahn, Wolf. "Uses of Painting Today." *Daedalus* 98, no. 3 (Summer 1969): 747–54.

David Kapp
NA 2004
Born New York City 1953

* *Coming out of the Subway*, 1998
Oil on linen, 50 ¼ × 50 ¼ in. (127.6 × 127.6 cm)
Gift of anonymous donor, accepted as NA diploma presentation, May 18, 2005

Kapp, David, and Robert Berlind. "In Conversation: Wolf Kahn with David Kapp and Robert Berlind." *Brooklyn Rail*, May 2007.

Edelman, Robert G. *David Kapp: Working the Grid; Paintings, 1980–2000.* West Stockbridge, MA: Hard Press Editions, 2001.

Hagen, Charles. *David Kapp*. New York: David Beitzel Gallery, 1991. Exh. cat.

Hagenberg, Roland, and Robert Pincus-Witten. *Untitled '84: The Art World in the Eighties*. New York: Pelham Press, 1984.

John Frederick Kensett
ANA 1848; NA 1849
Cheshire, CT 1816–1872 New York City

* *The Bash-Bish*, 1855
Oil on canvas, 36 ⅛ × 29 in. (91.8 × 73.7 cm)
Bequest of James A. Suydam, 1865

Driscoll, John Paul, and John K. Howat. *John Frederick Kensett: An American Master.* Edited by Susan E. Strickler. Worcester, MA: Worcester Art Museum; New York: Norton, 1985. Exh. cat.

Wilmerding, John. *American Light: The Luminist Movement, 1850–1875; Paintings, Drawings, Photographs.* Washington, DC: National Gallery of Art, 1980. Exh. cat.

Howat, John K. *John Frederick Kensett, 1816–1872.* New York: American Federation of Arts, 1968. Exh. cat.

Johnson, Ellen. "Kensett Revisited." *Art Quarterly* 20, no. 1 (Spring 1957): 71–92.

Jules Kirschenbaum
ANA 1962; NA 1965
New York City 1930–2000 Des Moines, IA

* *Dark in the Forest*, 1951–52
Oil on canvas, 36 × 29 ¾ in. (91.4 × 75.6 cm)
NA diploma presentation, October 2, 1967

Self-Portrait, 1963
Oil on Masonite, 23 ¾ × 19 ⅞ in. (60.3 × 50.5 cm)
ANA diploma presentation, April 1, 1963

Worthen, Thomas Fletcher. *Jules Kirschenbaum: The Need to Dream of Some Transcendent Meaning.* Iowa City: University of Iowa Museum of Art, 2006. Exh cat.

Burns, Jane. "Jules Kirschenbaum Contributed to Art World, Community." *Des Moines Register*, March 19, 2000.

Roberts, Charles W. "A Conversation with Jules Kirschenbaum." *Iowan*, Summer 1984, 20–25.

Weller, Allen S. "The New Romanticism." *Art in America* 48, no. 4 (Winter 1960): 34–45.

Albert Kresch
NA 2005
Born Scranton, PA 1922

* *North of Taos, N.M.*, 2005
Oil on canvas, 14½ × 46½ in. (36.8 × 118.1 cm)
NA diploma presentation, September 19, 2007

Weber, Bruce. *See It Loud: Seven Post-War American Painters*. New York: National Academy Museum, 2013. Exh. cat.

Hrbacek, Mary, Gabriel Laderman, and Martica Sawin. *Landscapes/Landshapes: Paintings by Albert Kresch*. New York: Lohin Geduld Gallery, 2010. Exh. cat.

Laderman, Gabriel, and Martica Sawin. *Albert Kresch: Paintings*. Dayton, OH: Wright State University, 2006. Exh. cat.

Goodrich, John, Stanley Lewis, and Denise Levertov. *Albert Kresch: Paintings*. New York: Salander-O'Reilly Galleries, 2002. Exh. cat.

Oliver Ingraham Lay
ANA 1876
New York City 1845–1890 Stratford, CT

* *Winslow Homer*, 1865
Oil on canvas, 20⅛ × 16⅛ in. (51.1 × 41 cm)
ANA diploma presentation, May 7, 1866

Oliver Ingraham Lay, Charles Downing Lay, and Lay Family Papers, 1789–2000. Archives of American Art, Smithsonian Institution, Washington, DC.

Hughie Lee-Smith
ANA 1965; NA 1967
Eustis, FL 1915–1999 Albuquerque, NM

* *Self-Portrait*, 1964
Oil on canvas, 24 × 20 in. (61 × 50.8 cm)
ANA diploma presentation, April 4, 1966

* *The Bridge*, before 1968
Oil on canvas, 25⅞ × 36 in. (65.7 × 91.4 cm)
NA diploma presentation, March 4, 1968

King-Hammond, Leslie. *Hughie Lee-Smith*. The David C. Driskell Series of African American Art 8. San Francisco: Pomegranate, 2010.

Marion, Sara L. *Stages of Influence: The Universal Theatre of Hughie Lee-Smith*. Albuquerque: University of New Mexico Art Museum, 2001.

Sims, Lowery S. *Hughie Lee-Smith Retrospective Exhibition*. Trenton, NJ: New Jersey State Museum, 1988. Exh. cat.

Three Masters: Eldzier Cortor, Hughie Lee-Smith, Archibald John Motley, Jr. New York: Kenkeleba Gallery, 1988. Exh. cat.

Porter, James A. *Modern Negro Art*. New York: Dryden Press, 1943.

Emanuel Leutze
HM 1843; NA 1860
Gmünd, Württemberg, Germany 1816–1868 Washington, DC

* *George Washington, Study for "Washington Crossing the Delaware,"* ca. 1850
Oil on canvas, 21 × 17 in. (53.3 × 43.2 cm)
NA diploma presentation, May 6, 1861

* *Worthington Whittredge*, 1861
Oil on canvas, 30 × 24⅝ in. (76.2 × 62.5 cm)
ANA diploma presentation, April 7, 1861

Wierich, Jochen. *Grand Themes: Emanuel Leutze, Washington Crossing the Delaware, and American History Painting*. University Park: Pennsylvania State University Press, 2012.

Groseclose, Barbara S. *Emanuel Leutze, 1816–1868: Freedom Is the Only King*. Washington, DC: Smithsonian Institution Press for National Collection of Fine Arts, 1975. Exh. cat.

Heiderstadt, Dorothy. *Painters of America*. New York: D. McKay, 1970.

Luigi Lucioni
ANA 1937; NA 1941
Malnate, Italy 1900–1988 New York City

William Whitehead, 1937
Oil on canvas, 17 × 14¼ in. (43.2 × 36.2 cm)
NA diploma presentation, November 3, 1941

Embury, Stuart P. *The Art and Life of Luigi Lucioni: A Contribution towards a Catalogue Raisonné*. N.p.: Stuart P. Embury, 2006.

Luigi Lucioni in the Collection of the Elizabeth De C. Wilson Museum. Manchester: Southern Vermont Arts Center, 2000.

Madorno, Nic, and Katurah Hutcheson. *Luigi Lucioni: Still Lifes*. New York: Richard York Gallery, 1991. Exh. cat.

"Luigi Lucioni." In *The Index of Twentieth Century Artists*, vol. 4, 675–76. New York: Research Institute of the College Art Association, 1937.

Reginald Marsh
ANA 1937; NA 1943
Paris, France 1898–1954 Dorset, VT

* *Barrel of Fun*, 1943
Oil on composition board, 24 × 29¾ in. (61 × 75.6 cm)
NA diploma presentation, April 3, 1944

Kenneth Hayes Miller, 1943
Oil on canvas, 30⅛ × 25¼ in. (76.5 × 64.1 cm)
ANA diploma presentation, April 20, 1943

Higginbotham, Carmenita. *The Urban Scene: Race, Reginald Marsh, and American Art*. University Park: Pennsylvania State University Press, 2015.

Haskell, Barbara, ed. *Swing Time: Reginald Marsh and Thirties New York*. New York: New-York Historical Society; London: D. Giles, 2012. Exh. cat.

Goodrich, Lloyd. *Reginald Marsh*. New York: Harry N. Abrams, 1972.

Marsh, Reginald. "Let's Go Back to Painting." *Magazine of Art* 37, no. 8 (December 1944): 293–96.

Louisa Matthíasdóttir
ANA 1981; NA 1988
Reykjavík, Iceland 1917–2000 Delhi, NY

* *Self-Portrait in Overalls*, ca. 1985
Oil on canvas, 68 × 38 in. (172.7 × 96.5 cm)
ANA diploma presentation, October 7, 1987

Pétursdóttir, Pétrún. *Louisa Matthíasdóttir: A Retrospective*. New York: American Scandinavian Foundation, 2004. Exh. cat.

Finnbogsdóttir, Vigdís, John Ashbery, Adalsteinn Ingólfsson, Martica Sawin, Jed Perl, and Lance Esplund. *Louisa Matthíasdottír*. Edited by Jed Perl. Reykjavík, Iceland: Nesútgáfan, 1999.

Ingólfsson, Adalsteinn. "Louisa Matthíasdóttir: Giantess in a Landscape." *Scandinavian Review* 82, no. 3 (Winter 1994): 56–60.

Sawin, Martica. "Louisa Matthíasdóttir: A Painter of the Figure." *Arts Magazine*, November 1961, 26–33.

Edward Harrison May
ANA 1849; NA 1876
Croydon, England 1824–1887 Paris, France

* *Frederic Edwin Church*, n.d.
Oil on canvas, 19 ⅞ × 15 ⅞ in. (50.5 × 40.3 cm)
ANA diploma presentation, May 7, 1849

The Grand Moving Panorama of Pilgrim's Progress. Montclair, NJ: Montclair Art Museum, 1999. Exh. cat.

Waters, Clara Erskine Clement, and Laurence Hutton. "Edward Harrison May." In *Artists of the Nineteenth Century and Their Works*, vol. 2, 100–101. Boston: Houghton Mifflin, 1896.

Tuckerman, Henry T. "Edward Harrison May." In *Book of the Artists*, 501–4. New York: G. P. Putnam and Son, 1867.

James McGarrell
ANA 1992; NA 1994
Born Indianapolis, IN 1930

* *Bison Self-Portrait*, 1987
Oil on canvas, 80 × 52 in. (203.2 × 132.1 cm)
ANA diploma presentation, September 22, 1993

The Painter, Young and Old (Edwin Dickinson), 1992
Oil on canvas, 80 × 60 in. (203.2 × 152.4 cm)
NA diploma presentation, December 14, 1994

Beasley, James M. *James McGarrell: Ten Years of Big Paintings with Smaller Canvases and Works on Paper*. Springfield, MO: Springfield Art Museum, 1994. Exh. cat.

Benton, William. *Young and Old: Double Portraits of 20th Century Artists*. Hanover, NH: Dartmouth College; New York: Frumkin/Adams Gallery, 1993. Exh. cat.

Geske, Norman A. "James McGarrell." In *Venice 34: The Figurative Tradition in Recent American Art*, 93–98. Washington, DC: Smithsonian Institution Press for National Collection of Fine Arts, 1968. Exh. cat.

Selz, Peter. "James McGarrell." In *New Images of Man*, 102–5. New York: Museum of Modern Art, 1959. Exh. cat.

Kenneth Hayes Miller
ANA 1942; NA 1944
Oneida, NY 1876–1952 New York City

Red Turban, 1930
Oil on wood panel, 24 × 20 in. (61 × 50.8 cm)
NA diploma presentation, October 2, 1944

Todd, Ellen Wiley. *The New Woman Revised: Painting and Gender Politics on Fourteenth Street*. Berkeley: University of California Press, 1993.

Marsh, Reginald. "Kenneth Hayes Miller." *Magazine of Art* 45, no. 4 (April 1952): 170–71.

Bishop, Isabel. "Kenneth Hayes Miller." *Magazine of Art* 45, no. 4 (April 1952): 169.

Burroughs, Alan. *Kenneth Hayes Miller*. American Artists Series. New York: Whitney Museum of American Art, 1931.

Richard E. Miller
ANA 1913; NA 1915
Saint Louis, MO 1875–1943 Saint Augustine, FL

* *Henry Ossawa Tanner*, n.d.
Oil on canvas, 30 × 25 in. (76.2 × 63.5 cm)
ANA diploma presentation, on or before May 11, 1910

Kane, Marie Louise. *A Bright Oasis: The Paintings of Richard E. Miller*. New York: Jordan-Volpe Gallery, 1997. Exh. cat.

Ball, Robert, and Max W. Gottschalk. *Richard E. Miller, N.A.: An Impression and Appreciation*. Saint Louis, MO: Longmire Fund, 1968.

Seares, Mabel Urmy. "Richard Miller in a California Garden." *California Southland*, no. 38 (February 1923): 10–11.

Thompson, Wallace. "Richard Miller: A Parisian-American Artist." *Fine Arts Journal* 27, no. 5 (November 1912): 709–14.

Felicie Waldo Howell Mixter
ANA 1922; NA 1945
Honolulu, HI 1897–1968 Boston

Self-Portrait, 1922
Oil on canvas, 30 × 25 in. (76.2 × 63.5 cm)
ANA diploma presentation, May 22, 1922

City Waterfront, between 1934 and 1946
Oil on canvas, 16 × 30 in. (40.6 × 76.2 cm)
NA diploma presentation, October 7, 1946

Sternberg, Paul E. "Felicie Waldo Mixter Howell [*sic*], N.A." In *Art by American Women: Selections from the Collection of Louise and Alan Sellars*, 99. Marietta, GA: Louise and Alan Sellars Collection of Art by American Women, 1991. Exh. cat.

Howell, Felicie Waldo. "The Use of the Flower for Decoration." *Country Life*, February 1923, 35.

"Pictures by Felicia [*sic*] W. Howell." *American Art News* 17, no. 27 (1919): 3.

Edgerton, Giles. "Is There a Sex Distinction in Art? The Attitude of the Critic toward Women's Exhibits." *Craftsman* 14, no. 3 (June 1908): 239–51.

Samuel F. B. Morse
FNAD 1826; PNAD 1826–45, 1861–62
Charlestown, MA 1791–1872 New York City

* *Self-Portrait*, ca. 1809
Watercolor on ivory, 3 ¼ × 2 ⅝ in. (8.3 × 6.7 cm)
Gift of Samuel P. Avery, John G. Brown, Thomas B. Clarke, Lockwood de Forest, Daniel Huntington, James C. Nicoll, and Harry W. Watrous, 1900

* *Benjamin West*, ca. 1811
Oil on canvas, 30 ¼ × 25 ⅜ in. (76.8 × 64.5 cm)
Purchase, 1944

Morse, Samuel F. B. *Lectures on the Affinity of Painting with the Other Fine Arts*. Edited by Nicolai Cikovsky, Jr. Columbia: University of Missouri Press, 1983.

Staiti, Paul J., and Gary A. Reynolds. *Samuel F. B. Morse*. New York: Grey Art Gallery and Study Center, New York University, 1982. Exh. cat.

Mabee, Carlton. *The American Leonardo: A Life of Samuel F. B. Morse*. New York: Alfred A. Knopf. 1943.

Morse, Samuel F. B. *Samuel F. B. Morse: His Letters and Journals*. Edited by Edward Lind Morse. 2 vols. Boston: Houghton Mifflin, 1914.

George Of
New York City 1876–1954

Abbot [sic] H. Thayer, n.d.
Oil on canvas, 20 × 16 in. (50.8 × 40.6 cm)
ANA diploma presentation, before April 1900

Fahlman, Betsy. "George F. Of (1876–1954)." In William Innes Homer, ed., *Avant-Garde Painting and Sculpture in America, 1920–25*, 106–7. Wilmington: Delaware Art Museum, 1975.

Pach, Walter. "Introducing the Paintings of George Of, 1876–1954." *ARTnews* 55, no. 6 (October 1956), 36–38, 62–63.

Maxfield Parrish
ANA 1905; NA 1906
Philadelphia 1870–1966 Plainfield, NH

* *Saint Valentine*, 1904
Tempera on gessoed panel, 20 × 15 ¾ in. (50.8 × 40 cm)
NA diploma presentation, May 8, 1907

Gilbert, Alma. *Maxfield Parrish: The Masterworks*. 3rd ed. Berkeley, CA: Ten Speed Press, 2001.

Yount, Sylvia. *Maxfield Parrish, 1870–1966*. Philadelphia: Pennsylvania Academy of the Fine Arts; New York: Harry N. Abrams, 1999. Exh. cat.

Cutler, Laurence S., and Judy Goffman Cutler. *Maxfield Parrish: A Retrospective*. San Francisco: Pomegranate Artbooks, 1995. Exh. cat.

Ludwig, Coy L. *Maxfield Parrish: A Retrospective*. Springfield, MA: George Walter Vincent Smith Art Museum, 1966. Exh. cat.

Philip Pearlstein
ANA 1980; NA 1988
Born Pittsburgh, PA 1924

* *Nude Torso*, 1963
Oil on canvas, 36 × 44 in. (91.4 × 111.8 cm)
NA diploma presentation, May 6, 1987

Kim, Byron, Graham Nickson, Linda Nochlin, Irving Sandler, and Robert Storr. *Philip Pearlstein: Just the Facts; Fifty Years of Looking and Drawing and Painting*. New York: New York Studio School of Drawing, Painting and Sculpture, 2014. Exh. cat.

Bowman, Russell. *Philip Pearlstein: The Complete Paintings*. New York: Alpine Fine Arts Collection, 1983.

Viola, Jerome. *The Painting and Teaching of Philip Pearlstein*. New York: Watson-Guptill, 1982.

Pearlstein, Philip. "Figure Paintings Today Are Not Made in Heaven." *ARTnews* 61, no. 4 (Summer 1962): 39, 51–52.

Ellen Emmet Rand
ANA 1926; NA 1934
San Francisco 1875–1941 New York City

* *Self-Portrait*, 1927
Oil on composition board, 30 × 24 in. (76.2 × 61 cm)
ANA diploma presentation, November 14, 1927

Boylan, Alexis L., ed. *Ellen Emmet Rand: Gender, Art, Business*. London: Bloomsbury Academic, forthcoming 2019.

Tappert, Tara Leigh. *The Emmets: A Generation of Gifted Women*. New York: Borghi, 1993. Exh. cat.

Cummings, Hildegard. *Good Company: Portraits by Ellen Emmet Rand*. Storrs, CT: William Benton Museum of Art, University of Connecticut, 1984. Exh. cat.

Curran, Grace Wickham. "Ellen Emmet Rand, Portrait Painter." *American Magazine of Art* 19, no. 9 (1928): 471–79.

Robert Reid
ANA 1902; NA 1906
Stockbridge, MA 1862–1929 Clifton Springs, NY

* *Daffodils*, n.d.
Oil on canvas, 42 × 44 in. (106.7 × 111.8 cm)
NA diploma presentation, October 25, 1906

* *Self-Portrait*, 1904
Oil on canvas, 27 ½ × 24 ⅝ in. (69.9 × 62.5 cm)
ANA diploma presentation, December 5, 1904

Weinberg, H. Barbara. "Robert Reid: Academic 'Impressionist.'" *Archives of American Art Journal* 15, no. 1 (1975): 2–11.

Stoner, Stanley. *Some Recollections of Robert Reid*. Colorado Springs, CO: Dentan Printing, 1934.

Goodrich, Henry W. "Robert Reid and His Work." *International Studio* 36, no. 144 (February 1909): 113–22.

Cortissoz, Royal. *In Summertime: Paintings by Robert Reid*. New York: R. H. Russell, 1900.

Paul Resika
ANA 1976; NA 1978
Born New York City 1928

* *The End of the Hurricane*, 1979
Oil on canvas, 24 × 29 in. (61 × 73.7 cm)
NA diploma presentation, February 4, 1980

Goldberg, Ira. "A Painter's Beginnings: An Interview with Paul Resika." *LINEA*, Spring 2010, 8–13.

Di Piero, W. S., and Karen Wilkin. *Paul Resika: Paintings*. New York: Salander-O'Reilly Galleries, 1993. Exh. cat.

Resika, Paul. "Forum Page: Must an Artist Know Landscape in Order to Paint It?" *American Artist* 40, no. 410 (September 1976): 410, 412–13.

White, Claire Nicholas. "Resika's Delectable Mountains." *ARTnews* 66, no. 2 (April 1967): 48–49, 78.

Albert Pinkham Ryder
ANA 1902; NA 1906
New Bedford, MA 1847–1917 Elmhurst, NY

★ *Marine*, 1907
Oil on wood panel, 8⅝ × 17¾ in. (21.9 × 45.1 cm)
NA diploma presentation, March 4, 1907

Novak, Barbara. "Albert Pinkham Ryder: Even with a Thought." In *American Painting of the Nineteenth Century: Realism, Idealism, and the American Experience*, 175–83. 3rd ed. Oxford: Oxford University Press, 2007.

Broun, Elizabeth, Eleanor L. Jones, et al. *Albert Pinkham Ryder*. Washington, DC: Smithsonian Institution Press for National Museum of American Art, 1989. Exh. cat.

Homer, William Innes, and Lloyd Goodrich. *Albert Pinkham Ryder, Painter of Dreams*. New York: H. N. Abrams, 1989.

Robinson, John. "Personal Reminiscences of Albert Pinkham Ryder." *Art in America* 13, no. 6 (June 1925): 176–87.

Paul Sample
ANA 1937; NA 1941
Louisville, KY 1896–1974 Hanover, NH

★ *Unemployment*, 1931
Oil on canvas, 36 × 40 in. (91.4 × 101.6 cm)
NA diploma presentation, December 1, 1941

★ *Self-Portrait*, 1937
Oil on canvas, 30 × 25 in. (76.2 × 63.5 cm)
ANA diploma presentation, January 18, 1938

Glick, Paula F. *Paul Sample*. New York: Gerold Wunderlich, 1997. Exh. cat.

McGrath, Robert L., and Paula F. Glick. *Paul Sample, Painter of the American Scene*. Hanover, NH: Hood Museum of Art, Dartmouth College, 1988. Exh. cat.

Sample, Paul. *Paul Sample, Ivy League Regionalist*. Coral Gables, FL: Lowe Art Museum, University of Miami, 1984. Exh. cat.

Lathrop, Churchill Pierce. *Paul Sample Retrospective Exhibition*. Manchester, NH: Currier Gallery of Art, 1948. Exh. cat.

John Singer Sargent
ANA 1891; NA 1897
Florence, Italy 1856–1925 London, England

★ *Claude Monet*, ca. 1887
Oil on canvas, 16 × 13 in. (40.6 × 33 cm)
NA diploma presentation, October 25, 1897

★ *Self-Portrait*, 1892
Oil on canvas, 21 × 17 in. (53.5 × 43.2 cm)
ANA diploma presentation, May 9, 1892

Ormond, Richard. *Sargent: Portraits of Artists and Friends*. London: National Portrait Gallery, 2015. Exh. cat.

Ormond, Richard, and Elaine Kilmurray. *John Singer Sargent: The Complete Paintings*. 8 vols. New Haven: Yale University Press, 1998–2014.

Kilmurray, Elaine, Richard Ormond, and Mary Crawford Volk. *John Singer Sargent*. London: Tate Gallery; Princeton: Princeton University Press, 1998. Exh. cat.

James, Henry. "John S. Sargent." *Harper's Magazine*, October 1887, reprinted in John L. Sweeney, ed., *The Painter's Eye: Notes and Essays on the Pictorial Arts by Henry James*, 216–28. Cambridge, MA: Harvard University Press, 1956.

Downes, William Howe. *John S. Sargent: His Life and Work*. Boston: Little, Brown, 1925.

Peter Saul
NA 2012
Born San Francisco 1934

★ *Self-Portrait*, 2013
Acrylic on canvas, 60 × 55 in. (152.4 × 139.7 cm)
NA diploma presentation, August 7, 2013

Weinhart, Martina, ed. *Peter Saul*. Frankfurt: Schirn Kunsthalle; Cologne: Snoeck, 2017. Exh. cat.

Byrne, Chris. *Peter Saul: 50 Years of Painting*. New York: Haunch of Venison, 2010. Exh. cat.

Cameron, Dan, Michael Duncan, and Robert Storr. *Peter Saul*. Ostfildern, Germany: Hatje Cantz, 2008. Exh. cat.

Carlozzi, Annette DiMeo, Peter Saul, and Robert Storr. *Peter Saul*. Aspen, CO: Aspen Art Museum, 1989. Exh. cat.

W. Lee Savage
ANA 1991; NA 1993
Charleston, WV 1928–1998 Tarrytown, NY

★ *Endangered Bobby*, 1992
Acrylic and mixed media on canvas, 54 × 54 in. (137.2 × 137.2 cm)
NA diploma presentation, May 26, 1993

★ *Self-Portrait with Cup and Narragansett Beer*, 1988
Acrylic on board, 25 × 25 in. (63.5 × 63.5 cm)
ANA diploma presentation, May 6, 1992

Danto, Arthur C., Bo Goldman, and Richard Ambrose. *W. Lee Savage: A Retrospective*. Charleston, WV: Sunrise Museum, 1994. Exh. cat.

Savage, W. Lee, dir. *The Hudson River and Its Painters*. Produced in association with Metropolitan Museum of Art, New York. Chicago: Home Vision, 1987. Videocassette (VHS), 57 min.

Aaron Shikler
ANA 1962; NA 1965
New York City 1922–2015

The Empire Coat, 1959
Oil on canvas, 35 × 25 in. (88.9 × 63.5 cm)
Gift of David Daniels, 1991

Shikler, Aaron. *Aaron Shikler: Recent Work*. New York: Davis and Langdale, 2003. Exh. cat.

Dobell, Byron. "Artist of the Portrait: Brooklyn-Born Aaron Shikler Is the Irresistibly Unfashionable Sargent of Our Times." *New York Magazine*, December 24–31, 1990, 99–100.

Aaron Shikler et David Levine. Paris: Galerie Claude Bernard, 1988. Exh. cat.

Levine, David, and Aaron Shikler. *Paintings and Drawings by David Levine and Aaron Shikler*. New York: Brooklyn Museum, 1971. Exh. cat.

Jaune Quick-to-See Smith
NA 2011
Born Saint Ignatius, Flathead Reservation, MT 1940

★ *Snake Dance*, 2011
Oil, collage, and mixed media on canvas, 72 × 48 in. (182.9 × 121.9 cm)
NA diploma presentation, November 7, 2012

Kastner, Carolyn. *Jaune Quick-to-See Smith: An American Modernist.* Albuquerque: University of New Mexico Press, 2013.

Kastner, Carolyn. "Jaune Quick-to-See Smith: Indigenous Bodies, Indigenous Stories in a Post-Columbian World." In Fear-Segal, Jacqueline, and Rebecca Tillett, eds., *Indigenous Bodies: Reviewing, Relocating, Reclaiming.* Albany: State University of New York Press, 2013.

Sasse, Julie. *Jaune Quick-to-See Smith: Postmodern Messenger.* Contemporary Southwest Images 19. Tucson, AZ: Tucson Museum of Art, 2004. Exh. cat.

Smith, Jaune Quick-to-See. *The Submuloc Show/Columbus Whos: A Visual Commentary on the Columbus Quincentennial from the Perspective of America's First People.* Phoenix, AZ: Atlatl, 1992. Exh. cat.

Moses Soyer
ANA 1964; NA 1966
Borisoglebsk, Russia 1899–1974
New York City

Self-Portrait, n.d.
Oil on canvas, 24 × 20 in. (61 × 50.8 cm)
ANA diploma presentation, May 3, 1965

Felix [Nussbaum], ca. 1930
Oil on canvas, 40 × 20 in. (101.6 × 50.8 cm)
NA diploma presentation, March 6, 1967

Werner, Alfred, and David Soyer. *Moses Soyer.* South Brunswick, NJ: A. S. Barnes, 1970.

Soyer, Moses. *Painting the Human Figure.* Edited by Robert W. Gill. New York: Watson-Guptill, 1964.

Willard, Charlotte, and Philip Evergood. *Moses Soyer.* Cleveland, OH: World, 1962.

Soyer, Moses. "Three Brothers." *Magazine of Art* 32, no. 4 (April 1939): 201–7, 254.

Raphael Soyer
ANA 1949; NA 1951
Borisoglebsk, Russia 1899–1987
New York City

Self-Portrait, 1950
Oil on canvas, 24 ½ × 20 ⅛ in. (62.2 × 51.1 cm)
ANA diploma presentation, March 6, 1950

Soyer, Raphael. "An Artist's Experiences in the 1930s." In Patricia Hills, *Social Concern and Urban Realism: American Painting of the 1930s.* Boston: Boston University Art Gallery, 1983. Exh. cat.

Soyer, Raphael. *Diary of an Artist.* Washington, DC: New Republic Books, 1977.

Goodrich, Lloyd. *Raphael Soyer.* New York: H. N. Abrams, 1972.

Gutman, Walter K., and Raphael Soyer. *Paintings and Drawings.* Newark, NJ: Rabin and Krueger Gallery; New York: Shorewood, 1960.

May Stevens
NA 2003
Born Boston 1924

* *Benny Andrews, the Artist, and Big Daddy Paper Doll*, 1976
Acrylic on canvas, 60 ¼ × 60 ¼ in. (153 × 153 cm)
NA diploma presentation, May 19, 2004

Hills, Patricia, and Phyllis Rose. *May Stevens.* San Francisco: Pomegranate, 2005.

Shapiro, Barbara Stern. *May Stevens: Images of Women Near and Far, 1983–1997.* New York: Mary Ryan Gallery, 1999. Exh. cat.

Stevens, May. *One Plus or Minus One.* New York: New Museum of Contemporary Art, 1988. Exh. cat.

Kuspit, Donald, Lucy Lippard, Moira Roth, Lisa Tickner. *May Stevens: Ordinary + Extraordinary; A Summation, 1977–1984.* With a foreword by Patricia Hills. Boston: Boston University Art Gallery, 1984. Exh. cat.

Altoon Sultan
NA 1995
Born New York City 1948

* *Tractor and Disc Harrow, Pawlett, Vermont*, 1987
Oil on canvas, 22 × 48 in. (55.9 × 121.9 cm)
NA diploma presentation, September 20, 1995

Tully, Judd. "The Weirdly Beautiful: Altoon Sultan's Agricultural Landscapes." In *Altoon Sultan: Recent Paintings.* New York: Tibor de Nagy Gallery, 2001. Exh. cat.

Sultan, Altoon. "Culture/Cultivation: Thoughts on Painting the Landscape." *Art Journal* 57, no. 4 (Winter 1998): 90–95.

Sims, Lowery Stokes. "Altoon Sultan." In Lisa M. Messinger, Robert Rosenblum, and Lowery Stokes Sims, *The Landscape in Twentieth-Century American Art: Selections from the Metropolitan Museum of Art*, 84–85. New York: American Federation of Arts; Rizzoli, 1991. Exh. cat.

Cutter, Jane. "Altoon Sultan." *American Artist* 47, no. 490 (May 1983): 37–47.

Reuben Tam
ANA 1975; NA 1987
Kapa'a, Kaua'i, HI 1916–1991

Monhegan Night, 1956
Oil on canvas, 34 × 46 in. (86.4 × 116.8 cm)
Gift of the artist's estate, 1991

**Monhegan Landform*, 1974
Oil on canvas, 36 × 30 in. (91.4 × 76.2 cm)
ANA diploma presentation, October 1, 1986

Price, Marshall N. "Reuben Tam." In *The Abstract Impulse: Fifty Years of Abstraction at the National Academy, 1956–2006*, 75. New York: National Academy Museum and School of Fine Arts; Hudson Hills Press, 2007. Exh. cat.

Saville, Jennifer, and Geraldine Tam. *Archipelago: Life Cycle of the Hawaiian Islands; A Portfolio of Paintings by Reuben Tam.* Honolulu: Honolulu Academy of Arts, 1998.

Tam, Reuben. *The Wind-Honed Islands Rise: Selected Poems of Reuben Tam.* Honolulu, HI: Manoa Books, 1996.

Henry Ossawa Tanner
ANA 1909; NA 1927
Pittsburgh, PA 1859–1937 Paris, France

* *The Miraculous Haul of Fishes*, ca. 1913–14
Oil on canvas, 38 × 47 ½ in. (96.5 × 120.7 cm)
NA diploma presentation, October 3, 1927

Woods, Naurice Frank. *Henry Ossawa Tanner: Art, Faith, Race, and Legacy.* New York: Routledge, 2018.

Marley, Anna O., ed. *Henry Ossawa Tanner: Modern Spirit.* Philadelphia: Pennsylvania Academy of the Fine Arts; Berkeley: University of California Press, 2012. Exh. cat.

Hartigan, Lynda Roscoe. "Henry Ossawa Tanner." In *Sharing Traditions: Five Black Artists in Nineteenth-Century America: From the Collections of the National Museum of American Art*, 99–116. Washington, DC: Smithsonian Institution Press for National Museum of American Art, 1985. Exh. cat.

Tanner, Henry Ossawa. "The Story of An Artist's Life." Pts. 1 and 2. *World's Work* 18, no. 2 (June 1909): 11661–66; 18, no. 3 (July 1909): 11769–75.

Abbott H. Thayer
ANA 1898; NA 1901
Boston 1849–1921 Dublin, NH

Winter Landscape, 1902
Oil on canvas, 29⅜ × 34⅞ in. (74.6 × 88.6 cm)
NA diploma presentation, May 5, 1902

Murphy, Kevin. *"Not Theories but Revelations": The Art and Science of Abbott Handerson Thayer.* Williamstown, MA: Williams College Museum of Art, 2016. Exh. cat.

Anderson, Ross. *Abbott Handerson Thayer.* Syracuse, NY: Everson Museum, 1982. Exh. cat.

Cortissoz, Royal. *American Painters*. New York: Charles Scribner's Sons, 1923.

Saint-Gaudens, Homer. "Abbott H. Thayer." *International Studio* 33, no. 131 (January 1908): 81–87.

Wayne Thiebaud
ANA 1985; NA 1987
Born Mesa, AZ 1920

* *Tennis Player (Self-Portrait)*, 1985
Oil on plywood panel, 12 × 11⅝ in. (30.5 × 29.5 cm)
ANA diploma presentation, October 1, 1986

Teagle, Rachel, ed. *Wayne Thiebaud, 1958–1968.* Davis: Jan Shrem and Maria Manetti Shrem Museum of Art, University of California, Davis, 2018. Exh. cat.

Baker, Kenneth, Nicholas Fox Weber, Karen Wilkin, and John Yau. *Wayne Thiebaud*. New York: Rizzoli, 2015.

Nash, Steven A., and Adam Gopnik. *Wayne Thiebaud: A Paintings Retrospective*. San Francisco: Fine Arts Museums of San Francisco, 2000. Exh. cat.

Maréchal-Workman, Andrée. "Wayne Thiebaud: Beyond the Cityscapes." *Smithsonian Studies in American Art* 1, no. 2 (1987): 35–51.

George Tooker
ANA 1968; NA 1970
New York City 1920–2011 Hartland, VT

* *Self-Portrait*, 1969
Egg tempera on gessoed panel, 24 × 19½ in. (61 × 49.5 cm)
ANA diploma presentation, March 3, 1969

* *Voice II*, 1972
Egg tempera on gessoed panel, 17½ × 11½ in. (44.5 × 29.2 cm)
NA diploma presentation, October 2, 1972

Moore, Bridget, et al. *George Tooker: Reality Recurs as a Dream*. New York: DC Moore Gallery, 2011. Exh. cat.

Cozzolino, Robert, Marshall N. Price, and M. Melissa Wolfe. *George Tooker*. London: Merrell, 2008. Exh. cat.

Spring, Justin, and George Tooker. "An Interview with George Tooker." *American Art* 16, no. 1 (Spring 2002): 60–81.

Garver, Thomas H. *George Tooker*. San Francisco: Pomegranate Artbooks, 1992.

Walter Ufer
ANA 1920; NA 1926
Louisville, KY 1876–1936 Albuquerque, NM

* *Self-Portrait*, n.d.
Oil on canvas, 30¼ × 25 in. (76.8 × 63.5 cm)
ANA diploma presentation, December 6, 1920

* *Jim*, 1918
Oil on canvas, 40⅛ × 36¼ in. (101.9 × 92.1 cm)
NA diploma presentation, October 4, 1926

Smith, Thomas Brent, ed. *A Place in the Sun: The Southwest Paintings of Walter Ufer and E. Martin Hennings*. Norman: University of Oklahoma Press, 2016.

Leslie, Mike, and Dean A. Porter. *Walter Ufer: Rise, Fall, Resurrection*. Oklahoma City: National Cowboy and Western Heritage Museum, 2014. Exh. cat.

Porter, Dean A., Teresa Hayes Ebie, and Suzan Campbell. *Taos Artists and Their Patrons, 1898–1950.* Notre Dame, IN: Snite Museum of Art, University of Notre Dame, 1999. Exh. cat.

Broder, Patricia Janis. *Taos: A Painter's Dream*. Boston: Little, Brown, 1980.

Elihu Vedder
ANA 1863; NA 1865
New York City 1836–1923 Rome, Italy

Andrew W. Warren, 1864
Oil on canvas, 30 × 25 in. (76.2 × 63.5 cm)
ANA diploma presentation, May 2, 1864

* *Jane Jackson*, 1865
Oil on canvas, 18 × 18 in. (45.7 × 45.7 cm)
NA diploma presentation, May 7, 1866

Taylor, Joshua C., Jane Dillenberger, and Richard Murray. *Perceptions and Evocations: The Art of Elihu Vedder.* Washington, DC: Smithsonian Institution Press for National Collection of Fine Arts, 1979. Exh. cat.

Soria, Regina. *Elihu Vedder: American Visionary Artist in Rome.* Rutherford, NJ: Fairleigh Dickinson University Press, 1970.

McSpadden, Joseph Walker. "Elihu Vedder, the Painter of the Mystic." In *Famous Painters of America*, 143–65. New York: Dodd, Mead, 1923.

Vedder, Elihu. *The Digressions of V. Written for His Own Fun and That of His Friends*. Boston: Houghton Mifflin, 1911.

J. Alden Weir
ANA 1885; NA 1886; PNAD 1915–17
West Point, NY 1852–1919 New York City

Self-Portrait, 1886
Oil on canvas, 21 × 17 in. (53.3 × 43.2 cm)
ANA diploma presentation, October 1, 1886

* *Albert Pinkham Ryder*, 1902–3
Oil on canvas, 24 × 20 in. (61 × 50.8 cm)
ANA diploma presentation, March 2, 1903

Dawson, Anne E., ed. *Rare Light: J. Alden Weir in Windham, Connecticut, 1882–1919.* Middletown, CT: Wesleyan University Press, 2016.

Cummings, Hildegard, Helen K Fusscas, and Susan G Larkin. *J. Alden Weir: A Place of His Own.* Storrs, CT: William Benton Museum of Art, University of Connecticut, 1991. Exh. cat.

Burke, Doreen B. *J. Alden Weir: An American Impressionist.* Newark: University of Delaware Press; New York: Cornwall Press, 1983.

Young, Dorothy Weir, and J. Alden Weir. *The Life and Letters of J. Alden Weir.* Edited by Lawrence W. Chisolm. New Haven: Yale University Press, 1960.

Charles White
ANA 1971; NA 1974
Chicago 1918–1979 Los Angeles

⋆ *Mother Courage II*, 1974
Oil on canvas, 49¾ × 39⅞ in. (126.4 × 101.3 cm)
NA diploma presentation, March 3, 1975

⋆ *Matriarch*, 1967
Oil on canvas, 20 × 17 in. (50.8 × 43.2 cm)
ANA diploma presentation, February 5, 1973

Oehler, Sarah Kelly, and Esther Adler. *Charles White: A Retrospective.* Chicago: Art Institute of Chicago, 2018. Exh. cat.

Gellman, Erik S. "Chicago's Native Son: Charles White and the Laboring of the Black Renaissance." In Darlene Clark Hine, John McCluskey, and Marshanda A. Smith, eds., *The Black Chicago Renaissance*, 147–64. Urbana: University of Illinois Press, 2012.

Jones, Kellie. "Charles White." In *Now Dig This! Art and Black Los Angeles 1960–1980*, 130–45, 152–53. Los Angeles: Hammer Museum, 2011. Exh. cat.

Barnwell, Andrea D. *Charles White.* David C. Driskell Series of African American Art. San Francisco: Pomegranate, 2002.

William J. Whittemore
ANA 1897
New York City 1860–1955
East Hampton, NY

⋆ *Charles Courtney Curran*, 1888–89
Oil on canvas, 17 × 21 in. (43.2 × 53.3 cm)
ANA diploma exchange presentation, May 7, 1934
Original ANA diploma presentation, May 6, 1889

Falk, Peter Hastings. *Who Was Who in American Art.* Madison, CT: Sound View Press, 1985.

Lockman, DeWitt McClellan. Interviews of artists and architects associated with the National Academy of Design, 1926–27. Microfilm. Archives of American Art, Smithsonian Institution, Washington, DC.

Guy C. Wiggins
ANA 1916; NA 1935
New York City 1883–1962
Saint Augustine, FL

⋆ *Manhattan*, 1929
Oil on canvas, 30 × 60 in. (76.2 × 152.4 cm)
NA diploma presentation, December 17, 1935

DePietro, Anne Cohen. *Wiggins, Wiggins and Wiggins: Three Generations of American Art.* New York: Joan Whalen Fine Art, 1998. Exh. cat.

Paintings by Three Generations of Wiggins, 1870's–1970's: Carleton Wiggins, N.A. (1848–1932), Guy C. Wiggins, N.A. (1883–1962), Guy A. Wiggins, (1921–). New Britain, CT: Loomis Chaffee School and New Britain Museum of American Art, 1979. Exh. cat.

Walt, Adrienne L. "Guy Wiggins: American Impressionist." *American Art Review* 4, no. 3 (December 1977): 100–113.

Wiggins, Guy C. *Guy C. Wiggins (1883–1962), American Impressionist.* Chicago: Campanile Galleries, 1970. Exh. cat.

Andrew Wyeth
ANA 1944; NA 1945
Chadds Ford, PA 1917–2009

⋆ *Self-Portrait*, 1945
Egg tempera on gessoed panel, 25 × 30 in. (63.5 × 76.2 cm)
ANA diploma presentation, February 5, 1945

Junker, Patricia, and Audrey Lewis. *Andrew Wyeth: In Retrospect.* Seattle: Seattle Art Museum, 2017. Exh. cat.

Cateforis, David, ed. *Rethinking Andrew Wyeth.* Berkeley: University of California Press, 2014.

Wyeth, Andrew, and Thomas Hoving. *Andrew Wyeth: Autobiography.* Kansas City, MO: Nelson-Atkins Museum of Art; Boston: Little, Brown, 1995.

Rodman, Selden. "Andrew Wyeth." In *Conversations with Artists*, 211–21. 1957. Reprint, New York: Capricorn Books, 1961.

N. C. Wyeth
ANA 1940; NA 1941
Needham, MA 1882–1945 Chadds Ford, PA

⋆ *Blubber Island, Maine*, 1938
Oil on gessoed panel, 25 × 40 in. (63.5 × 101.6 cm)
NA diploma presentation, February 17, 1942

⋆ *Self-Portrait*, 1940
Egg tempera on gessoed panel, 32¾ × 27½ in. (83.2 × 69.9 cm)
ANA diploma presentation, February 18, 1941

Podmaniczky, Christine B. *N. C. Wyeth: Catalogue Raisonné of Paintings.* 2 vols. Wilmington, DE: Wyeth Foundation for American Art, 2008.

Michaelis, David, and N. C. Wyeth. *N. C. Wyeth: A Biography.* New York: Alfred A. Knopf, 1998.

Wyeth, N. C. *The Wyeths: The Letters of N. C. Wyeth, 1901–1945.* Edited by Betsy James Wyeth. Boston: Gambit, 1971.

The Brandywine Heritage: Howard Pyle, N. C. Wyeth, Andrew Wyeth, James Wyeth. Chadds Ford, PA: Brandywine River Museum, 1971. Exh. cat.

CONTRIBUTORS

Jarrett Earnest is a writer and curator living in New York City. He is the author, most recently, of *What It Means to Write about Art: Interviews with Art Critics*.

Jennifer A. Greenhill is Associate Professor of Art History at the University of Southern California. Her forthcoming book explores the efforts of artists, magazine art directors, and advertisers to develop visual strategies of suggestive advertising circa 1900.

Kenneth Haltman is presently H. Russell Pitman Professor of Art History at the University of Oklahoma. He is coediting, with Richard Read, a volume of essays concerning and comparing antebellum American and nineteenth-century Australian landscape painting, to be published by the Terra Foundation for American Art.

Patricia Hills is Professor Emerita of History of Art and Architecture at Boston University. She is completing the Eastman Johnson catalogue raisonné database and writing a book on Joyce Kozloff.

Jeremiah William McCarthy is Associate Curator at the American Federation of Arts, New York. He is currently preparing a monograph on the artist Isabel Bishop.

Alexander Nemerov is Carl and Marilynn Thoma Provostial Professor in the Arts and Humanities at Stanford University. He is the author, most recently, of *Soulmaker: The Times of Lewis Hine*.

Susan Rather is Professor of Art History at the University of Texas, Austin. Her book *The American School: Artists and Status in the Late Colonial and Early National Era* received the 2018 Charles C. Eldredge Prize for Distinguished Scholarship in American art from the Smithsonian American Art Museum.

Akela Reason is Associate Professor of History and Director of the Museum Studies Certificate Program at the University of Georgia. Her current book project, *Politics and Memory: Civil War Commemoration in Gilded Age New York*, examines the history of building monuments to the Union in New York City.

Kimia Shahi is a PhD candidate in art history at Princeton University. Her dissertation investigates how artists devised new ways of seeing and modes of picturing the ocean and seacoasts in the United States during the second half of the nineteenth century.

Elizabeth A. Spear is a PhD candidate in art history at the University of Iowa. Presenting four case studies on paintings by Albert Bierstadt, George Catlin, Thomas Moran, and Dwight Tryon, her dissertation rethinks key examples of American landscape representation through the lens of collecting and display.

Diana Thompson is Director of Collections and Curatorial Affairs at the National Academy of Design, New York, where she is leading a multiyear initiative to digitize the entire permanent collection. This comprehensive online resource will include archival materials, biographies, and video documentation pertaining to the Academy's membership, history, and artworks.

Jonathan Frederick Walz is Director of Curatorial Affairs and Curator of American Art at The Columbus Museum, Georgia. He is researching and developing the national tour of *Alma Thomas: A Creative Life*, a retrospective set for 2021–22.

Alona Cooper Wilson is Director of Collections and Exhibitions and Chief Curator at the Museum of African American History, Boston and Nantucket.

CURATORS' ACKNOWLEDGMENTS

For America is the result of many people's determination, intellectual generosity, and passion.

This exhibition was co-organized by the American Federation of Arts and the National Academy of Design, and Pauline Willis provided unwavering enthusiasm for this creative endeavor. The devoted staff at our institutions worked tirelessly on various aspects of this project, and, at the AFA, we offer our deep gratitude to current colleagues Elizabeth Abbarno, Shawna Gallancy, Frances Wu Giarratano, Brian Keliher, Julija Lazutkaite, and Shelley Wilson, as well as former research assistant Pavla Berghen-Wolf; and, at the NAD, to Auzelle Epeneter and Mary Fisher, as well as former conservator Lucie Kinsolving. Rachel Kim deserves special thanks for her dedication to the realization of this book.

We wish to acknowledge the talented roster of catalogue contributors and Academicians who thought alongside us: Tom Burckhardt, Walter Chatham, Glenn Goldberg, Jennifer Greenhill, Barbara Grossman, Kenneth Haltman, David Humphrey, Joyce Kozloff, Robert Kushner, John Moore, Catherine Opie, Anthony Panzera, Akela Reason, Mira Schor, Jaune Quick-to-See Smith, Susan Rather, Judith Shea, Elizabeth Spear, Jonathan Walz, Leslie Wayne, Stephen Westfall, Alona Wilson, Fred Wilson, Alexi Worth; and those who looked alongside us: Jarrett Earnest, Patricia Hills, Alexander Nemerov, and Kimia Shahi. We wish, additionally, to acknowledge the many people who answered questions, offered suggestions and wise counsel, and in some cases, amity and encouragement, during this project's formative stages: Carol Aiken, Wendy Bellion, Sarah Burns, Bill Gerdts, Susan Howe, Angela Miller, Maura Reilly, Jeff Richmond-Moll, Elle Shushan, Howard Singerman, Eric Sutphin, Thayer Tolles, and Allan Wallach.

The creation of this ambitious catalogue was expertly guided with remarkable care and kindness by Audrey Walen. Jennifer Bernstein was an indefatigable and inspired editor. We offer particular thanks to gifted designer Takaaki Matsumoto, who, along with Amy Wilkins and Robin Brunelle, created a reading experience that surpassed any expectations. The team at Lucia | Marquand—Melissa Duffes, Leah Finger, Adrian Lucia, Meghann Ney, Kestrel Rundle, and Donna Wingate—produced this beautiful book, and additionally, we thank our colleagues at Yale University Press for ensuring its visibility. An art book is only as good as its images, and for lush photography we commend Anna Neighbor and Chad States of Neighboring States Photography and the team at Google Cultural Institute, led by Massimiliano D'Angelo. We also thank those who aided in securing images reproduced in this book: Barbara Bertucio, Eric Brown, J'Aimee Cronin and Julie Markey, Caroline Donadio and Marisa Bourgoin, Henry Duffy, Julie Dunn-Morton, Ian Gill, Brittany Gravely, Mark Johnson, Mike Kelly, Tommie Rodgers, Larissa Rubic, and Robert Vaszari. We gratefully acknowledge the following talented individuals who helped prepare work for this traveling exhibition: framer Ursula Hobson; conservators Kristin deGhetaldi and Brian Baade; and, at Atelier, Mati Bonetti de Buccini, Nik Flood, Shane Gebhard, Derek Jones, Stefan Schein, David Sigmund, and, especially, Adrianna Province.

Lastly, our research would not have been possible without the work of predecessors David Dearinger, who spearheaded publication of the first inventory of the Academy's paintings and sculpture; Lois Marie Fink and Joshua C. Taylor, who offered a lasting interpretation of the Academy's art; and especially Abigail Booth Gerdts, who accomplished the first systematic study of the Academy's collection.

INDEX

Note: Page numbers in *italics* refer to illustrations.

COPYRIGHTS AND CREDITS

Photographs of artworks are by Google and are courtesy of the National Academy of Design unless indicated below. The following list also acknowledges photographs from other sources. All works are copyright of the artist or the artist's estate unless otherwise specified.

© The Albertina Museum, Vienna: 262
Courtesy George Wesley Bellows Papers, Amherst College Archives & Special Collections, MA: 125, 129 left
© 2019 Emma Amos / Licensed by VAGA at ARS, NY. Courtesy of the artist and RYAN LEE Gallery, New York: 226–27, 239 left, 243
© 2019 Estate of Benny Andrews / Licensed by VAGA at ARS, NY. Courtesy Bridgeman Images: 213
© 2019 Estate of Benny Andrews / Licensed by VAGA at ARS, NY. Courtesy Michael Rosenfeld Gallery, LLC, New York, NY: 210, 212 right, 213, 219, 278–79
Courtesy Archives of American Art, Smithsonian Institution: 229
Worthington Whittredge papers, circa 1840s–1965, bulk 1849–1908. Archives of American Art, Smithsonian Institution: 49
Courtesy The Art Institute of Chicago / Art Resource, New York: 152 right
© Art Media Holdings, LLS: 188 left
Courtesy Art Resource, NY: 186 left
© 2019 The Associated Press: 190
© 2019 Will Barnet Trust / Licensed by VAGA at ARS, NY: 21
© The Rosemarie Beck Foundation. Courtesy of The Rosemarie Beck Foundation: 204, 205
© Estate of Isabel Bishop. Courtesy of DC Moore Gallery, New York: 248
© Estate of Aaron Bohrod / Licensed by VAGA at ARS, NY: 176, 177
Courtesy Colby College Museum of Art, Gift of Duncan Phillips, 1964.048: 123 right
Courtesy Courthouse Gallery Fine Art, Ellsworth, Maine: 203
Courtesy Curtis Licensing: 107 right
Courtesy Davis & Langdale Company, Inc.: 23
Courtesy David Diao and Postmasters Gallery, New York: 266, 267, 275
© 2019 Lois Dodd / Licensed by VAGA at ARS, NY: 198, 199
© Lois Dodd / Licensed by VAGA at ARS, NY. Courtesy Alexandre Gallery, New York: 235
Courtesy Richard Estes and Marlborough Gallery, New York, NY: 223
Courtesy Farnsworth Art Museum, Rockland, ME; Museum Purchase, 1991.9: 123 left
Courtesy Estate of Jane Freilicher and Paul Kasmin Gallery: 182–83, 196, 197
Courtesy of the Estate of Jane Freilicher and Tibor de Nagy Gallery, New York, NY: 186 right
Courtesy Ann Gale and the Dolby Chadwick Gallery: 257
© 2019 The Arshile Gorky Foundation / Artists Rights Society (ARS), NY. Courtesy Whitney Museum of American Art, New York; gift of Julien Levy for Maro and Natasha Gorky in memory of their father 50.17: 239 right
Courtesy Harvard Film Archive and the Woodberry Poetry Room: 185
Courtesy Walter Hatke and Gallery Henoch, New York: 2, 103
Courtesy Hurd La Rinconada Gallery and Guest Homes, San Patricia, NM: 159, 160 left
Courtesy The Hyde Collection, Glens Falls, NY, Bequest of Charlotte Pruyn Hyde, 1971.16: 87 left
© 2019 Wolf Kahn / Licensed by VAGA at ARS, NY. Courtesy of the artist and Miles McEnery Gallery, New York, NY: 79
Courtesy KHM-Museumsverband: 189
Courtesy Kiechel Fine Art: 8
© 2019 Estate of Hughie Lee-Smith / Licensed by VAGA at ARS, NY: 166–67, 169 right, 172, 173
© 2019 Estate of Hughie Lee-Smith / Licensed by VAGA at ARS, NY. Courtesy Bridgeman Images: 169 left, 170 left
© 2019 Estate of Hughie Lee-Smith / Licensed by VAGA at ARS, NY. Photo © 2019 Museum of Fine Arts, Boston: 170 right
© 2019 Estate of Reginald Marsh / Art Students League, New York / Artists Rights Society (ARS), New York: 164, 165 left
© Estate of Louisa Matthíasdóttir. Courtesy Tibor de Nagy Gallery, New York: 265, 273
Courtesy James McGarrell: 254, 255 left
© The Metropolitan Museum of Art. Courtesy Art Resource, NY: 32 right
Photo © 2019 Museum of Fine Arts, Boston: 231 left
Courtesy National Portrait Gallery, Smithsonian Institution: 34 right
Courtesy Philip Pearlstein and Betty Cuningham Gallery: 251
Courtesy Paul Resika and Bookstein Projects, New York: 201
© RMN-Grand Palais / Art Resource, NY: 193 right
Courtesy Saint Louis Art Museum, Bequest of Albert Blair, 48:1933: 84 right
© Peter Saul. Courtesy Mary Boone Gallery, New York: 258–59, 263, 277
© 2019 Scala Florence. Courtesy of the Ministero Beni e Att. Culturali e del Turismo. Courtesy Scala Archives: 193 left
Courtesy Jaune Quick-to-See Smith and Garth Greenan Gallery, New York: 261, 271
Courtesy Smithsonian American Art Museum, Gift of Allyn Cox: 236
Courtesy Smithsonian American Art Museum, Gift of the American Academy and Institute of Arts and Letters/Hassam and Speicher Fund: 265
© Estate of Moses Soyer / Licensed by VAGA at ARS, NY: 181
Courtesy May Stevens and RYAN LEE Gallery, New York: 206–7, 209, 211, 212 left, 217
Courtesy Reuben Tam papers, 1931–2006. Archives of American Art, Smithsonian Institution: 129 right
© and Courtesy Terra Foundation for American Art, Chicago, Daniel J. Terra Collection: 37
© 2019 Wayne Thiebaud / Licensed by VAGA at ARS, NY: 272
© Estate of George Tooker / Courtesy DC Moore Gallery, New York: 10–11, 18, 19
Courtesy University of Connecticut Libraries, Storrs, CT: 152 left
Courtesy US Department of Interior, National Park Service, Saint-Gaudens National Historic Site, Cornish, NH: 108 right
© The Charles White Archives: 26, 27
© 2019 Andrew Wyeth / Artists Rights Society (ARS), New York: cover, 7
Yale University Art Gallery: 32 left

Photographers
bpk Bildagentur / Art Resource, NY: 186 left
Mathew Brady: 49
Glenn Castellano, Collection of the Public Design Commission of the City of New York: 169 right
Joe Hazan: 186 right
Marty Lederhandler / March 6, 1970: 190
Joseph Levy, The Hyde Collection, Glens Falls, New York: 87 left
Becket Logan / Emma Amos Studio, New York: 226–27, 239 left, 243
Neighboring States: cover, 2, 7, 10–11, 18–19, 27–29, 40, 56, 74–75, 79–81, 89, 103, 138, 148–49, 155, 157, 165 left, 166–67, 172, 178–79, 253, 255 right, 258–59, 277
Richard Nichol: 257
Franck Raux: 193 right
Lee Stalsworth, Hirshhorn Museum and Sculpture Garden, Smithsonian Institution: 86 left
Natalia Zubko: 224

AMERICAN FEDERATION OF ARTS

This catalogue is published on the occasion of the traveling exhibition *For America: Paintings from the National Academy of Design*, organized by the American Federation of Arts for the National Academy of Design.

Curators
Jeremiah William McCarthy, Associate Curator, AFA
Diana Thompson, Director of Collections and Curatorial Affairs, NAD

Exhibition Itinerary
Dayton Art Institute, OH
February 20–June 2, 2019
New Britain Museum of American Art, CT
October 16, 2019–January 26, 2020
The Society of the Four Arts, Palm Beach, FL
February 15–April 26, 2020
Dixon Gallery and Gardens, Memphis, TN
July 19–September 27, 2020
New Mexico Museum of Art, Santa Fe
October 22, 2020–January 17, 2021
Figge Art Museum, Davenport, IA
February 20–May 9, 2021
Crocker Art Museum, Sacramento, CA
June 6–September 12, 2021

Support for the national tour of *For America: Paintings from the National Academy of Design* is provided by the JFM Foundation, Monique Schoen Warshaw, and Steph and Jody La Nasa.

First published in the United States of America in 2019 by
American Federation of Arts
305 East 47th Street, 10th Floor
New York, NY 10017
www.amfedarts.org

For the American Federation of Arts
Audrey Walen, Manager of Publications
Rachel Kim, Publications Assistant
Pavla Berghen-Wolf, Research Assistant
Kaitlyn Greenberg, Mary McClave, Karolina Sotomayor, Rebecca Wan, and Mizuho Yamazaki, Curatorial Interns

Produced by Lucia | Marquand, Seattle
www.luciamarquand.com

Copyedited by Jennifer Bernstein, Tenacious Editorial, Inc.
Designed by Matsumoto Incorporated
Typeset in Bembo
Proofread by Brynn Warriner
Indexed by David Luljak
Color management by iocolor, Seattle
Printed on Arctic volume ivory
Printed and bound in Turkey by Ofset Yapımevi

Distributed by
Yale University Press
302 Temple Street
P.O. Box 209040
New Haven, CT 06520-9040
www.yalebooks.com/art

Library of Congress Control Number: 2018964462
ISBN 978-1-885444-49-3 (American Federation of Arts)
ISBN 978-0-300-24428-1 (Yale University Press)

A CIP catalogue record for this book is available from the British Library.

Illustrations: Cover: detail of plate p. 6; front endpapers and flyleaf: details of plate p. 145; 2: detail of plate, p. 103; 10–11: detail of plate, p. 19; 28–29: detail of plate, p. 40; 44–45: detail of plate, p. 53; 62–63: detail of plate, p. 71; 80–81: detail of plate, p. 89; 104–5: detail of plate, p. 111; 120–21: detail of plate, p. 132; 148–49: detail of plate, p. 155; 166–67: detail of plate, p. 172; 182–83: detail of plate, p. 197; 206–7: detail of plate, p. 217; 226–27: detail of plate, p. 243; 258–59: detail of plate, p. 277; 278–79: detail of plate, p. 219; back endpapers and flyleaf: details of plate p. 135

AMERICAN FEDERATION OF ARTS

The American Federation of Arts is the leader in traveling exhibitions internationally. A nonprofit institution founded in 1909, the AFA is dedicated to enriching the public's experience and understanding of the visual arts through organizing and touring art exhibitions for presentation in museums around the world, publishing scholarly exhibition catalogues, developing innovative educational programs, and fostering better understanding among nations through the international exchange of art.

NATIONAL ACADEMY OF DESIGN

The National Academy of Design has a simple yet powerful mission: "to promote American art and architecture through exhibition and instruction." Founded in 1825, the NAD is an honor society of America's top artists and architects—the National Academicians—as well as a presenter of arts and an agent of arts education. Over the decades, the NAD has enriched and educated generations of artists and architects while preserving and sharing the work of the National Academicians with the public.